mypoliscilab ™

Where participation leads to action!

Welcome to MyPoliSciLab, where participation leads to action!

MyPoliSciLab is a state-of-the-art, interactive, and instructive online solution for introducing students to American Government. Designed to amplify and supplement a traditional lecture course or completely administer an online course, MyPoliSciLab combines multimedia — simulations, videos, news feeds and archives, quizzes and tests — to make teaching and learning more effective and fun!

WHAT STUDENTS ARE SAYING ABOUT ONLINE EXAMS AND QUIZZES

"I love it. I keep trying until I get a perfect grade and after a couple times you know the content like the back of your hand!"

"I liked being able to view the results of the quizzes immediately instead of having to wait for them to be graded by the instructor."

WHAT STUDENTS ARE SAYING ABOUT ONLINE ACTIVITIES

"The activities were my favorite part of the course. They took a different approach to an interesting subject, and made it more applicable to real-life situations. This made the subject seem even more real than before."

"I think they are a great tool to get students to interact with the material in a way you couldn't really do in class."

ONE PLACE.
Everything your students need to succeed.

MyPoliSciLab is a state-of-the-art, interactive, and instructive online solution for your American Government course.

❯ Pre-Test, Post Test, and Chapter Exam
For each chapter of the printed textbook, students will navigate through a pre-test, post-test, and a full-chapter exam — all fully integrated with the online E-book so students can assess, review, and improve their understanding of the material in each chapter.

❯ Chapter Review
For each chapter, students will find additional resources such as a complete study guide, learning objectives, a summary.

❯ E-book.
Matching the exact layout of the printed textbook, the E-book contains multimedia icons in the margins that launch a wealth of exciting resources.

❯ The *New York Times* Online Feed & The *New York Times* Search by Subject™ Archive
Both provide free access to the full text of The *New York Times* and articles from the world's leading journalists of the *Times*. The online feed provides students with updated headlines and political news on an **hourly** basis.

❯ Online Administration
Instructors can easily track students' work on the site and monitor their progress on each activity. The *Instructor Gradebook*, which now includes upgraded functionality, provides maximum flexibility for allowing instructors to sort by student, activity, or to view the entire class in spreadsheet view.

❯ Research Navigator™
This database provides thousands of articles from journals as well as popular periodicals, such as *Newsweek* and *USA Today*, that give students and professors access to scholarly and topical content from a variety of sources.

❯ Interactive Activities
Students will find over 100 simulations, interactive timelines, videos, comparative exercises, and more — all integrated with the online E-book through icons that appear in the margins. Now fully updated with brand-new activities!

SIMULATION. Students are given a role to play — such as congress member, lobbyist, or police officer — so they can experience the challenges and excitement of politics firsthand.

TIMELINE. With an abundance of media and graphics, students can step through the evolution of an aspect of our political system.

VISUAL LITERACY. Students interpret and apply data about intriguing political topics. Each activity begins with an interactive primer on reading graphs and charts.

PARTICIPATION. Bringing the importance of politics home, these activities appear as three types: 1) Debates, 2) Surveys, and 3) "Get Involved" activities.

COMPARATIVE. Students compare the U.S. political system to those of other countries.

CONTINUOUSLY UPDATED MULTIMEDIA MAPPED TO CHAPTER CONTENT

NEW FEATURES

Student Polling
Updated weekly with timely, provocative questions, this new feature allows students to participate in nationwide polls on hot topics. Students are asked to vote on questions such as "Should flag burning be permitted?" Results of student responses around the country are immediately displayed.

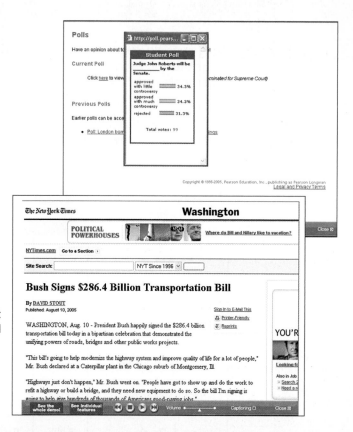

PoliSci News
PoliSci News contains 1) an online feed from The *New York Times* that is updated hourly, 2) an exclusive *New York Times* database that allows students to browse by subject area or search for a specific topic, and 3) PoliSci News Review — a series of articles selected by a political science professor that recap the previous week's most important political events and are followed by quizzes.

Roundtable Discussion Video Clips
Video clips consist of three professors discussing important concepts covered in the text. Key concepts such as campaign finance reform and critical questions such as "Is Federalism Dead?" are discussed from a wide range of perspectives and viewpoints — providing students with a balanced review of key course material. Each discussion is accompanied by critical thinking prompts, multiple choice questions, and a transcript for reference.

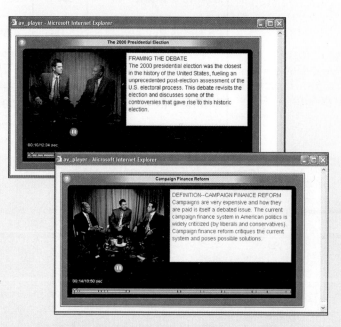

Debate Video Clips
Offering lively, challenging debates from two sides of an issue, these clips feature two professors discussing hot-button issues and answering pressing questions such as "Did George Bush steal the election?" Each discussion is accompanied by critical thinking prompts, multiple choice questions, and a transcript for reference.

INSTRUCTOR: WE CAN HELP YOU EASILY INTEGRATE THESE AMAZING ASSETS INTO YOUR COURSE...HOW?

Author's Choice
With so many incredible activities to assign, we have asked our authors to hand select one or two activities that best complement or amplify each chapter. You have the work done for you in easy-to-use, pre-packaged MyPoliSciLab assignments. If you only have time to assign and complete one activity for the chapter, the Author's Choice designation makes it easy!

Go to mypoliscilab.com to see a sample chapter!

Student Survey Results

Recently, Longman Publishers conducted a nationwide survey of students to determine just how useful they find MyPoliSciLab and its individual features. The sample included hundreds of students from both 2-year and 4-year schools.

The results are impressive. Not only do they show that students find MyPoliSciLab to be an effective supplement, but they show how each specific feature of MyPoliSciLab enhances students' learning experience and engages them with the course material. See for yourself!

Very low learning value →   Very high learning value

	1	2	3	4	5	4s & 5s
Online Quizzes	1.3%	1.3%	8.8%	26.8%	61.9%	88.7%
Chapter Exams	0.8%	5.0%	8.4%	18.4%	67.4%	85.8%
Debate Videos	2.2%	3.5%	15.8%	27.6%	50.9%	78.5%
Roundtable Videos	3.0%	3.0%	16.5%	32.0%	45.5%	77.5%
Chapter Activities	0.9%	5.2%	16.5%	23.9%	53.5%	77.4%
Online E-Book	5.4%	8.3%	15.1%	17.6%	53.7%	71.2%
PS News Review	5.0%	4.5%	23.2%	23.2%	44.1%	67.3%
Homepage Updates	8.0%	11.7%	16.9%	23.9%	39.4%	63.4%
Polling Questions	7.6%	9.0%	27.0%	20.9%	35.5%	56.4%

WHAT STUDENTS ARE SAYING ABOUT ONLINE E-BOOK

"It helped a lot, especially since you could magnify the words. Also, it was great to be able to type in a key word and see exactly where it appears in the text."

WHAT STUDENTS ARE SAYING ABOUT DEBATE VIDEOS

"All videos were fantastic and allowed each topic to be discussed from each viewpoint but was kept objective by the moderator."

WHAT STUDENTS ARE SAYING ABOUT POLISCI NEWS

"I really liked this feature. I don't get a chance to catch up on political news very often, so this was very helpful."

WHAT STUDENTS ARE SAYING ABOUT POLLING QUESTIONS

"The polling questions are fun. Sometimes I was very surprised at other students' responses."

PEARSON

Longman

The Struggle for
Democracy
EIGHTH EDITION

EDWARD S. GREENBERG
University of Colorado

BENJAMIN I. PAGE
Northwestern University

PEARSON
Longman

New York   San Francisco   Boston
London   Toronto   Sydney   Tokyo   Singapore   Madrid
Mexico City   Munich   Paris   Cape Town   Hong Kong   Montreal

About the Cover

The seven smaller cover snapshots give us a pictorial history of the creation of the Statue of Liberty. All but the front right shot were taken by photographer Albert Fernique and published in his 1883 book, *Album de las construction de la Statue de las Liberte.* From back left to front right: Work began on the statue in 1875. Here is a view of the workshop in Paris, with models of the statue in the background. Construction of the skeleton and plaster surface of the left arm and hand of the statue is shown. Men are seen at work on the construction of the statue. The snapshot of the exterior of the workshop shows the construction materials, the head of the statue, and a group of men gathered in front of the left foot of the statue. The head of the statue was displayed in a park in Paris before the entire statue was completed. The statue was assembled in Paris; this shot shows the erected bottom half of the statue under scaffolding, with the head and torch at its feet (the statue was then dismantled and shipped to America in 1885 in 350 pieces). The statue was uncrated and erected on Bedloe's Island (Liberty Island); it was completed in 1886.

EDITOR-IN-CHIEF	Eric Stano
DEVELOPMENT EDITOR	Diane Culhane
SENIOR MARKETING MANAGER	Elizabeth Fogarty
SUPPLEMENTS EDITOR	Brian Belardi
MEDIA EDITOR	Beth Crippen Strauss
PRODUCTION MANAGER	Donna DeBenedictis
PROJECT COORDINATION, TEXT DESIGN, AND ELECTRONIC PAGE MAKEUP	Elm Street Publishing Services, Inc.
COVER DESIGN MANAGER	Wendy Ann Fredericks
COVER DESIGNER	Kay Petronio
COVER PHOTOS	*Background:* Stockbyte/Getty Images, Inc., and Robert Llewellyn/Workbook. *Construction of the Statue of Liberty (all except front right):* Albert Fernique Photographer, 1883. Photography Collection, Miriam and Ira D. Wallach Division of Art, Prints and Photographs, The New York Public Library, Astor, Lenox and Tilden Foundations. *Front right:* Milstein Division of United States History, Local History & Genealogy, The New York Public Library, Astor, Lenox and Tilden Foundations.
CARTOGRAPHER	Michael D. Ward
PHOTO RESEARCHER	Photosearch, Inc.
MANUFACTURING BUYER	Lucy Hebard
PRINTER AND BINDER	Quebecor World Dubuque
COVER PRINTER	Coral Graphic Services, Inc.

For permission to use copyrighted material, grateful acknowledgment is made to the copyright holders on pp. C-1–C-2, which are hereby made part of this copyright page.

Library of Congress Cataloging-in-Publication Data
Greenberg, Edward S., 1942–
    The struggle for democracy / Edward S. Greenberg, Benjamin I. Page.—8th ed.
        p. cm.
    Includes bibliographical references and index.
    ISBN 0-321-42083-7 (alk. paper)—ISBN 0-321-44394-2 (alk. paper)
    1. United States—Politics and government. 2. Democracy—United States. I. Page, Benjamin I. II. Title.

JK276.G74 2006
320.473—dc22   2006050700

Please visit us at **www.ablongman.com/polisci**

ISBN 0-321-42083-7

1 2 3 4 5 6 7 8 9 10—QWD—09 08 07 06

Brief Contents

Detailed Contents

Note: Each chapter ends with the following sections: Summary, MyPoliSciLab Web Explorations, Internet Sources, and Suggestions for Further Reading. Red bullets designate special features within the chapter.

Preface

Critical Thinking and
The Struggle for Democracy

This eighth edition of *The Struggle for Democracy* strengthens the strong critical thinking focus of previous editions. In addition to a general updating and freshening of materials throughout the text—including results of the 2006 congressional elections; developments in the Bush presidency and policy agenda; the ongoing debate about immigration; new justices and new directions on the Supreme Court; the consequences of the continuing war and occupation in Iraq; disagreements over same-sex civil unions and marriage; the Katrina disaster and the politics of rebuilding the Gulf Coast; the growing role of religion in American politics; the lobbying scandal in Washington and congressional responses to it; the rise of the Internet as a location for the dissemination of political news and information; the persistence of federal budget deficits; and the growth of anti-Americanism in many parts of the world—there are three new features that advance our educational objectives in this textbook. The first feature, which we call "Mapping American Politics," uses cartograms (i.e., "weighted maps") to display political information in visually dramatic ways, making it easier for students to grasp some of the thorniest and most complex issues in American politics and public policy and to think about them in new ways. The second feature is a new section added to chapters called "How Exceptional?", which asks students to think about how the American political system differs from others and why those differences might matter. The third is a series of timelines to help students think more coherently about political and governmental developments over time. We will say more about these features later.

"Critical thinking" is the watchword for this eighth edition of *The Struggle for Democracy,* much as it has been for every edition since the first in 1993. Every element in this text is designed to promote critical thinking. In this revision, we have tried to pare away any and all materials that do not help students think critically about American government and politics and about their role as citizens, and we have added new information and features that encourage students to think about the way our political system works and how people are affected by what government does. In so doing, we have stayed true to our original vision for this book—responding to what we have learned from a multitude of instructors and students about what they want in an introductory textbook and conforming to what we, as experienced teachers of the introductory course, know works in the classroom. We have created a textbook that treats students as adults, engages their intellectual and emotional attention, and encourages them to be active learners. We hope that, in the process, we have also encouraged students to be the engaged, active, and informed citizens so vital to any democracy.

The critical thinking orientation of this edition of *The Struggle for Democracy* is organized around two principal themes: *Using the Democracy Standard* and *Using the Framework.* The first helps students come to grips with American government and politics in normative or value terms. The second helps students cut through the jumble of information about government and politics and bring some order out of the confusion, helping them make sense of *why* things happen. The critical thinking focus is supported, as well, by a number of specific offerings. These include MyPoliSciLab Web Explorations, at the end of each chapter, in which students do assignments on the Internet where they hone their evaluative and analytical critical thinking skills and, at the same time, have some fun. The "By the Numbers" exercises, a very popular feature according to adopter and student feedback, help students become better citizens by helping them become good, critical consumers of published numbers and statistics; this feature also invites students to apply the insights they have garnered from using this feature to current political problems and issues. And, as suggested earlier, "Mapping American Politics," "How Exceptional?" sections, and the timelines are also designed to help students become more analytical—and therefore more effective—citizens.

Using the Democracy Standard

Throughout this textbook, we help students think about the system as a whole, as well as particular political practices and institutions, using a clearly articulated, evaluative democracy "yardstick" for reaching judgments about the degree to which we have become, or are becoming, more or less democratic.

We develop this "evaluating democracy" theme in a number of places:

- Democracy is carefully defined in Chapter 1, and students learn there how they might use democracy to evaluate the performance of the American political system. The definition of democracy is broad and inclusive, built on the concepts of popular sovereignty, political equality, and liberty.

- In the opening pages of each chapter, students are reminded about the democracy "yardstick" and how it might be used to think critically about the subject matter to follow.

- Discussion of the relative democratic performance of the American political system, using the Chapter 1 definition as the yardstick, is laced throughout the text narrative.

- A chapter-ending "Using the Democracy Standard" box helps students think through the democracy issue once again, only this time they have the capacity to bring information and insights to bear that they have gained from reading the chapter, attending class and joining its discussions, and doing the MyPoliSciLab Web Explorations. This feature opens with a strongly stated proposition about the relative democratic character of the particular political or governmental institution under consideration in the chapter. The proposition is answered by two opposing views—brief but fairly stated "agree" and "disagree" statements. Finally, we ask students to think carefully about the opposing views, offering some guidelines on how to subject the statements to critical scrutiny. This feature helps students understand the complexity of many of the issues addressed in the book and learn how to formulate intellectually compelling arguments.

Using the Framework

In Chapter 1 we also provide a simple but powerful analytical framework that helps students understand how our complicated political system works. The framework makes clear that government, politics, and the larger society are deeply intertwined in recognizable patterns; that understanding what is going on requires a holistic focus; and that what might be called "deep structures"—the economy, society, political culture, and the constitutional rules—are particularly important for understanding how our system works. These deep structures have a great deal to do with the creation of the problems to which government must attend, the level of resources that is available to solve problems, the ideas that citizens and elected officials have in their heads as they go about using government to address problems, and the distribution of political power in society among individuals, groups, and organizations.

The framework appears in *The Struggle for Democracy* in the following places:

- The framework is discussed in detail in Chapter 1, and students are shown how it can be used to organize the large amounts of material they will encounter in the course of their reading. A powerful graphic associated with the discussion makes the framework more understandable and compelling.

- In the opening pages of each chapter, students are reminded about the framework and how it can be used to understand how government and politics work in the United States.

- Chapters in Part 2 examine the nature of American society, political culture, and economy; the United States's position in the world; and our constitutional rules—and why these issues matter for how government and politics work.

- Concepts and insights from the framework, as well as materials from the chapters in Part 2, are used throughout the text narrative.

- A "Using the Framework" box in each chapter shows students how the framework can help answer questions they might have about why things happen in American government and politics. Concepts and insights from the framework, as well as a graphical reminder, provide the tools to answer such questions as, "Why is out-of-state tuition more costly than in-state tuition?" and "Why can't we seem to get big money out of politics?" Teachers and students have told us repeatedly that this feature, which first appeared in the fifth edition, made the analytical framework come alive for them and helped them appreciate how the framework can be used to understand what is going on in American government and politics. This edition includes new "Using the Framework" boxes on the death penalty, the emergence of "big government" Republicanism, and the president's failure to win over Congress on private accounts in Social Security.

Mapping American Politics

In a visual sense, the most obvious addition to *The Struggle for Democracy* is "Mapping American Politics," which uses weighted maps to display and clarify statistical information about American politics and public policies. We use weighted maps—which display information that is organized on a geographical basis, with each unit (e.g., a county, state, or country) sized in various ways that are in proportion to the data being reported (e.g., votes or federal taxes collected)—to help students think more deeply about American politics using a tool they are likely to find pleasing and compelling. The maps illuminate a broad range of issues, including how the geographic bases of the political parties are changing, what the relative mix of Republican and Democratic voters is in each of the states, how the states compare with one another on federal taxes paid and federal monies received, how well people are represented in the

House and Senate, what the relationship is between violent crime incidence and capital punishment, where stories come from that appear in the news media, and where American economic and military assistance dollars go.

How Exceptional?

Since at least 1835 when Alexis deTocqueville published the first volume of his classic work *Democracy in America,* people have wondered whether and to what extent the United States might be exceptional, different in important ways from other countries. Throughout this edition of the textbook, we raise this question, describing both American political and governmental practices and institutions and comparing them with practices and institutions in another country or set of countries. We then invite students to think about the differences and assess whether these differences matter. We examine a broad range of comparisons, including the organization of executive and legislative powers, national political cultures, federalism, press freedoms, the role of political parties in legislative bodies, judicial review, the use of the death penalty, social insurance and social safety nets, and the extent and use of military power. Our hope and belief is that students will gain a deeper and more nuanced understanding of their own political system by comparing it with those of other countries, particularly with those that share our commitment to democracy.

Timelines

Timelines now appear throughout this book to help students develop a sense of historical context; they assist students in keeping track of and mentally organizing materials that are described in depth and detail in the body of the text. The timelines are numerous and cover many aspects of American politics and public policy. These include federalism milestones, development of the U.S. census, a history of the Internet, the rise and fall of labor unions, a history of the nonviolent civil rights movement, party caucus and primary schedules, steps in the federal budgetary process, the creation of executive departments and agencies, a history of free expression, and U.S. military operations abroad. We hope and expect that these timelines will not only help students better comprehend complex materials, but deepen their appreciation for how a range of political institutions and practices, as well as government policies, emerged over time.

By the Numbers

As teachers of the introductory course, we have grown increasingly concerned over the years by the inability of many students to understand the statistical information on government, politics, economy, and society that they encounter—including statistics such as the gross domestic product, the crime rate, voting turnout in presidential elections, and the level of poverty in the United States—or to distinguish between good and bad statistical information. Partly, this is the result of their general discomfort with statistics and numbers. Partly, this is the product of the failure of statistical reporting agencies and organizations to openly describe their operating assumptions and methods. All too often, moreover, interest and advocacy groups use statistics as instruments of political combat, leaving the impression that all statistics are "lies and damn lies," with one statistic no better than another. The news media are not all that helpful either, with their tendency to report social, economic, and political statistics in a haphazard, noncritical, and out-of-context fashion. Finally, statistics from the federal government, although generally more reliable and sensible than those calculated by interest groups, are themselves often the product of political negotiation and compromise—the poverty-line calculation is a good example. Although government statistics are incredibly useful, the consumer of such statistics must remain alert.

The "By the Numbers" feature appears throughout the text. A new one has been added ("Is America Becoming More Unequal?"), and the remainder have been updated and freshened. The goal of the feature is to help students become better consumers of statistical information and more analytical readers of social, economic, and political statistics reported by government, interest and advocacy groups, and academic researchers. Each box describes a particular statistic and tells why it is important—examples include voting turnout, the poverty line, the crime rate, the size of the federal government, interest group scoring of the performance of senators and representatives, and more. We then tell the story behind the statistic—why the statistic was first calculated, let us say, or what assumptions are embedded in it. We then show how the statistic is calculated and examine what critics and supporters say about its usefulness and validity. Finally, we ask students what they think, thus encouraging them to think in more depth about issues addressed by the statistic, whether it be poverty, voting turnout, or how the U.S. Census Bureau goes about doing the decennial census. If the "By the Numbers" feature works as we hope it does, students should become more sophisticated users of statistical information, but not cynical ones. We believe that in a world increasingly described by numbers, students who are armed with these skills can be better and more effective citizens.

MyPoliSciLab Web Explorations

We have designed a series of Web Explorations, housed within MyPoliSciLab, where students can explore and use the many riches of the Internet to put their critical thinking skills to work and have some fun at the same time. In these Web Explorations, which appear at the end of each chapter, we do not simply identify a website for students to visit, but give them a question or issue to investigate and ask that they report the results. These reports, tangible products of their investigations and analyses, may be for the students' own edification, enriching their experiences in the text, or may be assigned as a class activity. The Explorations are active and interactive in nature, never passive. Students are not casual visitors, browsing a site, but investigators and analysts using their critical thinking skills.

Organization and Coverage

Part 1 contains the introduction to the textbook and focuses primarily on describing the critical thinking tools to be used throughout: democracy and the analytical framework. Part 2 covers the structural foundations of American government and politics and also addresses subjects such as the economy, culture, and international system; the constitutional framework of the American political system; and the development of the federal system. Part 3 focuses on what we call *political linkage* institutions, such as parties, elections, public opinion, social movements, and interest groups, that serve to convey the wants, needs, and demands of individuals and groups to public officials. Part 4 concentrates on the central institutions of the national government, including the presidency, Congress, and the Supreme Court. Part 5 describes the kinds of policies the national government produces and analyzes how effective government is in solving pressing social and economic problems.

Although all of the standard topics in the introductory course are covered in the text, our focus on using democracy as a measuring rod to evaluate our system of government, and on using an analytical framework for understanding how things work, allows us to take a fresh look at traditional topics and to pay attention to topics that are not covered in detail in other textbooks:

- We pay much more attention than most other texts to *structural factors*—which include the American economy, social change in the United States, technological innovations and change, the American political culture, and changes in the global system—and examine how they affect politics, government, and public policy. These factors are introduced in Chapter 4—a chapter unique among introductory texts—and are brought to bear on a wide range of issues in subsequent chapters. For example, our discussion of interest group politics includes information about how the distribution of income and wealth affects the ability of different groups to form effective lobbying organizations.

- We attend very carefully to issues of *democratic political theory*. This follows from our critical thinking objective, which asks students to assess the progress of and prospects for democracy in the United States, and from our desire to present American history as the history of the struggle for democracy. For instance, we examine how the evolution of the party system has improved democracy in some respects in the United States but hurt it in others.

- We also include more *historical information* than is common among introductory texts, because the best way to understand the struggle for democracy and evaluate the progress of democracy in the United States is, in part, from a historical perspective. We show, for example, how the expansion of civil rights in the United States has been associated with important historical events and trends.

- We also include substantial *comparative information* because we believe that a full understanding of government and politics and the effect of structural factors on them is possible only through a comparison of developments, practices, and institutions in the United States with those in other nations. We understand better how our system of social welfare works, for example, when we see how other rich democratic countries deal with the problems of poverty, unemployment, and old age.

- Our approach also means that the subjects of *civil liberties* and *civil rights* are not treated in conjunction with the Constitution in Part 2, which is the case with many introductory texts, but in Part 5, on public policy. This is because we believe that the real-world status of civil liberties and civil rights, while partly determined by specific provisions of the Constitution, is better understood as the outcome of the interaction of structural, political, and governmental factors. Thus, the status of civil rights for gays and lesbians depends not only on constitutional provisions but also on the state of public opinion, degrees of support from elected political leaders, and the decisions of the Supreme Court. (Instructors who prefer to introduce their students to civil liberties and civil rights immediately after considering the Constitution can simply assign the liberties and rights chapters out of order.)

What's New in This Edition

A number of important changes have been made in this edition. They include the following:

- To reiterate a point already made: The most important change in this eighth edition of *The Struggle for Democracy* is the extension of the focus on critical thinking as the central organizing template. To get there, we have further refined and strengthened our discussions of democracy as a tool of evaluation and of the framework as a tool of analysis and understanding, paying special attention to drawing out these themes in every chapter.

- This edition of *The Struggle for Democracy* includes new exercises for the "By the Numbers" feature, described earlier in more detail, and updated and freshened MyPoliSciLab Web Explorations. We also have added a visually compelling cartogram feature "Mapping American Politics." These three features are unique among introductory American government and politics textbooks and add to the critical thinking tools available to students.

- This edition of *The Struggle for Democracy* includes two additional new features described earlier, aimed at enhancing the critical thinking orientation of the book: "How Exceptional?" and timelines.

- This edition pays more attention to "marginalized" groups in American society, including Hispanics and gays and lesbians. Combining this enhanced attention to marginalized groups with *The Struggle for Democracy*'s traditionally strong coverage of African Americans and women means that the current edition of this textbook reflects much of the cultural richness, diversity, and complexity of American society itself. These new materials are found throughout in the text narrative, in chapter-opening stories, and in boxed features. For example, Chapter 4 describes the rapid rise in the number of Americans of Hispanic origin and explores what this might mean for American politics. Chapter 15 considers the status of civil liberties protections for Arab Americans in the United States in the aftermath of 9/11. Chapter 16 discusses the current status of gay rights in the United States following the Supreme Court's landmark decision *Lawrence* v. *Texas* (2003) and the Massachusetts's high court ruling allowing same-sex marriage.

- We have expanded our coverage of websites in the Internet Sources sections—including more than a few of the most interesting political blogs—and integrated them even more tightly with *The Struggle for Democracy*. This is in addition to the very strong Internet presence found in the MyPoliSciLab Web Exploration features. Together, these will allow both students and instructors to have better access to timely information and alternative perspectives.

- In addition to expanded coverage of websites and the Web Explorations feature, we have made further strides to integrate the Web. Throughout the text, icons can be found in the margins referring readers to the interactive exercises and videos that are available in *MyPoliSciLab*, Longman's interactive website for American government. Each icon appears next to a particular topic and indicates that a simulation, visual literacy exercise, interactive timeline, participation activity, comparative government exercise, video roundtable discussion, or video debate related to that topic exists on the site. Activities pose critical thinking questions and provide feedback, helping the reader better understand the concepts presented in the text. Students will receive access to these interactive activities by redeeming the access code card bundled with this text. (Faculty must order an ISBN that includes both this textbook and the access card. Please contact your local Allyn & Bacon/Longman representative for more information.)

- Information has been updated throughout. There is not a single page in the text without fresh information. Timely subjects, such as the 2006 congressional elections; the actions and policies of the George W. Bush administration; the continuing impact on American politics of developments in the wars in Afghanistan and Iraq; important Supreme Court decisions involving federalism, civil liberties, and civil rights; emerging foreign policy problems in the Middle East and Latin America; and much more are covered throughout.

- We have continued our effort to make the text more user-friendly for students by paying more attention to the layout of text and the highlighting of key points, better defining of technical terms, presenting more detailed captions that explain tables and graphs, and providing more information in photo captions. Most importantly, we have tied the chapters together with critical thinking guideposts and exercises.

Supplements

Longman Publishers provides an impressive array of text supplements to aid instructors in teaching and students in learning. Each item in this extensive package works together to create a fully integrated learning system. Great care was taken to provide both students and professors with a supportive supplements package that accurately reflects the unique spirit of *The Struggle for Democracy*.

Instructor Supplements for Qualified College Adopters

Study Site for American Government
(www.longmanamericangovernment.com)   This online course companion provides a wealth of resources for students and instructors using Longman American government texts. Containing practice tests, flashcards, and Web explorations, the Study Site for American government helps students quickly master the fundamentals, review a subject for understanding, or prepare for an exam.

Instructor's Manual   (ISBN 0-205-51958-X) Written by Debra St. John of Collin County Community College District and Mary Carns of Stephen F. Austin State University, this comprehensive manual is designed to help instructors prepare lectures, classroom activities, and assignments. The manual features chapter outlines and summaries, a broad range of teaching suggestions, ideas for student research, and suggestions for discussion that complement text themes.

Test Bank   (ISBN 0-205-52959-8) Prepared by Dennis Plane of Juanita College, this manual is designed to reinforce and test students' knowledge of the themes and concepts of the text. The test bank contains hundreds of multiple-choice, short-answer, true/false, and essay questions with an answer key.

TestGen-EQ Computerized Testing System - (ISBN 0-205-51963-6) This flexible, easy-to-master computerized test bank includes all the test items in the printed test bank. The software allows professors to edit existing questions and to add their own items. Tests can be printed in several different formats and can include features such as graphs and tables. It is available for Windows and Macintosh computers.

PowerPoint® Presentations Available for downloading from Longman's Instructor Resource Center at **www.ablongman.com/IRC.** Written by Mary Carns at Stephen F. Austin State University and Terri Wright of California State University, Long Beach, these slides can also be easily modified using *PowerPoint®* software.

Transparencies This acetate package is comprised of 40 images taken from the text.

Instructor Resource Center (www.ablongman.com/IRC) A helpful Website where instructors can download supplements including: Instructor's Manuals, Test Banks, TestGens, and *PowerPoint®* presentations, as well as CourseCompass®, WebCT, and Blackboard materials. Instructors will need to request a password from their sales representative to gain access.

Digital Media Archive CD-ROM (ISBN 0-321-27068-1) This complete multimedia presentation tool for instructors includes more than 150 maps, graphs, and charts; 100 photos; and 50 video clips—all on one CD-ROM and ready for inclusion in an instructor's online course, *PowerPoint®* presentations, and websites. It was developed in consultation with Kurt Cline, California State University, Fresno; Martin S. Edwards, Texas Tech University; Scott R. Furlong, University of Wisconsin, Green Bay; James M. Lutz, Indiana University Purdue University, Fort Wayne; and John David Rausch, Jr., West Texas A&M University.

Longman Political Science Video Program Qualified adopters can peruse our list of videos for the American government classroom. Contact your local Allyn & Bacon/Longman representative for more information.

Student Supplements for Qualified College Adopters

MyPoliSciLab This state-of-the-art, interactive, online solution for the American government course, fully integrated in the course management system of your choice—CourseCompass®, WebCT, or Blackboard—or as an independent website, free of a course management system altogether, is available at no additional charge when bundled with a copy of *The Struggle for Democracy* and contains the following features:

- **Assessment.** For each chapter of the text, students will navigate through a comprehensive pre-test, post-test, and a full chapter exam, all fully integrated with an online e-book version of this text so students can assess, review, and improve their understanding of the text chapters.

- **Interactive Activities.** Developed and revised by a team of more than 15 political science faculty, *MyPoliSciLab* features more than 100 highly interactive activities, all updated and revised—including comparative activities, visual literacy exercises, interactive timelines, participation exercises, and **more than 30 simulations**—for all of the major topics in the course.

- **Roundtable Discussion Video Clips.** Added and updated throughout the semester, these 10- to 12-minute video clips consist of three professors discussing important concepts covered in the text. Dozens of key concepts (such as campaign finance reform) and critical questions (such as, "Is Federalism Dead?") are discussed from a wide range of perspectives and viewpoints, providing students with a balanced review of key course material. Each discussion is accompanied by critical thinking prompts, multiple-choice questions, and transcripts for reference.

- **Debate Video Clips.** Updated throughout the semester and offering lively, challenging debates from two sides of an issue, these 10- to 12-minute clips feature two professors discussing hot-button issues and answering pressing questions such as, "Did George W. Bush steal the election?" Each discussion is accompanied by critical thinking prompts, multiple-choice questions, and transcripts for reference.

- **Student Polling.** Updated weekly with timely, provocative questions, this new feature allows students to participate in nationwide polls on hot topics. Students are asked to vote on questions such as, "Should flag burning be permitted?" Results of the thousands of student responses around the country are immediately displayed.

- **PoliSci News.** PoliSci News contains an online feed from the *New York Times* that is updated hourly; an exclusive *New York Times* database that allows students to browse by subject area or search for a specific topic; and PoliSci News Review, a series of articles selected by a political science professor that recaps the previous week's most important political events and are followed by quizzes and critical thinking questions.

- **Author's Choice.** With so many incredible activities to assign, the authors of this book have hand selected one or two activities that best complement or amplify each chapter. You have the work done for you in easy-to-use, prepackaged *MyPoliSciLab* assignments. If you only have time to assign and complete one activity for the chapter, the Author's Choice designation makes it easy!

- **Research Navigator™.** The EBSCO ContentSelect Academic Journal Database content is collected from thousands of articles organized by discipline and fully searchable. Articles in popular periodicals such as *Newsweek* and *USA Today* are included as well, giving students and professors access to topical content from a variety of sources.

- **Link Library.** Offers editorially selected "Best of the Web" sites. Libraries are continually scanned and kept up-to-date, providing the most relevant and accurate links for research assignments.

- **Writing Resources.** Topics include Finding Sources, Using Your Library, Start Writing, Internet Research, and Citing Sources.

- **Online e-Book.** Matching the exact layout of the printed textbook, the online e-book contains multimedia icons in the margins that launch to exciting resources (e.g., simulations or videos), which expand on key topics students encounter as they read through the text.

- **Online Administration.** Instructors can easily track student work on the site and monitor students' progress on each activity. The *Instructor Gradebook,* which includes upgraded functionality to ensure a truly seamless experience for users, provides maximum flexibility allowing instructors to sort by student, activity, or to view the entire class in spreadsheet view.

See the advertisement at the front of this text for more information.

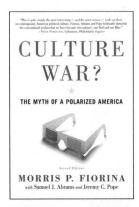

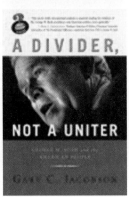

Great Questions in Politics Written by some of the most influential scholars and thinkers in political science, each book in this series examines a major question in American politics, offers a new perspective on our political system, and challenges conventional wisdom and prevailing attitudes.

Package any of the Great Questions in Politics books with *The Struggle for Democracy* and receive a 10 percent discount.

- *Culture War? The Myth of a Polarized America,* Morris. P. Fiorina, Stanford University; Samuel J. Abrams, Harvard University; and Jeremy C. Pope, Stanford University (ISBN 0-321-36606-9) This text combines polling data with a compelling narrative to debunk commonly believed myths about American politics—particularly the claim that Americans are deeply divided in their fundamental political views.

- *Governing by Campaigning: The Politics of the Bush Presidency,* 2007 Edition, George C. Edwards III, Texas A&M University (ISBN 0-205-52962-3) This brief volume, by one of the foremost experts on the presidency, explores how the Bush administration has attempted sweeping changes in public policy—without broad support for doing so—by taking its case to the American public more than any other president in history.

- *A Divider, Not a Uniter: George W. Bush and the American People: The 2006 Election and Beyond,* Gary C. Jacobson, University of California, San Diego (ISBN 0-205-52974-7) This brief, engaging book is rich in data and analyzes the reasons the public is so divided along party lines about George W. Bush.

- *Is Voting for Young People?* with New Postscript on New Forms of Citizen Engagement, Martin P. Wattenberg, University of California, Irvine (ISBN 0-205-51807-9) This accessible, provocative, and brief book explores the reasons the young are less and less likely to follow politics and vote in the United States, as well as many other established democracies, and suggests ways of changing that.

- *Seven Sins of American Foreign Policy,* Loch K. Johnson, University of Georgia (ISBN 0-321-41585-X) This brief, accessible book by renowned intelligence and foreign policy expert, Loch Johnson, examines seven major shortcomings—"sins"—in American foreign policy over several administrations that have generated pervasive negative attitudes toward the United States, cost us friendship and support, and impaired our ability to advance our international interests.

- *Congressional Travels: Places, Connections, and Authenticity,* Richard F. Fenno Jr., University of Rochester (ISBN 0-321-47071-0) This book argues that authenticity—knowing what a representative is like in his or her district and looking beyond mere roll-call voting—contributes significantly to understanding the full body of work done by our members of Congress. It further posits, by recounting Fenno's life's work, that the best way to gain a sense of authenticity is to do what Fenno is most famous for—making multiple trips and spending a great deal of time observing representatives at home, with their constituents, in their districts.

Study Site for American Government
(www.longmanamericangovernment.com) This online course companion provides a wealth of resources for students and instructors using Longman American government texts. Containing practice tests, flashcards, and Web explorations, the Study Site for American government helps students quickly master the fundamentals, review a subject for understanding, or prepare for an exam.

Study Guide (ISBN 0-205-51965-2) Written by George Gonzalez of the University of Miami and Mary Carns of Stephen F. Austin State University, this printed study guide includes chapter outlines, key terms, practice tests, and critical thinking questions.

Research Navigator and Research Navigator Guide Research Navigator is a comprehensive website comprising three exclusive databases of credible and reliable source material for research and for student assignments: EBSCO's ContentSelect Academic Journal Database, the *New York Times* Search by Subject Archive, and "Best of the Web" Link Library. The site also includes an extensive help section. The Research Navigator Guide provides your students with access to the Research Navigator website and includes reference material and hints about conducting online research. Available at no additional charge to qualified college adopters when packaged with the text.

Voices of Dissent: Critical Readings in American Politics, **Seventh Edition** (ISBN 0-205-56001-6) Edited by William F. Grover, St. Michael's College, and Joseph G. Peschek, Hamline University, this collection of critical essays goes beyond the debate between mainstream liberalism and conservatism to fundamentally challenge the status quo. Available at a discount when ordered packaged with the text.

Ten Things That Every American Government Student Should Read (ISBN 0-205-28969-X) We asked American government instructors across the country to vote for 10 things beyond the text that they believe every student should read and put them in this brief and useful reader edited by Karen O'Connor of the American University. Available at no additional charge when ordered packaged with the text.

Choices: An American Government Database Reader This customizable reader allows instructors to choose from a database of more than 300 readings to create a reader that exactly matches their course needs. Go to **www.pearsoncustom.com/database/choices.html** for more information.

Newsweek **Magazine Discount Subscription** Students receive 12 issues of *Newsweek* at more than 80 percent off the regular price. An excellent way for students to keep up with current events.

New York Times **Discount Subscription** A 10-week subscription for only $20! Contact your local Allyn & Bacon/Longman representative for more information.

Penguin-Longman Value Bundles Longman offers 25 Penguin Putnam titles at more than a 60 percent discount when packaged with any Longman text. A totally unique offer and a wonderful way to enhance students' understanding of concepts in American government. Please go to **www.ablongman.com/penguin** for more information.

Writing in Political Science, **Third Edition** (ISBN 0-321-21735-7) Written by Diane Schmidt, this guide takes students step-by-step through all aspects of writing in political science. Available at a discount when ordered packaged with any Longman textbook.

Longman State Politics Series

***Texas*, Fourth Edition**   (ISBN 0-321-38459-8) Written by Debra St. John, this is a 90-page primer on state and local government and issues in Texas. Available at no additional cost when shrink-wrapped with the text.

Annotated 1876 Texas Constitution   Annotated by Stefan D. Haag, Austin Community College, and Gary A. Keith, University of Texas, Austin, this supplement offers the full 1876 Texas Constitution integrated with a detailed primer examining the meaning and context of the Constitution's most significant language. This ancillary helps give students a deep understanding of what the 1876 Texas Constitution says, why it included the language it did, and what role this seminal document plays in the lives of Texans today.

***California*, Fifth Edition**   (ISBN 0-321-42764-5) Written by Barbara Stone, this is a 70-page primer on state and local government and issues in California. Available at no additional cost when shrink-wrapped with the text.

Florida   (ISBN 0-321-42763-7) Written by George Gonzalez, this is a 50-page primer on state and local government and issues in Florida. Available at no additional cost when shrink-wrapped with the text.

Georgia   (ISBN 0-321-42765-3) Written by Said L. Sewell and F. Carl Walton, this is a 70-page primer on state and local government and issues in Georgia. Available at no additional cost when shrink-wrapped with the text.

Acknowledgments

Writing and producing an introductory textbook is an incredibly complex and cooperative enterprise in which many people besides the authors play roles. We would like to take the opportunity to thank them, one and all. We start with the many wonderful people at Pearson Longman who worked on this edition, including development editor Diane Culhane, production manager Donna DeBenedictis, Sue Nodine and her colleagues at Elm Street Publishing Services for design and production work, photo researcher Shaie Dively, and senior marketing manager Elizabeth Fogarty. Special thanks go to Eric Stano, who has always believed in this book project and in us, and whose guidance helped make the fifth, sixth, and seventh editions so successful. We hope that his wise counsel on revisions for the eighth edition will have a similar result.

Professor Michael Ward of the University of Washington helped with the "Mapping American Politics" feature. Mike patiently taught us about cartograms and created the cartograms that appear in this edition of the book. We thank him for his contribution to the eighth edition and for his enduring friendship and support on this and other projects.

We would also like to thank our students for helping to shape this book. The undergraduates in our introductory courses in American government and politics at the University of Colorado, Boulder, and Northwestern University had much to say about what they liked and didn't like in the book, and they were more than willing to tell us how it might be improved. Our many graduate student TAs in these introductory courses, moreover, were extremely helpful in advising us about how the seventh edition was working or not working as a teaching tool in the classroom. Special thanks go to University of Colorado graduate student Tom McFarland, who worked diligently and effectively as Ed Greenberg's research assistant.

Over the years, Longman has enlisted the help of many political scientists on various aspects of this project. Their advice was especially valuable, and the final version of the book is far better than it would have been without their help. We would like to extend our appreciation to the following political scientists, who gave so generously of their time and expertise through the eight editions of *The Struggle for Democracy* and its supplements:

Ula Adeoye, *University of Illinois–Chicago*

Gordon Alexandre, *Glendale Community College*

John Ambacher, *Framingham State College*

Sheldon Appleton, *Oakland University*

Jeffrey M. Ayres, *Lake Superior State University*

Ross K. Baker, *Rutgers University*

Manley Elliott Banks II, *Virginia Commonwealth University*

Ryan Barrilleaux, *University of Miami*

Ken Baxter, *San Joaquin Delta College*

Todd Belt, *University of Hawaii*

Stephen Bennett, *University of Cincinnati*

Bill Bianco, *Duke University*

Joel Bloom, *University of Oregon*

Melanie J. Blumberg, *University of Akron*

Joseph P. Boyle, *Cypress College*

Richard Braunstein, *University of South Dakota*

Evelyn Brodkin, *University of Chicago*

James Bromeland, *Winona State University*

Barbara Brown, *Southern Illinois University–Carbondale*

Charles R. Brown, Jr., *Central Washington University*

Joseph S. Brown, *Baylor University*

Mark Byrnes, *Middle Tennessee State University*

David E. Camacho, *Northern Arizona University*

Mary Carns, *Stephen F. Austin University*

Cynthia Carter, *Florida Community College*

Jim Carter, *Sam Houston State University*

Gregory Casey, *University of Missouri*

Carl D. Cavalli, *North Georgia College and State University*

James Chalmers, *Wayne State University*

Paul Chardoul, *Grand Rapids Community College*

Mark A. Cichock, *University of Texas at Arlington*

Alan J. Cigler, *University of Kansas*

David Cingranelli, *State University of New York at Binghamton*

Natale H. Cipollina, *CUNY Baruch College*

Dewey M. Clayton, *University of Louisville*

John Coleman, *University of Wisconsin*

Ken Collier, *University of Kansas*

Lee Collins, *Monmouth College*

Edward Collins Jr., *University of Maine*

Richard W. Crockett, *Western Illinois University*

Lane Crothers, *Illinois State University*

Landon Curry, *University of Texas*

Paul B. Davis, *Truckee Meadows Community College*

Christine Day, *University of New Orleans*

Alan Draper, *St. Lawrence University*

Euel Elliott, *University of Texas*

Bob England, *Oklahoma State University*

Robert S. Erikson, *University of Houston*

Jasmine Farrier, *University of Louisville*

Thomas Ferguson, *University of Massachusetts, Boston*

M. Lauren Ficaro, *Chapman University*

Brian J. Fogarty, *University of North Carolina, Chapel Hill*

G. David Garson, *North Carolina State University*

John Geer, *Arizona State University*

Scott D. Gerber, *College of William and Mary*

Thomas Gillespie, *Seton Hall University*

Gregory Goldey, *Morehead State University*

Doris A. Graber, *University of Illinois*

John Green, *University of Akron*

Daniel P. Gregory, *El Camino Community College*

Eric E. Grier, *Georgia State University*

Mark F. Griffith, *The University of West Alabama*

Bruce E. Gronbeck, *University of Iowa*

Maria Guido, *Bentley College*

Robert Gumbrecht, *Merritt College*

Richard Haesly, *California State University–Long Beach*

Russell L. Hanson, *Indiana University*

Kevin R. Hardwick, *Canisius College*

Valerie Heitshusen, *University of Missouri*

Peter B. Heller, *Manhattan College*

Richard Herrara, *Arizona State University*

Roberta Herzberg, *Indiana University*

Seth Hirshorn, *University of Michigan*

Eugene Hogan, *Western Washington University*

John W. Homan, *Boise State University*

Marilyn Howard, *Columbus State Community College*

Ronald J. Hrebnar, *University of Utah*

David Hunt, *Triton College*

Jon Hurwitz, *University of Pittsburgh*

James Hutter, *Iowa State University*

Gary C. Jacobson, *University of California at San Diego*

William Jacoby, *University of South Carolina*

Willoughby Jarrell, *Kennesaw State College*

Jodi Jenkin, *Fullerton College*

Christopher B. Jones, *Eastern Oregon State University*

Mark R. Joslyn, *University of Kansas*

William Kelly, *Auburn University*

Fred Kramer, *University of Massachusetts*

Richard Lehne, *Rutgers University*

Jan E. Leighley, *Texas A&M University*

Joel Lieske, *Cleveland State University*

R. Philip Loy, *Taylor University*

Stan Luger, *University of Northern Colorado*

Maurice Mangum, *Southern Illinois University*

Dean E. Mann, *University of California*

Joseph R. Marbach, *Seton Hall University*

Michael D. Martinez, *University of Florida*

Peter Mathews, *Cypress College*

Louise Mayo, *County College of Morris*

Steve Mazurana, *University of Northern Colorado*

Michael W. McCann, *University of Washington*

Carroll R. McKibbin, *California Polytechnic State University*

William P. McLauchlan, *Purdue University*

Michael E. Meagher, *University of Missouri*

Stanley Melnick, *Valencia Community College*

Charles K. Menifield, *Murray State University*

Norma H. E. Miller, *South Carolina State University*

Neil Milner, *University of Hawaii*

Paul Moke, *Wilmington College*

Kristen R. Monroe, *Princeton University*

Mike Munger, *University of Texas*

Laurel A. Myer, *Sinclair Community College*

Albert Nelson, *University of Wisconsin, La Crosse*

David Nice, *Washington State University*

Charles Noble, *California State University at Long Beach*

Maureen Rand Oakley, *Mount St. Mary's College*

Colleen M. O'Connor, *San Diego Mesa College*

Daniel J. O'Connor, *California State University at Long Beach*

David J. Olson, *University of Washington*

Laura Katz Olson, *Lehigh University*

John Orman, *Fairfield University*

Marvin Overby, *University of Mississippi*

Elizabeth M. H. Paddock, *Drury College*

Kenneth T. Palmer, *University of Maine*

Toby Paone, *St. Charles Community College*

David Paul, *The Ohio State University–Newark*

Arthur Paulson, *Southern Connecticut State University*

Lisa Perez, *Austin Community College*

Joseph Peschek, *Hamline University*

Mark P. Petracca, *University of California*

Eric Plutzer, *Pennsylvania State University*

Larry Pool, *Mountain View College*

Amy Pritchett, *Cypress College*

John D. Redifer, *Mesa State College*

Richard Reitano, *Dutchess Community College*

Curtis G. Reithel, *University of Wisconsin, La Crosse*

Russell D. Renka, *Southeast Missouri State University*

Richard C. Rich, *Virginia Polytechnic Institute and State University*

Leroy N. Rieselbach, *Indiana University*

Sue Tolleson Rinehart, *Texas Tech University*

Phyllis F. Rippey, *Western Illinois University*

David Robinson, *University of Houston–Downtown*

Pamela Rogers, *University of Wisconsin*

David W. Romero, *University of California*

Francis E. Rourke, *Johns Hopkins University*

David C. Saffell, *Ohio Northern University*

Donald L. Scruggs, *Stephens College*

Jim Seroka, *University of North Florida*

L. Earl Shaw, *Northern Arizona University*

John M. Shebb, *University of Tennessee*

Mark Silverstein, *Boston University*

Morton Sipress, *University of Wisconsin, Eau Claire*

Henry B. Sirgo, *McNeese State University*

David A. Smeltzer, *Portland State University*

Neil Snortland, *University of Arkansas, Little Rock*

George Wade Swicord, *South Florida Community College*

David Tabb, *San Francisco State University*

C. Neal Tate, *University of North Texas*

James Lance Taylor, *University of San Francisco*

Robert Thomas, *University of Houston*

Richard J. Timpone, *State University of New York at Stony Brook*

Eric Ulsaner, *University of Maryland*

José M. Vadi, *California State Polytechnic University, Pomona*

Elliot Vittes, *University of Central Florida*

Charles Walcott, *University of Minnesota*

Benjamin Walter, *Vanderbilt University*

Susan Weissman, *St. Mary's College of California*

Jonathan P. West, *University of Miami*

Nelson Wikstrom, *Virginia Commonwealth University*

Leonard A. Williams, *Manchester College*

Daniel Wirls, *Merrill College*

Eugene R. Wittkopf, *Louisiana State University*

James Woods, *University of Toledo*

Teresa Wright, *California State University–Long Beach*

Jay Zarowitz, *Muskegon Community College*

Michele Zebich-Knos, *Kennesaw State University*

Finally, we thank you, the instructors and students who use this book. May it bring you success.

EDWARD S. GREENBERG
BENJAMIN I. PAGE

PART 1 Introduction: Main Themes

In Part 1, we explain the overall plan of the book, describe the main themes you will see in each chapter, and suggest why these topics are important for the study of American government and politics. We introduce the central dramatic thread that ties the book together: the struggle for democracy. We make the point that American political life has always involved a struggle among individuals, groups, classes, and institutions over the meaning, extent, and practice of democracy. Finally, in this part, we suggest that although democracy has made great progress over the course of U.S. history, it remains only imperfectly realized and is threatened by new problems that only vigilant and active citizens can solve.

CHAPTER 1

Democracy and American Politics

IN THIS CHAPTER

- What democracy means, and how it can be used as a standard to evaluate American government and politics

- A systematic way to think about how government and politics work

Robert Moses and the Struggle for African American Voting Rights

The right to vote in elections is fundamental to democracy. But many Americans won the right to vote only after long struggles. It took more than 30 years from the adoption of the Constitution, for instance, for most states to allow people without property to vote. Women gained the right to vote in all U.S. elections only in 1920, and young people ages 18 to 20 did so only beginning in 1971. African Americans in the South were not able to vote in any numbers until after 1965 despite the existence of the Fifteenth Amendment—which says that the vote cannot be denied to American citizens on the basis of race, color, or previous condition of servitude—adopted in 1870.

In Mississippi in the early 1960s, only 5 percent of African Americans were registered to vote, and none held elective office, although they accounted for 43 percent of the population. In Walthall County, Mississippi, not a single black was registered, although roughly 3,000 were eligible to vote.[1] What kept them away from the polls was a combination of exclusionary voting registration rules, economic pressures, and physical intimidation and violence directed against those brave enough to defy the prevailing political and social order. In Ruleville, Mississippi, Mrs. Fannie Lou Hamer was forced out of the house she was renting on a large plantation; fired from her job; and arrested, jailed, and beaten by police after she tried to register to vote.[2]

The Student Non-Violent Coordinating Committee (widely known by its initials, SNCC) launched its Voter Education Project in 1961 with the aim of ending black political isolation and powerlessness in the Deep South. Composed primarily of African American college students, SNCC aimed to increase black voter registration and to challenge exclusionary rules like the poll tax and the literacy test. SNCC also wanted to enter African American candidates in local elections. Its first step was to create "freedom schools" in some of the most segregated counties in Mississippi, Alabama, and Georgia to teach black citizens about their rights under the law and to encourage them to register to vote. Needless to say, SNCC volunteers tended to attract the malevolent attentions of police, local officials, and vigilantes.

The first of the freedom schools was founded in McComb, Mississippi, by a remarkable young man named Robert Parris Moses, who quit his job as a teacher in order to work with other young people in SNCC. Despite repeated threats to his life and more than a few physical attacks, Moses traveled the back roads of Amite and Walthall counties, meeting with small groups of black farmers and encouraging them to attend the SNCC freedom school. At the school, he showed them not only how to fill out the registration forms, but also how to read and interpret the constitution of Mississippi for the "literacy test" required to register to vote. Once people in the school gathered the courage to journey to the county seat

to try to register, Moses accompanied them to lend support and encouragement.

Moses paid a price. Over a period of a few months, he was arrested several times for purported traffic violations; attacked on the main street of Liberty, Mississippi, by the county sheriff's cousin and beaten with the butt end of a knife; assaulted by a mob behind the McComb County courthouse; hit by police and dragged into the stationhouse while standing in line at the voting registrar's office with one of his students; and jailed for not paying fines connected with his participation in civil rights demonstrations.

Despite the efforts of Bob Moses and other SNCC volunteers and the bravery of African Americans who dared to defy the rules of black political exclusion in Mississippi, African American voting registration barely increased in that state in the early 1960s. Black Americans in Mississippi would have to await the passage of the 1965 Voting Rights Act, which provided powerful federal government protections for all American citizens wishing to exercise their right to vote. The Voter Education Project, however, was one of the key building blocks of a powerful civil rights movement (see Chapter 8) that would eventually force federal action in the 1960s to support the citizenship rights (or civil rights) of African Americans in the South.

Robert Moses and many other African Americans in Mississippi were willing to risk all they had, even their lives, to gain full and equal citizenship in the United States. Likewise, throughout our history, Americans from all walks of life have joined the struggle to make the United States a more democratic country. The same thing is happening in many parts of the world today. We live in an age of democratic aspiration and upsurge; people the world over are demanding the right to govern themselves and control their own destinies. Americans are participants in this drama, not only because American political ideas and institutions have often provided inspiration for democratic movements in other countries but also because the struggle for democracy continues in our own society. Although honored and celebrated, democracy remains an unfinished project in the United States. The continuing struggle to expand and perfect democracy is a major feature of American history and a defining characteristic of our politics today. It is a central theme of this book. ■

Democracy

Why should there not be a patient confidence in the ultimate justice of the people? Is there any better, or equal, hope in the world?

—ABRAHAM LINCOLN, FIRST INAUGURAL ADDRESS

When people live together in groups and communities, it is generally understood that a governmental entity of some sort is needed to provide law and order; to protect against external aggressors; and to provide essential public goods such as roads, waste disposal, education, and clean water. If government is both necessary and inevitable, certain questions become unavoidable: Who is to govern? How are those who govern to be encouraged to serve the best interests of society? How can governments be induced to make policies and laws that citizens consider legitimate and worth obeying? In short, what is the best form of government? For most Americans—and for increasing numbers of people in other places—the answer is clear: democracy.

Democracy's central idea is that ordinary people want to rule themselves and are capable of doing so. This idea has proved enormously popular, not only with Americans, but with people all over the world.[3] To be sure, some people would give top priority to other things besides self-government as a requirement for the good society, including such things as safety and security, or the need to have religious law and values determine what government does. Nevertheless, the appealing notion that ordinary people can and should rule themselves has spread to all corners of the globe, and the number of people living in democratic societies has increased over the years.

In addition to its intrinsic appeal, there are other reasons democracy might be superior to other forms of political organization. Some political thinkers have argued, for example, that democracy is the form of government that best protects human rights because it is the only one based on a recognition of the intrinsic worth and equality of human beings. Others believe that democracy is the form of government most likely to reach rational decisions because it can count on the pooled knowledge and expertise of a society's entire population. Other thinkers have claimed that democracies are more stable and long-lasting because their leaders, elected by their citizens, enjoy a strong sense of legitimacy. Still others suggest that democracy is the form of government most conducive to economic growth and material well-being, a claim that is strongly supported by research findings. Others, finally, believe that democracy is the form of government under which human beings, because they are free, are best able to develop their natural capacities and talents.[4] There are many compelling reasons, then, why democracy has been preferred by so many people.

Americans have supported the idea of self-government and have helped make the nation more democratic over the course of our history.[5] Nevertheless, democracy remains a work in progress in the United States, an evolving aspiration rather than a finished product. Our goal in this book is to help you think carefully about the quality and progress of democracy in the United States. We want to help you reach your own independent judgments about the degree to

VIDEO DEBATE

American Democracy and Human Rights

which politics and government in the United States make our country more or less democratic. We want to help you draw your own conclusions about which political practices and institutions in the United States encourage and sustain popular self-rule and which ones discourage and undermine it. To do this, we must be clear about the meaning of democracy in the modern world.

Democratic Origins

Many of our ideas about democracy originated with the ancient Greeks. The Greek roots of the word *democracy* are *demos,* meaning "the people," and *kratein,* meaning "to rule." **Democracy,** then, is "rule by the people" or, to put it another way, self-government by the *many,* as opposed to the *few* or the *one.*

democracy
A system of rule by the people, defined by the existence of popular sovereignty, political equality, and political liberty.

Most Western philosophers and rulers before the eighteenth century were not friendly to the idea of rule that the *many* can and should rule themselves. Most believed that governing was a difficult art, requiring the greatest sophistication, intelligence, character, and training—certainly not the province of ordinary people. Aristotle expressed this view in his classic work *Politics,* where he observed that democracy "is a government in the hands of men of low birth, no property, and vulgar employments." Most preferred rule by a select *few* (such as an aristocracy, in which a hereditary nobility rules) or by an enlightened *one,* somewhat akin to the philosopher king described by Plato in his *Republic.* The idea that ordinary people might rule themselves represents an important departure from such beliefs.[6] In practice, throughout human history, most governments have been quite undemocratic.

Inherent in the idea of self-rule by ordinary people is an understanding that government must serve *all* its people and that ultimately none but the people themselves can be relied on to know and hence to act in accordance with their own values and interests. Power in any other hands will eventually lead to **tyranny,** a society where leaders abuse their power.

tyranny
The abuse of power by a ruler or a government.

Interestingly, democracy in the sense described here is more a set of utopian ideas than a description of real societies. Athens of the fifth-century BCE is usually cited as the purest form of democracy that ever existed. There, all public policies were decided upon in periodic assemblies of Athenian citizens—but many people, including women, slaves, and immigrants, were still excluded from such

Rule by the Few

Although President Mahmoud Ahmadinejab was elected to his office by the Iranian people and has been quite visible in defending the country's nuclear program, real power in the country is exercised by an un-elected clergy. Here, the president receives a certificate of appreciation from Supreme Leader Ayatollah Ali Khamenei.

Athenians Practice Direct Democracy

The essence of the classical Greek idea of democracy was face-to-face deliberations among citizens in open assemblies. This is difficult to achieve in societies with large populations where democracy depends instead on the election of representatives.

Comparing Political Landscapes

assemblies. Nevertheless, the existence of a society in Athens where "a substantial number of free, adult males were entitled as citizens to participate freely in government"[7] proved to be a powerful example of what was possible for those who believed that rule by ordinary people was the best form of government.

A handful of other cases of popular rule kept the democratic idea alive across the centuries. Beginning as early as the fifth-century BCE, for example, India enjoyed long periods marked by spirited and broadly inclusive public debate and discourse on public issues.[8] In the Roman Republic, male citizens elected the consuls, the chief magistrates of the powerful city-state. Also, in the Middle Ages in Europe, many cities were governed directly by the people (at least by men who owned property) rather than by nobles, church, or crown. Further, the Russian village, largely self-governing from the early Middle Ages to modern times, inspired democratic reformers in that autocratic society ruled by all-powerful czars. The short-lived but self-governing utopian communities founded by Robert Owen and Charles Fourier in the United States and France in the early nineteenth century also helped spread the democratic idea. And finally, the New England town meeting, where local people rule their communities directly, has inspired many democrats, as has the success of the Israeli Kibbutz, where assemblies of adult members directly decide all economic, social, and educational policies affecting their community.

Direct Versus Representative Democracy

direct democracy

A form of political decision making in which the public business is decided by all citizens meeting in small assemblies.

To the ancient Greeks, democracy meant rule by the common people exercised *directly* in open assemblies. They believed that democracy implied face-to-face deliberation and decision making about the public business. **Direct democracy** requires, however, that all citizens be able to meet together regularly to debate and decide the issues of the day. Such a thing was possible in fifth-century BCE Athens, which was small enough to allow all male citizens to gather in one place. In Athens, moreover, male citizens had time to meet and to deliberate because women provided household labor and slaves accounted for most production.

Because direct, participatory democracy is possible only in small communities where citizens with abundant leisure time can meet often on a face-to-face basis, it is an unworkable arrangement for a large and widely dispersed society such as the United States.[9] Democracy in large societies must take the representative form, since millions of citizens cannot meet in open assembly. By **representative democracy** we mean a system in which the people select others, called *representatives,* to act in their place.

Although representative (or indirect) democracy seems to be the only form of democracy possible in large-scale societies, some political commentators argue that the participatory aspects of direct democracy are worth preserving as an ideal and that certain domains of everyday life—workplaces and schools, for instance—could be enriched by more direct democratic practices.[10] It is worth pointing out, moreover, that direct democracy can and does flourish in some local communities today. In many New England towns, for example, citizens make decisions directly at town meetings. At the state level, the initiative process allows voters in many states to bypass the legislature to make policies or amend state constitutions. Some observers believe that the Internet will enable more people to become directly involved in political deliberations and decision making in the future.[11]

representative democracy

Indirect democracy, in which the people rule through elected representatives.

Democracy and the Internet

Fundamental Principles of Representative Democracy

In large societies such as our own, then, democracy means rule by the people, exercised indirectly through representatives elected by the people. Still, this definition is not sufficiently precise to use as a standard by which to evaluate the American political system. To help further clarify the definition of democracy, we add three additional benchmarks drawn from both the scholarly literature and popular understandings about democracy. These benchmarks are *popular sovereignty, political equality,* and *political liberty.* A society in which all three flourish, we argue, is a healthy representative democracy. A society in which any of the three is absent or impaired falls short of the representative democratic ideal. Let us see what each of them means.

Popular Sovereignty **Popular sovereignty** means that the ultimate source of all public authority is the people and that government does the people's bidding. If ultimate authority resides not in the hands of the *many* but in the hands of the *few* (as in an aristocratic order), or of the *one* (whether a benevolent sovereign or a ruthless dictator), democracy does not exist. Nor does it exist if government consistently fails to follow the preferences and serve the interests of the people.

How can we recognize popular sovereignty when we see it? The following six conditions are especially important.

popular sovereignty

The basic principle of democracy that the people ultimately rule.

Government Policies Reflect the Wishes of the People The most obvious sign of popular sovereignty is the existence of a close correspondence between what government does and what the people want it to do. It is hard to imagine a situation in which the people rule but government officials make policies contrary to the people's wishes.

This much seems obvious. However, does the democratic ideal require that government officials always do exactly what the people want, right away, responding to every whim and passing fancy of the public? This question has

You Are the Director of Economic Development for the city of Los Angeles, California

troubled many democratic theorists, and most have answered that democracy is best served when representatives and other public officials respond to what might be called the "deliberative will" of the people: what the people want after deliberating among themselves about an issue.[12] We might, then, want to speak of democracy as a system in which government policies conform to what the people want over some period of time.

Government Leaders Are Selected in Competitive Elections　The existence of a close match between what the people want and what government does, however, does not necessarily prove that the people are sovereign. In a dictatorship, for example, the will of the people can be consciously shaped to correspond to the wishes of the leadership. For the direction of influence to flow from the people to the leadership, some mechanism must exist for forcing leaders to be responsive to the people's wishes and to be responsible to them for their actions. The best mechanism ever invented to achieve these goals is the contested election in which both existing and aspiring government leaders must periodically face the people for judgment. (See the "Mapping American Politics" feature on pages 10–11 on competition in U.S. presidential elections.)

Elections Are Free and Fair　If elections are to be useful as a way to keep government leaders responsive and responsible, they must be conducted in a fashion that is free and fair. By free, we mean that there is no coercion of voters or election officials and that virtually all citizens are able to run for office and vote in elections. By fair, we mean, among other things, that election rules do not favor some over others and that ballots are accurately counted.

People Participate in the Political Process　Although government leaders may be elected in a balloting process that is free and fair, such a process is useful in conveying the will of the people and keeping leaders responsive and responsible only if the people participate. If elections and other forms of political participation only attract a minority of the eligible population, they cannot serve as a way to understand what the broad public wants or as an instrument forcing leaders to pay attention to it. Widespread participation in politics—including voting in elections, contacting public officials, working with others to bring matters to public attention, joining associations that work to shape government actions, and more—is necessary to ensure not only that responsive representatives will be chosen, but that they will have continuous incentives to pay attention to the people. Because widespread participation is so central to popular sovereignty, we can say that the less political participation there is in a society, the weaker the democracy. (See "By the Numbers: Is voting turnout declining in the United States?" on pages 12–13 to get a sense of how much Americans participate.)

High-Quality Information Is Available　If people are to form authentic and rational attitudes about public policies and political leaders, they must have access to accurate political information, insightful interpretations, and vigorous debate. These are the responsibility of government officials, opposition parties, opinion leaders, and the news media. If false or biased information is provided, if policies are not challenged and debated, or if misleading interpretations of the political world (or none at all) are offered, the people cannot form opinions in accordance with their values and interests, and popular sovereignty cannot be said to exist.

The Majority Rules　How can the opinions and preferences of many individual citizens be combined into a single binding decision? Since unanimity is unlikely—so the insistence that new policies should require unanimous

TIMELINE

The Initiative and Referendum

Getting Out the Student Vote

Democracy requires broad citizen participation in public affairs. Special efforts have been made in recent years—much like these at the University of Texas at Austin—to increase voting registration and turnout among young people, a group with especially low participation rates in American elections.

agreement for them to be adopted would simply enshrine the status quo—reaching a decision requires a decision rule. If the actions of government are to respond to all citizens, each citizen being counted equally, the only decision rule that makes sense is **majority rule,** which means that the government adopts the policy that the *most* people want.[13] In practical terms, what this means is that the popular will, formed in the best circumstances after careful deliberation, is discovered by ascertaining the positions on public issues of the majority of citizens. The only alternative to majority rule is minority rule, which would unacceptably elevate the *few* over the *many*.

majority rule

The form of political decision making in which policies are decided on the basis of what a majority of the people want.

Political Equality The second fundamental principle of democracy is **political equality,** the idea that each person carries the same weight in voting and other political decision making. Imagine, if you will, a society in which one person could cast 100 votes in an election, another person 50 votes, and still another 25 votes, while many unlucky folks had only 1 vote each—or none at all. We would surely find such an arrangement a curious one, especially if that society described itself as democratic. We would react in this way because equality of citizenship has always been central to the democratic ideal. Democracy is a way of making decisions in which each person has one, and only one, voice.

political equality

The principle that says that each person carries equal weight in the conduct of the public business.

Most people know this intuitively. Our sense of what is proper is offended, for instance, when some class of people is denied the right to vote in a society that boasts the outer trappings of democracy. The denial of citizenship rights to African Americans in the South before the passage of the 1965 Voting Rights Act is such an example. We count it as a victory for democracy when previously excluded groups win the right to vote.

Political equality also involves what the Fourteenth Amendment to the Constitution calls "equal protection," meaning that everyone in a democracy is

Mapping American Politics

Where the voters in America are purple

Introduction: Voting in elections in which people can choose among competing candidates and political parties is one of the hallmarks of democratic political systems. As we suggest in this chapter, democracy requires other things, such as political equality, civil liberties, and a free press, but competitive elections are essential. For the most part, at all levels of government in the United States, the most important public offices are filled by election, including that of the president. Both the map and the cartogram show the results from the 2004 presidential election won by Republican George W. Bush over Democrat John Kerry, focusing on turnout and competition between the candidates.

Different Maps; Different Stories: The standard geographic map of the United States on the left shows states won by George W. Bush (in red) and John Kerry (in blue). Election maps like this are widely distributed in newspapers, magazines, and television. However, they are misleading in a very fundamental way because they emphasize geographical space over people and overplay the partisan divisions in the country. They take no account of the relative populations of the states and exaggerate the political importance of large, underpopulated spaces. This map suggests a

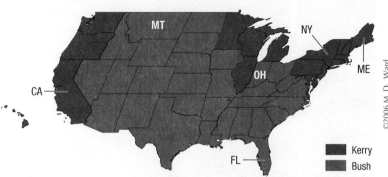

©2006 M. D. Ward

Standard U.S. Map, Red for Bush States, Blue for Kerry States

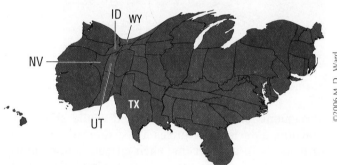

©2006 M. D. Ward

Size of States Adjusted to Reflect Voter Turnout; Mix of Red and Blue to Reflect Bush and Kerry Votes

country that is mostly red, or Republican, yet we know that the election contest in 2004 was very close. So is there a better way to visualize who voted and for whom in 2004?

---

treated the same by government. Government programs, for example, should not favor one group over another or deny benefits or protections to identifiable groups in the population, such as racial and religious minorities. Nor should people be treated better or worse than others by law enforcement agencies and the courts. Taken together, political equality and equal treatment are sometimes called **civil rights,** a subject we will address in more detail in Chapter 16.

Does democracy require that inequalities in the distribution of income and wealth not be too extreme? While many do not think this to be the case, thinkers as diverse as Aristotle, Rousseau, and Jefferson thought so, believing that great inequalities in economic circumstances are almost always translated into political inequality.[14] Political scientist Robert Dahl describes the problem in the following way:

civil rights

Guarantees by government of equal citizenship to all social groups.

The map on the bottom is called a *cartogram*. We will be using cartograms throughout this book to learn more about American politics. A cartogram is a way to visually present information that is organized on a geographical basis, with each unit (in this case, state) sized in proportion to the data being reported (in this case, number of voters). So rather than thinking of the cartogram as a "map," think of it as a figure displaying some aspect of American politics in a geographical fashion. Sometimes a cartogram shows geographical units in relation to one another in direct proportion to some simple measure, such as population size. Sometimes a cartogram shows geographical units drawn to reflect some measure on a per-capita basis (such as the distribution of homeland security defense dollars to states divided by population size). Sometimes a cartogram shows geographical units expanded or diminished from their "normal" geographical scale using mathematical transformations that enable the viewer to easily compare units (such as states and countries) while preserving the rough outlines of the normal shapes of these units. In each "Mapping American Politics" feature in this book, we will specify clearly what sort of cartogram we are using.

The cartogram here uses a simple and direct proportion; each state is sized according to the number of votes cast in the 2004 presidential election. By adjusting the size of the states to reflect the number of citizens who voted for president in 2004, this cartogram shows clearly that California, Florida, New York, Texas, and Ohio have lots of voters and Idaho, Wyoming, Montana, Nebraska, and Maine have relatively few.

Color is often used to convey additional information in cartograms, as we do here. The proportions of blue (for Democratic voters) and red (for Republican voters) in each state reflect the proportions of Democratic and Republican voters in that state. The result is a map with various shades of purple, as all states contain a mix of Democratic and Republican voters. The closer a state comes to the blue end of the spectrum, the more Democratic voters it has relative to Republicans; the closer a state comes to the red end of the spectrum, the more Republicans it has relative to Democrats. There are no pure red or blue states, no pure Republican or Democratic states. Even states that are deep purple (more blue), such as California, have many Republican voters, while states that are more red, such as Utah and Wyoming, have many Democratic voters.

What Do You Think? Does the cartogram convey more information than the conventional map about competition in the 2004 election and where the most voters are located? Do you see anything interesting in either the map or the cartogram that we have not mentioned here? How about your own state? Does anything about its portrayal in the cartogram surprise you?

Note: In these maps, and in all remaining maps in the "Mapping American Politics" feature, for reasons of presentation, Alaska is not shown (although information about Alaska is included in calculations where relevant), and Hawaii is moved closer to the mainland.

Source: **http://clerk.house.gov/members/electionInfo/2004/ Table.htm.** Details about methods for producing such cartograms can be found in the pioneering publication by Michael T. Gastner and Mark E.J. Newman, "Diffusion-Based Method for Producing Density-Equalizing Maps," *Proceedings of the National Academy of Sciences* 101 (May 18, 2004) pp. 7499–7504.

> *If citizens are unequal in economic resources, so are they likely to be unequal in political resources; and political equality will be impossible to achieve. In the extreme case, a minority of rich will possess so much greater political resources than other citizens that they will control the state, dominate the majority of citizens, and empty the democratic process of all content.*[15]

In later chapters, we will see that income and wealth are distributed in a highly unequal way in the United States and that this inequality is sometimes translated into great inequalities among people and groups in the political arena. In such circumstances, the norm of political equality is violated.

Political Liberty   The third element of democracy is **political liberty.** Political liberty refers to basic freedoms essential to the formation and expression of

political liberty

The principle that citizens in a democracy are protected from government interference in the exercise of a range of basic freedoms, such as the freedoms of speech, association, and conscience.

11

By the Numbers

Is voting turnout declining in the United States?

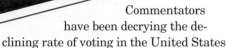

Commentators have been decrying the declining rate of voting in the United States for many years now. All sorts of explanations have been advanced to explain the decline; all sorts of remedies for the problem have been proposed. But what if there really hasn't been a decline in voting at all?

Why It Matters: We have argued in this chapter that widespread participation in voting and other civic activities is one measure of the health of democracy in any society. If the way we measure participation is inaccurate, we cannot do a good job of assessing the quality of democracy in the United States, or identify what problems and shortcomings in our political system need to be addressed to make it more democratic.

Behind the Traditional Voting Turnout Measure: Voter turnout in American elections *normally* is determined by a very simple calculation: the number of people who vote in a national election divided by the number of people in the United States who are of voting age, that is, 18 years of age and older. The denominator for this equation—voting age population, or VAP—is provided by the Census Bureau. But there is a problem: The denominator may be misleading, because it includes millions of people who are not eligible to vote at all: residents who are not citizens, felons (some states), people with past felonies (some states), and the mentally incompetent. If we calculated voting turnout as the number of voters divided by the number of people in the United States who *actually* are eligible to vote—the voting eligible population, or VEP—turnout would always be higher than is now reported because the denominator would be smaller.

Calculating a VEP-based Measure of Turnout: Two political scientists, Michael McDonald and Samuel Popkin, have done us the great service of transforming the Census Bureau's VAP (voting age population) number to a VEP (voting eligible population) number for every national election from 1948 to 2004, pulling out noncitizens and ineligible felons and former felons in states where they cannot vote. Using the voting eligible population rather than the resident population over the age of 18 as the denominator in the voting turnout equation, McDonald and Popkin's figures show the following:

- Voting turnout is actually 4 or 5 percentage points higher in recent elections than usually reported.
- Voting turnout declined between 1960 and 1972 regardless of which method was used. However, voting turnout appears to decline fur-

majority opinion and its translation into public policies. These essential liberties include the freedoms of speech, of conscience and religion, of the press, and of assembly and association, embodied in the First Amendment to the U.S. Constitution. Philosopher John Locke thought that individual rights and liberty were so fundamental to the good society that their preservation was the central responsibility of any legitimate government and that their protection is the very reason people agreed to enter into a **social contract** to form government in the first place.

Without these First Amendment freedoms, as well as those freedoms involving protections against arbitrary arrest and imprisonment, the other fundamental principles of democracy could not exist. Popular sovereignty cannot be guaranteed if people are prevented from participating in politics or if opposition to the government is crushed by the authorities. Popular sovereignty cannot prevail if the voice of the people is silenced and if citizens are not free

social contract

A philosophical device, used by Enlightenment thinkers such as Locke, Rousseau, and Harrington, to suggest that governments are only legitimate if they are created by a voluntary compact among the people.

ther after 1972 only when using the traditional VAP method; the VEP method shows no decline in voting turnout over the past 30 years.

- Voting turnout jumped substantially in 2004 for the hotly contested race between John Kerry and George W. Bush, whether using the VEP numbers or the VAP numbers, although the former were significantly higher.

The main reason voting turnout has declined in recent elections using the traditional VAP method is that the number of people who are residents of the United States but who are not eligible to vote in American elections has increased at every election, mostly due to the number of noncitizens living here.

Criticism of the VEP-based Measure of Turnout:
Some critics suggest that the old way of calculating voting turnout serves a very useful purpose, namely, pointing out how far short we fall in our claim to being a democratic society. The low turnout number reported by VAP, it is argued, helps focus attention on the issue of nonvoting in the United States and encourages efforts to reform voting rules to increase turnout.

What to Watch For:
When you come across voter turnout numbers, pay attention to whether the figure has been calculated based on the voting age population or on the voting eligible population. The latter will always be higher than the former. It is important to be aware that both methods of calculating turnout make sense in their own way; each has a slightly different story to tell.

What Do You Think?
Do you think we can and should try to increase the rate of voting turnout in

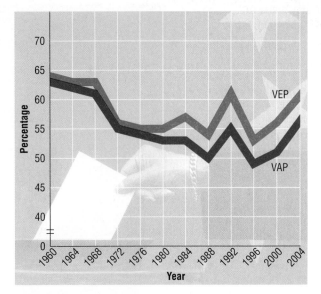

Voting Turnout in Presidential Elections, by Year

the United States, which is low in comparison to other democratic countries, regardless of which method of calculation we use? What do you think about making noncitizens—who pay taxes and are subject to U.S. laws—eligible to vote? How about former felons who have paid their debt to society?

Source: Michael P. McDonald and Samuel L. Popkin, "The Myth of the Vanishing Voter," *The American Political Science Review,* 95, no. 4 (December 2001), pp. 963–974; and Michael McDonald, "Voting-Age and Voting-Eligible Population Turnout Rates" (ElectioNexus, **http://elections.gmu.edu/VEP_VEP.htm;** 2005).

to argue and debate, based on their own ideas, values, and personal beliefs, and form and express their political opinions.[16] Political equality is violated if some people can speak out but others cannot.

For most people today, democracy and liberty are inseparable. The concept of *self-government* implies not only the right to vote and to run for public office, but also the right to speak one's mind, to petition the government, and to join with others in political parties, interest groups, or social movements.

Over the years, a number of political philosophers and practitioners have viewed liberty as *threatened* by democracy rather than as essential to it. We will have more to say about this subject later as we consider several possible objections to democracy. But it is our position that self-government and political liberty are inseparable, in the sense that the former is impossible without the latter.[17] It follows that a majority cannot deprive an individual or a minority group of its political liberty without violating democracy itself.

VIDEO ROUNDTABLE

Self-government

Women Insist on the Right to Vote

Although political equality is a cornerstone of American democracy, the nation's understanding of who is entitled to equal status has changed over the years. The right to vote was granted to all men regardless of race in 1870, although stringent registration rules made it very difficult for nonwhites to exercise that right. It wasn't until 1920 that the Nineteenth Amendment extended the right to vote to women; in 1971, a constitutional amendment lowered the voting age from 21 to 18. Here, suffragettes demonstrate for the right to vote in front of Woodrow Wilson's White House.

Objections to Majoritarian Representative Democracy

Not everyone is convinced that majoritarian, representative democracy is the best form of government. Here are the main criticisms that have been leveled against democracy as we have defined it.

"Majority Tyranny" Threatens Liberty   James Madison and the other Founders of the American republic feared that majority rule was bound to undermine freedom and threaten the rights of the individual. They created a constitutional system (as you will see in Chapter 2) that was in fact designed to protect certain liberties against the unwelcome intrusions of the majority. The fears of the Founders were not without basis. What they called the "popular passions" have sometimes stifled the freedoms of groups and individuals who have dared to be different. Until quite recently, for instance, a majority of Americans were unwilling to allow atheists or communists the same rights of free speech that they allowed others, and conscientious objectors were treated harshly during both world wars. In the 1950s, many people in the movie industry, publishing, and education lost their jobs because of the anti-left hysteria whipped up by Senator Joseph McCarthy and others.[18]

majority tyranny
Suppression of the rights and liberties of a minority by the majority.

Although there have been instances during our history of **majority tyranny,** in which the majority violated the citizenship rights of a minority—the chapter-opening story is a good example—there is no evidence that the *many* consistently threaten liberty more than the *few* or the *one*. To put it another way, the majority does not seem to be a special or unique threat to liberty. Violations of freedom seem as likely to come from powerful individuals and groups or from government officials responding to vocal and narrow interests as from the majority.

Liberty is essential to self-government, and threats to liberty, whatever their origin, must be guarded against by all who value democracy. But we must firmly reject the view that majority rule inevitably or uniquely threatens liberty. Majority rule is unthinkable, in fact, without the existence of basic political liberties.[19]

The People Are Irrational and Incompetent Political scientists have spent decades studying the attitudes and behaviors of citizens in the United States, and some of the findings are not encouraging. For the most part, the evidence shows that individual Americans do not care a great deal about politics and are rather poorly informed, unstable in their views, and not much interested in participating in the political process.[20] These findings have led some observers to assert that citizens are ill-equipped for the responsibility of self-governance and that public opinion (the will of the majority) should not be the ultimate determinant of what government does.

We will see in Chapter 5, however, that this evidence about individuals has often been misinterpreted and that the American public taken collectively is more informed, sophisticated, and stable in its views than it is generally given credit for.

Majoritarian Democracy Threatens Minorities We have suggested that when rendering a decision in a democracy, the majority must prevail. In most cases, the minority on the losing side of an issue need not worry unduly about its well-being because many of its members are likely to be on the winning side in future decisions about other matters. Thus, people on the minority and losing side of an issue such as welfare reform may be part of the majority and winning side on an issue such as educational spending. What prevents majority tyranny over a minority in most policy decisions in a democracy is that the composition of the majority and the minority is always shifting, depending on the issue.

Political Corruption

However, what happens in cases that involve race, ethnicity, religion, or sexual orientation, for example, where minority status is fixed? Does the majority pose a threat to such minorities? Many people worry about that possibility.[21] The worry is that unbridled majority rule leaves no room for the claims of minorities. This worry has some historical foundations, for majorities have trampled on minority rights with alarming frequency. Majorities long held, for instance, that Native Americans and African Americans were inferior to whites

Fear Can Undermine Democracy

Political hysteria has periodically blemished the record of American democracy. Fear of domestic communism, and anarchism, captured in this editorial cartoon, was particularly potent in the twentieth century and led to the suppression of political groups by federal and state authorities acting, in their view, in the name of a majority of Americans.

and undeserving of full citizenship. Irish, Eastern European, Asian, and Latin American immigrants to our shores, among others, have all been subjected to periods of intolerance on the part of the majority, as have Catholics and Jews. Gays and lesbians have been discriminated against in housing and jobs and have sometimes been violently victimized.

As Robert Dahl points out, however, there is no evidence to support the belief that the rights of minorities are better protected under alternative forms of political government, whether rule by the *few* (note the persecution of the Christian minority in China by the Communist ruling party) or by the *one* (note the persecution of Shia Muslims under the rule of Saddem Hussein in Iraq), and that given the other benefits of majority rule democracy, it is to be preferred.[22]

In any case, democracy, as we have defined it, requires the protection of crucial minority rights. Recall that majority rule is only one of the defining conditions of popular sovereignty and that popular sovereignty is only one of the three basic attributes of democracy, the others being political equality and political liberty. The position of minorities is protected in a fully developed democracy, in our view, by the requirements of equal citizenship (the right to vote, to hold public office, to be protected against violence, and to enjoy the equal protection of the law) and access to the full range of civil liberties (speech, press, conscience, and association). To the extent that a majority violates the citizenship rights and liberties of minorities, society falls short of the democratic ideal.

Democracy as an Evaluative Standard: How Democratic Are We?

After this discussion, it should be easy to see how and why the democratic ideal can be used as a measuring rod with which to evaluate American politics. We have learned that the fundamental attributes of democracy are popular sovereignty, political equality, and political liberty. Each suggests a set of questions that will be raised throughout this book to encourage critical thinking about American political life.

How to Satisfy Aunt Martha

- *Questions about popular sovereignty.* Does government do what citizens want it to do? Do citizens participate in politics? Can citizens be involved when they choose to be, and are political leaders responsive? Do political linkage institutions, such as political parties, elections, interest groups, and social movements, effectively transmit what citizens want to political leaders? What is the quality of the public deliberation on the major public policy issues of the day? Do the news media and political leaders provide accurate and complete information?

- *Questions about political equality.* Do some individuals and groups have persistent and substantial advantages over other individuals and groups in the political process? Or is the political game open to all equally? Do government decisions and policies benefit some individuals and groups more than others?

- *Questions about political liberty.* Are citizens' rights and liberties universally available, protected, and used? Are people free to vote? Can they speak openly and form groups freely to petition their government? Do public authorities, private groups, or the majority threaten liberty or the rights of minorities?

These questions will help us assess where we are and where we are going as a democracy. We do not believe that popular sovereignty, political equality, and political liberty are attainable in perfect form. They are, rather, ideals to which our nation can aspire and standards against which we can measure everyday reality.

A Framework for Understanding How American Politics Works

In addition to helping you answer questions about the quality of democracy in the United States, our goal in this textbook is to help you understand how American government and politics work. To help you do so, we describe in this section a simple way to organize information and to think about how our political system works.

Organizing the Main Factors of Political Life

If we are to understand why things happen in government and politics—for example, the passage of the 1965 Voting Rights Act that Robert Moses and his SNCC colleagues did so much to bring about—we must begin with what biologists call *taxonomy:* placing things in their proper categories. We believe that each and every actor, institution, and process that influences what our politics are like and what our national government does can be placed into four main categories: structure, political linkage, government, and government action.

- *Structure.* This category includes the economy and society, the constitutional rules, the political culture, and the international system: the most fundamental and enduring factors that influence government and politics. They form the foundation upon which all else is built. They are the most enduring parts of the American system, the slowest to change.[23] They determine, to a very large extent, what issues become a part of the political agenda, how political power is distributed among the population, what rules structure how government works, and what values Americans bring to their political deliberations.

- *Political linkage.* This category includes all of the political actors, institutions, and processes that transmit the wants and demands of people and groups in our society to government officials and that together help shape what government officials do and what policies they adopt. These include public opinion, political parties, interest groups, the news media, and elections.

- *Government.* This category includes all public officials and institutions (Congress, the president, the federal bureaucracy, and the Supreme Court) that have formal, legal responsibilities for making public policy.

- *Government action.* This category includes the wide range of actions carried out by government: making laws, issuing rules and regulations, waging war and providing national defense, settling civil disputes, providing order, and more.

This textbook is organized around these four categories. The chapters in Part 2 focus on structural level factors. The chapters in Part 3 are about political linkage processes and institutions. The chapters in Part 4 attend to government institutions and leaders. Finally, the chapters in Part 5 examine what government does.

Connecting the Main Factors of Political Life

To understand how government and politics work in the United States, we must appreciate the fact that the structural, political linkage, and governmental categories interact with one another in a particular kind of way to determine what actions government takes (see Figure 1.1). The best way to see this is to look at these categories in action, using the passage of the 1965 Voting Rights Act as an example. The main point of the exercise is to show how connecting and considering together the main factors of political life—structure, political linkage, and government—can help explain why government takes certain actions.

To understand passage of the landmark legislation, we might begin with *government,* focusing our attention on Congress and its members, President Lyndon Johnson (who was the most vigorous proponent of the voting rights legislation) and his advisers, and the Supreme Court, which was becoming increasingly supportive of civil rights claims in the mid-1960s.

Knowing these things, however, would not tell us all that we needed to know. To understand why Congress, the president, and the Court behaved as they did in 1965, we would want to pay attention to the pressures brought to bear on them by *political linkage* actors and institutions: public opinion (increasingly supportive of civil rights), the growing electoral power of African Americans in the states outside the South, and most important, the moral power of the civil rights movement inspired by people like Robert Moses and Martin Luther King.

Even knowing these things, however, would not tell us all that we needed to know about why the 1965 Voting Rights Act happened. Our inquiry would have to go deeper to include *structural* factors: economic, cultural, and social change; constitutional rules; and the international position of the United States. For example, economic changes in the nation over the course of many decades triggered a "great migration" of African Americans from the rural South to the urban North. Over the long run, this population shift to states with large blocks of **electoral college** votes, critical to the election of presidents, increased the political power of African Americans. Cultural change increased the number of Americans bothered by the second-class citizenship of African Americans,

electoral college

Representatives of the states who formally elect the president; the number of electors in each state is equal to the total number of its senators and congressional representatives.

Ready for Combat

African American combat service in World War II and in Korea helped transform white attitudes about racial equality in the United States and contributed to the emergence of a supportive environment for the civil rights movement. Shown here are six gunners from the 17th Bomb Wing night interdiction team that saw heavy action in Korea.

FIGURE 1.1 • The Analytical Framework

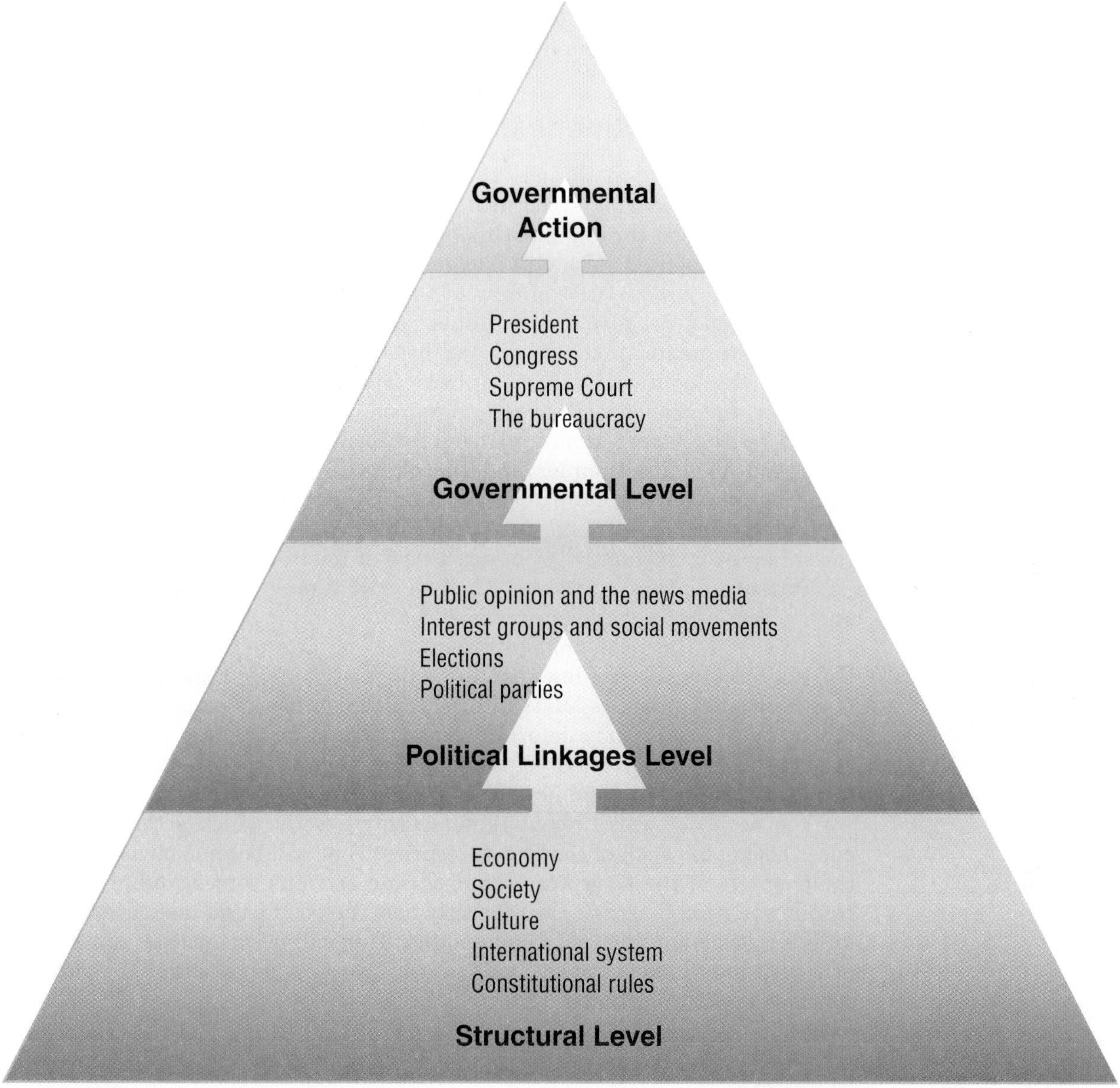

Various actors, institutions, and processes interact to influence what government does in the United States. Structural factors such as the economy, the political culture, the international system, and constitutional rules play a strong role in political events. They may influence the government directly, or, as is more often the case, through political linkages such as elections, parties, and interest groups. In a democratic society, the policies created by the government should reflect these influences.

even as combat service in World War II and the Korean War led many black Americans to insist on full citizenship rights. Finally, the **Cold War** struggle of the United States against the Soviet Union played an important role. Many American leaders, recognizing the contradiction between asking for the support of people of color in Third World countries in the struggle against communism while treating African Americans in the United States as second-class citizens, sought an end to the system of official segregation in the South (known as **Jim Crow**).[24]

Cold War
The period of tense relations between the United States and the Soviet Union from the late 1940s to the late 1980s.

Jim Crow
Popular term for the system of legally sanctioned racial segregation that existed in the American South until the middle of the twentieth century.

We see, then, that a full explanation of why the 1965 Voting Rights Act happened (government action) requires that we take into account how governmental, political linkage, and structural factors interact with one another to bring about significant change in American politics.

Understanding American Politics Holistically

This way of looking at things—that what government does can only be understood by considering structural, political linkage, and governmental factors—will be used throughout this book and will help bring order to the information presented. We will suggest throughout that action by public officials is the product not simply of their personal desires (although these are important), but also of the influences and pressures brought to bear by other governmental institutions and by individuals, groups, and classes at work in the political linkage sphere. Political linkage institutions and processes, in turn, can often be understood only when we see how they are shaped by the larger structural context, including such things as the national and global economies and the political culture. This way of understanding how American government and politics work is illustrated in the "Using the Framework" feature on the next page. This feature appears in each chapter to explore why particular government actions happen.

You should also keep in mind that, as in all complex systems, feedback also occurs. That is to say, influences sometimes flow in the opposite direction, from government to political linkage actors and institutions to structural factors. For example, federal tax laws influence the distribution of income and wealth in society, government regulations affect the operations of corporations, and decisions by the courts may determine what interest groups and political parties are able to do. We will want to pay attention, then, to these sorts of influences in our effort to understand how the American political system works.

You need not worry about remembering exactly which actors and influences belong to which of the four categories. That will become obvious because the chapters of the book are organized into sections corresponding to them. Nor do you need to worry about exactly how the people and institutions in the different levels interact with one another. This will become clear as materials are presented and learned and as you become more familiar with the American political process.

Summary

The struggle for democracy has played an important role in American history and remains an important theme in our country today, as well as in many other parts of the world. The struggle has involved the effort to make popular sovereignty, political equality, and political liberty more widely available and practiced. Because democracy holds a very special place in Americans' constellation of values and is particularly relevant to judging political processes, it is the standard used throughout this text to evaluate the quality of our politics and government.

The materials about politics and government are organized in a way that will allow us to make sense of the confusing details of everyday events and see *why* things happen the way they do. The organizing framework presented in this chapter visualizes the world of American politics as a set of interrelated *actors* and *influences*—institutions, groups, and individuals—that operate in three interconnected realms: the *structural, political linkage,* and *governmental* sectors. This way of looking at American political life as an ordered, interconnected whole will be used throughout the remainder of the book.

Using the Framework

The Voting Rights Act

How was Southern resistance to black political participation overcome?

Background: The Voting Rights Act of 1965 transformed the politics of the American South. Under federal government protection, the Act permitted African Americans to vote and run for elected office in states where a combination of violence, economic pressure, and state and local government rules made political participation difficult if not impossible prior to 1965. We can understand how such a momentous transformation happened by examining structural, political linkage, and governmental factors.

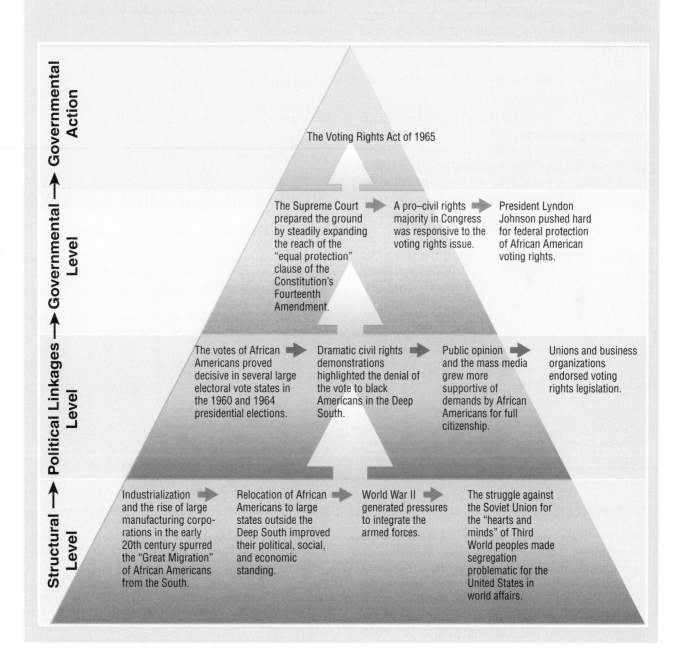

The Voting Rights Act of 1965

Governmental Level

The Supreme Court prepared the ground by steadily expanding the reach of the "equal protection" clause of the Constitution's Fourteenth Amendment. ➡ A pro–civil rights majority in Congress was responsive to the voting rights issue. ➡ President Lyndon Johnson pushed hard for federal protection of African American voting rights.

Political Linkages Level

The votes of African Americans proved decisive in several large electoral vote states in the 1960 and 1964 presidential elections. ➡ Dramatic civil rights demonstrations highlighted the denial of the vote to black Americans in the Deep South. ➡ Public opinion and the mass media grew more supportive of demands by African Americans for full citizenship. ➡ Unions and business organizations endorsed voting rights legislation.

Structural Level

Industrialization and the rise of large manufacturing corporations in the early 20th century spurred the "Great Migration" of African Americans from the South. ➡ Relocation of African Americans to large states outside the Deep South improved their political, social, and economic standing. ➡ World War II generated pressures to integrate the armed forces. ➡ The struggle against the Soviet Union for the "hearts and minds" of Third World peoples made segregation problematic for the United States in world affairs.

Governmental Action → Governmental → Political Linkages → Structural

Web Exploration
Democracy in the Former Communist Countries of Eastern and Central Europe

ISSUE: Creating democracy out of autocracy is never easy. After the fall of the Berlin Wall in 1989 and the collapse of the communist Soviet Union in 1991, people in each of the countries that had lived under Soviet-dominated communist governments in eastern and central Europe expressed a strong desire, as expressed in scores of public opinion polls, to become democratic. Each country chose its own path to this goal and each has moved towards it at a different pace.

SITE: Go to the Freedom House in MyPoliSciLab at **www.mypoliscilab.com.** In the "Web Explorations" section for Chapter 1, select "Democracy." Select "survey methodology" and read how Freedom House creates democracy ratings for each country; then select "Nations in Transit." From the pull-down menu "NIT Country Reports," choose two countries to read about.

WHAT YOU'VE LEARNED: After comparing these two countries, why do you think one is further along the road to democracy than the other? What factors central to democracy seem most difficult to put in place in the transition from autocracy? Press freedom? Civil liberties? Competitive elections? Are there lessons to be drawn from these cases that can be used by other countries trying to make a similar transition?

HINT: Some have argued that creating a system of elections is easier to do, and perhaps less important, than creating the institutions and practices in society that support freedom, such as the freedoms of speech, press, and conscience.

Internet Sources

A number of sites on the World Wide Web serve as "gateways" to vast collections of material on American government and politics. In subsequent chapters, we will indicate the location of sites on the Web to begin searches on the specific subject matter of the chapters. Here we concentrate on the general gateways, the starting points for wide-ranging journeys through cyberspace, geared to governmental and political subjects. Also included

are gateways to the multitude of political Web logs (blogs). Here are the gateways:

About.com US Politics Blogs
http://uspolitics.about.com/od/blogs/

The Corner; National Review (conservative Web log)
http://corner.nationalreview.com

The Daily Kos (liberal Web log)
http://www.dailykos.com

The Internet Public Library
www.ipl.org/div/subject/browse/law00.00.00/

New York Times, Politics Navigator
www.nytimes.com/library/politics/polpoints.html

Political Resources on the Web
www.politicalresources.net

American Politics Online
www.americanpoliticsonline.com

Yahoo/Government
www.yahoo.com/Government/

Suggestions for Further Reading

Dahl, Robert A. *Democracy and Its Critics.* New Haven, CT: Yale University Press, 1989.
   A sweeping defense of democracy against its critics by one of the most brilliant political theorists of our time.

Dahl, Robert A. *On Democracy.* New Haven, CT: Yale University Press, 1998.
   A brief yet surprisingly thorough examination of classical and contemporary democracy, real and theoretical.

Dryzek, John S. *Deliberative Democracy and Beyond: Liberals, Critics, Contestations.* Oxford: Oxford University Press, 2000.
   A spirited defense of deliberation in democratic political systems.

Putnam, Robert D. *Making Democracy Work: Civic Traditions in Modern Italy.* Princeton, NJ: Princeton University Press, 1993.
   A brilliant and controversial argument that the success of democratic government depends on the vitality of a participatory and tolerant civic culture.

Woodruff, Paul. *First Democracy: The Challenge of an Ancient Idea.* New York: Oxford University Press, 2006.
   A critique of modern forms of representative democracy in light of the direct, participatory form that existed in ancient Athens.

Zakaria, Fareed. *The Future of Freedom: Illiberal Democracy at Home and Abroad.* New York: Norton, 2004.
   The author suggests that majority rule democracy can only happen and be sustained in societies where individual freedom and the rule of law already exist, suggesting that democracy is unlikely to take hold in places such as Russia and Iraq.

PART 2 Structure

The chapters in Part 2 focus on structural influences on American government and politics. Structural influences are enduring features of American life that play key roles in determining what issues become important in politics and government, how political power is distributed in the population, and what attitudes and beliefs guide the behavior of citizens and public officials.

The constitutional rules are a particularly important part of the structural context of American political life. These rules are the subject matter of two of this part's chapters. Chapter 2 tells the story of the Constitution: why a constitutional convention was convened in Philadelphia in 1787, what the Founders intended to accomplish at the convention, and how specific provisions of the document have shaped our political life since the nation's founding. Chapter 3 examines federalism, asking what the framers intended the federal system to be and tracing how it has changed over the years.

The basic characteristics of American society also influence the workings of our political and governmental institutions, as well as the attitudes and behaviors of citizens and public officials. Chapter 4 looks in detail at the American economy, society, and political culture, as well as this country's place in the world, showing how these factors structure much of our political life.

CHAPTER **2**

The Constitution

IN THIS CHAPTER

- The enduring legacies of the American Revolution and the Declaration of Independence

- Our first constitution: The Articles of Confederation

- The Constitutional Convention

- What kind of constitution the framers created

- How the Constitution structures the rules of American politics

Shays's Rebellion

Artemas Ward, commander of American forces at Bunker Hill, a Revolutionary War hero, and a state judge, could not convince the crowd of several hundred armed farmers to allow him to enter the Worcester, Massachusetts, courthouse. For nearly two hours that day in September 1786, he pleaded and threatened, but to no avail. Unable to convince the local militia to come to his assistance, Ward left Worcester in a fury and carried word of the rebellion to Boston. Other judges trying to hold court in western Massachusetts in the summer and fall of 1786 had no better luck.[1]

The farmers of western Massachusetts were probably not a rebellious lot by nature, but desperate times pushed many of them to desperate actions. The end of the Revolutionary War in 1783 had brought the collapse of prices for agricultural products and widespread economic distress among farmers all over the new nation. Poor farmers sought relief from state governments, and for the most part, political leaders responded. Several states lent money (in the form of scrip, or paper money) to farmers to pay their taxes and debts. Other states passed stay laws, which postponed tax and mortgage payments for hard-pressed farmers.

In Massachusetts, however, the state legislature refused to help. Worse yet, the legislature and the governor had decided that all state debts must be paid in full to establish the creditworthiness of the state. The state's debt, accumulated to pay its share of the war costs, was owed primarily to a handful of the wealthiest Massachusetts citizens. To repay this debt, the legislature levied heavy taxes that fell disproportionately on farmers, especially those in the western part of the state. When the farmers could not pay their taxes—a distressingly common circumstance—the state collected its money through foreclosure: the public sale of farmers' lands, buildings, and livestock. Those who could not pay their debts, then, faced tax foreclosures and imprisonment under harsh conditions. Responding to these dire circumstances, many western Massachusetts farmers took up arms to close down the courts—the situation Artemas Ward faced in 1786.

By September 1786, Governor James Bowdoin had seen enough. He issued a proclamation against unlawful assembly and called out the militia to enforce it. Six hundred soldiers were sent to Springfield to ensure that the state supreme court could meet and issue the expected indictments against the leaders of the insurrection. The soldiers were met there by more than 500 armed farmers led by a former Revolutionary War officer, Captain Daniel Shays. After a long standoff, the militia withdrew, leaving the rebels in charge and the court unable to meet.

These events only hardened the governor's resolve to break the rebellion. He sent armed forces from Boston, which soon proved too much for the hastily organized and ill-equipped force under Shays. By the end of December 1786, the Boston militia had defeated the

rebels in two pitched battles, and Shays's Rebellion (as it was soon called) ended.

Although the insurrection was put down, most of the new nation's leading citizens were alarmed by the apparent inability of state governments to maintain public order under the Articles of Confederation. Shays's Rebellion realized the worst fears of national leaders about the dangers of ineffective state governments and popular democracy spinning out of control, unchecked by a strong national government. As George Washington said, "If government cannot check these disorders, what security has a man?"[2] It was in this climate of crisis that a call was issued for a constitutional convention to meet in Philadelphia to correct the flaws in our first constitution. Rather than amend the Articles of Confederation, however, the men who met in Philadelphia in the summer of 1787 wrote an entirely new constitution. ■

Thinking Critically About This Chapter

This chapter is about the founding of the United States (see Figure 2.1) and the formulation of the constitutional rules that structure American politics to this day.

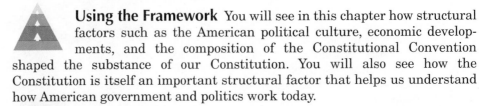 **Using the Framework** You will see in this chapter how structural factors such as the American political culture, economic developments, and the composition of the Constitutional Convention shaped the substance of our Constitution. You will also see how the Constitution is itself an important structural factor that helps us understand how American government and politics work today.

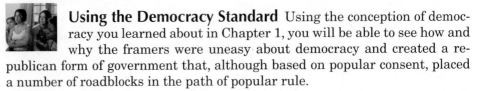 **Using the Democracy Standard** Using the conception of democracy you learned about in Chapter 1, you will be able to see how and why the framers were uneasy about democracy and created a republican form of government that, although based on popular consent, placed a number of roadblocks in the path of popular rule.

The Political Theory of the Revolutionary Era

Initially, the American Revolution (1775–1783) was waged more to preserve an existing way of life than to create something new. By and large, American colonists in the 1760s and 1770s were proud to be affiliated with Great Britain and satisfied with the general prosperity that came with participation in the British commercial empire.[3] When the revolution broke out, the colonists at first wanted only to preserve the English constitution and their own rights as

FIGURE 2.1 • Timeline of the Founding of the United States, 1774–1791

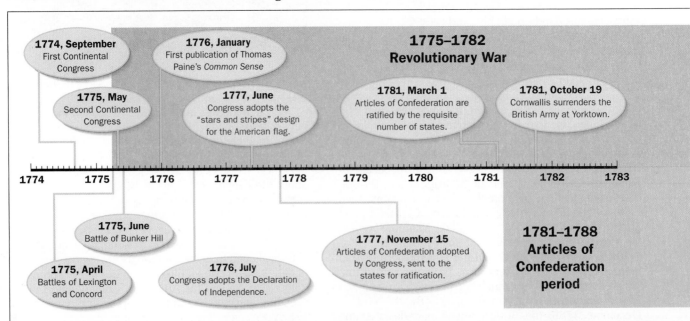

British subjects. These traditional rights of life, liberty, and property seemed to be threatened by British policies on trade and taxation. Rather than allowing the American colonists to trade freely with whomever they pleased and to produce whatever goods they wanted, for instance, England was restricting the colonists' freedom to do either in order to protect its own manufacturers. To pay for the military protection of the colonies against raids by Native Americans and their French allies, England imposed taxes on a number of items, including sugar, tea, and stamps (required for legal documents, pamphlets, and newspapers). The imposition of these taxes without the consent of the colonists seemed an act of tyranny to many English subjects in America.

Although the initial aims of the Revolution were quite modest, the American Revolution, like most revolutions, did not stay on the track planned by its leaders. Although it was sparked by a concern for liberty—understood as the preservation of traditional rights against the intrusions of a distant government—it also stimulated the development of sentiments for popular sovereignty and political equality. As these sentiments grew, so did the likelihood that the American colonies would split from their British parent and form a system of government more to the liking of the colonists.

The Declaration of Independence

When the Second Continental Congress began its session on May 10, 1775—the First had met only briefly in 1774 to formulate a list of grievances to submit to the British Parliament—the delegates did not have independence in mind, even though armed conflict with Britain had already begun with the battles of Lexington and Concord. Pushed by the logic of armed conflict, an unyielding British government, and Thomas Paine's incendiary call for American independence in his wildly popular pamphlet *Common Sense,* however, the delegates concluded by the spring of 1776 that separation and independence were inescapable.[4] In early June, the Continental Congress appointed a special committee, composed of Thomas Jefferson, John Adams, and Benjamin Franklin, to draft a declaration of independence. The document, mostly

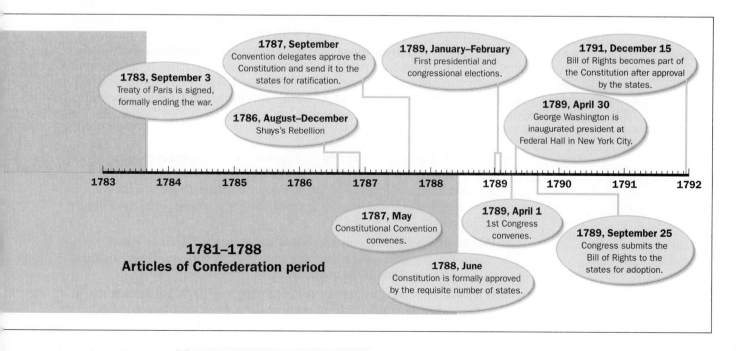

A Clarion Call for Independence

American leaders were reluctant at first to declare independence from Great Britain. One of the things that helped change their minds was Thomas Paine's wildly popular—it is said that a higher proportion of Americans read it than any other political tract in U.S. history—and incendiary pamphlet *Common Sense,* which mercilessly mocked the institution of monarchy and helped undermine the legitimacy of British rule.

THOMAS PAINE ESQ.ʳ

Late Secretary for Foreign Affairs to the American Congress.

Author of

The Rights of Man, Common Sense, &c.

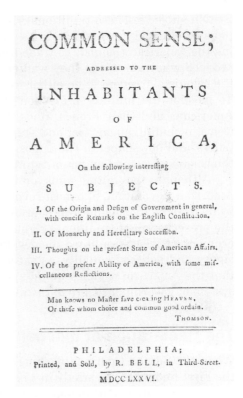

COMMON SENSE;

ADDRESSED TO THE

INHABITANTS

OF

AMERICA,

On the following interesting

SUBJECTS.

I. Of the Origin and Design of Government in general, with concise Remarks on the English Constitution.

II. Of Monarchy and Hereditary Succession.

III. Thoughts on the present State of American Affairs.

IV. Of the present Ability of America, with some miscellaneous Reflections.

Man knows no Master save creating HEAVEN,
Or those whom choice and common good ordain.
THOMSON.

PHILADELPHIA;

Printed, and Sold, by R. BELL, in Third-Street.

MDCCLXXVI.

Jefferson's handiwork, was adopted unanimously by the Second Continental Congress on July 4, 1776.

Key Ideas in the Declaration of Independence   The ideas in Jefferson's Declaration of Independence are so familiar to us that we may easily miss their revolutionary importance. In the late eighteenth century, most societies in the world were ruled by kings with authority purportedly derived from God, subject to little or no control by their subjects. Closely following John Locke's ideas in *The Second Treatise on Government,* Jefferson's argument that legitimate government can be established only by the people, is created to protect inalienable rights, and can govern only with their consent, seemed outrageous at the time. However, these ideas sparked a responsive chord in people everywhere when they were first presented, and they remain extremely popular all over the world today. Ideas articulated in the Declaration influenced the French Revolution of 1789, the 2004 "orange revolution" in Ukraine, and many revolutions in between. The argument as presented in the Declaration of Independence goes as follows:

- Human beings possess rights that cannot be legitimately given away or taken from them. *"We hold these truths to be self-evident, that all men are created equal, that they are endowed by their Creator with certain unalienable Rights, that among these are Life, Liberty, and the Pursuit of Happiness."*
- People create government to protect these rights. *"That to secure these rights, Governments are instituted among Men, deriving their just powers from the consent of the governed."*
- If government fails to protect people's rights or itself becomes a threat to them, people can withdraw their consent from that government and

create a new one, that is, void the existing **social contract** and agree to a new one. *"That whenever any Form of Government becomes destructive of these ends, it is the Right of the People to alter or to abolish it, and to institute new Government, laying its foundation on such principles, and organizing its powers in such form, as to them shall seem most likely to effect their Safety and Happiness."*

Important Omissions in the Declaration   The Declaration of Independence carefully avoided several controversial subjects, including what to do about slavery. Jefferson's initial draft denounced the Crown for violating human rights by "captivating and carrying Africans into slavery," but this was considered too controversial and was dropped from subsequent versions. The contradiction between the institution of slavery and the Declaration's sweeping claims for self-government, "unalienable" individual rights, and equality ("all men are created equal") was obvious to many observers at the time and is glaringly apparent to us today. The Declaration was also silent about the political status of women, Native Americans, and African Americans who were not slaves. Indeed, it is safe to assume that neither Jefferson, the main author of the Declaration, nor the other signers of the document had women, Native Americans, free blacks, or slaves in mind when they were fomenting revolution and calling for a different kind of political society. Interestingly, free blacks and women would go on to play important roles in waging the Revolutionary War against Britain.[5]

> **social contract**
> A philosophical device, used by Enlightenment thinkers, such as Locke, Rousseau, and Harrington, to suggest that governments are only legitimate if they are created by a voluntary compact among the people.

The Articles of Confederation: The First Constitution

The leaders of the American Revolution almost certainly did not envision the creation of a single, unified nation. At most, they had in mind a loose **confederation** among the states. This should not be surprising. Most Americans in the late eighteenth century believed that a government based on popular consent and committed to the protection of individual rights was possible only in small, homogeneous republics, where government was close to the people and where fundamental conflicts of interest among the people did not exist. Given the great geographic expanse of the colonies, as well as their varied ways of life and economic interests, the formation of a single unified republic seemed unworkable.

> **confederation**
> A loose association of states or territorial units formed for a common purpose.

Provisions of the Articles

Our first **constitution,** passed by the Second Continental Congress in the midst of the Revolutionary War in 1777 but not ratified by the requisite number of states until 1781, created a nation that was hardly a nation at all. The **Articles of Confederation** created in law what had existed in practice from the time of the Declaration of Independence: a loose confederation of independent states with little power in the central government, much like the United Nations today. Under the Articles, most important decisions were made in state legislatures.

The Articles provided for a central government of sorts, but it had few responsibilities and virtually no power. It could make war or peace, but it had no power to levy taxes (even customs duties) to pursue either goal. It could not

> **constitution**
> The basic framework of law that prescribes how government is to operate.
>
> **Articles of Confederation**
> The first constitution of the United States, adopted during the last stages of the Revolutionary War, created a system of government with most power lodged in the states and little in the central government.

regulate commerce among the states, nor could it deny the states the right to collect customs duties. It had no independent chief executive to ensure that the laws passed by Congress would be enforced, nor had it a national court system to settle disputes between the states. There were no means to provide a sound national money system. The rule requiring that all national laws be approved by 9 of the 13 states made lawmaking almost impossible. And, defects in the new constitution were difficult to remedy because amending the Articles required the unanimous approval of the states.

Shortcomings of the Articles

The Articles of Confederation did what most of its authors intended: to preserve the power, independence, and sovereignty of the states and ensure that the central government would not encroach on the liberty of the people. Unfortunately, there were also many problems that the confederation was ill-equipped to handle.

Most important, the new central government could not finance its activities. The government was forced to rely on each state's willingness to pay its annual tax assessment. Few states were eager to cooperate. As a result, the bonds and notes of the confederate government became almost worthless, and the government's attempts to borrow were stymied.

The central government was also unable to defend American interests in foreign affairs. Without a chief executive or a standing army, and with the states holding a veto power over actions of the central government, the confederation lacked the capacity to reach binding agreements with other nations or to deal with a wide range of foreign policy problems. These included the continuing presence of British troops in western lands ceded to the new nation by Britain at the end of the Revolutionary War, violent clashes with Native Americans on the western frontier, and piracy on the high seas.

The government was also unable to prevent the outbreak of commercial warfare between the states. As virtually independent nations with the power

VIDEO ROUNDTABLE

Articles of Confederation

Clashes on the Frontier

As settlers moved west, they inevitably came into conflict with Native Americans already living there. Many of the settlers were angry and distressed when the national government under the Articles of Confederation proved unable to protect them against the people being displaced. This painting shows a battle waged between settlers and Native Americans on the Kentucky frontier in 1785.

to levy customs duties, many states became intense commercial rivals of their neighbors and sought to gain every possible advantage against the products of other states. New York and New Jersey, for instance, imposed high tariffs on goods that crossed their borders from other states.

Factors Leading to the Constitutional Convention

Historians now generally agree that the failings of the Articles of Confederation led most of the leading citizens of the confederation to believe that a new constitution was desperately needed for the fledgling nation. What is left out of many accounts of the convening of the Constitutional Convention in Philadelphia, however, is the story of the growing concern among many of the most influential men in the confederation that the passions for democracy and equality among the common people set loose by the American Revolution were getting out of hand. During the American Revolution, appeals to the people for the defense of freedom and for the spread of the blessings of liberty were often translated by the people to mean their right to better access to the means of government and to the means of livelihood.[6] The common people were convinced that success would bring substantial improvements in their lives.[7]

The Republican Beliefs of the Founders

This fever for popular participation and greater equality is not what most of the leaders of the American Revolution had in mind.[8] The Founders were believers in a theory of government known as **republicanism.** Like all republicans of the eighteenth century, the framers were seeking a form of government that would not only be based on the consent of the governed but that would also make tyranny—the abuse of the inalienable rights of citizens by government—unlikely or impossible, whether the threat of tyranny came from the misrule of a single person (a king or military dictator, let us say), a small group of elites (an aristocracy, a clerical theocracy, or moneyed merchant class), or even the majority of the population. Their solution was threefold: to elect government leaders, to limit the power of government, and to place roadblocks in the path of the majority. The election of representatives, in their view, would keep potentially tyrannical kings and aristocratic factions from power while ensuring popular consent. Limiting the power of government, both by stating what government could and could not do in a written constitution and by fragmenting governmental power, would prevent tyranny no matter who eventually won control, including the majority. Limiting the influence of the majority was accomplished by making only one part of one branch of government subject to direct election of the people—the House of Representatives—leaving the other offices to indirect election (the Senate and the president) or appointment (the Supreme Court).

Although eighteenth-century republicans believed in representative government—a government whose political leaders are elected by the people—they were not sympathetic to what we might today call popular democracy. For the most part, they thought that public affairs ought to be left to men from the "better" parts of society; the conduct of the public business was, in their view, the province of individuals with wisdom and experience, capacities associated

republicanism, eighteenth century
A political doctrine advocating limited government based on popular consent, protected against majority tyranny.

The Roman Republic

The republican ideas of the framers were greatly influenced by the writings of Cicero and Cato on the Roman republic, which spanned the years 510 BCE to 27 BCE. They especially admired the Roman republic's commitment to the idea that the actions of rulers must be bound by laws created by an assembly. Here, members of the Roman senate debate an important public policy issue.

mainly with people of social standing, substantial financial resources, and high levels of education. Nor did eighteenth-century republicans believe that elected representatives should be too responsive to public opinion. Once in office, representatives were to exercise independent judgment about how best to serve the public interest, taking into account the needs and interests of society rather than the moods and opinions of the people.

Eighteenth-century republicans, then, did not believe that the people could or should rule directly. While they favored a system that allowed the common people to play a larger role in public life than existed in other political systems of the day, the role of the people was to be a far more limited one than we find acceptable today. They worried that too much participation by the people could only have a bad outcome. As James Madison put it in *The Federalist Papers*, "[Democracies] have ever been spectacles of turbulence and contention; have ever been found incompatible with personal security or the rights of property; and have in general been as short in their lives as they have been violent in their deaths."[9] (See Table 2.1 on the differences between democracy and eighteenth-century republicanism.)

Why the Founders Were Worried

An Excess of Democracy in the States   Worries that untamed democracy was on the rise were not unfounded.[10] In the mid-1780s, popular assemblies (called conventions) were created in several states to keep tabs on state legislatures and to issue instructions to legislatures concerning what bills to pass. Both conventions and instructions struck directly at the heart of the republican conception of the legislature as a deliberative body shielded from popular opinion.[11]

The constitution of the state of Pennsylvania was also an affront to republican principles. Benjamin Rush, a signatory to the Declaration of Independence, described it as "too much upon the democratic order."[12] This constitution

TABLE 2.1 • Comparing Eighteenth-Century Republicanism and the Democratic Ideal

18th-Century Republicanism	The Democratic Ideal
Government is based on popular consent.	Government is based on popular consent.
Rule by the people is indirect, through multiple layers of representatives.	Rule by the people may be direct or indirect through representatives.
The term *people* is narrowly defined (by education, property holding, and social standing).	The term *people* is broadly defined.
Office holding confined to a narrow and privileged stratum of the population.	Broad eligibility for office-holding.
Elected representatives act as "trustees" (act on their own to discover the public good).	Elected representatives act as "delegates" (act as instructed by the people; accurately reflect their wishes).
Barriers to majority rule exist.	Majority rule prevails.
Government is strictly limited in what it can do.	Government does what the people want it to do.
Government safeguards rights and liberties, with a special emphasis on property rights.	Government safeguards rights and liberties, with no special emphasis on property rights.

replaced the property qualification to vote with a very small tax (thus allowing many more people to vote), created a unicameral (single-house) legislative body whose members were to be elected in annual elections, mandated that legislative deliberations be open to the public, and required that proposed legislation be widely publicized and voted on only after a general election had been held (making the canvassing of public opinion easier).

To many advocates of popular democracy, including Tom Paine, the Pennsylvania constitution was the most perfect instrument of popular sovereignty. To others, like James Madison, the Pennsylvania case was a perfect example of popular tyranny exercised through the legislative branch of government.[13]

The Threat to Property Rights in the States   One of the freedoms that republicans wanted to protect against the intrusions of a tyrannical government was the right of the people to acquire and enjoy private property. Developments toward the end of the 1770s and the beginning of the 1780s seemed to put this freedom in jeopardy. For one thing, the popular culture was growing increasingly hostile to privilege of any kind, whether of social standing, education, or wealth. Writers derided aristocratic airs; expressed their preference for unlettered, plain-speaking leaders; and pointed out how wealth undermined equal rights.[14] Legislatures were increasingly inclined, moreover, to pass laws protecting debtors. For example, Rhode Island and North Carolina issued cheap paper money, which note holders were forced to accept in payment of debts. Other states enacted **stay acts,** which forbade farm foreclosures for nonpayment of debts. Popular opinion, while strongly in favor of property rights (most of the debtors in question were owners of small farms), also sympathized with farmers, who were hard-pressed to pay their debts with increasingly tight money, and believed—with some reason—that

PARTICIPATION

Explore Your State Constitution

stay acts

Enactments postponing the collection of taxes or mortgage payments.

many creditors had accumulated notes speculatively or unfairly and were not entitled to full repayment. Finally, Shays's Rebellion in western Massachusetts, where armed rebels tried to prevent the state courts from seizing farms for the nonpayment of debts, greatly alarmed American notables.

The Constitutional Convention

Concerned about these developments and shortcomings in the design of government under the Articles, most of America's economic, social, and political leaders were convinced by 1787 that the new nation and the experiment in self-government were in great peril. These concerns helped convince leaders in the states to select 73 delegates to attend the Constitutional Convention in Philadelphia (only 55 actually showed up for its deliberations). The goal was to create a new government capable of providing both energy and stability.

The convention officially convened in Philadelphia on May 25, 1787, with George Washington presiding. It met in secret for a period of almost four months. By the end of their deliberations, the delegates had hammered out a constitutional framework that has served as one of the structural foundations of American government and politics to the present day.

Who Were the Framers?

The delegates were not common folk. There were no common laborers, skilled craftspeople, small farmers, women, or racial minorities in attendance. Most delegates were wealthy men: holders of government bonds, real estate investors, successful merchants, bankers, lawyers, and owners of large plantations worked by slaves. They were, for the most part, far better educated than the average American and solidly steeped in the classics. The journal of the convention debates kept by James Madison of Virginia shows that the delegates were conversant with the great works of Western philosophy and political science; with great facility and frequency, they quoted Aristotle, Plato, Locke, Montesquieu, and scores of other thinkers. They were also a surprisingly young group, averaging barely over 40 years of age. Finally, they were a group with broad experience in American politics—most had served in their state legislatures—and many were veterans of the Revolutionary War.[15]

Intents of the Framers

Judgments about the framers, their intentions, and what they produced vary widely. Historian Melvin Urofsky wrote that "few gatherings in the history of this or any other country could boast such a concentration of talent."[16] Supreme Court Justice Thurgood Marshall, on the other hand, once claimed that the Constitution was "defective from the start" because the convention at which it was written did not include women or blacks.[17]

The most influential criticism of the framers and what they created was mounted in 1913 by the Progressive historian Charles Beard in his book *An Economic Interpretation of the Constitution*.[18] Beard boldly claimed that the framers were engaged in a conspiracy to protect their immediate and personal economic interests. Those who controlled the convention and the ratification process after the convention, he suggested, were owners of public securities who were interested in a government that could pay its debts, merchants interested in protections of commerce, and land speculators interested in the protection of property rights.

Beard has had legions of defenders and detractors.[19] Historians today generally agree that Beard overemphasized the degree to which the framers were

**The Framers Sign
the Constitution**

Members of the Constitutional
Convention sign their names
to the Constitution on
September 17, 1787. The
Constitution did not become
the law of the land, however,
until the ninth state, New
Hampshire, ratified it nine
months later.

driven by the immediate need to "line their own pockets," failed to give credit
to their more noble motivations, and even got many of his facts wrong. So a
simple self-interest analysis is not supportable. But Beard was probably on
the mark when he suggested that broad economic and social-class motives
were at work in shaping the actions of the framers. This is not to suggest that
they were not concerned about the national interest, economic stability, or the
preservation of liberty. It does suggest, however, that the ways in which they
understood these concepts were fully compatible with their own positions of
economic and social eminence. In conclusion, it is fair to say that the
Constitutional Convention was the work of American leaders who were au-
thentically worried about the instability and economic chaos of the confederation as well as the rise of a democratic and equalitarian culture among the
common people.

That being said, we must also acknowledge that the framers were
launched on a novel and exciting adventure, trying to create a form of government that existed nowhere else during the late eighteenth century. The success of their efforts was not guaranteed. They were, in effect, sailing in un-
charted waters, guided by their reading of history and of the republican
philosophers, their understanding of the nature of the English constitution,
and their experience with colonial governments before the Revolution and
state governments after.

Consensus and Conflict at the Convention

The delegates to the convention were of one mind on many fundamental
points. Most importantly, they agreed that the Articles of Confederation had to
be scrapped and replaced with a new constitution.

Most of the delegates also agreed about the need for a substantially
strengthened national government to protect American interests in the world,
provide for social order, and regulate interstate commerce. Such a government
would diminish the power and sovereignty of the states. Supporters of the idea
of a strong, centralized national government, such as Alexander Hamilton,

had long argued this position. By the time of the convention, even such traditional opponents of centralized governmental power as James Madison had changed their minds. As Madison put it, some way must be found "which will at once support a due supremacy of the national authority, and leave in force the local authorities so far as they can be subordinately useful."[20]

But the delegates also believed that a strong national government was potentially tyrannical and should not be allowed to fall into the hands of any particular interest or set of interests, particularly the majority of the people, referred to by Madison as the "majority faction." The delegates' most important task became that of finding a formula for creating a republican government based on popular consent but a government not unduly swayed by public opinion and popular democracy. As Benjamin Franklin put it, "We have been guarding against an evil that old states are most liable to, excess of power in the rulers, but our present danger seems to be a defect of obedience in the subjects."[21]

The Great Compromise   By far the most intense disagreements at the convention concerned the issue of representation in Congress, especially whether large or small states would wield the most power in the legislative branch. The **Virginia Plan,** drafted by James Madison, proposed the creation of a strong central government dominated by a powerful Congress controlled by the most populous states: Virginia, Massachusetts, and Pennsylvania. The Virginians proposed a government with a strong national legislature with seats apportioned to the states on the basis of population size and with the power to appoint the executive and the judiciary and to veto state laws. The smaller states countered with a set of proposals drafted by William Paterson of New Jersey (thereafter known as the **New Jersey Plan**), whose central feature was a unicameral national legislature whose seats were apportioned equally among the states. The New Jersey Plan envisioned a slightly more powerful national government than the one that existed under the Articles of Confederation, but one that was to be organized on representational lines not unlike those in the Articles, in which each of the states remained sovereign. The Virginia Plan, by contrast, with its strong national government run by a popularly elected legislature, represented a fundamentally different kind of national union, one in which national sovereignty was superior to state sovereignty.[22]

Debate over this issue was so intense that no decision could be reached on the floor of the convention. As a way out of this impasse, the convention appointed a committee to hammer out a compromise. The so-called Committee of Eleven met over the Fourth of July holiday while the convention was adjourned. It presented its report, sometimes called the Great Compromise and sometimes the **Connecticut Compromise** (because it was drafted by Roger Sherman of that state), on July 5, 1787. Its key feature was a bicameral (two-house) national legislature in which each state's representation in the House of Representatives was to be based on population (thus favoring the large states), while representation in the Senate was to be equal for each of the states (thus favoring the small states). The compromise, adopted on July 16, broke the deadlock at the convention and allowed the delegates to turn their attention to other matters.[23] (See the "Mapping American Politics" feature for more on the enduring effects of compromise.)

Slavery   Despite great distaste for the institution of slavery among many delegates—it is said that Benjamin Franklin wanted to insert a provision in the Constitution condemning slavery and the slave trade but was talked out of it for fear of splintering the convention[24]—slavery was ultimately condoned in the Constitution, although only indirectly; the word "slavery," in fact, does not ap-

---

Virginia Plan

Proposal by the large states at the Constitutional Convention to create a strong central government with power in the government apportioned to the states on the basis of population.

New Jersey Plan

Proposal of the smaller states at the Constitutional Convention to create a government based on the equal representation of the states in a unicameral legislature.

VISUAL LITERACY

The American System of Checks and Balances

Connecticut Compromise

Also called the *Great Compromise;* the compromise between the New Jersey and Virginia plans formulated by the Connecticut delegates at the Constitutional Convention; called for a lower legislative house based on population size and an upper house based on equal representation of the states.

pear in the Constitution at all. Rather, the legal standing of "involuntary servitude" is affirmed in three places. First, the delegates agreed, after much heated debate, to count three-fifths of a state's slave population (referred to as "three-fifths of all other Persons") in the calculation of how many representatives a state was entitled to in the House of Representatives (Article I, Section 2, paragraph 3). Much harm was done by this; counting noncitizen slaves for purposes of representation in the House increased the power of the slave states in Congress as well as the number of their electoral votes in presidential elections. This imbalance would continue until 1865, when the Civil War and the Thirteenth Amendment, ratified after the war, ended slavery in the United States. Second, it forbade enactments against the slave trade until the year 1808 (Article I, Section 9). Third, it required nonslave states to return runaway slaves to their owners in slave states (Article IV, Section 2, paragraph 3).

Many Americans today are bothered by the fact that a significant number of the delegates to a convention whose goal was to build a nontyrannical republic were themselves slaveholders (although a few, including George Washington, had provisions in their wills freeing their slaves upon their death). To understand more fully why the delegates did not abolish slavery, see the "Using the Framework" feature on page 40.

It would finally take a terrible civil war to abolish slavery in the United States. At the convention, Virginia delegate George Mason had a foreboding of such an outcome when he observed about slavery that "providence punishes national sins by national calamities."[25]

You Are Attempting to Revise the California State Constitution

The Presidency The Virginia Plan called for a single executive, while the New Jersey Plan called for a multi-person executive. In the spirit of cooperation that pervaded the convention after the Great Compromise, the delegates quickly settled on the idea of a single executive. They could not agree, however, on how this executive should be selected. Both sides rejected direct election by the people of the chief executive, of course, because this would be "too much upon the democratic order," but they locked horns over and could not agree to the Virginia Plan's method of selection: by the vote of state legislatures. The compromise that was eventually struck involved a provision for an **electoral college** that would select the president. In the electoral college, each state would have a total of votes equal to its total number of representatives and senators in Congress. Selection of electors was left to state legislatures. (Electoral college votes are determined today by popular vote in each state.) Elected members of the electoral college would then cast their votes for president. Should the electoral college fail to give a majority to any person, which most framers assumed would usually happen, the House of Representatives would choose the president, with each state having one vote (Article II, Section 1, paragraphs 2 and 3). The electoral college will be described in more detail in Chapter 10.

electoral college

Elected representatives of the states whose votes formally elect the president; the number of electors in each state is equal to the total number of its senators and representatives in the House.

What the Framers Created

What kind of government did the framers create? Let us examine the fundamental design for government laid out in the Constitution.

A Republican Form of Government
Recall that eighteenth-century republican doctrine advocated a form of government that, while based on popular consent and some popular participation, places obstacles in the path of majoritarian democracy and limits the purposes and powers of the government in order to prevent tyranny.

Mapping American Politics

Equal and unequal representation in the House and Senate

Introduction: One of the fundamental decisions made by the framers at the constitutional convention in Philadelphia in 1788 was to create a two-chamber legislative branch with each branch based on a different principle of representation. Each state's representation in the House of Representatives is based on its relative population size, with the proviso that no state shall have fewer than one representative. Representation in the House, because it very nearly mirrors the distribution of the American population among the states, then, can fairly be called democratic, based on the principle of one person, one vote. The Senate, on the other hand, is based on equal representation of the states—each state has two senators regardless of its population size—giving disproportionate political power

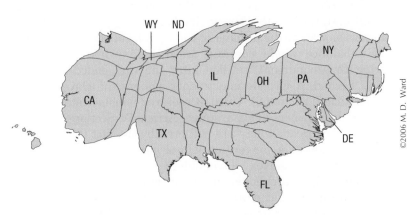

©2006 M. D. Ward

States in Proportion to Number of U.S. Representatives

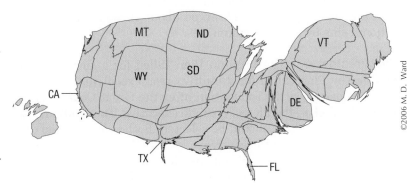

©2006 M. D. Ward

States in Proportion to Number of Residents per Senator

Election of Government Leaders Republican government is based on the principle of representation, meaning that public policies are made not by the people directly but by the people's elected representatives acting in their stead. Under the rules created by the Constitution, the president and members of Congress are elected by the people, although in the case of the presidency and the Senate, to be sure, they are elected only indirectly (through the electoral college and the state legislatures, respectively). The upshot, then, is that government policies at the national level are mostly made by either directly or indirectly elected officials. (The Seventeenth Amendment, ratified in 1913, transferred election of senators from legislatures to the people.) This guarantees a degree of popular consent and some protection against the possibilities of tyrannical government arising from misrule by the *one* or by the *few,* given the electoral power of the *many.*

Federalism The Articles of Confederation envisioned a nation structured as a loose union of politically independent units with little power in the hands of the central government. The Constitution fashioned a **federal** system in which some powers are left to the states, some powers are shared by the com-

federal

Describing a system in which significant governmental powers are divided between a central government and smaller territorial units, such as states.

to low-population states. We can see this by comparing the two cartograms.

Different Maps; Different Stories: The cartogram on the top shows states drawn in proportion to the number of representatives each has in the House of Representatives. Because representation in the House is based roughly on population size, the largest numbers of representatives come from more populous states, such as California, Texas, Florida, Ohio, Illinois, New York, and Pennsylvania, as one would expect in a democratic system. Equal representation of each state in the Senate, combined with vast population differences among the states, however, leads to serious representational distortions from a democratic theory point of view. In 2004, for example, almost 36 million people lived in California while only about a half-million people lived in Wyoming, yet each state had two senators. Thus, each California senator represented about 18 million people, while each Wyoming senator represented just over 250,000. In terms of representation, each person in Wyoming had 72 times the power in the Senate in 2004 as each person in California. The cartogram on the bottom reflects the representational power of the people in each state in the Senate, measured as the number of senators—always two—divided by state population size. The most populous states, such as California, New York, Texas, and Florida, almost disappear, while less populous states, such as Wyoming, Montana, Delaware, and the two Dakotas, loom large.

What Do You Think? For the most part, the framers of the Constitution were eighteenth-century republicans, distrustful of popular democracy. They created the Senate not only as a tactical maneuver to gain ratification of the Constitution by nine states, but to make the legislative branch more deliberative and less prone to follow the ebbs and flows of public opinion. Do you believe that the framers made a wise decision in giving equal representation to the states in the Senate? Or do you believe that the Senate's current design departs too far from the basic democratic principle of political equality? Would Congress likely make different kinds of policies if the Senate were organized to more closely reflect the size of state populations?

Sources: **www.house.gov**; **http://www.census.gov/ population/www/censusdata/apportionment.html**; and **www.senate.gov**.

ponent units and the central government, and some powers are granted to the central government alone.

The powers in the Constitution tilt slightly toward the center, however.[26] This recasting of the union from a loose confederation to a more centralized federal system is boldly stated in Article VI, Section 2, commonly called the **supremacy clause:**

> *This Constitution and the Laws of the United States which shall be made in Pursuance thereof; and all Treaties made, or which shall be made, under the Authority of the United States, shall be the supreme Law of the Land; and the Judges in every State shall be bound thereby, any Thing in the Constitution or Laws of any State to the Contrary notwithstanding.*

The tilt toward national power is also enhanced by assigning important powers and responsibilities to the national government: to regulate commerce, to provide a uniform currency, to provide uniform laws on bankruptcy, to raise and support an army and a navy, to declare war, to collect taxes and customs duties, to provide for the common defense of the United States, and more. (See

supremacy clause

The provision in Article VI of the Constitution that states that the Constitution and the laws and treaties of the United States are the supreme law of the land, taking precedence over state laws and constitutions.

Using the Framework

Slavery in the Constitution

Why was slavery allowed in the Constitution of 1787?

Background: Slavery was allowed in the Constitution until passage, after the Civil War, of the Thirteenth Amendment, which ended involuntary servitude in the United States. Although the words "slave" or "involuntary servitude" never appear in the document, slavery is given constitutional standing in the original document in Article I, Section 2, paragraph 3; Article I, Section 9; and Article IV, Section 2, paragraph 3. For Americans today, it seems almost inconceivable that such a thing could have happened. Taking a broader and more historical view makes the story clearer, though hardly more acceptable.

Governmental Action

The framers allowed the institution of slavery to continue in Article I, Section 2; Article I, Section 9; and Article IV, Section 2 of the Constitution.

Governmental Level

Slaveholders and merchants involved in the slave trade were well represented among the convention delegates.

Many other delegates, although personally opposed to slavery as an institution, feared that the introduction of a provision to end slavery would cause those states with high numbers of slaves to leave the convention and doom the effort to create a United States of America.

Political Linkages Level

Slaves and free blacks played no significant political role in America during the Articles of Confederation period. Their concerns about slavery had no political weight.

Few private organizations—interest groups, churches, or newspapers—were actively pressing for an end to slavery at the time of the Constitutional Convention.

Structural Level

The slave trade was a profitable business.

For the most part, individuals of European descent in America during the time of the constitutional convention did not believe that people of African descent were equal to whites in any respect, nor did they believe they were beings who possessed basic human rights.

Venerating the Constitution

Americans generally believe that the Constitution fashioned by the framers in Philadelphia in 1788 is one of the main reasons the American system of government has proved to be so enduring. Here, visitors wait to see the Constitution at the National Archives in Washington.

Article I, Section 8.) Especially important for later constitutional history is the last of the clauses in Section 8, which states that Congress has the power to "make all laws which shall be necessary and proper" to carry out its specific powers and responsibilities. We shall see later how this **elastic clause** became one of the foundations for the growth of the federal government in the twentieth century.

elastic clause

Article I, Section 8, of the Constitution, also called the *necessary and proper clause;* gives Congress the authority to make whatever laws are necessary and proper to carry out its enumerated responsibilities.

The Constitution left it up to each of the states, however, to determine qualifications for voting within their borders. This left rules in place in all the states that denied the right to vote to women, slaves, and Native Americans; it left rules untouched in many states that denied the vote to free blacks and to white males without substantial property. Most states removed property qualifications by the 1830s, establishing universal white male suffrage in the United States. It would take many years and constitutional amendments to remove state restrictions on the voting rights of women and racial minorities.

Limited Government The basic purpose of the U.S. Constitution, like any written constitution, is to define the purposes and powers of the government. Such a definition of purposes and powers automatically places a boundary between what is permissible and what is impermissible. By listing the specific powers (as in Article I, Section 8) of the national government and specifically denying others to the national government (as in Article I, Section 9, and in the first 10 amendments to the Constitution, known as the **Bill of Rights**), the Constitution carefully limited what government may legitimately do.

Bill of Rights

The first 10 amendments to the U.S. Constitution, concerned with basic liberties.

Checks on Majority Rule Afraid of unbridled democracy, the framers created a constitution by which the people rule only indirectly, barriers are placed in the path of majorities (see Figure 2.2), and deliberation is prized over conformity to majority opinion. As political philosopher Robert Dahl puts it, "To achieve their goal of preserving a set of inalienable rights superior to the majority principle . . . the framers deliberately created a framework of government that was carefully designed to impede and even prevent the operation of majority

FIGURE 2.2 • Amending the Constitution

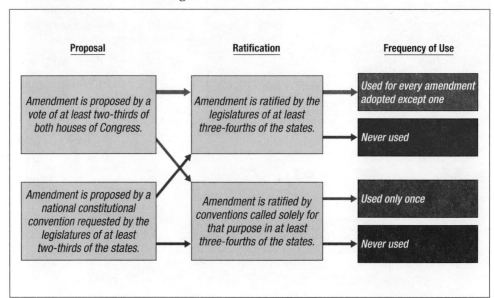

With two ways of proposing a constitutional amendment and two ways of ratifying one, there are four routes to changing the Constitution. In all but one case (the Twenty-First Amendment, which repealed Prohibition), constitutional amendments have been proposed by Congress and then ratified by the state legislatures.

rule."[27] Let us see what the framers did to try to dilute the power of the majority in the national government.

Of the three branches of government, only a part of one of them is selected by the direct vote of the people: the House of Representatives (Article I, Section 2, paragraph 1). As for the rest of the national government, the president is elected by the electoral college; the members of the Senate are elected by the state legislatures (since changed by the Seventeenth Amendment); and judges are appointed by the president and confirmed by the Senate. Representatives, senators, and presidents are elected, moreover, for different terms (two years for representatives, four years for presidents, and six years for senators), from different constituencies, and (often) at different times. These noncongruencies in elections were intended to ensure that popular majorities, at least in the short run, would be unlikely to overwhelm those who govern. Finally, the framers rejected the advice of radical democrats, such as Thomas Paine, Samuel Adams, and Thomas Jefferson, to allow the Constitution to be easily amended. Instead, they created an amending process that is exceedingly cumbersome and difficult (see Figure 2.2).

Thus, the framers designed a system in which majority opinion, although given some play (more than anywhere in the world at the time), was largely deflected and slowed, allowing somewhat insulated political leaders to deliberate at their pleasure.

Separation of Powers; Checks and Balances   During the American Revolution, American leaders worried mainly about the misrule of executives (kings and governors) and judges. As an antidote, they substituted legislative supremacy in state constitutions and in the Articles of Confederation, thinking that placing power in an elected representative body would make government effective and nontyrannical. The men who drafted the Constitution, however, though still leery of executive and judicial power, were more concerned by 1787 about the danger of legislative tyranny. To deal with this problem, the framers turned to the ancient notion of balanced government, popularized by the French philosopher Montesquieu. The central idea of balanced government is that concentrated power of any kind is dangerous and that the way to prevent tyranny is first to fragment governmental power into its constituent parts— executive, legislative, and judicial—then place each into a separate and independent branch. In the U.S. Constitution, Article I (on the legislative power), Article II (on the executive power), and Article III (on the judicial power) designate separate spheres of responsibility and enumerate specific powers for each branch. We call this the **separation of powers.**

To further ensure that power would not be exercised tyrannically, the framers arranged for the legislative, executive, and judicial powers to check one another in such a way that "ambition . . . be made to counteract ambition."[28] They did this by ensuring that no branch of the national government would be able to act entirely on its own without the cooperation of the others. To put it another way, each branch has ways of blocking the actions of the others. For instance, Congress is given the chief lawmaking power under the Constitution, but a bill can become a law only if the president signs it. The Supreme Court, moreover, has the power (although it is not specifically mentioned) to reject a law formulated by Congress and signed by the president if it is contrary to the Constitution. What is at work here was described nicely by Thomas Jefferson: "The powers of government should be so divided and balanced among several bodies of magistracy, as that no one could transcend their legal limits, without being effectually checked and constrained by the others."[29] We call the provisions that accomplish this objective **checks and balances.** Figure 2.3 shows in detail how each separate branch of the federal government can be checked by the other two. In this constitutional scheme, each branch has power, but none is able to exercise all of its powers on its own.

The Foundations for a National Free Enterprise Economy

The framers believed that the right to accumulate, use, and transfer private property was one of the fundamental and inalienable rights that governments were instituted to defend, so they looked for ways to protect it. They also believed that the obstacles to trade allowed under the Articles of Confederation were threatening to block the emergence of a vibrant national economy in which most of them were involved.

Property rights are protected in several places in the Constitution. Article I, Section 10, forbids the states to impair the obligation of contracts, to coin money, or to make anything but gold and silver coin a tender in payment of debts. In other words, the states could no longer help debtors by printing inflated money, forgiving debts, or otherwise infringing on the property of creditors, as had happened in such places as Rhode Island and North Carolina under the Articles of Confederation. Article IV, Section 1, further guarantees contracts by establishing that the states must give "full faith and credit" to the public acts, records, and judicial proceedings of every other state, which means that one could no longer escape legal and financial obligations in one state by moving to another. In addition, the Constitution guaranteed that the U.S. government would pay all debts contracted under the Articles of Confederation (Article VI, Section 1). Article IV, Section 2, paragraph 3, even protected private property in slaves by requiring states to deliver escaped slaves back to their owners.

Besides protecting private property, the framers took additional steps to encourage the emergence of a national free enterprise economy. Article I, Section 8, grants Congress the power to regulate interstate commerce (thus

separation of powers
The distribution of government legislative, executive, and judicial powers to separate branches of government.

checks and balances
The constitutional principle that government power shall be divided and that the fragments should balance or check one another to prevent tyranny.

FIGURE 2.3 • **Checks and Balances**

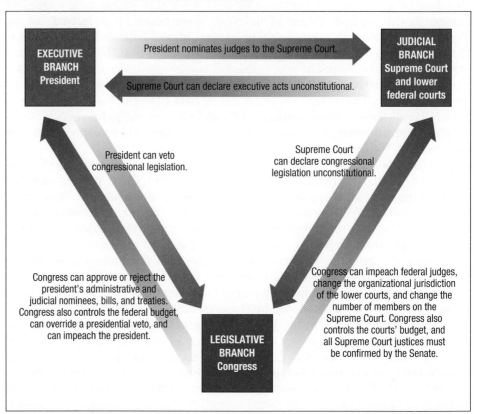

The framers of the Constitution believed that tyranny might be avoided if the power of government were fragmented into its executive, legislative, and judicial components and if each component were made the responsibility of a separate branch of government. To further protect against tyranny, they created mechanisms by which the actions of any single branch could be blocked by either or both of the other branches.

ending the chaos of individual states' regulations), to coin money and regulate its value (thus establishing a uniform national currency), to establish uniform laws of bankruptcy, and to protect the financial fruits of invention by establishing patent and copyright laws. At the same time, Article I, Sections 9 and 10, broke down barriers to trade by forbidding the states to impose taxes or duties on other states' exports, to enter into foreign treaties, to coin money, or to lay any imposts or duties on imports or exports.

The Struggle to Ratify the Constitution

Congress had instructed the delegates to the convention to propose changes to the Articles of Confederation. Under the provisions of the Articles of Confederation, such alterations would have required the unanimous consent of the 13 states. To follow such a course would have meant instant rejection of the new constitution, because Rhode Island, never friendly to the deliberations in Philadelphia, surely would have voted against it, and one or two additional states may well have joined Rhode Island. Acting boldly, the framers simply stated that ratification would be based on guidelines specified in Article VII of the unratified document they had just written, namely, approval by nine states meeting in special constitutional conventions. Congress agreed to this procedure, voting on September 28, 1787, to transmit the Constitution to the states for their consideration.

The battle over ratification was heated, and the outcome was far from certain. That the Constitution eventually carried the day may be partly attributed to the fact that the **Federalists** (those who supported the Constitution) did a better job of making their case than the **Anti-Federalists** (those who opposed the Constitution). Their intellectual advantages were nowhere more obvious than in the 85 articles written in defense of the Constitution for New York newspapers, under the name "Publius," by Alexander Hamilton (who wrote the most), James Madison (who wrote the best), and John Jay (who wrote only three). Collected later and published as *The Federalist Papers,* these articles strongly influenced the debate over ratification and remain the most impressive commentaries ever written about the U.S. Constitution. (Numbers 10 and 51, written by Madison, are reprinted in the Appendix, as is number 78, written by Hamilton.)

Anti-Federalist opposition to the Constitution was based on fear of centralized power and concern about the absence of a bill of rights.[30] Although the Federalists firmly believed that a bill of rights was unnecessary because of the protection of rights in the state constitutions and the many safeguards against tyranny in the federal Constitution, they promised to add one during the first session of Congress. Without this promise, ratification would probably not have happened. The Federalists kept their word. The 1st Congress passed a bill of rights in the form of 10 amendments to the Constitution (see Table 2.2 and the Appendix), and the amendments were eventually ratified by the required number of states by 1791.

Federalists

Proponents of the Constitution during the ratification fight; also the political party of Hamilton, Washington, and Adams.

Anti-Federalists

Opponents of the Constitution during the fight over ratification.

TABLE 2.2 ● The Bill of Rights

Amendment I	Freedom of religion, speech, press, and assembly
Amendment II	The right to bear arms
Amendment III	Prohibition against quartering of troops in private homes
Amendment IV	Prohibition against unreasonable searches and seizures
Amendment V	Rights guaranteed to the accused: requirement for grand jury indictment; protections against double jeopardy and self-incrimination; guarantee of due process
Amendment VI	Right to a speedy and public trial before an impartial jury, to cross-examine witnesses, and to have counsel
Amendment VII	Right to a trial by jury in civil suits
Amendment VIII	Prohibition against excessive bail and fines and against cruel and unusual punishment
Amendment IX	Traditional rights not listed in the Constitution are retained by the people
Amendment X	Powers not denied to them by the Constitution or given solely to the national government are retained by the states

Note: See the Appendix for the full text.

Ratification of the Constitution was a close call. Most of the small states quickly approved, attracted by the formula of equal representation in the Senate. Federalists organized a victory in Pennsylvania before the Anti-Federalists realized what had happened. After that, ratification became a struggle. Rhode Island voted no. North Carolina abstained because of the absence of a bill of rights and did not vote its approval until 1790. In the largest and most important states, the vote was exceedingly close. Massachusetts approved by a vote of 187–168; Virginia, by 89–79; and New York, by 30–27. The struggle was especially intense in Virginia, where prominent, articulate, and influential men were involved on both sides. The Federalists could call on George Washington, James Madison, John Marshall, and Edmund Randolph. The Anti-Federalists countered with George Mason, Richard Henry Lee, and Patrick Henry. Patrick Henry was particularly passionate, saying that the Constitution "squints towards monarchy." Although New Hampshire technically put the Constitution over the top, being the ninth state to vote approval, the proponents did not rest easily until approval was narrowly voted by Virginia and New York.

The Changing Constitution, Democracy, and American Politics

The Constitution is the basic rule book for the game of American politics. Constitutional rules apportion power and responsibility among governmental branches, define the fundamental nature of the relationships among governmental institutions, specify how individuals are to be selected for office, and tell how the rules themselves may be changed. Every aspiring politician who wants to attain office, every citizen who wants to influence what government does, and every group that wants to advance its interests in the political arena must know the rules and how to use them to their best advantage. Because the Constitution has this character, we understand it to be a fundamental *structural* factor influencing all of American political life.

Like all rules, however, constitutional rules can and do change over time. Their tendency to change with the times is why we sometimes speak of the "living Constitution." Constitutional changes come about in three specific ways: formal amendment, judicial interpretation, and political practices.

The Constitution may be formally amended by use of the procedures outlined in Article V of the Constitution (again, refer to Figure 2.2). This method has resulted in the addition of 27 amendments since the founding, the first 10 of which (the Bill of Rights) were added within three years of ratification. That only 17 have been added in the roughly 200 years since suggests that this method of changing the Constitution is extremely difficult. Over the years, proponents of constitutional amendments that would guarantee equal rights for women, ban same-sex marriages, and ban the burning of the American flag have learned how difficult it is to formally amend the Constitution; none of these amendments were added, despite polls reporting majorities in favor of them. Nevertheless, several formal amendments have played an important role in expanding democracy in the United States by ending slavery; extending voting rights to African Americans, women, and young people ages 18 to 20; and making the Senate subject to popular vote.

The Constitution is also changed by decisions and interpretations of the U.S. Supreme Court. For instance, in *Marbury* v. *Madison* (1803), the Court

Voicing Concerns at the Court

The Constitution has evolved over the years in three ways: through the amendment process, through evolving political practices, and through the Supreme Court's changing interpretation of the Constitution's meaning. Here antiabortion protesters demonstrate in front of the Supreme court building on the anniversary of the Court's *Roe* v. *Wade* decision to demand a reversal of that landmark decision.

claimed the power of **judicial review**—the right to declare the actions of the other branches of government null and void if they are contrary to the Constitution—even though such a power is not specifically mentioned in the Constitution. In *Griswold* v. *Connecticut* (1965), and later in *Roe* v. *Wade* (1973), to take another example, the Court supported a claim for the existence of a fundamental right of privacy even though such a right is not explicitly mentioned in the Constitution. Many conservatives believe that such actions by the Supreme Court are illegitimate because they go beyond the original intentions of the framers, or cannot be justified in the provisions of the Constitution. Many others disagree, believing that the Court has and must interpret the Constitution in light of changing circumstances that the framers could not have envisioned.

judicial review
The power of the Supreme Court to declare actions of the other branches and levels of government unconstitutional.

The meaning of the Constitution also changes through changing political practices, which end up serving as precedents for political actors. Political parties and nominating conventions are not cited in the Constitution, for example, but it would be hard to think about American politics today without them. It is also fair to say that the framers would not recognize the modern presidency, which is now a far more important office than they envisioned, a change that has been brought about largely by the political and military involvement of the United States in world affairs.

America's Constitution: How Exceptional?

The story of how formal amendments, judicial interpretations, and political practices have changed the constitutional rules in the United States will be told in more detail throughout this text. Having pointed out the various ways that the constitutional rules can and do change over the course of history should not detract, however, from the basic point about the degree to which the Constitution created a system of government that is quite exceptional when compared with other countries that might legitimately be called democracies. What is most exceptional about the American system of government that the Constitution shaped is the degree to which government authority and responsibilities are fragmented.[31] One can see this fragmentation when comparing our constitutional design to that of other countries.

First, the Constitution of 1787 created a system of separation of powers and checks and balances that is remarkably different from the **parliamentary systems** that characterize all other rich democracies. In our system, not only are executive, legislative, and judicial powers lodged in different institutions, but each institution is given tools both to influence the other branches and to protect itself from the encroachments of the others. There is no separation of executive and legislative power in parliamentary systems. In these systems, the prime minister is elected by the majority in the parliament and his/her cabinet (the heads of the executive branch departments) must be approved by parliament as well. In parliamentary systems, that is to say, executive and legislative powers are fused. In the United States, executive and legislative institutions were created to live in conflict, with gridlock an ever-present possibility. In some parliamentary systems, such as Great Britain and Finland, moreover, the judiciary is not co-equal to the other branches, as it is in the United States, lacking the power to overrule parliamentary or cabinet action as unconstitutional (although this judicial power exists in such parliamentary systems as India, Germany, France, and Japan).

Some countries with parliamentary systems—namely, those without a monarchy—elect a president, as we do in the United States. But, with the exception of the French president, they tend to fill the kinds of ceremonial roles that kings and queens do—christening new warships, opening parliament, greeting foreign dignitaries, and the like—without much independent power to shape national affairs. This is true, for example, in Germany and Israel.

Other countries have constitutions that created a system of separated powers—rather than a parliamentary system—but with not much in the way of checks and balances. The handful of democracies in Latin America, for example, have separately elected presidents and national legislatures, but in most of them the president has considerable power over the legislature because of emergency decree powers and can often remove judges without seriously consulting the legislature.[32]

Our Constitution further fragments government power by dividing the legislative power among two powerful and relatively independent chambers, each of which has somewhat independent responsibilities and constituencies, and relatively equal power in the legislative process. Although many parliamentary systems are bicameral in law, only Germany is bicameral in fact. In these other systems, the lower house has gained power over the legislative process (the House of Commons in Great Britain, the Knesset in Israel, the Diet in Japan), with the upper house becoming either entirely irrelevant or weak and easily circumvented.

The Constitution of 1787 also fragments power by creating a federal system, with powers and responsibilities distributed among the states and national government. To be sure, other countries, including Germany, India, and Brazil, have federal systems—a subject that will be explored in depth in Chapter 3—but the American states are unusually influential in national affairs because they are represented in an upper house in the national government that exercises real power (the Senate). Moreover, the states play an important role in the election of the president because of the state-based electoral college created by the framers, a way of electing the chief executive that exists nowhere else (to be described in more detail in Chapter 10).

parliamentary system

A system of government in which authority is lodged in a legislative body (the parliament) that chooses, usually from within its own ranks, a prime minister and a cabinet to run the day-to-day affairs of state.

Comparing Constitutions

Using the Democracy Standard

A republic or a democracy?

PROPOSITION   The Constitution created a republic, not a democracy, and we remain a republic today.

AGREE   The framers created a republic because they were worried about the possibility of majority tyranny in the new nation. Consequently, they wrote a number of provisions into the Constitution to control the purported excesses of democracy. These include the separation of powers into executive, legislative, and judicial branches; checks and balances to prevent any of the branches from governing on its own; federalism to fragment government powers between a national government and the states; an appointed federal judiciary with life tenure; selection of the president by the electoral college; and election of members of the Senate by state legislatures. Although some of these provisions have not worked precisely as the framers intended, the American system of government remains essentially "republican" in nature, with the majority finding it very difficult to prevail.

Although the framers had every intention of creating a **DISAGREE** republic and holding democracy in check, they were unable to do so. Over the years, as the nation became more egalitarian in its cultural, economic, and social life, the tide of democracy transformed the original constitutional design. By formal amendment, judicial interpretations, and changing political practices, government has been fashioned into a highly responsive set of institutions, heeding the voice of the people. For example, the Seventeenth Amendment created a Senate whose members are directly elected by the people. The Supreme Court, moreover, has extended civil rights protections to racial and ethnic minorities. And, the presidency has become both more powerful and more attentive to majority opinion. Today, the national government does pretty much what the American people want it to do, even if it sometimes takes a while for it to do so.

CONSIDER   • Which of the above arguments makes more sense to you?   • Does it appear to be the case that the American people pretty much get what they want from government?   • Can you think of issues where the majority does not, in fact, get its way with elected officials?   • If you can think of such cases, how would you explain the disconnect between people and government?   • Is it better explained by lack of responsiveness on the part of elected leaders or by the constitutional system designed by the framers?   • On the other hand, can you think of other areas of public life where elected leaders seem too responsive to the public?   • In these cases, why is it that the constitutional protections designed by the framers don't seem to be deflecting the influence of majority opinion?

The material in the remainder of this book will help you answer these questions more confidently, to be sure, but a preliminary consideration of them here will serve you well as you learn more about how American politics and government work.

While other countries, then, share bits and pieces of American constitutional design, ours is the only one that builds in fragmentation in so many ways. It is one of the reasons why American politics and government policy making are so often gridlocked and incoherent. It is, as we have suggested in this chapter, exactly what most of the framers had in mind.

Summary

The first constitution joining the American states was the Articles of Confederation. Under its terms, the states were organized into a loose confederation in which the states retained full sovereignty and the central government had little power. Because of a wide range of defects in the Articles of Confederation and fears among many American leaders that democratic and egalitarian tendencies were beginning to spin out of control, a gathering was called in Philadelphia to amend the Articles of Confederation. The delegates chose instead to formulate an entirely new constitution, based on the principles of republicanism (federalism, limited government, the separation of powers, checks and balances, and limitations on majority rule).

The Constitution was ratified in an extremely close vote of the states after a hard-fought struggle between the Federalists and the Anti-Federalists. The Federalists were supported primarily by those who believed in a more centralized republicanism; the Anti-Federalists were supported primarily by those who believed in small-scale republicanism. Despite its "close shave," the Constitution became very popular among the American people within only a few years of the ratification fight. Because of the continuing struggle for democracy by the American people, the Constitution has become far more democratic over the years than was originally intended by the framers.

mypoliscilab
Where participation leads to action!

Web Exploration
Delegates to the Convention

ISSUE: The Constitution was made by people who were not much like the average inhabitant of the United States in 1787.

SITE: Find out more about the delegates to the Convention by going to the National Archives in MyPoliSciLab at **www.mypoliscilab.com.** In the "Web Explorations" section for Chapter 2, open "delegates to the convention," then "delegates." Select a state and read the biographies of the delegates.

WHAT YOU'VE LEARNED: How would you describe the average delegate? How representative do you believe them to have been of the American people of the time?

HINT: There were no women; few artisans and small farmers; and no free blacks, indentured servants, slaves, or Native Americans at the proceedings. These groups together comprised the vast majority of the American population.

Internet Sources

Annotated Constitution
www.gpoaccess.gov/constitution/index.html
   An annotation of the Constitution in which each clause is tied to Supreme Court decisions concerning its meaning; done by the Library of Congress.

Biographical Sketches of the Delegates to the Constitutional Convention
www.archives.gov/national-archives-experience/charters/constitution_founding_fathers.html
   Profiles of the delegates to the Constitutional Convention.

Constitutional Finder
http://confinder.richmond.edu
   A site with links to constitutions for most nations of the world.

Cornell University Law School
www.law.cornell.edu/
   Pathways to the full text of U.S. Supreme Court decisions and opinions, articles on constitutional issues, and much more.

Political Science Resources: Political Thought
www.psr.keele.ac.uk/
   A vast collection of documents on democracy, liberty, and constitutionalism.

The U.S. Constitution Online
www.usconstitution.net
> *A very rich site that presents material on every aspect of the history and development of the Constitution.*

Suggestions for Further Reading

Amar, Akhil Reed. *America's Constitution: A Biography.* New York: Random House, 2005.
> *A detailed, lively, and passionate examination of the origins of the provisions of the U.S. Constitution, tracing each to its roots in the English legal tradition, experiences in the states during the colonial period, and the politics of the time.*

Ellis, Joseph J. *Founding Brothers: The Revolutionary Generation.* New York: Alfred Knopf, 2001.
> *An entertaining and accessible look at the intertwined lives of the men who wrote the Declaration of Independence, fought the Revolutionary War, fashioned the Constitution, and launched the new American government.*

Rossiter, Clinton, ed. *The Federalist Papers.* New York: New American Library, 1961.
> *Classic commentaries on the Constitution and its key provisions, written by Alexander Hamilton, John Jay, and James Madison.*

Storing, Herbert J. *What the Anti-Federalists Were For.* Chicago: University of Chicago Press, 1981.
> *The most complete collection available on the published views of the Anti-Federalists. Includes convincing commentary by Storing.*

Wood, Gordon S. *The Creation of the American Republic.* New York: Norton, 1972.
> *The most exhaustive and respected source on America's changing ideas during the period 1776–1787, or from the start of the American Revolution to the writing of the Constitution.*

Wood, Gordon S. *The Radicalism of the American Revolution.* New York: Knopf, 1992.
> *Examines and rejects the argument that the American Revolution was merely a political and not a social and economic revolution.*

CHAPTER 3

Federalism: States and Nation

IN THIS CHAPTER

- What federalism is and why we have it

- Conflicts over the meaning of federalism in the United States

- How our federal system differs from other systems of government

- Advantages and disadvantages of federalism

- The impact of terrorism on the national–state balance

- Federalism and democracy

Who's in Charge Here?

It didn't take very long for the "blame game" to begin.[1] Even as scenes of utter chaos and destruction in New Orleans caused by Hurricane Katrina were broadcast around the world in late August 2005, federal, state, and local officials started pointing fingers at each other. Democratic Louisiana Governor Kathleen Blanco asked why the Federal Emergency Management Agency (FEMA) was so slow to respond to the disaster and why active-duty military forces were not sent to help provide shelter, food and water, and order. Democratic Mayor Ray Nagin complained about the slow federal response in radio and television interviews and estimated that at least 10,000 people died from the flooding, violence, loss of power, and toxic wastes. FEMA Director Michael Brown said he hadn't known thousands of people were in the Superdome with little food, water, or sanitation, although conditions there were widely reported even before Katrina struck. Brown and some White House officials (although not President Bush) laid the blame squarely on state and local officials for failing to plan properly for the emergency, botching the evacuation, and failing to enforce law and order.

It will probably take investigators years to properly apportion the blame and begin to fix the problems Katrina revealed. One reason it will take so long is the complexity created by our federal system of government—the division of powers and responsibilities among the national and state governments (which, in turn, create and oversee local governments). In some matters, federal and state government powers and responsibilities are separate and clearly defined, but in others they are shared. Furthermore, the boundary lines for shared matters—including such crucial areas as law and order, disaster preparedness, and disaster relief—are not always clear and stable. The disaster resulted not just from the storm, but from the failure of all levels of government to fulfill their core responsibilities and to coordinate activities in areas of shared responsibilities. The failure to coordinate with other government jurisdictions may have been due to political rivalries, genuine confusion, or both.

Take core responsibilities. The federal government is in charge of maintaining the health and vitality of inland waterways used for transporting goods and people and for protecting river communities from floods. Over many years, the Army Corps of Engineers has built and maintained an elaborate system of levees on the lower Mississippi to straighten it and prevent flooding of low-lying cities, including New Orleans. Despite many warnings from scientists and engineers that the levee system was inadequate, Democratic and Republican presidents and Congresses failed to provide funds for a levee system that could adequately protect the city. For its part, FEMA failed to pre-position enough rescue teams and supplies and responded slowly when the levees broke. Finally, it

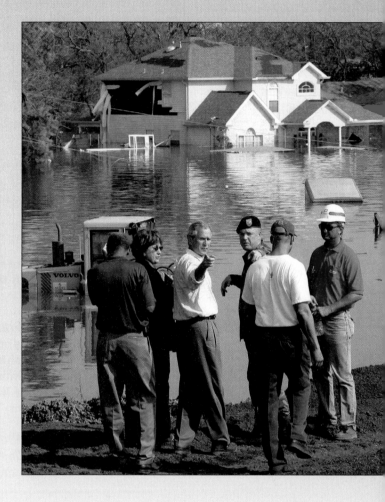

took the president and his team a few days to realize that state and local officials were simply overwhelmed.

The Louisiana state government also failed to meet some of its core responsibilities. It did not come close to implementing its own disaster mitigation and relief plan. Furthermore, over the years it had adopted a series of tax, subsidy, and regulatory policies that encouraged construction along low-lying coastal areas, putting people at risk and helping destroy wetlands that once protected populated areas from hurricane storm surges. Nor did local New Orleans officials meet their core responsibilities. The mayor delayed in ordering a mandatory evacuation, failed to provide transportation for people without cars once the order was given, and failed to provide adequate policing during and after the emergency. In addition, city officials had for years avoided upgrading and protecting vital infrastructure (pumps, sewage treatment facilities, emergency medical services, and more) or improving building codes for residential and commercial structures.

Some of the problems surrounding Katrina arose from very real confusion about who was to do what when. Traditionally, state and local governments have been the first responders to disasters, with the federal government providing backup, financial and logistical aid, and help with long-term recovery. The federal government will enter the picture earlier if state officials ask, or if federal officials determine that state and local officials cannot protect their citizens. At this writing, it is still unclear how the various governments communicated. White House officials claim, for example, that Governor Blanco refused to ask the federal government to take control of the Louisiana National Guard and New Orleans police. They also say they wanted to send the 82nd Airborne to restore order and coordinate logistics, but hesitated because the governor had not made a specific request. The governor said she told President Bush, "I need everything you have got." She never specified what kinds of troops she needed because "nobody told me that I had to request that. I thought that I requested everything they had. . . . We were in a war zone by then."

The Hurricane Katrina debacle shows that American federalism is a very complex system in which both cooperation and tension exist among the various levels of government. In this chapter, you will learn about the American system of federalism, where it came from, how it works, what strengths and weaknesses are associated with it, and how it contributes to or detracts from democracy. ■

Thinking Critically About This Chapter

This complex mixture of state and national government authority and responsibilities highlighted in the story of the response to Hurricane Katrina is an important characteristic of American federalism today and in the past.

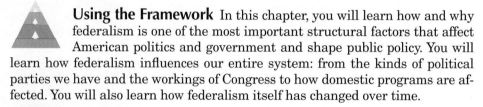 **Using the Framework** In this chapter, you will learn how and why federalism is one of the most important structural factors that affect American politics and government and shape public policy. You will learn how federalism influences our entire system: from the kinds of political parties we have and the workings of Congress to how domestic programs are affected. You will also learn how federalism itself has changed over time.

 Using the Democracy Standard Using the evaluative tools you learned in Chapter 1, you will be able to judge for yourself whether federalism enriches or diminishes democracy in the United States.

Federalism as a System of Government

The United States is full of governments. We have not only a federal government in Washington, D.C., but also governments in each of 50 states and in each of thousands of smaller governmental units, such as counties (about 3,000 of them), cities, towns and townships, school districts, and special districts that deal with such matters as parks and sanitation.

All these governments are organized and related to each other in a particular way. The small governments—those of counties, cities, towns, and special districts—are legal creations of state governments. They can be created, changed, or abolished by state laws, at the state's convenience. But state governments themselves have much more weight and permanence because of their prominent place in the Constitution. Together with the central government in Washington, D.C., they form what is known as a federal system. The *federal system* is part of the basic structure of U.S. government, deeply rooted in our Constitution and history. It is one of the most important features of American politics, since it affects practically everything else.

Sectarian Violence in Iraq

Deep divisions between Sunnis, Shias, and Kurds in Iraq made it inevitable that the nation's new constitution would take the form of a federation in which no single group could control the government. Widespread sectarian violence, as seen in this scene from a suicide bombing in Baghdad in 2005, underscored this point to constitution makers.

The Nature of Federalism

Federalism is a system under which significant government powers are divided between the central government and smaller units, such as states or provinces. Neither one completely controls the other; each has some room for independent action. A federal system can be contrasted with two other types of government: a confederation and a unitary government. In a **confederation,** the constituent states get together for certain common purposes but retain ultimate individual authority and can veto major central governmental actions. The United Nations, the European Union, and the American government under the Articles of Confederation are examples. In a **unitary system,** the central government has all the power and can change its constituent units or tell them what to do. Japan and France have this kind of government, as do a substantial majority of nations around the world. These three different types of governmental systems are contrasted in Figure 3.1.

American Federalism: How Exceptional?

Some of the elements of federalism go back in history at least as far as the Union of Utrecht in the Netherlands in 1579, but federalism as it exists today is largely an American invention,[2] although it has come to take on a variety of forms in the world today. Including the United States, 23 nations, with roughly 40 percent of the world's population, have federal systems today.[3]

Historical Origins of American Federalism   American federalism emerged from the way in which the states declared independence from Britain—becoming, in effect, separate countries—and then joined to form a confederation and then a single nation, as discussed in Chapter 2. Recall that the framers of the Constitution turned to federalism as a middle-ground solution between a confederation form of government—which was deemed a failed model based on the experience under the Articles of Confederation—and a unitary form of government—which a majority of states, jealous of their independence and

federalism

A system in which significant governmental powers are divided between a central government and smaller units, such as states.

confederation

A loose association of states or territorial divisions in which very little power is lodged in the central government.

unitary system

A system in which a central government has complete power over its constituent units or states.

Comparing Federal and Unitary Systems

FIGURE 3.1 • Types of Political Systems

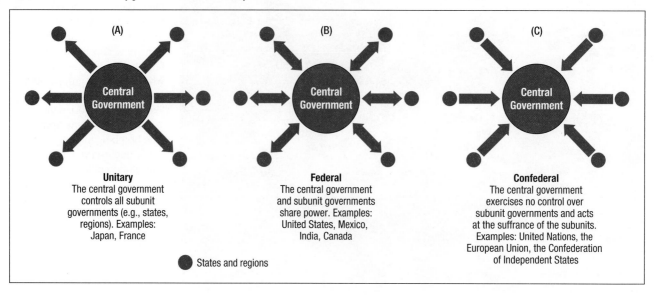

A majority of countries have unitary systems (A), in which the central government controls the state and local governments, which in turn exert power over the citizens. The United States, however, has a federal system (B), in which the central government has power on some issues, the states have power on other issues, and the central and state governments share power on yet others. In a confederation (C), the central institutions have only a loose coordinating role, with real governing power residing in the constituent states or units.

prerogatives, found unacceptable. Federalism was also a form of government that was consistent with the eighteenth-century republicanism of the framers because it helps fragment government power. But we can gain further insight into *why* the United States adopted and has continued as a federal system if we look at what other countries with similar systems have in common.

Role of Size and Diversity   Federalism tends to be found in nations that are large in a territorial sense and in which the various geographical regions are fairly distinctive from one another in terms of religion, ethnicity, language, and forms of economic activity. In Germany, for example, the Catholics of the south have traditionally been more conservative than the Protestants of the north and east, while the territories of the former Germany Democratic Republic have markedly lower living standards than those in the west. In Canada, the farmers of the central plains are not much like the fishers of Nova Scotia, and the French-speaking (and primarily Catholic) residents of Quebec differ markedly from the mostly English-speaking Protestants of the rest of the country. In Spain there are deep divisions along ethnic and language lines (as in the distinctive Basque and Catalan regions). Other important federal systems include such large and richly diverse countries as India, Pakistan, Russia, and Brazil. In all these countries, federalism gives diverse and geographically concentrated groups the degree of local autonomy they seem to want, with no need to submit in all matters to a unified central government. In Iraq, the relative degree of autonomy of Kurdish and Shiite provinces in a federal Iraq was the most important point of contention in the debate over a new Iraqi constitution in 2005.

The United States, too, is large and diverse. From the early days of the republic, the slave-holding and agriculture-oriented South was quite distinct from the mercantile Northeast, and some important differences persist today. Illinois is not Louisiana; the farmers of Iowa differ from defense and electronics workers in California. States today also vary in their approaches to public policy, their racial and ethnic composition, and their political cultures.[4] In *The Federalist Papers,* the Founders argued that this size and diversity made federalism especially appropriate for the new United States.

While the American system of federalism was truly exceptional at the founding, other large and important countries have taken on federal forms in the years since, especially since the end of World War II. To this extent, the United States is no longer the single exception or one among a handful of exceptions to the unitary nature of the majority of the world's governments.

Federalism in the Constitution

Federalism is embodied in the U.S. Constitution in two main ways: (1) Power is expressly given to the states, as well as to the national government, and (2) the states have important roles in shaping, and choosing officials for, the national government itself, and in amending the Constitution.

Independent State Powers

Although the Constitution makes the central government supreme in certain matters, it also makes clear that the state governments have independent powers. The **supremacy clause** in Article VI states that the Constitution, laws, and treaties of the United States shall be the "supreme law of the land," but Article I, Section 8, enumerates what kinds of laws Congress has the power to pass, and the Tenth Amendment declares that the powers not delegated to the central government by the Constitution or prohibited by the Constitution to the states are "*reserved to the states* [emphasis added] respectively, or to the people." This provision is known as the **reservation clause.**

In other words, the U.S. Constitution specifically lists what the national government can do. Its powers include authority to levy taxes, regulate interstate commerce, establish post offices, and declare war, plus make laws "necessary and proper" for carrying out those powers. The Constitution then provides that all other legitimate government functions may be performed by the states, except for a few things, such as coining money or conducting foreign policy, that are forbidden by Article I, Section 10. This leaves a great deal in the hands of state governments, including licensing lawyers, doctors, and dentists; regulating businesses within their boundaries; chartering banks and corporations; providing a system of family law; providing a system of public education; and assuming the responsibility for building roads and highways, licensing drivers, and registering cars. The reservation clause is unique to the United States and shows how important states are in American federalism. Other federal systems, such as Canada's and Germany's, reserve to the national government all functions not explicitly given to the states. Having said this, it remains the case that the Constitution is not crystal clear about the balance of powers and responsibilities between the state and national governments, leaving ample room for the meaning of federalism to change with the times.

supremacy clause

The provision in Article VI of the Constitution that the Constitution itself and the laws and treaties of the United States are the supreme law of the land, taking precedence over state laws and constitutions.

reservation clause

The Tenth Amendment to the Constitution, reserving powers to the states or the people.

Comparing State and Local Governments

The States' Roles in National Government

Moreover, the Constitution's provisions about the formation of the national government recognize a special position for the states. The Constitution declares in Article VII that it was "done in Convention by the unanimous consent of the *states* present" (emphasis added) and provides that the Constitution would go into effect not when a majority of all Americans voted for it but when the conventions of nine *states* ratified it. Article V provides that the Constitution can be amended only when conventions in or the legislatures of three-quarters of the states ratify an amendment. Article IV, Section 3, makes clear that no states can be combined or divided into new states without the consent of the state legislatures concerned. Thus, the state governments have charge of ratifying and amending the Constitution, and the states control their own boundaries.

The Constitution also provides special roles for the states in the selection of national government officials. The states decide who can vote for members of the U.S. House of Representatives (Article I, Section 2) and draw the boundaries of House districts. Each state is given two senators (Article V) who were, until 1913, to be chosen by the state legislatures rather than by the voters (Article I, Section 3; altered by the Seventeenth Amendment). And the states play a key part in the complicated electoral college system of choosing a president in which each state has votes equal to the number of its senators and representatives combined, with the president elected by a majority of *electoral* votes, not a majority of popular votes (Article II, Section 1).

Relations Among the States

horizontal federalism
Term used to refer to relationships among the states.

The Constitution also regulates relations among the states (these state-to-state relations are sometimes called **horizontal federalism**). Article IV of the Constitution is particularly important in this regard (see Table 3.1). For example, each state is required to give "full faith and credit" to the public acts, records, and judicial proceedings of every other state. This means that private contractual or financial agreements among people or companies in one state are valid in all the other states and that civil judgments by the courts of one state must be recognized by the others. Because of this constitutional provision, people in one state cannot evade financial obligations—for example, credit card or department store debts, alimony and child-support payments—by moving to another state.

Explaining Differences in State Laws

The "full faith and credit" provision is what worries many opponents of same-sex marriage about Massachusetts' legalization of the practice in 2004. When people of the same sex are married in Massachusetts, do they remain legally married if and when they move to another state? Currently five states—Connecticut, New Jersey, New York, New Mexico, and Rhode Island—and the District of Columbia have no law barring such marriages, but all other states have passed statutes or constitutional amendments doing so. A flurry of such statutes and state constitutional changes followed passage by Congress of the Defense of Marriage Act, which denied federal benefits (such as Medicaid and Medicare) to spouses in same-sex marriages and authorized states that wished to do so to enact legislation barring recognition of same-sex marriages from other states. However, the U.S. Supreme Court has yet to decide a case involving the "full faith and credit" obligations of the states on this issue. It will certainly do so if other states legalize same-sex marriage or if the practice remains legal in Massachusetts (its citizens will vote in late 2008 on a constitutional provision banning same-sex marriage).

TABLE 3.1 • Constitutional Underpinnings of Federalism

Provisions	Where to Find Them in the Constitution	What They Mean
Supremacy of the national government in its own sphere	Supremacy clause: Article VI	The supremacy clause establishes that federal laws and the Constitution take precedence over state laws and constitutions.
Limitations on national government powers and reservation of powers to the states	Enumerated national powers: Article I, Section 8 Limits on national powers: Article I, Section 9; Article IV, Section 3; Eleventh Amendment Bill of Rights: First through Tenth Amendments Reservation clause: Tenth Amendment	The powers of the federal government are laid out specifically in the Constitution, as are strict limitations on the power of the federal government. Powers not specifically spelled out are reserved to the states or to the people.
Limitations on state powers	Original restrictions: Article I, Section 10 Civil War Amendments: Thirteenth through Fifteenth Amendments	The Constitution places strict limitations on the power of the states in particular areas of activity.
State role in national government	Ratification of Constitution: Article VII Amendment of Constitution: Article V Election of representatives: Article I, Section 2 and Section 4 Two senators from each state: Article I, Section 3 No deprivation of state suffrage in Senate: Article V Choice of senators: Article I, Section 3 (however, see Seventeenth Amendment) Election of president: Article II, Section 1 (however, see Twelfth Amendment)	The states' role in national affairs is clearly laid out. Rules for voting and electing representatives, senators, and the president are defined so that state governments play a part.
Regulation of relations among states	Full faith and credit: Article IV, Section 1 Privileges and immunities: Article IV, Section 2	Constitutional rules ensure that the states must respect each other's legal actions

Article IV also specifies that the citizens of each state are entitled to all the "privileges and immunities" of the citizens in the several states. That means that whatever citizenship rights a person has in one state apply in the other states as well. For example, because of this provision, out-of-state residents have the same access to state courts as in-state residents, as well as an equal right to own property and to be protected by the police.

Agreements among a group of states to solve mutual problems, called **interstate compacts,** requires the consent of Congress. The framers inserted this provision (Article I, Section 10) into the Constitution as a way to prevent the emergence of coalitions of states that might threaten federal authority or the union itself. Interstate compacts in force today cover a wide range of cooperative state activities. For example, New York and New Jersey created and Congress approved a compact to create the Port of New York Authority. Other compacts among states include agreements to cooperate on matters such as pollution control, crime prevention, transportation, and disaster planning.

interstate compacts
Agreements among states to cooperate on solving mutual problems; requires approval by Congress.

The Evolution of American Federalism

It took a long time after the adoption of the Constitution for the present federal system to emerge. There were and continue to be ebbs and flows in the nature of the relationship between the states and national government and in the relative power of the states and the federal government as they interacted with one another.[5] Eventually, however, the national government gained ground.[6] There are many reasons for this:

- Economic crises and problems generated pressures on the government in Washington to do something to help fix the national economy. The Great Depression in the 1930s is the primary example, but even today, we expect the president, Congress, and the Federal Reserve to competently manage national economic affairs, something the states cannot do for themselves. Most Americans want the government in Washington to do something about lowering gasoline prices when they get too high.

- War and the preparation for war are also important spurs to national-level actions, rather than state-level ones, because it is only the government in Washington that can raise an army and a navy, generate sufficient revenues to pay for military campaigns, and coordinate the productive resources of the nation to make sustained war possible. It is no accident, then, that each of our major wars has served to enhance the power of government in Washington: the Civil War, World Wars I and II, the Korean War, the Vietnam War, and the new war on terrorism.

- Finally, a number of problems emerged over the course of our history that most political leaders and the public believed could be solved most effectively by the national government rather than by 50 separate state governments: air and water pollution; unsafe food, drugs, and consumer products; the denial of civil rights for racial minorities; anticompetitive practices by some large corporations; poverty; and more. When natural disasters such as Hurricane Katrina happen, for example, Americans want Washington to play a major role in recovery efforts.

The Perpetual Debate About the Nature of American Federalism

From the very beginnings of our nation, two political philosophies have contended with one another over the nature of American federalism and the role to be played by the central government. These are generally referred to as the nationalist position and the states' rights position.

The Nationalist Position   Nationalists believe that the Constitution was formed by a compact among the people to create a single national community, pointing to the powerful phrase that opens the preamble: "We the People of the United States" (not "We the States"). Nationalists also point to the clear expression in the preamble of the purposes for which "we the people" formed a new government, namely to "create a more perfect union . . . and to promote the General Welfare." Also important in the nationalist brief are provisions in the Constitution that point toward a strong central government with expansive responsibilities, namely, the "supremacy clause" in Article VI and the "elastic" or **"necessary and proper" clause** in Article I, Section 8. Not surprisingly, proponents of the nationalist position have advocated an active national government with the capacity and the will to tackle whatever problems might emerge to threaten the peace and prosperity of the United States or the general welfare of its people. Alexander Hamilton, Chief Justice John Marshall, Abraham Lincoln, Woodrow Wilson, and the two Roosevelts, Theodore and Franklin. Liberal Democrats tended to support this position for most of the post–World War II period—believing that social welfare, civil rights, and environmental pro-

nationalist position
The view of American federalism that holds that the Constitution created a system in which the national government is supreme, relative to the states, and that granted to it a broad range of powers and responsibilities.

necessary and proper clause
Article I, Section 8, of the Constitution, also known as the *elastic clause;* gives Congress the authority to make whatever laws are necessary and proper to carry out its enumerated responsibilities.

Border Stop

How to control illegal immigration across the U.S.–Mexican border, and what to do about those who make it across, have become contentious issues between several states and the federal government.

tection were safer in the hands of the federal government than the state governments—but have recently changed their tune on some issues, as you will see in the next section. Republican President George W. Bush, whom some call a "big government" conservative, has been the main author of several programs that have increased the size and reach of the federal government: the "No Child Left Behind" educational initiative, an expanding national defense budget, a subscription-drug benefit under Medicare, and a large expansion of the homeland security bureaucracy and budget.

The States' Rights Position   Proponents of the states' rights position argue that the Constitution was created as a compact among the states and that the framers meant for the states to be coequal with the national government. They base their argument on a number of foundations. They note, for instance, that the Constitution was written by representatives of the states; that it was ratified by the states and not by a vote of the public; and that the process for amending the Constitution requires the affirmative votes of three-fourths of the states, not three-fourths of the people. They also point out that the Constitution mandates equal representation of states in the Senate and requires that the president be elected by the electoral votes of the states. States' rights proponents say that the prominent role of the states in our system of government is also indicated in Article IV, Section 3 (which says that states are inviolate) and in the Tenth Amendment (the "reservation" clause, discussed above).

    Not surprisingly, proponents of the states' rights position have argued that the Constitution created a form of government in which the national government is strictly limited in size and responsibility and in which states retain broad autonomy in the conduct of their own affairs. Popular among states' rights proponents is the concept of **dual federalism,** which suggests that there are distinct, nonoverlapping areas of responsibility for the national government and the state governments and that each level of government is sovereign in its

states' rights position

The view of American federalism that holds that the Constitution created a system of dual sovereignty in which the national government and the state governments are sovereign in their own spheres.

dual federalism

Federalism in which the powers of the states and the national government are neatly separated like the sections of a layer cake.

own sphere. Thomas Jefferson, John C. Calhoun, the New England and Southern secessionists, the southern resistors to the civil rights revolution, and many contemporary conservatives are associated with this view of federalism. On several matters, many liberal Democrats have become "states rights" advocates; many now want the states to take the lead on stem cell research, physician-assisted suicide, and gay rights protections.

We shall see in the pages ahead that the nationalist view has prevailed over the long haul of American history. However, the states' rights view has always been and remains today a vital position from which to oppose too much power and responsibility in the government in Washington. (See Figure 3.2 for an overview of this history.)

Federalism Before the Civil War

In the late 1790s, during the administration of John Adams, Thomas Jefferson's Republicans deeply resented the Alien and Sedition Acts, which the Federalists used to punish political dissent by followers of Jefferson. In response, Jefferson and Madison secretly authored the Virginia and Kentucky Resolutions, which declared that the states did not have to obey unconstitutional national laws and left it to the states to decide what was unconstitutional. In this case, the Republicans, representing the more agricultural South, were advocating states' rights against a national government run by the more merchant-oriented Federalists of the Northeast. About a decade later, however, the merchants of New England used the southerners' own arguments to oppose President Madison's War of 1812 against Britain, which they felt interfered with their trade. Neither of these efforts at **nullification** prevailed.

nullification

An attempt by states to declare national laws or actions null and void.

The Pre–Civil War Supreme Court on Federalism One crucial question about federalism in the early years of the United States concerned who, if any-

FIGURE 3.2 • Timeline: Landmarks in the History of U.S. Federalism*

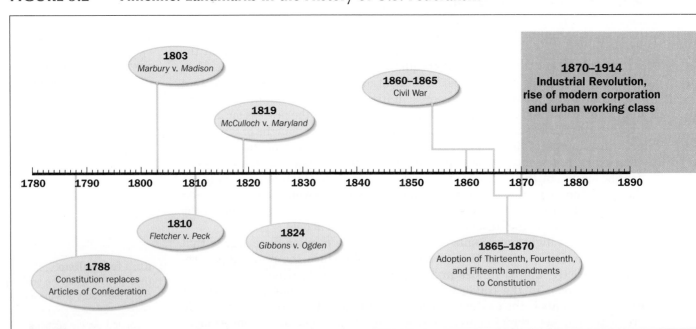

* Additional information provided only for items not discussed in the text.

one, would enforce the supremacy clause. Who would make sure that the U.S. laws and Constitution were actually the "supreme law of the land," controlling state laws? The answer turned out to be the U.S. Supreme Court, but this answer emerged only gradually and haltingly as the Court established its power within the federal system. Only after the strong-willed and subtle John Marshall became chief justice and, in 1803, established the Supreme Court's authority to declare *national* laws unconstitutional did the Supreme Court turn to the question of national power over the states. In *Fletcher* v. *Peck* (1810), it established the power of judicial review over the states, holding a state law unconstitutional under the U.S. Constitution.[7] Chief Justice Marshall cleverly avoided explicit discussion of the Court's power of judicial review over state laws. He simply took it for granted and used it.

The Supreme Court also provided crucial legal justification for the expansion of federal government power in the important case of *McCulloch* v. *Maryland* (1819). The case involved action by the state of Maryland to impose a tax on the Bank of the United States. The state of Maryland argued that the creation of the bank had been unconstitutional, exceeding the powers of Congress, and that, in any case, states could tax whatever they wanted within their own borders. But Chief Justice Marshall upheld the constitutionality of the bank's creation and its immunity from taxation and, in the process, made a major statement justifying extensive national authority.[8]

In his opinion for the Court, Marshall declared that the Constitution emanated from the sovereign people who had made their national government supreme to all rivals within the sphere of its powers, and those powers must be construed generously if they were to be sufficient for the "various crises" of the age to come. Congress, declared Marshall, had the power to incorporate the bank under the clause of Article I, Section 8, authorizing Congress to make all laws "necessary and proper" for carrying into execution its named powers. Moreover, Maryland's tax was invalid because "the power to tax involves the power to destroy," which would defeat the national government's supremacy. Justice Marshall's broad reading of the *necessary and proper* clause laid the

SIMULATION

You Are a Federal Judge

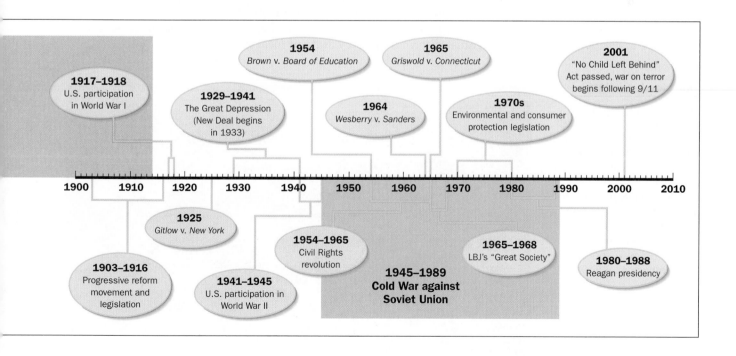

foundation for an expansion of what the national government could do in the years ahead. He made it clear that states would not be allowed to interfere.

The Supreme Court also ruled that provisions of the U.S. Constitution *excluded* the states from acting in certain areas where they might interfere with federal statutes or authority. According to this doctrine known as **preemption,** which remains in place today,[9] states cannot act in certain matters when the national government has done so.

In the first half of the nineteenth century, then, the Supreme Court played an important role in affirming the power of the national government relative to the states found in the supremacy clause. The Civil War accelerated this trend toward growing national power.

preemption
Exclusion of the states from actions that might interfere with federal authority or statutes.

The Civil War and the Expansion of National Power

The Civil War profoundly affected the relationship between the states and the national government. First, the unconditional southern surrender decisively established that the Union was indissoluble; states could not withdraw or secede. Hardly any American now questions the permanence of the Union.

Second, passage of what has become known as the **Civil War Amendments** resulted in constitutional changes that subordinated the states to certain new national standards, enforced by the central government. For example, the Thirteenth Amendment abolished slavery, and the Fifteenth gave former male slaves and their descendants a constitutional right to vote. (This right was enforced by the national government for a short time after the Civil War; it was then widely ignored until passage of the 1965 Voting Rights Act.)

Moreover, the Fourteenth Amendment (1868) included broad language going well beyond the slave issue: it declared that *no state* shall "deprive any person of life, liberty, or property, without due process of law; nor deny to any person within its jurisdiction the equal protection of the laws." The **due process clause** eventually became the vehicle by which the Supreme Court ruled that many civil liberties in the Bill of Rights, which originally protected people only against the national government, also provided protections against the states. And the **equal protection clause** eventually became the foundation for protecting the rights of blacks, women, and other categories of people against discrimination by state or local governments.

Civil War Amendments
The Thirteenth, Fourteenth, and Fifteenth Amendments to the Constitution adopted immediately after the Civil War.

due process clause
The section of the Fourteenth Amendment that prohibits states from depriving anyone of life, liberty, or property "without due process of law," a guarantee against arbitrary or unfair government action.

equal protection clause
The section of the Fourteenth Amendment that provides equal protection of the laws to all citizens.

Our Bloody Civil War

One important principle of American federalism was settled by the Civil War: The nation is indissoluble; no state or group of states can decide on its own to withdraw from it. Establishing that principle required a bloody contest of arms. Here Union dead litter the field at Gettysburg in 1863, a Union victory and a key turning point in the war.

Expanded National Activity Since the Civil War

Since the Civil War, and especially during the twentieth century, the activities of the national government expanded greatly, so that they now touch on almost every aspect of daily life and are thoroughly entangled with state government activities.

The Late Nineteenth Century to World War I   During the late nineteenth century, the national government was increasingly active in administering western lands, subsidizing economic development (granting railroads enormous tracts of land along their transcontinental lines), helping farmers, and beginning to regulate business, particularly through the Interstate Commerce Act of 1887 and the Sherman Antitrust Act of 1890. Woodrow Wilson's New Freedom domestic legislation—including the Federal Reserve Act of 1913 and the Federal Trade Commission Act of 1914—spurred even greater national government involvement in social and economic issues as did the great economic and military effort of World War I. During that war, for example, the War Industries Board engaged in a form of economic planning whose orders and regulations covered a substantial number of the nation's manufacturing firms.

The New Deal and World War II   Still more important, however, was Franklin Roosevelt's New Deal of the 1930s. In response to the Great Depression, the New Deal created many new national regulatory agencies to supervise various aspects of business, including communications (the Federal Communications Commission, or FCC), airlines (the Civil Aeronautics Board, or CAB), financial markets (the Securities and Exchange Commission, or SEC), utilities (the Federal Power Commission, or FPC), and labor-management relations (the National Labor Relations Board, or NLRB). The New Deal also brought national government spending to such areas as welfare and relief, which had previously been reserved almost entirely to the states, and established the Social Security pension system.

Putting People to Work

The Works Project Administration (WPA), created by Franklin Roosevelt as part of the New Deal, put many unemployed Americans to work on federal building projects during the Great Depression.

World War II involved a total economic and military mobilization to fight Germany and Japan. Not surprisingly, directing that mobilization, as well as collecting taxes to support it, planning for production of war materials, and bringing on board the employees to accomplish all of this, was centered in Washington, D.C., not in the states.

The Post-War Period   Ever since World War II, the federal government has spent nearly twice as much per year as all of the states and localities put together. Much of the money has gone in direct payments to individuals (through such items as Social Security benefits) and for national defense, especially during the height of the Cold War and during the years of the Vietnam conflict.

Two other trends in the last third of the twentieth century enhanced the role of the national government relative to the states. The first was the civil rights revolution (discussed in Chapters 8 and 16), and the second was the regulatory revolution, especially regulation related to environmental protection (discussed in Chapter 17). With respect to both, national standards, often fashioned by bureaucrats under broad legislative mandates and watched over by federal courts, were imposed on both states and localities. The civil rights revolution also had a great deal to do with the creation of Lyndon Johnson's Great Society program designed both to alleviate poverty and politically empower the poor and racial minorities. The Great Society not only increased the level of domestic spending but also increased the federal role in the political lives of states and localities.

TIMELINE

**Federalism and
the Supreme Court**

The Supreme Court's Support for the Nationalist Position   For several decades, beginning in the late nineteenth century, the U.S. Supreme Court resisted the growth in the federal government's power to regulate business. In 1895, for example, it said that the Sherman Antitrust Act could not forbid monopolies in manufacturing, since manufacturing affected interstate commerce only "indirectly." In 1918, the Court struck down as unconstitutional a national law regulating child labor. During the 1930s, the Supreme Court declared unconstitutional such important New Deal measures as the National Recovery Act and the Agricultural Adjustment Act.[10]

After 1937, perhaps chastened by President Roosevelt's attempt to enlarge the Supreme Court and appoint more friendly justices, the Court became a centralizing force, immediately upholding essential elements of the New Deal, including the Social Security Act and the National Labor Relations Act. Since that time, and until quite recently, the Court has upheld virtually every piece of national legislation that has come before it.

An important example is the Civil Rights Act of 1964, which rests on a very broad interpretation of the Constitution's commerce clause. In the 1964 act, the national government asserted a power to forbid discrimination at lunch counters and other public accommodations on the grounds that they are engaged in interstate commerce: They serve food imported from out of state. State economies are so closely tied to each other that by this standard, practically every economic transaction everywhere affects interstate commerce and is therefore subject to national legislative power.

Resurgence of the States in the 1990s   During the 1990s, there were a number of indications that the states were becoming more important in the American federal system. First, the states accounted for an ever-increasing share of public spending in the United States, suggesting that they were becoming more active in providing the wide range of government services the public demands. Second, the states accounted for an ever-increasing share of public employees in the United States; while state (and local) government employment grew during the 1990s, federal government employment shrank, suggesting that government service delivery was shifting to the states.

Behind the new vitality of the states within American federalism was the growing national consensus during the 1980s and 1990s about the virtues of **devolution,** the idea that became popular during the Reagan administration that more power in the federal system should be in the hands of the states. Public opinion surveys, for example, showed that a substantial majority of Americans believed that state governments were more effective and more trustworthy than the government in Washington and more likely to be responsive to the people. And Americans said that they wanted state governments to do more and the federal government to do less.[11]

President Clinton, a former governor of the state of Arkansas, was also an enthusiastic devotee of devolution, freely granting waivers from federal regulations to the states for experimenting with new forms of welfare, boasting of cuts in federal government employment, and touting the benefits of state government. And the Republican majority in the 104th Congress, working with President Clinton (but few from his party), passed legislation restricting "unfunded mandates" (about which we will have more to say later) and transferring welfare responsibility to the states.

For a time, the Rehnquist Court supported increasing the power of the states and decreasing that of the national government. It overruled a number of federal actions and laws on the ground that Congress had exceeded its constitutional powers, reversing more than half a century of decisions favoring an increased federal government role. In 1995, for example, the Court overturned

devolution

The delegation of power by the central government to state or local bodies.

Governors

Welfare to Work

During the 1990s, responsibility for several traditional federal programs was shifted to the states. The most important of these involved welfare. Working under broad federal guidelines and partially subsidized by welfare block grants, each of the states instituted its own "welfare to work" program.

federal legislation banning guns from the area around schools and legislation requiring background checks for gun buyers, arguing that both represented too broad a use of the commerce power in the Constitution. The Court used similar language in 2000 when it invalidated part of the Violence Against Women Act and in 2001 when it did the same to the Americans with Disabilities Act. However, in the last terms of Rehnquist's leadership, the Court retreated a bit from this states rights position, supporting federal law over that of the states on issues ranging from the use of medical marijuana to the juvenile death penalty, affirmative action, and gay rights.

Terrorism, the Bush Presidency, and the Resurgence of the Federal Government

The terrorist attacks of September 11, 2001, and the subsequent global struggle against terrorism refocused the nation's attention on national leaders in Washington, D.C. As in all wartime situations during our country's history, war and the mobilization for war require centralized coordination and planning. This tendency toward nationalism during war will probably be further exaggerated by the perceived need for homeland security, with the national government in Washington playing a larger role in areas such as law enforcement, intelligence gathering, bank oversight (to track terrorist money), public health (to protect against possible bioterrorism), and more.

While preserving his Republican conservative credentials on a number of fronts—cutting taxes, for example, and pushing for looser environmental regulations on businesses—George W. Bush also acted on a number of fronts to give a big boost to the power, cost, and scope of the federal government. Most important was his sponsorship of the "No Child Left Behind" educational reform, which imposed testing mandates on the states, and a prescription drug benefit under Medicare, which substantially increased the cost of the program. Mandatory spending by the states on Medicaid also expanded rapidly during the Bush presidency.

Changing American Federalism

Today's federalism is very different from what it was in the 1790s or early 1800s.[12] One major difference is that the national government is dominant in many policy areas; it calls many shots for the states. Another difference is that state and national government powers and activities have become deeply intertwined and entangled. The old, simple metaphor for federalism was a "layer cake": a system of **dual federalism** in which state and national powers were neatly divided into separate layers, with each level of government going its own way, unencumbered by the other. If we stay with bakery images, a much more accurate metaphor for today's federalism is a "marble cake," in which elements of national and state influence swirl around each other, without very clear boundaries.[13] Much of this intertwining is due to financial links among the national and state governments, which we address in the next section, as well as in the "Mapping American Politics" feature on pages 70–71.

VIDEO ROUNDTABLE

Contemporary Federalism

dual federalism

An interpretation of federalism in which the states and the national government have separate jurisdictions and responsibilities.

National Grants-in-Aid to the States

One of the most important elements of modern American federalism involves the granting of money from the national government to state and local governments. These **grants-in-aid** have been used to increase national government influence over what the states and localities do. The grants have grown from small beginnings to form a substantial part of state government budgets. In the following sections, you will learn how and why this trend began, what kinds of grants have and are being made, and how they affect national–state relationships.

grants-in-aid

Funds from the national government to state and local governments to help pay for programs created by the national government.

Origin and Growth of Grants

National government grants to the states began at least as early as the 1787 Northwest Ordinance. The U.S. government granted land for government buildings, schools, and colleges in the Northwest Territory and imposed various regulations, such as forbidding slavery there. During the early nineteenth century, the federal government provided some land grants to the states for roads, canals, and railroads, as well as a little cash for militias; after 1862, it helped establish agricultural colleges. Some small cash-grant programs were begun around 1900 for agriculture, vocational education, and highways.[14]

However, it was during the 1950s, 1960s, and 1970s, under both Republican and Democratic administrations, that federal grants to the states really took off. Such programs as President Dwight Eisenhower's interstate highway system and President Lyndon Johnson's Great Society poured money into the states.[15] After a pause during the Reagan presidency, grants began to increase again in the 1990s (see Figure 3.3). Federal grants to the states increased because presidents and Congress sought to deal with many nationwide problems—especially interstate highways, poverty, crime, and pollution—by setting policy at the

FIGURE 3.3 • The Growth in Federal Grants-in-Aid to States and Localities

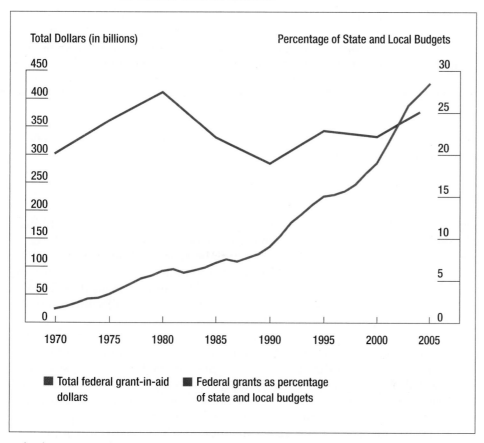

Federal grants-in-aid to state and local governments have grown steadily since 1970, the only exception being during the first half of the 1980s during the Reagan presidency. Because states and localities are doing more on their own, thus increasing their spending, the proportion of federal grants as a proportion of state and local budgets has increased only a little since 1970, even though there have been ups and downs over the years.

Source: Statistical Abstract of the United States, 2006.

Mapping American Politics

Federal dollars: Which states win and which ones lose?

Introduction: Our system of federalism involves a complex set of relationships between the federal government and the states. These relationships are spelled out in the text of the Constitution; decisions of the Supreme Court, interpreting the meaning of constitutional provisions concerning federalism; and bills passed by Congress and signed by the president, creating federal programs and imposing taxes and regulations. One aspect of federalism that often draws attention is the flow of money between the federal government and the states. The flow goes in two directions. Money flows from people and firms in the states to the federal government in the form of taxes (income, corporate, excise, and payroll). Money flows from the federal government to people and firms in the states in the form of grants-in-aid, block grants, and expenditures for specific

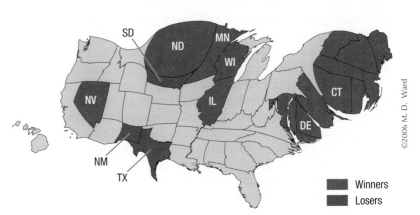

©2006 M. D. Ward

Winners
Losers

State Sizes Adjusted to Reflect Ratio of Federal Taxes Paid and Federal Monies Received per Capita

national level and providing money from national tax revenues, while having state and local officials carry out the policies.

Types of Grants

Over the years, many of the new programs were established through **categorical grants,** which give the states money but clearly specify the category of activity for which the money has to be spent and often define rather precisely how the program should work. For example, Lyndon Johnson's antipoverty initiatives—in the areas of housing, job training, medical assistance, and more—funneled substantial federal money to states and localities, but attached strict rules on how the money could be used.

As the new programs were developed and enacted, there was much talk about a new system of **cooperative federalism.** Soon, however, conflicts between the national and the state governments emerged. In some cases, when national rules and guidelines were vague, state and local governments used the money for purposes different from those Congress intended. When the rules were tightened up, some state and local governments complained about "red tape." And if state and local governments were bypassed, they complained that their authority had been undermined.

Responding to complaints from the states, and seeking to reduce federal government power to better fit their ideas about the proper role of government, Republican presidents Nixon and Ford succeeded in convincing Congress to loosen centralized rules and oversight, first instituting **block grants** (which

programs (such as payments to defense contractors) and projects (such as payments for highways and bridges). Given the nature of the political process and differences in the needs and resources of people and firms in the states, some states will inevitably come out ahead in this process (get more money from Washington than they pay in taxes), and some will come out behind, paying more than they receive.

The Story in the Cartogram: The cartogram shows winners and losers in the federalism money story. The size of each state has been adjusted using a mathematical formula based on a simple ratio: taxes paid by each state on a per-capita basis in 2002 divided by federal funds received by each state on a per-capita basis. If a state paid and received the same amount, the ratio would be 1, meaning that its size would not change in the cartogram. States that pay more in taxes than they receive from Washington have ratios higher than 1 and are expanded in the cartogram. States that pay less than they receive have ratios less than 1 and are reduced. It is readily apparent that a number of states pay

more taxes per capita than they receive back in federal program and grant dollars on a per-capita basis. These are in blue in the cartogram. North Dakota is a clear loser, as are Nevada, Minnesota, Wisconsin, Illinois, and the Middle Atlantic (especially Delaware) and New England (especially Connecticut) states. Texas, New Mexico, and South Dakota, in purple, do particularly well, receiving significantly more from Washington than they pay in.

What Do You Think?   Do you think the way monies flow between Washington and the states is fair? Should states all have similar money flow profiles? Or do you think that this is not a very important issue, that monies do and should flow to where they are needed? Why do you think some states stand out from others on this issue? How about your own state? Where does it fit in the overall picture?

Sources: IRS Data Book for FY 2002 (Tables 6 and 10) and *Statistical Abstracts of the United States, 2004–05* (Table 19).

give money for more general purposes such as secondary education and with fewer rules than categorical grant programs), then, for a short time, **general revenue sharing,** which distributed money to the states with no federal controls at all. President Nixon spoke of a "New Federalism" and pushed to increase these kinds of grants with few strings attached. They often provided money under an automatic formula related to the statistical characteristics of each state or locality, such as the number of needy residents, the total size of the population, or the average income level. (General revenue sharing ended in 1987 when even proponents of a smaller federal government realized that giving money to the states with "no strings attached" meant that elected officials in the federal government were losing influence over policies in which they wanted to have a say.)

> **general revenue sharing**
> Federal aid to the states without any conditions on how the money is to be spent.

Disputes frequently arise when these formulas benefit one state or region rather than another. Because statistical counts by the census affect how much money the states and localities get, census counts themselves have become the subject of political conflict. Illinois, New York, and Chicago sued the Census Bureau for allegedly undercounting their populations, especially the urban poor, in the 1990 census. (See "By the Numbers" for more information about how population counts are done and why it matters.)

Debates About Federal Money and Control

Most contemporary conflicts about federalism concern not just money but also control.

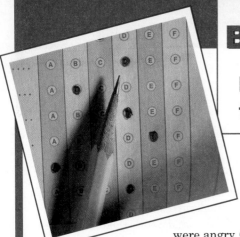

By the Numbers

How do we know how many people there are in each of the states?

Utah officials were angry. Convinced that the counting method used for the 2000 census had undercounted the number of people residing in the state, thereby "robbing" them of a congressional seat, they sued the U.S. Census Bureau.

How can something as simple as counting people become so controversial? And why are these census figures so important to states, anyway?

Why It Matters: The Constitution specifies that every 10 years, a census will be taken of the population of the United States. One purpose of the census is to determine how the finite number of seats in the House of Representatives (435) will be divided among the states, based on the size of their populations. A state's population also determines how much federal money (e.g., highway money) it will get. Moreover, counts of certain categories of people, like the poor, determine how much aid (e.g., Medicaid) the state will receive.

The Story Behind the Number: For most of our nation's history, the Census Bureau hired people to go door-to-door across the United States—from isolated farms to packed apartment buildings—to conduct a direct count of the population. Many people were missed in this process. Some were not home when the census takers came by; others lived in high-crime neighborhoods, where census takers did not want to venture; some had no home other than a crude shelter under a highway overpass. Recent immigrants had trouble communicating in English, and illegal aliens did not necessarily want to be found by census takers.

Indeed, the undercounted population in every recent census has been comprised mainly of racial minorities, recent immigrants, the homeless, and the undocumented. This pattern has generated complaints from a wide range of people and organizations: advocates of the poor who want more federal government monies directed to the problem of poverty in each state; civil rights organizations that believe that racial minorities are underrepresented in the House of Representatives; and Democratic Party politicians who believe that a more accurate count would benefit their party (the assumption being that lower income people, racial minorities, and recent immigrants tend to vote for Democrats).

In an attempt to remedy these undercount problems, the Census Bureau wanted to use "statistical sampling" of the population to fill in the gaps. However, the Supreme Court ruled in 1999 that the Bureau could not do so for purposes of reapportioning congressional seats, and President Bush announced that sampling could not be used to determine how much federal money the states would get. As an alternative, the Bureau has increasingly relied on a statistical procedure called "imputing."

Calculating Population Size and Characteristics:
Although Census Bureau statisticians have been using "imputing" in limited ways since the 1940s to fill in the gaps left by the inevitable undercounting, they relied much more on it for the 2000 census. In imputing, estimates are made about the characteristics of people living in a household where the Bureau has been unable to collect information. The estimates are based on what their neighbors are like (whether they are poor or rich, white or African American, and so on).

Conditions on Aid As we have seen, many categorical grant-in-aid programs require that the states spend federal money only in certain restricted ways. Even block grants—such as grants that support social welfare for the poor—have **conditions** attached. In theory, these conditions are "voluntary" because the states can refuse to accept the aid. But in practice, there is no clear line between incentives and coercion. Because the states cannot generally afford to give up federal money, they normally must accept the conditions attached to it.

conditions

Provisions in federal assistance requiring that state and local governments follow certain policies in order to obtain federal funds.

In the 2000 census, using imputing, almost 6 million people who had not actually been counted were included in the nation's population total. In some states, most notably in those with large numbers of racial minorities and immigrants (including California, Arizona, New Mexico, and Texas), more than 3 percent of the state's total population was imputed.

This brings us back to the state of Utah. Utah's suit claimed that the Census Bureau had illegally imputed tens of thousands of additional people to the state of North Carolina, resulting in North Carolina receiving the congressional seat that properly should have gone to Utah. Unfortunately for Utah, the Supreme Court approved imputing in 2002.

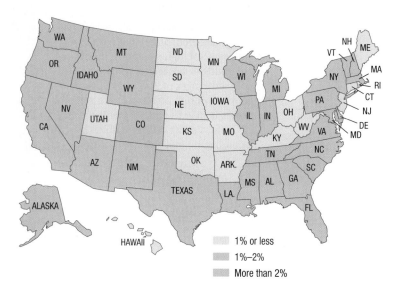

Percentage of People Imputed by the U.S. Census Bureau in Its Population Totals, by State

Source: The Wall Street Journal, August 30, 2001.

Imputing Criticized: Although most statisticians believe that imputing is a reasonable way to solve the problem of undercounting, the technique has its critics:

- The Utah suit pointed out, and others agree, that imputing—much like more standard sampling—makes statistical inferences about parts of the population rather than counting people directly, as implied by the wording in the Constitution (Article I, Section 2).

- Imputing assumes that neighborhoods are homogenous; it is based on the assumption that a household's characteristics can be estimated from the characteristics of its neighbors. Members of several minority groups who tend to live in less segregated circumstances—Asians and Pacific Islanders, for example—may find themselves undercounted.

What to Watch For: Official statistics are often published in both "adjusted" and "unadjusted" forms. "Adjusted" means that the raw information has been corrected in one way or another. Usually, the reasons for doing so are very reasonable and defensible. You might want to look at the documentation that is associated with all government statistical information to learn how the numbers have been "adjusted."

What Do You Think? In your view, does it make sense to depend on the census for methods of enumerating that were fashioned by the framers of the Constitution? Is there a reason to keep to traditional methods? Or does the greater accuracy introduced by advances in statistical computing—either imputing or sampling—argue for a different method for conducting the census?

Some of the most important provisions of the 1964 Civil Rights Act, for example, are those that declare that no federal aid of any kind can be used in ways that discriminate against people on grounds of race, gender, religion, or national origin. Thus, the enormous program of national aid for elementary and secondary education, which began in 1965, became a powerful lever for forcing schools to desegregate.

The national government uses its money to influence many diverse kinds of policies. During the energy crisis of the 1970s, all states were required to

Warning to Patrons

Federal money to the states usually has strings attached. States that wish to receive federal highway funds, for example, must set the age for drinking alcoholic beverages at 21 years of age or above. This sign on a bar in Los Angeles makes it clear to patrons that the state of California has agreed to abide by this federal guideline.

impose a 55-mile-per-hour speed limit or lose a portion of their highway assistance funds. The requirement was finally repealed in 1995. Similarly, in 1984, all states were required to set a minimum drinking age of 21 or have their highway aid cut by 15 percent.

mandate

A formal order from the national government that the states carry out certain policies.

Federalism and Regulations

Mandates   The national government often imposes a **mandate,** or demand, that the states carry out certain policies even when little or no national government aid is offered. (An "unfunded" mandate involves no aid at all or less aid than compliance will cost.) Mandates have been especially important in the areas of civil rights and the environment. Most civil rights policies flow from the equal protection clause of the Fourteenth Amendment to the U.S. Constitution or from national legislation that imposes uniform national standards. Most environmental regulations also come from the national government, since problems of dirty air, polluted water, and acid rain spill across state boundaries. Many civil rights and environmental regulations, therefore, are enforced by the federal courts.

Federal courts have, for example, mandated expensive reforms of overcrowded state prisons, most notably in Texas. National legislation and regulations have required state governments to provide costly special facilities for the disabled, to set up environmental protection agencies, and to limit

Spewing Pollution

Industrial pollution, such as these untreated emissions from this massive steel complex, often affects people of more than one state and requires the participation of the national government to clean up the mess and prevent recurrences.

the kinds and amounts of pollutants that can be discharged. The states often complain bitterly about federal mandates that require state spending without providing the money.

Cutting back on these "unfunded mandates" was one of the main promises in the Republicans' 1994 Contract with America.[16] The congressional Republicans delivered on their promise early in 1995 with a bill that had bipartisan support in Congress and that President Clinton signed into law. Because it did not apply to past mandates, however, and did not ban unfunded mandates but only regulated them (e.g., requiring cost-benefit analyses), unfunded mandates continue, as does the debate about their use. The main complaints coming from governors today concern the substantial costs imposed on the states by the No Child Left Behind testing program without sufficient federal funds to pay for it.

Preemption   The doctrine of preemption, based on the supremacy clause in the Constitution and supported by a series of decisions by the Supreme Court, says that federal statutes and rules must prevail over state statutes and rules when the two are in conflict. Recently, for example, several states have attempted to tax Internet purchases by people residing in their jurisdictions, but Congress has forbidden them to do so. Research suggests that the number of preemption statutes passed by Congress has increased substantially over the past three decades and has been unaffected by which political party is in control.[17]

**Is Federalism Dead
and Should It Be?**

U.S. Federalism: Pro and Con

Over the years, from the framing of the U.S. Constitution to the present day, people have offered a number of strong arguments for and against federalism, in contrast to a more unitary system. Let us consider some of these arguments.

Pro: Diversity of Needs   The oldest and most important argument in favor of decentralized government is that in a large and diverse country, needs and wants and conditions differ from one place to another. Why not let different states enact different policies to meet their own needs? California, New York, and New Jersey, for example, all densely populated, have tougher fuel mileage standards in place than those set by the federal government. (See the "Using the Framework" feature on why states can set their own tuition levels, including those for out-of-state students.)

Con: The Importance of National Standards   However, the needs or desires that different states pursue may not be worthy ones. Political scientist William Riker has pointed out that, historically, one of the main effects of federalism was to let white majorities in the southern states enslave and then discriminate against black people, without interference from the North.[18] Perhaps it is better, in some cases, to insist on national standards that apply everywhere.

You Are a Restaurant Owner

Pro: Closeness to the People   It is sometimes claimed that state governments are closer to the ordinary citizens, who have a better chance to know their officials, to be aware of what they are doing, to contact them, and to hold them responsible for what they do.

Con: Low Visibility and Lack of Popular Control   However, others respond that geographic closeness may not be the real issue. More Americans are better informed about the federal government than they are about state governments, and more people participate in national than in state elections. When more people know what the government is doing and more people vote, they are better able to insist that the government do what they want. For that reason, responsiveness to ordinary citizens may actually be greater in national government.

Pro: Innovation and Experimentation   When the states have independent power, they can try out new ideas. Individual states can be "laboratories." If the experiments work, other states or the nation as a whole can adopt their ideas, as has happened on such issues as allowing women and 18-year-olds to vote, fighting air pollution, reforming welfare, and dealing with water pollution. Recently, first California, then New Jersey, Connecticut, and Massachusetts, passed statutes allowing and offering state funding for stem cell research, given reluctance in Washington to vigorously explore this new area of scientific and technological inquiry. Massachusetts passed a law in 2006 mandating health insurance coverage for every person in the state.

Likewise, when the national government is controlled by one political party, federalism allows the states with majorities favoring a different party to compensate by enacting different policies. This aspect of diversity in policymaking is related to the Founders' contention that tyranny is less likely when government's power is dispersed. Multiple governments reduce the risks of

Using the Framework

Paying Out-of-State Tuition

I thought that attending a public university would save a lot of money, but it hasn't because I have to pay out-of-state tuition. Why do I have to pay so much money?

Background: All over the United States, students who choose to attend out-of-state public universities pay much higher tuition than state residents. Some educational reformers have suggested that the system be reformed so that students might attend public universities wherever they choose, without financial penalty. They have suggested that, over the long-haul and on average, such a reform would not have much impact on state budgets because students would randomly distribute themselves across state borders. Such proposals have never gotten very far. Taking a broad view of how structural, political linkage, and governmental factors affect this issue will help explain the situation.

Governmental Action

State legislatures decline to pass uniform tuition legislation.

The Supreme Court decides that different tuition rates for in-state and out-of-state residents do not violate the "privileges and immunities" section of Article IV, Section 2, of the Constitution.

Governmental Level

Elected leaders know that voters want access to low cost higher education for state residents. ➡ Elected leaders are not subject to political pressures to change tuition policy. ➡ Elected leaders are concerned with short-term budget issues; high out-of-state tuition allows them to raise part of the higher education budget out of such revenues.

Political Linkages Level

Voters in each state insist on access for their children and the children of their neighbors to low-cost public higher education. ➡ There is little political pressure on elected leaders within the states to lower or eliminate out-of-state tuition, whether from
– Public opinion and voters.
– Parties.
– The mass media.
– Interest groups.
– Social movements. ➡ Out-of-state students rarely vote in the states where they go to school; politicians have no incentive to think seriously about their tuition concerns.

Structural Level

The states are mainly responsible for education in our federal system; standardizing national tuition rates would require agreements among all the states.

Low Voter Turnout

A shift of power and responsibility from the federal level to the states and localities, given low voting turnout in state and local elections, may mean a decrease in the quality of American democracy.

bad policy or the blockage of the popular will; if things go wrong at one governmental level, they may go right at another.

Con: Spillover Effects and Competition Diversity and experimentation in policies, however, may not always be good. Divergent regulations can cause bad effects that spill over from one state to another. When factories in the Midwest spew out oxides of nitrogen and sulfur that fall as acid rain in the Northeast, the northeastern states can do nothing about it. Only nationwide rules can solve such problems. Similarly, it is very difficult for cities or local communities in the states to do much about poverty or other social problems. If a city raises taxes to pay for social programs, businesses and the wealthy may move out of town, and the poor may move in, impoverishing the city.[19]

What Sort of Federalism?

As the pros and cons indicate, a lot is at stake. It is not likely, however, that Americans will ever have a chance to vote yes or no on the federal system or to choose a unitary government instead. What we can decide is exactly *what sort* of federalism we will have—how much power will go to the states and how much will remain with the federal government. Indeed, we may want a fluid system in which the balance of power varies from one kind of policy to another. Over the long term of American history, of course, the nationalist position on federalism has generally prevailed over the states' rights position, but the states remain important, and there are many reasons to expect that the American people will continue to want the states to play an important role in fashioning policies that affect them.

It is important to keep in mind that arguments about federalism do not concern just abstract theories; they affect who wins and who loses valuable benefits. People's opinions about federalism often depend on their interests, their ideologies, and the kinds of things they want government to do.

Using the Democracy Standard

Does federalism advance or retard democracy?

PROPOSITION: Federalism undermines democracy by getting in the way of majority rule and political equality.

AGREE Federalism adds complexity to policymaking and makes it difficult for citizens to know which elected leaders to hold responsible for government actions. For example, it is not entirely clear whom citizens ought to hold responsible—state officials or federal government officials—when nothing is done to stop firms from polluting local air and water supplies. Also, citizens are much less informed about what goes on in state governments where many important policies are made. This is hardly surprising, because local news telecasts are more likely to carry news about the national government than state governments. In state-level politics, moreover, popular participation tends to be lower, politics tends to be less visible, and interest groups may have an easier time getting their way—precisely because media attention to such groups is limited. Because the well organized and the affluent have extra influence, political equality is impaired.

DISAGREE Federalism promotes popular democracy rather than undermining it. It does so by allowing a majority of citizens in each state to exercise control over a range of policies that directly affect them. This is especially important in a country where the populations of the states vary as widely as they do. With diverse populations, with their diverse needs and interests, federalism allows for diverse policies. This is especially true in those many states where citizens can bypass uncooperative legislatures and governors by using the initiative process to put into place new policy and constitutional changes they want. Citizens in many states, for example, forced term limits on officials, even though elected officials were mostly hostile to this reform. In other states, citizens forced changes in affirmative action policies in state colleges and universities.

CONSIDER • Where do you stand on these two competing positions? • Which level of government do you know more about? • Which public officials are you more familiar with, state or national? • Which kinds of elected officials, state or national, do you think you might have more influence with? • Have you ever contacted your member of Congress or your local representative or senator in the state legislature? • If so, which of them, national-level legislators or state-level legislators, were more responsive to your concerns? • If you have never been in touch with such officials, which level of government do you think would be more responsive to you or to a group to which you belong, perhaps on increasing college scholarship assistance in the future?

Summary

Federalism, a system under which political powers are divided between the state and federal governments, is a key structural aspect of American politics. Federalism in the United States was the product of both important compromises made at the Constitutional Convention and eighteenth-century republican doctrines about the nature of good government. Arguments in favor of federalism have to do with diversity of needs, closeness to the people, experimentation, and innovation. Arguments against federalism involve national standards, popular control, and needs for uniformity.

The U.S. Constitution specifies the powers of the national government and reserves all others (except a few that are specifically forbidden) to the states. The Constitution also provides special roles for the states in adopting and amending the Constitution and in choosing national officials. The precise balance of federalism has evolved over time, with the national government gaining ground as a result of U.S. Supreme Court decisions, the Civil War, expanding national domestic programs, two world wars, and the war against terrorism.

Contemporary federalism involves complex "marble cake" relations among the national and state governments, in which federal grants-in-aid play an important part. Grants for many purposes grew rapidly for a time but have now slowed down. The national government also influences or controls many state policies through mandates and through conditions placed on aid. Federalism has mixed implications for democracy.

mypoliscilab
Where participation leads to action!

Web Exploration
Regional Variation and Federalism

ISSUE: Federalism seems most appropriate where there is substantial variation among regions of a nation.

SITE: You can examine how much variation exists in the United States by going to the *Statistical Abstract of the United States* in MyPoliSciLab at **www.mypoliscilab.com.** In the "Web Explorations" section for Chapter 3, open "Regional Variation and Federalism," then open "states." Select "state rankings." Compare your own state with three or four others from different geographical regions of the United States on issues such as education, income, population growth, immigration, crime, and the like.

WHAT YOU'VE LEARNED: Given the profile of your state compared with others, are the differences great enough to support the need for greater autonomy for your state government, or would national rulemaking and policies make more sense?

HINT: If the differences are significant, from your point of view, federalism would make a lot of sense. Religious differences seem especially important to many people.

Internet Sources

Assessing the New Federalism
www.urban.org/center/anf/index.cfm
   News, essays, and research on the New Federalism and devolution.

National Center for State Courts
www.ncsconline.org
   Links to the home pages of the court systems of each of the states.

National Conference of State Legislatures
www.ncsl.org
   Information about state governments and federal relations, including the distribution of federal revenues and expenditures in the states.

Publius
www.oxfordjournals.org/our_journals/pubjof/ index.html
   Home page of the leading academic journal on federalism.

State Constitutions
www.findlaw.com/
   A site where the constitutions of all the states may be found.

Suggestions for Further Reading

Derthick, Martha. *Keeping the Compound Republic: Essays in American Federalism.* Washington, D.C.: Brookings, 2001.
   An examination of the enduring features of federalism, as well as its most important changes, in light of the framers original design, in Madison's words, of a compound republic.

Hero, Rodney E. *Faces of Inequality: Social Diversity in American Politics.* New York: Oxford University Press, 1998.
   An impressive argument with strong empirical evidence that the racial and ethnic composition of states matters for patterns of state politics.

Nagel, Robert. *The Implosion of American Federalism.* New York: Oxford University Press, 2002.
   Argues that American federalism has largely disappeared as power in the United States has flowed steadily to Washington, D.C.

Peterson, Paul E. *The Price of Federalism.* Washington, D.C.: Brookings Institution, 1995.
   Describes modern federalism and argues that the national government is best at redistributive programs, while the states and localities are best at economic development.

Riker, William H. *The Development of American Federalism.* Boston: Kluwer Academic, 1987.
   An influential discussion of what American federalism is and how it came about.

Walker, David B. *The Rebirth of Federalism,* 2nd ed. New York: Chatham House/Seven Bridges Press, 2000.
   Examination of the revitalization of the states and why it has happened.

CHAPTER 4

The Structural Foundations of American Government and Politics

IN THIS CHAPTER

- How population size, location, and diversity affect American politics

- How the American economy shapes government and politics

- Income and wealth distribution and why they matter

- How globalization affects the United States and its people

- What Americans believe about the nature of the good society

The Disappearing Highly Paid, Semiskilled Worker

Delphi, the giant auto-parts maker, filed for bankruptcy protection in October 2005 after failing to convince the United Auto Workers (UAW) to make massive contract concessions that would help stem losses at the company.[1] Robert Miller, Delphi's chief executive, claimed that the company was burdened by too many employees and excessively generous wages, medical coverage, and pensions. His post-bankruptcy plan to save the company included making big cuts in the size of the Delphi workforce, leaving the cheap auto-parts market to lower-cost producers abroad, concentrating its U.S. production on complex components such as electrical systems, and using the bankruptcy court to force concessions from the UAW.

The Delphi bankruptcy filing sent shock waves through the entire American automobile industry and its unions because it seemed to portend the future of the Big Three auto makers, Delphi's main customers. By late 2005, General Motors was on the brink of bankruptcy, having lost more than $4 billion in the first nine months of the year and saddled with more than $5 billion in annual health care obligations. Although the UAW agreed to substantial cuts in health care coverage just weeks later, GM soon announced that it would cut at least 30,000 jobs and close five plants, with more to follow. In early 2006, after reporting huge losses for the fourth quarter, GM announced deep cuts in health care coverage for retirees and future pension benefits for its employees, and offered buyouts for an additional 27,000 employees near retirement.[2] Ford's North American division was losing money by the middle of 2004, and the company as a whole reported massive losses in late 2005 and early 2006, and announced plans for substantial job reductions and plant closings. DaimlerChrysler remained profitable in 2005, but less so than in previous years, and experienced a substantial drop in sales in North America in the third and fourth quarters. The business press was reporting rising nervousness about the future of the company.

To be sure, many of the Big Three's troubles had been self-inflicted. The decreasing sales of the Big Three's high-profit-margin, gas-guzzling SUVs and light trucks in an era of escalating gasoline prices played a role, as did the growing popularity of cars from other companies (Toyota vehicle sales in the United States actually grew during this period). But some changes that have affected the auto industry have been affecting all manufacturing in the United States (as well as in Japan and western Europe) for some time. Most important, the number of manufacturing jobs has decreased even as overall manufacturing output has been growing briskly, putting pressure on unions to make concessions on wages, health care coverage, and pensions for remaining workers and retirees. While these trends first hit the steel, textile, and airline industries, the

transformation in the auto industry has been particularly noteworthy because the Big Three arguably were the foundation for the expansive American economy of the post-war era and middle-class living standards for high school–educated, semiskilled workers. From the 1950s through most of the 1970s, the Big Three, facing little foreign competition at home and enjoying a seemingly insatiable demand for cars to fill the new freeways linking booming suburbs to cities and to one another, enjoyed substantial and steady profits, and were willing to share this largesse with employees as well as investors. Over the years, the UAW, representing most Big Three workers, won contracts that gave them job security, high wages, full medical benefits, and substantial pensions.[3]

Why have things changed so dramatically? Experts point to several factors affecting manufacturing in general and the auto industry in particular. First, improvements in technology—information technology to manage supply chains and speed the design process, just-in-time manufacturing methods, robotic assembly, and more—have led to extraordinary gains in productivity, so more things (including cars) can be produced with far fewer workers. Second, as world markets have become more integrated and open, producers everywhere face stiffer foreign competition, forcing them to lower prices and look for ways to cut production costs, including labor. The end result in autos and other areas of manufacturing in the United States and other rich manufacturing countries is that fewer manufacturing workers are needed, those who remain need more education and technical skills, and unions are less able to protect the gains they had won earlier.[4]

These changes have dramatically reduced the living standards of semiskilled workers with a high school education or less. In the past, the road to the middle class for many of these people was paved by hard work in union-protected, high-wage, high-benefit jobs in industry. Today, there are proportionally fewer of these jobs for such people, who increasingly make do with low-wage service jobs with little job security and few guaranteed benefits. The loss of manufacturing jobs for those with only a high school education has had a particularly devastating impact on the African American community.[5]

These changes in the American economy are enormously consequential for American society and political life. Although unemployment is low by historical standards and mean household incomes have been rising, a very large group of people face hard circumstances and grim prospects. What to do about it—whether to provide more and better education and training, stronger social safety nets, and more incentives for companies to create jobs or leave it to the natural workings of the market economy—is part of the ongoing political debate today between Democrats and Republicans, liberals and conservatives. Other important changes in American society, culture, and economy, as well as America's position in the world, are also reshaping American politics and government. Tracking these many changes in the structural level of our analytical model, and examining how they are influencing American politics and what government does, is the focus of this chapter. ■

Thinking Critically About This Chapter

This chapter is about the structural foundations of politics and government in the United States; it is about how the nature of America's society, economy, culture, and place in the world shapes the political system.

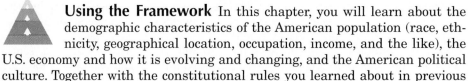 **Using the Framework** In this chapter, you will learn about the demographic characteristics of the American population (race, ethnicity, geographical location, occupation, income, and the like), the U.S. economy and how it is evolving and changing, and the American political culture. Together with the constitutional rules you learned about in previous chapters, you will see how these structural-level factors have a great deal to do with what issues dominate the political agenda, how political power is distributed in the population, and what ideas Americans bring to bear when grappling with complex public policy issues.

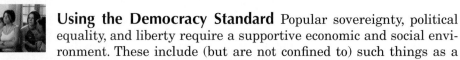 **Using the Democracy Standard** Popular sovereignty, political equality, and liberty require a supportive economic and social environment. These include (but are not confined to) such things as a well-educated population; a sizable middle class with access to resources, allowing its members to participate in public affairs; conditions of nondiscrimination against racial and ethnic minorities; and a culture that values and protects liberty. In this chapter you will learn whether or not such an environment exists.

America's Population

The typical American today is very different from the typical American of 1950, let alone 1790, when the first census was conducted. Where we live, how we work, our racial and ethnic composition, and our average age and standard of living have all changed substantially. Each change has influenced our political life.

Growing Diversity

Ours is an ethnically, religiously, and racially diverse society. The white European Protestants, black slaves, and Native Americans who made up the bulk of the U.S. population when the first census was taken in 1790 were joined by Catholic immigrants from Ireland and Germany in the 1840s and 1850s (see Figure 4.1). In the 1870s, Chinese migrated to America, drawn by jobs in railroad construction. Around the turn of the twentieth century, most emigration was from eastern, central, and southern Europe, with its many ethnic, linguistic, and religious groups. Today most emigration is from Asia and Latin America, with people from Mexico representing the largest single component. During the 1990s, according to the U.S. Census, there also was a significant increase in the number of immigrants from the Middle East and other locations with Muslim populations.

The rate of migration to the United States has been accelerating. During the 1990s, more immigrants arrived than in any decade in American history (9.1 million legal and 3.5 million illegal).[6] Since 2000, immigrants have been arriving at a rate of about 850,000 per year (78 percent for Latin America, according to the Bureau of Immigration and Customs Enforcement), drawn by the plentitude of jobs in the agricultural, hotel, construction, and restaurant

Understanding Who We Are

FIGURE 4.1 • Immigration to the United States, by Decade

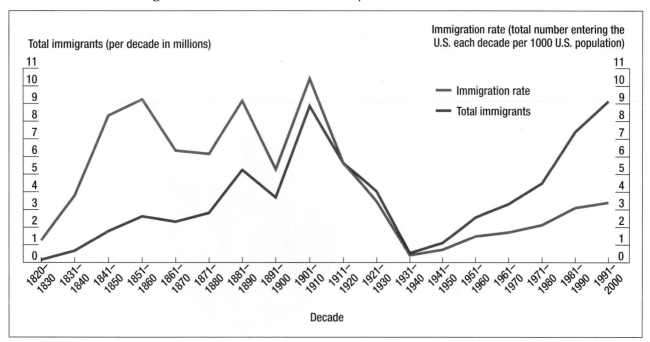

Measuring immigration to the United States in different ways gives rise to quite different interpretations of its scale. Measured in total numbers, the high points of immigration were the 1880s, the decade and a half after 1900, and the 1980s and 1990s. Measured in terms of the total U.S. population, however, immigration was an important factor in population change for much of the nineteenth century and the early part of the twentieth century, but not much after that. The rate of recent immigration, relative to the total U.S. population, remains historically low, although it is has been increasing steadily since its low point in the 1930s.

Source: U.S. Bureau of the Census.

industries. As a result of this and other immigration streams, the percentage of foreign-born people resident in the United States has almost tripled since 1970, reaching almost 12.4 percent of the population in 2005, up from 11.2 percent in 2000. Although the foreign-born population is concentrated in a handful of states—mainly California, New York, New Jersey, Florida, Illinois, and Texas—and a handful of cities and localities—mainly Miami, New York, Los Angeles–Long Beach, Orange County, Oakland, and Houston—the presence of new immigrants is being felt almost everywhere in America, including the Midwest (Ohio, Michigan, and Wisconsin) and the Deep South (North Carolina and Georgia, especially). In California, more than 27 percent of the population is foreign-born.[7]

Although the total number of current immigrants is substantial, it is worth noting that the immigration rate—that is, new immigrants as a proportion of the population (the red line in Figure 4.1)—is lower that it has been throughout much of our history. Furthermore, as a percentage of the total population, the foreign-born population of the United States today is lower today than it was in the late nineteenth and early twentieth centuries, when it reached almost 15 percent. For most people, of course, it is what has been happening recently that is most important to them, not historical comparisons.

The natural outcome of this history of immigration is substantial racial and ethnic diversity in the American population. Although the United States is still overwhelmingly non-Hispanic white (see Figure 4.2), its diversity is growing with every passing year. The Hispanic population has been growing

FIGURE 4.2 • Race and Hispanic Composition of the United States, 2005

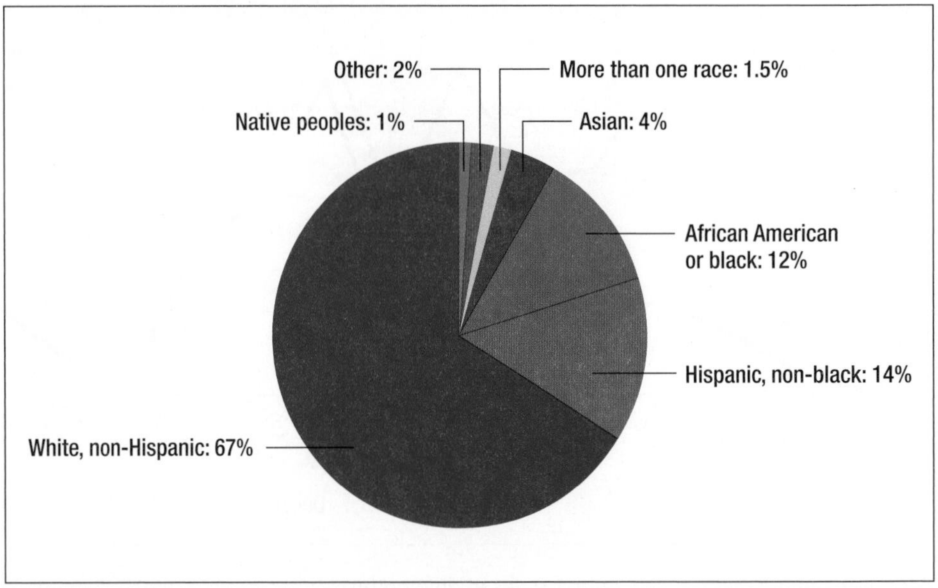

Other: 2%
More than one race: 1.5%
Native peoples: 1%
Asian: 4%
African American or black: 12%
Hispanic, non-black: 14%
White, non-Hispanic: 67%

The United States is a racially and ethnically diverse society and it is becoming more so every year, although non-Hispanic whites—who are themselves made up of many ethnic groups—are in the majority and will be for some time to come. It is important to note that Hispanics are defined by the Census Bureau as an ethnic group rather than a racial group, since Hispanics include people with different racial backgrounds. In this graph, we use data that combine Census Bureau figures on Hispanic ethnicity and U.S. racial composition. Native peoples include native Hawaiian and Pacific Islanders and American Indians and Alaska Natives.

Source: U.S. Bureau of the Census, 2006.

rapidly and is now the nation's largest minority group, accounting for a little more than 14 percent of America's resident population in 2005. African Americans are the next largest minority group, with a little more than 12 percent. The Asian-origin population is growing faster in a proportional sense than any other group, but it is still relatively small, accounting for about 4 percent of the U.S. population in 2004.

The most recent wave of immigration, like all previous ones, has added to our rich linguistic, cultural, and religious traditions; it has also helped revitalize formerly poverty-stricken neighborhoods in cities such as Los Angeles, New York, and Chicago. Immigrants from Asia and Europe especially have also made a mark in science and technology, earning a disproportionate share of PhDs in the sciences as well as technology patents, and are responsible for creating some of the hottest high-technology companies (e.g., one of the founders of Google, as well as the creators of Yahoo and Hotmail).[8] Because immigrants tend to be young, moreover, they have slowed the rate at which the American population is aging, particularly when compared with the rapidly aging populations of Russia, China, and most of Europe.

PARTICIPATION

The Debate Over Immigration

But immigration has also generated political and social tensions. The arrival of immigrants who are different from the majority population in significant ways has often sparked anti-immigration agitation and demands that public officials stem the tide. **Nativist** (antiforeign) reactions to Irish Catholic migrants were common throughout the nineteenth century. Anti-Chinese agitation swept the western states in the 1870s and 1880s. Alarm at the arrival of waves of immigrants from eastern, southern, and central Europe in the early part of the last century led Congress virtually to close the doors of the United States in 1921 and keep them closed until the 1950s. Wars have also triggered hostile actions against certain immigrant groups: German immigrants during World War I; Japanese Americans during World War II; and people from Middle Eastern and other Muslim countries after the September 11, 2001, terrorist attacks on the United States.

nativist
Antiforeign; applied to political movements active in the nineteenth century.

The current wave of Hispanic immigration, much of it illegal, has caused unease among many Americans. The respected Pew Foundation poll reported in 2006, for example, that 52 percent of Americans say that immigrants today are a burden "primarily because they take jobs and housing and receive public benefits," as compared with 41 percent who say that immigrants today

Google Founders

Many recent immigrants to the United States have played important roles in science, technology, and business. Here, Sergey Brin, from Russia, poses with Google co-founder Larry Page at their Silicon Valley Headquarters.

Multiethnic Shopping District

Immigration has helped to reinvigorate and revitalize neighborhoods in many cities across the United States, including this one in lower Manhattan.

VIDEO DEBATE

Illegal Immigration

"strengthen the United States because of their hard work and talents." Moreover, 53 percent said that illegal immigrants should be forced to return to their home countries, with only 40 percent willing to have them stay, although about one-half of those selecting the "force them to leave" option are willing to have a temporary guest worker program.[9]

These public attitudes have shaped the public debate about immigration—both legal and illegal—and affected a wide range of government policies. In 1998, for example, California voters approved a ballot proposition that banned the use of state funds for bilingual education. Political scientist Samuel Huntington caused a stir in 2004, but generated a great deal of sympathetic support as well, with the publication of his book *Who We Are,* which suggested that Hispanic immigration was damaging the Anglo-Protestant society that is, he claimed, the foundation for American economic and political freedom.[10] About the same time, angry anti-immigration activists founded the Minuteman Project to organize citizens to patrol the desert areas of the Mexican border in order to slow the flow of illegal immigrants. In 2005, several towns and counties on Long Island began requiring its public safety officers to report the presence of illegal immigrants to federal authorities. In that same year, the governors of Arizona and New Mexico declared "states of emergency" along the border, and beefed up state efforts to slow the flow. President Bush's proposal in 2006 for a temporary-worker program, granting stays of up to six years for Mexican workers not otherwise allowed in the United States and a road to citizenship for several million already here illegally, drew angry fire from conservatives in his own Republican Party.[11]

However, even though waves of immigration often trigger an initial negative response from the native population (among all races and ethnic groups, it is important to add) and opportunistic politicians, elected officials invariably begin to pay attention to immigrant groups as more become citizens and voters. Indeed, immigrants now represent the fastest growing voting bloc in the American electorate.[12] The upshot of this change is that elected officials at all levels of government are likely to become more responsive to the needs and interests of recent immigrant groups. The growing political importance of immigrants in the United States, especially Hispanics, reflects both sheer numbers and the geographic concentration of immigrants in states with very large or closely contested blocs of electoral votes in presidential elections.

Changing Location

Where the growing population of the United States is located also matters. Although we began as a country of rural farms and small towns, we rapidly became an urban people. By 1910, some 50 cities had populations of more than 100,000, and three (New York, Philadelphia, and Chicago) had more than 1 million. Urbanization, caused mainly by industrialization—the rise of large manufacturing firms required many industrial workers, while the mechanization of farming meant that fewer agricultural workers were needed—continued unabated until the mid-1940s. After World War II, a massive federal and state road-building program and government-guaranteed home loans for veterans started the process by which the United States became an overwhelmingly suburban nation (see Figure 4.3). Presently, "exurbia"—the areas beyond the older, first-ring of suburbia—is the fastest growing part of America's metropolitan areas. Meanwhile, rural communities across the country, but especially in the northern Rockies and western Great Plains states, are losing population.[13]

This shift in the location of the American population has had important political ramifications. The continued drain of population from rural areas, for instance, has diminished the power of the rural voice in state and national politics (with the exception of the Senate, where such rural, low-population states as Wyoming and Idaho have the same number of seats as large-population, highly urbanized states such as California and Florida). For their part, some central cities, burdened with populations of the poor and the less well-to-do, find it difficult to provide the level of public services considered normal only a few years ago. News footage of mostly poor African Americans being evacuated from the

FIGURE 4.3 • Where Americans Live

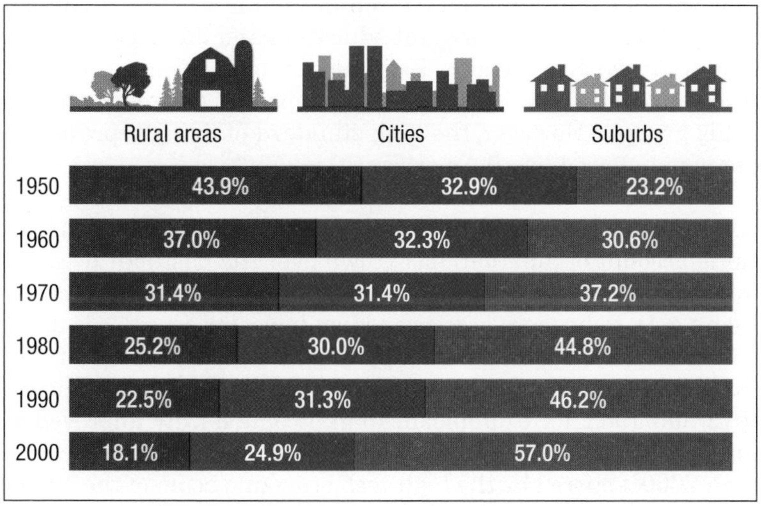

	Rural areas	Cities	Suburbs
1950	43.9%	32.9%	23.2%
1960	37.0%	32.3%	30.6%
1970	31.4%	31.4%	37.2%
1980	25.2%	30.0%	44.8%
1990	22.5%	31.3%	46.2%
2000	18.1%	24.9%	57.0%

In a relatively short period of time, the United States has changed from a society in which the largest percentage of the population lived in rural areas to one in which the largest percentage lives in suburbs. This development has produced several important changes in American politics and in the fortunes of our political parties.

Source: U.S. Bureau of the Census.

Katrina floodwaters in New Orleans was a stark reminder of the harsh reality of inner-city life in many parts of urban America. Heavily dependent on the assistance of the federal government, poor, central-city populations have become even more consistently Democratic in their voting preferences than in the past. Conversely, people living in the distant suburbs, mainly middle-class and working-class homeowners—who increasingly include among their number many members of minority and immigrant groups—have become less willing to support programs for central-city populations. They are more attuned to politicians who promise to pay attention to issues of traffic congestion and sprawl. In many big cities, higher-income people have been moving into newly gentrified sections. They tend to support politicians who promote public safety, support for the arts and culture, and environmental cleanup, but are lukewarm to candidates whose first priority is social welfare for the poor.

The U.S. population has also moved west and south over the course of time. The shift accelerated after World War II as people followed manufacturing jobs to these regions (many companies were attracted to the western and southern states because of their low taxes and anti-union policies). This population shift has led to changes in the relative political power of the states. Following each census from 1950 to 2000, states in the East and the upper Midwest lost congressional seats and presidential electoral votes. States in the West and the South—often referred to as the **Sun Belt** because of their generally pleasant weather—gained at their expense. Because a majority of Sun Belt states are more conservative than other states, their increasing importance in national politics may account for the Republican turn in national politics.

Sun Belt

States of the Lower South, Southwest, and West, where sunny weather and often conservative politics prevail.

Income, Wealth, and Poverty

The United States enjoys one of the highest standards of living in the world, consistently ranking first, second, or third in **gross domestic product (GDP)** per capita[14]—Luxembourg and Norway are the other countries always in the running for the top spot—and in the top group on the U.N.'s Human Development Index, which takes into account education and life expectancy as well as per-capita GDP (with Australia, Belgium, Canada, France, Norway, Iceland, the Netherlands, and Sweden), with little apparent difference among the members of this group.[15] However, the high standard of living represented by these numbers is not shared by all Americans.

gross domestic product, GDP

Monetary value of all goods and services produced in a nation each year, excluding income residents earn abroad.

Income   Overall, **median household income** in the United States (in constant dollars, taking account of inflation) has grown over the past four decades, meaning that the standard of living of most Americans has improved during that time (see Figure 4.4). To be more precise, median household income is up 25 percent from 1967, when the federal government began to collect this statistic. However, there have been periods of stagnation and even decline during this period. Between 1973 and 1983, for example, median income hardly improved at all. Income ramped up from 1984 to 1989, then dropped again through 1993. From 1994 through 2000, spurred by the high-tech economic boom of the 1990s, household income rose steadily among all demographic groups, including the least educated and least skilled. It fell from 2001 to 2004, however, rocked by the recession of 2001 and the slow job recovery that followed.[16] In 2005, median household income began slowly to rise again, a reflection of substantial economic and job growth in 2004 and 2005.[17] It is important to point out that median household income varies across demographic groups. African American

median household income

Household income number at which one-half of all households have more income and one-half have less income; the midpoint of all households ranked by income.

FIGURE 4.4 • Median Household Income, 1967–2004

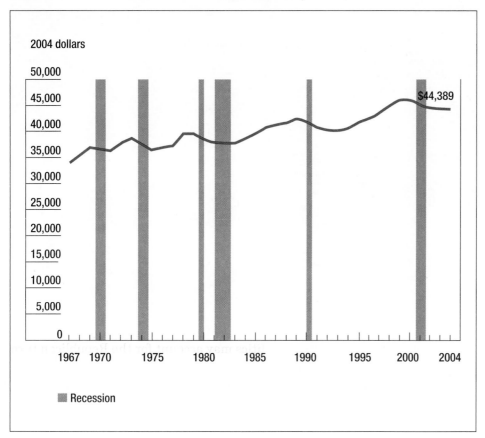

Median household income increased by 28 percent between 1967 and 2004. The increase came in spurts, with periods of stagnation and decline followed by sharp upturns. It is worth noting that income distribution has become more unequal over time, with more going to the top income earners, suggesting that median household incomes for many Americans did not increase at all over this time period.

Source: U.S. Census Bureau.

and Hispanic households have the lowest household incomes—although each made significant strides during the late 1990s—while Asian Americans and non-Hispanic whites have the highest.

Changes in household income can have important political effects. Not surprisingly, when household income is rising, Americans tend to express satisfaction with their situation and confidence in elected leaders. During periods of stagnation and decline, the opposite is evident. During the long 1973–1983 period of stagnation, for example, political observers talked about the rise of an "angry" middle class and the decline of the Democrats, capped in 1980 by the election of Ronald Reagan and a Republican Senate. Middle-class anger stoked by the post-1988 decline also seems to have played a role in the defeat of incumbent president George H. W. Bush in the 1992 election.[18]

Poverty In 1955, almost 25 percent of Americans fell below the federal government's official **poverty line.** The percentage dropped steadily until it reached in lowest point ever in 1973, 11.1 percent. It rose again from then until 1993, when it hit its recent high point of 15.1 percent. The 1990s boom

poverty line

The federal government's calculation of the amount of income families of various sizes need to stay out of poverty.

Down and Out in Beverly Hills

Poverty and homelessness have persisted in the face of strong economic growth in the 1990s and again after 2003. The contrast between rich and poor is evident on the streets of most large American cities, such as in this fashionable section of Los Angeles.

whittled away at the poverty rate (11.3 percent in 2000), but poverty is again on the increase. In 2004, in the wake of the 2001 recession and the slow jobs recovery, 12.7 percent of Americans lived below the poverty line, the highest percentage since 1998.[19]

The problem of poverty in the United States continues to concern many Americans. Here is why:

- A distressingly large number of Americans still live in poverty, 37 million in 2004.
- The official poverty rate is unlikely to fall much unless there is a sustained period of job growth in the next few years, or an increase in the scope and scale of government safety-net programs.
- The poverty rate in the United States remains substantially higher than in the other rich democracies.

The distribution of poverty is not random. It is concentrated among racial minorities and single-parent, female-headed households and their children.[20] Roughly 25 percent of African Americans and 22 percent of Hispanic Americans live in poverty, for example (although a sizable middle class has emerged in both communities), compared with almost 9 percent among non-Hispanic whites and 10 percent among Asians. Almost one in five children under the age of 18 live in poverty as do more than one in three people who live in single-parent, female-headed households.[21]

Obviously, the extent of poverty is politically consequential. Most importantly, poverty often is associated with a range of socially undesirable outcomes, including crime, drug use, and family disintegration,[22] all of which eventually draw the attention of other citizens who want government to do something about these problems. The cause of poverty reduction has also drawn the attention of many Americans who are offended on moral and other grounds by the extent of the poverty that exists in the world's largest economy. (See "Using the Framework" for insight into why it has been so difficult to further diminish poverty.)

Using the Framework

The Persistence of Poverty

Why didn't the tremendous economic growth of the 1990s make much of a dent in the number of poor people in the United States?

Background: Although the strong economy in the 1990s caused poverty rates to fall in the United States, there are still a surprisingly number of poor people in the United States, something brought vividly to life in scenes of poverty-stricken, African American evacuees from New Orleans in the wake of Hurricane Katrina. Surveys show that Americans would like government to do something to help the poor, although there is not much consensus on precisely what should be done to solve the problem of persistent poverty, except for a general unwillingness to go back to the traditional system of welfare that ended in 1996 (see Chapter 17). So, why doesn't the federal government do more to try to end poverty? Taking a look at how structural, political linkage, and governmental factors interact on this issue will help explain the situation.

Governmental Action

The national government provides small safety nets for the poor but does not institute programs to eliminate poverty.

Governmental Level

Proposals to eliminate poverty do not improve the electoral prospects of public officials at the present time.

Elected leaders in both parties tend to support the position that balanced budgets, deregulation, a friendly environment for investors, and encouragement of private enterprise is the best public policy.

Political Linkages Level

The poor are politically invisible; they represent a small minority of the electorate, have few organized groups to push their interests, and have not been able to build a social movement.

Wealthier Americans and large corporations make large contributions to candidates who promise to keep taxes low and government small.

Public opinion opposes big federal government programs to redistribute income.

The Democratic Party, historically the party championing the interests of the poor and near-poor, is often afraid of being tagged with the "liberal" and "tax-and-spend" labels.

Structural Level

American core beliefs about individualism, initiative, and opportunity make it difficult for proposals to assist the poor to gain recognition.

The economic boom of the 1990s, with its record levels of employment, reinforced the belief that anyone who wants to work, can.

The decrease in the number of high-wage, high-benefit jobs in manufacturing has diminished the economic prospects for unskilled, less-educated people.

FIGURE 4.5 • Household Income Distribution in the United States, by Quintiles, 1970 and 2000

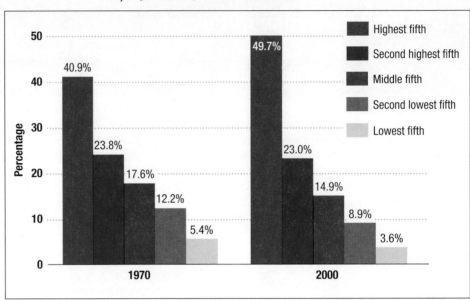

Income inequality has been increasing in the United States, reaching levels not seen since the 1920s. A standard way to measure income inequality is to compare the proportion of national income going to each 20 percent (*quintile*) of households in the population. Especially striking is the shrinking share of the bottom 60 percent and the increasing share of the top 20 percent.

Source: U.S. Bureau of the Census.

Inequality The degree of income and wealth inequality has always been higher in the United States than in the other rich democracies. Over the past two decades, income and wealth inequality have become even more pronounced; income and wealth inequality actually grew during the economic booms of the 1980s and 1990s. By 2000, the top quintile (the top 20 percent) of households took home almost 50 percent of national income (see Figure 4.5), the highest proportion ever recorded. Wealth (assets such as real estate, stocks and bonds, art, bank accounts, cash-value insurance policies, and so on) in the United States is even more unequally distributed than income. According to a study by economist Edward Wolff, the top 1 percent of households—with a net worth of at least $2.3 million—owned more than 42 percent of the nation's wealth by the mid-1990s, up from only 21 percent in 1975.[23] For more on how to conceptualize and measure inequality, and on what inequality might mean for American politics, see the "By the Numbers" feature.

The American Economy

Virtually everything we have discussed so far in this chapter is shaped by the American economy. The growth, diversification, and geographic dispersion of the American population, for example, can be traced directly to changes in the economy. Occupations, standards of living, and the distribution of income and wealth are closely connected to the operations of our economic institutions. Even important elements of the American political culture, as we shall soon see, are associated with our economy and how it works.

The Rise of Industrial Capitalism

At the time of the first census in 1790, almost three-quarters of all Americans worked in agriculture. Most of the remainder of the population worked in retail trade, transportation, and skilled trades closely connected to agriculture. About 80 percent of the working, male, nonslave population was self-employed, owning small farms, stores, wagons and horses, and workshops.[24] Until the Civil War, the American capitalist economy (except in the slave-holding South) was highly competitive, with many small enterprises, first tied to agriculture and then increasingly to manufacturing. After the Civil War, and partly as a result of it, the economy became increasingly industrialized and concentrated in giant enterprises.[25] By the turn of the twentieth century, the United States was the world's leading industrial nation, with many Americans working in manufacturing jobs.

Industrial enterprises grew to unprecedented size in the late nineteenth and early twentieth centuries, triggering mass migration to large industrialized cities from the rural parts of the nation. Partly, this change in scale was related to technology: The steam engine, electrical power, and the assembly line provided the means of bringing thousands of working people together for industrial production. Partly, this change in scale was tied to cost: Most of the new industrial technologies required unheard-of levels of investment capital. Large enterprises were also encouraged by changes in the laws of incorporation, which allowed competing corporations to merge into single, giant enterprises. A wave of mergers between 1896 and 1904 fashioned the corporate-dominated economy familiar to us today.[26]

The American economy and American corporations grew impressively during the first two-thirds of the twentieth century. Although thrown seriously off track for at least a decade by the Great Depression, the economy was pushed forward again by World War II and the Cold War that followed; both triggered rapid and substantial increases in government spending, research and development, and technological innovation. By 1975, 11 of the largest 15 corporations in the world were American; by 1981, 40 percent of

Mass Production Manufacturing

The principles of assembly-line, mass production manufacturing were honed to near perfection by Henry Ford in the early twentieth century at his Highland Park complex in Michigan. Here workers assemble a portion of a Model T, the first car to reach the mass public in the United States.

By the Numbers

Is America becoming more unequal?

Scholars and journalists have been claiming for some time now that economic inequality in the United States is not only the highest among all rich democracies, but is becoming steadily more pronounced. As the highly respected *Economist* put it recently, "Income inequality [in the United States] is growing to levels not seen since the Gilded Age, around the 1880s."[a]

Why It Matters: Rising economic inequality, if it is, in fact, happening, has troubling implications for the practice of democracy in the United States. It is undeniably the case that such inequalities all too often spill over into inequalities in politics. Those with substantially more income and wealth tend to have a stronger voice in politics and better access to political decision makers than people with lower incomes. Those at the top are more likely to vote; can and do make more contributions to candidates, parties, and advocacy groups; and have more information available to them than those on the bottom. The fundamental democratic principle of political equality is at risk when economic inequality is substantial.[b]

Calculating the Numbers: There are many ways to measure economic inequality. Each provides a slightly different angle for viewing the issue. We examine here two sets of numbers collected by international organizations that allow us to compare how the United States is doing on the distribution of earnings—money earned by working—with other rich countries. On the right is a graph based on data from the Organization of Economic Cooperation and Development (OECD) that reports ratios created by dividing the earnings among full-time employed individuals in the 90th percentile of the population by the earnings of working individuals in the 10th percentile. (These data, called P90/P10 ratios, were collected at two points in time, mostly in the early 1980s and the mid- to late 1990s.) Higher ratios mean higher levels of inequality. Thus, a ratio score of 2 means that individuals in the 90th percentile earn twice as much as individuals in the 10th percentile. A ratio score of 8 means that 90th percentile people earn eight times as

much. From the graph, several things are apparent. First, the more recent P90/P10 ratio is higher in the United States than in the other comparison countries, with the average individual in the 90th percentile earning about four-and-a-half times the average individual in the 10th percentile. Second, earnings inequality has increased in most of the rich countries (Japan, Finland, Norway, Switzerland, and Belgium are the exceptions). Third, the rise in earnings inequality over this time period has been most pronounced in the United States.

P90/P10 Ratios for Earnings Among Full-Time Employed Individuals, 1979–2000

Note: Countries are ordered by change in inequality (most recent observation minus earliest observation). Data for Norway include part-time employees.

On the right is a graph based on the Luxembourg Income Study of household earnings over time, that shows Gini coefficients of inequality. The Gini coefficient is a number between "0" and "1," where "0" is perfect equality (everyone has the same earnings) and "1" is perfect inequality (where one person or household takes all earnings, leaving nothing for anyone else). The higher the Gini coefficient, the higher the measured inequality. Several conclusions can be drawn from the graph. First, the United States does not have the highest level of inequality among the rich countries in the more recent observations—the United Kingdom (Great Britain) does—although we are very close. Second, the United States ranks third among these countries in how much inequality has increased, with Sweden, of all places, sneaking into the second spot. Third, and finally, with the exception of the Netherlands, earnings inequality among households is rising in all the rich countries shown.

What Do the Numbers Mean, Really?

Calculations using alternative data sources yield roughly the same result: The United States ranks very high on measures of economic inequality, and has been growing more unequal. But, does high and rising inequality mean that those at the bottom of the distribution are worse off? Not necessarily. During the 1990s, for example, even as earnings inequality was increasing in the United States, poverty rates were falling (poverty has increased in the last several years, however), the proportion of Americans owning their own homes increased, as did the inflation-adjusted income of the lowest 20 percent of the population. How can this be? The answer is that rising inequality can be the outcome of a number of income distribution processes, only one of which involves the worst off becoming even worse off: (1) The people on top become better off while those on the bottom become worse off; (2) the people on both the top and the bottom become worse off, but those on the bottom decline faster; (3) everyone is better off but incomes rise faster for those on the top than those on the bottom. Situation (1) is what many critics of American society and economy say is going on and what many people tend to think is going on when they see inequality statistics. Situation (3) is what many defenders of American society and economy say is going on.[c]

What Do You Think?

Some people think that inequality is inherently unjust and that rising inequality, even in cases where people on the bottom are better off in an absolute sense, is something that soci-

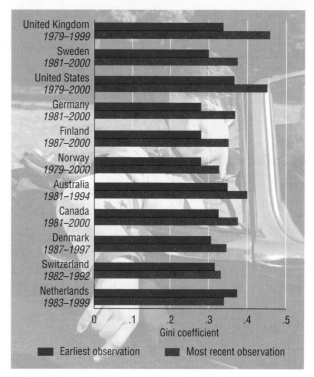

Gini Coefficients for Market Income Among Working-Age Households, 1979–2000

Note: Countries are ordered by change in inequality (most recent observation minus earliest observation).

Source: The 90/10 ratio graph and the Gini coefficient graph are from Lane Kenworthy and Jonas Pontusson, "Rising Inequality and the Politics of Redistribution in Affluent Countries," *Perspectives on Politics* 3, no. 3 (Washington, D.C.: The American Political Science Association, 2005), pp. 451–452.

ety must rectify. How do you feel about this? Is inequality acceptable if people in all parts of the income structure are better off? What do you think about the issue of inequality and democracy? If those on the top have relatively more income every year, won't they be able to exercise more and more political influence?

[a]"Ever Higher Society, Ever Harder to Ascend," *The Economist* (January 1, 2005), p. 22. Also see Kevin Phillips, *Wealth and Democracy: How Great Fortunes and Government Created America's Aristocracy* (New York: Broadway Books, 2002).

[b]"American Democracy in an Age of Rising Inequality," Report of the American Political Science Association's Taskforce on Inequality and American Democracy, *Perspectives on Politics,* vol. 2 (2004), pp. 651–666; Larry M. Bartells, "Is the Water Rising? Reflections on Inequality and American Democracy," *PS* (January, 2006), pp. 39–42.

[c]Gregg Easterbrook, *The Progress Paradox: How Life Gets Better While People Feel Worse* (New York: Random House, 2003).

the world's total foreign direct investment was still accounted for by the United States.[27]

This enormous growth in the wealth and reach of the American economy after World War II, fueled by the activities of the major corporations; by science-driven, productivity-enhancing technological change; and by the existence of strong unions in the manufacturing sector, made possible rapid improvements in the American standard of living, the growth of the middle class, and transformations in how Americans worked. By the mid-1970s, fewer than 1 in 7 Americans worked in agriculture, while more than 4 in 10 worked in **white-collar** and service jobs.[28]

white-collar worker
A person working at a service, sales, or office job.

Globalization and the New American Economy

Although the U.S. economy continued to grow in the 1970s and 1980s, its rate of growth began to fall behind that of western Europe and Japan, even as American corporations began to feel the pinch of intense competition from foreign corporations. Between the early 1970s and the late 1980s, the U.S. share of world manufacturing declined. The United States lost ground in steel, autos, machine tools, electronics, computer chips, and finance.

In the 1990s, however, the American economy rebounded with a vengeance, with its companies once again becoming the key players in crucial industries. The economies once seen as the principal threats to America's position—the European Union, Japan, and the so-called Asian tigers—began to lose ground; their rates of growth and technological innovation began to lag behind those of the United States. American companies emerged as the most important actors in the new global economy. Behind the apparent decline in the competitiveness of the American economy in the 1970s and 1980s, something startling seems to have been going on. Leaving older industries such as mining, steel, and shipbuilding to others, American companies proved to be particularly adept in areas such as computer software, biotechnology, business services (insurance, law, accounting, advertising, and so on), computer chips, Internet services, telecommunications, military and commercial aircraft, and popular entertain-

Globalization

The largest American corporations are also global corporations in the sense that they produce, market, and sell their products all over the world. This Microsoft advertisement is making its way across the harbor in Shanghai, China.

ment. In this emergent global economy, Apple, Microsoft, Intel, Dell, Disney, Amazon.com, Google, and eBay became (and remain) the companies that draw global attention and emulation efforts.

The reasons for the turnaround among American companies in particular and the American economy in general have been the subject of much debate among economists and business leaders. Some point to the lighter hand of government and labor unions in the United States (and the union hand is getting even lighter, as the chapter-opening story suggests), some point to stronger entrepreneurial traditions here, and still others credit the existence of freer markets,[29] but all seem to agree that American businesses were better positioned to succeed in the new global economy that blossomed in the 1990s.[30] To be sure, all the economic news has not been positive: There was a brief and shallow recession in 2001 coming on the heels of the dot-com bust, a slow jobs recovery in 2002 and 2003, growing federal government budget deficits after 2001, an ever-growing trade deficit (especially with China), and a decline in real estate. Airline companies and auto manufacturers also found themselves in difficulties. Iconic IBM was bought by a Chinese company. Nevertheless, from a comparative point of view, the American economy has been performing very well, and its companies are doing remarkably well, especially in light of the blows dealt by the 9/11 attacks, corporate accounting scandals, wars in Afghanistan and Iraq, oil price shocks, and Hurricane Katrina. In 2005, the United States remained the largest economy in the world measured by GDP, about as large as the combined economies of Japan, Germany, the United Kingdom, France, and Brazil.

America's involvement in a changing global economy has been politically consequential.[31] On the one hand, during good times, economic growth, low inflation, and soaring home valuations contribute to consumer confidence, rising living standards, and general satisfaction with government leaders. On the other hand, the new global economy is an incredibly competitive place, where companies in different countries are fighting for labor cost, technological, and price advantages over other firms, forcing companies to be, in the popular phrase, lean and mean, with many of them trimming health care plans, wage and salary schedules, and employees as part of their competitive strategies. Some companies, moreover, believe they must outsource to lower-cost suppliers, shift some operations to other locations, and constantly innovate. In this highly competitive economy, unions are being forced to make wage and benefit concessions, the number of manufacturing jobs is not growing (although manufacturing output is), and certain "creative class" skills are highly sought after and rewarded[32]—software engineers, portfolio managers, Web site creators, filmmakers, and business strategists, for example—while others are not—low-skilled manual and service workers, for example. For the former, work tends to be both exciting and lucrative. For the latter, work is routine, not very well paid, and characterized by frequent layoffs and part-time status. This may be why income inequality has increased despite a booming economy in the 1990s and a growing economy in 2003–2006.

Technological Innovations That Have Changed the Political Landscape

The United States in the World

In addition to its prominent role in the global economy, America's diplomatic, political, and military standing in the world is another important structural fact that shapes politics and government in the United States. In this section, we sketch the general outlines of that position over the course of U.S. history; in Chapter 18, we examine the foreign policies that have been forged in response to America's position in the world and how such policies are made.

Superpower: The First Stage

World War II thrust the United States into the leadership position that its economic position in the world had portended since 1900. The war stimulated a massive expansion of the entire industrial economy. At the same time, the financial and manufacturing infrastructures of our prewar economic rivals—Britain, France, Japan, and Germany—were devastated by the war.

The United States emerged from the war in 1945 with an expanded industrial economy, a large military establishment, and military superiority in most important areas. There was also a new belief among both Americans and their leaders that isolationism was dangerous and contrary to our long-term national interests.

Within a decade of the end of World War II, the United States stood as the unchallenged economic, political, and military power among the Western nations. For the first time in its history, the United States was willing and able to exercise leadership on the world level. It was the United States that organized the rich democracies into a political and economic partnership. It provided funds for rebuilding western Europe and for development projects in the Third World. It successfully pushed for free international trade and provided a stable dollar to serve as the basis of the international monetary system. And it organized and largely paid for the joint military defenses of them all. Is it any wonder, then, that *Life* magazine editor Henry Luce was moved to label the period the "American century"?

The fly in the ointment, of course, was the Soviet Union. Although badly crippled by the war (it is said that 20 million of its citizens died in the conflict), the Soviet Union entered the post-war era with the world's largest land army, superpower ambitions of its own, and a strong desire to keep the nations on its periphery in eastern and southern Europe in hands it considered friendly. In the ensuing **Cold War,** which began in the late 1940s and lasted for four decades, the two superpowers faced each other as leaders of conflicting political, economic, and ideological alliances; became engaged in a nuclear arms race; and fought surrogate wars with each other in various locations in the Third World, from Korea (where the Soviets were allied with the Chinese) and Vietnam, to the Belgian Congo, Central America, and Afghanistan (during the rebellion against Soviet occupation, 1980 to 1989).

Cold War

The period of tense relations between the United States and the Soviet Union from the late 1940s to the late 1980s.

Flexing Military Muscles in Moscow

During the Cold War, the United States and the Soviet Union avoided direct military conflict because their respective leaders feared mutual annihilation from a nuclear exchange if the disagreements between them ever turned from "cold" to "hot." Here, nuclear missiles are on display at the annual parade in Red Square in 1988 celebrating the 1917 Bolshevik Revolution.

America's superpower status had many implications for U.S. politics and government policies. For one thing, superpower status required a large military establishment and tilted government spending priorities toward national defense. For another thing, as we will see in later chapters, it enhanced the role of the president in policymaking and diminished that of Congress.

Superpower: The Second Stage

The 1990s saw startling changes in the world's military, political, and economic systems, all of which, at least nominally, heightened U.S. power in the world. Communism collapsed in eastern Europe. The Soviet Union ceased to exist. Communist China switched to a market economy. Most developing countries rejected the socialist development model, embraced "privatization," and welcomed foreign investment. Moreover, the United States took the lead in organizing the global economy. Many observers began to refer to the United States as the world's only superpower, without any real challengers to its political, diplomatic, military, and cultural preeminence. (For more on the United States in the world trading system, see the "Mapping American Politics" feature.)

Oddly, however, although the last superpower in a military sense, the United States has not necessarily had its way on all important matters, either with allies or enemies, nor is it likely to do so in the future. With the threat of the Soviet Union no longer supplying the glue to hold them together, U.S. allies feel freer to go their own way on a wide range of international issues. The United States could not agree with the Europeans for a very long time on what to do about the ethnic conflicts in Bosnia and Kosovo, for example. It also has differences with the European Union over trade issues, international treaties on the environment, land mines, and the international criminal court, and on the war with Iraq and the recovery effort there. Relations with France and Germany, long-time allies, became particularly strained over the war in Iraq. Disagreements about nuclear proliferation have strained U.S. relations with

VIDEO ROUNDTABLE

9-11-2001

Tough Times in Iraq

U.S. Army soldiers from the 1st Cavalry Division try to secure an area of Baghdad in 2004 during the coalition occupation. The high human and economic costs of operations in Iraq show that America's superpower status is not without its downside.

Mapping American Politics

The United States in the world trading system

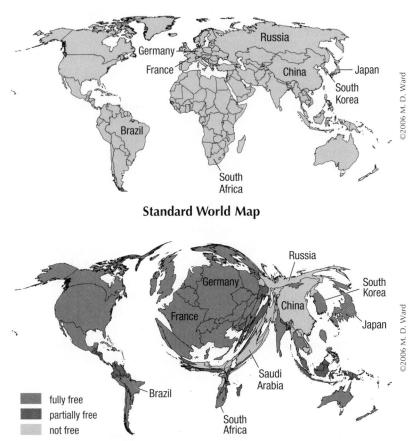

Introduction: What a government does is strongly influenced by the health and vitality of its economy. American political leaders recognize that their election or reelection to office depends a great deal on how well Americans are doing economically and strive to produce policies that contribute to economic growth and stability. Many of these policies have to do with the position of the United States in the world trading system. For the most part, government leaders, along with most economists, believe that participation in the global trading system benefits all countries that take part in it, a position that critics of globalization, including American trade unionists, dispute. Many political scientists and economists also believe that democracy and involve-

Standard World Map

©2006 M. D. Ward

fully free
partially free
not free

©2006 M. D. Ward

Nations of World Sized in Proportion to Trade

Russia, while security issues, human rights violations, trade imbalances, and protection of intellectual property have been an irritant in our relations with the emerging giant China. Nor has the United States been able, in spite of all of its power, to bring the Palestinians and Israelis together to encourage or force a solution to their decades-long conflict. And, perhaps most importantly, American citizens, officials, and companies, as well as American allies, remain vulnerable to terrorist attacks, with no end in sight to this danger.

Being the world's single military superpower is also very costly. The dramatic rise in the national defense and homeland security budgets—and a series of tax cuts passed during the first presidential term of George W. Bush—led to the reappearance of very large deficits in the national budget (which will be explored further in Chapter 17). Americans also discovered that fighting an insurgency in Iraq seriously stretched the manpower resources of the military, leading to a greater-than-normal reliance on reserve and National Guard units.

ment in the global economy are strongly associated, primarily because countries that engage in the global economy grow rich enough to generate a democracy-seeking middle class and cannot help but expose their people to a diverse set of ideas and cultural influences. So where does the United States stand in relationship to other countries in terms of its involvement in trade? And how democratic are trading nations?

Mapping Trade and Democracy: The cartogram shows countries sized in relationship to their total trade, the sum of their exports and imports, in 2004. The more trade a country engages in, the larger it is in the cartogram relative to its size on standard maps; the less trade a country engages in, the smaller it is relatively. The colors reflect levels of democracy based on Freedom House criteria that are similar to our definition of democracy in Chapter 1. Several things are immediately obvious. First, the United States is a major player in world trade, which most economists believe adds to its GDP and standard of living. Second, countries in western Europe are very big traders, as are Japan and South Korea. Third, some countries and regions play a relatively tiny role in world trade, including Central America,

South America, and, most dramatically, Sub-Sahara Africa (which, with the exception of South Africa, almost disappears from the cartogram). Russia also plays a surprisingly small role in the world trading system. Fourth and finally, the largest exporting countries tend to be democracies, although this is not true for China or Saudi Arabia, the former importing and exporting a wide range of products, the latter being the world's largest exporter of petroleum.

What Do You Think? Would it be a good thing if the United States further increased its level of trade? Why? Do you think American workers and consumers would be better off with more trade or less? Does the cartogram suggest that freedom and trade are associated? Or does the lack of freedom in China and Saudi Arabia suggest otherwise? If trade and democracy are linked, would you expect China and Saudi Arabia to become freer in the future?

Sources: Exports and imports in dollars taken from the World Bank: **http://stat.wto.org/StatisticalProgram/WsdbExport.aspx? Language=E;** democracy scoring from Freedom House online database at **www.freedomhouse.org.**

The American Political Culture: How Exceptional?

Americans' attitudes and opinions about what policies government should adopt, the performance and responsiveness of elected officials, and what the United States should do internationally are embedded in more fundamental beliefs about human nature, society, economic relations, and the role of government. Taken together, these fundamental or core beliefs make up the American *political culture.* In the next chapter on public opinion, we will examine the nature of American political attitudes and opinions; here, we will examine the core beliefs. These core beliefs can be understood as the raw material from which attitudes and opinions are built. Also in the next chapter, we will examine the processes—called **political socialization**—by which people come to have particular core beliefs, attitudes, and opinions.

political socialization
The process by which individuals come to have certain core beliefs and political attitudes.

Evidence strongly suggests that Americans share a common political culture that is very different from the political cultures of other societies.[33] To be sure, we are a vast, polyglot mixture of races, religions, ethnicities, occupations, and lifestyles. Nevertheless, one of the things that has always struck foreign observers of the American scene, ranging from Alexis de Tocqueville (*Democracy in America,* 1835 and 1840), to James Bryce (*The American Commonwealth,* 1888), and John Micklethwait and Adrian Wooldridge (*The Right Nation,* 2004), is the degree to which a broad consensus seems to exist on many of the core beliefs that shape our attitudes and opinions, our ways of engaging in politics, and what we expect of our government, and how different the elements of this consensus are from political cultural elements elsewhere. To be sure, consensus on core beliefs does not mean that people always agree on what government should do in particular situations. Thus, people who agree that government's role should be limited might disagree on what specific things government should do (say, national defense or school lunch programs). To be sure, people in other societies share some of the core beliefs of Americans, but the package of core beliefs is truly exceptional.

Understanding our political culture is important for understanding American politics and government. Why? Because the kinds of choices Americans make in meeting the challenges posed by a changing economy, society, and post–Cold War world depend a great deal on the core beliefs Americans hold about human nature, society, economic relations, and the role of government. Let's look, then, at the most important of these core beliefs.

Individualism

SIMULATION

What Are American Civic Values?

Americans believe that individuals have, as the Declaration of Independence puts it, inalienable rights, meaning that individual rights take priority over rights that might be attributed to society or government. Indeed, the very purpose of government, following John Locke's ideas in *The Second Treatise on Government* (1690) and Jefferson's in the Declaration (1776), is to protect these rights. In formal, legal terms, this has meant that Americans have worked hard to protect the constitutional rights of speech, belief, and association (among others). In a more informal sense, this has meant an abiding belief among Americans in the importance of personal ambition and choosing one's own life goals and way of life. (Thus, the appeal of the U.S. army's slogan "Be all that you can be.")

American individualism is also expressed as a belief that one's fate is (and ought to be) in one's own hands, rather than the product of impersonal social and economic forces beyond one's own control. In particular, one's fortunes are tied to one's own efforts. Those with talent, grit, and the willingness to work hard, Americans believe, are more likely than not to end up on top; those without at least some of these qualities are more likely to wind up at the bottom of the heap. Americans tend to assume that people generally get what they deserve in the long run.

Compared with people in other countries, Americans are also more likely to believe that people are naturally competitive, always striving to better themselves in relation to others. Popular literature in America has always conveyed this theme, ranging from the Horatio Alger books of the late nineteenth century to the many contemporary self-help books with keys to "getting ahead," "making it," and "getting rich." The French, particularly in the person of President Jacque Chirac, are fond of referring to this celebration of the com-

All for One, One for All

In Japan, commitment to the work team and the company are more important cultural values than they are in the United States. These Japanese supermarket workers start their day as a team.

petitive individual over the community as the "Anglo-Saxon disease" (thus including the English) and profess to want no part of it in continental Europe.

This core belief about individualism affects American attitudes toward many issues, including inequality and what should be done about it.[34] Americans overwhelmingly endorse the idea of "equality of opportunity" (the idea that people ought to have an equal shot in the competitive game of life), for instance, yet they also overwhelmingly reject the idea that people should be guaranteed equal rewards. Not surprisingly, Americans tend to look favorably on government programs that try to equalize opportunity—Head Start, education programs of various kinds, school lunch programs, and the like—but are generally against programs such as welfare, which seem to redistribute income from the hard-working middle class to individuals who are considered "undeserving."

Because Americans tend to assume that people get different rewards based on their own efforts, a belief in equality of opportunity is consistent with highly unequal outcomes. Another way to say the same thing is to point out that Americans seem to find inequality of income and wealth acceptable, so long as it is the outcome of a process in which individuals compete fairly with one another.[35] Not surprisingly, given this core belief, Americans are less likely to support government efforts to equalize matters than are people in other rich democracies, especially if efforts to equalize outcomes in society involve imposing limits on individual striving and achievement[36] (see Figure 4.6).

Private Property and Private Enterprise

More than people elsewhere, Americans tend to believe in the importance of private property and the efficiencies of the free market. Although many of these ideas come from and perhaps were best articulated by John Locke in his *Second Treatise,* they have been reinforced by the experience of fairly widespread property ownership in the United States compared with many other countries.[37]

FIGURE 4.6 • Freedom and Equality

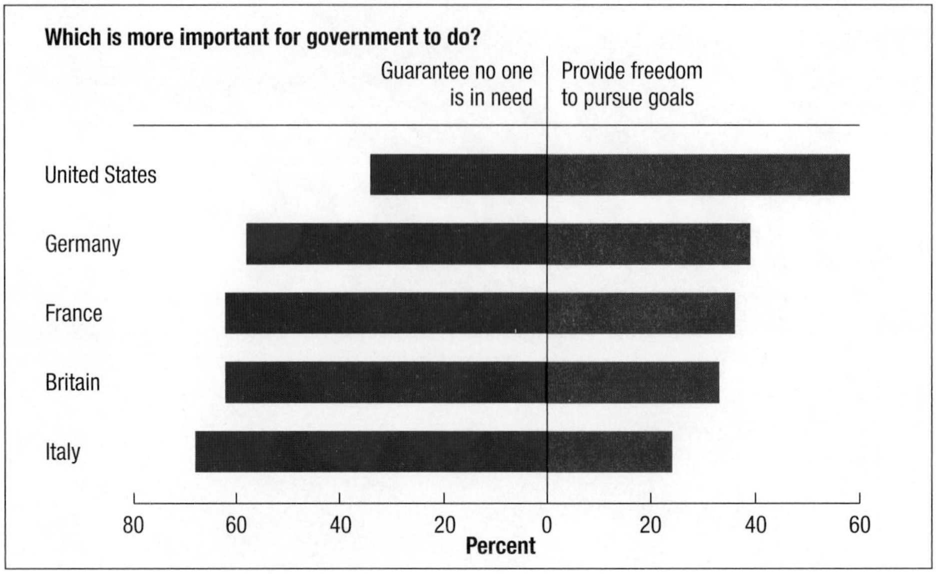

Which is more important for government to do?

| Guarantee no one is in need | Provide freedom to pursue goals |

United States

Germany

France

Britain

Italy

80   60   40   20   0   20   40   60
Percent

American beliefs about the role of government are remarkably different from those of people living in other rich democracies. Americans are much less likely to want government to do something about poverty and more likely to want to leave such an objective up to individuals.

Source: Pew Research Center, reported in *The Economist* (November 8, 2003), p. 4.

Locke argued that the Creator gave the earth and its resources in common to human beings and also gave human beings abilities that they have a right and an obligation to use. When they use these abilities, people turn common property into private property. By mixing their labor with the naturally occurring abundance of the earth, Locke argued, people are justified in taking the product of that effort for their own as private property. Because people are different in their abilities and their willingness to work, this process will always result in inequality. Inevitably, some will end up with more property than others.

The idea of private property is not only an economic concept in the American political culture. Equally important is the belief that ownership of property is the basis for the exercise of individual rights. Jefferson, for one, believed that a large, property-owning middle class was the essential foundation for a democratic society because people with property, even small amounts, were less likely to be intimidated by others, including those who govern society.

The basic theory of the free market was worked out by Adam Smith in his classic work, *The Wealth of Nations* (1776). Smith taught that if people were free to buy and sell in the marketplace, unfettered by government, the laws of supply and demand would perfectly and efficiently coordinate economic life; things that people wanted would be produced at prices that people could pay. Because the market is efficient and effective if left alone, he suggested, government should not interfere with its operations. Although few Americans now accept this "pure" free market ideal, most still believe that the private sector is usually more effective and efficient than the public sector. Given the esteem in which private property and the market are held, as well as the historical success of the American economy, it is entirely understandable that Americans tend to hold the business system (although not necessarily large corporations) in very high regard, more so than people in most other societies.

Distrust of Government

From the beginning, Americans have distrusted government. Indeed, as you will recall from the discussion in Chapter 2, the framers created a republican constitutional system precisely because they distrusted government and were trying to create a set of constitutional rules that would deny government the means to act in mischievous or evil ways. Americans have long believed that when governments are imbued with too much power, they are tempted to interfere with private property, individual rights, and economic efficiency. Distrust of government still remains attractive to most Americans today, even though most Americans expect government to do far more than the framers ever imagined. This core belief is not universally shared. In countries such as Germany, France, and Italy, where governments have always been powerful and have played an important role in directing society and the economy, people are much more likely to trust the intentions and trustworthiness of government.

This set of ideas about individualism, limited government, and the free market (what some people call *classical liberalism*)[38] influences many aspects of public policy in the United States. For example, the eminent economist John Kenneth Galbraith once decried the fact that ours is a society in which great private wealth exists side by side with public squalor. By that, he meant that Americans favor private consumption over public services and amenities and private over public initiatives.[39] In other rich democracies, citizens and political leaders tend to believe that extensive and high-quality public services in mass transit, health care, housing, and education are part and parcel of the good society. It is why government-funded high-speed bullet trains exist in Japan and France. It is why other rich democracies have a national system of health care or insurance. It is why Americans are so fond of consuming and so loath to increase their taxes.

Citizenship and the Nature of the Political Order

Certain beliefs about what kind of political order is most appropriate and what role citizens should play shape the actual daily behavior of citizens and political decision makers alike.

Democracy At the time of the nation's founding, democracy was not highly regarded in the United States. During our history, however, the practice of democracy has been enriched and expanded, and the term *democracy* has become an honored one.[40] While regard for democracy is one of the bedrocks of the American belief system today, Americans have not necessarily always behaved democratically. After all, African Americans were denied the vote and other citizenship rights in many parts of the nation until the 1960s. It is fair to say, nevertheless, that most Americans believe in democracy as a general principle and take seriously any claim that their behavior is not consistent with it. For example, public opinion surveys done during the past 25 years consistently show that about 60 to 70 percent of Americans want to abolish the Electoral College.

Freedom and Liberty Foreign visitors have always been fascinated by the American obsession with individual "rights," the belief that in the good society, government leaves people alone in their private pursuits. Studies show that freedom (also called *liberty*) is at the very top of the list of American beliefs and that it is more strongly honored here than elsewhere.[41] From the very beginning, what attracted most people to the United States was the promise of freedom in the New World. Many came for other reasons, to be sure: a great many came for strictly economic reasons, some came as convict labor, and some came in chains as slaves. But many who came to these shores seem to have done so to taste the freedom to speak and think as they chose, to worship as they pleased, to read what they might, and to assemble and petition the government if they had a mind to.

As in many cases, however, to believe in something is not necessarily to act consistently with that belief. There have been many intrusions on basic rights during our history. Later chapters address this issue in more detail.

Populism

The term *populism* refers to the hostility of the common person to concentrated power and the powerful. While public policy is not often driven by populist sentiments (for the powerful, by definition, exercise considerable political influence), populism has always been part of the American core belief system and has sometimes been expressed in visible ways in American politics.

One of the most common targets of populist sentiment has been concentrated economic power and the people who exercise it. Andrew Jackson mobilized this sentiment in his fight against the Bank of the United States in the 1830s. The Populist movement of the 1890s aimed at taming the new corporations of the day, especially the banks and the railroads. Corporations were the target of popular hostility during the dark days of the Great Depression and also in the 1970s, when agitation by consumer and environmental groups made the lives of some corporate executives extremely uncomfortable. Populism is a staple of contemporary conservatism in the United States with its attacks on Hollywood, the media, and academic elitists.

Populism celebrates the ordinary person. Elites and leaders of every stripe "shouldn't get too uppity," it is widely believed. Even the rich and powerful, it is said, put on their pants "one leg at a time" just like everyone else. Given this widespread belief, it behooves political candidates in America to portray themselves as ordinary folks, with tastes and lifestyles very much like everyone else's. How else might one explain private-school-educated and aristocratically born-and-bred George H. W. Bush expressing his fondness for pork rinds and country and western music during the 1988 presidential campaign. It is very different in France, where it is not considered a political liability to have gone to elite schools and authored important works of fiction, poetry, and biography as President Francois Mitterand (president from 1981 to 1995) and Jacque Chirac's foreign minister and Prime Minister Dominique de Villepin did.

VIDEO DEBATE

Church and State

Religious Belief

The United States is, by any measure, a strikingly religious society.[42] Polls conducted over the past three or four decades show that more Americans believe in God, regularly attend church, and say that religion is important in their lives, than people in any of the other rich democracies (see Figure 4.7). Levels of religiosity in the United States, in fact, approach those found in poor Muslim countries of the developing world.[43] This commitment to religion has existed from the beginning of the republic and is integrally related to the practice of politics in the United States, something that often baffles foreign observers.[44] Religious sentiments have been invoked by most important political leaders in the United States in their public pronouncements, and Americans have come to expect religious references when leaders talk about public matters.

FIGURE 4.7 • **Comparing Nations on Their Strength of Religious Belief**

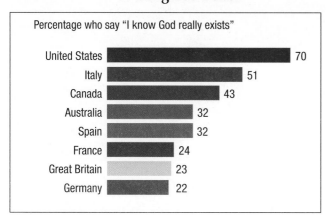

Percentage who say "I know God really exists"

Country	Percentage
United States	70
Italy	51
Canada	43
Australia	32
Spain	32
France	24
Great Britain	23
Germany	22

Compared with people in other rich democracies, a substantially higher proportion of Americans say they believe in God.

Source: International Social Survey, National Opinion Research Center, University of Chicago (1998).

Religious faith affects politics in important ways. For one thing, it affects which issues become part of political debate and election campaigns. Abortion, school prayer, and the teaching of evolution are not at the epicenter of politics in other countries, rich or poor, as they are in the United States. For another thing, religious belief has been important in drawing ideological lines. While churches and religious believers have often been on the liberal side of the political divide to be sure—note the substantial involvement of religious leaders, organizations, and believers in the civil rights and anti–Vietnam War movements—strong religious beliefs are most associated with conservative tendencies in American politics. Public opinion polls show

Mingling After Church

Americans are far more likely than people in the other rich democracies to say they believe in God and regularly attend religious services.

Using the Democracy Standard

Is real democracy possible in the United States?

PROPOSITION: **The kind of economy, society, and culture we have in the United States makes it difficult to have a real democracy because the key components of a working democracy—popular sovereignty, political equality, and political liberty—cannot flourish.**

AGREE The sort of economic system we have in the United States, although incredibly productive, distributes wealth and income in a highly unequal way, leaving the few at the top with the lion's share. At the same time, the middle class is stuck in place, and poverty prevails at a level unequaled by any of the other rich democracies. This leads to substantial inequalities in political power and influence among different income and wealth groups in the United States, because economic inequality always spills over into political inequality. Matters are made worse by the fact that Americans are dividing into racially and economically homogeneous housing areas, undermining the sense of community and shared sentiments that are the basis for democracy and for the sort of cooperation that is necessary for government to tackle serious social problems. To make matters worse, the American political culture celebrates an extreme form of individualism and antigovernment sentiments that makes it hard for Americans to cooperate in a way that makes it possible for the people to use government to serve public purposes.

American society is open, diverse, and filled with opportunity for those who are ambitious. Economic growth is raising the living standards of the population across the board, which bodes well for democracy; note the evidence that high living standards and democracy seem to go together. Also, economic, technological, and social changes—including the Internet, ease of travel, medical advances, and more—are allowing more and more people to develop their unique abilities and capacities, to become informed, to link together with others who share their public concerns, to get involved in community and political affairs, and to have their voices heard by public officials. Most importantly, perhaps, these developments make it possible for Americans to shape their own lives, improving their situations and those of their families, without the need of government. **DISAGREE**

CONSIDER There are two competing arguments discussed here. One focuses on structural developments that contribute to rising inequality, social fragmentation, and contempt for government. The other focuses on rising living standards, expanded opportunities, and the promise of technology for enriching democratic life in the United States.

• Which is closer to your own experience of life in this country and where you think American society is going? • Is it possible that there is some truth to each position, that some developments and conditions in American society, economy, culture, and world position are democracy-enhancing, while others are democracy-diminishing? • And, if the objective is to enrich democratic life in the United States, which of the barriers to democracy you have read about are most amenable to change?

that the most religious Americans (of all denominations) are also the most conservative Americans on issues ranging from abortion to prayer in the schools, social welfare, and military spending; church attendance, in the end, is a better predictor of party affiliation than income.

This combination of classical liberalism—individualism and individual rights, antigovernment sentiments, and belief in the primacy of private property and free enterprise—with populism and widespread religious belief is unique in the world. In this respect, the American political culture truly is exceptional.

Structural Influences on American Politics

We have examined a number of structural factors that influence American politics. Chapters 2 and 3 examined the constitutional rules, and this chapter considered the main features of American society, economy, political culture, and America's place in the world and how each influences important aspects of politics and government in the United States. These structural factors are interrelated. The constitutional rules are substantially shaped by our beliefs about the nature of the individual, society, and government that make up our political culture. The political culture, in turn, with its celebration of the market, competitive individualism, and private property, is perfectly attuned to a free enterprise economy. How the economy operates and develops has a lot to do with the life of the American people (where people live, what kind of work they do, and so on), as does the nation's place in the world. The characteristics of the American population trigger their own effects; the populace's level of education and skill has a lot to do with American economic performance, for instance.

These structural factors are used throughout this book to help explain how American politics and government work and what kinds of public policies we have—note especially the "Using the Framework" feature that appears in each chapter—but we want to focus on the importance of specific aspects of these structural factors even more in subsequent chapters. We believe that four structural factors are especially important today in shaping what is going on in the political system. They include the following: (1) the threat of terrorism, (2) the emergence of the United States as the world's single superpower, (3) rapid technological change, and (4) changes in the demographics of the American population. Each of these changes has altered the agenda of American politics, refashioned political coalitions and alliances, altered the balance of power among competing political interests and government institutions, and pushed public policies in different directions.

Summary

How politics and government work is shaped by such structural factors as the nature of society, the economy, the nation's place in the world, and the political culture.

The most important changes in the American population are its growth; its diversification along ethnic, religious, and racial lines; and its relocation from rural to urban and suburban areas and to the Sun Belt. Americans enjoy a very high standard of living, but inequality is substantial and poverty is surprisingly persistent. These factors affect the agenda of American politics and the distribution of political power.

The American economy is a market economy that has evolved from a highly competitive, small-enterprise form to a corporate-dominated one with a global reach. Economic change has had important political consequences.

The emergence of the United States as a superpower in the twentieth century changed the content of foreign policy, the balance of power between the president and Congress, the size of the federal government, and the priorities of the government's budget. The collapse of socialism in eastern Europe affirmed the position of the United States as the world's most important military power.

Americans believe strongly in individualism, limited government, and free enterprise. Beliefs about democracy, liberty, and the primacy of the common people also help define the political culture. The political culture shapes American ideas about what the good society should look like, the appropriate role for government, and the possibilities for self-government.

Web Exploration
Immigration and Immigrants

Issue: Immigration, and what to do about it and its social consequences, has become a contentious issue in American politics.

Site: Find out what Americans want to do about immigration by going to Public Agenda Online. Access MyPoliSciLab at **www.mypoliscilab.com.** In the "Web Explorations" section for Chapter 4, select "Immigration and Immigrants," then "Immigrants." Under Issue Guides, select "immigration." Then look at "people's chief concerns."

What You've Learned: What are Americans most worried about when it comes to immigration? What do they want to do about it? As you look at each survey question, ask yourself what immigration policies you favor. Are your views in line with the majority of Americans, or are you an "outlier?"

Hint: Note that people seem to worry not about immigration, as such, but about illegal immigration. They strongly support policies, moreover, that rapidly assimilate immigrants, including a focus on learning English.

Internet Sources

Fedstats
www.fedstats.gov/
Statistical information on the U.S. economy and society from more than 70 government agencies.

Pew Hispanic Center
http://pewhispanic.org
A rich site for data on Hispanic immigration to the United States and polling information on public opinion on immigration topics.

Statistical Abstract of the United States
www.census.gov/statab/www
A vast compendium of statistical information on the government, the economy, and society.

University of Texas Online, Statistics and Demographics
www.lib.utexas.edu/refsites/statistics.html#intl
A treasure trove of easily accessible U.S. and international statistical information.

Suggestions for Further Reading

Benjamin M. Friedman. *The Moral Consequences of Economic Growth.* New York: Knopf, 2005.
An argument for the existence of a powerful relationship between economic growth and democracy, tolerance, and generous social policies.

Hochschild, Jennifer L. *Facing Up to the American Dream.* Princeton, NJ: Princeton University Press, 1995.
A brilliant examination of the ideology of the American dream and how race and social class affect its interpretation and possibilities.

Phillips, Kevin. *American Theocracy: The Peril of Radical Religion, Oil, and Borrowed Money in the 21st Century.* New York: Viking, 2006.
A hard-hitting analysis of the role of fundamentalism in American government, politics, and public policies.

Veseth, Michael, *Globaloney: Unraveling the Myths of Globalization.* Lanham, MD: Rowman & Littlefield Publishers, 2005.
A compelling and entertaining argument suggesting that antiglobalists have exaggerated the harms arising from the new global economy and missed its many benefits.

PART 3 Political Linkage

In Part 2, we discussed a number of fundamental structural factors that affect how American politics works: the Constitution, our federal system, the nature of the American society and economy, the political culture, and the international system.

In Part 3, we turn to what we call political linkage factors: public opinion, the mass media, organized interest groups, political parties, elections, and social movements. These people and institutions are affected in many ways by the structural factors already discussed. They, in turn, strongly affect the governmental institutions that are the subject of the next portion of the book. They are not a formal part of government, but they directly influence what sorts of people are chosen to be government officials—who is elected president and who goes to Congress, for example. They also affect what these officials do when they are in office and what sorts of public policies result.

CHAPTER 5

Public Opinion

IN THIS CHAPTER

- What public opinion is and how it is related to democracy

- What sorts of government policies Americans favor or oppose

- How people acquire their political attitudes

- How opinions differ according to race, gender, age, income, and other factors

- How much effect public opinion has on what government does

The Vietnam War and the Public

On August 2, 1964, the Pentagon announced that the U.S. destroyer *Maddox,* while on "routine patrol" in international waters in the Gulf of Tonkin near Vietnam, had undergone an "unprovoked attack" by three communist North Vietnamese PT boats. Two days later, the Pentagon reported a "second deliberate attack" on the *Maddox* and its companion destroyer, the *C. Turner Joy.* In a nationwide television broadcast, President Lyndon Johnson referred to "open aggression on the high seas" and declared that these hostile actions required that he retaliate with military force. Air attacks were launched against four North Vietnamese PT boat bases and an oil storage depot.[1]

Years later, the *Pentagon Papers,* a secret Defense Department study leaked to the news media by defense analyst Daniel Ellsberg, revealed that the American people had been deceived. The *Maddox* had not been on an innocent cruise; it had, in fact, been helping South Vietnamese gunboats make raids on the North Vietnamese coast. The second "attack" apparently never occurred; it was imagined by an inexperienced sonar operator in dark and stormy seas. At the time, however, few skeptics raised questions. On August 7, 1964, by a vote of 88–2, the Senate passed the Tonkin Gulf Resolution, which approved the president's taking "all necessary measures," including the use of armed force, to repel any armed attack and to assist any ally in the region. A legal basis for full U.S. involvement in the Vietnam War had been established.

For more than a decade, the United States had been giving large-scale military aid to the French colonialists, and then to the American-installed but authoritarian South Vietnamese government, to fight nationalists and communists in Vietnam. More than 23,000 U.S. military advisers were there by the end of 1964, occasionally engaging in combat. On the other side of the world, the American public knew and cared little about the guerrilla war. In fact, few knew exactly where Vietnam was. Nevertheless, people were willing to go along when their leaders told them that action was essential to resist communist aggression.

After the Tonkin incident, people paid more attention. Public support for the war increased. When asked in August what should be done next in Vietnam, 48 percent said to keep troops there, get tougher, or take definite military action while only 14 percent said negotiate or get out.[2] Through the fall of 1964, more people wanted to step up the war than wanted to pull out, and many endorsed the current policy. In 1965, after the United States had begun the heavy "Rolling Thunder" bombing of North Vietnam, and after large numbers of U.S. troops had gradually engaged in combat in South Vietnam, public support of the war continued. Month after month, pollsters found that only a small minority wanted to withdraw from Vietnam; as many or more wanted to escalate the war further, and the majority favored continuing the current policy.

But the number of U.S. troops in Vietnam rose rapidly, from 184,300 at the end of 1965 to 536,100 at the end of 1968, and casualties increased correspondingly. A total of 1,369 Americans were killed in 1965; 5,008 in 1966; 9,377 in 1967; and 14,589 in 1968. Many thousands more were wounded, and others were captured or missing.[3] Television news began to display weekly casualty counts in the hundreds, with pictures of dead American soldiers going home in body bags. The war became expensive, as politicians put it, in "American blood and treasure." Senate hearings aired antiwar testimony. Peace marches and demonstrations, though resented by much of the public, nonetheless increased pressure to end the war.

By December 1967, about as many people (45 percent) agreed as disagreed with the proposition that it had been a "mistake" to send troops to fight in Vietnam. A large majority said they favored "Vietnamization," bringing U.S. troops home as South Vietnamese replaced them.

Then catastrophe struck. In January 1968, during Vietnam's Tet holidays, the North Vietnamese army launched what became known as the *Tet Offensive:* massive attacks throughout South Vietnam, including an assault on the U.S. embassy in Saigon. The American public was shocked by televised scenes of urban destruction and bloody corpses, of U.S. soldiers destroying Ben Tre village "in order to save it," of marines bogged down in the rubble of the ancient city of Hue, and of a 77-day siege of the American firebase at Khe Sanh. The chief lesson seemed to be that a U.S. victory in Vietnam, if feasible at all, was going to be very costly in terms of lives and dollars.

After Tet, criticism of the war—by politicians, newspaper editorials, and television commentators such as Walter Cronkite and others—mushroomed, and public support for the war diminished. President Johnson, staggered by a surprisingly strong vote for antiwar candidate Eugene McCarthy in the New Hampshire primary, announced that he would limit the bombing of North Vietnam, seek a negotiated settlement, and withdraw as a candidate for reelection. In March 1968, only 41 percent of Americans described themselves as hawks (supporters of the war), a sharp drop from the 61 percent of early February. Anger over Vietnam contributed to the election defeat of the Democrats the following November.

By January 1969, when the Nixon administration took office, a substantial majority of the public favored monthly reductions in the number of U.S. soldiers in Vietnam: 57 percent approved the idea, while only 28 percent disapproved. In June, Nixon announced the withdrawal of 25,000 troops, followed by announcements of 35,000 more in September, another 50,000 in December, and 150,000 during the following year. Large majorities of the public approved of the withdrawals. Most said they wanted to continue them even if the South Vietnamese government collapsed. There can be little doubt that public opinion influenced U.S. disengagement from the war.

This did not mean that a majority of Americans wanted to get out of Vietnam immediately; most disliked the idea of a communist victory. But antiwar marches and demonstrations continued during 1970 and 1971, and many people wanted a faster pace of withdrawal. Gradually, all U.S. troops left Vietnam; in January 1973, after the intensive Christmas bombing of North Vietnam, a peace agreement was finally signed. Two years later, the North Vietnamese army took control of Saigon and reunified Vietnam, a nation that had been divided since the end of World War II.

The Vietnam story shows how government officials can sometimes lead or manipulate opinion, especially when it concerns obscure matters in faraway lands, and how opinion is affected by events and their presentation in the mass media. The story also shows that public opinion, even on foreign policy matters, can sometimes have a strong effect on policymaking. This complex interaction between public opinion, the news media, elected officials, and foreign policy in Vietnam is not very different from what has been going on with respect to the war in Iraq. ∎

Thinking Critically About This Chapter

This chapter is about public opinion, how it is formed, and what effect it has on American politics and government.

 Using the Framework You will learn in this chapter how public opinion is shaped by a wide range of structural-level factors, including historical events, the political culture, family and community socialization, and economic and social change. You will also learn how public opinion influences the behavior of political leaders and shapes many of the policies of the federal government.

 Using the Democracy Standard Based on the standard of democracy described in Chapter 1, public opinion should be one of the decisive factors in determining what government does. You will see in this chapter, however, that while the influence of public opinion is important, public officials must pay attention to other political forces as well. They sometimes pay close attention to public opinion; at other times, they pay only slight attention to it.

---

core beliefs

Individual's views about the fundamental nature of human beings, society, and economy; taken together, they comprise the political culture.

Democracy and Public Opinion

Most Americans have **core beliefs** about the nature of human beings, society, and the political order. These core beliefs—including belief in individualism, limited government, and free enterprise, among others—make up the

American political culture, as described in Chapter 4. In addition to their over-arching core beliefs, most Americans also have attitudes about the specific political issues of the day, including attitudes about government policies, public officials, political parties, and candidates. When these **political attitudes** are expressed by ordinary people and considered as a whole—particularly as they are revealed by polling surveys—we refer to this as **public opinion.**

Public opinion is particularly important in a democracy if we understand democracy to be fundamentally about the rule of the people. For the people to rule, they must have their voice heard by those in government. To know whether or not the people rule, we require evidence that those in government are responsive to the voice of the people. The best evidence that those in power are responsive to the voice of the people is a strong showing that what government does reflects the wishes of the people. The wishes of the people can be discerned in elections, to be sure, but a particularly powerful way to know what the people want is to ask them directly in a polling survey. In a democracy, there will be a close match between public opinion and government policies and actions, at least in the long run.

Curiously, however, many leading political theorists, including some who say they believe in democracy, have expressed grave doubts about the wisdom of the public. James Madison, Alexander Hamilton, and other Founders of our national government worried that the public's "passions" would infringe on liberty and that public opinion would be susceptible to radical and frequent shifts.[4] Journalist and statesman Walter Lippmann declared that most people do not know what goes on in the world; they have only vague, media-provided pictures in their heads. Lippmann approvingly quoted Sir Robert Peel's reference to "that great compound of folly, weakness, prejudice, wrong feeling, right feeling, obstinacy and newspaper paragraphs which is called public opinion."[5]

Modern survey researchers have not been much kinder. The first voting studies, carried out during the 1940s and 1950s, turned up what scholars considered appalling evidence of public ignorance, lack of interest in politics, and reliance on group or party loyalties rather than judgments about the issues of

political attitudes
Individual's views about public policies, political parties, candidates, government institutions, and public officials.

public opinion
Political attitudes and core beliefs expressed by ordinary citizens as revealed by surveys.

Disengaged from Politics

These shoppers at a discount store in Mayfield Heights, Ohio, in October 2004 don't seem much interested in the televised presidential debate between John Kerry and George W. Bush, even though their state was a key battleground in that year's national election.

the day. Repeated surveys of the same individuals found that their responses seemed to change randomly from one interview to another. Philip Converse, a leading student of political behavior, coined the term *nonattitudes:* On many issues of public policy, many or most Americans seemed to have no real views at all but simply offered "doorstep opinions" to satisfy interviewers.[6]

What should we make of this? If ordinary citizens are poorly informed and their views are based on whim, or if they have no real opinions at all, it hardly seems desirable—or even possible—that public opinion should determine what governments do. Both the feasibility and the attractiveness of democracy seem to be thrown into doubt. When we examine exactly what sorts of opinions ordinary Americans have, however, and how those opinions are formed and changed, we will see that such fears about public opinion have been greatly exaggerated.

Measuring Public Opinion

Years ago, people who wanted to find out anything about public opinion had to guess, based on what their barbers or taxi drivers said, on what appeared in letters to newspaper editors, or on what sorts of one-liners won cheers at political rallies. But the views of personal acquaintances, letter writers, or rally audiences are often quite different from those of the public as a whole. Similarly, the angry people who call in to radio talk shows may not hold views that are typical of most Americans. To figure out what the average American thinks, we cannot rely on unrepresentative groups or noisy minorities.

Public Opinion Polls

sample survey
An interview study asking questions of a set of people who are chosen as representative of the whole population.

A clever invention, the public opinion poll, or **sample survey,** now eliminates most of the guesswork in measuring public opinion. A survey consists of systematic interviews conducted by trained professional interviewers who ask a standardized set of questions of a rather small number of randomly chosen Americans—usually about 1,000 or 1,500 of them for a national survey. Such a survey, if done properly, can reveal with remarkable accuracy what the rest of us are thinking.

The secret of success is to make sure that the sample of people interviewed is representative of the whole population, that is, that the proportions of people in the sample who are young, old, female, college-educated, black, rural, Catholic, southern, western, religious, secular, liberal, conservative, Democrat, Republican, and so forth are all about the same as in the U.S. population as a whole. This representativeness is achieved best when the people being interviewed are chosen through **random sampling,** which ensures that each member of the population has an equal chance of being chosen. Then survey researchers can add up all the responses to a given question and compute the percentages of people answering one way or another. Statisticians can use probability theory to tell how close the survey's results are likely to be to what the whole population would say if asked the same questions. Findings from a random sample of 1,500 people have a 95 percent chance of accurately reflecting the views of the whole population within about 2 or 3 percentage points.[7]

random sampling
The selection of survey respondents by chance, with equal probability, to ensure their representativeness of the whole population.

Perfectly random sampling is not feasible. Personal interviews have to be clustered geographically so that interviewers can easily get from one respondent to another. Telephone interviews—the cheapest and most common kind—are clustered within particular telephone exchanges. Still, the samples that sur-

Can I Ask About Your Vote?

Exit polls, which survey the opinions of people as they leave the polling place after voting, are a major source of information on who votes and how people make their voting decisions. They are also the basis for network election-night "who won" announcements, made well before all the ballots have been counted.

vey organizations use are sufficiently representative so that survey results closely reflect how the whole population would have responded if everyone in the United States had been asked the same questions at the moment the survey was carried out. Recently, some commercial polling organizations have tried to do polling on the Internet. For the most part, these attempts fall prey to the problem of nonrandom sampling. Not all Americans own computers; not all computer owners regularly use the Internet. So, polling people by Internet is going to capture a sample that is very unrepresentative of the American population.

Problems in Political Polling

Those who use poll results—including citizens encountering political polls in newspapers and on television—should be aware of the following problems with polls and what competent pollsters try to do about them:

You Are a Polling Consultant

- The wording of questions is important; it often makes a big difference exactly how questions are asked. For example, a question that asks "do you favor the death penalty?" is likely to get a higher proportion of people saying they are in favor than a question that asks "do you favor or oppose the death penalty?" because the former gives only one option.[8] Attaching the name of a popular president or an unpopular one to a survey question—as in "Do you support President X's proposal for Medicare reform?"—affects how people respond. Good survey questions try to avoid such "leading" wording.

- "Closed-ended" or "forced-choice" questions, which ask the respondents to choose among preformulated answers, do not always reveal what people are thinking on their own or what they would come up with after a few minutes of thought or discussion. So, in this sense, a survey may not always be capturing what people think is important or what choices they would make. Some scholars believe that such questions force people to express opinions about matters on which they really don't have an opinion, or even what the question means.[9] For these reasons, "open-ended" questions are sometimes asked in order to yield more spontaneous answers, and small discussion groups or

The Pollsters Get It Wrong

Harry Truman ridicules an edition of the *Chicago Tribune* proclaiming his Republican challenger, Thomas Dewey, president. Opinion polls stopped asking questions too early in the 1948 election campaign, missing Truman's last-minute surge. Top pollsters today survey likely voters right to the end of the campaign.

"focus groups" are brought together to show what emerges when people talk among themselves about the topics a moderator introduces.

Scholars and survey professionals worry about a number of things that can undermine the validity of survey research by making it difficult to draw a sample that is random, meaning representative of the entire population. In some cases, the problems seem to be getting worse. Here are the principal things they are concerned about:

- Because they are inundated by phone calls from advertisers who sometimes try to disguise themselves as researchers, Americans have become less willing to answer pollsters' questions.
- Finding themselves bothered by telephone solicitations that interrupt their lives, Americans are increasingly using answering machines and "caller ID" to screen their calls. Pollsters are finding it increasingly difficult to get past the screening.
- More and more Americans are turning to mobile phones and cutting their reliance on land lines. Because mobile phones are often turned off, survey researchers cannot always get through to people who are part of the prospective random sample.

The top academic and commercial polling firms claim they are taking steps to overcome these problems—using repeated call-backs and statistical methods to fill in for missing people, for example—but the problems are likely to get worse before they get better. For now, we will have to make do with polling results from quality researchers and firms.

Learning Political Beliefs and Attitudes

political socialization
The process by which individuals come to have certain core beliefs and political attitudes.

Political scientists use the term **political socialization** to describe the process by which individuals acquire their core beliefs about human nature, the country, the government, and the economy—which, taken together, form a society's political culture—and their attitudes about government officials, alternative public policies, the parties, candidates for elected office, and other political matters of the day. Agents of socialization—the instruments by which beliefs and attitudes are conveyed to individuals in society—include families, schools, churches, the mass media, and social groups with which individuals are most closely associated. This section will show how these agents of socialization shape the outlooks of Americans.

Some aspects of political socialization lead Americans to closely resemble one another. This alikeness is particularly striking with regard to the core beliefs of the American people explored in the last chapter: individualism, the sanctity of private property, distrust of government, populism, and piety. Other aspects of political socialization lead Americans to differ from one another in their basic outlook on the political world[10]—which, in turn, affects attitudes and opinions about specific political issues and people—in fairly significant yet understandable ways. We address this matter in a later section of this chapter titled "How People's Opinions Differ."

Agents of Socialization

Political Knowledge

Political socialization is a lifetime process in the sense that people engage in political learning throughout the life-course.[11] However, political learning in childhood and adolescence seems to be particularly important, as childhood is the period when people attain their core beliefs and general outlooks about the political world.

The *family* plays a particularly important role in shaping the outlooks of children. It is in the family—whether in a traditional or nontraditional family—that children pick up their basic outlook on life and the world around them. It is mainly from their family, for example, that children learn to trust or distrust others, something that affects a wide range of political attitudes later in life. It is from the family, and the neighborhood where the family lives, that children learn about which ethnic or racial group, social class or income group, and religion they belong to and begin to pick up attitudes that are typical of these groups. In dinner table conversations and other encounters with parents, children start to acquire ideas about the country—ideas about patriotism, for example—and their first vague ideological ideas: whether government is a good or bad thing, whether taxes are a good or bad thing, and whether certain people and groups in society are to be admired or not (welfare recipients, rich people, corporations, and the like). Most importantly, because it represents the filter through which a great deal of future political learning takes place, many children adopt the political party identifications of their parents, especially if the parents share the same party identification. Although the relationship between parent and child party identification is weaker now than it was in the 1940s and 1950s, a majority of adult Americans still identify with the same party as their parents.

Schools are also important as agents of political socialization. In the early grades, through explicit lessons and the celebration of national symbols—such as the flag in the classroom, recitation of the Pledge of Allegiance, pictures on the walls of famous presidents, patriotic pageants, and the like—schools convey lessons about American identity and patriotism. In the middle grades, schools teach children about the political process by sponsoring mock presidential elections and elections to student government. In the upper grades, most students in most school districts take courses in American history and American government and continue learning about participation through student government.

Learning About Democracy

Children gain many of their initial ideas about how the American political system works in their school classrooms. In the early grades, children gain impressions about the nation, its most important symbols (such as the flag), and its most visible and well-known presidents. They also learn the rudiments of democracy. Here elementary school students take part in a mock election.

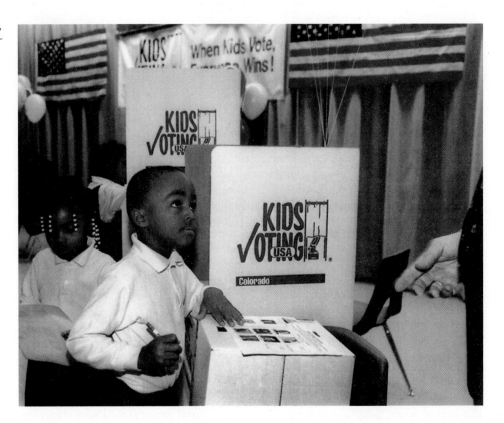

Popular culture—movies, music, and advertising—also shapes the budding political outlooks of young people.[12] To be sure, most of the messages coming from the popular culture have more to do with style, fashion, and attitude. But much in popular culture conveys political messages. Many rap-music performers, for example, embed political messages in their songs. Many Hollywood movies come with a political message; for example, themes of sleazy politicians and untrustworthy or corrupt elected officials are quite common.

Political socialization does not stop when children become adults. Substantial evidence shows that a *college education* affects people's outlooks about public policies and the role of government. People with a college education, for example, are more likely to support government programs to protect the environment. We know, moreover, that people's political outlooks are shaped by *major events* or developments that affect the country during their young adult years. In the past, such events have included the Great Depression, World War II, the civil rights movement and the countercultural revolution of the 1960s, the Reagan Revolution of the 1980s, and the 9/11 terrorist attacks on the United States. The effect of these events and developments seems most pronounced for young people who are just coming to a sense of political awareness. Political scientists identify this phenomenon as a *generational effect*. Thus, young people coming of age politically during the 1960s turned out to be much more liberal throughout their lives than young people coming of age during the 1950s or during the Reagan years.

Finally, a number of socializing agents affect people's attitudes and expressed political opinions throughout adulthood. *Jobs* and experiences at work can affect the confidence that people express about the future for themselves and their families. The *news media* affects people's attitudes by how they select and frame the issues they cover, as you will see in Chapter 6. Getting *married* and buying a home—because they bring with them new concerns with things such as the quality of local schools and neighborhoods, interest rates on home mortgages, and more—cause many people to alter their positions on political parties, candidates, and issues. So too does *retirement,* which often brings a new sense of urgency about government support for retirement and health care benefits.

How People's Opinions Differ

We have learned that agents of socialization are important in acquiring core beliefs as well as political attitudes about government, the parties, candidates, political leaders, and public policies. To a great extent, as you have seen in this chapter and in Chapter 4's section on the American political culture, the socialization of core beliefs in the United States is common to most Americans. Indeed, a broad range of socialization agents—from the news media and popular entertainment to government leaders and the schools—reinforce one another about what it means to be an American and to live in the United States. However, Americans also grow up and live in a variety of distinctive environments that shape general political outlooks and specific attitudes in distinctive ways. In this section, we explore some of the most significant circumstances that define and divide us in our political views.

Race and Ethnicity

Among the biggest differences are those between white and black Americans. Hispanics and Asian Americans also have some distinctive political opinions. Many white ethnic groups, however, are no longer much different from other members of the population.

African Americans   On most core beliefs about the American system, few differences are discernible between black Americans and other Americans.[13] Similar percentages of each group believe, for example, that people can get ahead by working hard, that providing for equal opportunity is more important than ensuring equal outcomes, and that the federal government should balance its budget. On a range of other political issues, however, the racial divide looms large.[14]

Partisanship is one important area where African Americans differ from whites. Blacks, who stayed loyal to the Republican party (the party of Lincoln and of Reconstruction) long after the Civil War, became Democrats in large proportions in the 1930s during the presidency of Franklin D. Roosevelt, whose New Deal greatly expanded the federal government's role in providing safety nets for the poor and unemployed. Most black Americans have remained Democrats, especially since the civil rights struggles of the 1960s. Today African Americans are the most solidly Democratic of any group in the population: Some 60 percent call themselves Democrats, while only about 2 percent call themselves Republicans (see Figure 5.1). In 2004, 88 percent of African Americans voted for Democrat John Kerry; only 11 percent supported Republican George W. Bush.[15]

Black Americans also tend to be much more liberal than whites on economic issues, especially on those involving government programs to provide assistance to those who need help in the areas of jobs, housing, medical care, education, and so on. This liberalism reflects African Americans' economically disadvan-

FIGURE 5.1 • Party Loyalties Among Various Social Groups, 2004

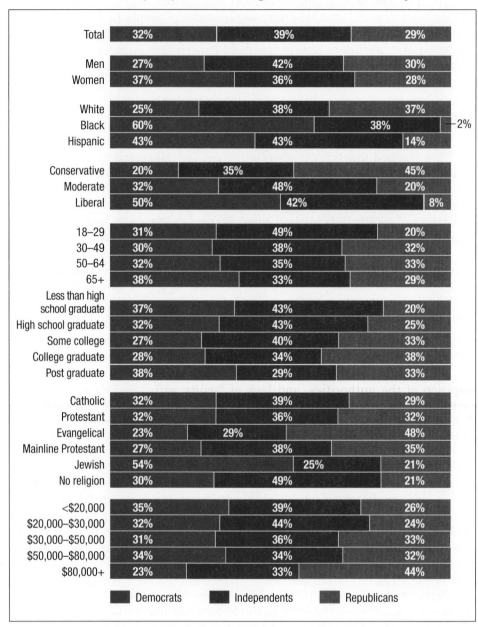

Blacks, city dwellers, women, and people of lower-income and educational levels tend to be Democrats, while whites, suburbanites, men, the college-educated, religious conservatives, and people with high incomes tend to be Republicans.

Source: American National Election Studies. 2004.

taged position in American society and the still-real effects of slavery and discrimination. However, blacks tend to hold strong religious values and to be rather conservative on some social issues. More are opposed to abortion, for example, than are whites. In general, however, African Americans are very liberal (i.e., favor an activist government to help solve social ills). More blacks identify themselves as liberals than as conservatives or moderates, a pattern that is almost exactly reversed among whites.[16] African Americans also are more likely than Americans in general to favor government regulation of corporations to protect the public (60 percent to 30 percent in 2003) and to favor protection of the environment and the consumer over the need to leave individuals free to act as they want (62 percent to 32 percent).[17] Black and white divisions are most apparent on issues related to affirmative action and who is responsible for the progress or lack of progress African Americans have experienced. For example, on affirmative action, 43 percent of whites agree with the statement "Affirmative action programs are needed as long as there are no rigid quotas," compared with 79 percent of black Americans.[18] Sixty-three percent of whites agree with the statement "Blacks who can't get ahead are responsible for their condition," compared with 43 percent of African Americans.[19]

Hispanics Hispanics—people of Spanish-speaking background—are the fastest-growing ethnic group in America and the largest minority group in the nation. As a whole, the Hispanic population identifies much more with the Democrats than the Republicans (see Figure 5.1). However, the Hispanic population itself is quite diverse. Cuban Americans, many of them refugees from the Castro regime, tend to be conservative, Republican, strongly anticommunist, and skeptical of government programs. The much more numerous Americans of Mexican or Puerto Rican ancestry, by contrast, are mostly Democrats and quite liberal on economic matters, although rather traditional on social questions—reflecting their predominant Roman Catholicism. For example, 77 percent of Hispanics say that abortion is unacceptable.[20]

Hispanics have been one of the least politically active groups in the United States, although they have begun to vote in increasing numbers. Low incomes, suspicion of the authorities, and lack of facility with the English language have long discouraged participation. Now, mobilized by social movement groups and increasingly wooed by both major parties, this sleeping giant of American politics seems to be awakening.[21]

Asian Americans Asian Americans, a small but growing part of the U.S. population—approximately 4 percent of the population in 2004—come from

Expanding the Number of Hispanic Voters

Both major political parties are trying to attract new voters among the rapidly growing Hispanic population. Here, two Hispanic men add their names to the voter rolls at a Democratic party registration drive in Texas during the 2004 presidential campaign.

quite diverse backgrounds in the Philippines, India, Vietnam, Korea, Vietnam, Thailand, China, and elsewhere. As a group, Asian Americans are more educated and economically successful than the general population but are less likely to vote and express an interest in politics than people of equal educational and financial status. One estimate suggests that only about 20 percent of Asian Americans are registered to vote, and that their political interest is lower than that of whites, blacks, and Hispanics.[22] On social issues, Asian Americans strongly support the death penalty and oppose same-sex marriage; on economic issues they are slightly more conservative than average. However, in recent elections they have leaned slightly toward the Democrats. They have also begun to win electoral office at the local level, primarily in large urban areas where the vast majority of Asian Americans live.

White Ethnics   Other ethnic groups are not so distinctive in their political opinions. Irish Americans and people of Italian, Polish, and other southern or eastern European ancestry, for example, became strong Democrats as part of the New Deal coalition. But as they achieved success economically, their economic liberalism tended to fade, and their social conservatism became more prominent. By the 1980s, these groups were not much different from the majority of other white Americans.

Social Class

Compared with much of the world, the United States has had rather little political conflict among people of different income or occupational groupings; in fact, rather few Americans think of themselves as members of a social "class" at all. When forced to choose, about half say they are "working class" and about half say they are "middle class."[23] In Great Britain, on the other hand, where the occupational structure is similar to that of the United States, 72 percent of the population calls itself "working class."[24]

Still, since the time of the New Deal, substantially more low- and moderate-income people have identified themselves as Democrats rather than as Republicans. This still holds true today;[25] in 2004, households in the lowest income quintile (lowest 20 percent) were twice as likely to call themselves Democrats as Republicans. Upper-income people—whether high-salaried business executives, doctors, accountants, and lawyers or asset-rich people with no need to hold a job—have identified with the Republican Party for a long time and continue to do so today. In 2004, those in the highest income quintile were almost twice as likely to call themselves Republicans rather than Democrats (see Figure 5.1).

People in union households—including both blue-collar and white-collar unions—have long favored the Democrats and continue to do so. In 2004, 59 percent of such said they favor the Democrats, roughly 11 percentage points higher than the party's support among all voters. This Democratic advantage in union households has changed hardly at all since the mid-1970s, although it is important to be aware that the proportion of Americans who are members of labor unions is quite low compared with other rich countries and has been steadily declining (see Chapter 7).

Researchers for the Pew Research Center have determined statistically, however, that income and union membership, while important in explaining party affiliation, are less important than other factors to be examined in this section, namely, race, religious commitment and church attendance, and, to a somewhat lesser degree, gender. Being a member of a racial minority, less reli-

On the Picket Line

Although a smaller proportion of American workers than in the past are in labor unions, union members, like these striking Boeing machinists in Seattle in 2005, remain an important part of the Democratic Party base in American elections.

gious or secular, and a woman better predicts Democratic party affiliation and vote than one's income or labor union membership.[26]

Lower-income people have some distinctive policy preferences. Not surprisingly, they tend to favor much more government help with jobs, education, housing, medical care, and the like, whereas the highest-income people, who would presumably pay more and benefit less from such programs, tend to oppose them.[27] To complicate matters, however, many lower-income people, primarily for religious reasons, favor Republican conservative positions on social issues such as abortion, law and order, religion, civil rights, education, and gay rights. Furthermore, many high-income people—especially those with postgraduate degrees—tend to be very liberal on lifestyle and social issues involving sexual behavior, abortion rights, free speech, and civil rights. They also tend to be especially eager for government action to protect the environment. We can see this manifested in recent elections where more high-income, high-education congressional districts in places such as California and Connecticut have elected Democrats, while low-income districts in Kentucky, Tennessee, and West Virginia are sending Republicans to Congress.[28]

Region

It is still true that "the South is different," although this is slowly changing. Regional differences have been reduced because of years of migration by southern blacks to northern cities, the movement of industrial plants and northern whites to the Sun Belt, and economic growth catching up with that of the North. But the legacy of slavery and segregation, a large black population, and late industrialization have made the South a unique region in American politics.

Even now, white southerners tend to be somewhat less enthusiastic about civil rights than northerners; only people from the Mountain West are as conservative on racial issues.[29] Southerners also tend to be conservative on social issues, such as school prayer, crime, women's rights, and abortion, and supportive of military spending and a strong foreign policy (although fairly liberal on economic issues, such as government-guaranteed jobs and health insurance).

These distinctive policy preferences have undercut southern whites' traditionally strong identification with the Democratic party, especially since the 1960s and 1970s, when the national Democrats became identified with liberal social policies and antiwar foreign policy. The white South's switch to the Republican party in the 1994 elections, in fact, is one of the major reasons Republicans were able to maintain control of Congress for a dozen years until the Democrats won back both houses in 2006. Though the South remains strongly Republican,[30] moderate Democrats like Jim Webb of Virginia have won important elections.

On many issues, northeasterners tend to be the most different from southerners, with midwesterners, appropriately, in the middle. Pacific Coast residents resemble northeasterners in many respects, but people from the Rocky Mountain states tend to be quite conservative, with strong majorities opposed to government job guarantees and health insurance assistance, for example.[31] The mountain states' traditions of game hunting in wide-open spaces have led them, like southerners, to cherish the right to bear firearms and to resist gun controls.

These regional differences should not be exaggerated, however. Long-term trends show a narrowing in regional differences on core beliefs and political attitudes.[32] This is the outcome of years of migration of Americans from one region to another and the rise of a media and entertainment industry that is national in scale, beaming messages and information across regional lines.

Education

The level of formal education that people reach is closely related to their income level because education helps people earn more and also because the wealthy can pay for more and better schooling for their children. But education has some distinct political effects of its own.

As we will see in Chapter 10, education is generally considered the strongest single predictor of participation in politics. College-educated people are much more likely to say that they vote, talk about politics, go to meetings, sign petitions, and write letters to officials than people who have attained only an elementary or a high school education. The highly educated know more about politics. They know what they want and how to go about getting it, joining groups and writing letters, faxes, and e-mail messages to public officials. Within every income stratum of the population, moreover, college-educated people are somewhat more liberal than others, being more in favor of, for example, increased domestic spending to combat poverty and provide national health insurance. They also are more likely than other people in their same income stratum to favor multilateralism in international affairs, favoring the use of diplomacy, multination treaties, and the United Nations to solve global problems.[33]

People who have earned postgraduate degrees also have some distinctive policy preferences. They are especially protective of the civil rights, civil liberties, and individual freedom of atheists, homosexuals, protesters, and dissenters. Education may contribute to tolerance by exposing people to diverse ideas or by training them in elite-backed norms of tolerance.

Gender

Women were prevented from participating in politics for a large part of our history; they got the vote, by constitutional amendment, only in 1920. Not all women immediately took advantage of this new opportunity. For many years, women voted and participated in politics at lower rates than men—about 10 or 15 percent lower in the elections of the 1950s, for example. And women are consistently less knowledgeable than men and say they are less interested than men in politics.[34] Only after the women's movement gained force during the 1970s did substantial numbers of female candidates begin to run for high office. Although an office-holding gap remains, the participation gap has disappeared.[35] We will explore this in more depth in Chapter 10.

A partisan "gender gap" first appeared in the 1980s and persists today, with the percentage of women who identify themselves as Democrats about 10 percentage points higher than men (see Figure 5.1). The difference between men and women is primarily a product of declining Democratic Party identification among men, particularly white southerners.[36] The differences show up in elections; in 2004, only 48 percent of women voted for George W. Bush, compared with 55 percent of men. However, although the partisan gender gap is real and persistent—women identify more with the Democrats and are more likely to vote for Democratic candidates—the scale of the gap remains in the single digits, leading some scholars to suggest that the gender gap issue has been exaggerated.[37]

Women also differ somewhat from men in certain policy preferences. Women tend to be somewhat more supportive of protective policies for the poor, the elderly, and the disabled. Women tend to be more opposed to violence, whether by criminals or by the state. More women over the years have opposed capital punishment and the use of military force abroad and favored arms control and peace agreements.[38] Interestingly, the gender gap on issues like defense spending, the use of military force abroad, and a missile-defense shield disappeared in the wake of terrorist attacks on the United States, as women shifted to a more defense-supportive position similar to that of men.[39] Equal numbers of men and women now endorse the principle of "peace through strength" (62 percent).[40] Perhaps surprisingly, there is no gender gap on the issue of abortion.[41]

Age

Younger citizens are less likely to identify with a political party than older cohorts and less likely to participate in or express an interest in politics. The young and the old also differ on certain matters that touch their particular interests: the draft in wartime, the drinking age, and, to some extent, Social Security and Medicare. Furthermore, people over the age of 60 tend to be more critical of government, perhaps because their expectations about what government can and should deliver are higher.[42] But the chief difference between old and young has to do with the particular era in which they were raised. Those who were young during the 1960s were especially quick to favor civil rights for blacks, for example. In recent years, young people have been especially concerned about environmental issues, and they are much more tolerant of homosexuality and more likely than their elders to support same-sex marriage. Often social change occurs by generational replacement. Old ideas, like the Depression-era notion that women should stay at home and "not take jobs away from men," die off with old people.

Religion

Although religious differences along denominational lines are and have always been important in the United States,[43] the differences between the religiously

Political Participation and the Young

Shoulder to Shoulder

Americans who came of age during the civil rights struggles of the 1960s are more likely than others to favor civil rights protections for African Americans. Here, white and black demonstrators march together in Selma, Alabama, in 1965 in support of voting rights for African Americans.

observant of all denominations and more secular Americans is becoming wider and more central to an understanding of contemporary American politics. We look first at denominational differences, then at what has come to be called the "culture wars."

Religious Denominations Roman Catholics, who constitute about 24 percent of the U.S. population, were heavily Democratic after the New Deal but now resemble the majority of Americans in their party affiliations—pretty evenly split between the Democrats and Republicans. Catholics' economic liberalism has faded somewhat with rises in their income, although this liberalism remains substantial. Catholics have tended to be especially concerned with family issues and to espouse measures to promote morality (e.g., antipornography laws) and law and order. But American Catholics disagree with many church teachings; they support birth control and the right to have abortions in about the same proportions as do other Americans, for example.

A majority of Americans (53 percent) are Protestant. Protestants come in many varieties—the relatively high-income (socially liberal, economically conservative) Episcopalians and Presbyterians; the generally liberal Unitarian-Universalists and middle-class northern Baptists; and the lower-income and quite conservative Southern Baptists and evangelicals of various denominations. The sharpest dividing line seems to be that between evangelical Protestants and mainstream Protestants. Evangelicals are more likely than mainstream Protestants to identify themselves as Republicans (48 percent compared with 35 percent) and voted much more decisively for George W. Bush in the 2004 election (78 percent compared with 55 percent). Approximately 2 percent of Americans are Mormons, members of the fast-growing Church of Jesus Christ of Latter-Day Saints. They are the most staunchly conservative and most solidly Republican of any major religious denomination in the country.

American Jews (about 2 percent of the U.S. population) began to join the Democratic Party in the 1920s and did so overwhelmingly in the 1930s, in response to Franklin D. Roosevelt's New Deal social policies and his foreign pol-

Praying for the Ten Commandments

Religiously committed people have become an important force in American politics. Here, demonstrators protest an Alabama state judicial ruling in 2003 that a Ten Commandments monument displayed at the Alabama Supreme Court building must be removed, a decision later upheld by the federal courts.

icy of resisting Hitler. Most Jews have stayed with the party. Next to African Americans, they remain the most Democratic group in the United States: About 49 percent identify themselves as Democrats and only 19 percent as Republicans. In the 2004 presidential election, Jews cast 74 percent of their votes for Kerry and only 25 percent for Bush. Jews are exceptionally liberal on social issues such as civil liberties and abortion. They also tend to be staunch supporters of civil rights. Although rising incomes have somewhat undercut Jews' economic liberalism, they remain substantially more supportive of social welfare policies than other groups.

Religiously Committed Versus the Less Committed and Secular   Among the factors that most differentiate Americans on political attitudes and partisanship is their degree of religious belief and practice.[44] The religiously committed, no matter the religious denomination, are the most likely Americans to vote Republican and to hold conservative views, particularly on social issues such as abortion, the death penalty, same-sex marriage, and stem cell research. Committed and observant Catholics, Jews, and Protestants are not only much more Republican and socially conservative than people who practice no religion and/or claim to be totally secular, but they are also more Republican and socially conservative than their less committed and observant co-religionists. As an example, 55 percent of committed white evangelicals identify as Republican compared with only 38 percent of other Evangelicals (and a miniscule 15 percent among people who say they are secular). Among mainstream Protestant denominations, the committed are 38 percent Republican, compared with 31 percent among the less committed. Taking all denominations together, to look at another example of how relative religious commitment matters, the "churched" are far more likely to vote Republican than those who are less "churched" or who don't go to church (or synagogue or mosque) at all (see Table 5.1).

The gap between the religiously committed and other Americans—particularly those who say they never or almost never go to church—on matters of party identification, votes in elections, and attitudes about social issues has

**TABLE 5.1 • Church Attendance and Vote
in 2004 Presidential Election**

	Bush	Kerry
More than once a week	64	35
Once a week	58	41
Monthly	50	49
A few times a year	45	54
Never	36	62

Source: National Election Pool, November 2004, reported in *Trends, 2005* (Washington, D.C.: The Pew Foundation, 2005), p. 35.

become so wide and the debates so fierce that many have come to talk about America's culture wars. On a range of issues—including Supreme Court appointments, abortion, the rights of gays and lesbians, prayer in the public schools, and the teaching of evolution—passions on both sides of the divide have reached what can only be called white-hot fever pitch. To be sure, much of the noise in the culture wars is being generated by leaders of and activists in religiously affiliated organizations and advocacy groups, exaggerating, perhaps, the degree to which most Americans disagree on most core beliefs and political attitudes.[45] But, the battle between the most and least religiously observant and committed has helped heat up the passions in American politics because each group has gravitated to one or the other political party—the former to the Republicans and the latter to the Democrats[46]—and become among the strongest activists and financial contributors within them.

Partisanship

Increasingly, what most differentiates how people feel and think about political matters is what party they identify with and how strongly they identify with it. The roots of people's party identification, or sense of belonging to a party, are not fully understood, but they seem to be related to the party identification of one's family, generational effects caused by major societal events such as the Great Depression and World War II, and other factors explored earlier, including race, religious affiliation, income, education, and region. Whatever the roots, many (though by no means all) Americans feel such an identification. When survey researchers ask people whether, generally speaking, they consider themselves Republicans, Democrats, independents, or something else, about 60 to 65 percent pick one of the two major parties,[47] although the exact numbers fluctuate a bit year to year, particularly around election time. Notably, 35 to 40 percent of Americans claim no party identification at all, or say they are independent.

In a later section, we will examine long-term trends in party identification in the United States. For now, in this section on how people differ on political attitudes, we would simply point out that one's party identification seems to be a strong determinant of political outlooks;[48] for about 6 in 10 Americans, party identity is a stable and powerful shaper of one's overall political identity. People use the party label to help organize their thinking about politics: to guide them in voting, judging new policy proposals, and evaluating the govern-

TABLE 5.2 • Partisanship and Issue Positions, 2003

Opinion Sought	Democrats	Republicans
Government should make every effort to help blacks and other minorities, even if it means giving them preferential treatment.	55	24
Government should guarantee every citizen enough to eat and a place to sleep.	81	46
We have gone too far in pushing equal rights in this country.	34	55
The best way to ensure peace is through military strength.	44	69
We all should be willing to fight for our country, right or wrong.	46	62
Government is really run for the benefit of all the people.	46	70
Business corporations make too much profit.	72	46

Source: Evenly Divided and Increasingly Polarized: The 2004 Political Landscape (Washington, D.C.: Pew Research Center, 2003).

ment's performance. People who consider themselves Republicans are much more likely than Democrats to vote for Republican candidates and approve of Republican presidents; they tend to belong to different social and economic groups; and they are more likely to favor policies associated with the Republican party. Republicans are much more likely than Democrats to support big business and an assertive national security policy; Democrats are much more likely than Republicans to support government programs to help the poor and help racial minorities get ahead. Table 5.2 shows some of these differences; on a wide range of issues on what government should do, Republicans and Democrats face each other across a wide chasm.

The evidence suggests that the partisan organization of political outlooks is becoming even more pronounced. Republicans are much more likely than in the past to vote across the board for Republicans and hold conservative economic and social beliefs; Democratic identifiers are much more likely than in the past to vote for Democrats and to hold liberal economic and social beliefs. So, among the 60 percent or so who identify with one of the two major parties, differences in public policy and ideological outlooks between Democrats and Republicans are becoming more and more pronounced (see Figure 5.2), and the intensity with which these preferences and outlooks are held by partisans is greater than in the past.[49]

While Democratic and Republican identifiers are moving farther apart, the distances are even greater between Democratic and Republican **active partisans,** those Republican and Democratic identifiers who not only vote but are engaged in other party, candidate, and party-support activities, such as making campaign contributions, attending candidate meetings, putting bumper stickers on their cars, and the like. Democratic active partisans are strongly liberal, with, for example, 78 percent supporting abortion, 70 percent

active partisan
People who identify with a party, vote in elections, and participate in additional party and party-candidate activities.

**FIGURE 5.2 • The Growing Ideological Homogeneity
of Party Identifiers, 1979–2004**

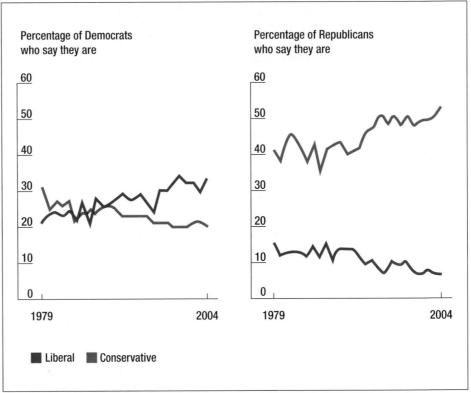

Party identification and political ideology are becoming more closely related. Republican identifiers, more conservative than Democratic Party identifiers anyway, are becoming even more conservative. At the same time, Democratic Party identifiers are becoming more liberal. The deep divide that reflects the confluence of parties and ideologies has become a key feature of modern American politics and contributes to much of the incivility and intensity of public affairs in recent years.

Source: New York Times/CBS News/Gallup Poll, 2004.

supporting the use of diplomacy over force in international relations, and 70 percent favoring environmental protection over job protection. For their part, Republican active partisans are a near mirror image, reporting only 41 percent, 11 percent, and 24 percent approval, respectively, for these things.[50]

The Contours of American Public Opinion:
Are the People Fit to Rule?

Now that we know more about how public opinion is measured and why people hold certain core beliefs and political attitudes, we can return to the issue raised in the opening pages of this chapter concerning the place of public opinion in a society that aspires to be a democracy. Recall from the earlier discussion that many observers of American politics in the past and today have had little confidence in the abilities of the average person to understand vital public issues or to rationally engage in public affairs. If, as they have feared, ordinary citizens are uninformed, prone to rapid and irrational changes in their political attitudes, and easily led astray, there is not much reason to assume that public opinion can or ought to play a central role in deciding what government should do. However, as we will see in this section, further examination of the opinions of ordinary Americans and how they change in response to events and new information will demonstrate that such fears about an uninformed and irrational public have been greatly exaggerated.

What People Know About Politics

Several decades of polling have shown that most ordinary Americans do not know or care a lot about politics.[51] Nearly everyone knows some basic facts, such as the name of the capital of the United States and the length of the president's term of office. But only about two-thirds of adults know which party has the most members in the House of Representatives. About one-half know that there are two U.S. senators from their state, and fewer can name their representative in the House. Only about 30 percent know that the term of a U.S. House member is two years. And barely one in four Americans can explain what is in the First Amendment.[52] Furthermore, people have particular trouble with technical terms, geography, abbreviations, and acronyms like NATO (the North Atlantic Treaty Organization) and NAFTA (the North American Free Trade Agreement).

The things that most Americans don't know may not be vital to their role as citizens, however. If citizens are aware that trade restrictions with Canada and Mexico have been eased, does it matter that they recognize the acronym NAFTA? How important is it for people to know about the two-year term of office for the U.S. House of Representatives, as long as they are aware of the opportunity to vote each time it comes along? Perhaps most people know as much as they need to know in order to be good citizens, particularly if they can form opinions with the help of better-informed cue givers (experts, political leaders, media sources, informed friends, interest groups, and so on) whom they trust or by means of simple rules of thumb.[53]

We do not mean to minimize the consequences of people's lack of political knowledge. It has some extremely important implications. As we will see in Chapter 7, for example, when policy decisions are made in the dark, out of public view, interest groups may influence policies that an informed public would oppose. Nor do we mean to encourage complacency, fatalism, or ignorance. Individuals should take the personal responsibility to be good citizens, and organized efforts to alert and to educate the public are valuable. But low levels of information are a reality that must be taken into account. It is unrealistic to expect everyone to have a detailed knowledge of a wide range of political matters.

By the same token, we should not expect the average American to have an elaborately worked-out **political ideology,** a coherent system of interlocking attitudes and beliefs about politics, the economy, and the role of government. You yourself may be a consistent liberal or conservative (or populist, socialist, libertarian, or something else), with many opinions that hang together in a coherent pattern. But surveys show that most people's attitudes are only loosely connected to each other. Most people have opinions that vary from one issue to another: conservative on some issues, liberal on others. Surveys and in-depth interviews indicate that these are often linked by underlying themes and values, but not necessarily in the neat ways that the ideologies of leading political thinkers would dictate.[54]

political ideology

A system of interrelated and coherently patterned beliefs and attitudes.

Ideological Combat

Most Americans do not have fully developed ideological positions, unlike many dueling heads they encounter on television and radio. Here, the very liberal James Carville and the very conservative Mary Matalin argue about a book on *Meet the Press*. As odd as it may seem, Carville and Matalin are husband and wife.

For the same reasons, we should not be surprised that most individuals' expressed opinions on issues tend to be unstable. Many people give different answers when the same survey question is repeated four years or two years or even a few weeks after their first response. Scholars have disagreed about what these unstable responses mean, but uncertainty and lack of information very likely play a part.

None of this, however, means that the opinions of the public, taken as a whole, are unreal, unstable, or irrelevant. The *collective whole* is greater than its individual parts. Even if there is some randomness in the average individual's expressions of political opinions—even if people often say things off the top of their heads to survey interviewers—the responses of thousands or millions of people tend to average out this randomness and reveal a stable **collective public opinion.** Americans' collective policy preferences are actually very stable over time. That is, the percentage of Americans who favor a particular policy usually stays about the same, unless circumstances change in important ways. Moreover, even if most people form many of their specific opinions by deferring to others whom they trust (party leaders, television commentators, and the like) rather than by compiling their own mass of political information, the resulting public opinion need not be ignorant or unwise because the trusted leaders may themselves take account of the best available information. Some recent research, moreover, indicates that Americans' collective policy preferences react rather sensibly to events, to changing circumstances, and to new information, so that we can speak of a "rational public."[55]

collective public opinion

The political attitudes of the public as a whole, expressed as averages, percentages, or other summaries of many individuals' opinions.

The Content of Collective Public Opinion

Americans have opinions about many different political matters, including the political system in general, the performance of our government, party identification, and specific policy preferences.

Showing Their Patriotism

Americans report very high levels of patriotism compared with people in other rich democracies, as well as higher levels of confidence in their fundamental government and economic institutions (although not necessarily confidence in their present leaders). Here, people in Washington celebrate George W. Bush's inauguration in 2005 with a display of American flags.

The System in General

At the most general level, Americans are satisfied with their lives and quite proud of their country and its political institutions. For example, one survey reports that only 4.8 percent of Americans agreed with the statement "There are some countries better than the United States." Well over three-quarters of Americans agreed with the statement "The American system of government is the best in the world."[56] In 2004, about 80 percent of Americans said they were proud to be an American; only 43 percent of British, 33 percent of French, and 23 percent of Germans said the same about their own countries.[57]

Long-term trust in the federal government to do the right thing is much lower than it was in the 1950s and 1960s,[58] despite surges in trust in the 1980s during the Reagan presidency; in the mid-to-late 1990s during the Clinton years, when the U.S. economy was in full bloom; and early in the first George W. Bush administration, immediately following the 9/11 terrorist attacks on the United States. The surge in trust in the federal government was widely commented upon by journalists and academics, with most attributing the surge to George Bush's popular and patriotism-inducing military effort to punish Osama bin Laden and Al Qaeda and to topple the Taliban regime in Afghanistan[59] and to a growing feeling among Republicans—the group historically most distrustful of the federal government—that it might want to trust a government in Washington that it now controlled.[60] The good feelings lasted only a short time, however, battered by the economic recession of the early 1990s, troubles in Iraq, rising energy prices, Washington scandals, and the poor governmental response to Katrina. Trust in the federal government fell after 2002, reaching only 29 percent in 2005 (see Figure 5.3).

Government Performance

One important aspect of happiness or unhappiness with government is a judgment about how well the president has been doing his job. For many decades,

FIGURE 5.3 ● Trust in Government, 1958–2005

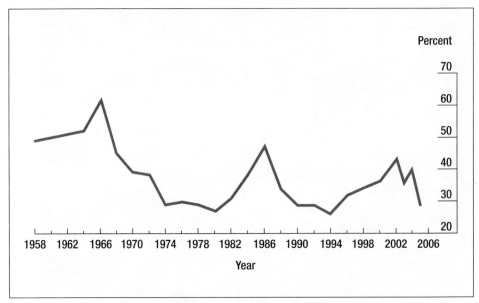

The graph shows the percentage of Americans who say they "trust the federal government to do the right thing" "almost always" or "most of the time." Several things about the trend line are interesting. First, trust in government today is much lower than it was in the 1950s and 1960s. Second, surges of trust happened during the Reagan and Clinton presidencies and in the period immediately following the 9/11 attacks on the United States, which generated strong feelings of patriotism and a desire for strong actions by the government to strike back at those deemed responsible. Trust in government subsequently fell back to its lowest levels, with public confidence battered by troubles in Iraq, increasing energy prices, and the confused federal response to Hurricane Katrina.

Source: American National Election Studies, 1956–2002; *New York Times*/CBS News polls, September 2003–2005.

presidential approval rating

A president's standing with the public, indicated by the percentage of Americans who tell survey interviewers that they approve a president's "handling of his job."

pollsters have been asking people whether they approve or disapprove of the president's handling of his job. The percentage of people saying that they approve—the **presidential approval rating**—is taken as a crucial indicator of a president's popularity. Approval tends to fluctuate up and down with particular events—Lyndon Johnson's approval fluctuated with events in Vietnam, and he decided not to run for reelection when his ratings fell to historic lows after the Tet Offensive—but in the current era, most presidents have come on hard times. Richard Nixon, Gerald Ford, and Jimmy Carter all had low approval ratings by the end of their terms. George H. W. Bush reached a then-record 89 percent approval in March 1991 in the aftermath of the Gulf War but fell below 30 percent by the summer, an unprecedented collapse. Oddly, Bill Clinton enjoyed the highest job approval ratings of any recent president for the final two years of the presidential term, in spite of the fact that he was impeached by the House of Representatives. George W. Bush's 90 percent job approval in late 2001 broke his father's record. By Spring 2006, however, Bush's approval had dropped to only 31 percent, the third lowest presidential approval rating in 50 years.[61]

The public's evaluations of presidents' handling of their jobs depend on how well things are actually going. The state of the economy is especially important: When the country is prosperous and ordinary Americans are doing well and feeling confident about the future, the president tends to be popular;

In the Rubble of the Twin Towers

The American public's approval of President Bush's job performance soared to historic highs after 9/11, but declined steadily after that as partisan bickering, economic uncertainty, and bad news from Iraq undermined his support. Presidents usually gain their highest levels of public support during national security emergencies and wars, especially if the news from the front lines is good.

when there is high inflation or unemployment or when general living standards remain stagnant, the president's popularity falls. George W. Bush's declining approval after his post–9/11 high point in 2001 was probably tied, in part, to the economic doldrums of 2002 and 2003 and rising gasoline prices in 2005. International crises may lead the public to rally and support the president (providing that leaders in both parties are doing so), but that solidarity lasts only a little while unless the crisis works out well. If bad news keeps coming, people begin to disapprove of the president's performance.[62] In 1980, for example, the long drawn-out Iran hostage crisis undermined President Carter's popularity and political influence and cost him the election against Ronald Reagan. Bad news from Iraq in 2005 and 2006 no doubt played a role in the erosion of President Bush's support, as well.

Party Identification

The distribution of **party identification** among the American people is important on a number of grounds. First, as you saw earlier in this chapter, party identification helps determine people's political attitudes on a wide range of issues. Second, how the parties stand relative to one another in the affections of the American people has a lot to do with which party controls the presidency, Congress, and, eventually, the federal courts. It has mattered a great deal, then, that the substantial lead that Democrats once enjoyed over the Republicans has virtually disappeared, and that the fastest growing and largest group among the American people are self-identified independents (see Figure 5.4).

Beginning at the time of Roosevelt's highly popular New Deal in the 1930s and continuing to the late 1980s, the Democratic lead over Republicans among party identifiers was substantial, making them the majority party. The Democrats still maintained a lead among party identifiers for most of the

party identification
The sense of belonging to one or another political party.

FIGURE 5.4 ● **Trends in Party Identification, 1952–2004**

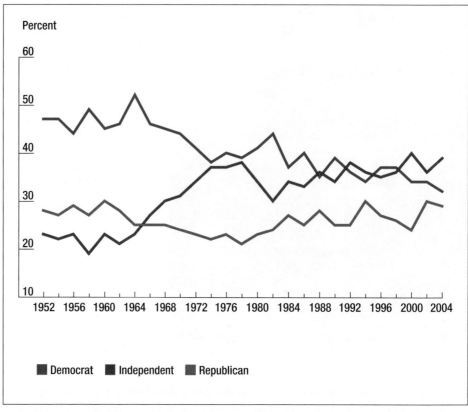

Over the years, the gap between the percentages of those who call themselves Democrats and those who call themselves Republicans has been getting smaller. This is happening because fewer Americans today identify as Democrats and more identify as independents. Oddly enough, the proportion of Americans identifying as Republicans has been very stable during this entire period.

Source: American National Election Studies.

Who Are Liberals and Conservatives?

1990s, but it was a small one, indeed, ranging from 2 to 7 percentage points. After 9/11, the Democrats and Republicans were dead even, with each accounting for 30 to 31 percent of the population. The country is now so evenly divided between party identifiers that even very small swings from election to election in Democratic and Republican voting turnout can have big effects on who wins and loses in presidential and congressional contests.

The proportion of people who say they are independents—including "leaners," or those who say they are independents but lean slightly to one party or another—has steadily increased, from the low 20s in the 1960s to the high 30s today (the remainder are respondents who choose "no preference" or "don't know"). Although some scholars maintain that these figures exaggerate the rise of independents because many leaners behave the same way as people who say they consider themselves Republicans or Democrats,[63] there has clearly been a decline in the proportion of Americans who identify with either of the two major parties. Scholars do not agree why this decline has occurred.[64] Oddly, then, while a growing proportion of the American population is calling itself independent, views about public policies in the United States are becoming increasingly polarized along partisan lines, primarily because partisans vote more than independents and partici- pate more in campaigns. Independents voted in larger numbers in 2006, however, tipping the elections to the Democrats.

Liberals and Conservatives

Although most Americans do not adhere to a rigid political ideology of the sort beloved by certain political philosophers or adhered to by many people around the world—for example, Marxism, communism, socialism, fascism, anarchism, radical political Islam, and the like—they do divide on the role they believe government should play. To complicate matters, Americans generally divide along two dimensions when it comes to government: one related to govern- ment's role in the economy, the other related to government's role in society. Some Americans—those we usually label **economic conservatives**—tend to put more emphasis on economic liberty and freedom from government interfer- ence; they believe that a free market offers the best road to economic efficiency and a decent society. Others—whom we usually label **economic liberals**— stress the necessary role of government in ensuring equality of opportunity, regulating potentially damaging business practices, and providing safety nets for individuals unable to compete in the job market. Government regulation of the economy and spending to help the disadvantaged are two of the main sources of political disputes in America; they make up a big part of the differ- ence between the ideologies of liberalism and of conservatism. However, this accounts for only one of the two dimensions. It is also useful to distinguish be- tween **social (or lifestyle) liberals** and **social (or lifestyle) conservatives,** who differ on such issues as abortion, prayer in the schools, homosexuality, pornography, crime, and political dissent. Those who favor free choices and the rights of the accused are often said to be liberals, while those preferring gov- ernment enforcement of order and traditional values are called conservatives.

It should be apparent that opinions on economic and social issues do not necessarily go together. Many people are liberal in some ways but conservative in others. A gay activist, for example, would likely be a social liberal, but he might also be an economic conservative when it comes to taxes and regulation of business. An evangelical minister preaching in a poor community might be a social conservative on issues such as homosexuality and pornography but an economic liberal when it comes to government programs to help the disadvan- taged. These combinations are real and play a role in American politics. The Pew Research Center surveys from 2005 show that people who combine eco- nomic (pro-business, pro-market) and social conservatism are 10 percent of the population, and 81 percent of them identify with the GOP. At the other end of the spectrum, people who are secular and socially liberal, as well as in favor of an activist government to deal with social problems, make up 19 percent of voters and support the Democrats at a rate of 59 percent.[65]

Policy Preferences

According to democratic theory, one of the chief determinants of what govern- ments do should be what the citizens *want* them to do, that is, citizens' **policy preferences.**

Spending Programs   As Figure 5.5 indicates, large and rather stable majori- ties of Americans (around 70 percent in recent years) think we are spending "too little" on education and fighting crime. The public also gives high and sta- ble support to Social Security, Medicare, and environmental programs.

economic conservatives
People who favor private enterprise and oppose gov- ernment regulations on spending.

economic liberals
People who favor govern- ment regulation of business and government spending for social programs.

social (lifestyle) liberals
People who favor civil liber- ties, abortion rights, and al- ternative lifestyles.

social (lifestyle) conservatives
People who favor traditional social values; they tend to support strong law-and-order measures and oppose abor- tion and gay rights.

Are You a Liberal or a Conservative?

policy preferences
Citizens' preferences con- cerning what policies they want government to pursue.

FIGURE 5.5 • Public Support for Spending Programs

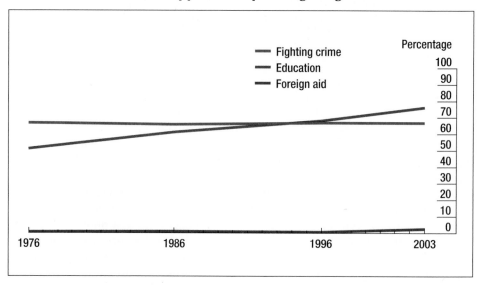

Large, fairly stable majorities of Americans have favored increased spending for fighting crime and aiding education, but very few have favored increased foreign aid over the years (though support increased after 2000).

Note: Year-to-year fluctuations have been averaged to create the trend line.
Source: American National Election Study, 2004.

Substantial majorities, moreover, want the federal government to help people pay medical bills and to pay for more research on diseases such as cancer and AIDS. About one-half of all Americans would increase spending on national defense.[66]

By contrast, few people think too little is being spent on foreign aid; many more think too much is being spent. Except for disaster relief, such as for the 2005 tsunami, foreign aid is generally unpopular. (The reason may be, in part, that few realize how little is spent on foreign aid—only about 1 percent of the annual federal budget is devoted to economic, humanitarian, and military assistance.) When this is made clear, support for economic aid rises sharply.[67] Large majorities of the public oppose military aid or arms sales abroad. The space program wins only slightly greater support.

Social Issues   As Figure 5.6 shows, Americans make distinctions among different circumstances when deciding whether they favor permitting abortions. For much of the past three decades, about 55 percent of Americans have reported that they support the legality of abortion under certain circumstances. Thus—as other reports show[68]—more are likely to find abortion acceptable if the life of the mother is in danger, but fewer support abortion when a women says she simply does not want another child. About 25 percent say abortion should be legal under all circumstances; about 20 percent believe that abortion always should be illegal.

Other surveys have revealed steadily growing support for civil liberties protections and for civil rights for women and minorities. Beginning in the 1940s or 1950s, for example, more and more Americans have come to favor having black and white children go to the same schools and integrating work, housing, and public accommodations. (At the same time, however, there is considerable opposition among whites to affirmative action.) And, there has been

FIGURE 5.6 • Public Approval for Allowing Abortions

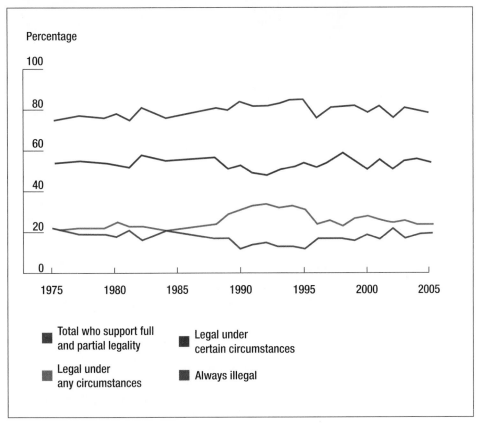

Only a minority of Americans supports or rejects abortion under any and all circumstances. For a long time now, a majority of Americans say they believe abortion should be legal, but only under certain circumstances.

Source: General Social Survey, 1965–2002.

a slow but steady increase in support of equal treatment for gays and lesbians, although substantial majorities oppose same-sex marriage. These issues are explored in depth in Chapter 16.

On a number of issues, Americans support positions favored by social conservatives. Large majorities, for example, favor allowing organized prayer in the public schools, banning pornography, preventing flag burning, penalizing drug use, punishing crimes severely, and imposing capital punishment for murder.

Foreign Policy In the realm of foreign policy, public opinion sometimes changes rapidly in response to crises and other dramatic events. Major international events affect opinions, as we saw in the chapter-opening story on public reactions to the Tet Offensive during the Vietnam War. The percentage of Americans saying we were wrong to invade Iraq steadily increased as the news from there got worse. But often foreign policy opinions are quite stable. Since World War II, for example, two-thirds or more of those giving an opinion have usually said that the United States should take an "active part" in world affairs. The exact percentage favoring an active role has varied somewhat, rising to a peak of about 83 percent in 1965, near the onset of the Vietnam War;

Saying "No" to the War in Iraq

Many Americans—including these demonstrators marching in New York City on March 23, 2003—opposed the decision to go to war in Iraq without the backing of the United Nations or the support of many traditional U.S. allies. Much to their disappointment, President Bush ignored their wishes and invaded Iraq in April.

War, Peace, and Public Opinion

isolationism

The policy of avoiding involvement in foreign affairs.

unilateralist

The stance toward foreign policy that suggests that the United States should "go it alone," pursuing its national interests without seeking the cooperation of other nations or multilateral institutions.

multilateralist

The stance toward foreign policy that suggests that the United States should seek the cooperation of other nations and multilateral institutions in pursuing its goals.

dropping to about 62 percent after the failure of that war; and recovering in later years. Today, those believing that the United States should play an active role in world affairs again hovers near 80 percent.[69] The percentage supporting a U.S. role has remained relatively high, not fluctuating much with alleged public moods.[70]

The public has been quite hesitant to use troops abroad, however, unless the threat to the United States is tangible. Just before U.S. troops were sent as peacekeepers to Bosnia in 1994, for example, 78 percent of the public opposed the idea and only 17 percent were in favor.[71] Opposition faded as the operation began to look less risky, but any substantial casualties abroad arouse large-scale public disapproval. The public strongly supported the use of the military to destroy Al Qaeda and the Taliban regime in Afghanistan[72] and initially supported President Bush's decision to invade Iraq in 2003, when only 23 percent of those surveyed said the United States "made a mistake sending troops to Iraq." By fall of 2005, with bad news from Iraq dominating the news, those thinking it was a mistake had soared to 54 percent.[73]

Although not many Americans embrace pure **isolationism**—the view that the United States should not be involved abroad and should only pay attention to its own affairs—the public (and political and economic leaders, as well) is divided over whether its involvement in the world should take a **unilateralist** or a **multilateralist** form. Unilateralists want to go it alone, taking action when it suits our purposes, and not necessarily seeking the approval or help of international organizations such as the United Nations or regional organizations such as NATO. Unilateralists are also uncomfortable with entering into too many international treaties. Multilateralists believe that the protection of American interests requires continuous engagement in the world, but do not think that the United States has the resources or ability to accomplish its ends without cooperating with other nations and with international and regional organizations. According to most surveys, roughly two out of three Americans are in the multilateralist camp, telling pollsters they oppose unilateral U.S. military intervention in most cases and support cooperation with the United Nations and NATO and international treaties on human rights, the environment, and arms control. In this regard, they are considerably more multilateralist than American legislative and executive branch officials.[74]

The People's "Fitness to Rule" Revisited

This examination of collective public opinion, its evident stability on a wide range of issues over time, and why it sometimes changes on some issues leads us to conclude that confidence in the role of the public in the American political system is warranted. The evidence demonstrates that collective public opinion is quite stable and sensible when it comes to core beliefs and attitudes about government, the parties, and policy preferences. The evidence further shows that when collective public opinion does change, it does so for perfectly understandable reasons: dramatic events, new information, or changes in perspective among American leaders. The conclusion we draw is a simple yet powerful one: The American people are fit to rule. The next question to address is whether the people, in fact, do rule.

Is Government Responsive to Public Opinion?

Public Opinion and Leadership

We have argued that a crucial test of how well democracy is working is how closely a government's policies match the expressed wishes of its citizens. Do the actions of the U.S. government match what collective public opinion says it wants government to do? Some scholars say yes, while some say no. Let's look at both sides.

"Yes, It Is"

Our opening story about the Vietnam War suggests that at least under some circumstances, public opinion does affect policymaking. We have encountered other examples that tell the same "government responsiveness" story in this book. We saw in Chapter 1, for example, that Congress passed the historic Civil Rights Act of 1964 after a period of time when public support for racial segregation was declining.

These stories about government responsiveness to public opinion have been buttressed by important statistical assessments.[75] Looking at many different policy issues—foreign and domestic—one scholar found, for example, that about two-thirds of the time, U.S. government policy coincides with what opinion surveys say the public wants. The same two-thirds correspondence has appeared when other scholars investigated how *changes* in public opinion relate to changes in federal, state, and local policies. Moreover, when public opinion changes by a substantial and enduring amount and the issue is prominent, government policy has moved in the same direction as the public 87 percent of the time within a year or so afterward.[76] Yet another influential study shows that substantial swings in the national political mood have occurred over the past half century or so and that public policy has followed accordingly. As the American people have moved first in a liberal direction, then a conservative direction, and back again over the years, elected leaders in Washington have shaped their policies to fit the public mood, being more activist in liberal periods and less activist in conservative periods.[77] Finally, one scholar concludes, after carefully reviewing the results of 30 studies, that public opinion almost always has some effect on what government does, and when an issue is visible and important to the people, public opinion is the decisive factor in determining the substance of government policy.[78]

"No, It's Not"

While these studies seem to lend substantial support for the idea that public opinion is a powerful determinant of what government does in the United States, this research has no shortage of critics. Showing a high correlation (i.e., a strong statistical relationship) between public opinion and government policy does not prove that public opinion causes government policies. There are any number of plausible reasons why a "causal relationship" may not really exist. Here is what the critics say:[79]

- It may be the case that public opinion and government policies move in the same direction because some third factor causes both of them to change. In this example, the true cause of government action is this third factor, not public opinion. There are many instances in the real world where this has happened. For example, the news media often play up a particular incident or situation and persuade both public opinion and government policymakers that action is needed. This is clearly what happened when the Hearst newspaper chain whipped up fervor among both the public and elected leaders for war against Spain in the wake of the sinking of the battleship *Maine* in Havana harbor. Or an interest group or set of interest groups might sway public opinion and government officials in the same direction at the same time, as medical, insurance, and hospital associations did when they launched a successful campaign to sink Bill Clinton's health care initiative in 1994.

- Even if public opinion and government actions are highly correlated, it may be the case that it is government that shapes public opinion. In statistical language, we might say that the causal arrow is reversed, going not from the public to government, but the other way around: that officials act to gain popular support for policies and actions these officials want.[80] Such efforts can range from outright manipulation of the public—the Tonkin Gulf incident described in the opening story in this chapter is such a case; some would claim that the use of the "weapons of mass destruction" rhetoric to raise support for the invasion of Iraq in 2003 is another compelling case—to the conventional public relations efforts carried out every day by government officials and agencies. This is why both the legislative and executive branches of the federal government are so well equipped with communications offices, press secretaries, and public liaison personnel.

So where does all of this leave us on the question of public opinion's influence on government? It is probably reasonable to say that public opinion plays an important role in shaping what government does, but so do a range of other political actors and institutions, including parties, interest groups, the news media, and social movements. It is probably reasonable to say, moreover, that the influence of public opinion on government is significantly less than the statistical studies suggest (e.g., the "two-thirds" rule) for the reasons given: the impact of third factors on both opinion and government and the significant

Using the Democracy Standard

What impact does public opinion have on American democracy?

PROPOSITION: **Public opinion is not very important in determining what the federal government does in the United States.**

AGREE Although the news media publish polls and talk a great deal about their meaning and effect on politics, public opinion is far less important than interest groups, business firms, large contributors, and periodic elections in determining what policies are enacted. There are simply too many examples of government acting contrary to the views of the public—including, for example, the disconnect between the expressed views of the public and government action on issues such as gun control, the impeachment of Bill Clinton, and health care—to plausibly argue for public opinion as a decisive tool of democracy. On most of the important issues of the day—whether regulating polluting companies or media empires, granting contracts to private companies for rebuilding Iraq, or fashioning trade legislation—powerful interest groups and large corporations generally get their way. Government leaders can get away with this because the public has no knowledge of or opinions about broad areas of public policy; with regard to other issues, like gun control, the public does not express very intense feelings; and with regard to still other issues, leaders can shape public opinion to fit what they want to do.

Political leaders pay very close attention to public opinion when they are in the midst of deciding on alternative courses of action. Some would argue that they do entirely too much of this, in fact, pandering to the whims of the public rather than exercising leadership. This desire to find out what the public thinks and what it wants is why congressional incumbents, candidates for office, presidents, and government agencies spend so much time and money polling their relevant constituencies. And it is no mystery why elected officials do this, as do their challengers: Public opinion is eventually translated into votes at election time. So, staying on the right side of public opinion—giving people what they want in terms of policies, as it were—is how people gain and keep elected offices. The result is that what the public wants generally becomes public policy; political scientists have shown that public opinion and government policy match up more often than not. **DISAGREE**

CONSIDER • Does the federal government generally do what you want it to do on most major issues? • If it doesn't, why do you think that might be the case? • Is it because your views are different from those of a majority of other Americans who generally get their way with government leaders? • Or is it because elected leaders are not likely to listen to people like you, even if your views are similar to a large majority of Americans, when powerful interest groups want these leaders to do something else? • If powerful interests are getting their way with government, rather than you and other Americans, what do you think people like you can do about it? • Are there alternative ways that you and the people who agree with you can be heard by government leaders? • Would more intense participation in electoral politics do the trick? • Or will getting your voice heard require different sorts of actions, perhaps petitions, or mobilizing like-minded people on the Internet, or marches, or disruptive demonstrations?

amount of influence government officials have over popular opinion.[81] And it is hard to avoid noticing the many times government acts almost exactly contrary to public opinion—Congress's decision to go ahead with the impeachment and trial of Bill Clinton in late 1998 and early 1999 in the face of strong public opposition comes to mind, as does inaction on gun control (see the "Using the Framework" feature).

Comparing Public Opinion

There is one more reason a simple, straightforward answer cannot be given to the question "How much influence does public opinion have on government policy?" Scholars have reported that opinion plays an important role in shaping government policy under certain conditions, but much less so under others. Public opinion seems to matter the most when issues are highly visible to the public (usually because there has been lots of political conflict surrounding the issue), are about matters that affect the lives of Americans most directly, and concern issues for which people have access to reliable and understandable information. When economic times are tough—during a recession, for example—no amount of rhetoric from political leaders, the news media, or interest groups is likely to convince people "that they never had it so good." People have a reality check in such circumstances. By the same token, many foreign policy questions are distant from people's lives and involve issues where information is scarce or incomplete. In this circumstance, government officials act with wide latitude and play an important role shaping what the public believes. After studying decades' worth of surveys of public and elite opinion on foreign policy issues collected by the Chicago Council on Foreign Relations, for example, Page and Bouton conclude that a deep disconnect exists between the public and elites, with the public much less eager than elites to use force in foreign affairs and more supportive of international cooperation—in the form of international treaties and the United Nations—to tackle global problems.[84] Additionally, some issues, such as the details of tax legislation or the deregulation of the telecommunications industry, are so obscure and complex that they become the province of interest groups and experts, with the public having but ill-formed and not very intense opinions.

Summary

Public opinion consists of the core political beliefs and political attitudes expressed by ordinary citizens; it can be measured rather accurately through polls and surveys. The democratic ideals of popular sovereignty and majority rule imply that government policy should respond to the wishes of the citizens, at least in the long run. An important test of how well democracy is working, then, is how closely government policy corresponds to public opinion.

People learn their political attitudes and beliefs from their families, peers, schools, and workplaces; they also respond to political events and the mass media. Structural factors in the society, the economy, and the international system strongly affect public opinion. Opinions and party loyalties differ according to race, religion, region, urban or rural residence, social class, education level, gender, and age. Blacks, Jews, city dwellers, women, and low-income people tend to be particularly liberal and Democratic; white Protestants, suburbanites, males, and the wealthy tend to be conservative and Republican.

Whether people are fit to rule depends a great deal on the quality of public opinion. Most people, of course, do not know a lot of facts about politics and do not have well-worked-out ideologies or highly stable policy preferences. Contrary to the fears of the Founders and others, however, the *collective* public opinion of Americans is real and stable, and it takes account of the available information.

Using the Framework

Gun Control

If a majority of Americans say they want gun control, why hasn't the federal government done much about it?

Background: Public opinion surveys have consistently indicated high public support for stricter federal gun control laws. At a general level, around two-thirds of Americans say they want stricter laws. Several specific proposals receive even higher levels of support. For example, about 80 percent of Americans say they want a nationwide ban on assault weapons, while 70 percent want the government to ban gun sales by mail-order and over the Internet. Although some laws, such as the Brady Bill–which requires background checks of gun buyers and a waiting period–have passed Congress, proposals for stricter control over the sale and distribution of weapons almost never get very far. Taking a broad look at how structural, political linkage, and governmental factors affect gun control legislation will help explain the situation.

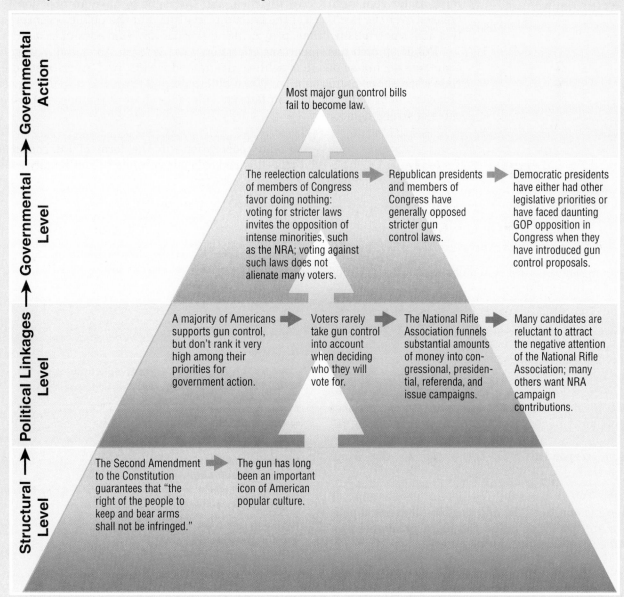

Governmental Action

Most major gun control bills fail to become law.

Governmental Level

The reelection calculations of members of Congress favor doing nothing: voting for stricter laws invites the opposition of intense minorities, such as the NRA; voting against such laws does not alienate many voters. ➡ Republican presidents and members of Congress have generally opposed stricter gun control laws. ➡ Democratic presidents have either had other legislative priorities or have faced daunting GOP opposition in Congress when they have introduced gun control proposals.

Political Linkages Level

A majority of Americans supports gun control, but don't rank it very high among their priorities for government action. ➡ Voters rarely take gun control into account when deciding who they will vote for. ➡ The National Rifle Association funnels substantial amounts of money into congressional, presidential, referenda, and issue campaigns. ➡ Many candidates are reluctant to attract the negative attention of the National Rifle Association; many others want NRA campaign contributions.

Structural Level

The Second Amendment to the Constitution guarantees that "the right of the people to keep and bear arms shall not be infringed." ➡ The gun has long been an important icon of American popular culture.

For the past four decades, Americans' trust in government and approval of the performance of political leaders have been declining, though there were significant up ticks during the Reagan and Clinton years and in the year or so following the 9/11 terrorist attacks on the United States. The public's regard for government and political officials rebounded dramatically in the aftermath of the terrorist attacks on the United States and the war on terrorism, then declined again. Party loyalty, although still widespread, has declined in strength. Most Americans strongly believe in freedom, economic liberty, capitalism, equality of opportunity, and democracy, but they disagree about the role of government in fostering these things. Economic liberals and conservatives disagree about economic regulation, taxes, government spending, and the need for safety nets for the unfortunate. Social liberals and conservatives disagree about the role of religion in American life, abortion, and the rights of gays and lesbians, among other things. Majorities of the public favor government action on crime, education, medical care, and the environment. Support is lower for defense and the space program and lower still for foreign aid. Support for civil rights, civil liberties, and the right to have an abortion increased over the last third of the twentieth century, but the public is conservative about patriotism, crime, prayer in the schools, and same-sex marriage.

Public opinion has important effects on what federal, state, and local governments do, but so do other political actors and events. And government officials often shape public opinion. When all is said and done, the responsiveness of government to public opinion falls considerably short of the hopes of advocates of strong democracy.

mypoliscilab
Where participation leads to action!

Web Exploration
The Gender Gap

ISSUE: There has been much talk of a "gender gap" in the United States.

SITE: Examine male and female political attitudes and behaviors by accessing the American National Election Study in MyPoliSciLab at **www.mypoliscilab.com.** In the "Web Explorations" section for Chapter 5, open "gender gap." Look at a few survey questions about public policies in Section 4. For each question you examine, select "percent among demographic groups who responded," and you will see how men and women have responded over the years to the same questions.

WHAT YOU'VE LEARNED: Is there a "gender gap"? If there is one, does the gap exist in all areas of politics and policy, or is the gap more pronounced on some issues compared with others?

HINT: As a measuring rod to determine the seriousness of the "gender gap," look at the differences between whites and blacks on the same survey questions.

Internet Sources

Doonesbury
www.doonesbury.com/arcade/strawpoll/index.cfm
  A daily online poll on current issues.

Gallup Organization
www.gallup.com/
  Access to recent Gallup polls as well as to the Gallup archives. Requires a paid subscription.

National Election Studies
www.umich.edu/~nes/nesguide/nesguide.htm
  Biennial survey of voters, focusing on electoral issues.

Pew Research Center for the People and the Press
www.people-press.org
  Complex, in-depth polls on domestic and foreign issues.

Political Compass
www.politicalcompass.org
  Determine where you stand in ideological terms by completing the online survey.

Polling Report
www.pollingreport.com
  A compilation of surveys from a variety of sources on politics and public affairs.

Suggestions for Further Reading

Erikson, Robert S., and Kent L. Tedin. *American Public Opinion,* 7th ed. New York: Longman Publishers, 2005.
A comprehensive survey of what we know about American public opinion and how we know it.

Garcia, John A. *Latino Politics in America.* Lanham, MD: Rowman and Littlefield Publishers, 2003.
Useful chapters on Hispanic public opinion and political socialization.

Page, Benjamin I., with Marshall Bouton. *The Foreign Policy Disconnect: What Americans Want from our Leaders but Do Not Get.* Chicago: University of Chicago Press, 2006.
Based on surveys of the public and elites sponsored by the Chicago Council on Foreign Relations, the authors demonstrate the existence of a deep disconnect between the public and elites on what kind of foreign policy the United States should have.

Stimson, James A. *Tides of Consent: How Public Opinion Shapes American Politics.* New York: Cambridge University Press, 2004.
Shows that public policies in the United States reflect long-range changes in American public opinion.

Weissberg, Robert. *Polling, Policy, and Public Opinion: The Case Against Heeding the "Voice of the People."* New York: Palgrave, 2002.
A passionate argument on why government officials should not be too responsive to public opinion.

CHAPTER 6

The News Media

IN THIS CHAPTER

- The role of the news media in a democracy

- How the news is gathered and disseminated

- Why government officials are key news sources

- Whether the news media have a liberal or a conservative bias

- Why some media are more regulated than others

- How the news media affect public opinion and policymaking

The Attack of the Blogs

Speaking at the annual gathering of luminaries at the World Economic Forum in Davos, Switzerland, on January 27, 2005, CNN chief news executive Eason Jordan reportedly said that U.S. military forces in Iraq had targeted journalists covering the war and its aftermath, killing 12.[1] Those in attendance later claimed not to remember the precise language Jordan used, but confirmed the nature of his remarks. Challenged by several people at the Forum, including Senator Barney Frank, Jordan reportedly said that, while journalists may not have been purposely targeted, American forces had been unduly reckless. Jordan cited as an example the shelling of the Palestine Hotel in Baghdad, where journalists from many countries were headquartered in April 2003 as the city was taken by U.S. forces.

Although several journalists from major news organizations were at the session, they did not report on Jordan's statement because the sessions were officially "off-the-record." Bothered by what he had heard at the conference, Rony Abovitz, a businessman from Florida, posted a story on the Forum's new blog—short for web log, an online journal where commentaries and news reports are posted with little or no editorial oversight—entitled "Do U.S. Troops Target Journalists in Iraq?" As a first-time blogger, Mr. Abovitz didn't expect much to happen, he said later. The posting, which appeared the day after Jordan spoke, was noticed by conservative talk-show host Hugh Hewitt, who mentioned it on his show on February 1. Hewitt's remark generated what's called a *blogswarm;* within days, hundreds of conservative blogs were attacking Jordan, calling him and CNN poster children of the liberal mainstream media.

Trying to stem the tide, CNN responded on February 2 to those who had contacted it about the incident, claiming, "Many bloggers have taken Mr. Jordan's remarks out of context. Eason Jordan does not believe that the U.S. military is trying to kill journalists . . . ." As the blogswarm increased, Jordan released a statement to the same effect, but the storm kept growing. Slowly, news organizations began to get on the story. Not surprisingly, the conservative-oriented ones jumped in first, starting with the *Weekly Standard* and the *Washington Times,* and continuing with the *New York Sun* and several cable news commentators, including Brit Hume. Several regional newspapers began to run the story, and a number of bloggers agreed to coordinate their efforts, forming a new blog called "Easongate." By February 10, *The New York Times* and *The Wall Street Journal* had picked up the story, although neither ran an extensive treatment. Feeling the pressure building and much to the surprise and distress of many in the news business, Eason Jordan resigned from CNN on February 11, 2005.

Although the "Easongate" bloggers were delighted with the outcome, others were alarmed. Steve Lovelady,

managing editor of the *Columbia Journalism Review Daily,* complained that "the salivating morons who make up the lynch mob prevailed." Jeff Jarvis, who publishes a widely read blog, "buzzmachine.com," and champions the democratic information role of the blogosphere, was nevertheless troubled, saying, "I wish our goal were not taking off heads but digging up truth." Even Ron Abovitz, who had started the ball rolling, was concerned. Noting bloggers should have higher goals than destroying people's careers, he observed, "At times it did seem like an angry mob, and an angry mob using high technology, that's not good."

The Jordan incident was not the first time bloggers played a central role in creating news and mobilizing partisans in American politics, nor will it be the last. In 2004 conservative bloggers accelerated the resignation of Dan Rather as CBS News's nightly anchor after uncovering inaccuracies in his critical reports on George W. Bush's National Guard service during the Vietnam War, and in 2005 they fueled the conservative firestorm that compelled Harriet Meirs to withdraw as a nominee for the Supreme Court. Liberal bloggers have their trophies as well, helping to force out Trent Lott as Majority Leader in the Senate in 2004, for example, over racially inflammatory remarks he had made at a 100th birthday celebration for Senator Strom Thurmond and organizing the effort to defeat incumbent-senator Joe Lieberman's bid in 2006 to win renomination for his seat in a race with antiwar candidate Ned Lamont.

Weblogs and bloggers are surely here to stay, given the low costs of entry into the blogosphere—anyone with a computer and a broadband connection to the Internet can create a blog at almost zero cost—and the sense among a wide range of people, some expert in some area, some merely passionate about some cause, that they have something to say and the constitutional right to say it. While most weblogs are apolitical, many are devoted to serious matters, and many of these are intended to affect the political debate in the nation.

What the blogosphere will mean for democracy remains to be seen. What it means for news organizations is that they can no longer dominate the information environment. In response, many are creating their own weblogs to be players in this new arena of news gathering and dissemination. ∎

Thinking Critically About This Chapter

In this chapter, we turn our attention to the diverse news media in the United States to learn how they are organized, how they work, and what effects they have on the quality of our political life.

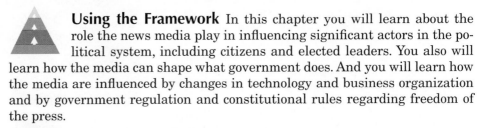

Using the Framework In this chapter you will learn about the role the news media play in influencing significant actors in the political system, including citizens and elected leaders. You also will learn how the media can shape what government does. And you will learn how the media are influenced by changes in technology and business organization and by government regulation and constitutional rules regarding freedom of the press.

Using the Democracy Standard Using the tools presented in Chapter 1, you will be able to evaluate the degree to which the news media advance democracy in the United States or retard it. You will be able to judge whether the media promote popular sovereignty, political equality, and liberty. Finally, you will see how certain changes in the media may be cause for concern in terms of the health of democracy.

Roles of the News Media in Democracy

The central idea of democracy is that ordinary citizens should control what their government does. However, citizens cannot hope to control officials, choose candidates wisely, speak intelligently with others about public affairs, or even make up their minds about what policies they favor unless they have good information about politics and policies. Most of that information must come through the news media, whether newspapers, radio, television, or, increasingly, the Internet. How well democracy works, then, depends partly on how good a job the news media are doing.

Watchdog Over Government: How Exceptional?

watchdog

The role of the media in scrutinizing the actions of government officials.

One role of the media in a democracy is that of **watchdog** over government. The idea is that the press should dig up facts and warn the public when officials are doing something wrong. Citizens can hold officials accountable for setting things right only if they know about errors and wrongdoing.

The First Amendment to the Constitution ("Congress shall make no law . . . abridging the freedom . . . of the press") helps ensure that the news media will be able to expose officials' misbehavior without fear of censorship or prosecu-

PUBLIC WATCHDOG

tion. This is a treasured American right that is not available in many other countries. Under dictatorships and other authoritarian regimes, the media are usually tightly controlled. Even in a democratic country such as Great Britain, strict secrecy laws limit what the press can say about certain government activities. In many countries, including France, Israel, and Sweden, the government owns and operates major television channels and makes sure that the programs are not too critical.[2] In Brazil, licenses for television and radio stations are awarded by the Ministry of Communications to political supporters of the government. In some Brazilian states, about one-half of the delegates to Congress own a TV or radio station. At the national level, several powerful politicians and party leaders run media empires that include television networks and newspapers in the major cities.[3] In Japan, although television, radio, and newspapers are formally independent of government, there is a widespread system of "press clubs" sponsored by politicians and government agencies, in which journalists and the people they write about come to know each other well, and membership among journalists is highly prized. Although freedom of the press is far from perfect in the United States, the news media enjoy greater freedom than their counterparts in other democratic countries. In many nondemocratic countries, moreover, press freedom hardly exists at all, with government censorship of the press and intimidation of journalists, all too common.[4]

Comparing News Media

But how well do the media in the United States fulfill their watchdog role? Even without formal censorship or government ownership of the media, various factors, including the way in which the news media are organized and their routines of news gathering, may limit how willing or able they are to be critical of government policies. In addition, the media may be too quick to blow scandals out of proportion and to destroy political leaders' careers.[5]

Clarifying Electoral Choices

A second role of the news media in a democracy is to make clear what electoral choices the public has: what the political parties stand for and how the candidates shape up in terms of personal character, knowledge, experience, and positions on the issues. Without such information, it is difficult for voters to make intelligent choices.

How much or how little attention do the media pay to candidates' stands on public policies? Do they devote too much coverage to the "horse race" (who is ahead? who is behind?) aspect of campaigns instead? In scrutinizing the character and personality of candidates, do the media go overboard in digging up dirt and reporting negative material even when it is very minor?

Providing Policy Information

A third role of the news media is to present a diverse, full, and enlightening set of facts and ideas about public policy. Citizens need to know how well current policies are working, as well as the pros and cons of the alternative policies that might be tried, to formulate sensible preferences. In a democracy, government should respond to public opinion, but that opinion should be reasonably well informed.

How much policy information do the U.S. media actually convey, and how accessible is it? How diverse and how accurate is that information? Is it biased—toward liberalism, for example, or toward conservatism? Are some voices heard and others ignored? We will address such questions in this chapter.

The Media Landscape

Three Hundred Years of American Mass Media

The media have changed greatly over our history and continue to change ever more rapidly. Today, the watchword is *fragmentation,* as the numbers and forms of news outlets proliferate and become more narrowly targeted at specific audiences.[6] Taken together, the various media represent, at least potentially, a multitude of ways for the public to gain access to political news, analysis, and commentary, although there are downsides as well.

Newspapers

yellow journalism

Sensational newspaper stories with large headlines and, in some cases, color cartoons.

By the mid-1830s, "penny papers" such as the *New York Herald* reached mass audiences of ordinary working people by means of low prices and human interest stories, written in a breezy and often sensational style. The invention of the telegraph allowed news to be gathered and distributed quickly, eventually to millions of people. In the 1840s, several New York newspapers formed the Associated Press (AP) to cooperate in gathering news and distributing it by telegraph. In the late nineteenth century, Joseph Pulitzer of the *New York World* (1883) and William Randolph Hearst of the *New York Journal* invented **yellow journalism,** a new sort of newspaper that combined sensationalism and political crusades with oversized headlines and full-color illustrations and comics. One Hearst crusade in 1898 helped provoke war against Spain over Spanish control of Cuba, a key step in the emergence of the United States as a world power. Today's tabloids, such as the *New York Post,* are less likely to start wars, but their journalistic techniques still resemble Hearst's yellow journalism.

The development of wire services such as the AP, the United Press International, and the Scripps-Howard Service (the last two are now defunct) meant that more political news could be spread much more quickly, to much bigger audiences, and, inevitably, in a much more nationally uniform way than ever before. Homogenization was accentuated by the development of large "chains" of newspapers, owned by the same company and pursuing uniform editorial policies. Most major metropolitan newspapers today are parts of such chains (which are themselves often parts of larger multimedia companies). They depend mainly on the AP for national and international news, on syndicated columnists for their editorial page, and on their own reporters to cover local affairs.

In addition to the chain-associated metropolitan dailies, newspapers come in three rough categories. First, there are newspapers that give serious, in-depth attention to domestic and international political affairs including, most notably, *The New York Times,* the *Washington Post,* and *The Wall Street Journal.* The *Los Angeles Times,* the *Miami Herald,* the *Boston Globe,* and the *Chicago Tribune* also fall on the serious end of the news continuum. Second, in a category all by itself, is *USA Today,* sold and marketed on a national scale, with some serious coverage of public affairs, but mostly devoted to lifestyle, personal finance, sports, and entertainment content. (*USA Today* sells about the same number of papers each day as *The Wall Street Journal* and about twice as many as *The New York Times.*[7]) Third, there are newspapers in urban areas that address minority communities of one kind or another and the issues that directly concern them, including gays and lesbians, African Americans, Hispanics, and Asian Americans.

Today, despite all of the innovations making newspapers accessible and entertaining, Americans are relying less and less on them for their information about the world in favor of television and, increasingly, the Internet, with radio a player as well[8] (see Figure 6.1). Among people ages 18 through 24, only 35 percent in 2004 followed political news in a newspaper (compared with 76 percent among those ages 50 through 64).[9] This may be a problem for democracy because television and radio have traditionally been less comprehensive and more shallow in their news coverage than the nation's top newspapers, although programs like the "Daily Show" with Jon Stewart can be quite insightful—and funnier than the normal television fare.

FIGURE 6.1 • Where People Get Their News

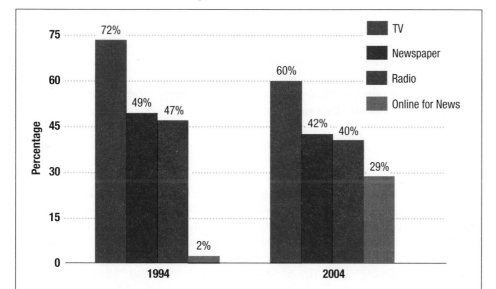

In recent years, people have turned increasingly to the Internet as a source of news, while decreasing somewhat their reliance on television, newspapers, and radio. Although the Internet still trails the other forms of news sources, it is catching up quickly.

Source: Trends, 2005 (Washington, D.C.: Pew Research Center, 2004), pp. 42, 44–45.

News with Laughs

For many Americans, particularly younger ones, alternative news sources, including *The Daily Show* on Comedy Central hosted by Jon Stewart, carry more credibility than the mainstream media.

Magazines

Several journals of political opinion and analysis that were founded in the nineteenth century are still published, such as *The Nation,* the *Atlantic Monthly,* and *Harper's,* and a wide range of other journals—liberal, conservative, radical, and reactionary—have entered the political debate. Among the most influential in political circles are the *Weekly Standard,* the *New Republic,* and the *New Yorker.* Beginning in the 1920s, Henry Luce's *Time,* a weekly newsmagazine, brought analysis and interpretation of the week's news, written in a brisk and colorful style, to hundreds of thousands and then millions of readers; it later drew competition from *Newsweek* and *U.S. News & World Report.* Increasingly, however, these newsmagazines carry less news and more content having to do with lifestyle issues, advice, and celebrities. Over the years, countless specialized journals (e.g., *Foreign Affairs* and *Foreign Policy* cover international affairs). Today hundreds, perhaps thousands, of special interest magazines are available to the reading public.

Radio

Radio, once thought vanquished by the television juggernaut, has been reborn. Besides music, AM and FM stations offer frequent news bulletins and call-in talk shows, on which all manner of political opinions, including the cranky and the outrageous, are voiced. Appealing disproportionately to the middle-aged, male, and politically conservative (both callers and listeners),[10] syndicated talk shows, hosted by people such as Rush Limbaugh (with an audience of almost 14 million), Sean Hannity (almost 13 million), and Michael Savage (about 8 million),[11] have become a political force, able to generate a flood of mail to Congress or the White House and even to force decisions on Washington policymakers. Liberal-oriented *Air America* started broadcasting in 2004, but its leading personalities, Ed Schultz and Al Franken, each attract an audience of less than 2 million.[12] Some talk has begun to appear on satellite radio, as well, with Howard Stern's program the most prominent.

Radio is not all sound and liberal and conservative populist fury, however, or simply fragmented, on-the-hour news sound bites. National Public Radio and local public radio stations provide extended news analysis and commentary, often thoughtful and occasionally unorthodox, on programs such as *Morning Edition* and *All Things Considered,* although many conservatives believe these outlets to be too liberal in their offerings. Many radio news and commentary offerings, from both serious and not-so-serious sources, increasingly are available as **podcasts.**

podcast
Digital audio and video files made readily available to interested people via computers and portable devices.

Television

According to a multitude of polls, Americans name television as their most important source of news, although it is decreasingly the case that television news means network news. The so-called Big Three (CBS, NBC, and ABC) national news broadcasts are losing their audience to cable rivals, such as FoxNews and CNN, but also to local news (59 percent of Americans say they watch local news), where the focus is on crime, sports, and weather, and to alternative news outlets, especially on the Internet. (See the "By the Numbers" feature to gain a sense of how accurate local television news is in informing people about crime.)

Another dramatic change in the news media landscape has been the loss of confidence in the historically most important sources of news about politics and public affairs: national news broadcasts, newspapers, and news magazines (see Figure 6.2 on page 162). The causes are largely unknown, but students of the media point to a number of possible causes, including the narrow targeting of audiences by media outlets, the rising partisanship of American politics (which plays out in the media), and the rise of niche audiences that tune in to news outlets that share their preexisting views, tuning out the others.

The Internet

The most important new development in the collection, organization, and distribution of information of all kinds is its digitalization and the easy access to this digitalized information by millions upon millions of computers and servers interconnected through the Internet. (See Figure 6.3 on page 163 for a timeline on the development of the Internet.) The rise in the use of the Internet, through broadband connections in homes, schools, libraries, and the workplace and increasingly through handheld devices such as PDAs and cellphones, has been stunning. In 2005, 73 percent of Americans said they used the Internet, including about one in three over the age of 65; 60 million claimed to have broadband connections in their homes in 2004, up from 6 million in 2000.[13] Ninety-seven million people have used government Web sites; 84 million have used the Internet to look for political news or for information about candidates and political campaigns. Here are a few other numbers from 2004 (keep in mind that most experts estimate a 10 to 20 percent increase annually in these numbers since then); on a typical day,[14]

- 70 million people went online, up from 52 million in 2000.
- 35 million people went online to get news, up from 19 million in 2000.
- 24 million people went online to look for political news or information, up from 9 million in 2000.

To be sure, most people use the Internet for such nonpolitical activities as sending and receiving e-mail, sharing photos, arranging travel and vacations, participating in online auctions, shopping for products, playing interactive

By the Numbers

How much serious crime is there in the United States?

"If it bleeds, it leads" seems to be the mantra of television news. Indeed, we are in danger in this country of being overwhelmed by news stories about crime, and the problem seems to be getting worse. While coverage of public affairs and foreign affairs has been falling, news coverage of crime has flourished, especially on local news telecasts.

Why It Matters: If television news broadcasts are accurately portraying real trends in crime, then they are doing a public service. If portrayals are inaccurate, then the public is being misled. This is problematic because public and official perceptions about the scale of particular social problems affect politics and government deeply. For example,

- When pressed by the public to address a perceived problem, government officials respond by redirecting resources at the problem and make budget and personnel decisions in light of it. If the problem is a false one, then government attention and resources get used ineffectively.

- Candidates campaign on issues that are most salient to the public. When the public misperceives the scale of a problem, it makes electoral choices based on irrelevant grounds.

- The more threatening the public finds a particular problem, the more it pushes aside other public priorities, such as education and health care.

The Story Behind the Crime Numbers: How accurately are the news media portraying the true state of affairs? To put it bluntly, not very well. Crime in general, and violent crime in particular, declined substantially during the 1990s, at precisely the same time that concerns about crime were at the forefront of media, popular attention, and political saliency. How do we know this to be the case?

The two most widely used measures of the incidence of crime in the United States are the Uniform Crime Report (UCR) of the FBI and the National Crime Victimization Survey (NCVS) of the Department of Justice. Each counts the incidence of crime in a different way. The UCR is based on reports from law enforcement agencies and is meant to help state and local police departments track their own performance and to plan their budgets. The NCVS is based on a survey of victims of crime and is used to assess how crime is experienced by Americans and how it affects them and their families.

Calculating the Crime Rate: The FBI's UCR, based on reports submitted voluntarily by state and local law enforcement agencies, counts the annual incidence of "violent crimes" (murder, forcible rape, robbery, and aggravated assault), "property crimes" (burglary, larceny-theft, motor vehicle theft, and arson), and "serious crimes" (all of the above). However, here is what is most important about the FBI's methodology: *It only counts crimes that come to the attention of police.*

The Justice Department's NCVS is based on an annual survey of roughly 50,000 randomly selected U.S. households. One person over the age of 18 in

blog

The common term for a weblog, a website on which an individual or group posts text, photos, audio files, and more, on a regular basis for others to view and respond to.

games, and more. But many millions use it, as the numbers suggest, to examine candidate, party, government, and advocacy group Web sites; read commentaries at political and ideologically oriented **blog** sites (where they can add their own comments); read materials on the Web sites of news organizations (newspapers, magazines, television networks and stations, and the like); make contributions to candidates, parties, and advocacy organizations; listen to political podcasts; access public affairs information from online university and public libraries, as well as from online encyclopedia-type sites such as Wikipedia and infoplease; and download news-related podcasts and videocasts.

each household is interviewed about any crimes that may have been committed against any member of the household during the previous year. The result is annual crime *victimization* information for more than 100,000 people, a very large number for a national survey. Because the NCVS includes crimes experienced by people that are never reported to the authorities, it tends to show higher rates of serious crime than the UCR.

Criticisms of Crime Rate Calculations: The experts generally prefer the NCVS numbers to those of the UCR for understanding the dimensions of the crime problem. The principal problems with the UCR concern the accuracy of recording and reporting crime. For example,

- Many serious crimes, especially rape, go unreported to police. The fact that the UCR came closer to the NCVS numbers starting in the 1990s may mean that more crimes are being reported than in the past.

- Ideas about what constitutes a serious crime may change as social mores change. Domestic violence was treated in the past by police as a family matter; now it tends to get recorded and reported by police.

- A small number of law enforcement agencies do not participate in the UCR reporting system or do not treat it with the seriousness that the FBI hopes for.

What to Watch For: Each way of measuring crime is valid and has its purposes. Although the UCR measure has some problems, it does a fairly good job of telling us what is going on year to year with respect to police encounters with crime. This, in turn, is useful to national, state, and local governments in deciding on budget and staffing issues for law enforcement. The NCVS does a very good job of

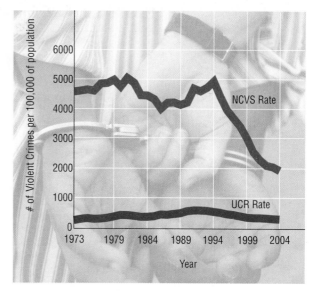

Serious Violent Crimes

Source: Crime Victimization 2004 and *Uniform Crime Reports,* Bureau of Justice Statistics, 2005.

telling us what is going on year to year with respect to overall victimization trends, and gives us a handle on the size of the underlying crime problem. The lesson here is to use the statistic that conforms most closely to the purposes of your inquiry.

What Do You Think? Do you believe that television news programs underplay or overplay the incidence of violent crime? Monitor local and national news for the next week or so and try to keep a running count of stories about crime. How does your count match what the UCR and NCVS numbers are telling us about crime?

The Internet has also become important in other ways that are relevant for politics. For one thing, e-mail has made it much easier for people to contact public officials to express their views. The Internet has also become a way for political activists of every persuasion to organize protests and demonstrations, publicize and raise money for their causes, and bring pressure to bear on public officials. It has also come of age in political campaigns. Howard Dean was a pioneer in this development in his run for the Democratic presidential nomination in 2004. Before then, no candidates had tapped the full potential of the Internet. Virtually all candidates for federal

FIGURE 6.2 • **Rising Mistrust of the News Media**

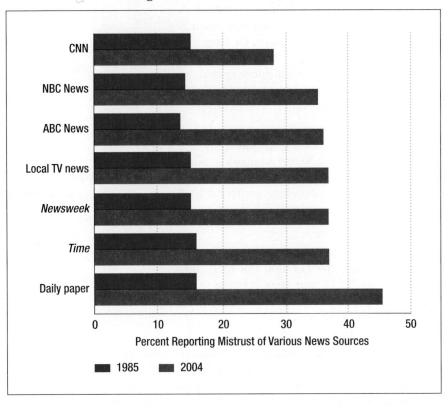

Americans' trust in the mainstream news media has dropped dramatically since the mid-1980s. It is not entirely clear why this has happened. Some blame the rise of "infotainment," which has arguably debased the news, while others blame the rise in bitter partisanship in American political life, which has increased distrust of national institutions across the board, including the news media.

Source: Pew Research Center poll, June 2004.

office had Web sites by the 2000 and 2002 electoral cycles, but the sites were mainly passive in character—places for posting policy papers and news of the candidate. Dean's campaign relied heavily on e-mail to contact and build a network of supporters, particularly among younger, computer-literate voters, asking for their help, attendance at rallies, and financial contributions. The response shocked the political pros and moved Dean to the front rank of contenders for the nomination months before the first primary in the snows of New Hampshire.

We will have more to say about these uses of the Internet as we examine social movements, interest groups, parties, and campaigns in later chapters. For now, we are interested in the Internet as a source of news and information, sometimes in competition with, sometimes in conjunction with, the news media: newspapers, television, magazines, and radio. The point to be made here is that the Internet is an incredibly vast source for political and public affairs news and information, some of it filtered by editorial processes typical of other news media outlets, but much of it uncontrolled, unconfirmed, speculative, passionate, and sometimes hysterical.[15] These characteristics make the medium quite compelling as a source of news and information, but one that must be used with great care.

FIGURE 6.3 ● **Timeline: The Internet**

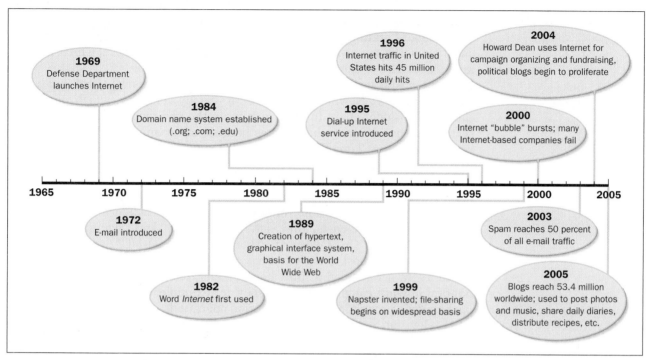

Sources: Infoplease, **www.infoplease.com**; "The Blogging Geyser," Perseus Research, **www.perseus.com/survey/news/releases** (April 8, 2005).

How the News Media Work

Whether citizens get from the news media the kinds of information they need for democracy to work properly depends on how the media are organized and function. In the remainder of this chapter, we focus on news media organizations and journalists, rather than on the various and exotic new forms of media, because, despite the rise of the Internet and the fragmentation of existing news media outlets, most people still get their news from fairly traditional sources.[16] Television remains, for example, the main source of news for most people—whether network or cable news stations or local news outlets—and much of what is on television news is, in turn, shaped by the treatment of the news in the nation's leading newspapers, particularly *The New York Times* and *The Wall Street Journal*. And much of the news content on popular Web sites, such as Yahoo, Google, and America Online (AOL), is provided by traditional news organizations. And, most political blogs contain links to the major news media outlets. So we want to know how the news media are organized, how they fashion the news, and what effects they have on politics and government.

Organization of the News Media

News media in the United States are privately owned businesses. Most are either very large businesses in their own right or, more typically, part of very large corporate empires.

Corporate Ownership Some television stations and newspapers—especially the smaller ones—are still owned locally, by families or by groups of investors, although they account for a rapidly declining share of the total. Most of the biggest stations and newspapers, however, as well as the television and cable networks, are owned by large media corporations, some of which, in turn, are subsidiaries of enormous conglomerates.

Each media sector is dominated by a few firms. Gannett (*USA Today* and 99 other dailies), Newhouse, and the McClatchy company (which purchased the Knight Ridder chain in 2006) dominate the newspaper business, a media sector that has fallen on hard times because of declining readership and advertising revenue. Time Warner dominates magazine publishing and owns the AOL Internet portal and Internet service. General Electric, Disney, News Corp., and Viacom dominate television. Six corporations receive more than half of all book-publishing revenues. Clear Channel, with 1,200 stations across the country, dominates radio (although it is losing audience to alternatives such as iPods, Pod-casts, and satellite radio[17]). And five firms (Warner Communications, Gulf+Western, Disney, Universal-MCA, and Columbia Pictures) receive most of the gross box office revenues from movies.[18]

Mergers across media lines have accelerated in recent years, leaving a handful of giant conglomerates. Disney, for example, owns not only its theme parks, movie production and distribution operations, and sports teams, but the ABC television network, local TV and radio stations in the nation's largest cities, cable television operations, and book publishers. In addition to magazines—including *Time, Fortune, Money, People,* and *Sports Illustrated*—Time Warner owns a major movie studio, its own cable TV network and cable production companies, theme parks, and AOL. Rupert Murdoch's News Corp. owns local TV stations in many of the nation's largest cities, cable and satellite operations (including Fox News and Direct TV), the 20th Century Fox film company, the *New York Post* and major newspapers in Great Britain and Australia, a stable of magazines and journals (including the conservative *Weekly Standard*), Harper Collins and Harper Morrow book companies, and radio and TV operations in Europe and Asia.

Merger Buzz

Walt Disney CEO Robert Iger, right, shakes hands with Pixar CEO Steve Jobs at the announcement in 2006 of Disney's purchase of the award-winning animation company. Jobs, the CEO of Apple as well as Pixar, agreed to join the Disney board, heightening investor confidence in Disney's animation and movie-making future.

Scholars disagree about the effect of corporate ownership and increased media concentration. A few see efficiency gains and an increase in the output and availability of information. But some critics maintain that the concentrated corporate control of our media adds dangerously to the already strong business presence in American politics. Others worry that increased concentration of media ownership may lead to less diversity of news and opinion. Still others worry that news organizations may pull their punches when reporting about the activities of their corporate parents or partners. Will ABC News go easy on problems at Disney, which owns ABC?

Uniformity and Diversity Whoever owns them, most newspapers and television stations depend largely on the same sources for news. Political scientist Lance Bennett points out that while there is a growing diversity of news outlets in the United States—more specialized magazines, television channels, and newspaper home pages on the Web—news sources are contracting. That is to say, much of what comes to us over a multitude of media avenues originates in fewer and fewer centralized sources.[19] Almost all major newspapers in the country subscribe to the AP wire service. Local radio stations increasingly buy headlines for their brief on-the-hour updates from a handful of headline service providers. Television news increasingly buys raw video footage, for in-house editing and scripting, from a handful of providers including Independent Television News (ITN), rather than having their own reporters and film crews on the ground. The AP supplies most of the main national and international news stories for newspapers and local news (although Reuter's is increasingly important)—even those that are rewritten to carry a local reporter's byline. Most of what appears on network and cable television news, too, is inspired by the AP wire, although they often take their lead from the major national newspapers such as *The New York Times, The Wall Street Journal,* and the *Washington Post.* National and local television news organizations depend on centralized news and video suppliers, with fewer of them using their own reporters. This is why viewers are likely to see the same news (and sports) footage on different stations as they switch channels, although each station adds its own "voiceover" from a reporter or news anchor. In most cases, the person doing the voiceover has no direct relationship to the story.

Profit Motives Media corporations, like other corporations, are in business primarily to make a profit. This fact has important consequences. It means, for example, that the major news media must appeal to audiences and get many people to buy their publications, the key to attracting advertising revenues. If most people are mainly interested in entertainment and want their news short, snappy, and sensational—what has come to be called **infotainment**—that is what they will get on network and cable television news and in *USA Today.* The process is especially well developed in evening local news broadcasts where coverage of politics and government have been "crowded out by coverage of crime, sports, weather, lifestyles and other audience-grabbing topics."[20]

Soft News vs. Hard News

infotainment
The merging of hard news and entertainment in news presentations.

Political Newsmaking

The kind of news that the media present is affected by the organization and technology of news gathering and news production. Much depends on where reporters are, what sources they talk to, and what sorts of video pictures are available.

The Limited Geography of Political News   Serious national news comes from a surprisingly few places. For the most part, the news comes from Washington, D.C., the seat of the federal government, and New York City, the center of publishing and finance in the United States. This is where most news media companies locate their reporters, though a few other areas get coverage as well. We show how the news is geographically concentrated in the "Mapping American Politics" feature.

The major television networks and most newspapers cannot afford to station many reporters outside Washington or New York. The networks usually add just Chicago, Los Angeles, Miami, and Houston or Dallas. When stories break in San Francisco or Seattle, news organizations can rush reporters to the area or turn to part-time "stringers" to do the reporting. Some significant stories from outside the main media centers simply do not make it into the national news. News-only channels, such as CNN, CNBC, and Fox News, have a big advantage on fast-breaking news, which they are ready to cover (through their own reporters or the purchase of local footage) and use immediately on their continuous newscasts.

While some newspapers have strong regional bureaus, the majority print mostly wire service reports of news from elsewhere around the country. The television networks' assignment editors also rely on the wire services to decide what stories to cover; during one month that was studied, NBC got the idea for 70 percent of its domestic film stories from the wire services.[21]

Because so much expensive, high-tech equipment is involved, and because a considerable amount of editing is required to turn raw video into coherent stories, most television news coverage is assigned to predictable events—news conferences and the like—long before they happen, usually in one of the cities with a permanent television crew. For such spontaneous news as riots, acci-

Putting Out the Day's Paper

Newspapers such as the Philadelphia *Evening Bulletin* tend to rely on wire services for source materials for their national and international news stories, although they will often have several of their own reporters in important cities such as Washington and New York. Much of their original journalistic efforts are aimed at local and regional issues.

dents, and natural disasters, special video camera crews can be rushed to the location, but they usually arrive after the main events occur and have to rely on "reaction" interviews or aftermath stories. This is not always true; occasionally television news organizations find themselves in the middle of an unfolding set of events and can convey its texture, explore its human meaning, and speculate about its political implications in particularly meaningful ways. This was certainly true of television coverage of the Hurricane Katrina disaster and its immediate aftermath in 2005.

Dependence on Official Sources

Dependence on Official Sources   Most political news is based on what public officials say. This fact has important consequences for how well the media serve democracy.

Beats and Routines   A newspaper or television reporter's work is usually organized around a particular **beat,** which he or she checks every day for news stories. Most political beats center on some official government institution that regularly produces news, such as a local police station or city council, the White House, Congress, the Pentagon, an American embassy abroad, or a country's foreign ministry.

In fact, many news reports are created or originated by officials, not by reporters. Investigative reporting of the sort that Carl Bernstein and Robert Woodward did to uncover the Watergate scandal in the early 1970s is rare because it is so time consuming and expensive. Most reporters get most of their stories quickly and efficiently from press conferences and the press releases that officials write, along with comments solicited from other officials. One pioneering study by Leon Sigal found that government officials, domestic or foreign, were the sources of nearly three-quarters of all news in *The New York*

beat
The assigned location where a reporter regularly gathers news stories.

Reporting from the White House

Much national television newsmaking takes place in Washington, D.C., where reporters have access to government officials and to a wide variety of dramatic visual backdrops. Brian Williams, for example, reported more than a few stories from in front of the White House before moving to the main anchor position on the NBC *Nightly News* telecast.

Mapping American Politics

The limited geography of national news

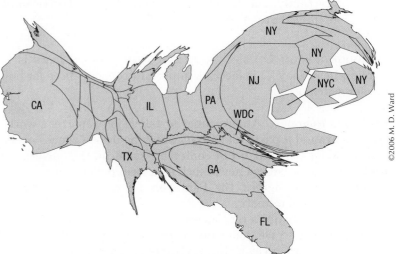

Introduction: Most national political reporters are located in and file their stories from two main locations: Washington, D.C., site of the federal government and most of the nation's most influential think tanks and interest group organizations, and New York City, the center of most media operations and key national and glo-bal financial institutions. For national news involving more than politics and governmental affairs or closely related economic issues, reporters tend to file stories from a broader range of geographical locations, although not equally from all areas around the United States. This is hardly surprising; maintaining reporters is expensive, so news organizations concentrate their news gathering where they will get the most bang for the buck: where the most important news occurs.

Headline News: Size of States in Proportion to Number of Headlines

Mapping the News: The cartogram depicts the states and the District of Columbia resized from normal in proportion to the number of headlines in wire-service stories originating from these locations in re-

©2006 M. D. Ward

Times and the *Washington Post*. Moreover, the vast majority, 70 to 90 percent of all news stories, were drawn from situations over which the newsmakers had substantial control: press conferences (24.5 percent), interviews (24.7 percent), press releases (17.5 percent), and official proceedings (13 percent).[22] Recent research suggests that the situation described by Sigal remains relatively unchanged.[23]

Beats and news-gathering routines encourage a situation of mutual dependence by reporters (and their news organizations) and government officials. Reporters want stories; they have to cultivate access to people who can provide stories with quotes or anonymous leaks. Officials want favorable publicity and want to avoid or counteract unfavorable publicity. Thus, a comfortable relationship tends to develop. Even when reporters put on a show of aggressive questioning at White House press conferences, they usually work hard to stay on good terms with officials and to avoid fundamental challenges of the officials' positions.

Leaking is in the news, of course, because of the perjury indictment in 2005 of "Scooter" Libby, a close advisor to Vice President Dick Cheney, by a federal grand jury investigating who had leaked Valerie Plame's identity as a CIA agent to friendly journalists. It was widely assumed that the **leak** was an administration attempt meant to put pressure on her husband, a prominent

leak, news
Inside or secret information given to a journalist or media outlet by a government official.

168

cent years. If news stories had originated in various states in proportion to their populations, the states' size would correspond to the relative sizes of their populations. In this cartogram, however, New York City, New York State, New Jersey, and California stand out as sites that generate a disproportionate share of news stores, as do Georgia, Florida, and, given its tiny geographic area (less than 10 miles square), Washington, D.C. New York City and its metropolitan area (which includes parts of New York State, New Jersey, and Connecticut) and Washington, D.C., generate so much news for the reasons cited earlier. Georgia's relatively large size may be due to the fact that both CNN and the federal government's Centers for Disease Control and Prevention are based there. Florida is in the news often because of tight and controversial political contests as well as more than its share of hurricanes. California generates many stories from the entertainment industry, much of which is centered there, as well as from Silicon Valley, the heart of the nation's high-tech industry. Some states virtually disappear, with very few news stories originating in the Mountain West, Southwest, Great Plains, and Midwest (other than Illinois), or the New England states of New Hampshire, Vermont, and Maine. News stories from Texas are less than one might expect, given the importance of the state in American politics, energy production, music, and the high-technology industry in Austin.

What Do You Think?   Do you think it is reasonable that news stories are concentrated in America's centers of governance, communications, finance, and entertainment? If this seems problematic, can you think of some way that news might be gathered to avoid such concentrations? Some people say that the news media are out of touch with the American people. Do you think this is true? If so, does the pattern in the cartogram showing the origins of news stories help explain the situation? Or doesn't it matter that news coverage is based in a few areas?

Map note: Alaska is not shown (although information about Alaska is included in calculations where relevant), and Hawaii is moved closer to the mainland.

Source: Data from Michael Gastner and described in M. T. Gastner and M. E. J. Newman, "Diffusion-Based Method for Producing Density-Equalizing Maps," *Proceedings of the National Academy of Sciences* 101 (May 18, 2004), pp. 7499–7504. Wire service news headlines from 1994 to 1998.

and credible critic of President Bush's weapons-of-mass-destruction rationale for going to war in Iraq, but it has since been shown that the White House was not involved. Nevertheless, leaking is common in Washington, part of the normal currency of journalist-official working relationships. Indeed, Woodward and Bernstein's Watergate story got its start with leaks from the anonymous "Deep Throat," revealed in 2005 to be Mark Felt, deputy director of the FBI during the Nixon administration. Most commonly, leaking is a way for officials to float policy ideas, get themselves noticed and credited with good deeds, undercut rivals in other government agencies, or report real or imagined wrongdoing. It is not yet clear whether the jailing of *New York Times* report Judith Miller for refusing to tell a federal prosecutor the name of her informant in the Plame leak investigation—she was released after revealing that it was "Scooter" Libby—will undermine journalists' ability to protect confidential sources. There is no federal "shield" law granting journalists a legal right to protect their sources, although more than one-half of the states have such laws. Virtually all the remaining states operate under court decisions that provide protection for journalists.[24]

The media's heavy reliance on official sources means that government officials are sometimes able to control what journalists report and how they report it. The Reagan administration was particularly successful at picking a

The Role of the Press

"story of the day" and having many officials feed that story to reporters, with a unified interpretation.[25] The Clinton administration tried to do the same but was not disciplined enough to make it work. President George W. Bush's administration pushed the news management envelope the farthest, eventually acknowledging that it had paid three journalists to write favorable stories, encouraged executive agencies to create news videos for media outlets without revealing the source of the videos, and allowed a political operative to be planted among the accredited White House press corps to ask questions at presidential news conferences.[26]

Military Actions   Dependence on official sources is especially evident in military actions abroad. Because it is wary of the release of information that might help an adversary or undermine public support for U.S. actions—as happened during the Vietnam conflict—the Defense Department tries to restrict access of reporters to military personnel and the battlefield and provide carefully screened information for use by the news media. Information management was especially evident during the 1991 Gulf War to expel Saddam Hussein from Kuwait, with its carefully stage-managed news briefings at U.S. military headquarters in Saudi Arabia featuring video of "smart" weapons, Defense Department organization of press pools to cover parts of the war, and tight restrictions on reporters' access to the battlefields in Kuwait and Iraq. Press management was even more highly developed during the post–9/11 conflict with the Taliban regime in Afghanistan, when reporters found it almost impossible to develop independent information. During phases of the Afghan operation, reporters had little access to military personnel, many of whom were located in scattered and inaccessible locations—often in countries where officials wanted to conceal the nature of U.S. involvement—and involved in special operations that required strict secrecy.

Embedded with the Troops

During the invasion and occupation of Iraq, U.S. military officials allowed journalists to accompany military units in the field. Here, *CBS News* reporter John Roberts reports after a fire fight on the road to Baghdad in 2003.

During the rapid advance to Baghdad to topple Hussein's regime in 2003, the Defense Department encouraged coverage of combat by journalists embedded in combat units, although administration officials continued to exercise control over information about the big picture during the initial stages of the war. In the end, however, the administration was unable to control news about military and civilian casualties during the long occupation, the difficulties of helping to create a new constitution and government for that country, and the abuse of Iraqi prisoners at Abu Ghraib and other prisons. There were simply too many journalists and news organizations from around the world reporting on events there—and too many American soldiers and Iraqi civilians posting what they were seeing and experiencing to weblogs—for the administration and military officials to be able to control the news.

Newsworthiness   Decisions about what kinds of news to print or to televise depend largely on professional judgments about what is **newsworthy.** Exactly what makes a story newsworthy is difficult to spell out, but experienced editors make quick and confident judgments of what their audiences (and their employers) want. If they were consistently wrong, they would probably not remain in their jobs very long.

In practice, newsworthiness seems to depend on such factors as novelty (man bites dog, not dog bites man), drama and human interest, relevance to the lives of Americans, high stakes (physical violence or conflict), and celebrity. Some trivial topics are judged newsworthy, such as the child-rearing practices of Britney Spears or Madonna. As the term *news story* implies, news works best when it can be framed as a familiar kind of narrative: an exposé of greed, sex, or corruption; conflict between politicians; or a foreign affairs crisis. On television, of course, dramatic or startling film footage helps make a story gripping. Important stories without visuals are often pushed aside for less important stories for which visuals exist.

Templates   On many important stories, a subtle "governing template" may prevail, a sense among both reporters and editors that news stories must take a generally agreed-upon slant to be taken seriously and to make it into the news broadcast or the newspaper. This is not because of censorship but because of the development of a general agreement among news reporters and editors that the public already knows what the big story looks like on a range of issues—filling in the details is what is important. Take reporting from China as an example. For many years, editors only wanted to hear about economic prosperity, emerging democratic freedoms, and happy peasants liberated from the economic and personal straightjacket of the Maoist collective farm system. After the pro-democracy demonstrations in Tiannanmen Square were brutally repressed by the People's Liberation Army, however, reporters say that it became almost impossible to write anything positive about China, because the prevailing template about China had changed.[27] Now that China has become a very important trading partner, stories about the Chinese economic miracle have proliferated (as well as some worrying about China as a potential economic, diplomatic, and military rival).

Episodic Foreign Coverage   Very few newspapers other than the *New York Times* can afford to station reporters abroad. Even the *Times* and the networks and wire services cannot regularly cover most nations of the world. They keep reporters in the countries of greatest interest to Americans—those that have big effects on American interests or enjoy close economic or cultural ties with the United States, such as Great Britain, Germany, Japan, Israel, Russia, and

newsworthy
Worth printing or broadcasting as news, according to editors' judgments.

You Are the News Editor

Orange Revolution

The American news media paid a great deal of attention to the "orange revolution" in Ukraine where, in late 2004, massive and peaceful demonstrations forced a rerun of rigged elections. In these elections, opposition leader Viktor Yushchenko became the first democratically elected president of the former Soviet republic. Soon after, news coverage of developments in Ukraine largely disappearred from the news media.

China—and they have regional bureaus in Africa and Latin America. In many countries, however, they depend on "stringers" (local journalists who file occasional reports). During major crises or big events, the media send in temporary news teams, such as the armies of reporters that swarmed to Bosnia and Kosovo during the conflicts with the Serbs and to the countries surrounding Afghanistan during the war to unseat the Taliban and find Osama bin Laden. The result is that most media devote the majority of their attention to limited areas of the world, dropping in only occasionally on others.

Foreign news, therefore, tends to be episodic. An unfamiliar part of the world, such as the Achea region of Indonesia or the Darfour region of the Sudan, suddenly jumps into the headlines with a spectacular story of a tsunami or ethnic cleansing, as with these two, or elsewhere a coup, an invasion, or a famine, which comes as a surprise to most Americans because they have not been prepared by background reports. For a few days or weeks, the story dominates the news, with intensive coverage through pictures, interviews, and commentaries. Then, if nothing new and exciting happens, the story grows stale and disappears from the media. Most viewers are left with little more understanding of the country than they began with. Thus, they find it difficult to form judgments about U.S. foreign policy.[28]

Interpreting

objective journalism

News reported with no evaluative language and with any opinions quoted or attributed to a specific source.

Political news may not make much sense without an interpretation of what it means. Under the informal rules of **objective journalism,** taught in university journalism schools and practiced by the nation's leading newspapers and network news programs, however, explicit interpretations by journalists are avoided, except for commentary or editorials that are labeled as such (some cable news operations, however, and without apology, freely mix commentary

and news). Thus, even if a reporter knows that an official is lying, he or she cannot say so directly but must find someone else who will say so for the record. Staged events—such as a news conference held in a national park to announce a bill to protect the environment—are rarely identified by reporters as staged events. In news stories, most interpretations are left implicit (so that they are hard to detect and argue with) or are given by so-called experts who are interviewed for comments. Often, particular experts are selected by print, broadcast, and telecast journalists because the position the experts will take is entirely predictable.

Experts are selected partly for reasons of convenience and audience appeal: Scholars and commentators who live close to New York City or Washington, D.C., who like to speak in public, who look good on camera, and who are skillful in coming up with colorful quotations on a variety of subjects, are contacted again and again. They often show up on television to comment on the news of the day, even on issues that are far from the area of their special expertise. In many cases, these **pundits** are simply well known for being on television often and are not experts on any subject at all. The experts and commentators featured in the media are often ex-officials. Their views are usually in harmony with the political currents of the day; that is, they tend to reflect a fairly narrow spectrum of opinion close to that of the party in power in Washington, D.C., or to the prevailing "conventional wisdom" inside the beltway.

pundits
Somewhat derisive term for print, broadcast, and radio commentators on the political news.

Is the News Biased?

Few topics arouse more disagreement than the question of whether the mass media in the United States have a liberal or conservative **bias**—or any bias at all. Many liberal critics believe the news media favor Republicans and the business establishment,[29] while many conservative critics believe the news media are unfair to Republicans and favor liberal social causes.[30] A small majority of Americans (53 percent in 2004) support the proposition that the news media are biased. Among this group, a majority of Republicans and independents say the news media are biased in a liberal direction, a position taken, as well, by a plurality of Democrats.[31]

bias
Deviation from some ideal standard, such as representativeness or objectivity.

Stunned by Katrina

Many conservative commentators charged that the news media focused on poor African Americans in New Orleans as the main victims of Hurricane Katrina when, in fact, the range of victims was much more diverse and living across a broad swath of Gulf Coast states.

PARTICIPATION

Are the Media Biased?

Liberal Reporters   Surveys of reporters' and journalists' opinions suggest that these individuals tend to be somewhat more liberal than the average American on certain matters, including the environment and such social issues as civil rights and liberties, affirmative action, abortion, and women's rights.[32] This is especially true of those employed by certain elite media organizations, including *The New York Times,* the *Washington Post,* and PBS. It is likely that reporters' liberalism has been reflected in the treatment of issues such as nuclear energy, global warming, and genetically engineered foods. In recent years, to be sure, more conservative reporters and newscasters have gained prominence, especially on cable news telecasts. Bill O'Reilly at Fox News is the most obvious example.

There is, however, little or no systematic evidence that reporters' personal values regularly affect what appears in the mainstream media.[33] Journalists' commitment to the idea of objectivity helps them resist temptation, as do critical scrutiny and rewriting by editors. And in any case, the liberalism of journalists may be offset by their need to rely on official sources, their reliance on experts who are either former officials or associated with centrist or conservative think tanks, and the need to get their stories past editors who are accountable to mostly conservative owners and publishers. So for every set of stories considered biased by conservatives—for example, reporting on the abuse of prisoners at Guantanamo Bay or focusing on the poor African American victims of Hurricane Katrina in New Orleans—there is a matching set of stories considered biased by liberals—for example, not carefully examining the Bush administration's claims about weapons of mass destruction in Iraq or the increase in income inequality in the United States.

Not-so-Liberal Owners and Corporations   The owners and top managers of most media corporations tend to be conservative and Republican. This is hardly surprising. The shareholders and executives of multi-billion-dollar corporations are not very interested in undermining the free enterprise system, for example, or, for that matter, increasing their own taxes, raising labor costs, or losing income from offended advertisers. These owners and managers ultimately decide which reporters, newscasters, and editors to hire or fire, promote or discourage. Journalists who want to get ahead, therefore, may have to come to terms with the policies of the people who own and run media businesses.[34]

The Marketplace The question of political bias in the news media is not so easily answered. Both reporters and news media owners have biases, but it is difficult to see that these views consistently move news reports in one direction or another. For another thing, the news media are now so diverse that pinning a political or partisan label on the "news media" as a whole makes no sense. Talk radio has an orientation different from that of network news. Network news organizations—the favorite whipping boys for both liberal and conservative critics—have lost their near monopoly over news distribution and find themselves in fierce competition for audience with cable news operations, Internet news sources, and news radio. Small journals of opinion, for their part, cover the gamut of political views, from extreme libertarian to socialist.

Media Bias

It is impossible, then, to support the claim that the news media are consistently biased in one partisan direction or another or in one ideological direction or another; all views can be found there. What can be said, however, is that the news media, being themselves business enterprises or part of larger corporate entities, are in business to make a profit for themselves or their corporate parents. This leads many of them to engage in certain practices in news gathering and presentation that may be harmful to their central role in a democratic society. We examine these practices in much of the remainder of this chapter.

Prevailing Themes in Political News

Even if we cannot be sure whether or how the media are biased, it is easy to identify certain tendencies in media coverage, certain beliefs that are assumed, and certain values and points of view that are emphasized.

Nationalism Although perhaps not terribly surprising, most news about foreign affairs takes a definitely pro-American, patriotic point of view, usually putting the United States in a favorable light and its opponents in an unfavorable light. This tendency is especially pronounced in news about military conflicts involving U.S. troops, as in Iraq, but it can be found as well in a wide range of foreign affairs news reports, including those concerning conflicts with other governments on trade, arms control, immigration, and intellectual property rights (patents and copyrights).

Self-censorship and the News

The news media also focus on subjects that interest and concern ordinary Americans, regardless of their importance in the larger picture. For example, in 1980 U.S. newspapers and television devoted intensive, year-long coverage to the fate of 49 Americans held hostage in the U.S. embassy in Tehran, Iran; in the early 1990s, they exhaustively covered a U.S. pilot, Scott O'Grady, who had been shot down over Bosnia. But much less attention was paid to the slaughter of millions of people during the same time in Indonesia, Nigeria, East Timor, Cambodia, and Rwanda.

This nationalistic perspective, together with heavy reliance on U.S. government news sources, means that coverage of foreign news generally harmonizes well with official U.S. foreign policy. Thus, the media tend to go along with the U.S. government in assuming the best about our close allies and the worst about official "enemies." When the United States was assisting Iraq in its war against Iran, for example, Saddam Hussein was depicted in a positive light; during the 1991 Gulf War and the Iraq war that started 12 years later, media characterizations of him changed dramatically.

In foreign policy crisis situations, the reliance on official news sources means that the media sometimes propagate government statements that are

Genocide in Rwanda

Media outlets in the United States did not devote much space or time to the terrible human tragedy that occurred in 1994 in Rwanda, where civil war and government-encouraged genocide resulted in the death of an estimated 1 million people. Here, tired refugees try to make their way to refugee camps in neighboring Zaire.

false or misleading, as in the announcement of unprovoked attacks on U.S. destroyers in the Gulf of Tonkin at the beginning of the Vietnam War (recall the chapter-opening story in Chapter 5). Secret information can also be controlled by the government. The widely reported "missile gap" that led to a big arms buildup during the Kennedy years and the "window of vulnerability" that preceded the Reagan defense budget increases both turned out to be illusions.[35]

It is important to point out that when the use of American armed forces abroad drags on beyond expectations and goals are not met (as in the conflicts in Vietnam and Iraq), the news media can and do become exceedingly negative in their coverage. This may simply reflect the mood change among nonadministration leaders and the public, or it might be a reaction among journalists and news organizations to their initial uncritical coverage of administration policies.

Approval of the American Economic System   Another tendency of the media is to run stories generally approving of free markets, free international trade, and minimal regulation. Our economic system wins approval, while variant or alternative systems, such as European social democracies with comprehensive social welfare programs, are generally portrayed more negatively. Countries whose economic policies mirror those of the U.S. economy, such as Poland and Chile, are praised, while countries trying to preserve a vibrant welfare state, such as France or Sweden, are criticized. Individual U.S. corporations are criticized for errors and misdeeds—for example, companies like Enron that file false earnings reports and accounting firms that help them deceive investors are likely to be hauled before the court of public opinion—but the economic system itself is rarely challenged. This stance is hardly surprising, since most Americans like the U.S. economic system (see Chapter 4), but it may sometimes discourage the consideration of alternative approaches to enduring problems.

Negativity and Scandal One sign that the news media are neither Republican nor Democratic, conservative nor liberal in their sympathies is the relish they take in covering and magnifying scandals involving political leaders and candidates of all stripes. Although the catalyst for these stories may be leaks from inside the government; negative ads aired by rival candidates, political parties, or advocacy groups; or postings to partisan and ideological blogs, they often are picked up by major news media outlets and developed further, occasionally with great relish.[36] These stories are especially compelling to the news media when even the appearance of wrongdoing in the personal lives of prominent people creates dramatic human interest stories. "Whitewater" allegations against President Clinton and First Lady Hillary Rodham Clinton—that they had dealt improperly with a real estate investment and a bank's campaign contributions while Clinton was governor of Arkansas and had obstructed justice while in the White House—were doggedly pursued by the *American Spectator, The New York Times,* and other media for most of Clinton's first term. Sex scandals dogged Bill Clinton for most of his presidency and contributed to his eventual impeachment (see more about this in the "Using the Framework" feature). Sex and financial scandals also claimed, among others, Senator Gary Hart, former House Speakers Jim Wright and Newt Gingrich, and House Speaker–elect Bob Livingston. Stories about Republican majority leader Tom DeLay's questionable campaign fundraising tactics were frequently in the news in the years before he resigned.

Infotainment   The prominent place of scandal in the news media is but one example of a larger and troubling trend: the massive invasion of entertainment values into political reporting and news presentation. As little as 15 to 20 years ago, news was monopolized by the three major television networks and the big-city daily newspapers, and the audiences for the news were fairly stable. In the intervening years, we have seen the media revolutionized by the growth of cable television and the Internet and the multiplication of news outlets. In this new world, the networks and the big-city dailies have lost audience, leaving the fragments of the old and new media to fight for audience share. The best way to do this, media executives have discovered, is to make the news more entertaining, for the worst sin of this brave new media world is to be boring.[37] All too often, "more entertaining" means that sensation and scandal replace consideration of domestic politics, public policies, and international affairs; short and snappy coverage displaces longer, more analytical coverage; dramatic visuals push aside stories that cannot be easily visualized; and stories that feature angry conflict displace stories in which political leaders are trying to make workable compromises.[38] As one student of the news media has put it, ". . . the economic imperative compelling news organizations [is] to find new dramatic stories to tell to fickle audiences who watch TV with the remote control in hand."[39]

The current "culture wars" between liberals and conservatives over the various legacies of the 1960s—involving issues such as abortion, affirmative action, religious values, teaching evolution in schools, same-sex marriage, and more—are perfect grist for the infotainment mill. Thus, a current staple of cable and broadcast television public affairs programming is the gathering of pundits from both sides of the cultural and political divide angrily shouting at one another for 30 or 60 minutes. And, because bringing together shouting pundits is far cheaper than sending reporters into the field to gather hard news, this form of news coverage is becoming more and more common, especially in the world of cable TV. It is highly unlikely that this emergent journalism of assertion and attack improves public understanding of the candidates, political leaders, or public policies.

Conflict and contest are also evident in coverage of campaigns, where the media concentrate on the "horse-race" aspects of election contests, focusing al-

Using the Framework

Monica All the Time

Why did the news media pay so much attention to the Monica Lewinsky story?

Background: President Clinton's sexual liaison with White House intern Monica Lewinsky and his affair with Paula Jones when he was governor of Arkansas dominated the nation's political news from the early summer of 1998 through the end of the Senate impeachment trial of the president in early 1999. It was almost as if nothing else of importance was happening in the nation or around the world. Why is that? Taking a look at how structural, political linkage, and governmental factors affected news coverage will help explain the situation.

Governmental Action

Impeachment hearings and vote in the House provided dramatic news material.

Senate deliberations and vote to remove the president from office provided dramatic news material.

Governmental Level

President Clinton engaged in behavior that was offensive to most Americans. → Many members of Congress believed that President Clinton had obstructed justice in the Paula Jones and Monica Lewinsky affairs. → A bitter partisan atmosphere permeated the 105th Congress. → The Republican Congress and Democratic President Bill Clinton were bitterly deadlocked on a wide range of issues; severe tensions existed between the two branches of government.

Political Linkages Level

Media television executives used "attack journalism," "infotainment," and scandal as a way to attract viewers from a highly fragmented set of media consumers. → The media fell into their "one big story at a time" syndrome. → Web-based and scandal-sheet papers fed leads to major mainstream news media. → The Republican Party used the Lewinsky scandal in advertising for the 1998 congressional elections. → Conservative interest groups also saw advantages in a weakened President Clinton and ran ad campaigns highlighting the Lewinsky matter.

Structural Level

Technological innovations multiplied the number of television channels, all of which require content to fill the hours. → As the Internet developed, it became (among other things) a medium for the distribution of information, opinion, and rumors.

most exclusively on who is winning and who is losing the race and what strategies candidates are using to gain ground or to maintain their lead. When candidates sometimes make a stab at talking seriously about issues, the media almost always treat such talk as a mere stratagem of the long campaign. The perpetual struggle between Congress and the president, built into our constitutional system, is also perfect for the infotainment news industry, especially if the struggle can be personalized, as it was in the years when House Speaker Newt Gingrich was doing battle with President Bill Clinton.

Limited, Fragmented, and Incoherent Political Information Most communications scholars agree that the media coverage of political news has certain distinctive features that result from characteristics of the mass media themselves, including the prevailing technology and organization of news gathering, corporate ownership, and the profit-making drive to appeal to mass audiences. These characteristics of the media mean that news, especially on television, tends to be episodic and fragmented rather than sustained, analytical, or dispassionate. Information comes in bits and pieces, out of context, and without historical background. Its effect is to entertain more than to inform. This may or may not be what people want, but it is what they get.

Effects of the News Media on Politics

The old idea that the mass media have only "minimal effects" on politics is now discredited. The contents of the media do make a difference; they affect public opinion and policymaking in a number of ways, including setting the agenda for public debate and framing how issues are understood.[40]

Agenda Setting

Several studies have demonstrated the effect known as **agenda setting.** The topics that get the most coverage in the news media at any point in time are the same ones that most people tell pollsters are the most important problems

agenda setting
Influencing what people consider important.

The Televised War

The Vietnam War was the first American war fully covered by television. Footage of American deaths and casualties, as well as visual reminders of the terrible consequences of the conflict on the Vietnamese civilian population, helped turn public opinion in the United States against the war. This still from television footage of children napalmed by an accidental American attack on a village of Trang Bang in 1972 is a particularly powerful example of the war coming home to American living rooms.

facing the country. This correlation does not result just from the media's printing what people are most interested in; it is a real effect of what appears in the media. In controlled experiments, people who are shown doctored television news broadcasts emphasizing a particular problem (e.g., national defense) mention that problem as being important more often than people who have seen broadcasts that have not been tampered with.[41]

Of course, media managers do not arbitrarily decide what news to emphasize; their decisions reflect what is happening in the world and what American audiences care about. If there is a war or an economic depression, the media report it. But some research has indicated that what the media cover sometimes diverges from actual trends in problems. Publicity about crime, for example, may reflect editors' fears or a few dramatic incidents rather than a rising crime rate. When the two diverge, it seems to be the media's emphasis rather than real trends that affects public opinion.[42]

When the media decide to highlight a human rights tragedy in "real time," such as "ethnic cleansing" in Kosovo, public officials often feel compelled to act, as Bill Clinton did when he was president. When the media ignore equally troubling human tragedies, such as the recent genocide in Darfour, public officials can attend to other matters. One scholarly study shows that in the foreign policy area, media choices about coverage shape what presidents pay attention to.[43]

Framing and Effects on Policy Preferences

framing

Providing a context for interpretation.

Experiments also indicate that the media's **framing,** or interpretation of stories, affects how people think about political problems and how they assign blame. Several commentators noticed during the Katrina disaster in New Orleans, for example, that TV news stories featuring whites talked of "foraging for food and supplies," while those featuring blacks talked of looting. There are reasons to believe that public impressions of what was going in the city were affected by this coverage. To take another example, whether citizens ascribe poverty to the laziness of the poor or to the nature of the economy, for example, depends partly on whether the media run stories about poor individuals (implying that they are responsible for their own plight) or stories about overall economic trends such as wage stagnation and unemployment.[44]

Use of Media by the American Public

What appears in the news media affects people's policy preferences as well. One study found, for example, that the public is more likely to favor government programs to help black Americans when the news media frame racial problems in terms of failures of society to live up to the tradition of equality in the United States. The public is less supportive of these programs when the news media frame the origins of racial problems in terms of individual failures to be self-reliant and responsible.[45] Another study found that changes in the percentages of the public that favored various policies could be predicted rather accurately by what sorts of stories appeared on network television news shows between one opinion survey and the next. News from experts, commentators, and popular presidents had especially strong effects.[46]

Fueling Cynicism

Americans are quite cynical about the political parties, politicians, and most incumbent political leaders. To some extent, this has been true since the founding of the nation. Nevertheless, scholars and political commentators have noted a considerable increase in negative feelings about the political system over the past two decades or so. Many commentators believe that news

media coverage of American politics has a great deal to do with this attitude change.[47] As the adversarial-attack journalism style and infotainment have taken over political reporting, serious consideration of the issues, careful examination of policy alternatives, and dispassionate examination of the actions of government institutions have taken a back seat to a steady diet of charges about personal misbehavior. When President George H. W. Bush joined a world leader at a press conference in 1992 to describe the nature of the agreement they had reached, reporters asked him instead about rumors of an extramarital affair a few years earlier. With the message being delivered by the mass media that political issues are really about special-interest maneuvering, that political leaders and aspiring political leaders never say what they mean or mean what they say, that all of them have something in their personal lives they want to hide, and that even the most admired of the lot have feet of clay, is it any wonder that the American people are becoming increasingly disenchanted with the whole business?

Government Regulation of the Media

Our Constitution protects freedom of the press, and the U.S. government has less legal control over the media than the governments of most other countries do (see Chapter 15 for more on press freedoms). But our government has the authority to make various technical and substantive regulations on the electronic media, if it wishes.

Print Media

Early in American history, government sometimes interfered with the press in a heavy-handed way. Under the Alien and Sedition Acts of 1798, for example, several Anti-Federalist newspaper editors were jailed for criticizing John Adams's administration. In recent years, however, the Constitution has been interpreted as forbidding government from preventing the publication of most kinds of political information or from punishing its publication afterward. The main exceptions involve national security, especially during wartime.

Prior Restraint

Several U.S. Supreme Court decisions, beginning in the 1920s and 1930s, have ensured the press a great deal of constitutional protection. The First Amendment provision that Congress shall make no law "abridging freedom of speech, or of the press" has been held by the Supreme Court to prevent the federal censorship of newspapers or magazines. Only under the most pressing circumstances of danger to national security can the government engage in **prior restraint** and prevent the publication of material to which it objects (see Chapter 15).

prior restraint

The government's power to prevent publication, as opposed to punishment afterward.

On June 30, 1971, for example, the Supreme Court denied a request by the Nixon administration to restrain *The New York Times* and the *Washington Post* from publishing excerpts from the *Pentagon Papers,* a secret Defense Department history of the United States' involvement in Vietnam. The Court declared that "the Government 'thus carries a heavy burden of showing justification for the enforcement of such a restraint.' . . . The Government had not met that burden." Justice Hugo Black's concurring opinion has become an important statement on freedom of the press.

Wartime Controls

In a sense, however, the *Pentagon Papers* case was an easy one because it concerned the right to publish a two-year-old history and analysis of past government policy, not information about current military or foreign policy actions that could jeopardize American lives. During wartime, the government has almost always asserted broad powers to control what reporters can see and what they can print. During World War II, for example, the Office of Censorship monitored all news entering and leaving the country, but it focused mainly on news about casualties and troop and ship movements rather than on political matters.

Relatively free news media access to the Vietnam War eventually brought a flood of negative stories.[48] U.S. officials, having learned their lesson, restricted journalists' access to the battlefield and American troops during the 1991 Gulf War with Iraq[49] and in the initial stages of the war against the Taliban regime in Afghanistan following 9/11. During the 2003 invasion of Iraq, embedded journalists had access to the battlefront—or, more accurately, the battlefront in the

From the Front

During the Vietnam War, journalists were generally able to go anywhere in the country to cover a story, provided they could find transportation and were willing to accept the risk of being in a war zone. Much of the reporting was highly critical of the war effort. As a result, later presidents and the Pentagon imposed much tighter controls on journalists reporting on U.S. military engagements in Panama, Grenada, Kuwait, Bosnia, and Iraq.

south of the country with the invasion launched from Kuwait—but the Pentagon and the administration tried to maintain control over reporting of the wider war and its implications.[50] They were not entirely successful, however, because European, Asian, and Arabic news organizations also were reporting the war, often from the point of view of the Iraqis. Although few Americans had access to these print and television news reports, many people around the world did, fueling the rise of anti-American feelings in many countries.[51] And, as you have seen, efforts to keep bad news from the American people about the occupation of Iraq were not successful.

The Electronic Media

The electronic media are more directly regulated by government than the print media, although such regulation has been diminishing.

VIDEO DEBATE

Censorship and the FCC

Government Licensing of the Airwaves   The federal government has broad powers to regulate the use of the airwaves, which are considered public property. Ever since the passage of the Radio Act of 1927 and the Communications Act of 1934, which established the Federal Communications Commission (FCC), the government has licensed radio and television stations and has required them to observe certain rules as a condition for obtaining licenses.

FCC rules specify the frequencies on which stations can broadcast and the amount of power they can use in order to prevent interference among broadcasters of the sort that had brought chaos to radio during the 1920s. Government regulations divide the VHF television band into 12 channels and allocate them in such a way that most major cities have three VHF stations—the main reason for the early emergence of only three major networks. The development of cable television greatly expanded variety and competition.

For a long time, to prevent monopolies of scarce channels, federal rules prohibited networks or anyone else from owning more than five local VHF stations around the country.[52] Deregulation during the 1990s loosened these rules. The most important step was passage of the Telecommunications Act of 1996, which, in addition to removing most restrictions on competition among telephone, cable, and broadcast companies and providing new frequencies for high-definition TV, removed most restrictions on the number of radio and television stations that a company could own nationally and within a single media market. The act also reduced restrictions on ownership across media sectors, nationally and locally, meaning that single giant companies could increase their holdings of radio and television stations, cable operations, and newspapers. To the surprise of no one, the industry experienced a wave of mergers in the years following passage of the act.

Concerns among many Americans about the increased availability of sexually suggestive materials on network and cable television and on radio have triggered increased scrutiny of media decency practices and standards by the FCC, as well as by congressional investigations. Public officials were especially sensitive to the public outcry over Janet Jackson's televised half-time performance at the Super Bowl in 2004. Worried by the FCC's renewed attention and increased willingness to levy fines for on-air indecency, some media corporations moved quickly to try to stem the tide. The major TV networks, for example, announced moves to beef up their standards departments and began to delay many live broadcasts for a few seconds so that potentially offensive material might be deleted. In 2004, Clear Channel Communications, worried about potential fines from the FCC, dropped

Howard Stern on the Air

Controversial talk show host Howard Stern, shown here doing his radio show in January 2006, has been able to escape the scrutiny of federal regulators worried about his use of indecent language by moving to Sirius Satellite Radio. Subscription-based satellite broadcasts fall outside the regular regulatory domain of the Federal Communications Commission.

"shock-jock" Howard Stern from its stations, who then migrated to satellite radio where little federal regulation exists. In 2005, major cable operators announced their intention to put together "family-friendly" channel plans and make them available as an option for their customers.

Public Service Broadcasting   The FCC was mandated by Congress to regulate the airwaves for the "public interest, convenience, or necessity." This vague phrase has been interpreted as including "the development of an informed public opinion through the public dissemination of news and ideas concerning the vital public issues of the day," with ideas coming from "diverse and antagonistic sources," and with an emphasis on service to the local community.

In practice, this requirement has mainly meant FCC pressure (backed up by the threat of not renewing stations' licenses) to provide a certain number of hours of news and "public service" broadcasting. Thus, government regulation created an artificial demand for news programming, before it became profitable, and contributed to the rise and expansion of network news and to the development of documentaries and news specials. In that way, government regulation presumably contributed to informed public opinion and to democracy. Recently, however, this public service requirement has been eroded and the amount of this kind of programming has declined.

fairness doctrine

The former requirement that television stations present contrasting points of view.

Fairness   For many years, the **fairness doctrine** of 1949 required that licensees present contrasting viewpoints on any controversial issue of public importance that was discussed. This requirement led to efforts at balance—presenting two sides on any issue that was mentioned—and sometimes to the avoidance of controversial issues altogether. It was left mostly up to broadcasters, however, to decide what was important or controversial and what constituted a fair reply and a fair amount of time to give it.

Fairness is not easy to define: Which of the unlimited number of possible opinions deserves a hearing? The FCC itself long ago made clear that it did not intend to make time available to "communist viewpoints," and both of the "two sides" that the media air are usually quite mainstream.

Equal Time Similarly, the **equal time provision** of the 1934 Communications Act required that except for news programs, stations that granted (or sold) air time to any one candidate for public office had to grant (or sell) other candidates equal time. This requirement threatened to cause the media great expense when minor party candidates insisted on their share of air time or when opponents wanted to reply to political speeches by incumbent presidents in election years. Contrary to its intent, therefore, this requirement led to some curtailment of political programming.

The equal time provision was suspended in 1960 to allow televised debates between candidates John F. Kennedy and Richard M. Nixon, and in 1976 and 1980, the FCC permitted the staging of the Ford–Carter and Carter–Reagan debates as "public meetings," sponsored by the League of Women Voters, to get around the provision. In 1983, the FCC declared that radio and television broadcasters were free to stage debates at all political levels among candidates of their own choosing.[53] Broadcasters and the Commission on Presidential Debates (a nonpartisan corporation created to sponsor presidential debates) decided to allow Independent candidate Ross Perot to join the debates in 1992 (Bush v. Clinton) and 1996 (Clinton v. Dole), but chose not to include Green Party candidate Ralph Nader in 2000 (W. Bush v. Gore), much to the chagrin of Nader and his supporters. In 2004, the presidential debates included only John Kerry and George W. Bush, the major party candidates.

The Internet When television and radio were introduced, the industries were regulated by the federal government almost immediately. This has not been the case for the Internet, despite its extraordinary growth and social impact. Although initially a product of government encouragement and financial support—it was first created to link together university and government defense researchers[54]—the Internet has been relatively free from regulation, although there have been calls for government to prevent certain content from appearing on it. The few attempts that have been made have not been successful. Congress, for example, tried to ban obscenity on the Net, but the Supreme Court in 1997 declared the statute an unconstitutional restriction of free speech. When the Clinton administration tried to prevent people from posting encryption codes, a federal court declared the effort as unconstitutional on the

equal time provision
The former requirement that television stations give or sell the same amount of time to all competing candidates.

Using the Democracy Standard

Do the news media help or hinder the practice of democracy?

PROPOSITION: **The news media are an important ingredient in making American politics democratic.**

AGREE   Without the information provided by the news media, ordinary citizens would have little hope of learning what is happening abroad; they could not begin to think about what sorts of policies the United States should pursue in foreign affairs. Nor, without the news media, could most Americans learn what their government is doing domestically, what sorts of candidates are running for office, or what kinds of public policies are being considered.

In these respects, the spread of the news media in the United States, and the penetration of millions of homes by newspapers, radio, television, and computers, has undoubtedly helped democracy. It has made it much easier for ordinary citizens to decide about alternative public policies, to judge the actions of government and elected leaders, and to make decisions about who should be elected to office. News media thus tend to broaden the scope of conflict and contribute to political equality. When citizens, rather than just political leaders or special-interest groups, know what is going on, they can have a voice in politics. Moreover, interactive media and media-published polls help politicians hear that voice.

Scholars and media critics who want the news media to   **DISAGREE**   be highly informative, analytical, and issue oriented are appalled by the personalized, episodic, dramatic, and fragmented character of most news stories, which do not provide sustained and coherent explanations of what is going on. Others worry about ideological biases they think arise from a leftist media elite or from a corporate-owned media industry. Some criticize the media's patriotic and ethnocentric tendencies to support official U.S. foreign policy and even to pass along deliberate untruths stated by government officials. If the news media regularly present one-sided or false pictures of politics, people may form mistaken policy preferences. Government responsiveness to manipulated preferences would not be truly democratic.

Still other critics worry that constant media exposés of alleged official wrongdoing or government inefficiency, and the mocking tone aimed at virtually all political leaders by journalists and talk radio hosts, have fueled the growing political cynicism of the public. If this is true, the media are not serving democracy as well as they might.

CONSIDER   • Which news media sources do you pay most attention to? Network or cable news programs? Talk radio? Websites of news organizations, advocacy groups, or nonpartisan policy organizations? Newspapers or magazines? Politically oriented blogs?   • Looking back on important recent actions by government leaders—for example, waging war and occupation in Iraq or the struggle in Congress to fashion a new national energy policy—do you think the news sources you most depend on did a good job in keeping you informed?   • Do you believe you were well served by the news sources you used?   • If not, why do you think this might be the case?   • What did these sources miss and why?   • What do you think they might do to improve their performance as a source of credible news and information for you and other American citizens?

Kids Surf the Web

As Internet usage has expanded in the United States, various and sundry individuals and groups have called for tighter federal regulation of the new medium, primarily to protect children from material with sexual content and to prevent dissemination of hate material. So far, none of the bills passed by Congress to achieve these regulatory goals has passed constitutional muster with the Supreme Court.

same grounds. In the view of the federal courts, at this writing, the Internet is an open medium where people are free to express their views, no different from dissemination of ideas by voice from atop a soap-box or by a pamphlet. Statute and case law in this area is sure to grow, however, as the Internet comes to play an ever-larger role in our lives. The story of Internet regulation is not yet finished. For example, Congress revisited the issue of Internet pornography when it passed the Child Online Protection Act of 1998 designed to block access to material on the Web that might be harmful to children. In 2004, however, the Supreme Court upheld a lower court's ruling blocking the law from taking effect, with the majority suggesting that the new law was an unconstitutional restriction on free speech.

Taken as a whole, then, government regulation of the media does not now amount to much. The trend has been toward a free market system with little government interference. Although the USA Patriot Act allows the federal government to more easily conduct surveillances of Internet and e-mail use by suspected terrorists, the overall conclusion about the light regulatory hand of the government still holds.

Summary

The shape of the news media in the United States has been determined largely by structural factors: technological developments; the growth of the American population and economy; and the development of a privately owned, corporation-dominated media industry.

The profit motive leads the major media to appeal to large audiences by limiting the quantity and depth of political news, by appealing to patriotism and other mainstream political values, and by emphasizing dramatic stories with visual impact and human interest.

News gathering is organized around New York City, Washington, D.C., and a handful of major cities in the United States and abroad. Most foreign countries are ignored unless there are crises or other big stories to communicate. Most news comes from government officials, who cultivate friendly relations with the press and provide accessible press conferences and information handouts.

Observers disagree about whether the media are biased in a liberal or a conservative direction. Reporters tend to be liberal, especially on social issues, but this tendency may be balanced or reversed by conservative owners and editors. The U.S. media tend to reflect ethnocentrism, support U.S. foreign policy, and celebrate American-style capitalism. They also broadcast negative campaign ads, publicize personal scandals, and sharply criticize officials who have lost popularity.

Media stories have substantial effects on the public's perceptions of problems, its interpretations of events, its evaluations of political candidates, and its policy preferences.

The media, especially the print media, are protected from many kinds of government interference by the First Amendment to the Constitution. But censorship occurs during wars and crises, and officials have indirect ways of influencing the news. The electronic media are legally open to direct regulation, but such regulation, including the fairness doctrine and the equal time provision, has mostly lapsed. The Internet remains relatively free from government regulation.

Web Exploration
Agenda Setting

ISSUE: Scholarly research shows that the news media help set the political agenda for both political leaders and ordinary citizens.

SITE: Access the Center for Media and Public Affairs in MyPoliSciLab at **www.mypoliscilab.com.** Go to the "Web Explorations" section for Chapter 6, open "agenda setting," then select "news media studies" on the home page of the MPA site. This will help you see what kinds of stories have received the most media attention in different years and how they have been covered. Look at the most recent studies.

WHAT YOU'VE LEARNED: Has the emphasis in the news changed over time? Are the same kinds of stories carried year after year or not? Is there more or less substantive news about government and politics? Is there more or less news about scandals and government wrong-doing? How well and fairly have news stories been reported?

HINT: Even a cynic might be surprised to learn how much news coverage is directed at scandal and sensation.

Internet Sources

The Center for Media and Public Affairs
www.cmpa.com
 Studies, commentaries, and forums on media and public affairs.

The State of the News Media
www.stateofthenewsmedia.org
 Annual scholarly review of the state of the news media, with attention to new developments.

The Columbia Journalism Review
www.cjr.org
 The website of the leading scholarly monitor of journalism and journalists; loaded with useful information about all aspects of newsmaking and dissemination.

The Pew Research Center for the People and the Press
www.people-press.org/
 The most complete public opinion surveys on citizen evaluations of the quality of media coverage of public affairs.

Suggestions for Further Reading

Alterman, Eric. *What Liberal Media? The Truth About Bias and the News.* New York: Basic Books, 2003.
 An impassioned yet well-documented answer to the charge that the news media are biased against conservatives.

Bagdikian, Ben H. *The New Media Monopoly,* Boston: Beacon Press, 2004.
 An analysis of the corporate structure of the media and its consequences.

Bennett, W. Lance. *News: Politics of Illusion,* 6th ed. New York: Longman, 2005.
 A critique of the news as trivial and uninformative.

Goldberg, Bernard. *Bias: A CBS Insider Exposes How the Media Distort the News.* New York: Harper Paperbacks, 2003.
 A conservative critique of the CBS News in particular and the mainstream news media in general.

Graber, Doris. *Mass Media and American Politics.* Washington, D.C.: CQ Press, 2006.
 A comprehensive examination of the news media's effect on American politics.

CHAPTER 7

Interest Groups and Business Corporations

Groups Face Off Over Social Security

President Bush pushed hard for reforming Social Security during the 2004 presidential campaign against John Kerry, and he began to carry through on his promise shortly after his reelection. In his 2005 State of the Union address, he told the assembled gathering in the Capitol and a large TV audience that "we must join together to strengthen and save Social Security." Bush proposed, among other changes, that younger workers be allowed to apply a portion of their Social Security payroll tax to individual retirement accounts. He urged Congress to adopt this change and urged the American people to let representatives and senators know they wanted it. Then the president set off on a campaign-style speaking tour around the country, featuring carefully controlled town meetings, to sell his ideas on Social Security reform in general and individual retirement accounts in particular.

The battle over Social Security was joined not only by the two major parties and by their representatives and senators, but by an impressive array of interest groups and advocacy organizations. The president was supported, for example, by the conservative advocacy organization Progress for America, which immediately launched a media advertising campaign in support of his plan (it had spent more than $35 million on campaign advertising for Bush in 2004). Also supporting the president was COMPASS—the Coalition to Modernize and Protect Social Security—an organization created by the Business Round Table, a group composed of the chief executive officers (CEOs) of many of America's largest corporations. COMPASS sponsored rallies and town meetings, spending about $20 million in the effort. USA Next, a conservative advocacy organization that had run harsh anti-Kerry ads during the 2004 presidential contest, ran advertising attacking the American Association of Retired Persons (AARP) for its opposition to the president's proposals, implying in its television advertising campaign that the AARP approved of same-sex marriage. The Club for Growth, a conservative advocacy organization that usually focuses its attacks on Democrats, took several Republican lawmakers to task in its advertising campaign for their purported willingness to raise the retirement age and the payroll tax.

The AARP, a 35-million-member organization representing older and retired Americans, led the campaign against individual retirement accounts within Social Security. It spent more than $10 million in advertising, mainly to inform its members about the pending legislation and encourage them to contact their representatives and senators. Americans United to Protect Social Security, an umbrella organization bringing together various labor unions and Democratic Party–affiliated groups, raised $35 million to oppose the president's plan and staged town hall meetings in Republican con-

gressional districts featuring an empty chair for the invited but absent Republican lawmaker. MoveOn.org, a liberal advocacy group and a notable player in the 2004 presidential and congressional campaigns on behalf of Democrats, ran a television ad on the day of the State of the Union that used Social Security cards to spell out the letters WMD (for weapons of mass destruction), with a voiceover warning, "Make sure you are not misled again." Finally, the AFL-CIO, representing 13 million unionized workers, focused on corporations supporting the president's proposal, staging rallies urging them to withdraw their support.

The president's proposal died quietly in Congress, never making its way out of the several House and Senate committees charged with considering it. Some observers say it was fated to fail because it did not address Social Security's real long-term problems (see more on this in Chapter 17) and that, as polls showed, the president was never able to convince a majority of Americans that it did. Others say that divisions among Republicans over the efficacy and necessity of the proposed changes in

Social Security doomed the proposal.[1] Still others say that Social Security reform was forced to take a back seat to other public concerns, including the war in Iraq, the ongoing threat of terrorism, recurring federal budget deficits, and the recovery effort following Hurricane Katrina. Still others say the plan, so closely identified with President Bush, could not succeed in the face of his declining popularity. Whatever the ultimate cause or causes and whatever the merits of the legislation proposed by the president, what is inescapable in this story is the range of interest groups involved in the battle.

A diverse array of interest groups is involved in all major legislative and executive proposals in the United States, just as they were in the debate over Social Security reform. Although different groups are involved in different policy struggles—business-oriented groups may be most involved in tax and regulatory issues, for example, while more ideological advocacy groups may be most involved in social issues such as abortion and affirmative action—interest groups are major players in American politics and key actors in the formation and execution of public policies in the United States. ■

Thinking Critically About This Chapter

This chapter is about the important role interest groups play in American government and politics, how they go about achieving their ends, and what effects they have in determining government policies in the United States.

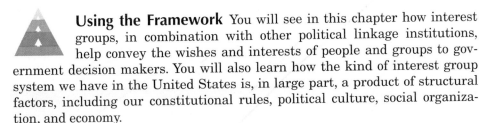 **Using the Framework** You will see in this chapter how interest groups, in combination with other political linkage institutions, help convey the wishes and interests of people and groups to government decision makers. You will also learn how the kind of interest group system we have in the United States is, in large part, a product of structural factors, including our constitutional rules, political culture, social organization, and economy.

 Using the Democracy Standard Interest groups have long held an ambiguous place in American politics. To some, interest groups are "special" interests that act without regard to the public interest and are the instruments of the most privileged parts of American society. To others, interest groups are simply another way by which people and groups in a democratic society get their voices heard by government leaders. Using the democracy standard described in Chapter 1, you will be able to choose between these two positions.

Interest Groups in a Democratic Society: Contrasting Views

Interest groups are private voluntary associations that try to shape public policy. They are made up of people or groups who share an interest or cause that they are trying to protect or advance with the help of government. To do this, interest groups try to influence the behavior of public officials, such as presidents, members of Congress, bureaucrats, and judges. These efforts are often perceived by officials as pressuring them, so interest groups are often called **pressure groups.** The term **lobby** is also commonly used—because of the practice of interest group representatives' talking to representatives and senators in the lobbies outside committee rooms—as in references to the

interest group

A private voluntary association that seeks to influence public policy as a way to protect or advance some interest.

pressure group

An interest group or lobby; an association that brings pressure to bear on government decision makers.

lobby

An interest or pressure group that seeks to convey the group's interest to government decision makers; also, an action by a group or association to influence the behavior of a public official.

Bosses of the Senate

In the late nineteenth century, most Americans thought of the Senate as the captive of large corporate trusts and other special-interest groups, as depicted in this popular cartoon, "Bosses of the Senate."

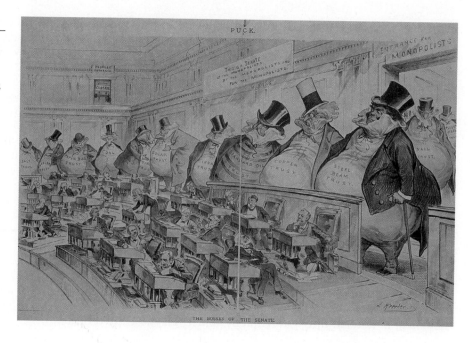

"dairy lobby" or the "gun lobby." *Lobby* is also a verb describing the actions of a group or association trying to influence the behavior of public officials.

The Evils of Factions

The danger to good government and the public interest from interest groups is a familiar theme in American politics. They are usually regarded as narrowly self-interested, out for themselves, and without regard for the public good.

This theme is prominent in *The Federalist,* No. 10, in which James Madison defined **factions** (his term for interest groups and narrow political parties) in the following manner: "A number of citizens, whether amounting to a majority or a minority of the whole, who are united and actuated by some common impulse of passion, or of interest, adverse to the rights of other citizens or to the permanent and aggregate interests of the community."[2] The "evils of faction" theme recurs throughout our history, from the writings of the "muckrakers" at the turn of the twentieth century to the Democratic presidential primary campaign of Howard Dean in 2004.

faction

Madison's term for groups or parties that try to advance their own interests at the expense of the public good.

Interest Group Democracy: The Pluralist Argument

According to many political scientists, however, interest groups do not hurt democracy and the public interest but are an important instrument in attaining both. The argument of these **pluralist** political scientists is shown in Figure 7.1 and goes as follows:[3]

- Free elections, while essential to a democracy, do not adequately communicate the specific wants and interests of the people to political leaders on a continuous basis. These are more accurately, consistently, and frequently conveyed to political leaders by the many groups and organizations to which people belong.

pluralist

A political scientist who views American politics as best understood in terms of the interaction, conflict, and bargaining of groups.

FIGURE 7.1 ● **The Pluralist View of American Politics**

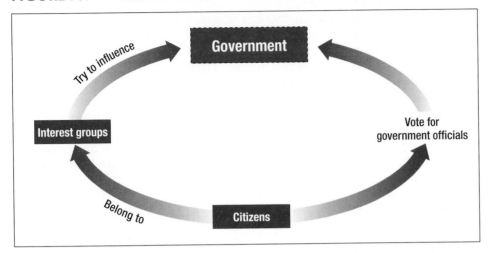

In the pluralist understanding of the way American democracy works, citizens have more than one way to influence government leaders. In addition to voting, citizens also have the opportunity to participate in organizations that convey member views to public officials. Because of weak political parties, federalism, checks and balances, and the separation of powers, access to public officials is relatively easy.

Pluralism

- Interest groups are easy to create; people in the United States are free to join or to organize groups that reflect their interests.

- Because of federalism, checks and balances, and the separation of powers, government power in the United States is broadly dispersed, leaving governmental institutions remarkably porous and open to the entreaties of the many and diverse groups that exist in society.

- Because of the ease of group formation and the accessibility of government, all legitimate interests in society can have their views taken into account by some public official. Because of this, the system is highly democratic.

Pluralists see interest groups, then, not as a problem but as an additional tool of democratic representation, similar to other democratic instruments such as public opinion and elections. We shall explore the degree to which this position is valid in this and other chapters.

Interest Group Formation: Structural, Political Linkage, and Governmental Factors

Nobody knows exactly how many interest groups exist in the United States, but there is wide agreement that the number began to mushroom in the late 1960s, that it has grown steadily ever since, and that it ranges today in the thousands. We have a more precise count, however, of the number of paid lobbyists who work for interest groups in Washington and try to affect government policies. In Washington today, more than 80,000 people work for private associations trying to influence the government, and thousands of others work for law firms whose main business is lobbying.[4] These associations and other lobbyists spent over $3 billion on lobby efforts in Congress in 2004.[5] Because lobbying Congress is only a part of what interest groups do, so these statistics show only the tip of the iceberg.

Much of the increase in the number of interest groups can be explained by the growing number of public interest or citizen groups organized around some cause or idea, rather than an economic or occupational interest, the traditional basis for forming interest groups. These include environmental, consumer protection, pro-life and pro-choice, family values, good government, civil rights, and women's organizations. Another set of important interest groups, long influential in American politics, includes small business associations, large corporations, business trade associations, and the professions. Although this set once dominated the interest group universe by sheer numbers, it is proportionally smaller in number today yet retains substantial influence in American politics and government at all levels,[6] as this chapter will show.

There are a number of reasons so many interest groups exist in the United States.

Diverse Interests

Being a very diverse society, there are simply lots of interests in the United States. Racial, religious, ethnic, and occupational diversity is pronounced. Also varied are the views about abortion, property rights, prayer in the schools, and environmental protection. Our economy is also strikingly complex and multifaceted, and becoming more so. In a free society, these diverse interests usually take organizational forms. Thus, the computer revolution has spawned computer chip manufacturers, software companies, software engineers, computer magazines, Internet services, technical information providers, computer component jobbers, Web designers, and countless others. Each has particular interests to defend or advance before government, and each has formed an association to try to do so. Thus, software engineers have an association to look after their interests, as do software and hardware companies, Internet access providers, digital content providers, industry writers, and so on.

Rules of the Game

The rules of the political game in the United States encourage the formation of interest groups. The First Amendment to the Constitution, for instance, guarantees citizens the right to speak freely, to assemble, and to petition the government, all of which are essential to citizens' ability to form organizations to advance their interests before government. Moreover, the government is organized in such a way that officials are relatively accessible to interest groups. Because of federalism, checks and balances, and the separation of powers, there is no dominant center of decision making, as there is in unitary states such as Great Britain and France. In unitary states (see Chapter 3), most important policy decisions are made in parliamentary bodies. In the United States, important decisions are made by many officials, on many matters, in many jurisdictions. Consequently, there are many more places where interest group pressure can be effective; there are more access points to public officials.

Comparing Interest Groups

The Growth in Government

Government does far more today than it did during the early years of the Republic. As government takes on more responsibilities, it quite naturally

Selling Security

New government programs, and the spending associated with such programs, often stimulate the formation of new companies to take advantage of opportunities and new organizations to represent these companies. Here, a company representative shows his firm's biohazards protective gear at a homeland security trade show in Washington, D.C.

comes to have a greater effect on virtually all aspects of economic, social, and personal life. People, groups, and organizations are increasingly affected by the actions of government, so the decisions made by presidents, members of Congress, bureaucrats, and judges are increasingly important. It would be surprising indeed if in response, people, groups, and organizations did not try harder to influence the public officials' decisions that affect them.

Some groups form around government programs in order to take advantage of existing government programs and initiatives. The creation of the Department of Homeland Security (DHS), with its large budget for new homeland defense technologies, stimulated the formation of new companies to serve this market, as well as new trade associations—including the Homeland Security Industries Association—to represent them. By mid-September 2003, there were already 108 registered lobbyists for homeland security, and most of the large lobbying firms in Washington had added a homeland security section. In 2004, almost 900 companies report having lobbied DHS.[7]

Disturbances

The existence of diverse interests, the rules of the game, and the importance of government decisions and policies enable and encourage the formation of interest groups, but formation seems to happen only when interests are threatened, usually by some change in the social and economic environment or in government policy. This is known as the **disturbance theory** of interest group formation.[8] To take one example, Focus on the Family, a conservative religious advocacy group, was formed when many evangelical Christians began to feel threatened by family breakdown, an increase in the number of abortions, the sexual revolution, and the growing visibility of gays and lesbians in American life.

disturbance theory
A theory that locates the origins of interest groups in changes in the economic, social, or political environment that threaten the well-being of some segment of the population.

Incentives

Some social scientists argue, however, that people are not inclined to form groups, even when their common interests are threatened, unless the group can offer a selective, material benefit to them.[9] A selective, material benefit is something tangible that is available to the members of an interest group but not to nonmembers. If someone can get the benefit without joining the group, then joining makes no sense as he or she can obtain the same benefit without contributing. This is known as the **free rider** problem, and it generally comes into play when a group is interested in a collective good, such as a government program or action that will be good for all the members of some category whether they belong to a formal organization or not. All women with young children gain when the National Organization for Women helps influence Congress to pass the Family Leave Act and are not required to join the organization to enjoy the benefit, for example. People join, it is argued, when an association has benefits that are available only to its members—for example, discounted life and health insurance programs for the members of the American Automobile Association.

This theory emphasizes how difficult and unlikely it is that interest groups will form at all. It cannot account very well, therefore, for the upsurge in group formation during the 1960s and 1970s, especially of the public interest and ideological variety.[10] The proliferation of such groups suggests that groups form not only around selective, material incentives but also around "purposive" (ideological, issue-oriented) incentives and around "solidaristic"

free rider

One who gains a benefit without contributing; explains why it is so difficult to form social movements and noneconomic interest groups.

Fundraising Blitz

Advocacy groups have become quite adept at raising money from the public to support their causes. Here, volunteers and employees of the Election Protection Nerve Center, a group committed to monitoring the fairness of elections, particularly in areas where racial and ethnic minorities are located, raise money from their offices in Washinton, D.C.

(in the sense of being part of something that one values) ones. People often join groups, for instance, because they believe in a particular cause (e.g., nuclear disarmament, civil rights, prayer in the public schools, or an end to legal abortion) or because they enjoy the companionship afforded by belonging to a group. The theory also fails to take into account how easy and relatively inexpensive it is for activists and political professionals to form advocacy groups today, using the telephone, direct mail, and the Internet to solicit members and contributions and to manage lobbying campaigns.[11]

What Interests Are Represented

What kinds of interests find a voice in American politics? A useful place to start is with political scientist E. E. Schattschneider's distinction between "private" and "public" interests. Although the boundaries between the two are sometimes fuzzy, the distinction remains important: **Private interest associations** try to gain protections or material advantages from government for their own members rather than for society at large.[12] For the most part, these represent economic interests of one kind or another. **Public interest associations** try to gain protections or benefits for people beyond their own members, often for society at large. These include a diverse set of associations. Some associations, for example, are motivated by an ideology or by the desire to advance a general cause—animal rights, let us say, or environmental protection—or by the commitment to some public policy—gun control or an end to abortion. Some represent the nonprofit sector, and some even represent government entities.

Private and public interest groups come in a wide range of forms. Some, including the AARP, are large membership organizations with sizable Washington and regional offices. Some large membership organizations have passionately committed members active in its affairs—such as the National Rifle Association—while others have relatively passive members who join for the benefits the organization provides—such as the American Automobile Association with its well-known trip assistance. Other groups are trade associations whose members are business firms. Still others are rather small organizations, without members, run by professionals and sustained by foundations and a sizeable mailing list for soliciting contributions—the Children's Defense Fund and the National Taxpayers Union come to mind. We examine these in more detail below (see also Table 7.1).

> **public interest association**
> An interest group that advocates for a cause or an ideology.
>
> **private interest association**
> An interest group that seeks to protect or advance the material interests of its members.

Interest Groups and Representation

Private Interest Groups

Many different kinds of private interest groups are active in American politics.

Business   Because of the vast resources at the disposal of business and because of their strategic role in the health of local, state, and national economies, groups and associations representing business wield enormous power in Washington. Large corporations such as Boeing and Microsoft are able to mount their own lobbying efforts and join with others in influential associations such as the Business Roundtable. Medium-sized businesses are well represented by organizations such as the National Association of Manufacturers and the U.S. Chamber of Commerce. Even small businesses have proved to be quite influential when joined in associations such as the National Federation of Independent Business, which helped stop the Clinton health plan in 1994. Agriculture and agribusinesses (fertilizer, seed, machinery, biotechnology, and food-processing companies) have more than held their own over the years

TABLE 7.1 • The Diverse World of Interest Associations

Interest	Interest subtypes	Association examples
Private Interests (focus on protections and gains for their members)		
Business	Corporations that lobby on their own behalf	Microsoft
		Boeing
	Trade Associations	Chemical Manufacturers Association
		National Cattlemen's Beef Association
	Peak Business Organizations	Business Round Table
		Federation of Small Businesses
Professions	Doctors	American Medical Association
	Dentists	American Dental Association
	Accountants	National Society of Accountants
	Lawyers	American Bar Association
Labor	Union	International Brotherhood of Teamsters
	Union Federation	AFL-CIO
Public Interests (focus on protections and gains for a broader public or society in general)		
Ideological and Cause	Environment	The Sierra Club
	Pro-choice	National Abortion Rights Action League
	Pro-life	Focus on the Family
	Anti-tax	Americans for Tax Reform
	Civil rights	National Association for the Advancement of Colored People
		Human Rights Campaign
Nonprofit sector	Medical	American Hospital Association
	Charitable	American Red Cross
Governmental entities	State	National Conference of State Legislatures
	Local	National Association of Counties

through organizations such as the American Farm Bureau Federation and the Farm Machinery Manufacturer's Association and through scores of commodity groups, including the American Dairy Association and the American Wheat Growers Association.

The Professions Several associations represent the interests of professionals, such as doctors, lawyers, dentists, and accountants. Because of the prominent social position of professionals in local communities and their ability to make substantial campaign contributions, such associations are very influential in the policymaking process on matters related to their professional expertise and concerns. The American Medical Association (AMA) and the American Dental Association (ADA), for instance, lobbied strongly against the Clinton health care proposal and helped kill it in the 103rd Congress. The Trial Lawyers Association has long been a major financial contributor to the Democratic Party and active in blocking legislation to limit the size of personal injury jury awards.

Labor Although labor unions are sometimes involved in what might be called public interest activities (such as supporting civil rights legislation), their main role in the United States has been to protect the jobs of their members and to secure maximum wages and benefits for them. Unlike labor unions in many parts of the world, which are as much political and ideological organizations as economic, American labor unions have traditionally focused on so-called bread-and-butter issues. Union lobbying activities are directed at issues that affect the ability of unions to protect the jobs, wages, and benefits of their members and to maintain or increase the size of the union membership rolls. As an important part of the New Deal coalition that dominated American politics well into the late 1960s, labor unions were influential at the federal level during the years when the Democratic party controlled Congress and often won the presidency.

Although organized labor is still a force to be reckoned with in electoral politics, most observers believe that the political power of labor unions has eroded in dramatic ways over the past several decades.[13] Organized labor's main long-range problem in American politics and its declining power relative to business in the workplace is its small membership base; in 2004, only 12.5 percent of American workers—and only 7.9 percent of private-sector workers—were members of labor unions compared with 35 percent in 1954[14] (see Figure 7.2). The long but steady decline in union membership is strongly associated with the decline in the proportion of American workers in manufacturing, the economic sector in which unions have traditionally been the strongest. Frustrated by what they see as organized labor leadership's unwillingness to put enough resources into efforts to unionize service workers (such as hospital, home-care, and hotel workers, and hourly employees at large retailers such as Wal-Mart and Home Depot), the fastest-growing segment in the American economy, a number of unions, following the lead of Andrew Stern's Service Employees International Union and James Hoffa's Teamsters Union, quit the AFL-CIO in 2005 to form a new labor federation, Change to Win. They were soon joined by the United Farm Workers, the carpenters' union, and others. Whether the new federation's competition with the AFL-CIO will revitalize or further damage organized labor remains to be seen.

Public Interest Groups

Public interest groups or associations try to get government to act in ways that will serve interests that are broader and more encompassing than the direct economic or occupational interests of their own members. Such groups claim to be committed to protecting and advancing the public interest.[15]

One type of public interest group is the **advocacy group.** People active in advocacy groups tend to be motivated by ideological concerns or a belief in some cause. Such advocacy groups have always been around, but a great upsurge in their number and influence has taken place since the late 1960s.[16] Many were spawned by social movements. In the wake of the civil rights and women's movements (see Chapter 8), it is hardly surprising that a number of associations have been formed to advance the interests of particular racial, ethnic, and gender groups in American society. The National Organization of Women advo-

advocacy group
An interest group organized to support a cause or ideology.

FIGURE 7.2 • Unionized Workers in the United States, 1945–2005

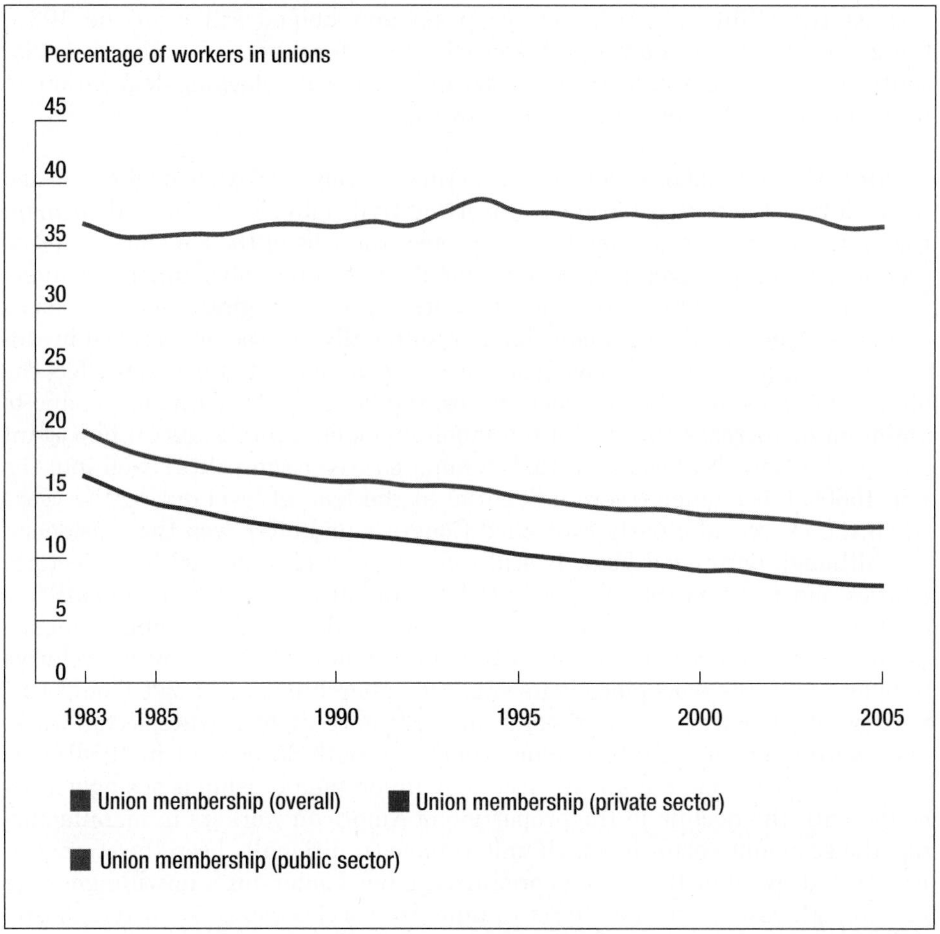

Percentage of workers in unions

(Graph showing union membership percentages from 1983 to 2005, with three lines: Union membership public sector near 35%, overall near 15% declining to 12%, and private sector near 15% declining to 7%)

■ Union membership (overall)   ■ Union membership (private sector)

■ Union membership (public sector)

Union membership in the United States has declined steadily since reaching its high point in the 1950s. Most of the decline is accounted for by declining employment in manufacturing and extractive industries, the traditional centers of labor union strength. Increasingly, the center of labor union strength has moved from the private sector to the public sector, where many schoolteachers, police, bus drivers, and firefighters are unionized.

Source: Bureau of Labor Statistics

SIMULATION

You Are an Environmental Activist

cates policies in Washington that advance the position of women in American society, for example; the League of Latin American Citizens has been concerned, among other things, with national and state policies that affect migrants from Mexico and other Latin American countries. Similarly, the NAACP and the Urban League are advocates for the interests of African Americans.

The environmental movement created organizations such as the Environmental Defense Fund, the Nature Conservancy, Clean Water Action, and the Natural Resources Defense Council, for example. The evangelical Christian upsurge led to the creation of such organizations as the Moral Majority, the Christian Coalition, the National Right-to-Life Committee, Focus on the Family, and the Family Research Council. The gay and lesbian movement eventually led to the creation of organizations such as the Gay and Lesbian Alliance Against Defamation (GLAAD). Some have been around for many years, such as the American Civil Liberties Union, committed to the protection of First Amendment freedoms, and the Children's Defense Fund, an advocate for poor children.

Religion in Politics

Evangelical Christian advocacy groups play a visible and important role in American politics. Here, a member of Focus on the Family makes a point about the unacceptability of homosexuality.

Most advocacy groups retain a professional, paid administrative staff and are supported by generous large donors (often foundations), membership dues, and/or donations generated by direct mail campaigns. While some depend on and encourage grassroots volunteers and some hold annual membership meetings where members play some role in making association policies, most advocacy associations are organizations without active membership involvement (other than check writing) and are run by lobbying and public education professionals.[17]

Two other types of public interest groups play a role in American politics, although usually a quieter one. First, associations representing government entities at the state and local levels of our federal system attempt to influence policies made by lawmakers and bureaucrats in Washington. The National Association of Counties is one example, as is the National Governors Association. Second, nonprofit organizations and associations try to influence policies that advance their missions to serve the public interests. Examples include the American Red Cross and the National Council of Non-Profit Associations.

What Interest Groups Do

Interest groups, whether public or private in nature, are in the business of conveying the policy views of individuals and groups to public officials. There are two basic types of interest group activity: the inside game and the outside game.[18] The inside game—the older and more familiar of the two—involves direct, personal contact between interest group representatives and government officials. In 2005, there were more than 26,000 registered lobbyists in Washington, D.C.—the main participants in the inside game—up from 10,000 as recently as 1996.[19] The outside game involves interest group mobilization of public opinion, voters, and important contributors in order to bring pressure to bear on elected officials.

The Inside Game

Lobbying and lobbyists have been in the news a lot lately, and the news has not been good. First, Congressman Randy "Duke" Cunningham resigned his congressional seat from California in late 2005 after pleading guilty to charges related to his having received more than $2.4 million from defense contractors. Then, in early 2006, "super lobbyist" Jack Abramoff pled guilty to three felony counts for fraud, tax evasion, and conspiracy to bribe public officials; prosecutors had amassed evidence that he had funneled millions on behalf of his clients to a long list of representatives and senators, mostly on the Republican side of the aisle, for campaign war chests and elaborate gifts, including vacations. It was revealed that Abramoff had especially close ties to then-Republican House Majority Leader Tom DeLay, not only raising campaign money for DeLay but paying for golfing vacations in Scotland. Finally, in 2005 and 2006, there was much talk about **ear-marking**—the practice of setting aside money in the annual appropriations bill for pet projects for constituents and private interests, many of them at the last minute with little chance for congressional review—that grew from 1,439 instances in the budget in 1995 to 13,997 in 2005, much of it in response to the pleadings of an army of lobbyists.[20]

The inside game of lobbying does not customarily involve bribing legislators. Rather, it is more the politics of insiders and the "old boy" network (although, increasingly, women are also part of the network). It is the politics of one-on-one persuasion, in which the skilled lobbyist tries to get a decision maker to understand and sympathize with the interest group's point of view or to see that what the interest group wants is good for the politician's constituents. Access is critical if one is to be successful at this game.

Many of the most successful lobbyists are recruited from the ranks of retired members of the House, the Senate, and high levels of the bureaucracy. More than half of the powerful drug industry's registered lobbyists, for example, are former members of Congress, former congressional staffers, or former employees of the executive branch.[21] By one estimate, about one-third of outgoing lawmakers are hired by lobbying firms or hang out their own lobbying shingle.[22] The promise of lucrative employment based on their skills—and especially on their many contacts—is what keeps so many of them around Washington after they leave office or quit federal employment.

The inside game seems to work best when the issues are narrow and technical, do not command much media attention or public passion, and do not stir up counteractivity by other interest groups.[23] This is not to say that interest groups play a role only on unimportant matters. Great benefit can come to an interest group or a large corporation from a small change in a single provision of the Tax Code or in a slight change in the wording of a regulation. Enron, for example, was very successful at getting Congress to remove federal oversight on many of its energy-trading and acquisitions activities. These stayed well out of public view until they came to light after Enron's spectacular collapse in 2001.

Lobbyists from citizens groups also play the inside game, often with great skill and effect. Many environmental regulations have been strengthened because of the efforts of skilled lobbyists from the Sierra Club, for example.

Political scientist E. E. Schattschneider has pointed out that the inside game—traditional lobbying—is pretty much outside the view of the public. That is to say, the day-to-day details of this form of lobbying are not the stuff of the evening news, nor the fodder of open political campaigns or conflict; such lobbying takes place behind closed doors. As such, it does not do much to advance democracy.

ear-marking

Practice of appropriating money for specific pet projects of members of Congress.

SIMULATION

You Are a Lobbyist

Lobbying a Member of the House

An important part of the job of the lobbyist is to convey the views and concerns of interest group members to representatives and senators. Here, a lobbyist for the Edison Institute buttonholes a member of the House to encourage a "yes" vote on the 2005 energy bill. The ability to hire and deploy lobbyists, however, is not randomly distributed among Americans. Those with the greatest economic resources tend to dominate the "inside game" of interest group politics.

Lobbying Congress   The essence of the inside game in Congress is the cultivation of personal relationships with people who matter—Senate and House leaders, other influential and well-placed legislators, chairpersons of important committees or subcommittees, and key staff members. Because much of the action in Congress takes place in the committees and because senators and representatives are busy with a wide range of responsibilities, cultivating relationships with important legislative and committee staff members is especially important for successful lobbyists. As one lobbyist put it, "If you have a staff member on your side, it might be a hell of a lot better than talking to the member [of Congress]."[24]

Lobbyists are also expected to make substantial contributions to the campaign war chests of representatives and senators and to persuade their clients to do the same.[25] One influential lobbyist is reported to have said recently that "about one-third of my day is spent raising money from my clients to give to people I lobby."[26]

Lobbying the Executive Branch   Career civil servants and political appointees in the executive branch have a great deal of discretionary authority because Congress often legislates broad policies, leaving it to bureaucratic agencies to fill in the details. Because of this, interest groups try to establish stable and friendly relationships with the agencies of the executive branch that are most relevant to their interests. The payoffs from these long-term relationships can be quite high. In 2003, for example, large media company and news organization leaders and lobbyists met with the top staff of the FCC in a successful effort to get the agency to loosen rules on ownership so that big companies could grow even bigger.

The key to success in lobbying the executive branch is similar to that in lobbying Congress: personal contact and cooperative long-term relationships. Interest group representatives can convey technical information, present the results of their research, help a public official deflect criticism, and show that what the group wants is compatible with good public policy and the political needs of the official.

Lobbyists

Lobbying the Courts   Interest groups sometimes lobby the courts, although not in the same way as they lobby the other two branches. A group may find that neither Congress nor the White House is favorably disposed to its interests and will bring a test case to the courts. Realizing that the improvement of the lot of African Americans was very low on the agenda of presidents and members of Congress during the 1940s and 1950s, for example, the NAACP turned to the courts for satisfaction. The effort eventually paid off in 1954 in the landmark *Brown* v. *Board of Education* decision.

Interest groups sometimes lobby the courts by filing *amicus curiae* ("friends of the court") briefs in cases involving other parties. In this kind of brief, a person or an organization that is not a party in the suit may file an argument in support of one side or the other in the hope of swaying the views of the judge or judges. Major controversies before the Supreme Court on such issues as abortion, free speech, or civil rights attract scores of *amicus curiae* briefs.

Interest groups also get involved in the appointment of federal judges. Particularly controversial appointments, such as the Supreme Court nominations of Robert Bork (whom many women's and civil rights interests considered too conservative) in 1987, Clarence Thomas (who was opposed by liberal and women's groups) in 1992, and Samuel Alito in 2005 (Democrats and liberals considered him much too conservative on a wide range of issues) drew interest group attention and strenuous efforts for and against the nominees.

The Outside Game

The outside game is being played when interest groups try to mobilize **grassroots,** constituency, and public opinion support for their goals and bring them to bear on elected officials. By all indications, the outside game has been growing steadily in importance in recent years compared to more traditional forms of lobbying.[27] This may be a good development for democracy, and here is why. Although groups involved in the outside game often try to hide their true identities—Americans for Fair Drug Prices, for example, may well be funded by the drug industry—and while some groups involved in the outside game have more resources than others, it is still the case that this form of politics has the effect of expanding and heightening political conflict, bringing issues out into the open and subjecting them to public scrutiny—what Schattschneider has called the "socialization of conflict."[28]

grassroots
The constituents, voters, or rank-and-file of a party.

Mobilizing Membership   Those interest groups with a large membership base try to persuade their members to send letters and to make telephone calls to senators and representatives when an important issue is before Congress. They sound the alarm, using direct mail and, increasingly, e-mail. They define the threat to members; suggest a way to respond to the threat; and supply the addresses, phone numbers, and e-mail addresses of the people to contact in Washington. Members are grouped by congressional district and state and are given the addresses of their own representatives or senators. The National Rifle Association (NRA) is particularly effective in mobilizing its considerable membership whenever the threat of federal gun control rears its

No to Guns

Mass demonstrations, designed to attract public attention through media coverage, are important tools in the arsenals of many interest groups. Here anti-gun groups show their displeasure with the National Rifle Association's opposition to gun control at the NRA's annual meeting in Denver in 1999, only weeks after the massacre at Columbine High School.

head. Environmental organizations such as the Sierra Club and Friends of the Earth sound the alarm to people on their mailing list whenever Congress threatens to loosen environmental protections.

Organizing the District   Members of Congress are especially attuned to the individuals and groups in their states or districts who can affect their reelection prospects. The smart interest group, therefore, not only will convince its own members in the state and district to put pressure on the senator or congressional representative but will also make every effort to be in touch with the most important campaign contributors and opinion leaders there.

Shaping Public Opinion   "Educating" the public on issues that are important to the interest group is one of the central features of new-style lobbying. The idea is to shape opinion in such a way that government officials will be favorably disposed to the views of the interest group. These attempts to shape public and elite opinion come in many forms. One strategy is to produce and distribute research reports that bolster the group's position. Citizen groups such as Environmental Defense and the Food Research and Action Center have been very adept and effective in this area.[29]

Another strategy is media advertising. Sometimes this takes the form of pressing a position on a particular issue, such as the Teamsters Union raising the alarm about open borders with Mexico, focusing on the purported unsafe nature of Mexican trucks roaming American highways. Sometimes it is "image" advertising, in which some company or industry portrays its positive contribution to American life.[30]

In the effort to shape public opinion, the well-heeled interest group will also prepare materials that will be of use to radio and television broadcasters and to newspaper and magazine editors. Many produce opinion pieces, magazine articles, television spots and radio "sound bites," and even television documentaries. Others stage events to be covered as news. The environmentalist group Greenpeace puts the news media on full alert, for example, when it tries to disrupt a whaling operation or a nuclear weapons test.

Finally, interest groups, using the latest computer technology, identify target groups to receive information on particular issues. Groups pushing for cuts

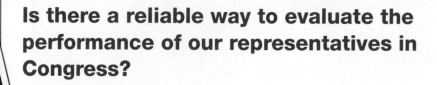

By the Numbers

Is there a reliable way to evaluate the performance of our representatives in Congress?

Imagine you are at the end of the semester and four different teachers give you a grade in your introductory political science course. One looks at your performance and gives you a grade of 100 percent. Your day is made! Teacher number 2 gives you an 83. OK, you might say, "I can live with that." Teachers 3 and 4 slam you with a 20 and a 10. Ouch! How to make sense of all of this? How come two teachers love you and two hate you? Surely they must be biased in some way.

This is exactly what happens to members of Congress when they are graded on their performance by interest groups. Unlike you, the confused student in the example above, congressional representatives expect the wide disparity in the grades they receive, understand what is going on, and are even proud of most of their grades, whether high or low. Note the wildly contrasting grades for Republican Senator Richard Shelby of Alabama and Democratic Senator Barbara Boxer of California given by four organizations in 2002: the Americans for Democratic Action (ADA), the American Conservative Union (ACU), the League of Conservation Voters (LCV), and the National Taxpayers Union (NTU).

Why It Matters: Having a consistent and reliable way to grade each member of Congress can help voters make more rational electoral choices. Without such grades, each citizen would have to investigate the record of his or her member of Congress, rely on news reports, or depend on information provided by the member.

Behind the Numbers: How are members of Congress graded? The answer is pretty straightforward. Each interest group in this example is strongly ideological or committed to a certain set of concerns, and each grades members of Congress in terms of these standards. The ADA is very strongly liberal—interested in civil liberties, civil rights, and economic and social justice—while the ACU is strongly conservative—in favor of capitalism, traditional moral values, and a strong national defense. The LCV supports legislation to protect the environment, while the NTU wants lower taxes, less wasteful government spending, and a balanced budget. So, members of Congress who vote to increase spending on child welfare programs, let us say, are likely to get high grades from the ADA, but low grades from the ACU and the NTU. Members who vote to open the Alaska

in the capital gains tax rate, for instance, direct their mail and telephone banks to holders of the American Express card or to addresses in ZIP code areas identified as upper-income neighborhoods. They are increasingly using the Internet, as well, in the effort to mobilize the public on issues of concern to them. For example, most have their own websites and publish position papers and other materials there. Many arrange postings to friendly weblogs in hopes of further disseminating their message. Some will use their websites and e-mail to organize e-mails to lawmakers from their constituents.[31] These activities are not always successful, to be sure; NARAL launched a multiple-front campaign in 2005, with heavy reliance on the Internet, to defeat John Roberts's nomination in the Senate for the seat of Chief Justice, but failed.

Getting Involved in Campaigns and Elections
Interest groups try to increase their influence by getting involved in political campaigns. Many interest groups, for example, rate members of Congress on their support for the interest group's position on a selection of key votes. The ratings are distributed

National Wildlife Reserve for oil exploration would surely receive a low grade from the folks at LCV.

Calculating Interest Group Scores:

Although each group uses a slightly different method to do its grading, at base, each approaches grading in pretty much the same way. For each interest group, its professional staff, sometimes in conjunction with outside experts, selects a set of key votes on which to assess members of Congress. The particular votes selected by each group will differ—a group interested solely in civil rights issues will not, for example, use a vote on the defense budget for its scorecard—but each identifies a set of votes it considers to be a good indicator of ideological or policy loyalty. On each vote, members of Congress are scored "with the group" or "against the group." The numbers are added up, then transformed to percentage terms, with 100 being the highest score and 0 the lowest.

What to Watch For:

Oddly enough, although not terribly sophisticated in either conceptual or computational terms, these are numbers you can trust. You can, as they say, "take them to the bank." Why? Because each interest group is clear about what it stands for, and each makes it clear that it is judging members of Congress from a particular perspective. When you are

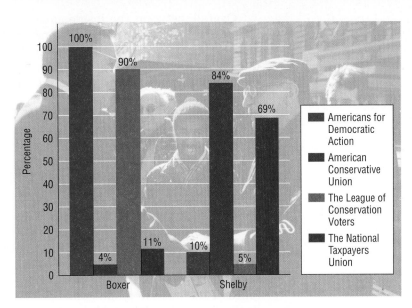

Interest Group Ratings of Senators Boxer and Shelby, 2005

Source: Project Vote Smart (**www.vote.smart.org**) for the year 2006.

considering whether to vote for or against an incumbent member of Congress, a good method would be to check member scores from organizations whose ideology and/or policy views you support.

What Do You Think?

How does your representative in Congress score with those groups whose values and policy position come closest to your own? You can investigate this at the Project Vote Smart website at **www.vote-smart.org** where you can find how your representative is evaluated by different interest groups.

to the members of the interest group and other interested parties in the hope that the ratings will influence their voting behavior. We show how groups do this in the "By the Numbers" feature in this section.

Interest groups also encourage their members to get involved in the electoral campaigns of candidates who are favorable to their interests. Groups often assist campaigns in more tangible ways—allowing the use of their telephone banks, mailing lists, fax and photocopy machines, computers, and the like. Some interest groups help with fund-raising events or ask members to make financial contributions to candidates.

Interest groups also endorse particular candidates for public office. The strategy may backfire and is somewhat risky, for to endorse a losing candidate is to risk losing access to the winner. Nevertheless, it is fairly common now for labor unions, environmental organizations, religious groups, and liberal and conservative ideological groups to make such endorsements.

Interest groups are also an increasingly important part of campaign fund-raising. This topic will be explored in more detail in the next section.

Overall, between the inside game and the outside game, interest groups have a diverse set of tools for influencing elected officials, bureaucrats, judges, and the public. And the number of groups capable of deploying these tools is large and growing every year. On the surface, it might look like the proliferation of interest groups has enhanced the democratic flavor of our country, allowing more and more Americans to have their interests represented. But not all agree that this is so. Let's take a look at the various viewpoints.

Possible Flaws in the Pluralist Heaven

Political scientist E. E. Schattschneider once observed that the flaw in the pluralist (or interest group) heaven is "that the heavenly chorus sings with a strong upper class accent." If his observation is accurate, then political equality is undermined by the interest group system, and democracy is less fully developed than it might be even taking into account the new importance of the outside game (which, as we have said, tends to "socialize conflict"). In this section, we look at inequalities in the interest group system and evaluate their effects.

Representational Inequalities

Not all segments of society are equally represented in the interest group system. The interest group inside lobbying game in Washington, D.C., is dominated, in sheer numbers and weight of activity, by business corporations, industry trade associations, and associations of the professions, although liberal and conservative advocacy groups lobby as well. Organized labor, we have seen, although still a powerful player in Washington, has lost much of its lobbying clout in recent years, mainly because of declining membership. Passage in 2005 of several pro-business bills that it strongly opposed—namely, bills making it more difficult to declare bankruptcy and to bring class action lawsuits in state courts—showcases labor's declining fortunes. For their part, the vast majority of advocacy groups, even those that perceive themselves as liberal and lean toward the Democrats, attract members and contributors who have much higher incomes, more elite occupations, and more education than the general public. Not surprisingly, given those whom these advocacy groups represent, they tend to focus less on issues of poverty and income inequality, the traditional purview of labor unions, let us say, and more on "quality of life" issues such as environmental protection, consumer protection, globalization, women's rights, racial and ethnic civil rights, gay and lesbian rights, and civil liberties.[32]

Resource Inequalities

Interest Groups and Campaign Finance

Business corporations and professionals are the most economically well-off parts of American society. It is hardly surprising that interest groups representing them can afford to spend far more than other groups to hire professional lobbying firms, form their own Washington liaison office, place advertising in the media, conduct targeted mailings on issues, mobilize their members to contact government officials, and pursue all of the other activities of old- and new-style lobbying. Lobbying in Washington is especially tilted toward business. Registered lobbyists for the various drug companies, for example, total more that the combined membership of the House and Senate.[33] (You can learn more about the influence of the drug industry, as well as the insurance industry, in the "Using the Framework" feature on the new Medicare drug prescription program.) The situation is highlighted by Table 7.2, which shows the amount of money spent by different sectors on lobbying activities. It is worth noting that nonbusiness groups and associations—listed as miscellaneous, single-issue, city/county, organized labor, and foreign countries—spend only a small fraction of what is spent by business (about $363 million versus more than $1.7 billion).

Corporate, trade, and professional associations also are important in campaign finance, with an especially prominent role played by **political action committees (PACs),** which are entities created by interest groups—whether business firms, unions, membership organizations, or liberal and conservative advocacy groups—to collect money and make contributions to candidates in federal elections. Corporate, trade, and professional PACs lead other groups in both sheer numbers and levels of spending, although labor unions and large and committed advocacy organizations such as the NRA and the Sierra Club are also important. During the 2003–2004 election cycle, for example, political action committees representing business and the professions accounted for 64 percent of the $310 million spent by all PACs on candidates for federal office, while labor unions accounted for only 16 percent. PACs representing the least-privileged sectors of American society are notable for their absence. As former Senator (R–KS) and presidential candidate Bob Dole once put it, "There aren't any poor PACs or food stamp PACs or nutrition PACs or Medicaid PACs."[34]

PACs briefly declined in scale and influence in the early 2000s because of the rise in importance of unregulated **soft money**—contributions to national party committees by groups and individuals to support "party-building"

PACs and The Money Trail

political action committee (PAC)

An entity created by an interest group whose purpose is to collect money and make contributions to candidates in federal elections.

soft money

Unregulated expenditures by political parties on general public education, voter registration, and voter mobilization; often used to indirectly influence campaigns for elective office, until banned after 2002.

TABLE 7.2 • Major Spending on Federal Lobbying in 2004, by Industry Sector ($ in millions)

1. Health care	$325.6
2. Communication, technology	280.3
3. Finance, insurance	272.5
4. Business—retail, services	164.6
5. Transportation	164.0
6. Energy, natural resources	157.2
7. Miscellaneous	141.4
8. Defense	93.8
9. Single-issue groups	89.3
10. Manufacturing	85.9
11. City/county	79.8
12. Agriculture	78.7
13. Real estate construction	58.5
14. Law	27.4
15. Organized labor	26.2
16. Foreign countries	26.1

Source: "Money in Politics Databases," PoliticalMoneyLine (**www.politicalmoneyline.com**) July 13, 2005.

Using the Framework

Prescription Drugs Under Medicare

How did a prescription drug benefit get added to Medicare in 2003 after so many years of failure?

Background: Democratic presidents and members of Congress had tried–but failed–for more then twenty years to add a prescription drug benefit to the Medicare program. In 2003, with Republicans in control of both the House and Senate, President George W. Bush was able to deliver on his campaign promise to the elderly. Although many elderly Americans continue to pay a substantial amount of money for their prescription drugs, most are now paying less than they would have without the new program. But others gained as well: Drug companies won provisions forbidding the importation of cheaper drugs from abroad and the negotiation of lower prices for drugs by the government, insurance companies were granted subsidies for providing drug benefit policies, and doctors won a provision in the bill loosening some of the restrictions on fees they receive under Medicare. How did all of this happen? Looking at how structural, political linkage, and governmental factors affected the political process will help us explain the outcome.

Governmental Action → Governmental Level → Political Linkages Level → Structural Level

The drug benefit under Medicare becomes law.

The House easily passed the bill that emerged from the Republican-controlled conference committee. → Senate Republicans won a close vote for the bill, after defeating a Democratic filibuster on the conference report. → President Bush signed the bill in an elaborate ceremony in the White House.

A Republican president, George W. Bush, was in the White House. His plan for a prescription drug benefit under Medicare was introduced in the House and the Senate. → Republicans controlled both houses of Congress; a slightly different version of the bill passed in each one.

Relative to other groups, the elderly vote in very high proportions in both presidential and congressional elections. These voters have said time and again that they want assistance with rising drug costs. → Drug and insurance companies, as well as the AMA, made very large campaign donations during the 2000 and 2002 election cycles. → Drug and insurance companies, as well as the AMA, mounted major lobbying efforts in the 108th Congress to ensure that the new program would take their interests into account.

During the 2000 presidential election campaign, both Al Gore and George W. Bush promised help to seniors with their rising drug costs. During the 2002 election campaign, many congressional candidates in both parties made similar promises. → Surprisingly, the most important interest group representing seniors, the usually Democratic-leaning American Association for Retired People (AARP), endorsed the plan fashioned by a Republican president and the Republican leaders of Congress.

The number of Americans over the age of 65 has been growing, and their prescription drug costs have been rising much faster than the cost of living. → Scientific innovation has helped create increasingly powerful, effective, and expensive drugs. → The drug industry is dominated by a handful of very large and economically powerful firms. → Insurance in the United States, including health care and medical insurance, is provided by a handful of very large and economically powerful firms.

activities, which invariably found their way into parallel campaigns supporting presidential and congressional candidates—but have made a comeback after passage of the Bipartisan Campaign Reform Act in 2002 (McCain-Feingold), which banned soft money contributions. Although McCain-Feingold imposes new limits on corporations' and labor unions' abilities to directly mount issue campaigns that mention candidates or officeholders in the period leading up to primary and general elections, the new law allows corporate and labor PACs to accept larger donations from individual contributors than in the past, contribute more to candidates and parties than under the old law, and run issue campaigns on television and radio right up to the day of primary and general elections, with no limitations on their aggregate or total expenditures (see Table 7.3).

The new law has dramatically enhanced the importance of 527 advocacy organizations, so named because of where they are defined in the Tax Code. Because McCain-Feingold places no limits on how much money can be contributed to them but bans soft money contributions to national party committees, "unregulated" money has flowed to 527s. In the 2003–2004 election cycle, it amounted to about $400 million.[35] These groups can use unregulated money to talk about issues, mobilize voters, and praise or criticize candidates and officeholders, the only restriction being the use of television and radio in the period immediately preceding primary and general elections (see Table 7.3 for details). Many new groups devoted to liberal or conservative causes and candidates sprouted up after passage of McCain-Feingold and played a very large role in the 2004 presidential election—Swift Boat Veterans for Truth (anti-Kerry) and MoveOn.org (anti-Bush) were the most prominent—and the 2006 congressional elections (see Chapter 11 opener). These groups depend on very large contributions from a handful of rich individuals; George Soros contributed more than $15 million to anti-Bush 527s in 2004, while Texas oilman T. Boone Pickens gave $4.6 million to anti-Kerry groups.

Interest groups don't contribute money to campaigns and to candidates without some expectation of a return on their investment. Advocacy groups want attention paid to the issues they care about; private interest groups want attention paid to their material interests. It has been argued that there are so many interest groups around that they tend to neutralize one another; hence, campaign contributions and expenditures don't really matter.[36] This may sometimes be true on high-visibility issues in which the public and an array of interest groups are engaged. Where interest groups seem to matter the most is in the small details of legislation, forged mainly in the committees and subcommittees of Congress: a small subsidy in a defense spending bill or a waiver of a regulation for a particular industry or company. Even major bills, if they are terribly complex, can take place without much public attention on the details, as was the case with the energy bill passed in 2005, which was loaded with tax breaks and subsidies for energy producers.

Political Action Committees

Access Inequality

Inequalities of representation and resources are further exaggerated by the ability of some groups to play a central role in the formation and implementation of government policies, based on the membership of these groups in informal networks within the government itself that are involved in policy areas of interest to them. These networks, often called **iron triangles,** customarily include a private interest group (usually a corporation or business trade association), an agency in the executive branch, and a committee or subcommittees in Congress, which act together to advance and protect certain government

iron triangle

An enduring alliance of common interest among an interest group, a congressional committee, and a bureaucratic agency.

TABLE 7.3 • Interest Group Political Fund-Raising and Spending Rules Under Terms of the Bipartisan Campaign Reform Act

hard money

Regulated campaign contributions to candidate and party committees, as well as to political action committees.

	Soft Money[a]	Hard Money[b]
Corporations and labor unions	• May not use funds from their *general treasuries* to make contributions to federal candidates or national political party organizations. • May not use funds from their *general treasuries* to pay for "electioneering communications" that mention a candidate or officeholder on television or radio 30 days prior to a primary election or 60 days prior to a general election. • Can make unlimited contributions to advocacy organizations.	• Can create Political Action Committees (PACs) to collect and contribute "regulated" money to federal candidates and party committees. • PACs can give up to $5,000 to a candidate for a federal office for each election (primary and general election). • PACs can give up to $15,000 per year to a national party committee. • One PAC can give up to $5,000 per year to another PAC. • No limits on a PAC's total contributions to federal candidates and national party committees. • No limits on a PAC's "electioneering communications" on television and radio.
Public interest/ advocacy groups, and other private associations (527s)	• No restriction on the size of individual contributions that the group or association can accept or how much money they can collect in the aggregate. • May not use "unregulated" money to pay for "electioneering communications" on television or radio 30 days prior to a primary election or 60 days prior to a general election. • No limits on "electioneering communications" prior to the pre-election "blackout" dates. • No limits on use of soft money for other electioneering activities including telephoning, targeted mailings, e-mail campaigns, door-to-door contact.	• Can create PACs to collect and contribute "regulated" money to candidates and party committees. • Same rules on collection and use of "regulated" money as for PACs created by corporations and labor unions.

[a]Money for use in campaigns collected *free of federal rules* limiting the size of allowable contributions; "unregulated" money.

[b]Money for use in campaigns collected *under strict federal rules* limiting the size of allowable contributions; "regulated" money.

Rebuilding the Levees

In addition to many members of the public, a wide range of interest groups support Army Corps of Engineers' water projects such as this one to rebuild the Industrial Canal levees in New Orleans in 2006.

programs that work to the mutual benefit of their members. Although some scholars say that iron triangles have become less important in American government,[37] they seem to be alive and well in shaping and carrying out public policies in the areas of agriculture, defense procurement, public lands, highway construction, and water. Large-scale water projects—dams, irrigation, and levees, for example—are supported by farm, real estate developer, construction, and barge-shipping interest groups; members of key Senate and House committees responsible for these projects, who can claim credit for bringing jobs and federal money to their constituencies; and the Army Corps of Engineers, whose budget and responsibilities grow apace as it builds the projects. Another iron triangle is shown in Figure 7.3.

The Special Place of Business Corporations

Economist and political scientist Charles Lindblom has argued that corporations wield such disproportionate power in American politics that they undermine democracy. He closes his 1977 book *Politics and Markets* with this observation: "The large private corporation fits oddly into democratic theory. Indeed, it does not fit."[38] Twenty years later, political scientist Neil Mitchell concluded his book *The Conspicuous Corporation,* which reported the results

FIGURE 7.3 • **Iron Triangle**

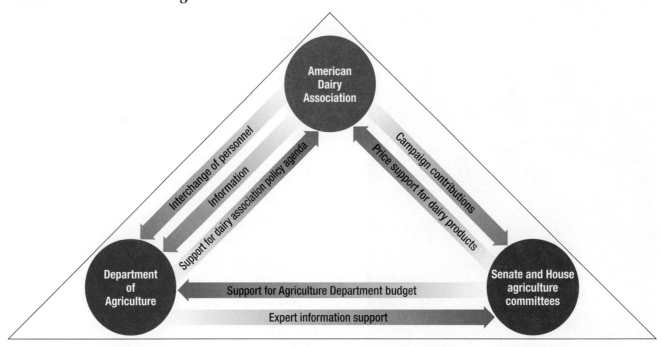

In an iron triangle, an alliance based on common interests is formed among a powerful corporation or interest group, an agency of the executive branch, and congressional committees or subcommittees. In this example from the dairy industry, an alliance is formed among parties that share an interest in the existence and expansion of dairy subsidies. Most scholars think iron triangles are less common today than in the past, though they are alive and well in a number of policy areas, including the one illustrated here.

of careful empirical testing of Lindblom's ideas, with the conclusion that "business interests (in the United States) are not routinely countervailed in the policy process. Their political resources and incentives to participate are usually greater than other interests."[39] Let's see why these scholars reached their somber conclusion about business corporations in American politics.

We have already learned about many of the advantages that corporations and business trade associations representing groups of corporations enjoy over others in the political process. The largest corporations are far ahead of their competitors in the number of lobbyists they employ, the level of resources they can and do use for political purposes, their ability to shape public perceptions and opinions through such instruments as issue advertising and subsidization of business-oriented think tanks like the American Enterprise Institute, and the ease of access they often have to government officials. When President George W. Bush in 2001 assigned Vice President Dick Cheney the task of fashioning a new national energy policy, for example, Cheney met almost exclusively with representatives from large energy companies and energy trade associations, including Enron and the Edison Electric Institute, as well as with members of the Business Roundtable, the association composed of the CEOs of the nation's most important business corporations. When a bill was finally passed in 2005, it was tilted heavily toward tax breaks and subsidies for large energy producers.

An additional source of corporate power is the high regard in which business is held in American society and the central and honored place of business

Learning About the Marketplace

Private enterprise is honored highly in the United States—where schools often give practical lessons on how a market economy is supposed to work, and business firms and organizations receive an advantage in their competition with other interests in American politics.

values in our culture. Faith in free enterprise gives special advantages to the central institution of free enterprise, the corporation. Any political leader contemplating hostile action against corporations must contend with business's special place of honor in the United States. To be sure, scandals involving large business enterprises such as Enron can tarnish big business now and then, but in the long run, as President Coolidge once famously said, "the business of America is business."

Business corporations are also unusually influential because the health of the American economy—and thus the standard of living of the people—is tied closely to the economic well-being of large corporations. It is widely and not entirely unreasonably believed that what is good for business is good for America. Because of their vital role in the economy, government officials tend to interpret business corporations not as "special interests" but as the voice of the national interest and to listen more attentively to their demands than they do to those of other sectors of American society. In this sense, corporations enjoy an especially privileged position in American politics.

Corporations are also powerful because their mobility is an important counterweight to any government effort (local, state, or national) to raise taxes or impose regulations that business deems especially onerous. Increasingly, large corporations are able to design, produce, and market their goods and services all over the world; they are not irrevocably tied to a single location. If government threatens their interests, large corporations can credibly counter with a threat to move all or part of their operations elsewhere. In this new global economic environment, political leaders are increasingly of a mind to maintain a friendly and supportive business climate.

Large corporations do not, of course, run the show entirely. Although they have the most resources, for instance, these resources do not translate automatically into real political influence. One interest group may have enormous resource advantages over other interest groups, for instance, but may use its resources ineffectively. Or an interest group with great resources may find itself opposed by other interest groups that together are able to mobilize impressive resources of their own. A powerful interest group may also find that an elected politician is not cooperative because the voters in the district are of a different mind from the interest group. So even with this immense set of resources, business power is not automatically and inevitably translated into political power.[40]

Nor does business always get its way in Washington. There are many issues of great importance on which business in general, or one corporation in particular, loses in the give-and-take of politics. There are times when business finds itself squared off against powerful coalitions of other interest groups (labor, consumer, and environmentalist groups, let us say). On occasion, corporations also find themselves at odds with one another on public policy issues. Thus, Internet service providers, computer and hand-held device makers, software developers, and the music and film industries, are locked in a battle over file-sharing.

Corporations are most powerful when they can build alliances among themselves. Most of the time, corporations are in competition with one another; they do not form a unified political bloc capable of moving government to action on their behalf. On those few occasions when corporations feel that their collective interests are at stake, however, they are capable of coming together to form powerful political coalitions. As political scientist David Vogel put it, "When business is both mobilized and unified, its political power can be formidable."[41] For example, in 2005 several bills long advocated by business trade groups were signed into law: one restricting class action law suits against companies; the other tightening up bankruptcy laws to make it more difficult for individuals to avoid paying creditors.[42]

In our view, the best way to think about corporations in American politics is to see their power waxing and waning within their overall privileged position. Corporate power may be greater at certain times and weaker at other times, but always in a game in which corporations enjoy advantages over other groups. If corporations feel that their collective interests are at stake—as when labor unions are particularly aggressive or when government's regulatory burden is perceived to be too heavy—and they are able to present a united front, they are simply unbeatable. This cannot be said about any other sector of American society.[43]

Successful Interest Groups

Curing the Mischief of Factions

Americans have worried about the "mischief of factions" ever since James Madison wrote about them in *The Federalist,* No. 10 (see the Appendix). Over the years, various things have been tried to control the purported negative effects of these special interests. Disclosure has been the principal tool of regulation. In 1946, Congress imposed a requirement (in the Federal Regulation of Lobbying Act) that all lobbyists working in Congress be registered. The Lobby Disclosure Act of 1995 requires a wider range of political actors to register as lobbyists and makes them report every six months on which policies they are trying to influence and how much they are spending to do it.

Reformers have also tried to regulate some of the most troublesome abuses of the politics of factions. Sections of the Ethics in Government Act (1978) aim at the so-called revolving door in which former government officials become lobbyists for interests with whom they formerly dealt in their official capacity. The act forbids ex-officials from lobbying their former agency for a year or lobbying at all on any issue in which the former officials were substantially involved. Finally, the 1995 Act says that former U.S. trade representatives and their deputies are banned for life from lobbying for foreign interests.

Using the Democracy Standard

Do interest groups help or hinder American democracy?

PROPOSITION: Because they represent narrow and special interests, the proliferation of interest groups has made American politics less and less democratic.

AGREE The interest group system is by and for the privileged. The democratic principle of "political equality" is violated because powerful interest groups that play the largest role in shaping public policies in the United States represent, by and large, wealthier and better-educated Americans, corporations, and other business interests and professionals, such as doctors and lawyers.

DISAGREE The interest group system enhances democracy because it gives individuals and groups another tool to keep elected and appointed officials responsive and responsible to their needs, wants, and interests. Political parties are important for making popular sovereignty work, to be sure, but being broad and inclusive umbrella organizations, they often ignore the interests of particular groups. And, although elections are essential for keeping public officials on their toes, they happen only every two to four years. The day-to-day work of popular sovereignty is done by interest groups. Additionally, the rise of citizen groups, supported by thousands of ordinary people with ordinary incomes, has made the interest group system less unequal; a wider range of groups representing a broad swath of the population, is now a key player in the political game.

CONSIDER There is no doubt that the interest group system plays an important role in shaping what government does in the United States; elected officials pay lots of attention to them, for all the reasons explored in this chapter. Whether the interest group system advances or retards democracy, however, can only be determined by knowing which sectors of the American population are represented by interest groups and how well interest groups represent the people they claim to be representing. After examining the materials in this chapter, consider how you would answer these questions.

• Is any sector left out or underrepresented by interest groups? • How about your personal experience with interest groups? • Have any of them been in contact with you? • Are you involved with any of them, perhaps participating in some activity sponsored by interest groups? • Have you made financial contributions to any of them? • If you have some association with some interest group—perhaps a student government group representing the interests of students at your school before state and national government bodies—how would you rate its effectiveness? • What made this group effective or ineffective?

Reformers have also tried to control the effects of interest group money in politics. The McCain-Feingold bill, passed in 2002 and designed to put limits on the use of soft money office, is the latest attempt. It is too soon to tell how effective this reform will be, but early indications suggest that political money has been redirected to PACs and 527 advocacy organizations.

There was also much talk about cleaning up lobbying in Congress in the wake of the Abramoff indictment and revelations of widespread influence peddling. Congress did not do much on this front, however. Reforms were confined to limiting trips paid for by lobbyists, expanding reporting requirements, and extending to two years the time limit on when former legislators can lobby their former colleagues.

While such steps are to be applauded, many observers worry that these reforms have not gone to the heart of the problem. Some political scientists have suggested that we focus our efforts instead on strengthening the institutions of majoritarian democracy. The key institution of majoritarian democracy, at least in theory (as you will see in Chapter 9), is the political party. Parties can, as political scientist Walter Dean Burnham put it, "generate countervailing collective power on behalf of the many individually powerless against the relatively few who are individually—or organizationally—powerful."[44] Others believe that the narrowness of interest group politics might be tempered by strengthening the presidency, our only nationally elected office.[45]

Summary

Americans have long denigrated special interests as contrary to the public good. Some political scientists, however, see interest groups as an important addition to the representative process in a democracy.

The United States provides a rich environment for interest groups because of our constitutional system, our political culture, and the broad responsibilities of our government.

A number of interests are accommodated in our interest group system. The most important private interests include business, agriculture, labor, and the professions. Public interest or citizens' groups try to advance some issue or ideological interest that is not connected to the direct material benefit of their own members. There has been a significant expansion in the number of such groups since 1968.

Interest groups attempt to influence the shape of public policy in a number of ways. In the inside game, interest group representatives are in direct contact with government officials and try to build influence on the basis of personal relationships. In the outside game, interest groups attempt to apply indirect pressure to officials by mobilizing other groups, the members of their own group, public opinion, elite opinion, and the electorate to support their positions on policy matters.

Business, trade, and professional associations dominate the interest group system, although citizens groups are also influential. They enjoy clear advantages over other groups in terms of resources and access to public officials. The business corporation holds an especially privileged place in the interest group system because of the support of business values in our culture and the perceived importance of the corporation to the economic well-being of Americans.

Efforts to control the "mischief of factions" have mainly been regulatory in nature. Some reformers believe that interest groups will only cease to be a problem if the parties and presidency are strengthened.

Web Exploration
Corporations and Political Money

Issue: It has been suggested that corporations and business and professional associations dominate the campaign finance system, adding to their political influence.

Site: See who contributed what during the 2004 elections by accessing the Center for Responsive Politics in MyPoliSciLab at **www.mypoliscilab.com.** Go to the "Web Explorations" section for Chapter 7, select "Corporations and Political Money," then "corporate money." Select "Who Gives" then look at "Industries" and "All-Time Donors." Categorize the contributors in this list and the amounts spent.

What You've Learned: Is the claim of corporate and business dominance supported by the evidence?

HINT: Pay attention to the flow of dollars to each party, while there is some overlap, each has distinct sets of contributors.

Internet Sources

Center for Responsive Politics
www.opensecrets.org/
  Follow the money trail—who gets it? who contributes?—in American politics.

National Taxpayers Union
www.ntu.org
  Conservative group that advocates for lower taxes.

National Organization for Women
www.now.org
  The women's organization that has long been a "player" in Washington politics.

National Rifle Association
www.nra.org/
  Home page of one of America's most politically successful interest groups.

Project VoteSmart
www.vote-smart.org/
  Information on interest group campaign contributions to and ratings for all members of Congress.

Student Environmental Action Committee
www.seac.org/
  A grassroots coalition of student environmental groups.

Townhall
www.townhall.com
  A portal to scores of conservative organizations and citizen groups.

Yahoo/Organizations and Interest Groups
www.yahoo.com/Government/Politics/
  Direct links to the home pages of scores of public and private interest groups as well as to Washington lobbying firms.

Suggestions for Further Reading

Ainsworth, Scott H. *Analyzing Interest Groups: Group Influence on People and Policies.* New York: W. W. Norton, 2002.
  Shows how economic forms of reasoning can be used to better understand how interest groups work and what effect they have on politics and government.

Berry, Jeffrey M. *The New Liberalism: The Rising Power of Citizen Groups.* Washington, D.C.: Brookings, 1999.
  A controversial book that argues that liberal citizen groups representing consumer, civil rights, and environmental interests are more influential in the halls of Congress than either business or conservative citizens groups.

Cigler, Al J., and Burdett A. Lommis. eds. *Interest Group Politics,* 6th ed. Washington, D.C.: CQ Press, 2002.
  A collection by leading scholars that focuses on diverse aspects of interest group activities in American politics and their effects on public policies.

Dahl, Robert A. *A Preface to Democratic Theory.* Chicago: University of Chicago Press, 1956.
  The leading theoretical statement of the pluralist position and the democratic role of interest groups.

Davidson, Roger H., and Walter J. Oleszek, *Congress and Its Members,* 10th ed. Washington, D.C.: CQ Press, 2006.
  A comprehensive book on Congress that carefully examines the role of organized interests in the legislative process.

Lindblom, Charles. *Politics and Markets.* New York: Basic Books, 1977.
  A controversial and widely commented-on book in which one of the leading pluralist theorists concludes that the modern corporation is incompatible with democracy.

Skocpol, Theda. *Diminished Democracy: From Membership to Management in American Civil Life.* Norman, OK: University of Oklahoma Press, 2003.
  An analysis of the decline of mass membership associations and how it hurts American civic life.

Smith, Mark A. *American Business and Political Power: Public Opinion, Elections, and Democracy.* Chicago: University of Chicago Press, 2000.
  An argument, counter to that of Lindblom, that business corporations are not as powerful in American politics as often perceived.

CHAPTER 8

Social Movements

IN THIS CHAPTER

- Why social movements develop

- Where social movements fit in a democratic society

- What social movements do in politics

- How social movements influence what government does

Women Win the Right to Vote

The struggle for women's suffrage (e.g., the right to vote) was long and difficult. The main instrument for winning the struggle to amend the Constitution to admit women to full citizenship was a powerful social movement that dared to challenge the status quo, used unconventional tactics to gain attention and sympathy, and demanded bravery and commitment from many women.[1] One of these women was Angelina Grimké.

Abolitionist Angelina Grimké addressed the Massachusetts legislature in February 1838, presenting a petition against slavery from an estimated 20,000 women of the state. In doing so, she became the first woman to speak before an American legislative body. Because women at this time were legally subordinate to men and shut out of civic life—the life of home and church were considered their proper domains—Grimké felt it necessary to defend women's involvement in the abolitionist movement to end slavery. She said the following to the legislators:

> Are we aliens because we are women? Are we bereft of citizenship because we are mothers, wives and daughters of a mighty people? Have women no country—no interests staked in public weal—no partnership in a nation's guilt and shame? . . . I hold, Mr. Chairman, that American women have to do this subject [the abolition of slavery], not only because it is moral and religious, but because it is political, inasmuch as we are citizens of the Republic and as such our honor, happiness and well-being are bound up in its politics, government and laws.

Although this bold claim of citizenship for women did not fall on receptive ears—Grimké was derided as ridiculous and blasphemous by press and pulpit—it helped inspire other women who had entered political life by way of the abolitionist movement to press for women's rights as well. Meeting at Seneca Falls, New York, in 1848, a group of women issued a declaration written by Elizabeth Cady Stanton stating that "all men and women are created equal, endowed with the same inalienable rights." The declaration, much like the Declaration of Independence on which it was modeled, then presented a long list of violations of rights.

The Seneca Falls Declaration remains one of the most eloquent statements of women's equality ever written, but it failed to have an immediate effect because most politically active women (and men) in the abolitionist movement believed that their first order of business was to end slavery. Women's rights would have to wait.

After the Civil War destroyed the slave system, women's rights leaders such as Stanton, Susan B. Anthony, and Lucy Stone pressed for equal citizenship rights for all, white or black, male or female. They were bitterly disappointed when the Fourteenth Amendment, ratified after the war, declared full citizenship rights for all males born or naturalized in the United States, including those who had been slaves, but failed to include women. Women's rights activists realized that they would have to fight for rights on their own, with their own organizations.

Women's rights organizations were formed soon after the Civil War. For more than two decades, though, the National Woman Suffrage Association (NWSA) and the American Woman Suffrage Association (AWSA) feuded over how to pressure male politicians. Susan B. Anthony (with the NWSA) and Lucy Stone (with the AWSA) were divided by temperament and ideology. Anthony favored pressing for a broad range of rights and organized dramatic actions to expose men's hypocrisy. At an 1876 centennial celebration of the United States in Philadelphia, Anthony and several other women marched onto the platform, where the emperor of Brazil and other dignitaries sat, and read the declaration aloud. Stone favored gaining the vote as the primary objective of the rights movement and used quieter methods of persuasion, such as petitions.

In 1890, the two main organizations joined to form the National American Woman Suffrage Association (NAWSA). They dropped such controversial NWSA demands as divorce reform and legalized prostitution in favor of one order of business: women's suffrage. The movement was now focused, united, and growing more powerful every year.

In 1912, the NAWSA organized a march to support a constitutional amendment for suffrage. More than 5,000 women paraded through the streets of Washington before

Woodrow Wilson's inauguration. The police offered the marchers no protection from antagonistic spectators who pelted the marchers with rotten fruit and vegetables and an occasional rock, despite the legal parade permit they had obtained. This lack of protection outraged the public and attracted media attention to the suffrage movement.

Almost immediately after the United States entered World War I in April 1917, with the express purpose of "making the world safe for democracy," women began to picket the White House, demanding that full democracy be instituted in America. One demonstrator's sign quoted directly from President Wilson's war message—"we shall fight . . . for the right of those who submit to authority to have a voice in their own government"—and asked why women were excluded from American democracy. As the picketing at the White House picked up in numbers and in intensity, the police began arresting large groups of women. Other women took their place. The cycle continued until local jails were filled to capacity. When suffragists began a hunger strike in jail, authorities responded with forced feedings and isolation

cells. By November, public outrage forced local authorities to relent and free the women. By this time, public opinion had shifted in favor of women's right to vote.

In the years surrounding U.S. entry into the war, other women's groups worked state by state, senator by senator, pressuring male politicians to support women's suffrage. After two prominent senators from New England were defeated in 1918 primarily because of the efforts of suffragists and prohibitionists, the political clout of the women's groups became apparent to most elected officials. In June 1919, Congress passed the Nineteenth Amendment, and the necessary 36 states ratified it the following year. By uniting around a common cause, women's organizations gained the right to vote for all women.

Although few social movements have been as effective as the women's suffrage movement in reaching their primary goal, other social movements have also played an important role in American political life. This chapter is about what social movements are, how and why they form, what tactics they use, and how they affect American political life and what government does. ∎

Thinking Critically About This Chapter

This chapter is about the important role of social movements in American government and politics.

 Using the Framework You will see in this chapter how social movements are a response to structural changes in the economy, culture, and society and how they affect other political linkage actors and institutions—parties, interest groups, and public opinion, for example—and government. You will learn, most importantly, under what conditions social movements most effectively shape the behavior of elected leaders and the content of government policies.

 Using the Democracy Standard At first glance, because social movements are most often the political instrument of minorities, it may seem that they have little to do with democracy. You will see in this chapter, however, that social movements play an especially important role in our democracy, principally by broadening public debate on important issues and bringing outsiders and nonparticipants into the political arena.

What Are Social Movements?

secularization
The spread of nonreligious values and outlooks.

Social movements are loosely organized collections of people and groups who act over time, outside established institutions, to promote or resist social change. Today's Christian conservative movement, for example, is a broad collection of people, churches, and other organizations that have come together to resist the **secularization** of American society and to promote their version of religious values in American life.

Although they share some similarities, social movements are different from political parties and interest groups. Unlike political parties, for example, the sole aim of social movements is not to elect their own members to public office, although they may sometimes try to do so. Unlike interest groups, the sole aim of social movements is not to lobby political decision makers about legislative matters, although they may sometimes try to do this as well. What sets social movements apart from parties and interest groups is their focus on broad, societywide issues and their tendency to act outside the normal channels of government and politics, using unconventional and often disruptive tactics.[2] Some scholars call social movement politics "contentious politics."[3] When suffragists disrupted meetings, went on hunger strikes, and marched to demand the right to vote, they were engaged in contentious politics.

This general definition of social movements requires further elaboration if we are to understand their role in American politics. Here we highlight some important things to know about them:

- *Social movements are generally the political instruments of political outsiders.* Social movements often help people who are outside the mainstream gain a hearing from the public and from political decision makers. The women's suffrage movement forced the issue of votes for women onto the public agenda. The civil rights movement did the same for the issue of equal citizenship for African Americans. Gays and lesbians forced the country to pay attention to issues that had long been left "in the closet." Insiders don't need social movements; they can rely instead on interest groups, political action committees (PACs), lobbyists, campaign contributions, and the like to make their voices heard.

- *Social movements are generally mass grassroots phenomena.* Because outsiders and excluded groups often lack the financial and political resources of insiders, they must take advantage of what they have: numbers, energy, and commitment.

- *Social movements often use unconventional and disruptive tactics.* Officials and citizens almost always complain that social movements are ill-mannered and disruptive. For social movements, that is precisely the point. Unconventional and disruptive tactics help gain attention for movement grievances.

- *Social movements are populated by individuals with a shared sense of grievance.* People would not take on the considerable risks involved in joining others in a social movement unless they felt a strong, shared sense of grievance against the status quo and a desire to bring about social change. Social movements tend to form when a significant number of people come to define their own troubles and problems not in personal terms but in more general social terms (the belief that there is a common cause for all of their troubles) and when they believe that the government can be moved to take action on their behalf. Because this is a rare combination, social movements are very difficult to organize and sustain.

- *Social movements often generate interest group organizations.* Although particular social movements eventually fade from the political scene, for reasons we explore below, the more successful ones create organizations that carry on their work over a longer period of time. Thus, the women's movement spawned the National Organization for Women, while the environmental movement created organizations such as the Sierra Club and the Nature Conservancy. The movement of Christian evangelicals spurred the creation of groups such as the Family Research Council and the National Right to Life Committee.

SIMULATION

You Are the Leader of Concerned Citizens for World Justice

Major Social Movements in the United States

Many social movements have left their mark on American political life and have shaped what government does in the United States. Here we describe some of the most important.

The *abolitionists* aimed to end slavery in the United States. They were active in the northern states in the three decades before the outbreak of the Civil War. Their harsh condemnation of the slave system helped bring on the war that ended slavery.

The *Populist* movement was made up of disaffected farmers of the American South and West in the 1880s and 1890s who were angry with business practices and developments in the American economy that were adversely affecting them. Their aim was to force public ownership or regulation of banks, grain storage companies, and the railroads. For a short time, they were quite successful, winning control of several state legislatures, sending members to Congress, helping to nominate William Jennings Bryan as the Democratic candidate for president in 1896, and forcing the federal regulation of corporations (e.g., in the Interstate Commerce Commission Act).

The *women's suffrage* movement, active in the late nineteenth and early twentieth centuries, aimed to win the right to vote for women. As we saw in the chapter-opening story, the movement won its objective when the Nineteenth Amendment to the Constitution was ratified in 1920.

The *labor* movement represents efforts by working people over the years to protect jobs, ensure decent wages and benefits, and guarantee safe work-

FIGURE 8.1 • Timeline: The Nonviolent Civil Rights Movement

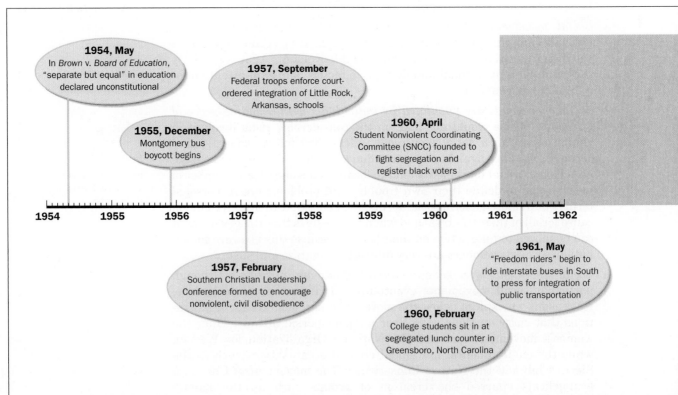

places. The periods of greatest militancy—when working people took to the streets and the factory floors to demand recognition of their unions—were in the 1880s, the 1890s, and the 1930s. The labor movement eventually forced the federal government to recognize the right of working people to form labor unions to represent them in negotiations with management.

The *civil rights* movement began in the mid-1950s, reached the peak of its activity in the mid-1960s, and gradually lost steam after that (see Figure 8.1). The movement, which was committed to nonviolent civil disobedience as one of its main tactics, remains one of the most influential on record, having pressed successfully for the end of formal segregation in the South and discriminatory practices across the nation (see Chapters 1 and 16). The main weapons of the movement were nonviolent civil disobedience and mass demonstrations.

The *anti–Vietnam War* movement was active in the United States in the late 1960s and early 1970s. Its aim was to end the war in Vietnam. It used a wide variety of tactics in this effort, from mass demonstrations to voting registration and nonviolent civil disobedience. Fringe elements even turned to violence, exemplified by the Days of Rage vandalism along Chicago's Gold Coast mounted by a wing of Students for a Democratic Society and the bombing of a research lab at the University of Wisconsin in which a graduate student was killed.

The *women's* movement has been important in American life since the late 1960s. Its aim has been to win civil rights protections for women and to broaden the participation of women in all aspects of American society, economy, and politics. Although it did not win one of its main objectives—passage of the **Equal Rights Amendment (ERA)** to the U.S. Constitution—the broad advance of women on virtually all fronts in the United States attests to its overall effectiveness.

Equal Rights Amendment (ERA)
Proposed amendment to the U.S. Constitution stating that equality of rights shall not be abridged or denied on account of a person's gender.

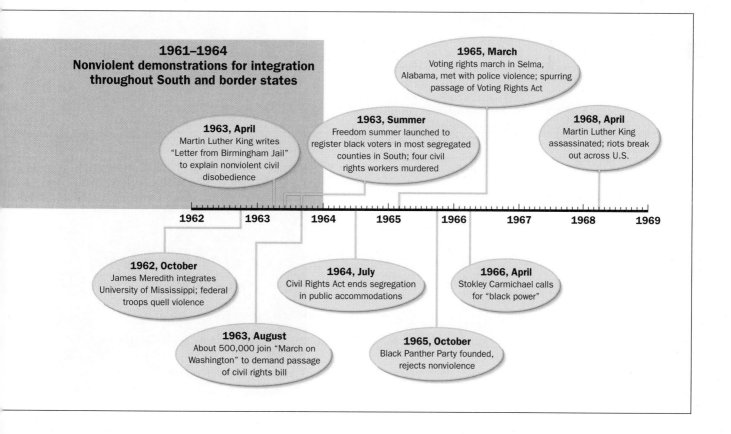

1961–1964
Nonviolent demonstrations for integration throughout South and border states

1965, March
Voting rights march in Selma, Alabama, met with police violence; spurring passage of Voting Rights Act

1963, April
Martin Luther King writes "Letter from Birmingham Jail" to explain nonviolent civil disobedience

1963, Summer
Freedom summer launched to register black voters in most segregated counties in South; four civil rights workers murdered

1968, April
Martin Luther King assassinated; riots break out across U.S.

1962   1963   1964   1965   1966   1967   1968   1969

1962, October
James Meredith integrates University of Mississippi; federal troops quell violence

1964, July
Civil Rights Act ends segregation in public accommodations

1966, April
Stokley Carmichael calls for "black power"

1963, August
About 500,000 join "March on Washington" to demand passage of civil rights bill

1965, October
Black Panther Party founded, rejects nonviolence

The *environmental* movement has been active in the United States since the early 1970s. Its aim has been to encourage government regulation of damaging environmental practices and to raise the environmental sympathies of the public. While the vitality of the movement has waxed and waned over the years, the public's strong support for environmental regulation suggests that it has been unusually successful. Although disruptive and even violent tactics have sometimes been used, the movement has depended more on legal challenges to business practices and the creation of organizations to lobby in Washington.

The *gay and lesbian* movement began in earnest in the late 1960s. Its aim was to gain the same civil rights protections under the law enjoyed by African Americans and other minority groups and to gain respect from the public. Ranging from patient lobbying and voting to mass demonstrations and deliberately shocking actions by groups such as ACT-UP, the movement's efforts have been only partially successful (see Chapter 16 for more details), but have also sparked strong counterattacks by groups such as the Christian Coalition and Focus on the Family that are opposed to its objectives.

Religious fundamentalist movements have occurred at several different moments in American history and have been very influential. These movements have brought together strongly religious people trying to infuse American society and public policies with their values. The contemporary movement of Christian conservatives falls within this tradition and has become very important in American politics, especially on the issues of abortion, school prayer, educational curriculum, and censorship of the media. The *pro-life (anti-abortion)* movement is part of the current larger religious fundamentalist movement. Its main objective is to end the legal availability of abortion in the United States.

An emergent *antiglobalization* movement announced itself to the public with demonstrations in Seattle in late 1999 targeted at the World Trade

Anti-Abortion Demonstrators

In recent years, many religious Americans have become politically active because of their objection to the general secularization of American life and social trends such as gay rights and abortion, which they consider contrary to traditional family values. Here a group of fundamentalist Christians demonstrates against the legal protection of abortion.

Organization (WTO), whose trade ministers were meeting in the city to fashion an agreement to further open national borders to trade and foreign investment.[4] The demonstrations were mostly peaceful, but some demonstrators turned violent. This movement is extremely diverse and includes people who are worried about the effects of globalization on the environment, income inequality in the United States and Third World countries, food safety, labor rights, sweat shops, unfair trade, and national sovereignty. The movement remains active, with protesters showing up at most large WTO gatherings, as well as those put on by the World Bank, the International Monetary Fund, the World Economic Forum (which meets annually in Davos, Switzerland), and the G-8 summit meetings of the leaders of the major industrial democracies.

An *anti-Iraq war* movement quickly formed in the months leading up to the U.S. invasion of Iraq in 2003. The movement's most dramatic political act was the organization of massive demonstrations across the world on February 15, 2003. In the United States, demonstrations took place in 150 cities; in New York, the crowd converging on the U.N. headquarters building filled a space 20 blocks long, along First and Second Avenues.[5] The massive demonstrations did not convince President Bush to put off the Iraq invasion, however. The movement lost support after the invasion of Iraq in April 2003, as patriotic feelings rose as troops went into battle, but the subsequent insurgency, and the high cost to the United States of the insurgency in lives and money, rekindled the movement in late 2005. It, as well as changing public opinion on the war, set the stage for increased calls from representatives and senators in Congress, even from some Republicans, for the administration to settle on an exit date from Iraq.

A series of massive demonstrations in the spring of 2006 in cities across the nation signaled the rise in the United States of an *immigrants' rights movement*. Although the goals of movement leaders, activists, and joiners were quite diverse, they were joined by a wish to give legal status to those presently living and working in the United States illegally, to allow more legal immigration from Mexico, and to increase Americans' understanding of the positive role played by immigrants—legal and illegal—in the American economy. Demonstration participants included not only legal immigrants, American citizens of Mexican

Anti-Iraq War Demonstrators

As the human and financial costs of the Iraq occupation mounted, thousands of Americans joined demonstrations such as this one in New York in April 2006 to protest the war and occupation and to demand that the troops be brought home.

descent, and sympathizers from many other ethnic and racial groups but, remarkably, tens of thousands of undocumented people subject to deportation if they came to the attention of the authorities.

Social Movements in a Majoritarian Democracy

At first glance, social movements do not seem to fit very well in a democracy. First, social movements usually start out with only a small minority of people, whereas democracy requires majority rule. Second, social movements often use disruptive tactics, when it seems that many channels already exist (e.g., voting, petitioning and writing to policymakers, and writing letters to newspapers) for people to express their grievances. In this section, we talk about how social movements can (and often do) help make American politics more democratic.

Encouraging Participation

Gun Rights and Gun Control

Social movements may increase the level of popular involvement and interest in politics. In one sense, this is true simply by definition: Social movements are the instruments of outsiders. Thus, the women's suffrage movement showed many middle-class women that their activities need not be confined exclusively to home, family, church, and charity work and encouraged them to venture into political life by gathering petitions or joining demonstrations demanding the vote for women. The civil rights movement in the 1960s encouraged southern African Americans, who had long been barred from the political life of their communities, to become active in their own emancipation. The religious fundamentalist movement spurred the involvement of previously politically apathetic evangelicals. The pro-immigration movement may yet spur increased political participation by Hispanic Citizens.

Social movements also encourage popular participation by dramatizing and bringing to public attention a range of issues that have been ignored or have been dealt with behind closed doors. The reason is that their contentious actions make these movements' members highly visible. They offer irresistible fare for the television camera. This ability to make politics more visible—called broadening the **scope of conflict** by political scientist E. E. Schattschneider[6]—makes politics the province of the many rather than the few.

scope of conflict

The number of groups involved in a political conflict; few groups mean a narrow scope of conflict, and many groups mean a wide scope of conflict.

Overcoming Political Inequality

Social movements also sometimes allow individuals and groups without substantial resources to enter the game of politics. Many social movements are made up of people who do not have access to the money, time, contacts, or organizational resources that fuel normal politics.[7] The ability of those without resources to disrupt the status quo by mobilizing thousands to take to the streets to voice their demands—what sociologists call **mass mobilization**—is a powerful political tool for people on the outside looking in. In the right circumstances, the disruptive politics of social groups can become as politically useful as other resources such as money and votes. Seemingly politically powerless women were able to mobilize to win the vote in the early part of the twentieth century; seemingly politically powerless blacks in the Deep South were able to secure full citizenship rights in the 1960s.

mass mobilization

The process of involving large numbers of people in a social movement.

Creating New Majorities

Over time, social movements may also help create new majorities in society. Social movements are the province of minorities, of course, and in a majoritarian democracy, minorities should have their way only if they can convince enough of their fellow citizens that what they want is reasonable. Before the 1930s, for instance, only a minority of Americans may have been convinced that labor unions were a good idea. The **Great Depression** and a vigorous, militant labor movement changed the opinion climate in the nation and created the basis for federal laws protecting the right of working people to form labor unions. Such issues as gender-based job discrimination and pay inequity, to take another example, were not important to the general public until they were brought center stage by the women's movement.

Great Depression

The period of economic crisis in the United States that lasted from the stock market crash of 1929 to America's entry into World War II.

Overcoming Gridlock

Sometimes it takes the energy of a social movement to overcome the antimajoritarian aspects of our constitutional system (see Chapter 2) and get anything done at all. As political scientist Theodore Lowi describes the issue:

> *Our political system is almost perfectly designed to maintain an existing state of affairs. . . . Our system is so designed that only a determined and undoubted majority could make it move. This is why our history is replete with social movements. It takes that kind of energy to get anything like a majority. . . . Change comes neither from the genius of the system nor from the liberality or wisdom of its supporters and of the organized groups. It comes from new groups or nascent groups—social movements—when the situation is most dramatic.*[8]

It is important to note that many of the social reforms of which most Americans are most proud—women's right to vote, equal citizenship rights for African Americans, Social Security, collective bargaining, and environmental protection—have been less the result of "normal" politics than of social movements started by determined and often disruptive minorities.

Factors That Encourage the Creation of Social Movements

A certain combination of factors, mainly structural, is apparently necessary for a social movement to develop.[9] We review the most important ones here.

The Existence of Social Distress

People who are safe, prosperous, and respected generally have no need of social movements. By contrast, those whose lives are difficult and unsafe or whose way of life or values are threatened, or whose way of life is disrespected, often find social movements an attractive means of calling attention to their plight and of pressing for changes in the status quo.[10]

Social distress caused by economic, social, and technological change helped create the conditions for the rise of most of the major social movements in American history. For example, the Populist movement occurred after western and southern farmers suffered great economic reverses during the latter part of the nineteenth century. The labor movement during the 1930s was spurred by the Great Depression—the virtual collapse of the industrial sector of the

Marching for Equal Rights

Social movements are a response to a real, immediate social distress or injustice. When women began to enter the job market in increasing numbers during the 1960s and 1970s, discriminatory hiring, barriers to career advancement, and unequal pay were unspoken realities of the business world. As more and more women refused to accept these conditions, the women's movement emerged. Here, a group demonstrates in favor of the Equal Rights Amendment, which did not receive passage in enough states to make it part of the U.S. Constitution.

American economy, historically unprecedented levels of unemployment, and widespread destitution. The rise of the Christian conservative movement seems to be associated with the perception among conservatives that religious and family values have declined in American life. For many women, distress caused by discriminatory hiring, blocked career advancement—in the form of the "glass ceiling" and the "mommy track"—and unequal pay at a time when they were entering the job market in increasing numbers during the 1960s and 1970s made participation in the women's movement attractive.[11] Discrimination, police harassment, and violence directed against them spurred gays and lesbians to turn to "contentious politics."[12] The AIDS epidemic added to their sense of distress and stimulated further political participation.[13]

Availability of Resources for Mobilization

Social strain and distress are almost always present in society. But social movements occur, it seems, only when the aggrieved group has the resources (including skilled leaders) sufficient to organize those who are suffering strain and distress.[14] The grievances expressed by the labor movement had existed for a long time in the United States, but it was not until a few unions developed—generating talented leaders, a very active labor press, and widespread media attention—that the movement began to take off. The women's movement's assets included a sizable population of educated and skilled women, a lively women's press, and a broad network of meetings to talk about common problems[15] (generally called *consciousness-raising groups*). The Christian conservative movement could build on a base of skilled clergy (for instance, Jerry Falwell and Pat Robertson), an expanding evangelical church membership, religious television and radio networks, and highly developed fund-raising technologies. The antiglobalization and anti-Iraq war movements, highly decentralized and organizationally amorphous, skillfully used the Internet to spread information, raise money, and organize demonstrations here and abroad.[16] Spanish-language radio stations played a big role in mobilizing people to join pro-immigrant marches and rallies in spring 2006.

A Supportive Environment

The rise of social movements requires more than the existence of resources for mobilization among aggrieved groups. The times must also be right, in the sense that a degree of support and tolerance must exist for the movement among the public and society's leaders.[17] The civil rights movement took place when overt racism among the public was declining (even in the then-segregated South) and national leaders were worried about the bad effects of segregation in the South on American foreign policy. Christian conservatives mobilized in an environment in which many other Americans were also worried about changes in social values and practices and when the Republican party was looking for a way to detach traditional Democratic voters from their party. The labor movement's upsurge during the 1930s coincided with the electoral needs of the Democratic party.[18] The women's movement surged at a time when public opinion was becoming much more favorable toward women's equality.[19] In 1972, for example, two out of three Americans reported to pollsters that they supported the proposal for an Equal Rights Amendment; the same proportion said they believed that the issues raised by the women's movement were important.[20] Gays and lesbians have benefited from the more tolerant attitudes toward homosexuality that have developed in recent years. Asked whether school boards should have the right to fire teachers who are homosexuals, only 33 percent of Americans agreed with the statement in 2003, compared with 51 percent as recently as 1987.[21]

Suspect Classifications and Gay Marriage

A Sense of Efficacy Among Participants

Some scholars believe that to develop an effective social movement, people who are on the outside looking in must come to believe that their actions can make a difference, that other citizens and political leaders will listen and respond to their grievances.[22] Political scientists call this "I can make a difference" attitude a sense of **political efficacy.** Without a sense of efficacy, grievances might

political efficacy
The sense that an individual can affect what government does.

Gay Pride Parade

Gays and lesbians have become much more politically visible and assertive since the "Stonewall" incident and riots in 1969. Here a gay-pride parade in San Francisco calls attention to the gay and lesbian communities and to the issues members of these communities want placed on the political agenda, including more funding for AIDs research.

explode into brief demonstrations or riots, but they would not support a long-term effort requiring time, commitment, and risk.

It may well be that the highly decentralized and fragmented nature of our political system helps sustain a sense of efficacy, because movements often find places in the system where they will be heard by officials. Christian conservatives have had little effect on school curricula in unitary political systems like that of Great Britain, for instance, where educational policy is made centrally, so few try to do anything about it. In the United States, however, they know they can gain the ear of local school boards and state officials in parts of the country where conservative religious belief is strong. Gays and lesbians have been able to convince public officials and local voters to pass antidiscrimination ordinances in accepting communities, such as San Francisco, California, and Boulder, Colorado, and to win cases in several state courts.

Some scholars have suggested that a strong sense of common identity among protest groups contributes to efficacy. Knowing that one is not alone, that others see the world in common ways and have common concerns, is often the basis for people's willingness to commit the time and energy and to take the risks that social movements require. Growing gay and lesbian identity seems to be an important component of the rising political self-confidence of this movement.[23]

A Spark to Set Off the Flames

Social movements require, as we have seen, a set of grievances among a group of people, the resources to form and sustain organization, a supportive environment, and a sense of political efficacy among the potential participants in the movement. But they also seem to require something to set off the mix, some dramatic precipitating event (or series of events), sometimes called a *catalyst,* to set them in motion. Passage of the Fourteenth Amendment, protecting the citizenship rights of males, galvanized the early women's suffrage movement, as we saw in the chapter-opening story. The gay and lesbian movement seems to have been sparked by the 1969 "Stonewall rebellion"—three days of rioting set off by police harassment of the patrons of a popular gay bar in Greenwich Village in New York City. The most important catalyst for the civil rights movement was Rosa Parks's simple refusal to give up her seat on a Montgomery, Alabama, bus in 1957. In 2006, Latinos were moved to action when the House passed a bill sponsored by James Sensenbrenner (R–WI) making illegal immigrants felons, subjecting long-time undocumented immigrants to deportation, and beefing up control of the U.S.–Mexican border.

Tactics of Social Movements

Social movements tend to use unconventional tactics to make themselves heard. Such tactics depend on the dramatic gesture and are often disruptive. As you saw in the opening story, the women's suffrage movement used mass demonstrations and hunger strikes to great effect. The labor movement invented **sit-down strikes** and plant takeovers as its most effective weapons in the 1930s. Pro-life activists added to the protest repertoire clinic blockades and the harassment of clinic patients, doctors, employees, and their families. More extreme elements within these groups have even added violence against clinics and doctors, including murder.

sit-down strike
A form of labor action in which workers stop production but do not leave their job site.

The most effective tool of the civil rights movement was nonviolent **civil disobedience,** a conscious refusal to obey a law that a group considers unfair, unjust, or unconstitutional, courting arrest by the authorities and assault from others, without offering resistance, as a way to highlight injustice and gain broader public sympathy. Dr. Martin Luther King was the strongest advocate for and popularizer of this strategy, having borrowed it from Mahatma Gandhi, who used it as part of the campaign that ended British colonial rule in India after the Second World War.[24] A particularly dramatic and effective use of this tactic took place in Greensboro, North Carolina. Four black students from North Carolina Agricultural and Technical State University sat down at a "whites only" lunch counter in a Woolworth's store on February 1, 1960, and politely asked to be served. When requested to leave, they refused. They stayed put and remained calm even as a mob of young white men screamed at them, squirted them with ketchup and mustard, and threatened to lynch them. Each day, more students from the college joined them. By the end of the week, more than 1,000 black students had joined the sit-in to demand an end to segregation. These actions ignited the South. Within two months, similar sit-ins had taken place in nearly 60 cities across nine states; almost 4,000 young people, including a number of white college students from outside the South, had tasted a night in jail for their actions. Their bravery galvanized blacks across the nation and generated sympathy among many whites. The student sit-in movement also spawned a new and more impatient civil rights organization, the Student Non-Violent Coordinating Committee (SNCC). (See the story of SNCC in Chapter 1.)

For his part, Dr. King led a massive nonviolent civil disobedience campaign in Birmingham, Alabama, in 1963 demanding that the city abide by the Supreme Court's decision in *Brown* v. *Board of Education* (1954) to end the segregation of schools and demanding the more broadly based **integration** of public services, especially public transportation. Nonviolent demonstrators, many of them schoolchildren, were assaulted by snarling police dogs, electric cattle prods, and high-pressure fire hoses that sent demonstrators sprawling. Police Commissioner Eugene "Bull" Connor filled his jails to overflowing with hundreds of young marchers, who resisted only passively, alternately praying

civil disobedience

Intentionally breaking a law and accepting the consequences as a way to publicize the unjustness of the law.

Civil Rights Movement

integration

Policies encouraging the interaction between different races in schools or public facilities.

Sit-Down Strike at GM

The sit-down strike was invented by labor movement activists in the American auto industry in the 1930s. Here, union members strike but stay put on the job site, daring management to use violence to end the work stoppage at General Motors in 1937.

Braving the Mob

Nonviolent civil disobedience proved the most effective tool of the civil rights movement. By violating unjust laws quietly and nonviolently, protesters alerted outsiders to the injustice of their situation. A sit-in at a "whites only" lunch counter in Greensboro, North Carolina, in 1957 by black college students, and publicity about the ill treatment they received at the hands of locals, sparked a wave of sit-ins by black college students and a few white sympathizers across the South. The arrest of nonviolent demonstrators generated sympathetic interest among previously apathetic whites across the nation.

and singing civil rights songs, including "We Shall Overcome." The quiet bravery of the demonstrators and the palpable sense among public officials and private sector leaders in the nation that matters were quickly spinning out of control convinced President John Kennedy on June 11, 1963, to introduce his historic civil rights bill for congressional consideration.

Why Some Social Movements Succeed and Others Do Not

Social movements have had a significant effect on American politics and on what government does. Not all social movements are equally successful, however. What makes some more successful than others seems to be

- The proximity of the movement's goals to American values.
- The movement's capacity to win public attention and support.
- The movement's ability to affect the political fortunes of elected leaders.

Low-Impact Social Movements

A social movement will have little effect if it has few followers or activists, has little support among the general public, and is unable to disrupt everyday life significantly or to affect the electoral prospects of politicians. The poor people's movement, which tried to convince Americans to enact policies that would end poverty in the United States, failed to make much of a mark in the late 1960s.

A social movement is particularly unlikely to have an effect on policy when it stimulates the formation of a powerful countermovement. The rational politician may find it prudent to take no action at all when he or she has difficulty calculating the relative weight of the two sides in a dispute between movements. This is one of several things that happened to the proposed Equal

A "Day Without Immigrants"

Marchers took to the streets across the nation on May 1, 2006, many taking time off from work, to show how important legal and illegal immigrants are for the American economy and to demand a path to citizenship for many more immigrants. These demonstrators are in Los Angeles.

Rights Amendment banning discrimination on the grounds of gender. The ERA failed to receive the approval of the necessary three-fourths of the states after anti-ERA forces (mainly Christian conservatives) rallied to block action during the 1970s.[25]

Repressed Social Movements

Social movements committed to a radical change in the society and the economy tend to threaten widely shared values and the interests of powerful individuals, groups, and institutions.[26] As a result, they rarely gain widespread popular support and almost always arouse the hostility of political leaders. Such movements very often face repression of one kind or another.[27] In the late nineteenth and early twentieth centuries, for instance, the labor movement was hindered by court injunctions forbidding strikes and boycotts, laws against the formation of labor unions, violence by employer-hired armed gangs, and strikebreaking by the National Guard and the U.S. armed forces. In 1877, 60,000 National Guardsmen were mobilized in 10 states to break the first national railroad strike. The strike against Carnegie Steel in 1892 in Homestead, Pennsylvania, brought the mobilization of 10,000 militiamen, the arrest of 16 strike leaders on conspiracy charges, and the indictment of 27 labor leaders for treason. The Pullman strike of 1894 was abruptly ended by the use of federal troops and by the arrest and indictment of union leaders.

Partially Successful Social Movements

Some social movements have enough power and public support to generate a favorable response from public officials but not enough to force them to go very far. In these situations, government may respond in a partial or half-hearted way. President Franklin D. Roosevelt responded to the social movements pressing for strong antipoverty measures during the Great Depression by proposing the passage of the Social Security Act, which fell far

Protesting Same-Sex Marriage

The 2004 decision by the Massachusetts Supreme Court that the state must provide ways for same-sex couples to marry sparked a furious reaction among religious conservatives. Here a group of evangelical Christians prays that the state legislature will reverse the state's high court decision. By 2006, over a score of states had enacted constitutional provisions prohibiting same-sex marriage as a way to forestall action similar to that of Massachusetts by their own state courts.

You Are a State Legislator

short of movement expectations.[28] The pro-life movement discovered that President Reagan was willing to use movement rhetoric to appoint sympathetic judges but was unwilling to submit anti-abortion legislation to Congress. Christian conservatives enjoyed some legislative successes during the height of their power in the 1990s and were important voices in the nominations of John Roberts and Samuel Alito to the Supreme Court by President Bush in 2005, but they failed to achieve some of their primary objectives: enact a law to ban late-term (in their words "partial birth") abortions, pass a constitutional amendment banning same-sex marriages, and remove Bill Clinton from the presidency by impeachment and trial. Gays and lesbians enjoyed some important successes, but encountered setbacks as well. (For more on gay and lesbian advances and setbacks, see the "Using the Framework" feature, as well as Chapter 16.)

Successful Social Movements

Social movements that have many supporters, win wide public sympathy, do not challenge the basics of the economic and social orders, and wield some clout in the electoral arena are likely to achieve a substantial number of their goals. The women's suffrage movement, described in the chapter-opening story, is one of the best examples. The civil rights movement is another, yielding, after years of struggle, the Civil Rights Act of 1964—which banned segregation in places of public accommodations such as hotels and restaurants—and the Voting Rights Act of 1965—which put the might of the federal government behind efforts to allow African Americans to vote and hold elected office. These enactments helped sound the death knell of the "separate but equal" doctrine enunciated in the infamous *Plessy* decision (1896), engineered the collapse of legal segregation in the South, and made the guarantee of full citizenship rights for African Americans a reality. The Voting Rights Act was particularly important in transforming the politics of the South. Black registration and voting turnout

Using the Framework

"Don't Ask, Don't Tell, Don't Pursue"

Why didn't Bill Clinton deliver on his promise to drop all restrictions on gays and lesbians in the military?

Background: Almost immediately after he was elected to office in 1992, Bill Clinton announced that, in his constitutional capacity as Commander-in-Chief, he intended to lift restrictions on gays and lesbians in the armed forces of the United States. In doing so, he was delivering on a campaign promise he had made to gay and lesbian organizations. After only a few weeks, however, he backed off from his promise and instituted a policy that came to be called "don't ask, don't tell, don't pursue." This policy of "turning a blind eye," yet allowing dismissal of gay and lesbian military personnel once discovered, satisfied no one, although it remains in force today. Taking a broad view at how structural, political linkage, and governmental factors affected Clinton's ultimate policy on gays and lesbians in the military will shed light on this situation.

Governmental Action

Bill Clinton announces that he will institute a "don't ask, don't tell" policy for gays and lesbians in the military.

Governmental Level

Members of Congress from both parties strongly oppose lifting restrictions on gays and lesbians in the military. ➡ The Chiefs of each of the branches of the military vehemently and publicly oppose lifting restrictions. ➡ The president, though committed to lifting restrictions on gays and lesbians, realizes that pushing the policy will lead to tension with Congress and the military services, and get his new administration off to a shaky start, so he retreats.

Political Linkages Level

The gay and lesbian movement creates a backlash, particularly among religious conservatives in all denominations. ➡ The Republican Party makes rolling back the so-called gay agenda a major part of its platform. ➡ Public opinion is conflicted; Americans support nondiscrimination against gays and lesbians in principle, but oppose gays and lesbians on a wide range of specific proposals.

Gays and lesbians form and effectively use social protest groups beginning in the 1970s. ➡ Gays and lesbians play an increasingly open role in political campaigns, as candidates, financial contributors, and party activists. ➡ The Democratic Party increasingly welcomes gay and lesbian support and participation. ➡ The mass media and entertainment industries become more sympathetic to gays and lesbians.

Structural Level

Higher levels of education among the population increases toleration of alternative lifestyles. ➡ Urbanization creates enclaves where gays and lesbians build communities, create social networks, and develop economic and political resources. ➡ The individualistic component of American culture and the Fourteenth Amendment to the Constitution favor a nondiscriminatory environment. ➡ However, the strongly religious component of American culture is also the foundation for widespread antihomosexual attitudes among religious conservatives.

Using the Democracy Standard

How do social movements affect democracy?

PROPOSITION: Social movements make American politics more democratic.

AGREE Our constitutional system favors the *status quo*. Federalism, separation of powers, and checks and balances make it extremely difficult to institute fundamentally new policies or to change existing social and economic conditions. The primacy of the status quo is further enhanced by the political power of economically and socially privileged groups and individuals who generally resist changes that might undermine their positions. Social movements represent a way—a difficult way, to be sure—by which political outsiders and the politically powerless can become players in the political game. Movements are a way such groups and individuals can gain a hearing for their grievances, work to win over a majority of their fellow citizens, and force elected leaders to take action. Equal citizenship for women and for African Americans, for example, would not have happened at all, or would have been much longer in coming, if not for existence of social movements demanding change.

DISAGREE Social movements are the tool of small minorities who force elected officials to respond to their demands because of the tangible threat of social disruption. Based on the age-old notion that "the squeaky wheel gets the grease," troublesome and disruptive groups can often get their way, even though the majority does not favor such action. In addition, because social movements often defy the law and social conventions, they tend to tear at the foundations of a stable democracy. A society that depends on social movements to bring needed change, moreover, is in a pretty sorry state; the normal tools to bring change in a democracy are sufficient.

CONSIDER Think about the most important changes brought about by government action in the United States over the course of our history.

• Which of them do you most admire? Perhaps Social Security and Medicare? Perhaps equal citizenship for disadvantaged minorities? Perhaps the expansion of civil liberties protections? • Which of the most important changes do you admire the least? Perhaps annual budget deficits? Perhaps domestic programs that don't work? • As best as you are able to tell, did social movements play an important role in forcing the policies that you most admire? Or in the policies that you least admire? • Based on your answers to these questions, what do you think the overall role of social movements ought to be in American politics? • Are they a good thing or a bad thing for American democracy? • Do leaders listen too much to them or too little?

increased dramatically all over the region during the late 1960s and the 1970s. Elected black officials filled legislative seats, city council seats, the mayors' offices in large and small cities, and sheriffs' offices. Between 1960 and 2001—the last year for which this statistic is available—the number of elected black officials in the United States increased from a mere 40 to more than 9,000.[29]

Elected white officials, tacking with the new winds of change, began to court the black vote in the years after passage of the Voting Rights Act. George Wallace, who first became famous by "standing in the schoolhouse door" to prevent the integration of the University of Alabama and who once kicked off a political campaign with the slogan "Segregation Today, Segregation Tomorrow, Segregation Forever," actively pursued the black vote in his last run for public office.

Movements can be successful even if no new laws are passed. Other measures of success include increased respect for members of the movement, changes in fundamental underlying values in society, and increased representation of the group in decision-making bodies. The women's movement has had this kind of success. Although the Equal Rights Amendment (the movement's main goal) failed, women's issues came to the forefront during these years, and, to a very substantial degree, the demands of the movement for equal treatment and respect made great headway in many areas of American life.[30] Issues such as pay equity, family leave, sexual harassment, and attention to women's health problems in medical research are now a part of the American political agenda. Women have made important gains economically and are becoming more numerous in the professions, corporate managerial offices (although there is some evidence that a glass ceiling remains in place), and political office.

Summary

Social movements emphasize rather dramatically the point that the struggle for democracy is a recurring feature of our political life. They are mainly the instruments of political outsiders who want to gain a hearing in American politics. Social movements often contribute to democracy by increasing the visibility of important issues, by encouraging wider participation in public affairs, and sometimes by providing the energy to overcome the many antimajoritarian features of our constitutional system.

Social movements try to bring about social change through collective action. Their rise is tied to the availability of organizational and leadership resources to a group of people who have a strong sense of grievance. Successful social movements happen, moreover, only if the political environment is supportive, in the sense that at least portions of the general population and some public officials are sympathetic to the movements' goals. The decline of particular social movements is associated with a number of things, including goal attainment, factional splits, the exhaustion of movement activists, and the replacement of grassroots activity by formal organization.

Social movements have had an important effect on our political life and in determining what our government does. Some of our most important legislative landmarks can be attributed to them. However, social movements do not always get what they want. They seem to be most successful when their goals are consistent with the central values of the society, have wide popular support, and fit the needs of political leaders.

mypoliscilab
Where participation leads to action!

Web Exploration
Movements and Political Participation

ISSUE: A common claim for social movements as a democratic instrument is that they increase political participation by outsiders.

SITE: Access the American National Election Study in MyPoliSciLab at **www.mypoliscilab.com.** Go to the "Web Explorations" section for Chapter 8, select "movements and political participation," then "participation." Select "Political Involvement and Participation in Politics." Choose various questions related to political participation, including voting. At the bottom of the page where you find general results for each question, the results are broken down by racial groups and gender in the section "percentage among demographic groups that responded."

WHAT YOU'VE LEARNED: Did the Civil Rights movement and the women's movement increase political participation among African Americans and women? Did participation increase in the period during and immediately after the social movements were at their height?

HINT: For African Americans, the relevant dates are the early 1960s to the present; for women, the relevant dates are the early 1970s to the present.

Internet Sources

African American News and Issues
www.aframnews.com /
A website devoted to materials on African American political, social, economic, and cultural life.

Christian Coalition
www.cc.org/
Information and links from the nation's most influential Christian conservative organization.

The Lesbian and Gay Alliance Against Defamation
www.glaad.org
News, issues, and links related to the gay and lesbian movement.

Pew Hispanic Center
http://pewhispanic.org
A rich site for data on Hispanic immigration to the United States and polling information on public opinion on immigration topics.

The Smithsonian Exhibits: Disability Rights
http://americanhistory.si.edu/disabilityrights/welcome.html
A Smithsonian online exhibit featuring the history of the disability rights movement.

Yahoo!Society and Culture
www.yahoo.com/Society_and_Culture/
A gateway with links to a multitude of social movements, issues, and groups.

Suggestions for Further Reading

Branch, Taylor. *Parting the Waters: America in the King Years, 1954–1963*. New York: Simon & Schuster, 1988.
A detailed and compelling description of the civil rights movement, with a particular focus on Martin Luther King, Jr.; winner of the National Book Award and the Pulitzer Prize.

Chafe, William H. *The Unfinished Journey: America Since World War II,* New York: Oxford University Press, 2003.
A justly celebrated history of America since 1945, with a particular focus on the civil rights and women's movements.

Dudziak, Mary L. *Cold War Civil Rights*. Princeton, NJ: Princeton University Press, 2002.
A compelling history of how the Cold War struggle with the Soviet Union provided a supportive environment for the civil rights movement.

Evans, Sarah M. *Born for Liberty: A History of Women in America*. New York: Free Press, 1997.
A compelling and widely used history of women in America, both substantively rich and a joy to read.

Horton, Carol A. *Race and the Making of American Liberalism*. New York: Oxford University Press, 2005.
Suggests that American liberalism has been useful in ending discrimination and expanding diversity, but much less useful in diminishing dramatic racial inequalities in status, power, and wealth.

Martin, Mart. *The Almanac of Women and Minorities in American Politics*. Boulder, CO: Westview Press, 2002.
A detailed, in-depth compendium about every aspect of women's and minorities' places in American political life.

Rimmerman, Craig A. *From Identity to Politics*. Philadelphia: Temple University Press, 2002.
An analysis of the gay and lesbian movement, using social movement theory to clarify how it has developed and changed, and a political agenda for the future.

Tarrow, Sidney. *Power in Movement: Social Movements and Contentious Politics*. Cambridge, U.K.: Cambridge University Press, 1998.
The leading academic treatment of social movements; analytically sophisticated and loaded with useful information about a broad range of movements.

CHAPTER 9

Political Parties

IN THIS CHAPTER

- Why political parties are important in a democracy

- How American political parties differ from parties elsewhere

- Why we have a two-party system

- How our party system has changed over the years

- What role third parties play

- How the Republican and Democratic parties differ

The Parties at War

As the war in Iraq dragged on, arguments between Democrats and Republicans over prewar intelligence about Saddam Hussein's alleged weapons of mass destruction program and ties to terrorist organizations burst out into the open in late 2005. The issue of how the Bush administration had used prewar intelligence resurfaced after vice presidential advisor "Scooter" Libby was indicted for lying to a grand jury investigating who had revealed the name of a covert CIA operative whose husband had questioned the existence of such a program. In a speech on November 11, 2005, shortly after the indictment, President Bush claimed that critics of prewar intelligence were undermining the war effort and the broader war on terrorism. Republican National Chairman Ken Mehlman chimed in a few days later that criticism of administrative actions leading up to the invasion of Iraq was unjustified and immoral: "This kind of political doublespeak sends exactly the wrong message to our troops, to the Iraqis and to our terrorist enemies." Vice President Dick Cheney similarly accused the administration's critics of being "dishonest and reprehensible," and continued, "Any suggestion that prewar information was distorted, hyped, or fabricated by the leader of the nation is utterly false. . . . This is revisionism of the most corrupt and shameless variety. It has no place anywhere in American politics, much less in the United States Senate."

The Democrats responded in kind. Democratic Senate Leader Harry Reid of Utah pointed out, "Rather than giving our troops a plan to move forward in Iraq and changing their failed course, they [administration supporters] continue to ignore the facts and lash out at those who raise legitimate questions about how the administration misused intelligence in its rush to war." Senator Ted Kennedy said, "The only thing dishonest and reprehensible is the way the administration distorted, misrepresented, and manipulated the intelligence to justify a war America never should have fought." Senator John Kerry, who had lost to President Bush in 2004, claimed that the Vice President was "still misleading the American people about the war and how we got into it."[1]

Democratic and Republican sparring over how we got into Iraq and how best to end our involvement there illustrates the partisan rancor that now characterizes American politics. In 2005 and 2006, for example, the two parties wrangled bitterly—both in Washington and across the country—over abortion, same-sex marriage, Social Security reform, the Medicare prescription drug program, extension of tax cuts, changes in bankruptcy and tort law, extension of the USA Patriot Act, and the causes of and solutions for mounting federal budget deficits. Incivility has become the order of the day when party leaders and elected officials deal with one another.

Opponents in Congress are accused of being scoundrels, liars, or cowards. Conference committees to iron out differences between Senate and House versions of important bills increasingly freeze out members of the minority party. Presidents are accused by their partisan opponents of plotting to undermine civil liberties, squash religious freedom, or enrich their friends. Federal judicial nominees are reviled by partisan opponents in the Senate and subjected to public castigation by advocacy groups associated with the opposition. In this environment, it is hardly surprising that cooperation across party lines is increasingly rare, not only in Congress but in state legislatures and city councils as well.

American politics is no stranger to partisan politics and nasty relations between the parties; to one extent or another, Democratic and Republican leaders and activists have always been in the business of making the other party look bad. It's good politics. However, things seem to be getting worse, at least according to most veteran observers of American politics. Most say they have not seen this level of partisan acrimony in a very long time and worry that bitter interparty combat is infusing nearly every aspect of political life in the United States.

What accounts for the intense partisanship of American politics today? The consensus of political scientists, journalists, and commentators is that the near–dead heat that exists between the parties across the nation—in expressed party identification among voters, the close division of seats between Democrats and Republicans in Congress and in many state legislatures, and the very tight results in recent presidential elections—has convinced party leaders that the best way to win elections at all levels is to unite and mobilize the party's base and get

243

it to the polls. Muting ideological and policy messages in a bid to win the votes of independents, most have concluded, risks alienating their own partisans and decreasing their turnout. It remains to be seen whether the Democratic success in the 2006 congressional elections in attracting independent voters by running moderate candidates in tightly contested areas will eventually change things.

So the first order of business for the parties has become the care and feeding of the party's base. And what better way to do this than to get partisans angry at the other party and worried about what it would do if it were to win? Democrats try to increase turnout among racial minorities, labor union members, hourly workers, environmentalists, and women by attacking Republicans for opposing affirmative action, being too friendly to large corporations, supporting unfair tax policies, rolling back environmental regulations, and undermining the right to abortion. Republicans try to mobilize their base of evangelical Christians, social conservatives, farmers, white southerners, people in the Mountain West, and the economically better-off by accusing Democrats of undermining the traditional family, blocking economic prosperity by supporting inefficient regulations and higher taxes, and sapping American strength abroad and thereby weakening the country in the fight against terrorism.

Political parties are an important part of democratic political systems. How well they function and fulfill their responsibilities has a lot to do with determining the health and vitality of democratic polities. We will examine political parties in this chapter and ask whether heightened levels of interparty conflict make our system more or less responsive to the people and our government more or less able to fashion coherent and workable public policies.   ■

Thinking Critically About This Chapter

This chapter is about American political parties, how they evolved, what they do, and how their actions affect the quality of democracy in the United States.

 Using the Framework You will see in this chapter how parties work as political linkage institutions connecting the public with government leaders and institutions. You will see, as well, how structural changes in the American economy and society have affected how our political parties function.

 Using the Democracy Standard You will see in this chapter that political parties, at least in theory, are one of the most important instruments for making popular sovereignty and majority rule a reality in a representative democracy, particularly in a system of checks-and-balances and separated powers such as our own. Evaluating how well our parties carry out these democratic responsibilities is one of the main themes of this chapter.

The Role of Political Parties in a Democracy

political party

An organization that tries to win control of government by electing people to office who carry the party label.

Political parties are organizations that try to win control of government by electing people to office who carry the party label. In representative democracies, parties are the principal organizations that recruit candidates for public office, run their candidates against the candidates of other political parties in competitive elections, and try to organize and coordinate the activities of government officials under party banners and programs.

Many political scientists believe that political parties are essential to democracy.[2] They agree with E. E. Schattschneider that "political parties created democracy and . . . modern democracy is unthinkable save in terms of the parties."[3] What Schattschneider and others see in the political party is the main instrument of popular sovereignty and, especially, majority rule: "The parties are the special form of political organization adapted to the mobilization of majorities. How else can the majority get organized? If democracy means anything at all it means that the majority has the right to organize for the purpose of taking over the government."[4]

In theory, political parties can do a number of things to make popular sovereignty and political equality possible:[5]

- *Keep elected officials responsive.* Competitive party elections help voters choose between alternative policy directions for the future. They also allow voters to make a judgment about the past performance of a governing party and decide whether to allow that party to continue in office. And, a party can adjust its **party platform**—the party's statement of its position on the issues—to reflect the preferences of the public as a way to win elections.

- *Include a broad range of groups.* Political parties can enhance political equality in a democracy because they tend to include as many groups as they possibly can. Parties are by nature inclusive, as they must be if they are to create a winning majority coalition in elections. It is customary for parties in the United States to recruit candidates for public office from many ethnic and racial groups and to include language in their platforms to attract a diversity of groups.

- *Stimulate political interest.* When they are working properly, moreover, political parties stimulate interest in politics and public affairs and increase participation. They do this as a natural by-product of their effort to win or retain power in government; they mobilize voters, bring issues to public attention, and educate on the issues that are of interest to the

party platform

A party's statement of its positions on the issues of the day.

Deciding on a Political Party

The Government is Closed

Struggles over the budget between the Republican-led Congress and President Clinton (a Democrat) led to temporary closures of all nonessential government departments and agencies in 1995.

party.[6] Party competition, by "expanding the scope of conflict," attracts attention and gets people involved.[7]

- *Ensure accountability.* Parties can help make officeholders more accountable. When things go wrong or promises are not kept, it is important in a democracy for citizens to know who is responsible. Where there are many offices and branches of government, however, it is hard to pinpoint responsibility. Political parties can simplify this difficult task by allowing for collective responsibility. Citizens can pass judgment on the governing ability of a party as a whole and decide whether to retain the incumbent party or to throw it out of office in favor of the other party.

- *Help people make sense of complexity in politics.* Party labels and party positions on the issues help many people make sense of the political world. Few people have the time or resources to learn about and reach decisions on every candidate on the ballot or the issues before the public at any period in time. Party labels and policy positions can act as useful shortcuts enabling people to cut through the complexities and reach decisions that are consistent with their own values and interests.

- *Make government work.* In a system like ours of separation of powers and checks and balances, designed to make it difficult for government to act decisively, political parties can encourage cooperation across the branches of government among public officials who are members of the same party. Parties can help overcome gridlock, an all too common feature of our constitutional system.

Political parties, then, can be tools of popular sovereignty. Whether our own political parties fulfill these responsibilities to democracy is the question we explore in the remainder of this chapter as well as in Chapter 10.

History of the Two-Party System

Declining Political Parties

The United States comes closer to having a "pure" two-party system than any other nation in the world. Most Western democracies have multiparty systems. In the United States, however, two parties have dominated the political scene since 1836, and the Democrats and the Republicans have controlled the presidency and Congress since 1860. Minor or third parties have rarely polled a significant percentage of the popular vote in either presidential or congressional elections (more will be said later about third parties and independent candidates), although they are sometimes successful at the state and local levels. Jesse Ventura, for example, was elected governor of Minnesota in 1998 as the nominee of the Reform Party.

Although the United States has had a two-party system for most of its history, the system has not been static. It has, in fact, changed a great deal, both mirroring and playing a central role in the dynamic and sometimes chaotic story of the development of the United States, as described in Chapter 4. Scholars have identified six relatively stable periods in the history of the two-party system in the United States, each different in one or more important ways from the others. These periods have lasted between 30 and 40 years, separated by periods of **realignment,** after which a new party period has emerged. Realignments take several forms: two of them, 1896 and 1932, were relatively sudden; two stretched over a decade or so (the ones beginning around 1816 and 1860); and one was even longer, leading into our current sixth party system described below.[8] Figure 9.1 shows this history in graphic form.

realignment

The process by which one party supplants another as the dominant party in a political system.

The First Party System: Federalists Versus Democratic Republicans

Although the Founders were hostile to parties in theory, they created them almost immediately. The first was formed in the 1790s by George Washington's energetic secretary of the treasury, Alexander Hamilton. In a successful effort to push through the administration's ambitious legislative program, Hamilton persuaded sympathetic members of Congress to form a loosely organized party that eventually took the name Federalist.

Thomas Jefferson, James Madison, and others formed a party in Congress and in state and local communities to oppose the Hamilton domestic program and Federalist foreign policy. They called it the Democratic-Republican Party—later, simply the Democratic Party—and found their main supporters among small farmers, artisans, hired employees, and the less-privileged. The new party played a key role in the election of Thomas Jefferson to the presidency in 1800.

The Federalist party gradually disappeared, unable or unwilling to copy the grassroots organizing strategy of the Democratic-Republican Party, and tainted by its pro-British sympathies during the War of 1812 and its image as a party of the wealthy and the aristocratic in an increasingly democratic America. By 1816, the first two-party system had evolved into a one-party or no-party system, generally known (because of the absence of party competition) as the Era of Good Feelings.

The Second Party System: Democrats Versus Whigs

The Era of Good Feelings gave way in the late 1820s to a strong two-party system that grew out of the disputed presidential election of 1824. In that election, Andrew Jackson won a plurality of the popular and electoral votes

Rallying the Troops

The second party system was characterized by well-organized parties, skilled in the use of methods (such as this parade) to mobilize the "common man" to participate in electoral politics.

FIGURE 9.1 • Timeline: Party Systems in the United States

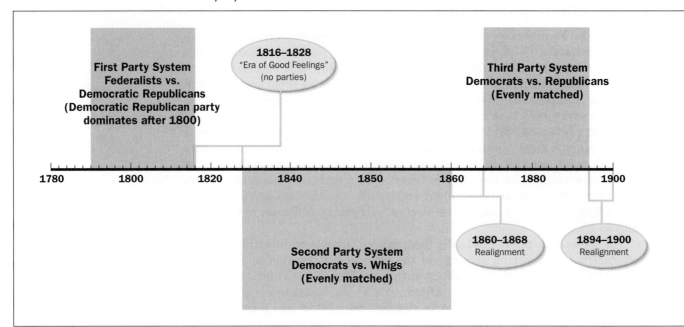

American politics has been characterized by a series of stable political party eras punctuated by periods of transition—some sudden, others more sustained—from one party era to another. The present party system, characterized by near parity between the parties and a large block of independent voters, is unique in American history.

but failed to win a majority of either. The House of Representatives chose John Quincy Adams president. Supporters of Jackson formed an opposition from one wing of the Democratic-Republican Party, taking the name Democratic Party. The Jacksonian Democrats were the first broadly based popular party, building on the rapid expansion of white, male suffrage, and were opposed to high tariffs and big business. Adams and his supporters, assisted by the powerful Speaker of the House Henry Clay, organized as the Whig Party (sometimes called the Democratic Whig Party), favoring legislative supremacy and support for business interests.

Each of the parties split apart along sectional lines as the nation drifted toward civil war. The Whig party simply disintegrated and disappeared. Several of its fragments came together with *Free-Soilers* (who opposed the expansion of slavery into the western territories) and antislavery Democrats to form a new Republican party—the ancestor of the present-day Republicans—which ran its first presidential candidate, John Frémont, in the election of 1856. The Democrats survived but could not agree on a single candidate to run against Republican Abraham Lincoln in 1860, so the southern and northern wings of the party each nominated its own candidate.

From the Civil War to 1896: Republicans and Democrats in Balance

Once the southern states had reentered the Union after Reconstruction, the Republicans and the Democrats found themselves roughly balanced in national politics. Between 1876 and 1896, the Democrats managed to control the

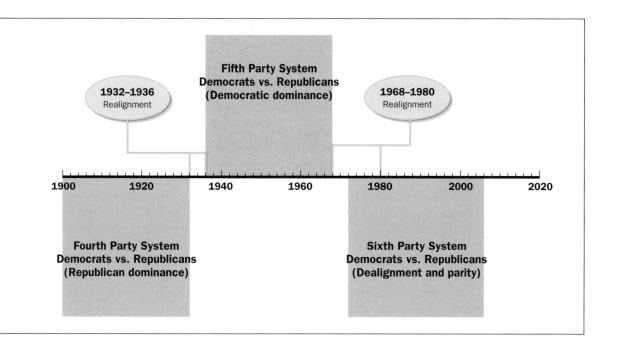

presidency for 8 of 20 years, the Senate for 6 years, and the House of Representatives for 14 years. Each party had a strong regional flavor. The Democratic party was primarily a white southern party, although Catholics and many workers in northern urban areas also supported it. The Republicans (also known as the "Grand Old Party," or GOP) became a party of business, the middle class, and newly enfranchised male African Americans.

The Party System of 1896: Republican Dominance

Beneath the apparent calm of a balanced two-party system, however, a storm was brewing. The late nineteenth century was a time of rapid economic and social change and disruption, one effect of which was to spawn a host of protest movements and third parties. The Populist party, the most important of them, garnered 8.5 percent of the total vote in the 1892 election and won four states in the electoral college, running on the slogan, "Wealth belongs to him who creates it." During the 1890s, Populist party candidates also won governorships in eight states and control of at least as many state legislatures.

In 1896, the Populist party joined with the Democratic party to nominate a single candidate for the presidency, the charismatic orator William Jennings Bryan, who urged "free coinage of silver" to help debtors with cheaper currency. The threat of a radical agrarian party, joining blacks and whites, farmers and labor unionists, proved too much for many Americans and contributed to one of the most bitter electoral campaigns in U.S. history. Conservative Democrats deserted their party to join the Republicans. Businesses warned each other and their workers in no uncertain terms about the dangers of a Populist-Democratic victory. Newly formed business organizations, such as the National Association of Manufacturers, spread the alarm about a possible Democratic victory. In the South, efforts to intimidate potential black voters increased dramatically.[9]

The Republicans won handily and dominated American politics until the Great Depression and the election of 1932. Between 1896 and 1932, the Republicans won control of both houses of Congress in 15 out of 18 elections and of the presidency in 7 out of 9.

The New Deal Party System: Democratic Party Dominance

New Deal

The programs of the administration of President Franklin D. Roosevelt.

New Deal coalition

The informal electoral alliance of working-class ethnic groups, Catholics, Jews, urban dwellers, racial minorities, and the South that was the basis of the Democratic party dominance of American politics from the New Deal to the early 1970s.

The Great Depression, the **New Deal,** and the leadership of President Franklin D. Roosevelt ushered in a long period of Democratic party dominance. From 1932 through 1964, the Democrats won seven of nine presidential elections, controlled the Senate and the House of Representatives for all but four years, and prevailed in a substantial majority of governorships and state legislatures across the nation. Democratic dominance was built on an alliance of workers, Catholics, Jews, unionists, small- and medium-sized farmers, urban dwellers, white ethnics, southerners, and blacks that came to be known as the **New Deal coalition.** The New Deal coalition supported an expansion of federal government powers and responsibilities, particularly in the areas of old age assistance, aid for the poor, encouragement of unionization, subsidies for agriculture, and regulation of business.

The Sixth Party System: Dealignment and Parity

The New Deal coalition began to slowly disintegrate in the 1968 election (won by Republican Richard Nixon) and finally collapsed in 1980 with the Republican capture of the presidency and the Senate.[10] The change in the party system was triggered by three major developments. First, strong support by the Democratic Party for the civil rights revolution—which brought new antidiscrimination laws, busing to achieve school integration, and, eventually, minority set-asides for government jobs and contracts and affirmative action programs in higher education—caused many white southerners and

FDR Adds to His Coalition

The wealthy and patrician Franklin D. Roosevelt attracted a wide range of common people to his Democratic Party, including industrial workers, poor farmers, and farm laborers. Here he talks with Georgia farmers during his campaign for the presidency in 1932.

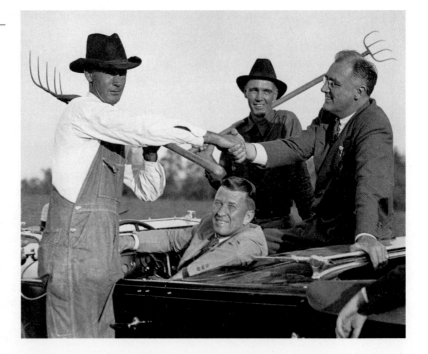

blue-collar workers to switch their loyalties from the Democrats to the Republicans, even while African Americans became more loyal to the Democrats.[11] Second, the tendency of the Democrats to openly welcome feminists and gays and support their bid for equal rights, as well as the growing identification of Democrats with the doctrine of strict separation of church and state, caused religious conservatives to abandon the party. Third, perceived Democratic Party opposition to the Vietnam War, especially during the Nixon years 1969 through 1973, caused many Americans who favored a strong national defense and an aggressive foreign policy to drift away as well.

After 1980, the pace of Democratic decline began to pick up, with Democrats losing their big advantage in control of governorships and state legislatures, as well as in party identification among the electorate. They also began to lose control in Congress, first in the Senate and then the House after the 1994 elections. Despite Democratic losses and Republican gains, the overall picture of the post-1980 period has been one of divided government at both the federal and state levels, a situation in which one party controls the executive and the other controls all or part of the legislative branch.

The transition from the fifth party system to the sixth was not the classic party realignment that occurred after the elections of 1896 and 1932. In those earlier elections, a system dominated by one party was replaced in rather short order by a system dominated by the other. This time, however, while the dominant Democratic Party lost its overall lead, the Republican Party did not emerge as the unchallenged, across-the-board leader in politics and governance, although some saw the seeds of a possible new Republican majority in the return of unified government to Washington after the 2002 congressional elections. The Democratic victory in 2006 ended such talk. This form of change in which a dominant part declines without another taking its place is **dealignment**.[12] The resulting sixth party system is one of near parity in which the Republican and Democratic parties are evenly divided in terms of elected offices held, the distribution of votes among the electorate, and party identification among Americans. In party terms, the United States had become a 50–50 nation.[13]

As explained in the chapter-opening story, the sixth party system is highly volatile, given the parity between the parties, higher levels of partisanship among party activists and strong identifiers, and a large block of voters who consider themselves independents, without enduring loyalties to either party (see Chapter 5). Because the parties are so close in the number of elected offices they hold, even small swings in turnout can change which party controls the presidency and Congress. Because Democratic and Republican identifiers are divided so deeply on issues and ideology, **partisan** voters and party activists and leaders believe more is at stake in elections, increasing the emotional intensity of elections. And because there are so many more independent voters than in the past, more voters swing toward the Democrats in one election, then toward the Republicans in the next. Or they now and again support a maverick independent candidate or insurgent third party, upsetting the fine balance between Democrats and Republicans. The "Mapping American Politics" feature illustrates the geographical shift in party strength between the fifth and sixth party periods and the present situation of partisan parity.

Poverty and Political Parties

dealignment
A gradual reduction in the dominance of one political party without another party supplanting it.

partisan
A committed supporter of a political party; seeing issues from the point of view of a single party.

Why a Two-Party System?

Most Western democracies have multiparty systems, with more than two major parties. Why are we so different from other countries? There are several reasons.

Mapping American Politics

The shifting geography of the parties

Introduction: The centers of strength of each of the major political parties changed during the last third of the twentieth century. In 1960 the Democrats tended to dominate in the southern states and in the industrial states of the Middle Atlantic and upper Midwest, while Republicans were particularly strong in parts of New England, the Great Plains, the Mountain West, and the Pacific Coast. In recent presidential elections, not only have the Plains and Mountain West states become more reliably Republican, but the South has moved solidly into the Republican column. At the same time, the Pacific Coast and New England have become more reliably Democratic. Because of population shifts, moreover, the distribution of electoral votes has shifted among the

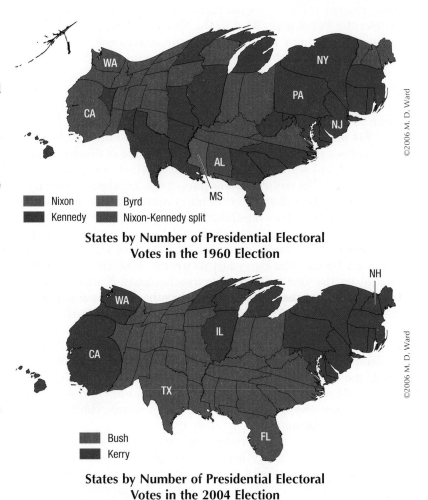

©2006 M. D. Ward

States by Number of Presidential Electoral Votes in the 1960 Election

- Nixon
- Kennedy
- Byrd
- Nixon-Kennedy split

©2006 M. D. Ward

- Bush
- Kerry

States by Number of Presidential Electoral Votes in the 2004 Election

Electoral Rules: How Exceptional?

The kinds of rules that organize elections help determine what kind of party system exists.[14] Which rules are chosen, then, have important consequences for a nation's politics.

proportional representation

The awarding of legislative seats to political parties to reflect the proportion of the popular vote each party receives.

Proportional Representation Most other democratic nations use some form of **proportional representation** (PR) to elect their representatives. In PR systems, each party is represented in the legislature in rough proportion to the percentage of the popular vote it receives in an election. In a perfect PR system, a party winning 40 percent of the vote would get 40 seats in a 100-seat legislative body, a party winning 22 percent of the vote would get 22 seats, and so on. In such a system, even very small parties would have a reason to main-

states, changing the calculations of those who plan and wage presidential campaigns.

Mapping Party Electoral Votes: The states in the two cartograms are sized in proportion to their electoral votes in presidential elections and colored by whether they cast their electoral votes for Democrats (blue) or Republicans (red) in 1960 (the cartogram on the top) and 2004 (the cartogram on the bottom). Because each state's electoral votes are the total of their representatives and senators in Congress, they are roughly proportional to the size of their populations. We can see at least two important things in the cartograms. First, between 1960 and 2004, electoral votes of the Middle Atlantic states, New England, and the upper Midwest decreased while they increased in California, the Southwest, and the South (particularly in Florida and Texas), reflecting the shift in the populations of the states over this time period. Second, both elections were extremely close, but the states that came together to elect Democrat John F. Kennedy in 1960 and those that combined to elect George W. Bush in 2004 were quite different, although there is some overlap. These changes have changed the strategies of the parties. The Democrats today can pretty much count on winning California, Washington, Illinois, the New England states, New York, and New Jersey;

Republicans can count on the South outside of Florida and the Southwest, Mountain West, and Plains states. (Alabama and Mississippi in 1960 were beginning their transition from the Democratic column to the Republican, with Mississippi choosing Harry Byrd's "States Rights" Party and Alabama splitting its votes between the Democrats and the Republicans). The remaining states—often called battleground states—are where presidential campaigns are waged today and where presidential elections are won and lost.

What Do You Think? Does it make sense to you to elect presidents by electoral votes rather than direct popular vote, especially when so many states are safe for one party or the other? Some critics argue that having so many noncompetitive states in the electoral college, with the bulk of the electioneering going on in the handful of states where the outcome is in doubt, deprives the majority of Americans of being fully engaged in the process of electing the president. What do you think?

Map note: Mississippi electoral votes were cast for Harry Byrd, an independent candidate, in 1960. Alabama split its 11 electoral votes: 6 for Kennedy and 5 for Nixon.

Source: Election data are from historical tables, U.S. Bureau of the Census, *Statistical Abstract of the United States,* 2006.

tain their separate identities, for no matter how narrow their appeal, they would win seats as long as they could win a proportion of the popular vote. Voters with strong views on an issue or with strong ideological outlooks could vote for a party that closely represented their views. A vote for a small party would not be wasted, because it would ultimately be translated into legislative seats and, perhaps, a place in the governing coalition.

Israel and the Netherlands come closest to having a pure PR system, organized on a national basis; most western European nations depart in various ways from the pure form. Most, for instance, vote for slates of party candidates within multimember electoral districts, apportioning seats in each district according to each party's percentage of the vote. In Germany, seats in the Bundestag (the lower house of the national parliament) are filled by a combination of elections from single-member districts and a party's share of the nationwide vote. Russia

Comparing Political Parties

has a similar system for elections to the lower house of the state Duma. Most democracies that use proportional representation also have a minimum threshold (often 5 percent) below which no seats are awarded to a party. In the Russian parliamentary elections in 2004, so many parties were on the ballot that only a handful were able to cross the minimum-vote threshold for parliamentary seats.

SIMULATION

You Are Redrawing the Districts in Your State

Winner-Take-All, Plurality Election, Single-Member Districts Elections in the United States are organized on a winner-take-all, single-member-district basis. Each electoral district in the United States—whether it is an urban ward, a county, a congressional district, or a state—elects only one person to a given office and does so on the basis of whoever wins the *most* votes (not necessarily a majority). This is why our way of electing leaders is sometimes called a "first past the post" system, analogous to a horse race. This arrangement creates a powerful incentive for parties to coalesce and for voters to concentrate their attention on big parties. Let's see why.

From the vantage point of party organizations, this type of election discourages minor-party efforts because failure to come in first in the voting leaves a party with no representation at all. Leaders of such parties are tempted to merge with a major party. By the same token, a disaffected faction within a party is unlikely to strike out on its own because the probability of gaining political office is very low.

From the voter's point of view, a single-member, winner-take-all election means that a vote for a minor party is wasted. People who vote for a minor party may feel good, but most voters have few illusions that such votes will translate into representation and so are not inclined to cast them.

Note that the most important office in American government, the presidency, is elected in what is, in effect, a single-district (the nation), winner-take-all election. The candidate who wins a majority of the nation's votes in the electoral college wins the presidency (see Chapter 10). A party cannot win a share of the presidency; it is all or nothing. In parliamentary systems, the executive power is lodged in a cabinet, however, where several parties may be represented.

Tracking Electoral Votes

A presidential election is decided by which candidate has won a majority in the electoral college, *not* by a majority of the total votes cast. That is why on election night every four years the television networks focus on state-by-state victories and defeats.

Restrictions on Minor Parties

Once a party system is in place, the dominant parties often establish rules that make it difficult for other parties to get on the ballot.[15] A number of formidable legal obstacles stand in the way of third parties and independent candidates in the United States. While many of these restrictions have been eased because of successful court challenges by recent minor-party and independent presidential candidates such as Ross Perot, the path to the ballot remains tortuous in many states, where a considerable number of signatures are required to get on the ballot. Moreover, the requirements for ballot access are different in every state. While the two main parties, with party organizations in place in each of the states and well-heeled national party committees, are able to navigate this legal patchwork, new and small parties find it quite difficult.

The federal government's partial funding of presidential campaigns has made the situation of third parties even more difficult. Major-party candidates automatically qualify for federal funding once they are nominated. Minor-party candidates must attract a minimum of 5 percent of the votes cast in the general election to be eligible for public funding, and they are not reimbursed until after the election. In recent decades, only the Reform Party among the legion of minor parties has managed to cross the threshold to qualify for federal funding. Because the Green Party's candidate, Ralph Nader, won only 2.7 percent of the national vote in the 2000 election, it was not eligible for federal funding for the 2004 election. David Cobb, the Green Party's presidential candidate in 2004, hardly registered at the polls, winning about 0.1 percent of the vote. (Nader, the candidate of the Independent and Reform Parties, also organizations without federal funding, garnered only 0.4 percent of the vote.)

The Role of Minor Parties in the Two-Party System

Minor parties have played a less important role in the United States than in virtually any other democratic nation.[16] In our entire history, only a single minor party (the Republicans) has managed to replace one of the major parties. Only six (not including the Republicans) have been able to win even 10 percent of the popular vote in a presidential election, and only seven have managed to win a single state in a presidential election.

Minor parties have come in a number of forms:

Third Parties

- *Protest parties* sometimes arise as part of a social movement. The Populist party, for instance, grew out of the western and southern farm protest movements in the late nineteenth century. The Green Party was an offshoot of the environmental and antiglobalization movements.

- *Ideological parties* are organized around coherent sets of ideas. The several Socialist parties have been of this sort, as has the Libertarian party. The Green Party ran in the 2000 elections on an anticorporate, antiglobalization platform.

- *Single-issue parties* are barely distinguishable from advocacy groups. What makes them different is their decision to run candidates for office. The Prohibition party and the Free-Soil party fall into this category as did Perot's "balanced budget" Reform Party in 1996.

- *Splinter parties* form when a faction in one of the two major parties bolts to run its own candidate or candidates. An example is the Bull

Nader Seeks Votes

Candidates such as Ralph Nader and third parties such as the Green Party often bring up issues the main parties are unable or unwilling to address.

Third Parties in American History

Moose Progressive party of Teddy Roosevelt, formed after Roosevelt split with Republican party regulars in 1912.

Minor parties do a number of things in American politics. Sometimes they articulate new ideas that are eventually taken over by one or both major parties. Ross Perot's popular crusade for a balanced budget during his 1992 campaign helped nudge the major parties toward a budget agreement that, for a while, eliminated annual deficits in the federal budget.

It is also the case that third parties can sometimes change the outcome of presidential contests by changing the outcome of the electoral vote contest in the various states: in 1992, a substantial portion of the Perot vote was comprised of people who otherwise would have voted Republican, allowing Bill Clinton to win enough states to beat George H. W. Bush; in 2000, a substantial portion of the Nader vote in Florida was composed of people who otherwise would have voted Democratic, allowing George W. Bush to win Florida's electoral votes and the presidency over Al Gore.

Democrats and Republicans

The Democratic and Republican parties don't look much like parties in other rich democratic countries. In most of them, the political parties are hierarchically structured organizations led by full-time party professionals and traditionally committed to a set of ideological principles. They also tend to have clearly defined membership requirements, centralized control over party nominations and electoral financing, and disciplinary authority over elected party members in the national parliament and cabinet ministries. The major American parties have almost none of these qualities, although the Republicans have become much more ideologically cohesive than has traditionally been the case in American politics.

The Organization of American Political Parties

The Republican and Democratic parties are not organizations in the usual sense of the term, but rather loose collections of local and state parties, campaign committees, candidates and officeholders, and associated interest groups that get together every four years to nominate a presidential candidate. Unlike a corporation, a bureaucratic agency, a military organization, or even a political party in most other countries, the official leaders of the major American parties cannot issue orders that get passed down a chain of command. Even popular, charismatic, and skillful presidents, including George Washington, Abraham Lincoln, Woodrow Wilson, Franklin Roosevelt, Harry Truman, John Kennedy, and Ronald Reagan, have had nearly as much trouble controlling the many diverse and independent groups and individuals within their own parties as they have had dealing with the opposition. George W. Bush discovered this in 2005 and 2006 when a significant number of Republican members of the House and Senate, loyal followers throughout his first term, began to abandon him on Iraq, his plan to change Social Security, and immigration reform.

The ill-defined nature of Republican and Democratic party membership is another indicator of how different American political parties are from political parties in other countries, as well as from private organizations. What does it mean, in fact, to be a Republican or a Democrat in the United States? Americans do not join parties in the sense of paying dues and receiving a membership card. To Americans, being a member of a party may mean voting most of the time for the candidate of a party or choosing to become a candidate of one of them. Or it may mean voting in a party primary. Or it may mean contributing money to, or otherwise helping in, a local, state, or national campaign of one of the party candidates. Or it may just mean generally preferring one party over another most of the time. These are loose criteria for membership, to say the least—looser than for virtually any other organization that might be imagined.

Unlike a traditional organization and unlike political parties in other democracies, the various elements of the Democratic and Republican parties are relatively independent from one another and act in concert not on the basis of orders, but on the basis of shared interests, sentiment, and the desire to win elections,[17] which can be quite powerful coordinators of party activities, to be sure. (See Figure 9.2 for a graphical representation of these ideas.) Most important, perhaps, the parties do not control the nomination of candidates running under the party label—their most vital political role—or the flow of money that funds electoral campaigns or the behavior of its officeholders once elected. In the past, party candidates were usually nominated in district, state, and national conventions, where party regulars played a major role. They are now almost exclusively nominated in primaries or grassroots caucuses in the states, where the party organizations help but do not run the show. Nomination comes to those who are best able to raise money, gain access to the media, form their own campaign organizations, and win the support of powerful interest and advocacy groups (such as the National Rifle Association in the GOP and the National Education Association in the Democratic Party). To a very large extent, Democratic and Republican party organizations are there to help candidates in these efforts, not order them about.[18] It is because of this that many commentators have come to describe American political parties as being "candidate-centered."

Nominees are so independent they sometimes oppose party leaders and reject traditional party policies, and there is not much the party can do about it. Republicans were embarrassed, for example, when David Duke, former Grand

The Differences Between Democrats and Republicans

FIGURE 9.2 • Political Party Organization in the United States

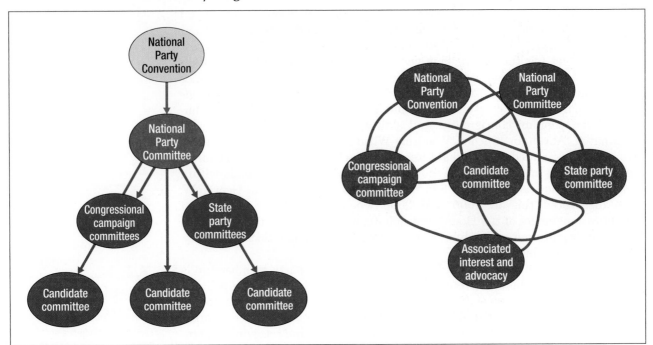

The graphic on the left shows a hypothetical organizational chart of the Republican and Democratic parties as if they were structured hierarchically like many other organizations you are familiar with. It would be a mistake, however, to think of our national parties this way. The drawing on the right, which depicts our national parties as network or weblike organizations, where there is neither central authority nor a chain of command, is closer to reality. The ties between elements of the parties include money, ideology, sentiment, and common interests.

Wizard of the Ku Klux Klan, was elected to the Louisiana state legislature in 1988, where he proposed bills concerning race that made other Republicans extremely uncomfortable. He then campaigned for and won the Republican nomination for governor in 1990 (he lost in the general election), despite the opposition of state and national Republican officials. None of this could have happened in other rich democracies.

None of this is meant to suggest, however, that Democrats and Republicans are entirely devoid of tools to encourage coordination and cooperation among their various levels. Here are the most important ones.

Party Conventions   The national party conventions are the governing bodies of the parties (see Chapter 10). Convention delegates meet every four years not only to nominate presidential and vice presidential candidates but also to write a party platform and revise party rules.

Although the national convention is the formal governing body of each of the parties, it cannot dictate to party candidates or party organizations at other levels of jurisdiction. The presidential nominee need not adhere to either the letter or the spirit of the party platform, for instance, although most nominees stay fairly close to the platform most of the time (usually because the winning candidate's supporters control the platform-writing committee). State and local party organizations may nominate whomever they choose to run for public office and may or may not support key planks in the national party's platform.

Party First

In most European countries, people vote for parties rather than individual candidates. These party activists are urging British voters to cast their ballots for the Labour party, for example, rather than for the rival Conservative party.

National Party Committees The Democratic and Republican national committees conduct the business of the parties during the four years between national conventions. The national committees are made up of elected committeemen and committeewomen from each of the states, a sizable staff, and a chairperson, but they rarely meet. The real business of the committee is run by the party chair, assisted by the committee staff. The chair exercises little power when a president from the party is in office because the party chair is compelled to take direction from the White House. When the opposition controls the presidency, the party chair exercises more influence in party affairs, although the extent of that power is still not very great.

Although the national committees have little direct power, they have become increasingly important as campaign service organizations for party candidates running for national and state offices.[19] In addition to substantial financial contributions to candidate campaign organizations, they do a wide variety of things to help. Out of their Washington, D.C., in-house TV and radio studios come attack ads aimed at the other party and its candidates, tailored to the particular district or state in which the ads will be used. Other ads extol the sponsoring party and its achievements. Direct mail campaigns are mounted to disseminate information and party positions on the issues and to make appeals for campaign contributions, increasingly using sophisticated data-mining techniques to allow very narrow targeting of messages to different groups of people.[20] News releases are prepared for the media, as are campaign-oriented sound and video bites to be used as news clips on local radio and television. Each party also produces training courses for potential candidates, complete with "how-to" manuals and videos. Each has a website where people can access information about the party, get news about the nefarious behavior of the opposition, and make monetary contributions to the party and party candidates.

To carry out these activities, both the Republican and Democratic national committees have steadily increased the number of employees in their

Stirring Up the Party Faithful

National party conventions serve several purposes for American political parties. Every four years, delegates choose presidential and vice presidential candidates, revise party rules, write the party platform, repair or build political coalitions, and, as shown here, attempt to whip up enthusiasm for their nominees.

national offices, especially in the areas of finance, advertising, information technology, campaign planning, and video specialist and support personnel, and they have expanded their budgets to carry out an ever-broader range of campaign activities for party candidates. Each of the national committees has become a highly professionalized campaign organization, filled with highly skilled people able to provide party candidates with what they need to wage first-rate electoral campaigns.

The consensus among political professionals, as well as political scientists, is that the Republicans have been more successful at building these campaign service machines than Democrats.[21] While the Democrats have been trying to catch up, they still lag behind.[22]

Congressional Campaign Committees Almost as old as the national party committees, but entirely independent of them, are the congressional campaign committees that aid members of Congress in their campaigns for re-election. They help raise money, provide media services (making short videotapes of the members of Congress for local television news shows, for instance), conduct research, and do whatever else the party members in Congress deem appropriate. These committees are controlled by the party members in Congress, not the party chair, the national committees, or even the president. Much as with the national committees, the congressional campaign committees have become highly professionalized and well funded.[23]

State Control and National Platforms

State Party Organizations As expected in a federal system, separate political party organizations exist in each of the states. Although tied together by bonds of ideology, sentiment, and campaign money and constrained in what they can do by rules set by the national party committees and conventions—rules on how and when to choose delegates to the national convention, for example—the state party organizations are relatively independent of one another and of the national party.

Associated Interest and Advocacy Groups Although not technically part of the formal party organizations, some groups are so closely involved in the affairs of the parties that it is hard to draw a line between them and the political parties. Focus on the Family, founded and run by James Dobson, for example, is barely distinguishable from the Republican party; it contributes campaign money almost exclusively to GOP candidates, runs its own candidates in the Republican primaries, and counts many of its members among the delegates to the Republican National Convention. Organized labor has had a similar relationship with the Democratic party since the Great Depression and the New Deal.

Some new advocacy groups with strong ties to the party have been created as a way to get around the ban on soft money to national party organizations.[24] These 527 groups—described in Chapter 7—can accept donations of any size and are free to collect as much money as they can for use in issue and candidate campaigns: making hard money contributions to the parties and candidates, mobilizing voters, and educating the public about issues in ways that are compatible with the views of party candidates. Although theoretically independent of the parties, several have been created by prominent Democrats and Republicans to bolster party electoral fortunes. MoveOn.com, for example, is a liberal campaign and issues organization that works closely with the Democrats; the Club for Growth is a conservative organization that works closely with Republican candidates, and its 527 arm spends considerable sums on their campaigns.

Core Supporters

The Republican and Democratic parties each have a set of core supporters—often called the party base—upon which it can count for votes, campaign contributions, and activists to advance the fortunes of the parties and their candidates for elected office. Much of the material on core supporters was examined in Chapter 5 but is worth repeating here. We saw earlier that the strongest Republican supporters may be found among whites (particularly in the South and Rocky Mountain West), conservative Christians and the most religiously committed (those who express a belief in God and say they regularly attend religious services) among all denominations, businesspeople (whether small business owners or top executives in large corporations), ideological conservatives, people in rural areas, and those with the highest incomes. The strongest Democratic supporters may be found among African

Mobilizing Core Voters

Political parties try to energize their core supporters at election time, usually by raising issues dear to the hearts of particular core groups. All Democratic presidential candidates, for example, must be sure that African Americans are on board. Here, John Kerry speaks at the Shiloh Baptist Church in Dayton, Ohio, during his 2004 campaign.

Americans, Jews, non-Cuban Hispanics, people who are secular in belief, people with postgraduate degrees, union households, ideological liberals, people living on the West Coast and the Northeast, and lower-income people. Democrats find strong support, as well, among teachers and other government employees at the local, state, and national levels,[25] and people living in university towns and science and technology research centers such as the Silicon Valley (stretching from San Jose to San Francisco), Austin, Seattle, Boulder, the Research Triangle area in North Carolina, and the Route 128 economic corridor around Boston and Cambridge.[26]

Increasingly in recent years, Republicans and Democrats have tried to win elections by first mobilizing these core supporters—often called "rallying the base"—by focusing on issues and symbolic gestures that will bring them to the polls, then trying to win a majority among those voters not automatically predisposed to one party or the other (Catholics are a good example, as are self-identified independents). In our 50–50 nation, where the numbers of Republican and Democratic core supporters are equal in strength, winning even a small majority among these less partisan groups while mobilizing one's own partisans is the key to winning elections. Issue and ideological appeals are important in these efforts, a subject we examine in the next section.

Ideologies and Policies

Because the Republican and Democratic parties have traditionally organized themselves as fairly broad coalitions, seeking to attract as many voters as possible in order to prevail in winner-take-all, single-member-district elections, there always have been strong pressures on them to tone down matters of ideology.[27] However, each party also has a core of loyal supporters and party activists, such as delegates to the party convention and caucus attendees, contributors to election campaigns, and closely allied advocacy groups, who are more ideologically oriented than the general public. Each party, moreover, has a stable core set of voters from groups concerned about particular issues and problems and committed to particular government policies. The result is a party system composed of parties with significant and growing ideological and policy differences between them.[28]

Ideology may be understood as a coherently organized set of beliefs about the fundamental nature of the good society and the role government ought to play in achieving it. Traditionally, political parties in many other Western democracies have been closely associated with an ideology with which activists, members, and officeholders identify and that provides the themes for election campaigns and a guide for the actions of party members who hold offices in the government. Until recently in Europe, for example, Social Democratic or Labor parties often lined up in elections against Liberal, and Conservative parties, with Marxist, Christian Socialist, Nationalist, and other parties entering into the contests as well. (Ideology has become less pronounced among European parties in the last few years, however.)

Ideological contests in the traditional European manner are not the norm in U.S. elections because both American parties share many of the same fundamental beliefs: free enterprise, individualism, the Constitution, the Bill of Rights, and so on. Nevertheless, the differences between Democrats and Republicans on many ideological issues are significant; Republicans tend to believe that government should play a limited role in managing the economy and providing public services for its citizens, whereas Democrats tend to believe that government programs and regulations can and should tame the excesses of the market economy and try to make society more equal. Not surprisingly, given the ideological differences between the two parties, disagreements about a wide range of issues—especially on taxes and business regulation, but also on affirmative action, abortion, environmental protection, and gay rights—are real, important, enduring, and becoming much more distinctive. Indeed, ideological and policy differences between the Democrats and Republicans are becoming so marked, and the tendency of the Republicans to become a more internally cohesive conservative party so pronounced, that a number of observers now talk about the "Europeanization" of the American party system.[29]

Let's see how ideological and policies differences manifest themselves in our political parties.

Ideology and Party in Public Perceptions   For one thing, the Democratic and Republican parties differ in the electorate's perceptions of them; 64 percent of Americans, for example, report that they see the parties as different on a whole range of issues.[30] Most accurately see the Democrats as the more **liberal** party (in the sense of favoring an active federal government, helping citizens with jobs, education, medical care, and the like) and the Republicans as the more **conservative** party (opposing such government activism and supporting business).[31] Democrats, moreover, are much more likely to say they are liberals; Republicans are much more likely than others to say they are conservative. Additionally, those Americans who classify themselves as liberals overwhelmingly support Democratic candidates; self-described conservatives overwhelmingly support Republicans. In 2004, for example, 93 percent of self-identified Republicans voted for George W. Bush for president, while 89 percent of Democrats voted for John Kerry. This association of liberalism with the Democrats and conservatism with the Republicans is growing stronger all the time.[32]

liberal

The political position that holds that the federal government has a substantial role to play in economic regulation, social welfare, and overcoming racial inequality.

conservative

The political position that holds that the federal government ought to play a very small role in economic regulation, social welfare, and overcoming racial inequality.

Ideology and Policies in Party Platforms   Our parties also tend to write political platforms at their conventions that differ significantly from one another. Scholars have discovered persistent differences in the platforms of the two parties in terms of rhetoric (Republicans tend to talk more about opportunity and freedom), issues (Democrats worry more about poverty and social welfare), and the public policies advocated.[33] There were especially dramatic differences between the parties on key issues in their 2004 convention platforms, a reflection of the high partisanship existing then.

The Ideologies of Party Activists   The activists of one party are quite different in their views from activists and voters in the other party, as well as the general public. Republican delegates to the 2004 Republican National Convention, for example, as in all recent conventions, were more conservative than Republican voters and much more conservative than the average registered voter (see Table 9.1). They were also much more hostile to affirmative action, same-sex marriage, social spending programs, and gun control than Republican voters and registered voters in general. Analogously, delegates to the Democratic National Convention were more liberal than Democratic voters and registered voters and much more favorable to gun control, affirmative action, gay rights, and a woman's right to an abortion than the other two groups.[34]

Party Ideologies in Government   Finally, the parties differ in what they do when they win control of government. Republican members of Congress tend to vote differently from Democrats, the former being considerably more conservative on domestic issues. This difference translates into public policy. Republicans and Democrats produce different policies on taxes, corporate regulation, and social welfare when they are in power.[35] These differences will be

TABLE 9.1 • Comparing Delegates to the 2004 National Party Conventions with Other Americans*

	Delegates to Democratic National Convention	Democratic Voters	All Voters	Republican Voters	Delegates to Republican National Convention
Very or somewhat liberal	41	33	20	6	2
Very or somewhat conservative	3	19	35	56	60
Believe government should do more to solve national problems	79	48	42	35	7
Believe gay couples should be allowed to marry	45	36	26	11	3
Believe abortion should be generally available to those who want it	75	49	34	17	13
Believe that when it comes to regulating the environmental and safety practices of business, the federal government should do more	85	71	59	45	15
Believe that it is extremely important for the United States to work through the United Nations to solve international problems	79	66	49	31	7

*All numbers indicate the percentage of people agreeing with the statement.

Source: New York Times/CBS News polls. June 16–July 17, 2004, and August 3–23, 2004.

explored further in Chapter 11 on Congress, Chapter 17 on domestic policies, and Chapter 18 on foreign and national defense policies.

Divisions Within the Parties While differences between Democrats and Republicans have become more pronounced, and while ideological and policy cohesion within the parties has been increasing, especially in the GOP, there are still important disagreements within each of the parties.[36] There is not perfect unity, as one might have found in the past within communist and socialist parties, let us say, or as exists today in Islamist parties such as the Muslim Brotherhood in Egypt. The division in the Democratic Party is between a very liberal wing—found among Democratic activists and advocacy groups and among most officeholders in the West Coast and northeastern states—and a more "centrist" wing—typified by the Democratic Leadership Council and moderates elected in traditionally Republican areas (see Virginia's Jim Webb). The liberal wing supports traditional Democratic Party programs in which government plays a central role in societal improvement, leveling the playing field for minorities and women, protecting union jobs, providing substantial social safety nets, protecting civil liberties, and avoiding the use of military power in foreign affairs. (Liberal, antiwar Democrats succeeded in 2006 in denying the party nomination in Connecticut to Senator Joe Lieberman.) The centrist wing opposes racial preferences and supports lower taxes, free trade, deregulation, a crackdown on crime, and a strong military supported by a large defense budget.

Perhaps because it has become America's governing party at the national level with responsibility for putting real policies into place, a number of fissures have appeared in recent years within Republican ranks.[37] There is a division, for example, between traditional "small government" Republicans, worried about the size of the federal budget and new intrusive programs, and "big government" Republicans, who support important new programs such as No Child Left Behind and the Medicare prescription drug benefit. Libertarian-oriented Republicans, who detest government interference in private lives, disagree with many socially conservative Republicans about the role government should play in abortion and end-of-life decisions. Many business-oriented Republicans want government to support scientific research, including stem cell initiatives, appoint people to the courts who are concerned first and foremost about property rights and federal overregulation of business, and ease up on immigration restrictions, while the more socially conservative tend to worry most about judicial nominees' stances on gay rights and abortion and want the federal government to tighten up American borders. Finally, neoconservative Republicans want the United States to be expansive in foreign affairs, using American economic and military power to spread democracy and American values, while more traditional Republicans, worried about the size and cost of such policies and lacking confidence in the ability of government to achieve desired results, believe a more modest foreign policy is appropriate.

The Parties in Government and in the Electorate

Fearful of the tyrannical possibilities of a vigorous government, the framers designed a system of government in which power is so fragmented and competitive that effectiveness is unlikely. One of the roles that political parties can play in a democracy such as ours is to overcome this deadlock by persuading officials of the same party in the different branches of government to cooperate with one another on the basis of party loyalty.[38] The constitutionally designed conflict between the president and Congress can be bridged, it has been argued, when there is **unified government**—when a single party controls both houses of Congress and the presidency—as the Democrats did during much of the 1960s and the Republicans did between 2001 and 2006. (See "Using the Framework" feature on the return of unified government during this period.) On the other hand, the existence of strong parties during periods of **divided government,** when Republicans and Democrats each controlled a branch of the federal government—as in 1995–2000 when Democrat Bill Clinton was president and the Republicans controlled both houses of Congress—often leads to gridlock.[39] We will learn more about what parties do in government and what happens when government is unified or divided in later chapters on Congress (Chapter 11), the president (Chapter 12), the executive branch (Chapter 13), and the courts (Chapter 14).

Parties are not only political organizations and sets of officeholders in government, but also images in the minds of voters and potential voters, mental cues that affect the behavior of the electorate. This aspect of the parties was discussed in Chapter 5 and will be considered in greater detail in Chapter 10. We will simply reiterate here that fewer Americans than in the past are inclined to identify with or to have confidence in a party, but that those who still identify themselves as Republicans or Democrats feel much more strongly about this identification and divide more clearly along the lines of ideology and policy preferences. This odd combination of growing indifference toward

unified government
Control of the executive and legislative branches by the same political party.

divided government
Control of the executive and legislative branches by different political parties.

Using the Framework

Ending Gridlock

How did Republicans manage to break the gridlock in Washington after they took power in 2001?

Background: In the 1990s, official Washington seemed to grind to a screeching halt. Divided government was the rule. Not only was major legislation tough to come by, but partisan warfare between a Republican-dominated Congress and a Democratic president (Clinton) led to a budget crisis that twice closed the federal government (except for essential services) and to the impeachment of Bill Clinton on a straight party-line vote in the House. After the election of George W. Bush in 2000, however, new bills were passed with a fair degree of regularity: three

different tax cuts, No Child Left Behind, a new prescription drug benefit under Medicare, creation of the Department of Homeland Security, the USA Patriot Act, restrictions on class action lawsuits, the Energy Policy Act of 2005, the Bankruptcy Act of 2005, and the Sarbanes-Oxley Act regulating corporate accounting practices. Taking a look at how structural, political linkage, and governmental factors affect policy making in Washington will help explain the changed situation from 2001 through 2005.

Governmental Action

Major bills are passed by Congress and signed into law by President Bush.

Governmental Level

From 1995 through 2000, divided government was the rule, with Republican majorities in the House and Senate and a Democratic president, Bill Clinton.

The elections of 2000, 2002, and 2004 resulted in unified government, with Republicans in control of Congress (with the exception of 2002, when Democrats temporarily regained the majority in the Senate after one Republican senator defected) and the presidency.

Because of their extremely high levels of party unity and discipline in both houses of Congress, but especially in the House of Representatives, Republicans were able to control the legislative agenda without much need of help from the Democrats, even though they did not enjoy a large majority of seats in either chamber.

Political Linkages Level

Neither party enjoyed a commanding lead in party identification nationally during the 1990s or 2000s.

Congressional elections became very close and hotly contested, with control of Congress hanging in the balance every two years, so partisanship increased.

The political parties became more ideological, with the virtual disappearance of conservative Democrats in the South and Mountain West and liberal Republicans in New England.

Partisan warfare and scandals became standard fare in the mass media, making cooperation and civility in public affairs, in general, and between the parties, in particular, less likely.

Structural Level

Separation of powers and checks and balances in the Constitution make gridlock the "default" condition in Washington.

The end of the Cold War ended the semi-crisis atmosphere that encouraged the political parties in Congress, and the Congress and the president, to cooperate with one another on a wide range of issues.

The sense of patriotism and shared threat arising from the 9/11 attacks created a brief period of Democratic-Republican and presidential-congressional cooperation in late 2001/early 2002.

Using the Democracy Standard

How do our major political parties affect democracy?

PROPOSITION: **American political parties don't ensure that government is responsive and responsible to the people.**

AGREE Our parties are so loose and fragmented in an organizational sense, and often so mushy in an ideological sense, that voters do not know what they are getting when they put a party in office and cannot be assured that the majority party will be able to carry out its program, even if it wanted to do so. Democrat Bill Clinton, for example, campaigned as a liberal in the 1992 presidential campaign but ended up advocating free trade, balanced budgets, and a cautious approach to affirmative action. In addition, parties don't seem to be able to do much to overcome the constraints on bold initiatives created by our system of separation of powers and checks and balances, even when one party is in control of several branches of government. For example, George W. Bush's attempt to add private accounts to Social Security failed in Congress in 2005–2006, despite the fact that his party—the Republicans—controlled both the House and the Senate. Things are even worse when Republicans control one branch of government and the Democrats control the other. Partisan warfare and gridlock in Washington are the most common result of this division of power between the parties.

DISAGREE Our parties are the only mechanism we have for allowing voters to decide on a program for the government and to hold a group or team of elected officials responsible for their actions. Although flawed, parties are the only instrument that people have for doing this. Interest groups and social movements are much too narrow; only parties seek to be inclusive and present broad programs for public approval. Moreover, the parties are becoming better organized and more ideologically distinctive, so voters increasingly know what they are getting when they put a party in office. To be sure, divided government often leads to gridlock when strong parties exist, but this is simply an argument that people ought to vote along party lines and have a single party control the entire government.

CONSIDER Political scientists tend to believe that strong political parties are an essential part of democracy.

• Are you persuaded that political parties are important for democracy? • If you believe they are important for democracy, how well do you think our existing parties carry out their responsibilities? • Does the increasing intensity of partisan conflict in the United States appeal to you as a way to simplify electoral and policy choices, or do you find yourself turned off, wishing that the overlap between Democrats and Republicans were greater and that bipartisanship might play a larger part in American politics today? • If you believe that parties are important in a democracy, but they are not fulfilling their role very well, what would you do to change what they do? • Are we stuck with parties as they are, or can they be changed to better serve citizens?

the parties and withdrawal from active participation among one group of Americans (mainly independents) and intensified commitment and partisanship among party identifiers and activists is contributing to a more volatile and conflict-ridden politics in the United States, a theme we will return to over the course of this text.

Summary

The American party system is unique among the Western democracies in several respects. First, ours is a relatively pure two-party system and has been so since the 1830s. Second, our major parties are candidate centered, having very little power in their national party organizations to affect the behavior of individual candidates, officeholders, or state and local party organizations. American parties are less ideologically coherent than parties in many other democracies, but the enduring and important differences between Democrats and Republicans are very important and becoming much more pronounced.

Although American politics has been dominated by the same two parties for almost a century and a half, the two-party system has not been stagnant. It has undergone a series of realignments, spurred by structural changes in society and the economy, in which the relative power of the parties has shifted, as have the voting alignments of the public, the dominant political coalitions, and government policies.

The parties play an important role in government, sometimes contributing to governmental effectiveness and policy coherence. At other times, during periods of divided government, parties often contribute to gridlock.

mypoliscilab
Where participation leads to action!

Web Exploration
Third Parties in the United States

Issue: We have a two-party system, but many minor parties exist here.

Site: Learn more about these minor, or third, parties at Politics1 in MyPoliSciLab at **www.mypolyscilab.com.** Go to the "Web Explorations" section for Chapter 9, select "Third Parties in the United States," then "third parties." Examine the platforms and activities of several minor parties.

What You've Learned: Do any of the parties you examined address issues that neither of the major parties has tackled? Do you find any of them appealing? If you like one of the parties, and that party appears on the ballot, will you vote for that party or not? What are your reasons?

HINT: People with very strong views on a handful of issues are often unhappy with the two main parties.

Internet Sources

Democratic National Committee
www.democrats.org/
Information about Democratic party candidates, party history, convention and national committees, state parties, stands on the issues, affiliated groups, upcoming events, and more.

National Political Index
www.politicalindex.com/
Links to state and local parties and affiliated organizations and interest groups, as well as news and information about the parties.

Political Resources on the Web
www.politicalresources.net/
Information about political parties in all democratic countries.

Republican National Committee
www.rnc.org/
Information about Republican party candidates, party history, convention and national committees, state parties, stands on the issues, affiliated groups, upcoming events, and more.

Suggestions for Further Reading

Gould, Lewis. *Grand Old Party: A History of the Republicans.* New York: Random House, 2003.
A comprehensive history of the Republican party in the United States.

Greenberg, Stanley B. *The Two Americas: Our Current Political Deadlock and How to Break It.* New York: Thomas Dunne Books, 2004.
A bold plan for breaking the politics of parity by one of the Democratic Party's leading strategists.

Hershey, Marjory. *Party Politics in America,* 11th ed. New York: Pearson Longman Publishers, 2005.
A new edition of the leading political parties textbook in the United States; comprehensive, detailed, yet engaging.

Witcover, Jules. *Party of the People: A History of the Democrats.* New York: Random House, 2003.
A comprehensive history of the Democratic party in the United States.

CHAPTER 10

Participation, Voting, and Elections

IN THIS CHAPTER

- What the role of elections is in a democracy

- How African Americans, women, and young people won the right to vote

- Why many Americans don't vote

- How to run for the presidency

- What part money plays in presidential elections

- How voters decide

- Why elections matter

Bush Wins the 2004 Presidential Election

After a bruising and bitter race with Democrat John Kerry, Republican George W. Bush was reelected to the presidency in 2004. The campaign was one of the most intense in recent American history—and certainly the longest and most expensive. Unlike the disputed election of 2000 (when he received about 500,000 fewer votes than Al Gore), Bush won both electoral college and popular vote majorities in 2004; roughly 3.5 million more people voted for him than for Kerry.

To many Americans, the campaign seemed to go on forever. Bush and Kerry battled for almost eight months; they opened their campaigns against each other in early March 2004 and carried on through election day on November 2. Typically, presidential contests come up to full speed in the days following the late-summer Republican and Democratic nominating conventions. In this election, however, each of the parties' presidential nominees was known early: Bush because he was running unopposed for the presidential nomination in the Republican Party and Kerry because he had enough primary wins by early March to virtually sew up the Democratic Party nomination. Knowing that Kerry was to be the eventual Democratic nominee, the Bush campaign and associated advocacy groups were concentrating on him by mid-March. Assured of the nomination, Kerry ignored the handful of Democratic presidential hopefuls who remained on primary ballots in states that had not yet voted and turned his full attention to attacking the Bush record.

The two campaigns were able to launch into full-scale attack mode because the official campaign organizations, state and national party organizations, and associated advocacy groups were loaded with money. Bush had amassed a war chest of more than $200 million for his uncontested nomination campaign; Kerry, who had to mortgage his house to keep his campaign going in February, recovered nicely by mid-March and managed to raise more than $100 million for his preconvention campaign against the president, 30 percent of the total coming from Internet donations. Counting additional funds for the postconvention period, the Bush campaign raised $367 million; Kerry raised almost as much—$326 million[1]—making him the best-financed challenger ever.

In part, the Bush and Kerry campaigns were able to raise these enormous sums because of changes in the campaign finance system under the McCain-Feingold law, which doubled the amount of money individuals could contribute to federal candidates and increased what they could give to party organizations. Adding to the money glut were so-called 527 advocacy organizations, such as Swift Boat Veterans for Truth (anti-Kerry) and MoveOn.org (anti-Bush), able to raise and spend unlimited amounts of money for the expression of political views, helped by huge contributions from superwealthy individuals such as Texas homebuilder Bob Perry ($10 million to anti-Kerry organizations) and financier George Soros (more than $15 million to anti-Bush groups).[2] Union, corporate, and interest group PACs, moreover, raised more money for the campaign than they ever had before, adding to the flood. In the end, spending on the presidential campaigns by all concerned was conservatively estimated to have topped $1.2 billion—30 percent greater than in 2000—making it the most expensive presidential election in American history.[3]

Changes in the campaign finance rules were only part of the reason for the surge in campaign giving. What drove the process more than anything else was the fierce partisanship that has come to characterize American political life. Each side of the partisan divide was convinced that the stakes were very high in the 2004 election. For many Democrats, Bush was an illegitimate president, chosen in 2000 not by the American people, but by the Supreme Court. He was even less worthy of support, in the eyes of many Democrats, because of what they perceived to be the president's unilateralist foreign policy, which had alienated allies; record tax cuts for the wealthy and the return of massive federal government deficits; an unnecessary and botched war in Iraq; and growing dangers to civil liberties by the antiterrorism steamroller. A Bush victory, moreover, seemed to portend further erosions in the wall separating church and state and a new Supreme Court that would overturn *Roe* v. *Wade*. For many Republicans, a Kerry victory seemed to portend the creation of massive new government programs, increases in taxes, more support for gay rights and abortions, additional regulations hampering business, and, perhaps most important of all, weakness and lack of resolve in the war on terrorism.

It is hardly surprising—given the level of partisan rancor; the widespread sense that the outcome of the election would determine the shape of American domestic and foreign policy for years to come; generous campaign war chests on both sides; and the proliferation of well-funded, single-issue, and ideological 527 organizations—that 2004 proved to be one of the nastiest and most uncivil races in recent memory.

Not surprisingly—given the high level of partisanship; the widespread sense that this election would have important consequences for the future of the nation; and the unprecedented effort by the campaigns, the parties, and 527 organizations to get their base to the polls—voting turnout was very high. More than 120 million Americans cast ballots, roughly 60 percent of voting-age-eligible Americans, the highest percentage since the 1968 election.

Finally, the 2004 election demonstrated once again that presidents are chosen by electoral votes, not popular votes, which explains why the campaigns focused almost all their efforts in a handful of so-called battleground states, where the contest between Kerry and Bush was close. States strongly in the camp of one party or the other—California and New York for the Democrats, for example, and Texas, Utah, and Indiana for the Republicans—hardly saw a television campaign ad or had a visit from either of the candidates. Closely contested states, especially Florida, Pennsylvania, Ohio, Michigan, Minnesota, Wisconsin, Iowa, and New Mexico, were inundated. In the end, the 2004 campaign was waged primarily in this handful of states. ∎

Thinking Critically About This Chapter

The story of the 2004 presidential election focuses our attention on the issue of democratic control of the national government through the electoral process and on the degree to which the public participates in this key activity of the representative democratic process.

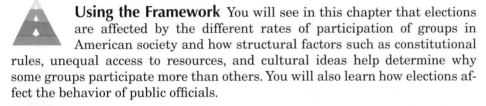 **Using the Framework** You will see in this chapter that elections are affected by the different rates of participation of groups in American society and how structural factors such as constitutional rules, unequal access to resources, and cultural ideas help determine why some groups participate more than others. You will also learn how elections affect the behavior of public officials.

 Using the Democracy Standard We suggest in this chapter that elections are the lynchpin of any discussion about the democratic quality of any system of government because they are, in theory, what makes popular sovereignty possible. You will see in this chapter that while elections in the United States do much to make our system democratic, they fall short of their democratic promise.

Elections and Democracy

Elections are fundamental to democratic politics, the chief means by which citizens control what their government does. Many important struggles for democracy in the United States have involved conflicts over the right to vote. But can elections actually ensure that governments will do what their people want?

Democratic theorists have suggested several ways that elections in a two-party system like that found in the United States can bring about popular control of government. We will briefly discuss three of these ways, indicating how they might work in theory and what might go wrong in practice.[4] The rest of this chapter is concerned with what actually happens in American national elections and with the question of whether these elections really bring about popular control of government.

The Prospective (or Responsible Party) Voting Model

The idea of **responsible party** elections is based on the old commonsense notion that elections should present a "real choice": Political parties should stand for different policies, the voters should choose between them, and the winning party should carry out its mandate. Political scientists call this the **prospective voting model,** meaning that voters are interested in and capable of deciding what government will do in the future.

Theory For this system to work perfectly, each of the two parties must be cohesive and unified; each must take clear policy positions that differ significantly from the other party's positions; citizens must accurately perceive these positions and vote on the basis of them; and the winning party, when it takes office, must do exactly what it said it would do. If all these conditions are met, then the party with the more popular policy positions will win and enact its program. In such an electoral system, government will do what the majority of the voters want.[5]

Problems Even if an election were to work exactly as the responsible party ideal dictates, however, a serious problem arises. There is no actual guarantee that either party would take policy positions that pleased the voters, only that the winning party's stand is less *unpopular* than the loser's. Also, crucial decisions about what the parties stand for and what choices they present to the voters would be made by someone other than ordinary citizens—by party leaders or perhaps by interest groups and big contributors.

Moreover, the conditions under which responsible party government is supposed to work do not fully exist in the United States. American voters, for example, do not vote solely on the issues or on ideology, as the prospective voting model requires them to do, because they take other things into account when casting their ballots, including candidate personalities. Moreover, the parties do not always keep their promises once in office. Even if the parties fully intend to keep their promises, they sometimes fail to do so because they are unable to win control of the entire government in our system of separated powers—a precondition of any effort to transform campaign promises into policies. And, when there is divided government—for example, when there is a Democratic President and a Republican-controlled Congress—the existence of distinctive and highly competitive political parties will almost always lead to gridlock, so that few policies promised in an election campaign can be put into effect.

There is an additional problem with the prospective voting model that its adherents did not anticipate: As the Republican and Democratic parties become more internally coherent in terms of policy preferences and ideology—which we suggested in Chapter 9 is happening—political conflict becomes more intense and impassioned because the stakes for each party in the outcome of elections become much more important than in a less partisan environment. If the other party wins control of the government, even if it does so by a razor-thin margin, the party out of power has more to lose. The party in power can make policies to which the party out of power objects very strongly. This is one of the reasons contemporary politics in the United States increasingly is characterized by intense partisanship and incivility.

Clearly, then, the responsible party idea does not correspond exactly to what happens in American elections. But we will see that it comes close enough to the truth to describe at least a part of reality. Also, theories about responsible parties provide some useful standards for judging what may be wrong with U.S. elections and how they might be improved, particularly with respect to the clarity of stands on issues.

The Electoral Competition Voting Model

A very different, and less obvious, sort of democratic control can be found in what political scientists call the **electoral competition,** or median voter, **model** of democratic elections. In this sort of electoral model, unified parties compete for votes by taking the *most popular* positions they can. They do so by trying to take positions that will appeal to the **median voter** at the exact midpoint of the political spectrum. Both parties are therefore likely to end up standing for the *same* policies: those favored by the most voters.

Theory   Scholars have proved mathematically that if citizens' preferences are organized along a single dimension (such as the liberal–conservative continuum shown in Figure 10.1), and if parties purely seek votes, both parties will take positions exactly at the *median* of public opinion, that is, at the point where exactly one-half the voters are more liberal and one-half are more conservative. If either party took a position even a bit away from the median, the other party could easily win more votes by taking a position closer to the median.[6]

If electoral competition drives parties together in this way, and if they keep their promises, then, in theory, it should not matter which party wins; the winner enacts the policies that the most voters want. Democracy is ensured by the hidden hand of competition, much as efficiency is ensured by competitive markets, according to standard economic theory.

electoral competition model

A form of election in which parties seeking votes move toward the median voter or the center of the political spectrum.

median voter

Refers to the voter at the exact middle of the political spectrum.

FIGURE 10.1 • Electoral Competition Model

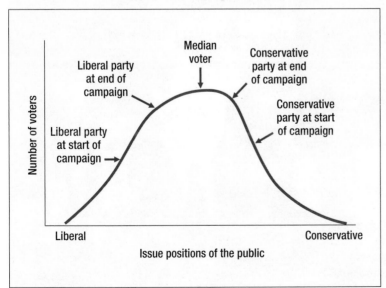

This model suggests that in the interest of winning the election, parties will move toward the median voter (where most votes are to be found) as the campaign progresses.

Problems   Again, however, the conditions needed for electoral competition to work perfectly are not likely to be met in the real world. Electoral competition ensures democratic control only if the parties are unified and take stands on the issues for pure and direct vote-seeking reasons; it can break down if the parties are fragmented or ambiguous, if they care about policies for ideological reasons rather than for reasons of securing the most votes, or if they seek contributors' dollars rather than citizens' votes. Moreover, the voters must consider nothing but the issues (e.g., not being distracted by candidates' personalities or images) and must know exactly where the parties stand. And the parties have to keep their promises. There are reasons to doubt that any of these things will happen flawlessly.[7]

Still, we will see that these conditions are close enough to the truth so that electoral competition does work, to a significant extent, in real elections. Indeed, electoral competition is probably one of the main reasons that government policy is significantly influenced by public opinion.

electoral reward and punishment

The tendency to vote for the incumbents when times are good and against them when times are bad.

retrospective voting

A form of election in which voters look back at the performance of a party in power and cast ballots on the basis of how well it did in office.

The Retrospective (or Reward and Punishment) Voting Model

A third process by which elections might bring about democratic control of government is **electoral reward and punishment,** a form of election in which voters judge how well a group in power has governed and decide if they want this group to continue in office.

Theory   Here the idea is that the voters simply make **retrospective,** backward-looking judgments about how well incumbent officials have done in the past, rewarding success with reelection and punishing failure by throwing the incumbents out. The result, in theory, is that politicians who want to stay in of-

Accepting Defeat

Some presidential elections are retrospective in nature, meaning that the electorate makes its decision based on an incumbent's performance in office. The electorate's concern about the poor performance of the American economy was a major factor in George H. W. Bush's defeat at the hand's of challenger Bill Clinton in 1992. Here, the Republican president concedes the election to his Democratic rival.

fice have strong incentives to bring about peace and prosperity and to solve problems that the American people want solved. Politicians' ambitions force them to anticipate what the public wants and to accomplish it.[8]

The reward-and-punishment process of democratic control has the advantage of simplicity. It requires very little of voters: no elaborate policy preferences, no study of campaign platforms, just judgments of how well or how badly things have been going. Also, like electoral competition, it relies on politicians' selfishness rather than their altruism. It allows time for deliberation, and it lets leaders try out experimental or temporarily unpopular policies, as long as the results work out well and please the public in time for the next election.

Problems   However, reward and punishment may be a rather blunt instrument. It gets rid of bad political leaders only after (not before) disasters happen, without guaranteeing that the next leaders will be any better. It relies on politicians *anticipating* the effects of future policies, which they cannot always do successfully. Moreover, the reward-and-punishment process focuses only on the most prominent issues and may leave room for unpopular policies on matters that are less visible. It may also encourage politicians to produce deceptively happy but temporary results that arrive just in time for election day and then fade away.

Imperfect Electoral Democracy

We will see that each of the three processes of democratic control we have discussed works, to some extent, in American elections. On occasion, even, the three processes converge and help produce an election that is enormously consequential for the direction of the nation. The 1932 election was one of these occasions and is described in the "Using the Framework" feature.

But none of the three processes works well enough to guarantee perfectly democratic outcomes most of the time. In certain respects, they conflict: Responsible parties and electoral competition, for example, tend to push in opposite directions. In other respects, all three processes require similar conditions that are not met in reality.

For example, none of the three can ensure government responsiveness to all citizens unless *all* citizens have the right to vote and exercise that right. Unfortunately, millions of Americans cannot or do not go to the polls. Their voices are not heard; political equality is not achieved.

Another problem with our system of elections was brought to public attention by the chaos and uncertainty of the 2000 presidential election in Florida: Not all ballots cast by voters are actually counted. For a variety of reasons, ranging from lack of voter education to confusing ballot layouts and malfunctioning voting machines, a number of ballots in every election in the United States are disqualified and not included in the final vote tally. In 2000, from 4 to 6 million votes of the roughly 100 million cast nationally were not counted.[9] Worse yet, especially for the democratic norm of political equality, the votes of poor people and members of racial minorities were three times more likely than those of other Americans to be uncounted in the 2000 election.[10] In 2004, 32 percent of the 1.2 million **provisional ballots** cast nationwide—used when poll workers cannot immediately confirm that a person is registered to vote—were judged to be invalid and were not counted in the final election tally,[11] and widespread concerns were raised about the accuracy of registration lists and the reliability of voting machines.[12]

provisional ballot
A vote that is cast but not counted until determination is made that the voter is properly registered.

Using the Framework

Elections Bring the New Deal

Have elections ever changed the course of American government?
Do elections ever really change what government does?

Background: Occasionally in American history, a national election is so consequential that it alters the overall direction of government policy and the role of government in the United States. The election of Franklin Delano Roosevelt and an overwhelmingly Democratic Congress in the 1932 elections was just such a moment. In the first 100 days of his administration, Roosevelt launched his New Deal, convincing Congress to pass bills to regulate the banking and securities industries, to bail out failing banks and protect the deposits of the public, to launch public works and relief efforts, and to provide price supports for farmers. This revolution in the role of the federal government was made possible by the 1932 elections, but to fully understand what happened, structural, political linkage, and governmental factors have to be taken into account.

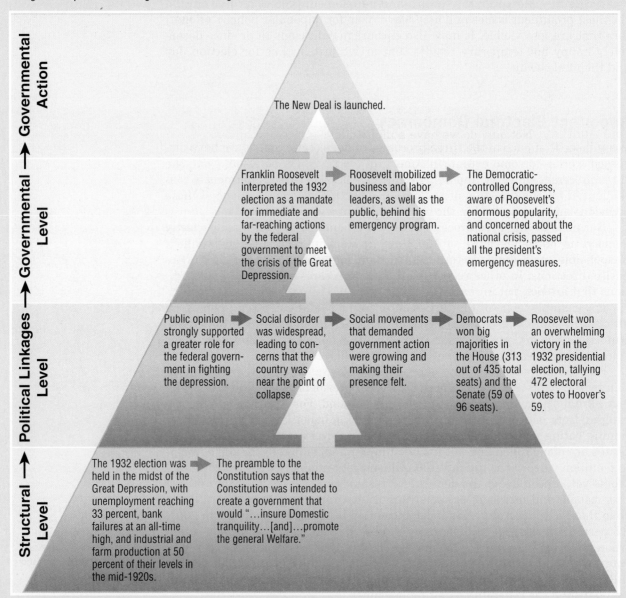

Governmental Action

The New Deal is launched.

Governmental Level

Franklin Roosevelt interpreted the 1932 election as a mandate for immediate and far-reaching actions by the federal government to meet the crisis of the Great Depression. ➡ Roosevelt mobilized business and labor leaders, as well as the public, behind his emergency program. ➡ The Democratic-controlled Congress, aware of Roosevelt's enormous popularity, and concerned about the national crisis, passed all the president's emergency measures.

Political Linkages Level

Public opinion strongly supported a greater role for the federal government in fighting the depression. ➡ Social disorder was widespread, leading to concerns that the country was near the point of collapse. ➡ Social movements that demanded government action were growing and making their presence felt. ➡ Democrats won big majorities in the House (313 out of 435 total seats) and the Senate (59 of 96 seats). ➡ Roosevelt won an overwhelming victory in the 1932 presidential election, tallying 472 electoral votes to Hoover's 59.

Structural Level

The 1932 election was held in the midst of the Great Depression, with unemployment reaching 33 percent, bank failures at an all-time high, and industrial and farm production at 50 percent of their levels in the mid-1920s. ➡ The preamble to the Constitution says that the Constitution was intended to create a government that would "…insure Domestic tranquility…[and]…promote the general Welfare."

American Elections: How Exceptional Compared with Others?

American elections differ quite dramatically from those of most other democratic countries. The differences are the result of rules—mainly found in the Constitution but also in federal statutes and judicial decisions—that define offices and tell how elections are to be conducted. Here are the distinguishing features of elections in the United States:

Comparing Voting and Elections

The United States Has More Elections Than Any Other Democratic Country   In some sense, we are "election happy" in the United States. We not only elect the president and members of Congress (senators and representatives), but also, being a federal system, we elect governors, state legislators, and (in most states) judges. In addition, state constitutions allow autonomy for counties, cities, and towns, and all of their top officials are elected by the people. We also elect school boards in most places, and the top positions in special districts (e.g., water or conservation districts). And then there are the many state and local ballot initiatives that add to the length and complexity of the ballot at election time. No other country holds so many elections, covering so many offices and public policy issues.

Elections in the United States Are Separate and Independent from One Another   Not only do we have a multitude of elections, but the election to fill each particular office is separate and independent from the others. In parliamentary systems, one votes for a party, and the party that wins a majority gets to appoint a whole range of other officials. The majority party in the British parliament (the legislative branch), for example, chooses the prime minister and cabinet ministers (the executive branch), who run the government. The government, in turn, appoints officials to many posts that are filled by elections here. In the United States, the president and members of

A Garden of Yard Signs

The United States depends more on elections to fill its many public offices than other democratic countries, contributing to more frequent elections and longer ballots than elsewhere.

Congress are elected independently from one another, as are governors, state legislators, mayors of cities, city councils, and school boards.

Elections Fill Government Positions That Have Fixed Terms of Office

The office of president of the United States is fixed at four years, representatives serve for two years, and senators for six. At the state level, terms of office for all important elected positions are fixed, whether for governors or legislators. The same holds true for county, city, and town elected offices. In parliamentary systems, the government can call an election at any time within a certain number of years (in Britain, it is five years), timing the election to maximize chances for reelection. One implication of fixed elections in the United States is that presidents cannot call for new elections in hopes of changing the party mix in Congress to their advantage. It also means that an unpopular president can stay in office until the next election, since there is no method to remove him other than by impeachment and trial. In parliamentary systems, elections customarily are held when the majority party or majority coalition in parliament loses support among its members, shown in a defeat on a major bill proposed by the government (the prime minister and cabinet) or on a "vote of confidence" called by the opposition. In 2005, Chancellor Gerhardt Schroeder's Social Democratic Party and its Green Party coalition partner lost a confidence vote in the German parliament. New elections brought the Christian Democratic Union (CDU) and its leader, Angela Merkel, to the chancellorship, with the Social Democratic Party acting as junior partner in the new coalition government.

VIDEO ROUNDTABLE

Mid-Term Elections 2006

National (and Statewide) Elections Are Held on a Fixed Date

In 1845, Congress determined that elections for president and members of Congress will occur on the Tuesday after the first Monday in November (the Constitution only requires that national elections be held on the same day throughout the country). States have generally followed suit for election of governors and members of the legislature. One implication, related to the fixed terms of offices described earlier, is that neither presidents nor governors can time elections to their political advantage as we have seen can happen in parliamentary systems. Another implication is that Tuesday elections may cut down on participation. In other democracies, elections are held either on the weekend or on days that are declared a national holiday.

Elections in the United States Are Almost Always of the "First Past the Post" Type, in Which Only a Single Person Is Elected

Winners in most elections in the United States are those who win the most votes—not necessarily a majority—in a particular electoral district. This type of election is often called "first past the post," as in a horse race where the winner is the first past the finish line. This includes Congressional elections and presidential contests for electoral votes in each of the states. We do not have proportional representation in national level races, nor do we have "run-off" elections between the top two vote-getters in presidential or congressional elections to ensure a majority victor. In 2004, as a matter of fact, George W. Bush became the first president since the election of his father in 1988 to win a majority of the national popular vote (all elected presidents come to office based on winning a majority in the electoral college). In France and Finland, by way of contrast, a second election is held if no candidate wins a majority in the first round of voting for the president. This type of election ensures that the person who is elected comes to office with majority support.

Political Participation

In this section, we turn our attention to political participation. For elections to be democratic—whether in the prospective, electoral competition, or retrospective voting models—participation in elections and campaign activities must not only be at high levels, but also must not vary substantially across social groups in the population (i.e., by race, gender, income, occupation, religion, ethnicity, region, and so on), or else the principle of political equality would be violated.

Political **participation** is political activity by individual citizens. It includes **unconventional participation,** such as demonstrating, boycotting, and the like (discussed in Chapter 8), and also **conventional participation,** such as writing letters to the editor on political issues, contacting officials, going to public meetings, working in campaigns, and giving money, which we focus on here. The most basic form of conventional political participation, the one that plays the most central part in theories of democratic control through elections, is the act of voting.

Expansion of the Franchise

Until passage of the Fourteenth and Fifteenth Amendments after the Civil War, it was up to each state to determine who within its borders was eligible to vote. In the early years of the United States, many of the states limited the legal right to vote—called the **franchise**—quite severely. In fact, a majority of people could not vote at all. Slaves, Native Americans, and women were excluded altogether. In most states, white men without property or who had not paid some set level of taxes were not allowed to vote. In some states early on, white men with certain religious beliefs were excluded.

One of the most important developments in the political history of the United States, an essential part of the struggle for democracy, has been the expansion of the right to vote. The extension of the franchise has been a lengthy and uneven process, spanning 200 years.

White Male Suffrage
The first barriers to fall were those concerning property and religion. So strong were the democratic currents during Thomas Jefferson's presidency (1801–1809) and in the years leading up to the election of Andrew Jackson in 1828 that by 1829, property, tax-paying, and religious requirements had been dropped in all states except North Carolina and Virginia. That left universal **suffrage,** or the ability to vote, firmly in place for most adult white males in the United States.[13] Most of Europe, including Britain, did not achieve this degree of democracy until after World War I.

Blacks, Women, and Young People
Despite this head start for the United States compared with the rest of the world, the struggle to expand the suffrage to include African Americans, women, and young people proved difficult and painful. Ironically, universal white male suffrage was often accompanied by the withdrawal of voting rights from black freedmen, even in states that did not permit slavery.[14] It took the bloody Civil War to free the slaves and the Fifteenth Amendment to the U.S. Constitution (1870) to extend the right to vote to all black males, in both North and South. Even so, most blacks were effectively disfranchised in the South by the end of the nineteenth century and remained so until the 1960s civil rights movement and the Voting Rights Act of 1965 (see Chapter 1).

participation
Political activity, including voting, campaign activity, contacting officials, and demonstrating.

unconventional participation
Political activity in the form of demonstrations or protests.

conventional participation
Political activity related to elections (voting, persuading, and campaigning) or to contacting public officials.

franchise
The right to vote.

suffrage
The right to vote.

At the Polls

Early U.S. elections were poorly organized and hard to get to. In addition, only a small proportion of the population was eligible to vote. Here a group of white men, the only people with the right to vote in most places in the United States at the time, wait to vote in the presidential election of 1824 at a polling station near Boston.

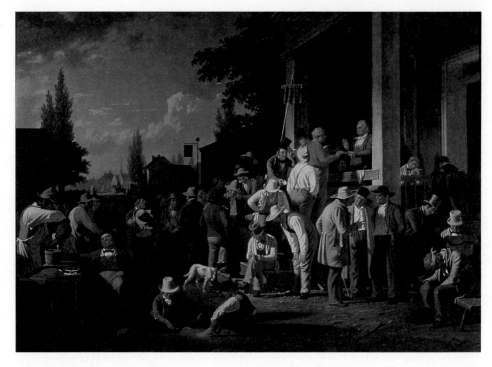

Women won the right to vote in 1920 in all the states with the Nineteenth Amendment to the Constitution, after a long political battle. (See the chapter-opening story in Chapter 8 for details of this struggle.) Residents of the District of Columbia were allowed to vote in presidential—but not congressional—elections after 1961, and 18- to 20-year-olds gained the franchise only in 1971.

The result of these changes at the state and national levels was an enormous increase in the proportion of Americans who were legally eligible to vote: from about 23 percent of the adult population in 1788–1789 to nearly 98 percent by the beginning of the 1970s—practically all citizens except people who have recently moved, people in mental institutions, and incarcerated felons. However, the proportion of the voting-age population that is eligible to vote has dropped a bit in recent years, primarily because of the large influx of immigrants into the United States over the past two decades who cannot vote until they become citizens.

Direct Partisan Elections   A related trend has involved the more direct election of government officials, replacing the old indirect methods that insulated officials from the public. At the same time, the development of a two-party system has clarified choices by focusing citizens' attention on just two alternatives for each office.

electoral college

Representatives of the states who formally elect the president; the number of electors in each state is equal to the total number of its senators and congressional representatives.

The election of the president, even with the existence of the **electoral college,** has become more directly democratic. By the time of the Jefferson–Adams presidential campaign of 1800, which pitted the new Republican and Federalist parties against each other, most state legislatures had stopped picking the presidential electors themselves (as the Constitution permits). Instead, the legislatures allowed a popular vote for electors, most of whom were pledged to support the presidential candidate of one party or the other.

This is the same system we use today: In practically every state, there is a winner-take-all popular vote for a slate of electors—positions usually awarded by each of the political parties to loyal party workers and contributors—who are pledged to a particular presidential candidate. In fact, only the name of the candidate and the party to whom the electors are pledged, not the names of the electors we are actually voting for, appear on the ballot. Thus, when the winning electors meet as the electoral college in their respective states and cast ballots to elect the president, their actions are generally controlled by the popular vote that chose them. This system, odd and cumbersome as it is, almost always ensures that American citizens choose their president more or less directly (though not in the 2000 Bush–Gore election when Bush won the electoral college vote—and thus the presidency—and Gore won the popular vote).

By 1840, the parties had started nominating presidential candidates in national conventions instead of in congressional party caucuses. Later still, the parties began letting voters select many convention delegates directly in state **primary elections** instead of having party activists choose them in political party conventions in each of the states. Today, most delegates to the Republican and Democratic national conventions are selected in primary elections, although a handful of states, including Iowa, use a **caucus nominating system** in which party supporters and activists hold neighborhood and areawide meetings to select delegates. These innovations have probably increased the democratic control of government, although we will see that each of them has antidemocratic features, too.

The direct popular election of U.S. senators did not replace their being chosen by state legislatures until 1913, with the Seventeenth Amendment to the Constitution. Since 1913, all members of the Senate have been subject to direct choice by the voters.

Taken together, the expansion of the franchise and the development of direct, two-party elections have represented major successes in the struggle for democracy. But victory is not yet complete.

Low Voting Turnout

During the first 100 years or so of the United States' existence, not only did more and more people gain the right to vote but also higher and higher proportions of eligible voters actually turned out on election day and voted. It is not easy to be sure of the exact **turnout** percentages because of data inaccuracies and voting fraud, but in presidential elections, the figure of roughly 11 percent of eligible voters who turned out in 1788–1789 jumped to about 31 percent in 1800 (when Thomas Jefferson was first elected) and to about 57 percent in 1828 (Andrew Jackson's first victory). By 1840, the figure had reached 80 percent, and it stayed at about that level until 1896.[15]

The disturbing fact is that today, despite the big increase in 2004, a much smaller proportion of people vote than did during most of the nineteenth century. Since 1912, only about 50 to 65 percent of Americans have voted in presidential elections (see Figure 10.2) and still fewer in other elections: 40 to 50 percent in off-year (non-presidential-year) congressional elections and as few as 10 to 20 percent in primaries and minor local elections. In recent years, the turnout rate as a percentage of the voting age population has dropped to the lower end of those ranges (it is higher if we calculate turnout in terms of eligible voters), although there was a big jump in 2004, no doubt because of the strong partisan nature of the contest and the huge and expensive effort by the parties and associated campaign and advocacy groups to turn out their respective party bases. Turnout here, moreover, is much lower than in most other rich democracies; in western Europe, turnout rates regularly top 75 percent.

The Electoral College

primary election

Statewide elections in which voters choose delegates to the national party conventions; virtually all delegates are pledged to a specific candidate for the party's nomination.

caucus nominating system

A system for selecting delegates to the national party conventions characterized by neighborhood and areawide meetings of party supporters and activists; used in only a handful of states.

turnout

The proportion of eligible voters who actually vote in a given election.

FIGURE 10.2 • The Rise and Fall of Turnout in Presidential Elections, 1789–2004

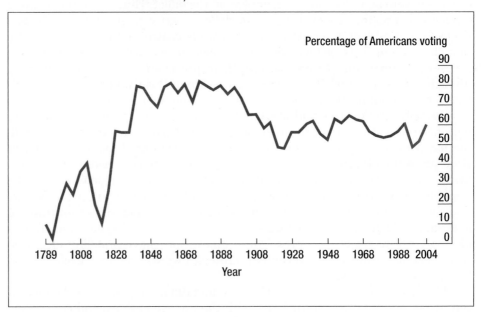

Turnout in presidential elections rose sharply during the nineteenth century—except during the "era of good feelings" when there was no party competition and little interest in politics among the public—but declined in the twentieth century. In 2004, turnout increased dramatically, but only to a level typical of the 1950s and 1960s.

Sources: U.S. Bureau of the Census; "Biggest Turnout of Voters Since 1968," The Associated Press, November 3, 2004. From 1920, the Census Bureau has calculated voting turnout as the percentage of the voting age population voting.

The Prepared Voter Kit

Causes of Low Turnout Why do so few Americans participate in elections? Scholars have identified several possible factors; most are related to whether they are allowed to vote, whether they are interested in voting, and whether anyone asks them to vote.[16]

Barriers to Voting In the United States, only citizens who take the initiative to register in advance are permitted to vote in an election. Many people do not make the extra effort to register, or circumstances make it difficult. For example, people who move, either within a state or to another state, must find out where and when to register in their new location. Many procrastinate and do not register in time, lowering turnout, according to one study, by 9 percentage points.[17]

In most European countries with high turnout rates, the government, rather than individual citizens, is responsible for deciding who is listed as eligible to vote and registers them automatically. In some countries, such as Belgium and Italy, moreover, citizens are *required* to vote and may be fined if they don't. Also, in most countries, election days are holidays on which people don't have to go to work.

The United States might increase political equality and popular sovereignty by making voting easier. One way to do so would be to ease registration requirements,[18] perhaps allowing registration by postcard or same-day registration at polling places. It is worth noting that voting turnout in the United States among those who have registered to vote hovers at about 85 percent

Voting Day in France

Voting day is a national holiday in many democratic countries, such as France. Here, voters cast their ballots in a voting center in Marseille in the first round of the 2002 presidential election.

and that voting participation in states that allow same-day registration is significantly higher than in other states.[19] These findings suggest that the registration requirement for voting is probably a significant barrier to participation, because participation rates go up when such barriers are lowered. The federal "motor voter" law passed in 1993, providing for registration in motor vehicle bureaus and other government offices, represents an important step in lowering the registration barrier in the United States.

Another way to increase participation would be to ease the voting act itself. Suggestions include making every election day a legal holiday, as is done in most western European countries; allowing an extended voting period, which several states have instituted in recent elections; or expanding the use of mail balloting over a period of several weeks, which Oregon does.

Too Much Complexity   As we suggested earlier, when voters go to the polls in the United States, they must make voting choices for a multitude of federal, state, and local offices and often decide on constitutional and policy measures put on the ballot by state legislatures (called **referenda**) or the public (called **initiatives**), especially in states such as California and Colorado where these are common. Research demonstrates that many potential voters are simply overwhelmed by the complexity of the ballot and stay home.[20]

Alienation   That many Americans felt apathetic toward or alienated from politics and government may have contributed to the declines in turnout that began in the late 1960s.[21] Such unsettling events as the assassination of popular leaders (John F. Kennedy, Robert Kennedy, Martin Luther King, Jr.), the Vietnam War, urban unrest, and the Watergate and Iran-Contra scandals surely played a role in the decline in voting.[22] More recently, the turn of the mass media to "infotainment" and scandals as staples of what they do has probably discouraged potential voters. Some scholars blame the increase in negative campaign advertising as a leading culprit, although other scholars disagree, saying that such ads sometimes even spur people to vote.[23] One scholar suggests that the recent rise

referenda

Procedures available in some states by which proposed state laws or constitutional amendments are submitted to the voters for approval or rejection.

initiatives

Procedures available in some states for citizens to put proposed laws and constitutional amendment on the ballot for voter approval or rejection.

in partisan conflict as our parties become more ideologically coherent is also a part of the low voter turnout story, as those who are repelled by the incivility choose to distance themselves from the political system.[24] High turnout in 2004, especially in the hotly contested battleground states, suggests, however, that intensely fought election contests might actually attract additional people to the polls,[25] especially those who are highly partisan. There may be a limit to this competition effect, however, if the same methods that bring out the partisans keep independents from the voting booth.[26]

Lack of Voter Mobilization of the Public by the Parties   Another reason voting turnout is low may be tied to the failure of the political parties to rouse people and get them to the polls to vote. The parties have always been interested, of course, in getting their own supporters to the polls, to rally the base, as it were, and doing what they could to keep the opposition away. They have never been in the business of increasing the vote turnout in general as a sort of civic duty. The problem is that aiming at your own voters with highly partisan appeals delivered by mail, telephone, and, increasingly, by e-mail, by highly professionalized but distant party organizations and advocacy groups does not increase turnout among the noncommitted public[27] and may even persuade many of them to stay home, as we suggest in the previous section. As well, old-style, door-to-door canvassing in neighborhoods seems to have been far more effective in raising turnout than modern methods, but it is used less often than in the past (although the parties have recently redoubled their door-to-door canvassing efforts).[28]

Campaign Involvement and Contacting Public Officials

Despite the relatively low voter turnout levels in the United States, however, Americans are actually more likely than people in other countries to participate actively in campaigns.[29] During the 2004 presidential campaign, some 31 percent of adults said they gave money to a party or candidate, 13 percent attended a political meeting or rally, and 4 percent worked actively in a campaign organization.[30] Much the same thing is true of contacting public officials; 22 percent of Americans say

Ready to Go Door-to-Door

Although turnout in American elections is relatively low compared with turnout in other democratic countries, Americans tend to participate more in campaigning than people elsewhere.

they did so during the past year, most often with local elected officials. Americans are also far more likely than citizens in other democracies to be involved in organizations, of both the private and public variety (see Chapter 7), that play such an important role in our electoral politics.[31]

Who Participates?

Not all Americans participate equally in politics; the evidence shows that political participation varies a great deal according to people's income, education, age, and ethnicity. This means that some kinds of people have more representation and influence with elected officials than others, and, other things being equal, they are more likely to have their preferences and interests reflected in what government does.

Voting Turnout: Who Votes?

Income and Education

For the most part, politically active people tend to be those with higher-than-average incomes and more formal education.[32] These people are also more likely to vote. In 2004, 75 percent of those with incomes of $75,000 or above said they had voted, but only 49 percent of those with incomes under $35,000 said they had done so. In 2004, 78 percent of college graduates reported that they had voted, but only 56 percent of high school graduates and 40 percent of those who had not graduated from high school had done so (see Figure 10.3).

Some statistical analyses have indicated that the crucial factor in voter turnout is level of formal education. When other factors are controlled, college-educated people are much more likely to tell interviewers that they have voted than are the less educated. There are several possible reasons: People with more education learn more about politics, are less troubled by registration requirements, and are more confident in their ability to affect political life.

At the same time, citizens with lower incomes are also less likely to work in campaigns, give money, contact officials, and the like. Wealthier Americans, who have more time, more money, and more knowledge of how to get things done, tend to be much more active politically. As a result, they may have more political clout than their fellow citizens.

Race and Ethnicity

In the past, fewer black people than whites voted, but now the proportions are more nearly equal: 67 percent of non-Hispanic whites and 60 percent of blacks voted in 2004, according to the U.S. Bureau of the Census (see Figure 10.3). The remaining differences result from blacks' lower average levels of income and education. Blacks are at least equally likely to vote, and sometimes more likely, than non-Hispanic whites of similar educational and income backgrounds.

Hispanics, however, have historically had very low participation rates, but things may be changing; although only 47 percent voted in 2004, this was a significant jump from 1996 when only 27 reported voting. Many Hispanics are discouraged from participating by low incomes, language problems, or suspicion of government authorities. This recent jump in the turnout rate for Hispanics has made a difference in states where Hispanic voters are concentrated: California, Texas, and Florida. And, both George W. Bush and John

FIGURE 10.3 • 2004 Presidential Election Turnout by Social Group

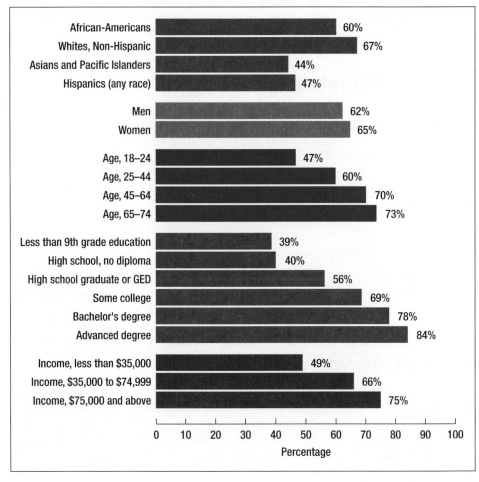

Age, education, race, ethnicity, income, and gender all affect voting behavior. Members of certain social groups are more likely to vote in elections than others. The Census Bureau warns that these numbers may be inflated because of people's tendency to want to report positive citizen behavior to interviewers. What is important here, however, is not necessarily the accuracy of the turnout totals but the comparison between groups of people. The relative turnout comparisons between groups fits the general picture available from other academic research and government sources.

Source: U.S. Bureau of the Census.

Kerry made special efforts to win over this group in their 2004 campaigns, demonstrating its rising importance.

Voting has also been relatively low among Asian Americans; only 44 percent reported voting in 2004. However, Asian American individuals and organizations have become more active in local politics and have increased campaign contributions to candidates and parties.

Age

Age is one of the most important variables when explaining why some people vote and others do not. The youngest groups of eligible voters go to the polls much less often than older voters: Only 47 percent of 18- to 24-year-olds did so in 2004, compared with 73 percent of 65- to 74-year-olds. The reasons may be that young people tend to be less rooted in communities, less familiar with registration and voting procedures, less in the habit of voting, and less clear about what stake they have in elections.[33] Or, it may be that no recent candidates or issues have appealed to them. In the 2004 Democratic presidential nomination contest, however, Howard Dean struck a chord among many young Americans who supported and worked for the Dean campaign, and many young people said they were very interested in the war in Iraq and what Bush and Kerry intended to do about it.[34] This may account for the jump in the youth vote which increased to 47 percent in 2004 from only 36 percent in 2000.

Gender

The gender gap in voting and other forms of political participation, which had favored men for most of our history, disappeared in the United States by the end of the 1980s.[35] Indeed, in the 2004 presidential election, women voted at slightly higher rates than men (again, see Figure 10.3). This marks a dramatic change over the past two decades and may be traced to the improvement in the educational attainments of women, the entrance of more women than ever into the paid workforce, and the increased importance of issues such as pay equity and abortion on the American political agenda.

Does It Matter Who Votes?

Some observers have argued that it doesn't matter if many people don't vote because their preferences aren't much different from those who do; the results would be about the same if everyone voted. In some elections, nonvoters have shown support for the same candidate who won, so their votes would apparently have changed nothing,[36] and some surveys have indicated that nonvoters' policy preferences differ little from those of voters.

Patrolling the Neighborhood

The massive increase in the size of the African American electorate in the South after passage of the 1965 Voting Rights Act resulted in the election of many African Americans to state and local offices and the integration of many government agencies, including police and sheriff's departments. Here, an officer patrols an urban neighborhood.

However, we should not be too quick to accept these arguments, just as few now accept the nineteenth-century view that there was no need for women to vote because their husbands could protect their interests. Even when the expressed preferences of nonvoters or nonparticipators do not look very distinctive, their objective circumstances, and therefore their needs for government services, may differ markedly.[37] Latinos, the young, and those with low incomes might benefit from government programs that are of less interest to other citizens. A political system that included and mobilized these people vigorously might produce quite different government policies. A large body of research, for example, shows that government efforts to compensate people with low incomes in the rich democracies is associated with the degree to which low income people vote, with the United States, where low income people participate at far lower rates than others, doing the least in this area of government activity.[38]

Compulsory Voting

Comparing Political Campaigns

Campaigning for Office

The ideas we discussed about how elections might ensure democratic policy-making all depend in various ways on what sorts of choices are presented to the voters. It makes a difference what kind of people run for office, whether they take clear policy stands, whether those stands differ from each other, and whether they stand for what the average voter wants. In evaluating how democratic our elections are, therefore, we need to examine what kinds of alternatives are put before the voters in campaigns. In this chapter, we focus on presidential campaigns. Congressional campaigns are addressed in Chapter 11.

Contending for the Party Presidential Nomination

The major party candidates for president of the United States are formally chosen well before the November election and are effectively chosen even before the parties hold nominating conventions. Candidates are drawn from a rather small pool. Despite what some parents tell their children, not every American has a significant chance of becoming president or of being nominated for president by a major party.

Who Has a Chance   In any given presidential election, only a handful of candidates are serious possibilities. So far in American history, these have virtually always been middle-aged or elderly white Protestant men with extensive formal educations, fairly high incomes, and substantial experience as public figures—usually as government officials (especially governors or senators) or military heroes. Movie stars, media commentators, business executives, and others who would be president almost always have to perform lesser government service before they are seriously considered for the presidency. Ronald Reagan, for example, most of whose career was spent acting in motion pictures and on television, served as governor of California before being elected president.

In recent years, the presidency has been practically monopolized by former governors such as Bill Clinton and George W. Bush (who have demonstrated executive ability) and vice presidents (who have a great deal of public visibility and name recognition). The single best stepping-stone to becoming president is clearly the vice presidency, which is usually filled by former senators or governors. Since 1900, 5 of the 18 presidents have succeeded from the vice presidency after the president's death or resignation, and two others, Nixon and Bush (the elder), were former vice presidents elected in their own right.

Serious candidates for president almost invariably represent mainstream American values and policy preferences. Seldom does an "extreme" candidate get very far. Serious candidates are also generally acceptable to the business community and have enthusiastic support from at least some sectors of industry or finance. They also must be considered "presidential" by the news media. And they must be attractive to those individuals and groups that fund campaigns.

Getting Started   A person who wants to run for the presidency usually begins at least two or three years before the election by testing the waters, asking friends and financial backers if they will support a run, and observing how people react to the mythical "Great Mentioner." A friendly journalist may write that Senator Blathers "has been mentioned" as a smart, attractive, strong candidate; Blathers waits to see whether anyone agrees. The would-be candidate may commission a national survey to check for name recognition and a positive image. He or she may put together an exploratory committee to round up private endorsements, commitments, and financial contributions, perhaps setting up private political action committees to gather money.

You Are a Professional
Campaign Manager

If all goes well in the early stages, the presidential aspirant becomes more serious, assembling a group of close advisers, formulating strategy, officially announcing his or her candidacy, forming a fund-raising operation, and putting together organizations ("Draft Blathers" or "Citizens for Blathers" committees) in key states. Early money is crucial to finance organization and advertising and to qualify for federal matching funds later.[39] And it is a clear sign that party bigwigs and associated interest and advocacy groups take the candidacy seriously. For all of these reasons, those who fail to raise early money almost always fail in the first primaries and eventually drop out. By October 1999, months before the first primary, candidate George W. Bush had already gathered $57 million, discouraging several potential rivals, including Elizabeth Dole; running unopposed for renomination as the Republican Party's candidate in the 2004 presidential election, President George W. Bush had collected almost $100 million by the end of 2003 before the primary season had even begun. Entering the 2004 primary season, insurgent Democratic candidate Howard Dean had amassed more than $30 million in his war chest; Senator Bob Graham of Florida, considered at one time to be among the most serious candidates for the Democratic nomination, dropped out of the race well before the start of the primaries after he was able to raise only $4.5 million.

Another important early decision is whether to be a part of the public campaign finance system—in which the federal government matches the first $250 from each individual donor on condition that candidates limit preconvention campaign spending to no more than $44.6 million—or to go it alone, raise hard money contributions from individuals (limited to $2,000) and PACs (limited to $5,000), and spend what they wish. In the 2004 election cycle, Bush, Dean, and John Kerry were able to raise enough money to fund their campaigns for their parties' nominations outside the public system, so each decided to forgo public money with its attendant spending limits.

Public Campaign Financing

Another important early decision involves which state primaries and caucus contests to enter. Each entry takes a lot of money, energy, and organization, and any loss is damaging; many candidates drop out after just a few early defeats, as Dick Gephardt, Wesley Clark, and Joe Lieberman did in 2004. To win the nomination, it is generally necessary to put together a string of primary victories.

Deciding on the theme of the campaign and the strategy to deliver the message is increasingly in the hands of hired pollsters and campaign consultants.[40] Alternative approaches to themes, messages, and issues are proposed; tested with the public in focus groups and surveys; and then crafted into stump

You Are a Media Consultant
to a Political Candidate

speeches, television and radio spots, and Web pages. Of course, candidates with strong views on the issues—such as Howard Dean's on the wrong-headedness of the invasion and occupation of Iraq—always have the final word on campaign themes.

Primaries and Caucuses   Party nominees for president are officially selected every four years at national party **conventions,** made up of state party delegations from around the country. Since the 1970s, most of the delegates to the conventions have been chosen in state primary elections, with direct voting by citizens. (Some primaries are open to all voters, as in the 2000 GOP primaries in South Carolina and Michigan; others are closed, reserved for those who register with the party whose primary election it is.) The Democrats' popularly elected delegates are supplemented by "superdelegates," usually members of Congress or local officials. A few states use caucuses, where active party members and officials gather in meetings around the state to choose delegates to state conventions, which in turn select the delegates to the national convention.

Because the states and the parties—not the federal government—control this nominating process, the system is a disorganized, even chaotic one, and it changes from one election to the next. Some states have primaries for both parties on the same day (including the all-important New Hampshire primaries); others hold primaries for the parties on separate dates. States are particularly anxious that they are not ignored, so an increasing number of them have moved their primary and caucus dates forward in the calendar. States with late primaries, even very large ones such as California, discovered in recent elections that the winners of early primaries had, for all intents and purposes, sewed up the party nominations, discounting the importance of their own primaries and caucuses. As a result, the primary and caucus season was "front-loaded" in 2004, with the bulk of delegates selected for both parties between the Iowa caucuses and the New Hampshire primaries in late January and the Kansas primaries in mid-March.

convention

A gathering of delegates who nominate a party's presidential candidate.

Not Much Help

The endorsement of his candidacy for the Democratic Party presidential nomination by former Vice President and Democratic presidential nominee Al Gore didn't do Howard Dean much good. The Vermont governor, the front-runner at the end of 2003, dropped out of the nomination race after suffering a string of stinging primary and caucus defeats to John Kerry early in 2004.

It is especially important for a candidate to establish momentum by winning early primaries and caucuses. Early winners get press attention, financial contributions, and better standings in the polls as voters and contributors decide they are viable candidates and must have some merit if people in other states have supported them. All these factors—attention from the media, money, and increased popular support—help the candidates who win early contests go on to win more and more contests.[41]

Since 1952, no national party convention has taken more than one ballot to nominate its candidate for the presidency, and the preconvention front-runner has always been the nominee. Now the trick is to win delegates in primaries and caucuses, which, in reality, decide the nomination before the convention ever takes place.[42] In 2004, the nominee for each party was known by early March. For the GOP, George W. Bush ran virtually unopposed, and his nomination was never in doubt. For the, Democrats, John Kerry's sweeping victory in the Super Tuesday primaries, coupled with his earlier primary and caucus victories, all but served up the nomination for the senator from Massachusetts by March 2.

The Convention Because the front-runner now comes to the national convention with enough delegates to win on the first ballot, the gathering has become a coronation ceremony in which prepledged delegates ratify the selection of the leading candidate, accept that candidate's choice for the vice presidency, and put on a colorful show for the media and the country. Enthusiasm and unity are staged for the national television audience; it is a disaster if serious conflicts break out or the timing goes wrong.

The evidence from polls indicates that at virtually all recent national conventions, the party nominee has been the surviving candidate who has had the most support from rank-and-file party identifiers in the nation as a whole.[43] The candidates who have survived the hurdles of raising money, mobilizing activists, and winning primary votes do not, of course, necessarily

The Public Face of Party Conventions

The impression conveyed by political conventions can have an important impact on elections. The apparent unhappiness of many anti–Vietnam War delegates with their party's selection at the 1968 Democratic convention in Chicago severely damaged the campaign of nominee Hubert Humphrey. In contrast, the 1984 Republican convention that selected Ronald Reagan as its nominee more nearly resembled a coronation and gave Reagan and the GOP a fast start in the fall campaign.

include the most popular potential presidents in the country; if they did, Colin Powell would probably have won the Republican presidential nomination in 1996. And the big differences between the delegates of the two parties tend to push the two parties' nominees and issue positions away from each other, in a responsible party rather than a purely electoral competition process. Still, the parties not only use the convention as a gathering of activist partisans to nominate one of their own but usually try to make an appeal for support from more centrist voters around the country. Sometimes this balancing act works; sometimes it doesn't. Conservative Barry Goldwater was the darling of the 1964 Republican convention, but he failed miserably in the general election; liberal and antiwar candidate George McGovern was the favorite of Democratic convention delegates in 1972, but he was badly defeated by Richard Nixon in the general election.

Nomination Politics and Democracy   What does all this have to do with democratic control of government? Several things. On the one hand, as we have indicated, the nomination process has some success in coming up with candidates who take stands with wide popular appeal, much as electoral competition theories dictate. On the other hand, as the sharp differences between Republican and Democratic convention delegates suggest (see Table 9.1 on page 264), Republican and Democratic nominees tend to differ in certain systematic ways, in responsible party fashion. Party platforms—the parties' official statements of their stand on issues—tend to include appeals to average voters but also distinctive appeals to each party's constituencies.

Both these tendencies might be considered good for democracy. However, the crucial role of party activists and money givers in selecting candidates means that nominees and their policy stands are chosen partly to appeal to party elites, financial contributors, and strong partisans rather than to ordinary voters. Thus, neither party's nominee may stand for what ordinary citizens want, the result being voter dissatisfaction and no ideal democratic outcome.

Incumbents   We have been focusing on how outsiders and political challengers try to win party nominations. Things are very different for incumbent presidents seeking reelection, like Bill Clinton in 1996 or George W. Bush in 2004. These candidates must also enter and win primaries, but they have the machinery of government working for them and, if times are reasonably good, a unified party behind them. They also have an easier time getting campaign contributions, especially for the primaries when incumbent presidents only occasionally meet serious competition. They campaign on the job, taking credit for policy successes while discounting or blaming others, such as Congress, for failures. Winning renomination as president is usually easy, except in cases of disaster such as the 1968 Vietnam War debacle for Lyndon Johnson.

The Autumn Campaign

You Are a Presidential Campaign Consultant

Incumbents and challengers alike, having won a party nomination, must face the autumn campaign. For the general election, if not before, the candidates set up a campaign organization in each state, sending aides to coordinate backers and local party leaders. Intense money-raising continues, and a new round of public financing kicks in. Candidates plan itineraries to make three or four speeches in different media markets each day, concentrating on so-called battleground states where the contest between the presidential candidates is deemed to be very close and could go either way (see the "Mapping American Politics" feature on campaign ad buys). In all of this, hired pollsters and campaign consultants are deeply involved, playing a role in virtually all tactical and strategic decision making.[44]

A new media blitz begins, with many brief spot commercials on television, including "attack" ads such as Democrat Bill Clinton's in 1992 mocking George H.W. Bush's "read my lips, no new taxes" pledge (which he did not keep) and Republican Robert Dole's in 1996 pointing to Clinton's flawed character (with the Gennifer Flowers and Monica Lewinsky sex scandals center-stage). Political consultants use voter focus groups to identify hot-button emotional appeals. Negative advertising has been heavily criticized as simplistic and misleading, but it has often proved effective and is difficult to control or counteract.

Another element of strategy is to get potential supporters registered and to the polls. Organized labor and 527 organizations such as MoveOn.org work on turning out Democrats, while conservative Christian groups and business-oriented organizations work on Republican turnout. As we have noted, low-income and minority citizens have sometimes been ignored by both major parties.

Television and Presidential Campaigns

Informing Voters   What kinds of information do voters get in presidential campaigns? Among other things, voters get information on the candidates' stands on the issues, their past performances, and their personal characteristics.

Issues   Some of the information voters get concerns issues. In accord with electoral competition theories, both the Republican and the Democratic candidates usually try to appeal to the average voter by taking similar, popular stands on policy, especially foreign policy. Kerry and Bush both stayed close to the center in 2004. But as responsible party theories suggest, Republican and Democratic candidates usually do differ on a number of issues, such as medical care, federal aid to education, prescription drug programs, tax cuts, social welfare, civil rights, the environment, abortion, and the use of the military in foreign policy. On these issues, the Democratic candidate tends to take a more liberal stand than the Republican, just as Democratic party identifiers, activists, money givers, and convention delegates tend to be more liberal than their Republican counterparts.

While Democratic and Republican presidential candidates generally differ on a range of issues that are fairly predictable and that tend to appeal to party identifiers, they also try to appeal to independent voters and a few in

Getting "Swift Boated"

In the 2004 presidential campaign, 527 advocacy organizations became very important, mostly by running attack ads. One of the most effective was the Swift Boat group, which attacked Democratic candidate John Kerry's war record, calling his wartime awards and citations "dishonest and dishonorable."

Mapping American Politics

Ad buys and battleground states

Introduction: As you have seen, presidents are selected not by the people directly, but by votes in the electoral college. The winner is that candidate who wins a majority of electoral votes. (In all but a few presidential elections, one exception being the 2000 election of George W. Bush over Al Gore, the candidate who won a majority of the electoral college also won the highest popular vote across the country.) Campaigns are conducted on a state-by-state basis in a bid to put together a majority of electoral votes. With the exception of Nebraska and Maine, states use winner-take-all systems in which the candidate with the most votes (not necessarily a majority) wins all the state's electoral votes. Knowing this, campaign managers and their candidates focus on a relative handful of

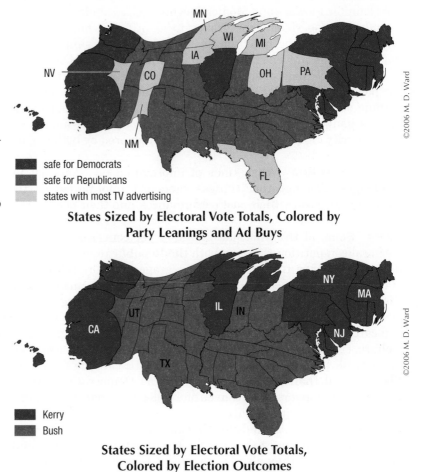

safe for Democrats
safe for Republicans
states with most TV advertising

States Sized by Electoral Vote Totals, Colored by Party Leanings and Ad Buys

Kerry
Bush

States Sized by Electoral Vote Totals, Colored by Election Outcomes

©2006 M. D. Ward

the opposition party by using vague and ambiguous "feel good" themes. No one, for example, could object to George H. W. Bush's 1988 promises to be an "education president" and an "environmental president" or to Clinton's 1996 promise to "build a bridge to the twenty-first century."

Past Performance Often candidates talk about past performance and future goals. The "outs" blame the "ins" for wars, recessions, and other calamities. The "ins" brag about how they have brought peace and prosperity and paint a warm picture of a glorious future, without saying exactly how it will come about.

Incumbent presidents, of course, can do things that accurately or inaccurately suggest successful performance. They can try to schedule recessions for off years, pumping up the economy in time for reelection. Or they can make dramatic foreign policy moves just before election day, like Nixon's 1972 trips to the Soviet Union and China.

states where the contest is too close to call and where winning might affect the outcome of the presidential contest. They virtually ignore states that are not "in play," where the outcome is a foregone conclusion. In the 2004 election, for example, Democrats were in such a commanding position in California, New York, and Massachusetts that neither Democrats nor Republicans thought it wise to use scarce funds to campaign there. Republicans were so far ahead in Texas, Utah, and Indiana that neither party thought it worthwhile to campaign there.

Mapping Ad Buys: The cartogram on the top, with the size of the states reflecting the number of electoral votes, highlights the states where the parties and campaign organizations bought the greatest number of television ads urging votes for their candidate in the month or so before the 2004 election. You can see that significant television ad buys occurred in only 10 states, but those 10 accounted for 88 percent of all such ads bought across the entire country. The focus of the campaign on battleground states is very evident. Note that several of the very largest electoral college states were not among those 10, including California, Illinois, New Jersey, and New York (reliably Democratic) and Texas (reliably

Republican). Ad buys occurred overwhelmingly in states where party and campaign professionals believed either party's presidential candidate had a chance to win. The cartogram on the bottom shows the final electoral vote outcome.

What Do You Think? Taking a look at how the vote turned out in the battleground states, whose campaign seems to have done a better job of using ad buys effectively? If you lived in a nonbattleground state, did it seem that there was very little campaign advertising on television? If you lived in a battleground state, did it seem that there was too much advertising? Do you think the presidential contest should be waged on a nationwide basis, rather than on a state-by-state basis? Is there any way to convince parties and presidential campaigns to do this so long as we use the electoral college system for selecting presidents?

Note: In cartograms, Alaska is not shown (although information is included in calculations), and Hawaii is moved closer to the mainland.

Source for top left cartogram: "Presidential TV Advertising Battle Narrows to Just Ten Battleground States," Nielsen Monitor-Plus and the University of Wisconsin Advertising Project (press release, October 12, 2004).

Personal Characteristics   Most of all, however, voters get a chance to learn about the real or alleged personal characteristics of the candidates. Even when the candidates are talking about something else, they give an impression of either competence or incompetence. Jimmy Carter, for example, emphasized his expertise as a "nuclear engineer," whereas Gerald Ford was haunted by films of him stumbling on airplane ramps.

Candidates also come across as warm or cold. Dwight D. Eisenhower's radiant grin appeared everywhere in 1952 and 1956, as Reagan's did in 1984, but Richard Nixon was perceived as cold and aloof in 1968, despite clever efforts at selling his personality.

Still another dimension of candidates' personalities is strength or weakness. George H. W. Bush overcame the so-called wimp factor in 1988 with his tough talk about crime and the flag. Merely by surviving many personal attacks in 1992 and 1996, Clinton appeared strong and resilient.

The sparse and ambiguous treatment of policy issues in campaigns, as well as the emphasis on past performance and personal competence, fits better with ideas about electoral reward and punishment than with responsible parties or issue-oriented electoral competition. Candidate personalities are not irrelevant to the democratic control of government. Obviously, it is useful for voters to pick presidents who possess competence, warmth, and strength. And citizens may be more skillful in judging people than in figuring out complicated policy issues.

Voters can be fooled, however, by dirty tricks or slick advertising that sells presidential candidates' personalities and tears down the opponent. Moreover, the focus on personal imagery may distract attention from policy stands. If candidates who favor unpopular policies are elected on the basis of attractive personal images, democratic control of policymaking is weakened. By the purchase of advertising and the hiring of smart consultants, money may, in effect, overcome the popular will.

Money and Elections

Most observers agree that money creates problems in U.S. presidential elections. The main problem is probably not that too much money is spent but that the money comes from private sources that may influence government policymaking after the election is over.

The Cost of Presidential Campaigns   Presidential campaigns cost a great deal of money, although the system is so complex that even seasoned observers can make only educated guesses about the total. Expenditures by the official presidential campaigns and party committees are fairly easy to keep track of, to be sure, because of reporting requirements to the Federal Election Commission. During the 2003–2004 election cycle, the official Bush campaign spent about $345 million on pre- and postconvention electioneering, while John Kerry spent about $310 million for his. Republican and Democratic national committees spent an additional $1.4 billion from January 2003 through December 2004 (this includes spending on congressional races as well).[45] Where the numbers get tricky is keeping track of money spent by private associations and advocacy groups on activities that closely parallel presidential, congressional, and party campaigns. It is anyone's guess what these organizations spend on things such as "get out the vote" drives, issue advertising on television and radio, door-to-door campaigning for candidates and issues, appeals to organization members, and more, because most of these expenditures do not have to be reported. The Center for Responsive Politics estimates that 527 groups spent $386 million on federal elections (presidential and congressional races) and PAC's about $384 million during the 2003–2004 campaigns.[46]

Where Does the Money Come From?   Since 1971, most of the money spent in the fall presidential campaign by the two presidential candidates has come from the federal treasury, paid by the taxpayers. Taxpayers can check off a box on their tax returns to authorize a $3 contribution from public funds. The government uses these taxpayer contributions to provide matches for money contributors give to candidates during the primary and general election campaigns of those candidates who agree to spending limits. In 2004, the Kerry and Bush campaigns each received $74.4 million in public funds for the general election in the fall. Although Kerry and Bush refused public money for their nomination campaigns, both accepted it for the general election contest.

But why would they do such a thing, given that accepting public funding for their campaigns limited what they could spend?

- Because publically provided funds are not inconsiderable.
- Because the two party presidential candidates get lots of free publicity simply by being the standard bearer of one of the two major parties.
- Because various state, local, and national party committees spend generously on the campaigns.
- Because interest groups and advocacy organizations spend lavishly on independent parallel campaigns (see Chapter 7).

Does Money Talk?   Money matters a great deal in the presidential nomination process—aspirants for party nominations who cannot raise sizeable funds always drop out of the race—but not so much during the postconvention run for the White House.[47] As we pointed out earlier, once a presidential campaign is under way, each of the major party candidates has at his or her disposal all of the organizational resources of the party organization and money from traditional party contributors and allied interest groups as well as matching funds from the government; each candidate generally has enough money to run a credible campaign.

Money may talk at a later stage, however. It is widely believed, although difficult to prove, that contributors of money often get something back.[48] The point is not that presidential candidates take outright bribes in exchange for policy favors. Indeed, exchanges between politicians and money givers are complex and varied, sometimes yielding little benefit to contributors. Undeniably, however, cozy relationships do tend to develop between politicians and major money givers. Contributors gain access to, and a friendly hearing from, those whom they help to win office.

It is clear that money givers are different from average citizens. They have special interests of their own. As we have indicated, a large amount of campaign money comes from large corporations, investment banking firms,

Raising Money

Under the McCain-Feingold campaign finance rules that bar soft money contributions to national party committees, advocacy groups with close ties to the parties have become increasingly important. Cecile Richards is president of America Votes, an organization that pays for issue campaigns in favor of abortion rights, environmental protection, worker rights and protections, and other issues close to the hearts of Democrats. Here she chats with actor Robert Redford at a fund-raising event in Hollywood during the 2004 presidential election campaign.

wealthy families, labor unions, professional associations (e.g., doctors, lawyers, or realtors), and issue-oriented groups such as the National Rifle Association, the Christian Coalition, and the National Abortion Rights Action League. The big contributors generally do not represent ordinary workers, consumers, or taxpayers, let alone minorities or the poor. Surveys show that the individuals who give money tend to have much higher incomes and more conservative views on economic issues than the average American.[49]

The result is political inequality. Those who are well organized or have a lot of money to spend on politics have a better chance of influencing policy than ordinary citizens do, and they tend to influence it in directions different from those the general public would want. The role of money in presidential nomination and election campaigns (and in congressional campaigns, as we show in Chapter 11) is a major problem for the working of democracy in the United States.

Campaign Finance Reform

Election Outcomes

After the parties and candidates have presented their campaigns, the voters decide. Exactly how people make their voting decisions affects how well or how poorly elections contribute to the democratic control of government.

How Voters Decide

Years of scholarly research have made it clear that feelings about the parties, the candidates, and the issues have substantial effects on how people vote.[50]

Social Characteristics People's socioeconomic status, religion, and ethnic background are significantly related to how they vote. Since the 1930s, for example, African Americans, Jews, and lower-income citizens have tended to vote heavily for Democrats, while white Protestants and upper-income Americans have voted mostly for Republicans. In 2004, 88 percent of blacks, but only 41 percent of whites, voted for John Kerry against George W. Bush; 55 percent of people with household incomes under $50,000, but only 41 percent of those with incomes over $100,000, voted for Kerry; and 74 percent of Jews, but only 38 of Protestants, voted for him. Regular attendees at religious services voted 2:1 for Bush over Kerry. Recently, women have voted for Democrats in greater numbers than have men, although the differences were not as marked in 2004; 51 percent of women, but only 44 percent of men, voted for Kerry. Older people have traditionally supported Democratic candidates more often, and at higher rates, than other age groups, but this is no longer true. In 2004, 54 percent of those over 60 voted for Bush (see Figure 10.5).

Party Loyalties To some extent, these social patterns work through long-term attachments to, or identification with, political parties. As indicated earlier, a majority of Americans—between 60 and 65 percent—still say they consider themselves Republicans or Democrats. Party loyalties vary among different groups of the population, often because of past or present differences between the parties on policy issues, especially economic and social issues.[51] For this reason, when people use their party identification as a shortcut for choosing a candidate, they are likely choosing a candidate who is close to them on the issues. The ability of party identification to serve as a useful tool for people to choose candidates that are close to them on the issues is further enhanced by the close linkages between the parties and ideologies,

FIGURE 10.5 • Presidential Vote in 2004, by Social Group

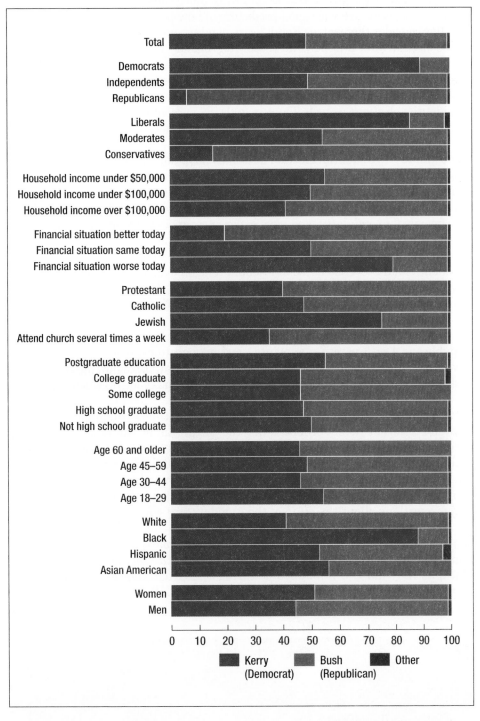

Minorities, lower-income voters, and women tended to vote for John Kerry in the 2004 election, while Protestants, regular church-goers, higher-income people, and men tended to favor George W. Bush.

Source: "Edison/Mitofsky Exit Poll, 2004 Presidential Election," CNN.com, **www.cnn.com/ELECTION/2004,** November 2, 2004.

with Democrats generally more liberal (including party identifiers, activists, and candidates) and Republicans generally more conservative.[52]

Party loyalties are very good predictors of how people will vote.[53] Those who say they consider themselves Republicans tend to vote for Republican candidates in one election after another, and those who consider themselves Democrats vote for Democratic candidates. This is especially true in congressional elections and in state and local races, where most voters know little more about the candidates than their party labels, but the party loyalty factor is extremely important in presidential elections as well. Thus, in 2004, 89 percent of Democratic identifiers voted for Kerry, and 93 percent of Republican identifiers voted for Bush.

Candidates   Presidential election outcomes have not simply reflected the party balance in the country; if that were true, Democrats would have won most presidential elections during the post–World War II period. Voters also pay a lot of attention to their perceptions of the personal characteristics of candidates. They vote heavily for candidates who have experience, appear strong and decisive, and convey personal warmth. The Republican candidate in 1952 and 1956, Dwight D. Eisenhower, had a tremendous advantage in these respects over his Democratic opponent, Adlai Stevenson;[54] so did Ronald Reagan over Walter Mondale in 1984, and George H. W. Bush over Michael Dukakis in 1988. Only in 1964 did the Democratic candidate (Lyndon Johnson) appeal to voters substantially more than the Republican candidate (Barry Goldwater). In elections between 1952 and 1972, the contrast between Republican and Democratic candidates typically gained the Republicans 4 or 5 percentage points—just enough to overcome the Democrats' advantage in what political scientists call the **normal vote:** how votes would be cast if only party identification determined voters' choices for president.

normal vote

The proportion of the votes that each party would win if party identification alone affected voting decisions.

Issues   Voters also pay attention to issues. Sometimes this means choosing between different policy proposals for the future (as in the responsible party voting model), such as Reagan's 1980 promises to cut back federal government activity or Clinton's 1992 pledges of jobs and a middle-class tax cut. More often, however, issue voting has meant retrospective voting (the electoral reward and punishment model), making judgments about the past, especially on major questions about the state of the economy and war or peace.

The voters tend to reward the incumbent party for what they see as good times and to punish it for what they see as bad times. In especially bad economic times, for example, Americans tend to vote the incumbent party out of office, as they did the Republicans during the Great Depression in 1932. In 1992 the electorate punished Republican George H. W. Bush for the poor state

An Unfortunate Tank Ride

News photos and video of Democratic presidential candidate Michael Dukakis taking a ride in a new M1-A-1 battle tank during the 1988 campaign did not convince very many people that he was strong on national defense, which was his apparent objective. Much to the chagrin of his campaign team, the ride became the butt of jokes by late-night comedians and editorial cartoonists.

of the economy and in 1996 it rewarded Bill Clinton for being president during good economic times. This did not happen in 2004, however, when protection against terrorism seemed to trump people's concerns about slow job growth. Several scholars and pollsters believe that cultural issues—such as gay and lesbian rights, abortion, civil rights and affirmative action, law and order, and the like—may have become more important than retrospective judgments about economic issues in determining voter choices. This may help explain why increasing numbers of affluent and educated Americans are voting Democratic, while lower-income, less-educated, and church-going whites are increasingly casting their ballots for Republicans.[55]

Foreign policy can be important as well, especially when war and peace are at issue. Bitter disillusionment over the Korean War hurt the Democrats in 1952, just as the Vietnam War cost them in 1968, and unhappiness about American hostages in Iran and the Soviet intervention in Afghanistan hurt Jimmy Carter in 1980. During nearly all of the past half-century, in fact, Republican candidates have been seen as better at providing foreign policy strength and at keeping us out of war. In most elections, however, foreign policy concerns take a back seat to domestic ones for most voters.

The Electoral College

As many Americans learned for the first time in 2000, the outcome of presidential elections is determined not by the number of popular votes cast for each candidate; it depends on the votes in the electoral college. (See "By the Numbers" feature for more information on the 2000 election.)

When Americans vote for a presidential candidate whose name appears on the ballot, they are actually voting for a slate of **electors** in their state—equal to the number of the state's U.S. senators and representatives—who have promised to support a party's presidential candidate. (Very rarely have electors reneged on their promises and cast ballots for someone else; there was one so-called faithless elector in 2000.) Nearly all states now have winner-take-all systems in which the winner of the popular vote wins the state's entire allotment of electoral votes; Maine and Nebraska, in slight variations, choose electors on a winner-take-all basis for each congressional district.

The "college" of electors from the different states never actually meets; instead, the electors meet in their respective states and send lists of how they have voted to Washington, D.C. (see the Twelfth Amendment to the Constitution). The candidate who receives a majority of all the electoral votes in the country is elected president. Not since 1824 has it been necessary to resort to the odd constitutional provisions that apply when no one gets a majority of electoral votes: The House of Representatives chooses among the top three candidates, by majority vote of state delegations.

Most of the time, this peculiar electoral college system works about the same way as if Americans chose their presidents by direct popular vote, although this was not true in 2000 when Bush won the electoral vote while losing the popular vote. The old idea that electors would exercise their independent judgments is long gone. But the system does have certain consequences:

- *It magnifies the popular support of winners*. A candidate who wins in many states, by a narrow margin in each, can win a "landslide" in the electoral college. In 1996, for example, Bill Clinton's 49 percent of the popular vote translated into 379 electoral votes, or 70 percent of the total. Ordinarily, this magnification just adds legitimacy to the democratic choice, especially when the winner has only a **plurality** of the popular vote, that is, more than anybody else but less than a majority of all votes.

VISUAL LITERACY

Electoral Rules: How Do They Influence Campaigns?

electors
Representatives who are elected in the states to formally choose the U.S. president.

VIDEO DEBATE

The 2000 Presidential Election

plurality
More votes than any other candidate but less than a majority of all votes cast.

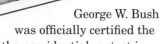
By the Numbers

Did George W. Bush really win the 2000 presidential vote in Florida?

George W. Bush was officially certified the winner of the presidential contest in Florida on December 12, 2000, thirty-five days after the November election. Florida's 25 electoral votes brought his national total to 271, just barely enough to win the White House.

Interestingly, however, a comprehensive review of Florida ballots has come up with several other possible outcomes to the Florida vote, depending on different ways the ballots could have been counted. In fact, the possible outcomes vary from Bush winning by 537 votes to Gore winning by 200!

Why It Matters: Elections must be fair if they are to play the role assigned to them in democratic theory. Part of a fair election is an accurate count of votes cast. Without an accurate count, voter wishes will not be conveyed to public officials, and the legitimacy of elected officials is at risk, making governance more difficult.

Behind the Vote Count Numbers: A consortium of eight leading news organizations—including *The Wall Street Journal, The New York Times, The Washington Post,* the Associated Press, and CNN—sponsored a 10-month study by the widely respected National Opinion Research Center at the University of Chicago. Center researchers examined every uncounted "under-vote" ballot (where no vote for president was recorded by the voting machine), with an eye toward determining each voter's intent. Only ballots that showed evidence of clear voter intention were included in the consortium's recount.

These included ballots with "hanging" and "pregnant" chads which the machines failed to record and optical scan ballots where voters indicated their vote with a check mark or an "x" rather than filling in the bubble as instructed.

Calculating the Winner's Margin of Victory: The official tally concluded that Bush won by 537 votes. However, Center investigators found that different counting methods would have yielded the results shown on page 303. There are some incredible ironies in these numbers.

- **Scenario 1** Had the Gore team gotten everything it asked for from election officials and the courts, Gore still would have lost to George W. Bush.

- **Scenario 2** The U.S. Supreme Court did not steal the election, as many Gore supporters claimed, for had it allowed the Florida Supreme Court's solution to stand, Bush would have won anyway.

- **Scenario 3** A majority of Florida voters went to the polls on November 8 to cast a vote for Al Gore for president. The method proposed by the U.S. Supreme Court shows this; recounting all "under-count" disputed ballots on a statewide basis using consistent standards yields a Gore victory. The upshot: Gore was badly advised by his team of lawyers, who insisted on recounts in only certain counties.

Because of the enormous boost in George W. Bush's popularity following the terrorist attack on the United States and the widely supported attack on the Taliban regime in Afghanistan that followed,

Many of our presidents have been elected by a plurality but with less than 50 percent of the popular vote—most recently, Clinton (1992 and 1996), Richard Nixon (1968), John Kennedy (1960), and Harry Truman (1948).

- *It may let the less popular candidate win.* A president can be elected who had *fewer* votes than an opponent, if those votes happened to produce narrow margins in many states. Such a result has occurred three times: in 1876, when Rutherford Hayes defeated Samuel Tilden; in 1888, when Benjamin Harrison beat the more popular Grover Cleveland; and in 2000, when George W. Bush defeated Al Gore. (Gore beat Bush by more

And the Winner Is . . . Close Calls in Presidential Elections

most Americans ignored the consortium's findings when it was published after 9/11. Most seemed perfectly content to have Bush as president, no matter what had happened in Florida.

Criticisms of the Florida "Recount":
Some have argued that the consortium's recount was flawed in two major ways:

- First, it did not include "over-votes" in its estimates—those ballots where more than one name for president was indicated or where the same name was entered more than once—which were also ruled invalid by election officials in Florida. For the most part, these involved ballots where voters made two punches on very confusing ballots (the infamous "butterfly ballots") or where voters wrote in the same name as the candidate they had punched or marked, presumably to make clear to election officials who they had voted for. A substantial majority of over-vote ballots had Gore as one of the choices.

- Second, there is the issue of absentee ballots from overseas armed forces personnel. Had they been counted in the same way other ballots were counted—that is, not counting ballots kicked out because of "under-vote" or "over-vote" problems—Bush would have lost hundreds of votes to Gore and probably lost Florida and the White House.

What to Watch For:
When counting votes, as in all other counts, the rules for doing so matter. This is

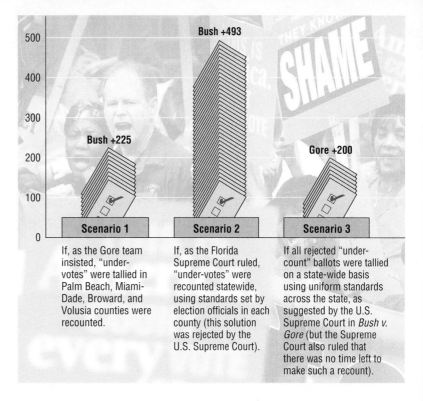

Bush +493

Bush +225

Gore +200

500
400
300
200
100
0

Scenario 1
If, as the Gore team insisted, "under-votes" were tallied in Palm Beach, Miami-Dade, Broward, and Volusia counties were recounted.

Scenario 2
If, as the Florida Supreme Court ruled, "under-votes" were recounted statewide, using standards set by election officials in each county (this solution was rejected by the U.S. Supreme Court).

Scenario 3
If all rejected "under-count" ballots were tallied on a state-wide basis using uniform standards across the state, as suggested by the U.S. Supreme Court in *Bush v. Gore* (but the Supreme Court also ruled that there was no time left to make such a recount).

why the lawyers from the Gore and Bush teams fought so ferociously following the Florida election about how to do the recount. Whenever you run across a statistic that involves counting, in one form or another, you might want to look further into what counting rules were used.

What Do You Think?
Can you think of any other way to decide the winner of an election when, for all intents and purposes, the race ends up in a dead heat? Some countries use a "run-off" system in which the two top people run against each other to determine who has won a majority of popular votes before a winner is declared. In the 2000 presidential elections, this would have meant a run-off election between Gore and Bush, without Ralph Nader or Pat Buchanan on the ballot.

than a half million votes nationally.) Several early-nineteenth-century presidents were probably chosen with only small fractions of the popular vote, although we cannot be sure because some of the statistics are unreliable. Most notably, in 1824, John Quincy Adams defeated the very popular Andrew Jackson in the House of Representatives.

- *It discourages third parties.* Our constitutional arrangements for a single president and single-member congressional districts (rather than proportional representation) already discourage third parties; if candidates cannot win a plurality, they get nothing. The electoral college

Using the Democracy Standard

Do elections matter?

PROPOSITION: Elections don't matter much in determining what government leaders do. It's probably the reason so many Americans don't bother to vote.

AGREE Elections don't do much to help the people control the government, mainly because U.S. political parties undermine the ability of elections to play the democratic role reserved for them in responsible party government, electoral competition, and electoral reward-and-punishment theories of democratic elections. Each of these democratic election models requires that the parties be cohesive organizations, with clear programmatic and ideological positions that distinguish them from competing parties. U.S. parties are not like this; they are too "candidate centered," sacrificing coherence and unity to the electoral needs of a diverse set of individual candidates. When candidates feel that their election or reelection depends on their own fund-raising and campaigning, and that siding with their party may be risky, they all too easily abandon party loyalty. Parties of this sort, internally contradictory and ambiguous, do not allow voters to choose a governing party team that will takes responsibility for government performance. They do not provide the tools by which the public can cut through the confusion and complexity of politics and government, make sense of how things work, and magnify its voice in public affairs. To make matters worse, many Americans are aware that enormous influence is exercised over parties and their candidates by powerful interest groups and large campaign contributors. Feeling that their vote doesn't matter much in the end, potential voters stay away from the polls in droves.

Scholars have shown that government officials, in the **DISAGREE** long run, do what the American people want them to do about two-thirds of the time. Although a variety of instruments help convey what the people want to officials—public opinion polls, interest groups, and social movements—it is ultimately the fact that officials must face the voters that keeps them in line. And, it is the political parties that organize electoral contests and help people sort out the candidates and make sense of their electoral promises, allowing people to cast votes in a relatively rational manner. Elections matter, that is to say, and it is the political parties that make elections function in a way that allows the people to control what goes on in government. The problem of nonvoting is exaggerated, moreover. People are free to participate or not participate; it is a free country. If they choose not to, it is probably because they are not terribly unhappy about the direction that government is taking.

CONSIDER College-age people vote less often than any other age group. Indeed, age is a better predictor of voting than income, education, or gender.

• Why do you think young people participate at such low levels? • Is it because many young people are not yet rooted in a community and job? • Or do you think that young people are turned off by electoral politics, not seeing it as a mechanism for changing the direction of the country in domestic and foreign affairs? • Or do you think that people your age tend to be pretty well satisfied by the way things are going and stay away from the polls because they don't feel that anything is amiss or needs to be changed? • How about you? • Do you vote? • If not, why is that? • And, if not, what would get you to the voting booth? • If you don't vote, are you active in politics in other ways, such as being part of a social movement or advocacy group? • If so, why do you find this to be a more satisfying way to participate in politics?

adds symbolically to this discouragement: A third party with substantial support may get no electoral votes at all if its support is scattered among many states. In 1992, for example, Ross Perot's impressive 19 percent of the popular vote translated into zero electoral votes because he failed to win a plurality in any single state.

People who would like to abolish the electoral college point to its narrowing of choices and the possibility of undemocratic outcomes. Those who like it claim that it discourages fraud by limiting the votes that any one state can cast, that the two-party system it encourages is good, and that the added legitimacy of electoral college "landslides" is helpful—or at least harmless.

The Electoral College

Summary

Elections are the most important means by which citizens can exert democratic control over their government. Voters can choose *responsible parties* to carry out their distinctive programs. *Electoral competition* forces vote-seeking parties and candidates to appeal to the center of public opinion. *Electoral reward and punishment* gives officials incentives to carry out policies that will win public approval. However, none of these processes guarantees a perfectly democratic outcome.

Political participation can be conventional (voting, helping in campaigns, and contacting officials) or unconventional (protesting or demonstrating). The right to vote, originally quite limited, was expanded in various historical surges to include nearly all adults and to apply to most major offices. Turnout has declined, however, and in recent years only about half the eligible voters have cast ballots for the presidency.

Candidates for president start by testing the waters, raising money, and forming campaign organizations; in a series of state primaries and caucuses, they seek delegates to the national nominating conventions, which generally choose a clear front-runner or the incumbent president. During the campaign, the candidates are generally vague about issues; they concentrate on building personal images and emphasizing past performance.

Money matters most in the struggle for each party's presidential nomination. Much of the money is regulated "hard money" raised by the candidate and party committees, as well as political action committees representing private interests and advocacy organizations. The remainder is unregulated money spent by individuals and associations on independent issue campaigns that favor one candidate or another. Candidates who cannot raise money or have money raised for them by others do not become serious contenders in the party nomination contests. Money differences between the candidates in the presidential contest in the fall are less important in determining the outcome because of public financing and intense and costless press coverage of the election.

Voters' decisions depend heavily on party loyalties, the personal characteristics of the candidates, and the issues, especially the state of the economy and of U.S. foreign policy. After recessions and unsuccessful wars, the incumbent party generally loses. The electoral college does not always accurately reflect popular votes. Elections matter not only when there is a clear choice but also when electoral reward or punishment occurs or when electoral competition forces both parties to take similar popular stands.

Web Exploration
Party Platforms and Electoral Theory

ISSUE: According to democratic theorists, elections can ensure popular accountability in representative democracies in three ways: by allowing the public to choose between future courses of action (responsible party government), by allowing voters to render judgments about a party's performance in office (electoral reward and punishment), and by forcing parties and candidates to offer platforms that conform to what the public wants (electoral competition).

SITE: Access the Democratic and Republican National Committees in MyPoliSciLab at **www .mypoliscilab.com.** Go to the "Web Explorations" section for Chapter 10, open "Party Platforms and Electoral Theory," then the national committee sites for each party. At each party site, look at the official platforms passed at their respective 2004 conventions.

WHAT YOU'VE LEARNED: How did each party present itself during the 2004 national election cycle in terms of the models of electoral democracy described in this chapter? Did Republicans and Democrats ask voters to choose a future direction for government or ask them to simply make a judgment about the party's past performance? Or did the parties simply try to position themselves in terms of where they judged the voters to be?

HINT: You will probably discover that each of the parties shows signs of trying to do all three, although the emphasis will probably be on one.

Internet Sources

The Center for Public Integrity
www.publicintegrity.org/
An especially good site for following the money trail—how campaign money is gathered and spent.

Democratic National Committee
www.democrats.org/
Official site of the Democratic party with information on party positions and candidates, how to work as a volunteer or contribute money, and more.

The National Archives Electoral College Site
www.archives.gov/federal_register/electoral_college/index.html
Everything there is to know about the law and practices of the electoral college and the process by which it elects the president.

Project Votesmart
www.vote-smart.org/
A political portal loaded with links to information about candidates, parties, election rules, and issues.

Republican National Committee
www.rnc.org/
Official site of the Republican party with information on party positions and candidates, how to work as a volunteer or contribute money, and more.

Suggestions for Further Reading

Hacker, Jacob S., and Paul Pierson, *Off Center: The Republican Revolution and the Erosion of American Democracy.* New Haven: Yale University Press, 2005.
A lively and controversial book about the recent domination of American politics by Republicans and how they have been able to refashion a broad range of government policies despite holding a very slim governing majority.

Polsby, Nelson W., and Aaron Wildavsky. *Presidential Elections,* 12th ed. Lanham, MD: Rowman and Littlefield, 2005.
A comprehensive textbook on the presidential nominating process, campaigning, and voting.

Verba, Sidney, Kay Lehman Schlozman, and Henry E. Brady. *Voice and Equality: Civic Volunteerism in American Politics.* Cambridge, MA: Harvard University Press, 1995.
A comprehensive analysis of inequalities in political participation and their meaning for the quality of democracy in the United States.

Wattenberg, Martin P., *Where Have All the Voters Gone?* (Cambridge, MA: Harvard University Press, 2002).
A clear-headed and accessible a look at this perennial and complex question.

PART 4 Government and Governing

The chapters in Part Four examine how federal government institutions operate and how and why public officials, both elected and appointed, behave as they do in office. Part Four includes chapters on Congress, the presidency, the executive branch, and the Supreme Court.

The chapters in this part assume that government institutions and public officials can be understood only in their structural and political contexts. What government does is influenced strongly by structural factors such as the constitutional rules, the economy, the political culture, society, and the nation's place in the world. What government does is also shaped by political linkage institutions such as elections, parties, interest groups, public opinion, and social movements that transmit the preferences of individuals and groups to public officials.

Democracy is the evaluative thread that runs through each chapter. We ask about the degree to which federal government institutions and public officials advance or retard the practice of democracy in the United States.

CHAPTER 11

Congress

The Democrats Retake Congress

Democrats regained control of Congress from Republicans in the 2006 mid-term elections, winning majority control of both houses for the first time since 1994. In the House, Democrats had hoped to squeeze out 15 seats to ensure a majority but ended up with almost twice that number. Overall, 331 House districts voted more Democratic than they had in 2004, while only 75 districts became significantly more Republican. The Democrats took 29 districts from the Republicans, including 19 that had gone for President Bush in 2004, mostly in white, suburban areas. For the first time since 1970, Republicans failed to pick up a single Democratic seat. In the Senate, Democrats took control by winning 6 of the 33 contested Republican Senate seats and holding on to all their own. GOP casualties included George Allen in Virginia, an aspirant for the 2008 Republican presidential nomination, and Rick Santorum in Pennsylvania, chairman of the Republican Senate Conference.

Although it is often said that "all politics is local," there are congressional elections that become nationalized—that is, elections where voters respond primarily to national rather than local issues. This was true in the Republican mid-term election victories in 1994, when Newt Gingrich's "Contract with America" captured public attention, and in 2002, when issues of homeland security preoccupied voters in the aftermath of 9/11. One indicator of the national character of elections in 2006 was the scope of the Democratic victory; the Democrats not only captured control of both houses of Congress but won an additional 275 seats in state legislatures across the country, gaining control of both houses in 23 states, up from 19 (as against 15 controlled by Republicans), and won an additional 8 governorships, for a 28–22 advantage.

Another indicator was the degree to which voters reported being primarily concerned about national issues. According to preelection and exit polls, a substantial majority were deeply dissatisfied with the war in Iraq, believed that the country was moving in the wrong direction, and were distressed about corruption and impropriety in Washington (the Jack Abramoff affair and the House Republican leadership's slow response to reports of inappropriate sexual communications from Congressman Mark Foley to several House pages). Polls also showed that a substantial number of voters cast their vote to express dissatisfaction with President George W. Bush, whose job performance rating, battered in the year before the election by poor federal government performance in the Katrina recovery effort, high gasoline prices, and bad news from Iraq, was the lowest of any president's at the time of a mid-term election since 1950. In the end, those expressing dissatisfaction with the president favored Democrats by a 2-to-1 margin.

The 2006 mid-term congressional elections were notable on a number of other counts. Not surprisingly, given recent trends, campaign spending reached record levels. The Center for Responsive Politics, a nonpartisan research group, estimates that overall spending for the 2005–2006 congressional election cycle by House and Senate candidates, national and state party committees, and outside advocacy groups, was $2.8 billion, almost 20 percent more than the last mid-term election cycle in 2001–2002. Winning House candidates spent almost $1 million in their races; winning Senate candidates spent almost $8 million. While Republicans spent more overall, Democrats managed to narrow the spending gap in the last three months of the campaign.[1]

Also notable was the success of women, who increased their numbers in the House from 67 to 73; in the Senate, from 14 to 16. Although women remain substantially underrepresented in Congress (only 17 percent of the House and 16 percent of the Senate), they have assumed unprecedented positions of power in the 110th Congress. Hillary Rodham Clinton (D–NY) is one of the Senate's most visible members, for example, and a leading candidate for the Democratic Party's presidential nomination in 2008. Most importantly, the Democratic victory in the House allowed Nancy Pelosi (D–CA) to become Speaker of the House, arguably the most visible and influential position in Congress. As Speaker, Pelosi serves as the principal congressional voice in negotiations with President Bush over the national agenda and the public face of the Democratic Party. She is the first woman in American history to attain the Speakership.

309

Total turnout and the partisan division among voters were also quite revealing. Perhaps not surprisingly, given the intensity of the campaigns, turnout was relatively high compared with recent mid-term elections, 40.4 percent according to Herbert Gans of the Center for the Study of the American Electorate, up from 39.7 percent in 2002 and 36 percent in 1998. While each party managed to win the votes of party identifiers—91 percent of self-identified Republicans voted for Republican congressional candidates in 2006, while 93 percent of Democratic identifiers voted for Democratic candidates—Democrats won the House and Senate by winning over self-identified independents, often by running moderate candidates in areas where they had not enjoyed much success in the past. Independents, who had split their vote evenly between Democrats and Republicans in the 2004 presidential election, favored Democrats over Republicans by 14 percent in 2006 and voted in substantially higher numbers than before.

What about the larger meaning of the 2006 mid-term elections? Although it is still too early to tell what the elections will mean in terms of complex, lingering problems such as the Iraq war, the threat of terrorism, the persistence of poverty, global warming, and issues of health care coverage and cost, it is not too early to suggest that Republican hopes of a long-term partisan realignment in favor of the GOP have been at least temporarily sidetracked. Influential Republican strategist Karl Rove has long believed that the main building blocks for such a realignment include a tax-hostile middle and upper-middle class, men, religious conservatives, and a rapidly growing, family-oriented Hispanic population. In 2006, however, Democrats made significant gains in predominantly white suburbs, among men, among people who attend church (including mainstream Protestants, Catholics, Jews, and Muslims, but not Protestant evangelicals, who continued to vote Republican), and especially among Hispanics. Seventy percent of Hispanics cast their ballots for Democrats in 2006, compared with 44 percent who voted for President Bush in 2004. Republican hopes for adding Hispanics to their base surely were dashed by anti-immigration rhetoric among many Republican officeholders and candidates and by House Republicans' rejection of the president's proposal to allow a path to citizenship for undocumented immigrants. And Rove's base-building-first strategy was dealt an additional blow by the swing of a majority of independents to the Democrats. As Republican National Chairman Tom Reynolds put it after the election, addressing the possibility of a party realignment, "we're going to take a two-year hiatus."[2]   ∎

Thinking Critically About This Chapter

In this chapter, we turn our attention to the Congress of the United States, examining how Congress works as both a representative and governing institution.

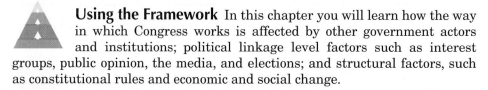

Using the Framework In this chapter you will learn how the way in which Congress works is affected by other government actors and institutions; political linkage level factors such as interest groups, public opinion, the media, and elections; and structural factors, such as constitutional rules and economic and social change.

Using the Democracy Standard Using the concept of democracy developed in Chapter 1, you will be able to evaluate how well Congress acts as a democratic institution. You will see that the story of Congress and democracy is a mixed one: Congress is, at times and under certain circumstances, highly responsive to the American public; at other times and under other circumstances, it is most responsive to special interest groups and large contributors.

Constitutional Foundations of the Modern Congress

As we saw in Chapter 2, the framers of the Constitution were concerned about the possibility of government tyranny. Yet they also wanted an energetic government capable of accomplishing its assigned tasks. These multiple objectives and concerns are reflected in the constitutional design of Congress.

Empowering Congress

The framers began by empowering Congress, making the legislative branch the center of lawmaking in the federal government. In Article I, Section 1, of the Constitution, they gave Congress the power to make the laws: "All legislative power herein granted shall be vested in a Congress of the United States." For the framers, Congress was the main bearer of federal governmental powers. In listing its powers and responsibilities in Article I, Section 8—the **enumerated powers**—they were largely defining the powers and responsibilities of the national government itself.[3] The framers enhanced the enumerated powers by adding the **elastic clause,** granting broad power to Congress to pass whatever legislation was necessary to carry out its enumerated powers.

Constraining Congress

Worried that too strong a legislative branch would lead to tyranny, the framers also limited congressional power. As we learned in Chapter 2, they made Congress a **bicameral** body—divided into two chambers—so that legislation could occur only after patient deliberation. Single-house legislative bodies, they believed, would be prone to rash action. They then added provisions—Article I, Section 9—specifically to prohibit certain kinds of actions: **bills of attainder, ex post facto laws,** the granting of titles of nobility, and the suspension of the right of **habeas corpus.** In the 1st Congress, additional constraints on congressional action were added in the form of the Bill of Rights. Note that the First Amendment, perhaps the most important constitutional provision protecting political liberty, begins with the words "Congress shall make no law . . . "

We also learned in Chapter 2 that the national government was organized on the basis of a "separation of powers" and "checks and balances" so that "ambition might check ambition" and protect the country from tyranny. This means that although the framers envisioned the legislative branch as the vital center of a vigorous national government, they wanted to make sure that Congress would be surrounded by competing centers of government power. We will see that this fragmentation of governmental power in the United States affects how Congress works and often makes it difficult for it to fashion coherent and effective public policies.

Bicameralism and Representation

Congress is organized into two legislative chambers, each with its own principles of representation and constitutional responsibilities. While we often use the word "Congress" and think of it as a single institution, it is worth remembering that the House and Senate are very different from one another and are "virtually autonomous chambers."[4] In what came to be known as the Great Compromise, the framers decided to apportion the House of Representatives on the basis of population and the Senate on the basis of equal representation of the states (see Chapter 2 for details). The terms of office of the members of the House of Representatives were set at two years. The terms of the members of the Senate were set at six years, with only one-third of the seats up for election in each two-year election cycle. We learn in this chapter how these differences affect the legislative process.

The Constitution called for the election of senators by state legislatures, not by the people. The objective was to insulate one house of Congress from popular pressures and to make it a seat of deliberation and reflection. As James

enumerated powers
Powers of the federal government specifically mentioned in the Constitution.

elastic clause
Article I, Section 8, of the Constitution, also called *the necessary and proper clause;* gives Congress the authority to make whatever laws are necessary and proper to carry out its enumerated responsibilities.

bicameral
As applied to a legislative body, consisting of two houses or chambers.

bill of attainder
A governmental decree that a person is guilty of a crime that carries the death penalty, rendered without benefit of a trial.

ex post facto law
A law that retroactively declares some action illegal.

habeas corpus
The legal doctrine that a person who is arrested must have a timely hearing before a judge.

TABLE 11.1 • **Constitutional Differences Between the House and the Senate**

	Senate	House of Representatives
Term	6 years	2 years
Elections	One-third elected in November of even-numbered years	Entire membership elected in November of even-numbered years
Number per state	2	Varies by size of state's population (minimum of 1 per state)
Total membership	100	435 (determined by Congress; at present size since 1910)
Minimum age for membership	30 years	25 years
Unique powers	Advice and consent for judicial and upper-level executive branch appointments	Origination of revenue bills
	Trial of impeachment cases	Bringing of impeachment charges
	Advice and consent for treaties	

Madison put it, "The use of the Senate is to consist in its proceeding with more coolness . . . and with more wisdom than the popular branch."[5] The election of senators by the state legislatures could not survive the democratizing tendencies in the country, however. The Seventeenth Amendment, passed in 1913 after years of agitation for reform pressed by labor and farm groups and progressive reformers, gave the people the power to elect senators directly.

In addition to its general grants of power to Congress, the Constitution assigns particular responsibilities to each of the legislative chambers (see Table 11.1). For example, the House of Representatives has the power to impeach the president for "high crimes and misdemeanors," which it did in the case of Bill Clinton; the Senate has the power to conduct the trial of the president and remove him from office, if the impeachment charges are proved to its satisfaction (which they were not for Clinton).

Federalism

Congress is also greatly affected by the federal design of the Constitution. As we learned in Chapter 3, in our federal system, some powers and responsibilities are granted to the national government, some are shared between the national government and the states, and some are reserved for the states. It is inevitable in such a system that conflicts will occur between state governments and the national government and its legislative branch. Such conflicts sometimes reach the Supreme Court for resolution. In *United States* v. *Lopez* (1995), for instance, the Court ruled that Congress had gone too far in the use of its commerce clause powers when it passed a law banning firearms in and around public schools. Although the goal of the law might be worthy, such a matter, in the opinion of the Court, was the business of the states, not Congress.

Federalism also infuses "localism" into congressional affairs.[6] Although Congress is charged with making national policies, we should remember that the members of the Senate and the House come to Washington as the representatives of states and districts. They are elected by and are beholden to the voters at home and have voters' interests and opinions in mind even as they struggle with weighty issues of national importance.

Representation and Democracy

Members of Congress serve as our legislative representatives. But do they carry out this representative responsibility in a way that can be considered democratic?[7] To answer this question, we need to look at several aspects of representation: styles of representation, how closely the demographics of members of Congress match the demographics of the population in general, and the electoral process.

Styles of Representation

In a letter to his constituents written in 1774, English politician and philosopher Edmund Burke described two principal styles of representation. As a **delegate,** the representative tries to mirror perfectly the views of his or her constituents. As a **trustee,** the representative acts independently, trusting to his or her own judgment of how to best serve the public interest. Burke preferred the trustee approach: "Your representative owes you, not his industry only, but his judgment; and he betrays you, instead of serving you, if he sacrifices it to your opinion."[8]

Campaigning for Congress in Illinois several decades later, Abraham Lincoln argued otherwise: "While acting as [your] representative, I shall be governed by [your] will, on all subjects upon which I have the means of knowing what [your] will is."[9] (If only he had access to public opinion polls!)

Every member of the House and Senate chooses between these two styles of representation. Their choice usually has less to do with their personal tastes than it has to do with the relative safety of their seats and how often they must face the electorate. Senators with six-year terms face the electorate less often than members of the House, so they are generally freer than representatives to assume the trustee style. As they get closer to the end of their term and the prospect of facing the voters, however, senators edge toward the delegate style. Because members of the House must run for reelection every two years, and tend to be in campaign mode at all times, they are pushed almost inexorably toward the delegate style.[10]

delegate

According to the doctrine articulated by Edmund Burke, an elected representative who acts in perfect accord with the wishes of his or her constituents.

trustee

According to the doctrine articulated by Edmund Burke, an elected representative who believes that his or her own best judgment, rather than instructions from constituents, should be used in making legislative decisions.

Race, Gender, and Occupation in Congress

Representation also implies that elected officials are like us in important ways—that they represent us because they are similar to us. Which raises the question: Is the makeup of Congress in a demographic sense similar to that of the nation as a whole? This is often called **descriptive representation.** From the point of view of descriptive representation, the views of significant groups—let us say, women and African Americans—will only be taken into account in policymaking if members of these groups hold seats in a legislative body in rough proportion to their size in the population. From this perspective,

descriptive representation

Sometimes called *statistical representation;* means that the composition of a representative body reflects the demographic composition of the population as a whole.

a perfectly representative legislative body would be similar to the general population in terms of race, sex, ethnicity, occupation, religion, age, and the like. In this sense, the U.S. Congress is highly *unrepresentative.*

Gender and Race   Both women and racial minorities are significantly underrepresented in Congress, particularly in the Senate, despite important recent gains. We can see this in Figure 11.1, which compares the distribution of women and minorities in the 109th Congress (2005–2006) with their distribution in the country as a whole.

Black representation reached its peak during the post–Civil War Reconstruction period, when blacks played an important political role in several southern states. African Americans disappeared from Congress for many years after the reimposition of white supremacy in the South at the end of the nineteenth century. Although a handful of black representatives from northern cities served during the first half of the twentieth century—Oscar De Priest from Chicago's predominantly black South Side and Adam Clayton Powell from New York City's Harlem, for example—very few African Americans were elected to Congress until the late 1960s. While there has been some improvement in representation of African Americans in the House of Representatives—from 26 to 42 between the 102nd (1991–1992) and 109th

FIGURE 11.1 • Women and Minorities in the 109th Congress, 2005–2006

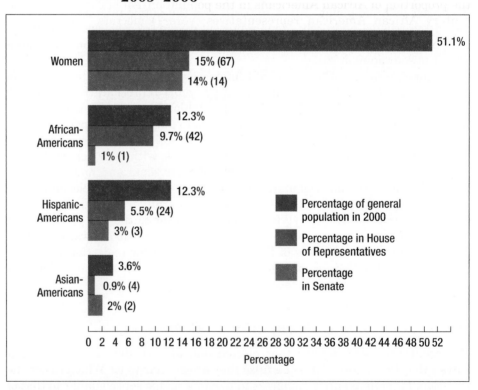

Although their numbers in Congress have increased in recent years, women and racial minorities are still substantially underrepresented compared with their proportion in the American population. This graph compares the percentage of women and racial minorities in each house of the 109th Congress with their percentages in the population in 2000.

Source: U.S. Bureau of the Census; the website of the U.S. Senate at **www.senate.gov;** the website of the House of Representatives at **www.house.gov.**

Congresses—their numbers are still well below what might be expected, given the proportion of African Americans in the population. All but four twentieth-century African American representatives were Democrats. There is one African American in the Senate today, Barak Obama (D–IL).

Hispanics are even more poorly represented than African Americans relative to their proportion of the population, but the increase in their number in recent years has given the Hispanic caucus a greater voice in legislative affairs than in the past. Interestingly, while Hispanics have now replaced African Americans as the largest minority group in the population, they are less well represented than African Americans in Congress. Twenty-four served in the House and two in the Senate in the 109th Congress following the election in 2004 of Ken Salazar (D–CO) and Mel Martinez (R–FL). Other minority groups are represented in small numbers among members of the House. There were five Arab Americans in the 109th Congress, for example. The last Native American senator, Ben Nighthorse Campbell (R–CO), retired in 2004.

The first woman to sit in Congress was Jeannette Rankin of Montana, a suffragist and pacifist, elected in 1916. The number of women in Congress increased during the 1990s, with a big gain coming in the 1992 elections (often called the "year of the woman"), which sent 48 women to the House and 7 to the Senate in the 103rd Congress (compared with only 29 and 2, respectively, in the 102nd Congress). Proportionally, however, female representation in Congress is quite low, given that slightly more than half of all Americans are female; however, the proportion of women in the House of Representatives is about average for national legislative bodies around the world, although it lags seriously behind countries such as Sweden, Norway, the Netherlands, New Zealand, and Germany, where women hold 45, 38, 37, 32, and 32 percent of legislative seats, respectively.[11] Fourteen women served in the Senate in the 109th Congress and 16 in the 110th. Although leadership posts in Congress are overwhelmingly held by men, a few women have gained party leadership posts. Most notable is Nancy Pelosi (D–CA), who became the first female Speaker of the House in American history after the Democrats won the House in 2006.

Occupation   Members of Congress are far better educated than the rest of the population. They also tend to come from high-income families, have personal incomes that are substantially above average, and lean heavily toward legal or business occupations. In 2005, for example, 360 members of the House had legal or business backgrounds, while only 15 came from the ranks of the working class, whether of the blue-collar or white-collar service variety, and there was no one who had been a farm laborer.[12]

Does it matter that descriptive representation is so low in Congress, that its members are so demographically unrepresentative of the American people? Some political scientists and close observers of Congress think not. They suggest that the need to face the electorate forces lawmakers to be attentive to all significant groups in their **constituencies.** A representative from a farm district tends to listen to farm **constituents,** for example, even if that representative is not a farmer.

Nevertheless, many who feel they are not well represented—women, African Americans, Asian Americans, Hispanics, blue-collar workers, gays and lesbians, those with disabilities, and the poor—often believe that their interests would get a much better hearing if their numbers were substantially increased in Congress. There is some tentative evidence to support this view: Women members of the House introduce more bills related to women's and children's issues than do their male colleagues.[13] The demographic disparity between the American population and the makeup of Congress, then, suggests a violation of the norm of political equality, an important element of democracy.

The Electoral Connection

The election is the principal instrument in a democracy for keeping representatives responsive and responsible to citizens. Let's see how congressional elections affect the quality of representation in the United States.

Electoral Districts   Each state is entitled to two senators. This has important implications for politics in the United States, as well as the quality of democratic representation here. Equal representation gives extraordinary power in the Senate to states with small populations. Wyoming, our least populous state, for example, has exactly the same number of senators as California, but it has less than one-seventieth of California's population; two senators in Wyoming in 2004, for example, represented only 506,000 people, while the two senators from California represented almost 36 million. This means that a coalition of 51 senators from the 26 smallest population states, representing a mere 18 percent of the American population, can pass a bill in the Senate. (Recall the "Mapping American Politics" feature in Chapter 2, which graphically shows the disproportionate share of power in the Senate held by the nation's smallest states.)

Representation in the House of Representatives is determined by a state's population, with the proviso that each state must have at least one congressional district. The House of Representatives decided that, beginning in 1910, its upper limit would be 435 members (the House can change this number at any time, although it is highly unlikely). Because the American population is constantly growing in size and changing where it lives, the 435 House representatives must be periodically redistributed among the states. **Reapportionment,** the technical name for this redistribution, occurs every 10 years, after the national census (see Figure 11.2 for the most recent changes). Based

constituency
The district of a legislator.

constituent
A citizen who lives in the district of an elected official.

You Are an Informed Voter

reapportionment
The reallocation of House seats among the states, done after each national census, to ensure that seats are held by the states in proportion to the size of their populations.

FIGURE 11.2 • States Gaining and Losing Congressional Seats Following the 2000 Census

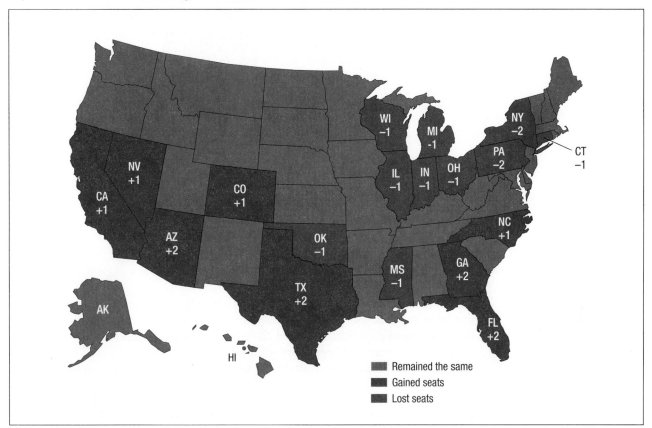

The number of representatives for each state in the House of Representatives is based on the size of its population. Because the relative sizes of the states' populations change over time while the number of representatives is fixed, the number of representatives from each state is recalculated after each census. This process is called reapportionment. This map shows which states gained and lost representatives after the 2000 census.

Source: U.S. Bureau of the Census.

on the official census, some states keep the same number of seats; others gain or lose them depending on their relative population gains or losses.

States gaining or losing seats must redraw the boundary lines of their congressional districts so that they are of roughly equal population size. Redrawing district lines within a state is known as **redistricting** and is done primarily by state legislatures, although the courts have been playing a more active role lately in cases where legislatures are unable to decide (redistricting is the job of a nonpartisan commission in five states). Very often in the past, because it was then legal to do so, legislatures created congressional districts of vastly different population sizes—in New York in the 1930s, some congressional districts had 10 times the population of others—and a significantly overrepresented rural population. The Supreme Court ruled in *Wesberry* v. *Sanders* (1964), however, that the principle of one person, one vote applies to congressional districts, meaning that congressional districts within a state must be of roughly equal population size. Because the distribution of the population changes in many states over the course of 10

redistricting

The redrawing of congressional district lines within a state to ensure roughly equal populations within each district.

The Dreaded Gerrymander

The term *gerrymander* is derived from this 1812 Elkanah Tinsdale cartoon, which lampoons a Massachusetts district drawn to ensure the election of a Republican candidate. The "Gerrymander" was named after Massachusetts Governor Elbridge Gerry, who signed the bill that created the salamander-shaped district.

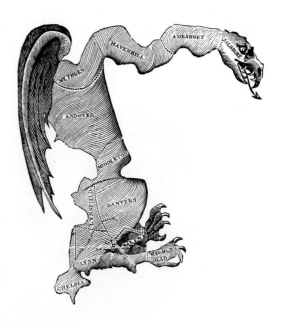

VIDEO ROUNDTABLE

Redistricting

gerrymandering

Redrawing electoral district lines to give an advantage to a particular party or candidate.

years—some people moving from the cities to the suburbs; some people moving from rural areas to cities—many congressional district boundaries must be redrawn even in those states that have neither gained nor lost congressional seats because of reapportionment.

Although congressional districts must hold approximately equal numbers of citizens, state legislatures are relatively free to draw district lines where they choose. The party that controls the state legislature and governorship usually tries to draw the lines in a way that will help its candidates win elections.[14] The results are often strange indeed. Rather than creating compact and coherent districts, neighborhoods, towns, and counties can be strung together in odd-looking ways in order to take full partisan advantage of the redistricting process. Taken to an extreme, the process is known as **gerrymandering,** after Governor Elbridge Gerry of Massachusetts, who signed a bill in 1811 that created a district that looked like a salamander. It made wonderful raw material for editorial cartoonists.

The Supreme Court has tried to prevent the most flagrant abuses, especially when some identifiable group of voters—for example, a racial or ethnic group—is disadvantaged, but it has turned a blind eye to partisan redistricting in which parties in power try to draw district lines to their own advantage, although it came close to overturning Pennsylvania's extremely partisan district map in 2004.[15] The Court, along with most politicians, seems to accept the notion that "to the victor belongs the spoils." Partisan redistricting happens when the same party controls both houses of the state legislature and the governor's office, although even here there are sometimes conflicts if one or another of the party's incumbent House members feels that he or she has been hurt by the redrawn district lines. But this situation of unified party control existed in only 15 states when the states began to redistrict after the 2000 census. One of these unified states was Texas, where Republicans gained control of the governorship and the state legislature in the 2002 elections. In an unprecedented action in 2003—unprecedented in the sense that states always redistrict once every ten years—the Texas legislature overturned a redistricting plan put in place after the 2000 census by a federal judicial panel and imposed a new redistricting plan favorable to the GOP. Tom DeLay, at the time the powerful majority leader of the U.S. House of Representatives and a member of Congress from Texas, was widely considered to have been the key player in this process. The redistricting carved out an additional five safe congressional seats for his party. The Supreme Court later ruled in *United Latin American Citizens* v. *Perry* (2006) that, with the exception of one redrawn district with a large Hispanic population, the Texas partisan-based, second-time-in-a-decade, redistricting was constitutionally acceptable. Ironically, perhaps, Republicans lost Tom DeLay's own redrawn House district to a Democrat in 2006.

Divided party control of the redistricting process, however, was the rule in 30 states—recall that five states use nonpartisan commissions—during the normal redistricting period following the census. Needless to say, intense partisan conflict and deadlock were often the result, with resolution coming in many states only after the matter was turned over to the courts. In states with divided party control, where neither party has sufficient strength to get its way, the two parties have increasingly made bipartisan redistricting arrangements that protect their own incumbents, presumably on the grounds that the best each party can do is to protect hard-won gains. In large states such as California, Illinois, Michigan, New York, and Ohio, there is hardly a district anymore where the incumbent faces serious competition in the general election. Across the nation, incumbent-protection redistricting has become so extensive that only about 35 seats in elections to the House of Representatives are actually competitive. In 2004, when 98 percent of incumbents running for election won their races, only 10 races for congressional seats were decided by less than 5 percentage points.[16]

Amendments to the 1965 Voting Rights Act passed in 1982 encouraged the states to create House districts in which racial minorities would be in the majority. Sponsors of the legislation hoped that this would lead to an increase in the number of members of racial minority groups elected to the House. The result was the formation of 24 new **majority-minority districts,** 15 with African American majorities and 9 with Hispanic American majorities.[17] The creation of some of these districts has taken great imagination. North Carolina's Twelfth District, for instance, created after the 1990 census, linked a narrow strip of predominantly African American communities along 160 miles of Interstate 85 connecting Durham and Charlotte. After first encouraging the creation of majority-minority districts, the Supreme Court had second thoughts about districts that are highly irregular in form, noncontiguous (not compact), unconnected to traditional political jurisdictions (*Shaw* v. *Reno,* 1993), or drawn with race as the sole criterion (*Miller* v. *Johnson,* 1995). In *Hunt* v. *Cromartie* (2001), and much to the surprise of legal and political observers, the Court approved a slightly redrawn North Carolina Twelfth District map, ruling that race can be a significant factor in drawing district lines "so long as it is not the dominant and controlling one." This ruling suggests that most of the other majority-minority districts will probably survive legal challenges, even if their lines are slightly redrawn in the end. (For more insight into how district lines are drawn, see the "By the Numbers" feature).

The creation of these special majority-minority districts has contributed to the increase in the number of racial minority representatives in Congress; each of the districts has consistently elected a member of a racial minority group to the House. Ironically, however, the creation of such districts has undermined Democratic Party strength in other districts by taking traditionally Democratic-oriented minority group voters away from previously Democratic-dominated districts in order to form majority-minority ones. (One political scientist reports that after 1991 Republicans won and held every congressional

VIDEO DEBATE

Congressional Partisanship

majority-minority districts

Districts drawn to ensure that a racial minority makes up the majority of voters.

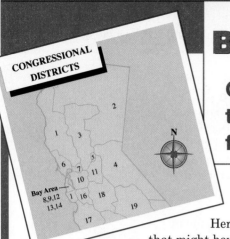

CONGRESSIONAL DISTRICTS

By the Numbers

Can congressional districts be drawn to include equal numbers of voters yet favor one party over the other?

Here is a headline that might have appeared in any city newspaper in late 2001 or early 2002: "Legislature fails to reach agreement on congressional district lines; Issue to be decided by the state courts." What's going on? How difficult can it be to count people and draw congressional district lines? Actually, it is difficult and the issues are important.

Here is what is going on. Every 10 years, immediately after the census is conducted, a complicated process of redrawing congressional district lines goes on in the states. In six of them (Arizona, Hawaii, Idaho, Montana, New Jersey, and Washington), redistricting is done entirely by a special commission; in the remainder, legislatures and governors must do the job. Agreement becomes especially difficult in states with divided government—those with a legislature controlled by one party and the governorship held by the other party, or those where the two houses of the legislature are controlled by different parties. Often, the courts are called upon to break the deadlock.

Why It Matters: How congressional district lines are drawn has a lot to do with which political party will control the House of Representatives, at least until the next census.

Behind Redistricting: In the House of Representatives, seats are apportioned to each state based on the state's population. Thus, after a new census is taken, a state may gain or lose seats based on the current count of people residing there. To gain a seat means that a new congressional district must be carved out of the state; to lose a seat means that lines must be redrawn to fill in the gap. Even in states where the size of its congressional delegation has not changed, lines must always be redrawn because of population shifts within state boundaries (e.g., more people moving to the suburbs). They must make such adjustments because the Supreme Court ruled in *Wesberry* v. *Sanders* (1964) that each congressional district within a state must be of roughly the same population size.

How District Lines Are Drawn: In theory, as long as district lines create congressional districts of roughly equal size, and as long as district lines do not unduly disadvantage racial and ethnic groups, congressional district lines can be drawn in any way that politicians choose. The politicians can be very imaginative in doing so, as they try to ensure that their own party and favored members of Congress are advantaged by the outcome.

Where the district lines are drawn is extremely important in determining the composition of the con-

seat where redistricting had reduced the African American population by 10 percentage points or more.[18]) Naturally, Republicans have been eager to support minority group efforts to form their own districts. Concentrating black voters in homogeneous districts has tipped the balance to Republicans in many congressional districts in the South. One result is that policies favored by a majority of African American citizens are less likely to be enacted because of the decreased strength of Democrats in the House, this despite an increase in the number of African American representatives.[19]

Money and Congressional Elections Running for the House or the Senate is a very expensive proposition, and it keeps getting more expensive. During the 2003–2004 election cycle, the average Senate race cost $5.2 million—about $2.6 million per candidate—while the price tag for a House race—where most

gressional delegation from each state. Note the following hypothetical example, which shows how easily district lines can be used to effect different outcomes. Let "D" stand for 100,000 Democratic voters; let "R" stand for 100,000 Republican voters; and let "A" stand for 100,000 African Americans, most of whom vote for Democrats. Taking the same number and locations of voters, district lines can be drawn to yield three Democratic seats and no Republican seats (map on left) or to yield two Republican seats and one Democratic seat (map on right).

Comment on the Process for Drawing District Lines:
These alternative outcomes are somewhat exaggerated in order to make a point about how politicians strive for maximum flexibility in the redistricting process. In real life, the Court has also demanded that district lines not deviate too much from their historical patterns and that they be relatively compact, putting people who live near each other in the same district. The map on the right shows a majority-minority district sought at first by African American organizations and leaders as a way to increase their representation in Congress. The formation of such districts, especially in the South, was supported by Republicans because GOP leaders believed that draining traditional Democratic districts of supporters into new majority-minority districts would enhance their party's fortunes. This is how things actually worked out in the end; majority-minority districts increased the number of African Americans in Congress, but the process of concentrating black voters in these districts made the other districts in these states more homogeneously white and Republican, increasing the GOP advantage.

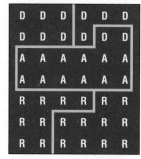

Result: districts equal in size (1.4 million each); three Democratic seats, zero Republican seats.

Result: districts equal in size (1.4 million each); one Democratic seat carved out to create a position for an African-American and two Republican seats.

D = 100,000 white Democrats   R = 100,000 white Republicans
A = 100,000 African Americans, mostly Democrats

Different Congressional District Lines, Different Party Outcomes

What to Watch For:
Redistricting is one of the most important things that goes on in our political system, yet it is virtually invisible to the general public. Pay attention to the debates over redistricting in your state and determine what political alliances appear and what political bargains are being struck.

What Do You Think?
Do you think there might be some nonpartisan, scientific method to draw district lines that would avoid the sometimes unseemly process of reshaping congressional districts to suit political parties and interested groups? If there was such a method, do you think it would be better than our current system? Why or why not?

races are not very competitive, as you've seen—was about $530,000 per candidate (or a bit more than $1 million for the race). Total spending by candidate committees in 2003–2004 was $1.2 billion, double the cost of congressional races just 25 years ago, even taking inflation into account.[20] This spending by the candidate's campaign—or hard money—is but the tip of the iceberg, however. To the grand totals above we must add the dollars raised and spent by national, state, and local political party organizations on congressional campaigns and money spent by private groups on various forms of advertising and get-out-the-vote efforts designed to assist candidates for congressional office. Although new campaign finance rules came into effect after 2002 under terms of the McCain-Feingold legislation (see Chapters 7 and 10 on the rule changes and their effects), individuals and groups have found innovative ways to pump money into congressional campaigns. The doubling of the maximum limit on

open-seat election

An election in which there is no incumbent officeholder.

The Debate over Campaign Finance Reform

the amount of money that candidates can accept from individuals under the new law—from $1,000 per election campaign to $2,000—is important. So too is the tendency of 527 advocacy groups to find ways around the restrictions on campaign communications discussed earlier.

Incumbents in the House, have an easier time raising money than their challengers and spend more. **Open-seat election** races, in which no incumbent is involved, also attract and use lots of money, especially in the Senate (see Figure 11.3). Moreover, being a member of the majority party in Congress serves as a magnet for money because contributors generally want to be able to have access to those in power.[21]

Congressional campaign hard money comes from four main sources: individuals, political action committees (PACs), political parties, and the candidates themselves. Individuals contribute the largest amount, accounting for 56 percent of contributions to House candidates and 65 percent to Senate candidates in the 2004 election cycle. PACs are the next largest, accounting for 32 percent of campaign contributions in the House contributions and 13 percent in the Senate. PACs are allowed to contribute up to $5,000 per candidate per election, and they can give to as many candidates as they wish. Many especially wealthy candidates support their election campaigns out of their own pockets. In the record to date, Jon Corzine (D–NJ)—now governor of New Jersey—spent $62 million in his bid for a Senate seat in 2000. He only barely won.

Congressional candidates also receive campaign money from national, congressional, and state party committees. Party committees are allowed to make a $5,000 contribution per campaign to each House candidate. National

FIGURE 11.3 • Campaign Money Raised by Incumbents, Challengers, and Open-Seat Candidates, 2003–2004 Election Cycle

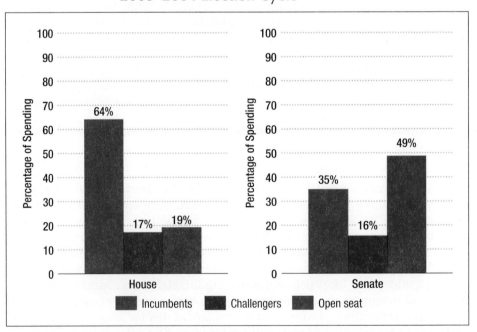

Because campaign contributors want access to important decision makers in Congress, contributors tend to give a disproportionate share of campaign contributions to incumbents and to those open-seat candidates who have a good chance to win their elections.

Source: Federal Election Commission.

and senatorial party committees are allowed to give $17,500 to each candidate for each stage of the electoral process. Many congressional candidates also receive campaign contributions from PACs associated with congressional party leaders such as Dennis Hastert (R–IL), when he was the House Speaker, and Senate Majority Leader Harry Reid of Nevada.

Republicans raise more money than Democrats, although this advantage has been narrowing. They are able to do so for several reasons. First, Republican party identifiers generally have higher incomes than Democratic identifiers. Second, the sympathies of large business firms and their top executives lean toward the Republicans. Third and finally, money tends to flow toward incumbents in congressional races—whether they be Democrats or Republicans—and the GOP was the majority party in Congress in recent years. This Republican advantage may diminish with the Democrats now in power in Congress.

The Incumbency Factor Incumbents—current officeholders—win at much higher rates than in the past, especially in the House (see Figure 11.4). In 2004, 98 percent of House and 96 percent of Senate incumbents won reelection. In 2006, 95 percent of House incumbents running for reelection won their races, while 79 percent of Senate incumbents won (unusually, all incumbent losers in the House and Senate were Republicans). High incumbency reelection rates, especially in the House of Representatives, mean that the overwhelming majority of electoral contests for Congress are not really competitive; almost all seats in the House today are considered "safe," with the incumbent facing little serious challenge from the opposition party candidate.

There are several reasons incumbents almost always win when they seek reelection. The most important, of course, is that the redistricting process in

Why Is It so Hard to Defeat an Incumbent?

FIGURE 11.4 • Rates of Incumbent Reelection in Congress

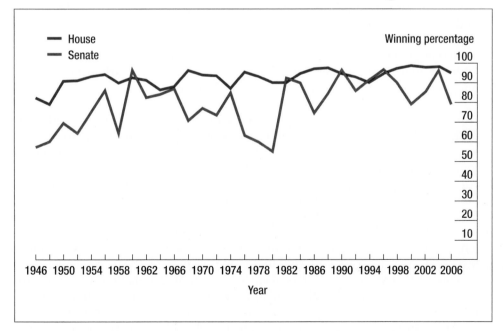

The probability that incumbents will be reelected remains at historic highs. This does not mean, however, that the membership of Congress is stagnant. Turnover in membership is substantial because of retirements and the defeat of incumbents in primary elections.

Source: Calculations by the authors from various issues of the *Congressional Quarterly Weekly Report* and *The New York Times.*

many states in recent years—reviewed earlier in this chapter—has been fashioned to protect incumbents in each of the parties. On the face of it, this process has been very effective.

Incumbents also have the advantage of attracting and spending much more campaign money than their rivals. Many contributors look at campaign contributions as an "investment" in access to key members of Congress.[22] To contribute to a challenger is to jeopardize access if the challenger loses, which is most often the case.

Incumbents also use the congressional machinery to help their reelection chances.[23] Already well known to voters because they garner so much free media coverage, members of Congress have many ways to advertise their accomplishments and keep their names before the public. For example, the **franking privilege** allows them to mail newsletters, legislative updates, surveys, and other self-promoting literature free of charge. The House and the Senate also provide travel budgets for lawmakers to make periodic visits to their states or districts. Because members believe that time spent in their districts helps their electoral chances—a belief supported by a great deal of research[24]—they spend lots of time back home.[25] Some manage to spend three or four days a week in their districts or states, meeting constituents, giving speeches, raising money, and keeping in the public eye. The congressional leadership helps by scheduling important legislative business for the Tuesday-to-Thursday period and cutting down the number of hours Congress is in session.

Incumbents also use their offices to "service the district." One way is through **casework,** helping constituents cut through the red tape of the federal bureaucracy, whether it be by speeding up the arrival of a late Social Security check or expediting the issuance of a permit for grazing on public land.[26] Generous budgets for establishing and staffing offices in the constituency help representatives and senators do casework. Another way to service the district is to provide **pork**—federal dollars for various projects in the district or state. In 2005, for example, Congress passed a massive $300 billion highway and mass transit bill that, in addition to whatever improvements it might bring for the safety and convenience of Americans, poured lots of federal construction money into the constituencies of senators and representatives for highway and bridge projects, rail and bus improvements, urban bike paths, and more. (See the "Using the Framework" feature.)

How Representative?   Representatives and senators pay a great deal of attention to the interests and the preferences of the people in their districts and states. Because they are worried about being reelected—even incumbents tend to run scared, perhaps afraid of being the exception that proves the rule—they try to see as many people as they can during their frequent visits home, and they pay attention to their mail and the public opinion polls. Moreover, they vote on and pass laws in rough approximation to public opinion. Members of Congress vote in a manner that is consistent with public opinion in their districts about two-thirds of the time,[27] and Congress produces laws that are consistent with national public opinion at about the same rate.[28] Having said that, however, it is also the case that members of Congress are very skilled at shaping public opinion in their districts[29] and at shaping legislation in ways that seem to address public concerns without actually doing so.[30] For example, responding to the widespread public concern about the state of private pension plans, Congress set about reforming the system in 2006. In the end, it gave companies more leeway in escaping pension obligations and lowered the amount of money companies had to contribute to the federal pension bailout program.

franking privilege

Public subsidization of mail from the members of Congress to their constituents.

casework

Services performed by members of Congress for constituents.

pork

Also called *pork barrel;* projects designed to bring to the constituency jobs and public money for which the members of Congress can claim credit.

Using the Framework

Big Government Republicans

If Republicans favor small government, why did they push through an enormous highway spending bill?

Background: The Republican-controlled Congress passed a massive highway and transportation bill amounting to almost $300 billion in the late summer of 2005, despite warnings of a veto from President George W. Bush, who said he was worried about adding to the growing federal government deficit. A little over a week after Congress sent the bill to him, however, he signed it at a ceremony at a large Caterpillar manufacturing plant in Illinois, saying that with this new legislation "there's going to be more demand for the machines you make." Scores of editorial writers heaped scorn on Republicans for passing this "pork"-laden legislation—literally thousands of projects requested by individual members of Congress for their states and

districts were included—and small-government proponents such as the conservative Cato Institute expressed keen disappointment. As if this were not enough for critics, the Republican-controlled Congress and a Republican president legislated other expensive, government-expanding legislation, including a Medicare prescription drug benefit and a subsidy-filled energy bill. So how could such a thing have happened? We can see how by taking a broader view of the emergence of the Republicans as the party of government, despite small majorities in the House and Senate, and considering how structural, political linkage, and governmental factors shaped this outcome.

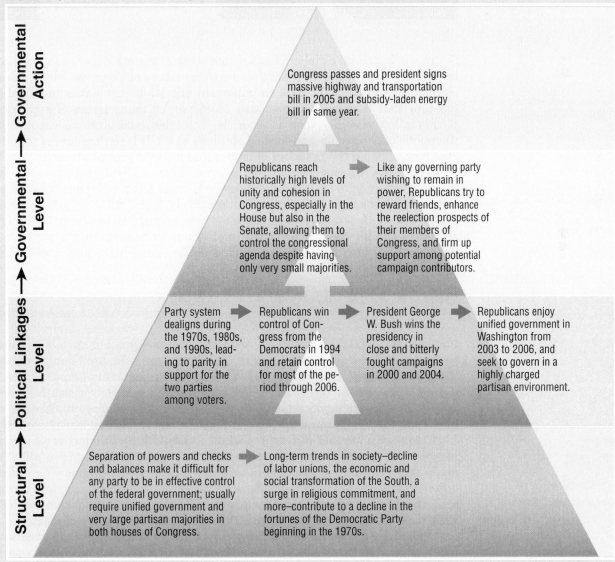

Governmental Action

Congress passes and president signs massive highway and transportation bill in 2005 and subsidy-laden energy bill in same year.

Governmental Level

Republicans reach historically high levels of unity and cohesion in Congress, especially in the House but also in the Senate, allowing them to control the congressional agenda despite having only very small majorities.

Like any governing party wishing to remain in power, Republicans try to reward friends, enhance the reelection prospects of their members of Congress, and firm up support among potential campaign contributors.

Political Linkages Level

Party system dealigns during the 1970s, 1980s, and 1990s, leading to parity in support for the two parties among voters.

Republicans win control of Congress from the Democrats in 1994 and retain control for most of the period through 2006.

President George W. Bush wins the presidency in close and bitterly fought campaigns in 2000 and 2004.

Republicans enjoy unified government in Washington from 2003 to 2006, and seek to govern in a highly charged partisan environment.

Structural Level

Separation of powers and checks and balances make it difficult for any party to be in effective control of the federal government; usually require unified government and very large partisan majorities in both houses of Congress.

Long-term trends in society—decline of labor unions, the economic and social transformation of the South, a surge in religious commitment, and more—contribute to a decline in the fortunes of the Democratic Party beginning in the 1970s.

In the Home District

Members of Congress must spend a considerable amount of their time staying in touch with their constituents. Here, Representative Rosa DeLauro (D–CT) visits a computer class in a public school during one of her many weekend trips back to her home district in Connecticut.

In a substantial number of cases, moreover, Congress does *not* follow public opinion, even on highly visible issues. If members of Congress follow public opinion two-thirds of the time on important bills, that still leaves one-third of the time that they go their own way. Moreover, on many issues of high complexity or low visibility, such as securities and telecommunications regulation, the public may have no well-formed opinions at all. It is in these areas that we can most fully see the influence of money and interest groups at work.

One of the reasons members of Congress have some latitude in representing public opinion in their districts—indeed, in the nation—is that, as we have shown, most come to Congress from relatively "safe" districts where being turned out by the voters is not common. Consequently, House elections do not adequately fulfill the role assigned to elections in democratic theory: as the principle instrument for keeping elected leaders responsive and responsible.

How Congress Works

Congress is a vital center of decision making and policymaking in our national government. It is not a place where the executive's bills are simply rubber-stamped, as it is in legislative bodies in many parliamentary systems. By all accounts, Congress is the most influential and independent legislative body among the Western democratic nations. In this section, we turn our attention to how Congress is organized and how it functions as a working legislative body.

There are a number of very important things to keep in mind as we examine how Congress is organized and operates. First, while they are alike in many ways, the House and Senate are very different institutions. The bodies differ in size, the kinds of constituencies House members and senators represent, the terms of office of their members, and their constitutional responsibilities; together, these differences give each chamber a distinctive character.

Second, both the House and Senate have had a tendency over the years to succumb to centrifugal forces, always seemingly on the verge of flying apart, with each representative and senator tempted to go his or her own way. The

COMPARATIVE

Comparing Legislatures

task of running each body has been likened to "herding cats." The reasons are fairly obvious: Representatives and senators in some sense are like independent contractors. Congressional leaders lack the normal tools of organizational leadership to force compliance with their wishes; they cannot order members about, they cannot hire or fire them (this is the role of voters), nor can they control the size of their paychecks or benefits. Moreover, in our candidate-centered form of politics, congressional leaders traditionally have had little control over the reelection of representatives and senators who run their own campaigns. Between 1995 and 2007, Republicans used party resources and leadership positions to gain a great deal of control over legislative affairs, especially in the House of Representatives. Republicans not only granted more formal powers to the office of the Speaker but learned to channel campaign money from their own PACs, party campaign committees, and conservative groups and individuals to maintain discipline among members who might be tempted to stray too far from where legislative party leaders want them to be on important matters. The process of centralization of leadership in the Senate did not advance as far as in the House but, given leadership influence over the flow of campaign money from diverse sources, some centralization occurred there as well.[31] It remains to be seen if the Democrats, now in control of the House and Senate, are willing to similarly empower their leaders.

Political Parties in Congress: How Exceptional?

Political parties have a very strong presence in Congress. Its members come to Washington, D.C., as elected candidates of a political party. At the start of each session, they organize their legislative business along political party lines. At the start of each new Congress, each **party conference**—all the members of a political party in the House or the Senate (although House Democrats use the term **caucus** rather than conference)—meets to select its leaders, approve committee assignments, including committee and subcommittee chairs, and reach agreement on legislative objectives for the session. The majority party in the House selects the Speaker of the House, while the majority party in the Senate selects the president pro tempore (usually its most senior member) and the majority leader. The minority party in each chamber also selects its leaders. Political parties, as we shall see, also are influential in what policies representatives and senators support and how they cast their votes on important bills. So, political parties are at the very core of legislative business in the United States. Nevertheless, as important as they are, legislative political parties here are less decisive in governance than political parties in parliamentary systems, where they not only determine the organization and operations of the legislative body, but select the executive as well. The majority party or coalition in parliamentary system such as Great Britain, Australia, France, and Sweden, as suggested earlier, selects the prime minister and the cabinet to run the day-to-day affairs of the country.

party conference
An organization of the members of a political party in the House or Senate.

caucus
A regional, ethnic, racial or economic subgroup within the House or Senate.

The Party Composition of Congress
From the 1932 elections in the midst of the Great Depression until the 1994 elections, with brief interludes of Republican control along the way, Congress was dominated by the Democratic party. Democratic domination of House elections during this period is especially notable, even surviving GOP landslide wins in the presidential elections of 1980 (Reagan), 1984 (Reagan), and 1988 (G. H. W. Bush). In the Senate, Republicans were in the majority for only 10 years during this same period. Democratic party domination ended with the 1994 elections, however, when

Republicans won control of both houses of Congress for the first time in 40 years. Because Republicans were unusually unified from 1995 through 2006, especially in the House, they were very successful in controlling the congressional agenda. The Democrats regained control of both houses of Congress after winning the 2006 mid-term elections.

Party Voting in Congress The political parties provide important glue for the decentralized fragments of Congress and the legislative process. Party labels are important cues for members of Congress as they decide how to vote on issues before the committees and on the floor of the House and the Senate. Indeed, it has been shown that party affiliation is the best predictor of the voting behavior of members of the Congress and that it is becoming ever more important.[32] That is to say, both houses of Congress are becoming more **partisan,** although not as partisan as in parliamentary systems, where, in votes on important issues like the budget and confidence motions, the government normally enjoys 100 percent of majority party or majority coalition support. The reason is simple: If the government loses such votes in a parliamentary system, it is dissolved and new elections are called, putting the seats of members of parliament at risk.

One way to track partisanship is a statistic calculated by congressional scholars Davidson and Oleszek showing how often the average Democrat and Republican voted with his or her party in partisan votes in Congress (see Figure 11.5).[33] You can see that partisanship has been rising steadily since the early 1970s and is evident today in 9 out of 10 votes. This partisanship has played out in ever-more-frequent battles between the parties in Congress. Under Newt Gingrich's leadership in 1995, for example, Republicans in the House pushed through every provision of their congressional campaign platform (largely written by Gingrich and his aides)—the Contract with America—with no input from the Democratic side of the aisle. Extraordinary levels of partisanship were also evident in the House on votes to impeach President Clinton in December 1998; in the votes associated with his trial in the Senate in December 1999; in the House vote in 2001 on President George

---

partisan

A committed member of a party; seeing issues from the point of view of the interests of a single party.

Out in the Cold

The majority party organizes the House at the beginning of each session of Congress and generally has its way if its members remain disciplined. Here, the leadership of the minority Democrats in Congress protest their exclusion from House deliberations by holding mock sessions outside on the Capitol lawn in early 1995. Things got even worse after that for the Democrats. In the 109th Congress, 2005–2006, Republicans ran House affairs virtually alone although they had only a small majority at the time, something that was possible because of the GOP's unprecedented unity.

FIGURE 11.5 • Party Voting in Congress

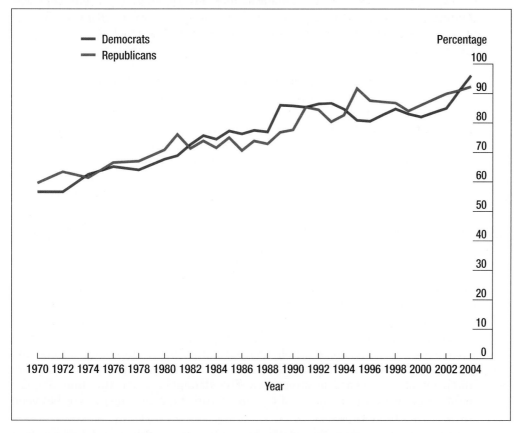

Partisanship has been growing in Congress. One indicator is the increase in the percentage of times the average Democrat and Republican in the House and Senate sided with his/her party on partisan votes—those votes when a majority of Democrats voted against a majority of Republicans.

Source: Roger H. Davidson and Walter J. Oleszek, *Congress and Its Members* (Washington, D.C.: CQ Press, 2006), p. 285.

W. Bush's proposed $1.6 trillion tax cut; in both houses of Congress in 2005 and 2006 on President Bush's proposals for private accounts under Social Security and extension of previous tax cuts; and in the debate over the use of intelligence in the run-up to the Iraq war.

One result is that reaching bipartisan agreements is becoming more difficult. As Maine Republican Senator Olympia Snowe has observed, "The whole Congress has become far more polarized and partisan so it makes it difficult to reach bipartisan agreements. The more significant the issue, the more partisan it becomes."[34]

There are a number of reasons partisanship is increasing. One factor is the changing regional bases of the parties, particularly the historic transformation of the Deep South from a solidly Democratic region at the congressional level to a solidly Republican one.[35] In the 2004 elections, for example, five Republicans were elected to Senate seats previously held by Democrats in the Deep South. Four of these seats had been held by southern Democratic moderates—John Breaux of Louisiana, Bob Graham of Florida, Zell Miller of Georgia, and Fritz Hollings of South Carolina, all of whom retired—and one had been held by 2004 Democratic vice presidential nominee John Edwards (D–NC). The resulting transformation in party regional representation was stunning; in the 109th Congress, only four Democrats were left in the Senate from the 11 states of the former Confederacy. Democrats took back a southern seat in 2006 when Jim Webb defeated George Allen in Virginia.

Another reason that partisanship is on the rise in Congress is that partisan conflict and division is happening across the board in the country—a subject we have looked at several times in this book—especially among party activists and committed party voters. Members of Congress, facing an ever-more partisan-divided electorate and hearing from increasing numbers of party-associated advocacy groups—helped along, for the GOP, by the so-called K Street project that filled lobbying firms with former Republican congressional staffers[36]—are pressured strongly to act as partisans as they go about their legislative tasks.[37] (Refer again to the "Using the Framework" feature on page 325 to learn more about this.)

It is not entirely clear whether party voting differences are caused directly by party affiliation or indirectly by the character of constituencies or by the preexisting ideological commitments of members of Congress. Some scholars have found strong independent party effects regardless of constituency or ideology. Others argue that the tendency of people in the same party to vote together is simply a reflection of the fact that Democratic lawmakers tend to come from districts and states that are similar to one another and that Republican lawmakers come from places that are different from the constituencies of Democrats. Republicans generally come from higher-income districts than Democrats. Democratic districts, in turn, tend to contain more union members and racial minorities. The strongest tie, in this line of argument, is between the member of Congress and the constituency, not between the member and the party.[38]

Increasingly, however, internal party unity and conflict between the parties seem attributable to ideology. Both in the electorate and among the members of Congress and other political elites, Democrats have become somewhat more liberal, while Republicans have become much more consistently conservative.[39] Political scientist and former Democratic representative from Oklahoma Mickey Edwards observes the following about the ideological tendencies of members of Congress: ". . . most people who run for office have . . . [strong] feelings not only about specific issues but about general philosophical concepts, such as the proper role of government, the impact of taxation on investment and savings, and the reasons for crime and poverty."[40]

Differences from Parliamentary Parties Although America's two major parties have become more unified internally and more distinctive from each other on policy and ideological grounds, they remain, nevertheless, different from the main parties in parliamentary systems in a number of ways. First, and most important, because of the candidate-centered nature of our parties (described in Chapter 9), senators and representatives can and do stray from the party reservation, even on important matters—something that is exceedingly rare in parliamentary systems on important matters. Neither President Bush nor Senate and House leaders were able in 2005, for example, to gain strong support from Republicans on the president's plans to change Social Security. Nor were Republican legislators willing in 2006 to support President Bush on his proposal for a road to citizenship for millions of undocumented immigrants. Several prominent Republican senators abandoned the president on Iraq in 2006 and on the rules for questioning terrorism suspects. Second, because candidates for congressional office are largely self-selected and self-starting—their ability to run for office does not depend, as it does in political parties in parliamentary systems, on decisions of party leaders and committees—members of Congress need not spend years working for the party and moving up the ranks within the party organization, where they become groomed for higher office, as British, German, and French parliamentarians must. The American parties, that is to say, do not require a long apprenticeship.[41] Third and finally, one must always return to what it means to have disciplined parties in a system of separation of powers and checks and balances, as in the United States, compared with having disciplined parties in a parliamentary system. In the latter, party discipline tends toward effective action, there being no institutional separation between the executive and the legislative branches, for they are one and the same. In the former, more disciplined parties—as the Republicans, in particular, are becoming—may lead to effective action when the president, the House, and the Senate are held by the same party, but lean toward gridlock during times of divided government.[42]

Congressional Leadership

The political parties work through the leadership structure of Congress because the leaders of the majority political party are, at the same time, the leaders of the House and the Senate.[43] As Congress becomes more partisan, party becomes ever more important in shaping the actions of House and Senate leaders.[44]

Congressional Leadership

Leadership in the House   The leader in the House of Representatives is the Speaker of the House. This position is recognized in the Constitution and stands in the line of succession to the presidency, immediately after the vice president.

Until 1910, the Speaker exercised great power over the House legislative process. The bases of his power were his right to appoint committees and their chairs and his position as chair of the powerful Rules Committee, which controls the flow of legislation in the House. The revolt of the rank-and-file against Speaker "Uncle Joe" Cannon in 1910 resulted in the Speaker's removal from the Rules Committee and the elimination of the Speaker's power to appoint committees and their chairs.

From 1910 until the early 1970s, the weakened Speaker competed with a handful of powerful committee chairs for leadership of the House. A few Speakers, such as Sam Rayburn of Texas, were able to lead by sheer dint of their personalities and legislative skills, but power tilted toward the committee chairs most of the time.

The Democratic Caucus staged a revolt against the committee system after 1974 and restored some of the powers of the Speaker, especially in making committee assignments. The Democratic Conference also gave the Speaker more power to refer bills to committee, control the House agenda, appoint members to select committees, and direct floor debate. This change gave Speakers Tip O'Neill, Jim Wright, and Tom Foley considerable leadership resources.

In 1995, the Republican Caucus gave even more power to control the House legislative process to their first Speaker since 1954, Newt Gingrich. Some scholars suggest that Gingrich's speakership was the most powerful one since Cannon's.[45] Unexpected losses of Republican House seats in the 1998 elections, after a campaign featuring a Gingrich-designed advertising blitz to impeach the president, led to his resignation of the speakership and from the House. He was succeeded as Speaker by Dennis Hastert. Hastert eventually

The Power of the Speaker of the House

was criticized for lack of leadership in the Mark Foley Capitol pages scandal, which drew headlines and lost votes for Republicans in 2006.

The majority party in the House also selects a majority leader to help the Speaker plan strategy and manage the legislative business of the House, and a majority **whip.** Neither House nor party rules spell out their precise responsibilities. The nature of these jobs depends very much on what the Speaker wants, on the majority leader's talents and energy, and on what the Speaker and majority leader want the whip to do. In general, however, the Speaker may be likened to the Chairman of the Board in a business corporation, while the majority leader may be likened to the Chief Executive Officer, responsible for the day-to-day operations of the enterprise.[46] The whip is the majority leader's deputy, carrying out many of the tasks of getting bills passed, including counting votes and twisting arms. Tom DeLay of Texas was a particularly effective Republican whip, serving in that post from 1999 to 2002, and an even more effective Republican majority leader from 2002 to 2005 (he did not run for reelection to the party post in 2006 because of his indictment for campaign finance irregularities in Texas and troubles over ties to lobbyist Jack Abramoff). During these years, it seemed to many that Tom DeLay was the real leader of Republicans in the House, not Speaker Dennis Hastert. Called "the Hammer" because of his hard-nosed, hard-ball style, he appealed to fellow Republicans because of his intense partisanship, unmatched parliamentary skills, and legendary fund-raising abilities.

The minority party elects a minority floor leader, who acts as the chief spokesperson and legislative strategist for the opposition. The minority leader not only tries to keep the forces together but also seeks out members of the majority party who might be willing to vote against the House leadership on key issues. Nancy Pelosi was elected minority leader in 2005 and was very effective in managing her party's legislative affairs (she became the first female Speaker of the House in 2007 after the Democrat's 2006 election victory). Like the majority party, the minority party elects a whip to help the minority leader count and mobilize votes.

whip

A political party member in Congress charged with keeping members informed of the plans of the party leadership, counting votes before action on important issues, and rounding up party members for votes on bills.

Party Leader on the Campaign Trail

Then–minority whip Nancy Pelosi talks to the party activists about the need to recapture the House in 2004. Although they did not win in 2004, they did so in 2006, thanks to the efforts of Pelosi, Congressional Chairman Rahm Emanuel of Illinois, and others. Pelosi became Speaker of the 110th Congress in 2007.

A Senate Legend in Action

Later president of the United States, Lyndon B. Johnson of Texas was one of the most effective majority leaders in the history of the United States Senate. Here, he urges Senators Kennedy, Smathers, Humphrey, and Proxmire to vote for an important civil rights bill in 1957.

Leadership in the Senate Leadership in the Senate is less visible. Senators with formal leadership titles, such as the president pro tempore, exercise little influence. The Senate majority leader is as close as one comes to a leader in this body, but the powers of the office pale before those of the Speaker of the House. The Senate majority leader has some influence in committee assignments, office space designation, and control of access to the floor of the Senate. The majority leader is also important in the scheduling of the business of the Senate. The degree of actual influence is based less on formal powers, however, than on skills of personal persuasion, the respect of colleagues, visibility in the media as majority party spokesperson, and a role at the center of many of the various communication networks. In addition, campaign contributors often take the advice of the majority leader in how they allocate money for incumbents seeking reelection, giving the majority leader additional influence. In 2005, moreover, the Republican conference increased the formal powers of the office by allowing the majority leader to appoint one-half of the members of the most important committees.[47]

Despite this change, the power of the position is thus personal and not institutional; it cannot be passed on to the next leader. The Senate remains a body of independent, relatively equal members loosely tied together by threads of party loyalty, ideology, and mutual concern about the next election. It is not an environment conducive to decisive leadership, although a few, such as Lyndon Johnson, managed to transcend the limits of the office.

Congressional Committees

Most of the work of Congress takes place in its many committees and subcommittees. Committees are where many of the details of legislation are hammered out and where much of the oversight of the executive branch takes place.

Contemporary Legislative Process

Why Congress Has Committees Committees serve several useful purposes. For one thing, they allow Congress to process the huge flow of business that comes before it. The committees serve as screening devices, allowing only a small percentage of the bills put forward to take up the time of the House and the Senate.

Committees are also islands of specialization, where members and staff develop the expertise to handle complex issues and to meet executive branch experts on equal terms. The Ways and Means Committee of the House can go toe-to-toe with the Treasury Department, for instance, on issues related to taxation. Committee expertise is one of the reasons Congress remains a vital lawmaking body.

Members of Congress also use their committee positions to enhance their chances for reelection. Rational lawmakers usually try to secure committee assignments that will allow them to channel benefits to their constituents or to advance an ideological agenda popular in their district or state.

Types of Committees in Congress

There are several kinds of committees, each of which serves a special function in the legislative process.

Standing committees are set up permanently, as specified in the House and Senate rules. These committees are the first stop for potential new laws. The ratio of Democrats to Republicans on each committee is set for each house through a process of negotiation between the majority and minority party leaders. The majority party naturally enjoys a majority on each of the committees and controls the chair, as well as a substantial majority on the most important committees, such as the Budget and Finance Committee in the Senate and the Rules Committee and the Ways and Means Committee in the House. Not surprisingly, the ratio of Democrats and Republicans on committees is a point of considerable contention between the two parties, especially when they are evenly divided.

The avalanche of legislative business cannot be managed and given the necessary specialized attention in the full House and Senate standing committees. For most bills, **hearings,** negotiations, and **markup** take place in subcommittees. It is in the subcommittees, moreover, that most oversight of the executive branch takes place.

Select committees are usually temporary committees created by congressional leaders to conduct studies or investigations. Their distinguishing feature is that they have no power to send bills to the House or Senate floor. They exist to resolve matters that standing committees cannot or do not wish to handle. Often the issues before select committees are highly visible and gain a great deal of public attention for their members. Select committees investigated the Watergate scandal, the Iran-Contra affair, and intelligence failures regarding the 9/11 attacks and the run-up to the war in Iraq.

Joint committees, with members from both houses, are organized to facilitate the flow of legislation. The Joint Budget Committee, for instance, helps speed up the normally slow legislative process of considering the annual federal budget.

Before a bill can go to the president for signature, it must pass in identical form in each chamber. The committee that irons out the differences between House and Senate versions is called a **conference committee,** and one is created as needed for each piece of major legislation. While it is probably an exaggeration to call conference committees the "third house of Congress," as some political observers do, there is no denying their central role in the march of bills through the legislative labyrinth. Although they are supposed to reconcile versions of bills coming out of the House and the Senate, conference committees sometimes add, subtract, or amend provisions that are of great consequence. Much of the power of conference committees comes from the fact that

standing committees
Relatively permanent congressional committees that address specific areas of legislation.

hearings
The taking of testimony by a congressional committee or subcommittee.

markup
The process of revising a bill in committee.

select committees
Temporary committees in Congress created to conduct studies or investigations; they have no power to report bills.

joint committees
Congressional committees with members from both the House and the Senate.

conference committees
Ad hoc committees, made up of members of both the Senate and the House of Representatives, set up to reconcile differences in the provisions of bills.

bills reported by them to the House and Senate must be voted up or down; no new amendments are allowed. During the early and mid-2000s, Republican leaders often excluded their Democratic counterparts from conference committees considering important bills, making conference a place to work out differences among House and Senate Republicans.

How Members of Congress Get on Committees Because committees are so central to the legislative process, getting on the right one is important for reelection and for achieving policy and ideological goals. Committee assignments are determined by party leaders in each house, guided (but not determined) by the members' **seniority** and preferences. Each party in each chamber goes about the assignment process in a slightly different way. House Democrats use their Steering Committee, chaired by their floor leader, to make assignments. House Republicans have their own Steering Committee on which the Speaker (when Republicans are in the majority) has direct control of one-fourth of the votes. The Republican leader also appoints GOP members to the elite Rules and Ways and Means Committees. In the Senate, both parties use small steering committees made up of party veterans and leaders to make assignments. Lawmakers have traditionally tried to land positions on committees that will help them serve their constituents and better their prospects for reelection. Thus, they will try to join a committee that directly serves their constituency—Agriculture if the member is from a farm district or state, or Interior if the member is from a mining or oil district—or one of the elite committees, such as Rules, Ways and Means, Finance, or Appropriations. Appointment to an elite committee gives a lawmaker not only high visibility and a central role in policymaking, but also a strategic vantage point from which to help the constituency, advance personal and party policy and ideological goals, and attract campaign contributions—all of which help his or her reelection prospects. There is a long waiting list for assignments to the most powerful committees, so new members are unlikely to be appointed to them. Lawmakers are more likely to gain a position on one of the elite committees if they make significant contributions to the

seniority

The principle that one attains a position on the basis of length of service.

Attending to the Major Players

Representatives and senators try to get on committees that are responsible for legislation affecting major economic interests in their district or state. Those from Montana, where cattle ranching is a major part of the state economy, angle to get an agriculture-related committee appointment.

national party committees or to other party congressional candidates from their own campaign funds.[48] For assignments to nonelite standing committees, congressional leaders try to accommodate the wishes of their members, within the constraints of the seniority system.[49]

For most of the twentieth century before the 1970s, appointment by seniority was an unbreakable rule. The most senior committee member of the majority party automatically became chair of the committee; the most senior member of the minority party automatically became the **ranking minority member.** After 1974, however, both Republicans and Democrats in the House instituted the secret ballot among party members for the election of chairs, and seniority was occasionally ignored. Once again, Speaker Gingrich broke long tradition when, in the 104th and 105th Congresses (1995–1998), he often bypassed the most senior committee members in favor of members who would support his conservative legislative program. Appointment of committee chairs in the House remains firmly in the hands of majority party leaders today. In the Senate, however, seniority continues to be an important criterion for appointment to a chairmanship position.

The Role of Committee Chairs

Not long ago, chairs of committees were the absolute masters of all they surveyed. From 1910, when substantial power was stripped from the Speaker of the House and distributed to committee chairs, until the early 1970s, when the Democrats reined in the autocratic chairs they had created, the heads of congressional committees went unchallenged. Committee chairs hired and assigned staff, controlled the budget, created or abolished subcommittees at will, controlled the agenda, scheduled meetings, and reported (or refused to report) bills to the floor.

Things are different today. Committee chairs now exercise more power over subcommittees and their resources than they did in the 1970s and 1980s, but they have seen much of their power migrate to the party leadership in each house.[50] Republicans in the House and Senate even imposed term limits of six years on committee chairs. The upshot is that decisions that were entirely the province of the chair in the past have now been greatly diminished and are shared with others.[51] Still, committee chairs remain the most influential and active members within their committees. They cannot command obedience, but they are at the center of all of the lines of communication, retain the power to schedule meetings and control the agenda, control the committee staff, manage committee funds, appoint members to conference committees, and are usually the most senior and experienced members of their committees, to whom some deference is owed.

Rules and Norms in the House and Senate

Like all organizations, Congress is guided by both formal rules and informal norms of behavior.[52] Rules specify precisely how things should be done and what is not allowed. Norms are generally accepted expectations about how people ought to behave and how business ought to proceed.

Traditionally, members of the House have been expected to become specialists in some area or areas of policy and to defer to the judgment of other specialists on most bills. This mutual deference is known as **reciprocity.** While reciprocity is still common, deference to specialists—usually chairs or ranking members of committees—is declining in favor of deference to the wishes of party leaders. In the Senate, the norm of reciprocity was always less prevalent than it was in the House. Because there are fewer members in the Senate, because senators are elected on a statewide basis, and because the Senate has

ranking minority member

The highest ranking member of the minority party on a compressional committee.

reciprocity

Deferral by members of Congress to the judgment of subject-matter specialists, mainly on minor technical bills.

been the breeding ground for many presidential candidacies, a senator has more prestige, visibility, and power than a member of the House. As a result, senators are generally unwilling to sit quietly for a term or two, waiting their turn. It is not unusual for a first-term senator to introduce major bills and make important speeches. In the House, such a thing was very unusual in the past. There the old rule held sway: "To get along, go along."

Legislative life is much more rule-bound in the House of Representatives, because of its large size, than in the Senate; it tends to be more organized and hierarchical (see Table 11.2). Leaders in the House have more power, the majority party exercises more control over legislative affairs, the procedures are more structured, and the individual members have a harder time making their mark. It is geared toward majority rule, with the minority playing a lesser role. The Senate tends to be a more open and fluid place, and it lodges less power in its leaders than the House does. Each senator is more of an independent operator than his or her House colleagues. The Senate is a much more relaxed place, one that accommodates mavericks, tolerates the foibles of its members, and pays more attention to members of the minority party. It is a place where the minority and individual senators play important roles in the legislative process.

Differences between the House and the Senate are especially apparent in floor debate. Bills are scheduled for floor debate in the Senate, for instance, not by a powerful committee but by **unanimous consent,** meaning that business can be blocked by a single dissenter. In the Senate, moreover, each senator has the power to place a hold on a bill or nomination to delay consideration by the whole body. While holds cannot be found in the formal rules of the Senate, they have become part of the many informal customs of the body. Their use is regulated only by the majority leader who can decide on whether to grant holds and how long they can be in effect. Unlike the House, where debate on a bill is strictly regulated as to the number and kinds of amendments, as well as time limits for debate (determined by the Rules Committee with the agreement of

VIDEO DEBATE

Congressional Term Limits

unanimous consent

Legislative action taken "without objection" as a way to expedite business; used to conduct much of the business of the Senate.

TABLE 11.2 ● Differences Between House and Senate Rules and Norms

Senate	House
Informal, open, nonhierarchical	Rule-bound, hierarchical
Leaders have only a few formal powers	Leaders have many formal powers
Members may serve on two or more major committees	Members restricted to one major committee
Less specialized	More specialized
Unrestricted floor debate	Restricted floor debate
Unlimited amendments possible	Limited amendments possible
Amendments need not be germane	Amendments must be germane
Unlimited time for debate unless shortened by unanimous consent or halted by invocation of cloture	Limited time for debate
More prestige	Less prestige
More reliance on staff	Less reliance on staff
Minority party plays a larger role	Minority party plays a smaller role

filibuster

A parliamentary device used in the Senate to prevent a bill from coming to a vote by "talking it to death," made possible by the norm of unlimited debate.

cloture

A vote to end a filibuster or a debate; requires the votes of three-fifths of the membership of the Senate.

the Speaker), the Senate's tradition allows for unlimited numbers of amendments—that need not be germane to the bill under consideration—and unlimited debate. Senators in the minority have periodically used this tolerance of unlimited amendments and debate to good effect. Because limiting debate is so difficult in the Senate, the opponents of a bill can tie up legislative business by refusing to stop debating its merits. This practice is known as the **filibuster.** During a filibuster, senators opposing a bill have been known to talk for hour upon hour, often working in shifts. The only requirement is that they say something; they cannot hold the floor without speaking. During a filibuster, senators need not even talk about the bill itself; Senate rules do not require remarks to be germane. Senators have read from novels or quoted verse, have told stories about their children, and have quoted long lists of sports statistics. The purpose is to force the majority to give up the fight and move on to other business. While the filibuster remains part of the Senate tradition and is unlikely to be changed on most matters, Republicans forced Democrats in 2005 to agree to use the filibuster only rarely and only under extraordinary circumstances when the matter before the body is a presidential judicial nomination. Without such an agreement, the then-majority Republicans threatened use of the "nuclear option," ending the use of the filibuster entirely on matters of judicial appointments.

When a very strong majority favors a bill or when a bill that has great national import and visibility is before the body, the Senate can close debate by invoking **cloture.** Cloture requires support by three-fifths of those present and voting. It is very rarely tried; it very rarely succeeds. Many observers believe that the increasing use of the filibuster threat—which is leading to a situation where passage of major bills increasingly requires 60 votes (three-fifths of the Senate)—circumvents majority rule and therefore undermines democracy. Cloture is so difficult to invoke that the mere threat of a filibuster by a determined minority party, a growing trend in the Senate, often forces the majority in the Senate to comply with the wishes of the minority. For more on the status of the majority and the minority in filibusters and cloture, see the "Mapping American Politics" feature.

Legislative Responsibilities: How a Bill Becomes a Law

We can put much of what we have learned to work by seeing how a bill moves through the legislative labyrinth to become a law. The path by which a bill becomes a law is so strewn with obstacles that few bills survive; in fact, only about 6 percent of all bills that are introduced are enacted. To make law is exceedingly difficult; to block bills from becoming laws is relatively easy. At each step along the way (see Figure 11.6), a "no" decision can stop the passage of a bill in its tracks. As one account points out, members of the House or the Senate have "two principal functions: to make laws and to keep laws from being made. The first of these [they] perform only with sweat, patience, and a remarkable skill in the handling of creaking machinery; but the second they perform daily, with ease and infinite variety."[53]

What follows describes how major bills become law most of the time. Minor bills are often considered in each house under special rules that allow shortcuts. Thus, in the House, the "suspension calendar" and the "corrections calendar" set aside certain times for consideration of minor matters. It is also worth noting that bills involving the federal budget—authorization and appropriations bills—have several unique aspects to them, which need not concern us here.

FIGURE 11.6 • How a Bill Becomes a Law

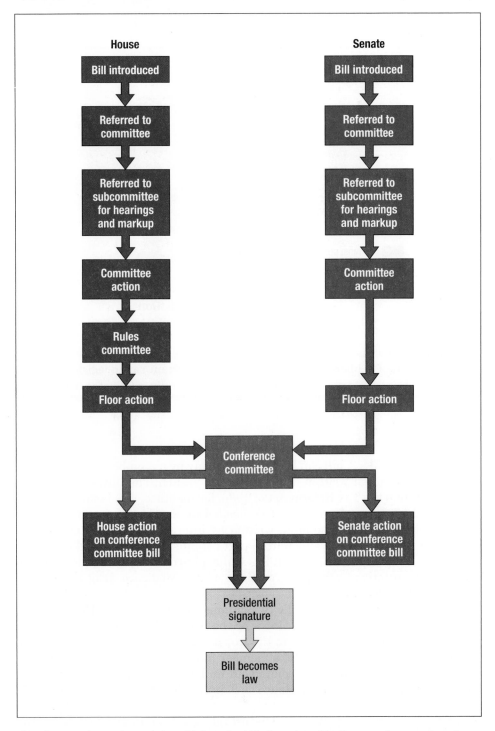

This diagram shows the path by which major bills introduced in Congress become law. As explained in the text, the road that bills must travel is complex and difficult, and few bills survive it. A bill can be derailed at any stop in its passage. A subcommittee can refuse to report a bill; a bill may be defeated on the floor of each chamber; a conference committee may fail to reach an agreement on a compromise; the conference bill may be defeated in either chamber; or the president may veto the bill.

Mapping American Politics

Majorities, minorities, and Senate filibusters

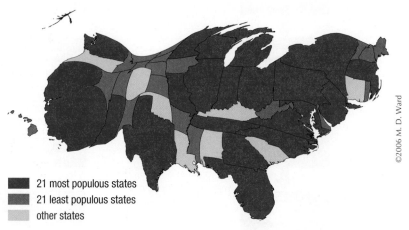

States Sized by Population

Legend:
- 21 most populous states
- 21 least populous states
- other states

©2006 M. D. Ward

Introduction: Unlimited debate is a tradition in the U.S. Senate. Senate rules make it very difficult to end debate on a proposed bill and bring it to a vote if a number of senators wish to continue deliberations. Occasionally senators try to kill a bill by "filibustering," talking it to death, if you will, by not allowing other business to be taken up on the floor of the Senate. Filibusters can only be ended by passage of a "cloture" motion, which requires 60 votes, so the votes of only 41 senators can keep a filibuster going. The filibuster is often defended as an important instrument of deliberative democracy, as it allows the minority in the Senate to have an important say in legislative mat-

---

SIMULATION

You Are a Member of Congress

hopper

The box in the House of Representatives in which proposed bills are placed.

Introducing a Bill A bill can be introduced only by a member of Congress. In reality, bills are often written in the executive branch. The initial draft of the bill that became the Tax Reform Act of 1986, for instance, was fashioned in the Treasury Department by a committee headed by the department's secretary, James Baker. Bills are also often written by interest groups. Industry trade groups, for example, wrote substantial parts of bills designed to roll back timber and mining regulations in 1995, while pharmaceutical industry trade group representatives wrote key portions of the Medicare drug benefit bill that went into effect in 2006.

With the exception of tax bills (which must originate in the House), a bill may be introduced in either the House or the Senate. In the House, a member introduces a bill by putting it into the **hopper** (a box watched over by one of the House clerks). In the Senate, a member must announce a bill to the body after being recognized by the presiding officer. The bill is then assigned a number, with the prefix *H.R.* in the House or *S.* in the Senate.

Committee Action on a Bill The presiding officer in the Senate or the Speaker in the House refers the bill to the appropriate standing committee. In the majority of cases, referral to committee is routine; the subject matter of the bill clearly indicates the appropriate committee. Revenue bills go automatically to the Ways and Means Committee in the House and to the Finance Committee in the Senate, for instance. In a small but still significant number of cases, however, the relevant committee is not so obvious because of overlapping committee jurisdictions. For example, the House Committee on International Relations is in charge of "international policy," whereas the

ters and not be steamrolled by the majority. Critics of the filibuster, whether Democrats or Republicans, liberals or conservatives, usually claim that filibusters are contrary to the principle of majority rule. Who is right?

Different Maps; Different Stories:

Both are right and wrong. The filibuster can be be considered to serve the minority or the majority, depending on who we think the senators represent. Sustaining a filibuster, while requiring the votes of only 41 of 100 senators, may involve senators representing a large majority of the American population, a small minority, or anything in between. A filibuster sustained by a coalition of 41 senators from the most populous states would represent about 75 percent of Americans (red states on the cartogram), but a filibuster sustained by a coalition of 41 senators from the least populous states would represent only about 11 percent of Americans (green states). The cartogram, with states drawn to reflect the sizes of their populations, shows this very clearly.*

What Do You Think?

Republicans have been saying for awhile now that they want to change the filibuster rule, especially on votes that involve judicial appointments on which the Senate has constitutional "advise and consent" responsibilities. Their argument is that a minority should not be able to block this important constitutional role. But what if the minority in the Senate actually represents states with a majority of the population? Some have suggested that a filibuster should be sustained only when the 41 senators supporting it represent a majority of Americans. What do you think about this idea?

*41 senators represent 20 1/2 states, but there is no way reasonably to draw one-half of a state. In this cartogram, the large-state bloc and the small-state block each is composed of 21 states.

Commerce Committee is in charge of "foreign commerce generally." In such cases, the Speaker can make multiple referrals, that is, send a bill to more than one committee for consideration. In the Senate, bills must go to a single committee, regardless of any ambiguity that may exist about its exact content. Needless to say, the more bills there are without an obvious committee destination, the more discretionary power there is in the hands of the Speaker of the House and the Senate majority leader. Where they decide to send such bills often determines whether bills will survive the legislative process and what form they will take in the end.

Committee chairs normally pass the bill on to the appropriate subcommittee for hearings. Many a bill dies at this stage, when either the subcommittee or the full committee declines to consider it further. A bill quietly killed in committee can reach the floor only by a device called a **discharge petition,** which is rarely successful.

If a bill is accepted for consideration, the subcommittee generally holds hearings, taking testimony from people for and against it. Subcommittee staff not only help prepare representatives and senators for the questioning but also often take part in the questioning themselves. The subcommittee may then forward the bill as rewritten by the staff and subcommittee members to the full committee, or it can decide to allow the bill to go no further.

Rewriting the bill in committee is called the *markup* (discussed earlier), which usually occurs amid very intense bargaining and deal making, with an eye toward fashioning a bill that will muster majority support in the full committee and on the floors of the House and the Senate and that will gain the support of the president. The staff plays a central role in the markup.

discharge petition

A petition signed by 218 House members to force a bill that has been before a committee for at least 30 days while the House is in session out of the committee and onto the floor for consideration.

The subcommittee reports its action to the full committee. The committee chair, in consultation with other important members of his or her committee, may opt for the committee to hold its own hearings and markup sessions, may decide to kill the bill outright, or may simply accept the action of the subcommittee. If the subcommittee has done its job well and has consulted with the most important players on the full committee (especially the chair), the committee will simply rubber-stamp the bill and move it along for floor action.

Floor Action on a Bill   If a bill is favorably reported from committee, congressional leaders schedule it for floor debate. In the House, major bills must first go to the Rules Committee, which decides where bills will appear on the legislative calendar and the terms under which bills will be debated by the House. A rule specifies such things as the amount of time for debate and the number (if any) and nature of amendments allowed. The Rules Committee may choose not to issue a rule at all or to drag its feet, as it did with civil rights bills until the mid-1960s. This has happened less often in recent years because both Democratic and Republican Speakers have had more power over Rules Committee appointments. The committee can also grant a "closed rule," allowing only a yes or no vote without amendments, as it generally does with tax bills.

Floor debate in the Senate, where rules do not limit debate as in the House, is much more freewheeling. Floor debate is also more important in the Senate in determining the final form a bill will take because Senate committees are less influential than House committees. Senators are also less likely to defer to committee judgments. Also, the threat of a filibuster means that the minority in the Senate plays an important role in determining the final shape of legislation.

After floor debate, the entire membership of the chamber votes on the bill, either as reported by the committee or (more often) after amendments have been added. If the bill receives a favorable vote, it then goes through the same

Making a Point on the Floor

Although much of the action on legislation and confirmation of appointments takes place in the offices of the party leaders in each house and in House and Senate committees and subcommittees, debate on the floor, when it is widely reported by the news media and telecast by C-SPAN, can affect the views of the public. Here, Robert Byrd (D–WV) makes a point on the Senate floor in 2005 in the debate over the nomination of Condoleezza Rice as Secretary of State.

obstacle course in the other chamber or awaits action by the other house if the bill was introduced there at the same time.

Conference Committee   Even if the bill makes it through both houses, its journey is not yet over. Bills passed by the House and the Senate almost always differ from one another, sometimes in minor ways and sometimes in quite substantial ways. Before the bill goes to the president, its conflicting versions must be rewritten so that a single bill gains the approval of both chambers of Congress. This compromise bill is fashioned in a conference committee made up of members from both the House and the Senate appointed by the Speaker and the Senate majority leader, customarily from the relevant committees.

A bill from a conference committee must be voted up or down on the floors of the House and the Senate; no amendments or further changes are allowed. If, and only if, both houses approve it, the bill is forwarded to the president for consideration.

Presidential Action   Because the president plays an important constitutional role in turning a bill into a law, he or his assistants and advisers are usually consulted throughout the legislative process. If the president approves the bill, he signs it and it becomes law. If he is not particularly favorable but does not want to block the bill, it becomes law after 10 days if he takes no action. He can also **veto** the bill and return it to Congress. A bill can still become law by a two-thirds vote of each house, which will override the president's veto. A president can also kill a bill at the end of a congressional session if he takes no action and Congress adjourns before 10 days pass. This is known as a **pocket veto.** We will have more to say about the presidential veto in Chapter 12.

Legislative Oversight of the Executive Branch

Oversight is another important responsibility of Congress. Oversight involves keeping an eye on how the executive branch carries out the provisions of the laws that Congress has passed and on possible abuses of power by executive branch officials, including the president.

Oversight is primarily the province of the committees and subcommittees of Congress, and it is among Congress's most visible and dramatic roles. High-profile examples of legislative probes of alleged administrative malfeasance or incompetence include Watergate, the Iran-Contra affair, the savings-and-loan collapse and bailout, corporate accounting scandals, intelligence failures and prisoner abuse in Iraq, Afghanistan, and Guantanamo Bay, and the federal response to the Hurricane Katrina disaster in New Orleans and along the Gulf Coast.

Hearings are an important part of the oversight process. Testimony is taken from agency officials, outside experts, and congressional investigatory institutions such as the Government Accounting Office and the Office of Technology Assessment. The hearings are not simply information-gathering exercises, however. As often as not, they are designed to send signals from committee members to the relevant part of the bureaucracy. Hearings that focus on the overly aggressive efforts of Internal Revenue Service agents to collect taxes, for example, are a clear signal to IRS officials that they had better rein in their agents before the next round of hearings on the budget.

During periods of unified government, however, oversight sometimes is scaled back when hearings might embarrass a president of one's own party. Critics claimed in 2006 that the relevant committees in the House and Senate

veto
Presidential disapproval of a bill that has been passed by both houses of Congress. The president's veto can be overridden by a two-thirds vote in each house.

pocket veto
Rejection of a bill if the president takes no action on it for 10 days and Congress has adjourned during that period.

oversight
Congressional responsibility for monitoring the actions of executive branch agencies and personnel to ensure conformity to federal statutes and congressional intent.

took a pass on investigating the administration's domestic eavesdropping, for
example, for precisely this reason, despite a report from the nonpartisan
Congressional Research Service that warrantless searches were "inconsistent
with the law."[54] Back in power in 2007, Democrats conducted wide-ranging
oversight hearings.

Congress's most powerful instrument of oversight of the Executive Branch
is **impeachment** (responsibility of the House) and trial and removal from office
(responsibility of the Senate) of high executive officials, including the president.
This is a blunt tool, rarely used, except in the most partisan atmosphere or in
cases involving truly egregious executive behavior. Over the course of American
history, only seven executives have been removed from office by the Senate. No
president has ever been convicted and removed from office, but the impeachment processes in the House of presidents Andrew Johnson, Nixon, and Clinton
were deeply divisive, so Congress treads very cautiously in this area.

impeachment

House action bringing formal
charges against a member
of the executive branch on
the federal judiciary that may
or may not lead to removal
from office by the Senate.

Congress and the American People

Although Americans tend to approve of their own representatives and senators, they hold Congress in very low esteem as an institution. Except in rare
instances, fewer Americans say they believe Congress is doing a good job than
believe that the president is doing a good job. Fewer report having "a great
deal of confidence" in Congress as an institution than for the Supreme Court
or the president. This pattern has endured for a long time and shows no sign
of abating.[55] Approval and confidence ratings, much as those for the president,
tend to track the economy and confidence about the future among Americans,
being higher in good times and lower in bad times. But it is inescapable that
when it comes to national institutions, Congress does not fare well.

Scholars and journalists have advanced a number of reasons for this state of
affairs, including rising incivility and blatant partisanship in Congress, the purported influence of powerful special interests in the fashioning of legislation,
and a perceived inability of representatives and senators to fashion policies that

Using the Democracy Standard

Is Congress out of touch with the American people?

PROPOSITION: Congress is out of touch with the American people and doesn't do what the people want it to do.

AGREE   Although representatives and senators must ultimately face the voters, their reelection prospects are strongly related to how much money they can raise for their campaigns. With a healthy campaign war chest, as well as the advantages they have as incumbents, representatives and senators can get their message to voters and make the case that they should remain in office. Building a healthy campaign war chest also depends heavily on money from special interests and wealthy individuals. It is not surprising, then, that the candidates pay particular attention to what these contributors want. Moreover, the way Congress is organized and works—the power of small states in the Senate, for example, and the power that flows to the minority in the Senate by virtue of the filibuster—makes it very difficult to turn the wishes of the majority into concrete laws, even if members of Congress are inclined to be responsive. Finally, because of redistricting that favors incumbents by creating safe, noncompetitive districts, House members need not worry unduly about elections. This means that one of the most important tools for keeping representatives responsive and responsible to citizens is absent.

DISAGREE   Although they have to attend to the interests of big contributors, representatives and senators are ultimately accountable to the voters. For example, unlike members of the House, Senators cannot create safe districts because their constituency is their entire state. The result is that incumbent reelection rates are lower in the Senate than in the House. There are also more voluntary retirements, meaning that there is considerable turnover in the Senate following congressional elections. So the wishes of the electorate are reflected in the composition of the Senate. In the House, although incumbents almost never lose, they act as if their congressional seats are at risk and work hard to retain them. For this reason, they pay a great deal of attention to their constituent mail, spend substantial time in their home districts talking to the voters, and invest heavily in polling to stay in touch. In the end, because senators and representatives pay careful attention to the electorate, they are responsive to the wishes and needs of the people. The result is that Congress legislates in ways that match what the American people want on most major issues.

CONSIDER   If you believe, as the framers did, that Congress ought to be a deliberative body, free from popular pressures, acting in the public interest as representatives and senators define it, then the failure to legislate exactly as the public would want will cause you no great anxiety. If you believe that Congress ought to be democratically responsive, then you might take solace in the evidence that shows that Congress follows public opinion to a substantial degree in the long run.

• What is your position on this issue? • Do you believe that Congress is too responsive or not responsive enough? • What would you do to make Congress fit your conception of the proper role of Congress in the American political system? • Would you further insulate Congress from the voice of the people? • Make it more accessible and responsive to public opinion? • Or leave it as is?

solve national problems. There is a great deal of merit in these complaints. There is no doubt, as we have shown in these pages, that Congress has become the site for partisan warfare. There is no doubt, moreover, that narrow interests prevail on a range of important issues, including the 2005 Energy Bill, filled with subsidies for large energy companies. Finally, there is no doubt that Congress has not adequately addressed problems such as rising income inequality, failing private pension systems, and large gaps in health care insurance coverage. But it may also be the case, as two scholars have suggested, that people's reaction to the sheer messiness of the give-and-take of the legislative process may be a factor in congressional unpopularity. As they put it,

> *People do not wish to see uncertainty, conflicting opinions, long debate, competing interests, confusion, bargaining, and compromised, imperfect solutions. They want government to do its job quietly and efficiently, sans conflict and sans fuss. In short . . . they often seek a patently unrealistic form of democracy.*[56]

These scholars of Congress may or may not be correct in this judgment; it may be that the more typical criticisms of Congress are to blame and that popular discomfiture with the messiness of the legislative process, highlighted so persistently by the harsh glare of the mainstream and alternative news media, has little to do with Congress's low standing with the public. Nevertheless, it is worth noting that the national institution that is held in highest regard by the public is the Supreme Court, which fashions its decisions behind closed doors, without the public or news media privy to the bargains and compromises that accompany the making of rulings and writing of opinions.

Summary

The framers of the Constitution wanted to fashion a legislative branch that was both energetic and limited. They granted Congress legislative power, gave it an existence independent of the executive branch, and enumerated an impressive range of powers. They also gave the other branches powers to check legislative excesses, created a bicameral body, and strictly denied certain powers to Congress.

Structural change in the nation has shaped Congress, influencing it to increase in size, expand the volume and complexity of its business, and become more institutionalized and professional.

Congress is a representative institution. Its members are constantly balancing the preferences of the people in their constituencies and important interest groups and contributors. Because elections are the most important mechanism for representation, and because they are the way in which members attain office, elections dominate the time and energy of lawmakers and shape how Congress organizes itself and goes about its business.

To conduct its business, Congress depends on an elaborate set of norms and rules and a web of committees and subcommittees, political parties, legislative leaders, and an extensive staff. Several of these elements encourage fragmentation, decentralization, and occasional gridlock but also allow the development of the specialized expertise that enables Congress to meet the executive branch on equal terms. Other tools help the members coordinate and expedite legislative business.

Web Exploration
Parties and Leaders in Congress

ISSUE: Much of what Congress does is determined by the parties and the leadership in the House and Senate.

SITE: Access the home pages of the Speaker of the House and of the Senate Majority Leader in MyPoliSciLab at **www.mypoliscilab.com.** Go to the "Web Explorations" section for Chapter 11. Select "Parties and leaders in Congress," then "leaders" for each house of Congress. For the House, select "leadership offices," then "Office of the Speaker." For the Senate, select "Senators," then "Senate Leadership." At these sites, you will be able to examine not only the biographies of the present leaders, but also the party legislative programs each has fashioned for his institution.

WHAT YOU'VE LEARNED: What do you think of these programs? Where are the major areas of agreement and disagreement between the parties?

HINT: Your answer will probably depend a great deal on whether you identify with one of the parties and its agenda.

Internet Sources

CongressLink at the Dirksen Center
www.congresslink.org
Designed for teachers of American government, history, and civics, this is a very rich information site on Congress. Features include access to information on pending legislation, legislative schedules and ways to contact members of Congress, caucuses, committees, rules, histories of the House and Senate, and much more.

Federal Election Commission
www.fec.gov
Information on campaign finance for presidential and congressional elections.

PoliticalMoneyLine
www.fecinfo.com/
Everything you might want to know about campaign fund-raising and spending in congressional races.

Thomas
http://thomas.loc.gov/
Expansive repository of information on the House of Representatives, including the full text and progress of bills, the Congressional Record, legislative procedures and rules, committee actions, and more.

U.S. House of Representatives Home Page
www.house.gov
House schedule, House organization and procedures, links to House committees, information on contacting representatives, and historical documents on the House of Representatives.

U.S. Senate Home Page
www.senate.gov
Similar to the House of Representatives home page, focused on the Senate. One exciting new feature is a virtual tour of the Capitol.

Suggestions for Further Reading

Adler, E. Scott, and John S. Lapinski, eds. *The Macropolitics of Congress.* Princeton: Princeton University Press, 2006.
A collection of recent research by leader scholars on the impact of congressional lawmaking on American society.

Caro, Robert. *The Years of Lyndon Johnson.* New York: Knopf, 1982.
This classic and award-winning biography of Lyndon Baines Johnson of Texas reveals more about how Congress worked in the "old days" than virtually any academic treatise.

Davidson, Roger H., and Walter J. Oleszek. *Congress and Its Members,* 10th ed. Washington, D.C.: Congressional Quarterly Press, 2006.
The classic textbook on Congress, now in its 10th edition.

Oleszek, Walter J. *Congressional Procedures and the Policy Process,* 6th ed. Washington, D.C.: Congressional Quarterly Press, 2004.
The most comprehensive compilation yet published of the rules and operations of the legislative process in Congress, written by a scholar who served as the policy director of the Joint Committee on the Organization of Congress.

Quirk, Paul J., and Sarah A. Binder. *The Legislative Branch.* New York: Oxford University Press and the Annenberg Foundation Trust, 2005.
A very accessible compendium of essays by leading scholars on every aspect of Congress and the legislative process.

Sinclair, Barbara. *Unorthodox Lawmaking: New Legislative Processes in the U.S. Congress.* Washington, D.C.: Congressional Quarterly Press, 1997.
Argues that the traditional textbook rendition of "how a bill becomes a law" has dramatically changed over the past two decades.

Specialized newspapers and journals: *The Hill, Roll Call, Congressional Quarterly, National Journal.*
Valuable sources for up-to-the-minute, in-depth coverage of what is happening in Congress.

CHAPTER **12**

The Presidency

IN THIS CHAPTER

- Why the presidency grew to be a powerful office

- How presidents play many roles

- Why presidents often disagree with Congress

- How democratic the presidency is— whether presidents listen and respond to the public

- Why different presidents often pursue similar policies

The War Presidency of George W. Bush

George W. Bush did not necessarily intend being a war president. But war and national defense have come to define much of his presidency, and the long-term outcome of events in Iraq, as well as in the broader Middle East, will have much to do with how historians judge his presidency. And, the extraordinarily broad powers he has claimed as commander-in-chief charged with defending the nation—including warrantless surveillance of American citizens and activists groups by the National Security Agency (the NSA) and the FBI—may have long-term implications for the office itself.

Oddly enough, on the campaign trail and in his first major addresses as president following the closely contested and disputed election of 2000, George W. Bush conveyed modest foreign policy and national defense goals for his presidency. In his October 12, 2000, debate with Democratic candidate John Kerry, Bush talked of humility and limited goals in foreign policy: "If we're an arrogant nation, [people of other countries will] resent us; if we're a humble nation, but strong, they'll welcome us . . . that's why we've got to be humble, and yet project strength in a way that promotes freedom." In his inaugural address on January 20, 2001, President Bush spoke mostly about domestic policy issues, talking hardly at all about foreign and national defense policies, and then in the most general terms. In his first State of the Union address, on February 27, the president again had much to say—and in far greater detail than he had in his inaugural speech—about his domestic policy priorities, talking a great deal about the need for "compassionate conservatism," with hardly a word about what he had in mind for foreign policy or possible looming threats to the United States or its interests.

All this changed, of course, with the 9/11 terrorist attacks on the United States. Responding swiftly to the attacks, Bush used the several powers of his office to form an international coalition against Al Qaeda and the Taliban regime in Afghanistan and initiate measures by executive order to protect the home front against possible terrorism. He issued executive orders, for example, to freeze the financial assets of charitable organizations purported to be tied to terrorism, establish military tribunals for the trial of foreign nationals accused of terrorism, and interrogate thousands of Middle Easterners and Muslims who might have information about terrorism. The American public responded favorably to these military, diplomatic, home-front measures, giving the president, by the end of the year, the highest sustained approval ratings in the history of public opinion polling, a considerable improvement over the historically low support he had in the polls during the first part of the year.

With the overthrow of the Taliban regime in Afghanistan, President Bush's attention turned to Iraq, a nation he claimed was developing weapons of mass de-

struction and cooperating with terrorist organizations. Using his popular standing with the public, the president gradually built support for the invasion of Iraq and the overthrow of Saddam Hussein and his Baathist regime. Although the president's plans were supported only lukewarmly by congressional Democrats, met with skepticism and anger by allied governments and publics around the world, resisted by the U.N. Security Council, and the object of large antiwar demonstrations here and abroad, he nevertheless managed to win a resolution in Congress supporting an attack on Iraq, the support of the American people once the invasion had begun in spring 2003, and several appropriations from Congress to support the occupation.

Although the ground war was swift and successful, the military victory soon turned into an occupation of a restive and resentful population (especially in the predominantly Sunni Arab areas of the country). By late 2005, President Bush, Vice President Dick Cheney, and other administration officials were pointing to signs of progress—namely, an elected provisional government, a new constitution ratified in a national election, national parliamentary elections, and a host of successful reconstruction projects—but news from and about Iraq was mainly bad. A fierce insurgency was raging in significant parts of the country, replete with terrorist attacks against soft civilian targets, the killing of foreign contractors and police and other officials working for the new Iraq government, roadside bombings of U.S. military convoys, and mortar attacks against American encampments and outposts (the American death toll passed 2,000 by fall 2005). There was also a domestic

349

political debate over the nature and use of intelligence leading to the war (on weapons of mass destruction and Iraq's ties to the 9/11 terrorists), controversy surrounding the treatment of prisoners held by the United States, and worries that administrative zeal in defending the country was compromising civil liberties at home.

By early 2006, a substantial majority of Americans believed that invading Iraq had been a mistake, and only about 40 percent agreed that the president was doing a good job.[1] The Republican-controlled Senate approved a resolution designating 2006 a year of transition in Iraq, requesting periodic reports from the president on progress there. The Supreme Court ruled that the president had exceeded his authority in using military tribunals for enemy combatants held at Guantanamo. Public anger about Iraq contributed to the Democratic takeover of Congress in the 2006 elections.

There is much in these events that sheds light on the nature of the American presidency. For one thing, American presidents enjoy considerable freedom of action in waging war. President Bush's polices in Iraq are rooted in both the Constitution and the wartime practices of other presidents; both historical precedent and the constitutional responsibilities of the office grant presidents enormous powers when the United States faces what is perceived to be a national security crisis and engages in war. The Constitution makes the president the commander-in-chief of the armed forces, in charge of the deployment and use of American military power in defense of the United States. The Constitution also makes the president the chief diplomat of the United States, responsible for conducting relations with other countries and, by extension, for fashioning foreign policy. We need only to look back to the wartime presidencies of Abraham Lincoln, Woodrow Wilson, and Franklin Delano Roosevelt to see that the people and other government officials generally look to presidential leadership during war and national security emergencies—and give presidents enormous latitude to act.

However, we also know from historical experience that presidents can run into trouble on the domestic front if bad news from the battlefront begins to accumulate and if the military enterprise comes to be seen by the public, the press, and other public officials as a failed or flawed effort. Abraham Lincoln barely won renomination by his party for the presidency in 1864 as Civil War deaths rose to stunning levels, Harry Truman lost congressional and public support as the Korean War dragged on in the early 1950s, and Lyndon Johnson announced he would not seek the Democratic Party's presidential nomination in 1964 because of rising public anger and deep divisions in the country over the war in Vietnam. Similar to George W. Bush, each of these presidents had enjoyed wide support in the initial stages of war, and each had lost much of this support by the end (Lincoln's support rallied, however, when news of Union victories at Gettysburg and Vicksburg seemed to herald the end of the bloody conflict).

As this story shows, the president has enormous powers under certain circumstances; however, at other times, the president is constrained by the powers of competing branches of government—especially Congress—news organizations, advocacy groups, and public opinion. Using this review of the Bush presidency as a backdrop, this chapter will look at the office of the president, with special attention to how it has evolved over time and how its nature at any particular time is the result of the interaction of constitutional rules, historical precedent, current events, and the qualities of the person who sits in the Oval Office. Because of the constitutional rules and historical precedent, every presidency is, in some respects, similar to every other presidency. On the other hand, because of the importance of contemporary events and the personal qualities of each president, every presidency is also unique.   ■

Thinking Critically About This Chapter

This chapter is about the American presidency, how it has evolved, and what role it plays in American politics and government.

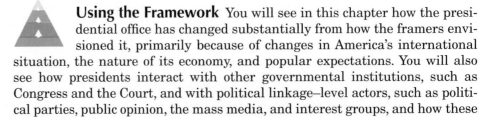

Using the Framework You will see in this chapter how the presidential office has changed substantially from how the framers envisioned it, primarily because of changes in America's international situation, the nature of its economy, and popular expectations. You will also see how presidents interact with other governmental institutions, such as Congress and the Court, and with political linkage–level actors, such as political parties, public opinion, the mass media, and interest groups, and how these interactions influence what government does.

Using the Democracy Standard You will see in this chapter how the presidential office, although not envisioned by the framers to be a democratic one, has become more directly connected to and responsive to the American people. On the other hand, you will be asked to think about whether presidents' growing ability to influence the thinking of the public and shape their perceptions of public events undermines democracy.

The Expanding Presidency

The American presidency has grown considerably since our nation's beginning. The increase has occurred in presidential responsibilities, burdens, power, and impact.

The Earliest and Latest Presidencies Compared

When George Washington took office as the first president, he had a total budget (for 1789–1792) of just over $4 million. Washington had only a handful of federal employees. Even by 1801, there were only about 300 federal officeholders in the capital. Washington's cabinet consisted of only five officials: the secretaries of state, war, and the treasury; a postmaster general; and an attorney general (who acted as the president's personal attorney, rather than as head of a full-fledged Justice Department). The entire Department of State consisted of one secretary, one chief clerk, six minor clerks, and one messenger. In 1790, only about 700 Americans were in uniform, and they had no way to project force around the world. Federal government functions were few. The entire United States consisted of the 13 original eastern and southeastern states, with only 864,746 square miles of land area; the population was only about 4 million persons, most living on small farms.[2]

When George W. Bush was first sworn into office more than 200 years later, he presided over a federal budget with more than $1.8 trillion in annual expenditures and a federal bureaucracy with approximately 2.4 million civilian employees. He was commander-in-chief of the armed forces, with about 1.4 million men and women in uniform; hundreds of military bases at home and scattered throughout the world; and perhaps 20,000 deliverable nuclear warheads, enough to obliterate every medium-sized or large city in the world

Washington Reviews the Troops

The presidency has grown in scale and responsibility. As commander-in-chief of the armed forces, President George Washington, here reviewing his troops during his first year as president, commanded an army of just over 700 soldiers and had little to do with affairs outside the United States. Today the president commands a force of about 1.4 million stationed all over the world.

Source: Washington Reviewing the Western Army at Fort Cumberland, Maryland by Frederick Kemmelmeyer. The Metropolitan Museum of Art, Gift of Edgar William and Bernice Chrysler Garbish 1963. (63.201.2) Photograph © 1983 The Metropolitan Museum of Art.

many times over. The United States in 2001 had a population of almost 278 million diverse people; a gross domestic product of more than $9.5 trillion; and a land area of some 3.8 million square miles, stretching from Alaska to Florida and from Hawaii to Maine.[3]

The Founders' Conception of the Presidency

The Founders certainly had in mind a presidency more like Washington's than Bush's. As discussed in Chapter 2, Article II of the Constitution provided for a single executive who would be strong, compared with his role under the Congress-dominated Articles of Confederation, but the Constitution's sparse language declaring that "The executive power shall be vested in a President of the United States," barely hinted at the range of things twenty-first-century presidents would do.[4] The Constitution made the president "commander-in-chief" of the armed forces, for example, without any suggestion that there would be a vast standing army that presidents could send abroad to fight without a declaration of war. It empowered presidents to appoint and to "require the opinion in writing" of executive department heads without indicating that a huge federal bureaucracy would evolve. The Constitution provided that presidents could from time to time "recommend . . . measures" to Congress without specifying that these proposals would very often (especially in the twentieth century) come to dominate the legislative agenda. Still, the vague language of the Constitution proved flexible enough to encompass the great expansion of the presidency.

The Dormant Presidency

From the time of George Washington's inauguration at Federal Hall in New York City to the end of the nineteenth century, the presidency, for the most part, conformed to the designs of the Founders. The presidency did not, by and large, dominate the political life of the nation. Presidents saw their responsibility as primarily involving the execution of policies decided by Congress. Congress was a fully equal branch of government, or perhaps more than equal. But the office changed after that.

Structural Factors   Why does the early presidency seem so weak in comparison with the contemporary presidency? Surely it is not because early presidents were less intelligent, vigorous, or ambitious; some were and some were not. A more reasonable answer is that the nation did not often require a very strong presidency before the twentieth century, particularly in the key areas of foreign policy and military leadership. Only in the twentieth century did the United States become a world power, involved in military, diplomatic, and economic activities around the globe. With that *structural* development came a simultaneous increase in the power and responsibility of the president.

It was not until the late nineteenth century, moreover, that the economy of the United States was transformed from a simple free market economy of farmers and small firms to a corporate-dominated economy, with units so large and interconnected that their every action had social consequences. This transformation eventually led to demands for more government supervision of the American economic system. As this role of government grew, so did the president's role as chief executive of the federal government.

Although the presidency was largely dormant until the end of the nineteenth century, events and the actions of several presidents during the early period anticipated what was to happen to the office in our own time. Precedents were set; expectations were formed; rules were changed.

Important Early Presidents The war hero George Washington solidified the prestige of the presidency at a time when executive leadership was mistrusted.[5] Washington also affirmed the primacy of the president in foreign affairs and set a precedent for fashioning a domestic legislative program. Thomas Jefferson, although initially hostile to the idea of a vigorous central government, boldly concluded the Louisiana Purchase with France, which roughly doubled the size of the United States and opened the continent for American settlement. Andrew Jackson, elected with broader popular participation than ever before, helped transform the presidency into a popular institution, as symbolized by his vigorous opposition to the Bank of the United States (which was seen by many ordinary Americans as a tool of the wealthy).

James Polk energetically exercised his powers as commander-in-chief of the armed forces, provoking a war with Mexico and acquiring most of what is now the southwestern United States and California. Abraham Lincoln, in order to win the Civil War, invoked emergency powers based on his broad reading of the Constitution: He raised and spent money and deployed troops on his own initiative, with Congress acquiescing only afterward; he temporarily suspended the right of **habeas corpus** and allowed civilians to be tried in military courts; and he unilaterally freed the slaves in the Confederate states by issuing the Emancipation Proclamation.

habeas corpus
The legal doctrine that a person who is arrested must have a timely hearing before a judge.

The Twentieth-Century Transformation

More enduring changes in the presidency came only in the twentieth century, when new structural conditions made an expanded presidency both possible and necessary. Theodore Roosevelt vigorously pushed the prerogatives and enhanced the powers of the office as no president had done since Lincoln. Roosevelt was happiest when he was deploying the troops as commander-in-chief or serving as the nation's chief diplomat to protect American economic and political interests. On the domestic front, Roosevelt pushed for regulation of the new and powerful business corporations, especially by

VIDEO DEBATE

Presidential Power

TR Makes His Point

Popular presidents can use the office, in Teddy Roosevelt's words, as a "bully pulpit" to move the nation to action on a broad range of fronts, even in noncrisis times. Roosevelt was very effective in using the "bully pulpit" to establish the national park system, build a more powerful navy, and move vigorously against the powerful "trusts" that dominated the American economy in the early years of the twentieth century.

trusts

Large combinations of business corporations.

breaking up **trusts,** and he established many national parks. In Teddy Roosevelt, we see the coming together of an energetic and ambitious political leader and a new set of structural factors in the United States, particularly the nation's emergence as a world power and an industrialized economy. The interplay of these three factors expanded the power and responsibilities of the presidency.

Woodrow Wilson's presidency marked further important steps in the expansion of the federal government and the presidency. Wilson's "New Freedom" domestic program built on the Progressive Era measures of Teddy Roosevelt, including further regulation of the economy by establishment of the Federal Reserve Board (1913) and the Federal Trade Commission (1914). Under Wilson, World War I brought an enormous increase in activity: a huge mobilization of military personnel and a large, new civilian bureaucracy to oversee the production and distribution of food, fuel, and armaments by the American "arsenal of democracy."

It was Franklin D. Roosevelt, however, who presided over the most significant expansion of presidential functions and activities in American history and changed American expectations about the office. In response to the Great Depression, Roosevelt and the Democratic majority in Congress pushed into law a series of measures for economic relief that grew into vast programs of conservation and public works, farm credit, business loans, and relief payments to the destitute. Roosevelt's New Deal also established a number of independent commissions to regulate aspects of business (the stock market, telephones, utilities, airlines) and enacted programs such as Social Security, which provided income support for retired Americans, and the Wagner Act, which helped workers join unions and bargain collectively with their employers.

Even bigger changes, however, resulted from World War II when the government mobilized the entire population and the whole economy for the war effort. With the end of World War II, the United States was established as a military superpower. Since the time of Franklin Roosevelt, all U.S. presidents

JFK in His Element

President John F. Kennedy was a master of public performance, not only on television, but in front of crowds of citizens or gatherings of reporters. This skill enhanced the formal powers of his office, increasing his influence with other government leaders.

Reagan and Gorbachev in Red Square

Whether rightly or wrongly, Ronald Reagan—whose foreign policies included a dramatic arms buildup followed by proposals to refashion the basic relationship between the two superpowers—is often given credit for ending the Cold War and nurturing the collapse of the Soviet Union. Here, President Reagan and Soviet leader Mikhail Gorbachev enjoy the sun and meet people in Red Square.

have administered a huge national security state with large standing armed forces, nuclear weapons, and bases all around the world.

Although he accomplished little on the legislative front during his brief time in office—he did introduce the 1964 Civil Rights Act, passed after his death—John F. Kennedy was the first president to appreciate the importance of television as both a campaign tool and as an instrument for influencing the public and political actors in Washington, the states, and other countries. His televised speeches and press conferences, where his charm, intelligence, and sense of humor were clearly evident, became one of his most effective governing tools. Presidents after him tried to follow his lead, but only Ronald Reagan and Bill Clinton came close to Kennedy's mastery of the medium.

In the 1980s, Ronald Reagan managed to bring many of the main items of the conservative agenda to fruition: a massive tax cut to stimulate the economy, cutbacks in the number of regulations that affect business, cuts in a wide range of domestic social programs, and a substantial buildup of U.S. armed forces. Perhaps more importantly, he showed the American people and others around the world that a vigorous and popular presidency was still possible after the failed presidencies of Richard Nixon, Gerald Ford, and Jimmy Carter.

How Important Are Individual Presidents?

We cannot be sure to what extent presidents themselves caused this great expansion of the scope of their office. Clearly, they played a part. Lincoln, Wilson, and Franklin Roosevelt, for example, not only reacted vigorously to events but also helped create events; each had something to do with the coming of the

Presidential Greatness

wars that were so crucial in adding to their activities and powers. Yet these great presidents were also the product of great times; they stepped into situations that had deep historical roots and dynamics of their own.

Lincoln found a nation in bitter conflict over the relative economic and political power of North and South and focused on the question of slavery in the western territories; war was a likely, if not inevitable, outcome. Wilson and Franklin Roosevelt each faced a world in which German expansion threatened the perceived economic and cultural interests of the United States and in which U.S. industrial power permitted a strong response. The Great Depression fairly cried out for a new kind of presidential activism. Kennedy faced an international system in which the Soviet Union had become especially strident and menacing. George W. Bush was president when the 9/11 terrorist attacks on the United States occurred. Thus, the great upsurges in presidential power and activity were, at least in part, a result of forces at the *structural* level and the result of developments in the economy, American society, and the international system.

We see, then, that it is this mixture of a president's personal qualities (personality and character) and deeper structural factors (such as the existence of military, foreign policy, or economic crises) that determines which presidents transform the office.

The Powers and Roles of the President

Presidential Leadership: Which Hat Do You Wear?

The American presidency has assumed powers and taken on roles unimaginable to the Founders. Each touches on the daily lives of everyone in the United States and affects tens of millions of people around the world as well.

Ceremonial Responsibilities

The president is both the chief executive of the United States—responsible for the executive branch of the federal government—and the chief of state, a symbol of national authority and unity. In contrast to European parliamentary democracies such as Britain or Norway, where a monarch acts as chief of state while a prime minister serves as head of the government, in the United States the two functions are combined. It is the president who performs many ceremonial duties (attending funerals, proclaiming official days, honoring heroes, celebrating anniversaries) that are carried out by members of royal families in other nations. Jimmy Breslin, an irreverent New York newspaper columnist, once wrote, "The office of President is such a bastardized thing, half royalty and half democracy, that nobody knows whether to genuflect or spit."[6] Because it adds to their prestige and standing with other government officials and the public, presidents have always found the chief of state role to be a useful tool in their political arsenal, enabling them to get their way on many important issues.

Comparing Chief Executives

Domestic Policy Leader

The president has taken on important responsibilities on the domestic front that were probably not anticipated by the framers. These include his role as the nation's legislative leader and manager of the economy.[7]

The president's role as chief of state involves many seemingly mundane tasks—such as lighting the national Christmas tree, as Bill Clinton is doing—that nevertheless add to the prestige of the office.

Legislative Leader While the Constitution seems to give responsibility for the legislative agenda to Congress, over time, the initiative for public policy has partly shifted to the president and the executive branch. The bases of this change may be found in the Constitution, statutes passed by Congress, and the changing expectations of the American people. The Constitution, for example, specifies that the president must, ". . . from time to time give the Congress information on the state of the union, and recommend to their consideration such measures as he shall judge necessary and expedient." Until Woodrow Wilson's presidency, the "state of the union" took the form of a written report sent every year or every two years to Congress for its consideration. These reports often gathered dust in the House and Senate clerks' offices. Wilson, a strong believer in the role of the president as chief legislative leader similar to the prime minister in a parliamentary system, began the practice of delivering the State of the Union to Congress in an address to a joint session of the House and Senate, in which the president sets out his agenda for congressional legislation. Wilson correctly sensed that the American people were in the mood for vigorous legislative leadership from the president, given the enormous technological, economic, and social changes that were happening in the United States and the problems that were being generated by these changes. In modern times, the State of the Union address has become the most important tool by which presidents gain the attention of the public and other public officials for what they want to accomplish. The state of the nation is now a very dramatic and visible event, delivered before a joint session of Congress, with members of the Supreme Court, the president's cabinet, and the military joint chiefs in attendance, and a national television audience. In the State of the Union, presidents, much as Wilson did, set out what issues they hope Congress will address, with a promise that detailed proposals for legislation will be forthcoming. In doing so, presidents now have the biggest say in defining the political agenda for the nation.

The president's legislative role also was enhanced by the Budget Act of 1921, which requires the president to submit an annual federal government

The President as National Policy Leader

Presidents use the annual State of the Union address to outline their legislative agenda for the nation, as George W. Bush is doing here in 2005. He asked Congress, among other things, to add private accounts to Social Security and tighten up the nation's bankruptcy laws.

budget to Congress for its consideration, accompanied by a budget message setting out the president's rationale and justifications. We will have more to say about the federal budget in Chapter 17.

Although the House and Senate often take action on their own with regard to the nation's legislative agenda, what is striking is the degree to which Congress waits for and acts in response to presidential State of the Union addresses, budgets, and legislative proposals to meet various national problems. Indeed, the twentieth century is dotted with presidential labels on broad legislative programs: Wilson's New Freedom, Roosevelt's New Deal, Truman's Fair Deal, Kennedy's New Frontier, and Johnson's Great Society.

Manager of the Economy   We now expect presidents to "do something" about the economy when things are going badly. The Great Depression taught most Americans that the federal government has a role to play in fighting economic downturns, and the example of Franklin Roosevelt convinced many that the main actor in this drama ought to be the president. Congress recognized this in 1946 when it passed the Employment Act, requiring the president to produce an annual report on the state of the economy, assisted by a new Council of Economic Advisors, with a set of recommendations for congressional action to maintain the health of the American economy. (See "By the Numbers" to see how we can tell how well the economy is performing). The role is now so well established that even conservative presidents, such as Ronald Reagan and George H. W. Bush, felt compelled to involve the federal government in the prevention of bank failures, the stimulation of economic growth, and the promotion of exports abroad.

In the rapidly expanding global economy, moreover, presidents have become increasingly engaged in the effort to open world markets on equitable terms to American goods and services. The first President Bush helped push through an agreement with Japan on semiconductors. President Clinton was especially active as a spokesperson for the benefits of the American way of doing business and pushed hard to expand a global free trade regime, negotiating and gaining congressional approval for the North American Free Trade Agreement (NAFTA) treaty and the creation of the World Trade Organization. The second President Bush entered into several bilateral and multilateral free trade agreements with Latin American countries.

Foreign Policy and Military Leader

Although the framers gave a role to Congress in fashioning foreign and military policies—note congressional control of the federal purse strings, its role in declaring war, and the Senate's "advice and consent" responsibilities with respect to treaties and appointment of ambassadors—they wanted the president to be the major player in these areas. What they could not have anticipated was that the United States would develop into the world's superpower, with global responsibilities and commitments, a development that enormously expanded the power of the presidency in the federal government.[8]

Foreign Policy Leader   In a case decided in 1936, the Supreme Court confirmed the president's position as the nation's preeminent foreign policy maker, saying: ". . . the president is the sole organ of the federal government in the field of international relations."[9] The president's role as foreign policy leader is rooted in the diplomatic and treaty powers sections of Article II of the Constitution, as well as in his role as commander-in-chief of the armed forces.[10]

The Constitution specifies that the president shall have the power to appoint and receive ambassadors and to make treaties. Although these formal constitutional powers may seem minor at first glance, they confer on the president the main responsibility for fashioning American foreign policy. Take the power to appoint and receive ambassadors. From the very beginning of the American republic, presidents have used this provision as a tool for recognizing or refusing to recognize foreign governments. In 1793, for example, George Washington refused to accept the credentials of the French ambassador Citizen Edmond Genet, signaling that the United States did not recognize the legitimacy of the French revolutionary government. In the twentieth century, Woodrow Wilson refused to recognize or have dealings with the revolutionary government of Mexico. Presidents Wilson, Harding, Coolidge, and Hoover refused to recognize the revolutionary communist government of the Soviet Union, a policy that was reversed by Franklin D. Roosevelt. The Chinese communist government went unrecognized by the United States for 23 years after it came to power, a policy that was eventually reversed by Richard Nixon. The president's sole power to proclaim U.S. policy in this area is suggested by the following: Neither Franklin D. Roosevelt nor Richard Nixon required the permission of any other government institution or public official—whether Congress or the courts or state legislatures, for example—to change American policy with respect to the Soviet Union or Communist China. The decision was the president's alone to make.

The power to initiate the treaty-making process is also a powerful tool of presidential diplomacy and foreign policymaking. By virtue of this power, the president and the foreign policy officials in the state, treasury, commerce, and defense departments that report to him consult, negotiate, and reach agreements with other countries. Sometimes the agreements with other countries take the form of treaties—the Paris Treaty ending the Revolutionary War is an example, as are the various arms control, human rights, trade, and environmental treaties to which the United States is a party. More often, however,

By the Numbers

How well is the American economy performing?

Is the economy getting better or worse, and by how much? Seem like easy questions to answer, but consider the two examples graphed here from official U.S. government reports during a time in the early 2000s when liberals and conservatives, and Democrats and Republicans, were arguing bitterly about how well the economy was doing.

Why It Matters: Government reports on the state of the American economy are very important. Such reports affect the mood of the public and their sense of confidence in the direction the country is moving and how much they support and trust elected leaders. These reports also influence investors' confidence in the American economy and their willingness to invest, thus shaping the future direction of the economy. They also are important pieces of information for government leaders—including the Federal Reserve Board, Congress, and the president—as they fashion policies to keep the economy on course. Finally, the reports trigger automatic changes in a wide range of government benefits and financial instruments, including Social Security checks and inflation-adjusted bonds. So it is important to get the numbers right and correctly interpret the numbers the government reports.

The Story Behind the Numbers: Let's look at the jobs numbers first. The Bureau of Labor Statistics (BLS)—which reported a drop in nonfarm payrolls of 30,000 in June 2003—bases its payroll numbers on reports by businesses and governments that are compared with unemployment insurance records in the states, which are fairly comprehensive and current. Total employment—which increased by 251,000 according to the BLS—is based on a sampling of households that is compared with household employment figures from the census taken every 10 years. Most economists suggest nonfarm payroll is the better of the two measures of short-term job gains and losses because of the total employment number's dependence on census numbers as the base for calculations in a society whose household numbers are changing year to year.

The second type of number—quarterly economic growth—is reported in three ways because the data

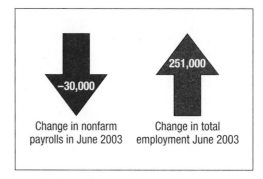

Change in nonfarm payrolls in June 2003   Change in total employment June 2003

Job Growth or Job Loss? June 2003

---

executive agreement
An agreement with another country signed by the president that has the force of law, like a treaty; does not require Senate approval; originally used for minor technical matters, now an important tool of presidential power in foreign affairs.

international agreements take the form of **executive agreements** entered into by the president and one or more foreign governments. Originally understood to be agreements about minor or technical details associated with a treaty, executive agreements eventually began to be used for very important matters, such as regulation of truckloads and safety standards on Mexican truckers under the North American Free Trade Agreement. President George W. Bush, to take another example, entered into an executive agreement in 2002 with Russia committing the two countries to a reduction in the size of their nuclear stockpiles.[11]

Commander-in-Chief Article II, Section 2, of the Constitution specifies that the president is the commander-in-chief of U.S. armed forces—without saying

to make firmer calculations come only in bits and pieces. Thus, the Commerce Department reports an advance number, a preliminary number, and a final number. The advance and preliminary numbers are particularly troublesome because they depend a great deal on incomplete information—businesses don't always get their quarterly government reports done on time, and reports in some areas of the economy, most notably the service sector, are not made on a quarterly basis. So government statistical agencies have to do a substantial amount of statistical guesswork, inferring some numbers from more solid ones. As an example, the total amount of money paid in commissions for financial transactions—a component in the calculation of overall economic activity—is inferred from the total volume of stock market activity.

What to Watch For: It is important to understand how important government statistics are collected and reported. This may seem like a pretty hard thing to do, but each statistical reporting agency in the federal government includes this information in its reports, although you may sometimes have to dig for it. The average person, of course, doesn't necessarily have the time or inclination to perform such investigations. It is probably reasonable to pay attention to professional economists and financial analysts as they discuss the meanings of competing numbers, especially to the ones who have been the most consistently on the mark over the years. It is also worth remembering that many government statistical agencies report preliminary and final numbers, and that the final numbers—taking advantage of the fact that they are based on more complete information—are worth waiting for.

What Do You Think? In your view, can we depend on government statistical reports to accurately reflect what they purport to measure? Should we depend on statistics that are based on incomplete information and that depend on a great deal of statistical inference? If not, whose statistical reports can we depend on to be more accurate? Industry trade groups? Economic consulting firms? Do we have any other choice but to depend on government trend data, perhaps insisting that they gather the best information available and on a timely basis?

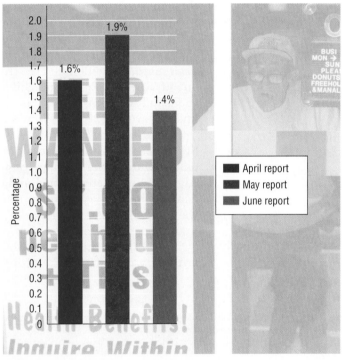

GDP Growth, First Quarter, 2003

anything at all about what this actually means. On the other hand, Article I, Section 8, specifies that Congress has the power to declare war. What the framers seemed to have in mind was a distinction between defensive war and offensive war, with the president the primary decision maker with respect to the former and Congress preeminent with respect to the latter. Thus, the president was given the power to deploy and use the armed forces in order to protect the United States against external invasions and internal insurrections; Congress was given the power to declare war against another country.[12] Over the years, this distinction between offensive and defensive war has been blurred; American forces increasingly have been sent into hostilities abroad, deployed by presidents without a formal declaration of war by Congress (the last such declaration, in fact, came in December 1941 after the Japanese attack on Pearl Harbor, and there have been only five such declarations in American history), in the name of defending the United States. Here is what seems to have been going on: As the United States became a global power, presidents, other American leaders, and the public came to believe that defending the United States required more than simply defending against cross-border invasions from other countries. Other threats seemed to many to be equally dangerous, including communism, nationalist threats to American economic interests, drug trafficking, and, most recently, terrorism.

Presidents have used American military power, without an explicit declaration of war, to protect the United States against each of these threats. Thus, in the early 1950s, Harry Truman fought a bitter war in Korea against North Korean and Chinese forces, without a declaration of war from Congress, in the name of halting communist aggression. Presidents Eisenhower, Kennedy, Johnson, and Nixon did the same in Vietnam. Ronald Reagan used American forces in Grenada and Nicaragua to fight communism and launched an air attack against Libya to punish it for its involvement in terrorism. George H. W. Bush launched an invasion of Panama to capture its president and alleged drug lord Manuel Noriega, and in 1991 used more than 500,000 U.S. troops in Operation Desert Storm to push Iraq out of Kuwait. President Bill Clinton claimed the power to send several thousand American troops as peacekeepers to Bosnia in 1995, Haiti in 1996, and Kosovo in 1999 and to wage an air war against Serbia to try to prevent "ethnic cleansing." For his part, George W. Bush, in the months after the September 11, 2001, attacks on the United States, launched a military campaign against the Taliban regime and the Al Qaeda terrorist network in Afghanistan, then invaded and occupied Iraq in 2003 to protect the country against the Iraqi regime's purported weapons of mass destruction and ties to the 9/11 terrorists. In none of these or related cases was Congress called upon to pass a formal declaration of war.

To be sure, when presidents choose to use American military power, they ordinarily consult widely with Congress and other government and opinion

Opening Days in Kuwait

President George H. W. Bush gained congressional and popular support to push invading Iraqi troops out of Kuwait in 1991. Although he said at the time that he did not require congressional approval for this action, given his constitutional role as commander-in-chief, he recognized that such approval would help legitimize his use of American forces.

leaders. They do everything they can, moreover, to enlist the support of the public. They may even at times ask that Congress pass a resolution of support authorizing presidential use of the armed forces to defend the national security of the United States, although they are not legally bound to do so. Thus, President George H. W. Bush asked Congress to pass a resolution supporting Desert Storm in 1991, which it did. Likewise, in 2002, his son, President George W. Bush, asked Congress for a resolution supporting military action against Saddam Hussein's Iraq, which it did. Tellingly, each of the Bush presidents let it be known that military action would be forthcoming no matter the outcome of congressional deliberations.

Some presidents also have claimed that the office's commander-in-chief powers allow them to take extraordinary actions on the home front that seemingly violate civil liberties of some Americans if such actions are required to defend the nation. Thus, Abraham Lincoln used military tribunals to try a number of southern sympathizers during the Civil War, Woodrow Wilson censored the press during World War I, Franklin Roosevelt ordered placement of Japanese Americans into internment camps during World War II, and George W. Bush detained without trial American citizens he defined as "enemy combatants" (which the Supreme Court has disallowed) and authorized domestic eavesdropping by the National Security Agency to find terrorists.

The President's Staff and Cabinet

Each of the president's functions is demanding; together, they are overwhelming. "Passive" presidents such as Chester Arthur or Calvin Coolidge may well be a vanishing breed. Of course, presidents do not face their burdens alone; they have gradually acquired many advisers and helpers. The number and responsibilities of these advisers and helpers have become so extensive, and the functions they perform so essential, that they have come to form what some call the **institutional presidency.**[13]

The White House Staff

The White House staff, for example, which is specially shaped to fit the particular needs of each president, includes a number of close advisers.

One top adviser, usually designated **chief of staff,** tends to serve as the president's right hand, supervising other staff members and organizing much of what the president does. Presidents use their chiefs of staff in different ways. Franklin Roosevelt kept a tight rein on things himself, granting equal but limited power and access to several close advisers in a *competitive* system. Dwight Eisenhower, used to the *hierarchical* army staff system, gave overall responsibility to his chief of staff, Sherman Adams. In the George W. Bush White House, Joshua Bolten runs the show with a firm hand, having replaced the somewhat ineffectual Andrew Card in 2006.

Another important staff member in most presidencies is the **national security adviser,** who is also head of the president's National Security Council, operating out of the White House. The national security adviser generally meets with the president every day to brief him on the latest events that might affect the nation's security and offer advice on what to do. Several national security advisers, including Henry Kissinger (under Nixon) and Zbigniew Brzezinski (under Carter), have been strong foreign policy managers and active, world-hopping diplomats who sometimes clashed with

institutional presidency
The permanent bureaucracy associated with the presidency, designed to help the incumbent of the office carry out his responsibilities.

chief of staff
A top adviser to the president who also manages the White House staff.

national security adviser
A top foreign policy and defense adviser to the president who heads the National Security Council.

the secretaries of state and defense. Most recent presidents, however, have appointed team players who have closely reflected the president's wishes and quietly coordinated policy among the various executive departments. Condoleezza Rice followed this pattern in George W. Bush's first administration and Steven Hadley does so in the second.

Most presidents also have a top domestic policy adviser who coordinates plans for new domestic laws, regulations, and spending, although this role is often subordinate to that of the chief of staff and is not usually very visible. Close political advisers, often old comrades of the president from past campaigns, may be found in a number of White House or other government posts (e.g., James Baker served as George H. W. Bush's secretary of state, while Karen Hughes served as White House Counselor to the younger Bush during his first term) or may have no official position at all (such as Republican consultant Dick Morris, who crafted Clinton's 1996 reelection strategy). Prominent in every administration is the press secretary, who holds press conferences, briefs the media, and serves as the voice of the administration. Nearly all presidents have a legal counsel (a hot seat for Bill Clinton's counsel, given the Whitewater, campaign finance, and Monica Lewinsky inquiries and his impeachment and trial in Congress). There are also one or more special assistants who act as a liaison with Congress, deal with interest groups, handle political matters, and consult on intergovernmental relations. In George W. Bush's administration, political strategist Karl Rove wore most of these hats at the same time, until Joshua Bolten convinced the president that Rove should focus his efforts on the 2006 congressional elections.

However, the exact shape of the White House staff changes greatly from one presidency to another, depending on the preferences and style of the president. What is particularly striking about President George W. Bush's management style is his penchant for setting overall goals and policies but giving his staffers a great deal of freedom and latitude in getting the job done.[14] Supporters claim that this contributes to business-like efficiency in the White House; critics worry that it contributes to the president's isolation, notable, for example, in his slow response to the Hurricane Katrina disaster.

Rove Leads the Way

Karl Rove, generally credited with crafting the strategies that allowed George W. Bush to win two presidential elections and the Republicans to retain control of Congress between 2001 and 2006, has played a wide range of roles in the White House. Most famously, until early 2006, he simultaneously held advisory positions as electoral strategist and domestic policy adviser to the president.

The Executive Office of the President

One step removed from the presidential staff, and mostly housed in the Executive Office Building next door to the White House, is a set of organizations that forms the **Executive Office of the President (EOP).**

Most important of these organizations is the **Office of Management and Budget (OMB).** The OMB advises the president on how much the administration should propose to spend for each government program and where the money will come from. The OMB also exercises legislative clearance; that is, it examines the budgetary implications of any proposed legislation and sometimes kills proposals it deems too expensive or inconsistent with the president's philosophy or goals.

The **Council of Economic Advisers (CEA)** advises the president on economic policy. Occasionally, the head of the council exercises great influence, as Walter Heller did during the Kennedy administration. More often, the head of the CEA is inconspicuous.

The Executive Office of the President also includes the **National Security Council (NSC),** a body of leading officials from the Departments of State and Defense, the Central Intelligence Agency (CIA), the military, and elsewhere who advise the president on foreign affairs. The NSC has been particularly active in crisis situations and covert operations. The NSC staff, charged with various analytical and coordinating tasks, is headed by the president's national security adviser. At times, the NSC staff has gone beyond analysis to conduct actual operations, the most famous of which was the Iran-Contra affair, under the direction of Lieutenant Colonel Oliver North, when weapons were secretly sold to Iran in the hope of freeing U.S. hostages and some of the proceeds were illegally diverted to the Nicaraguan Contra rebels fighting the leftist Sandinista regime.

The Vice Presidency

The vice presidency itself, however, has not always been highly regarded. John Nance Garner, Franklin Roosevelt's first vice president, has been quoted as saying in his earthy Texan way that the office was "not worth a pitcher of warm piss."[15] Within administrations, vice presidents used to be fifth wheels, not fully trusted (since they could not be fired) and not personally or politically close to the president. Vice presidents used to spend much of their time running minor errands of state, attending funerals of foreign leaders not important enough to demand presidential attention, or carrying out limited diplomatic missions. Some vice presidents were virtually frozen out of the policymaking process. For example, while vice president, Harry Truman was never informed of the existence of the Manhattan Project, which built the atomic bomb. He learned of the bomb only months before he was obligated to make a decision on using it to end the war against Japan, soon after he became president on the death of Franklin D. Roosevelt.

Recent presidents, however, have involved their vice presidents more.[16] Bill Clinton gave Al Gore important responsibilities, including the formulation of environmental policy, coping with Ross Perot's opposition to NAFTA, and the ambitious effort to "reinvent government." More than any other vice president in American history, Dick Cheney is at the center of the policymaking process in the White House, serving (by all accounts) as President George W. Bush's principal advisor on both domestic and foreign policy, the key player within the administration on long-range policy planning, the main liaison to Republicans in Congress,[17] and an important consumer of information from the intelligence community.[18]

Executive Office of the President (EOP)
A group of organizations that advise the president on a wide range of issues; includes the Office of Management and Budget, the National Security Council, and the Council of Economic Advisers.

Office of Management and Budget (OMB)
An organization within the Executive Office of the President that advises on the federal budget, domestic legislation, and regulations.

Council of Economic Advisers (CEA)
An organization in the Executive Office of the President made up of a small group of economists who advise on economic policy.

National Security Council (NSC)
An organization in the Executive Office of the President made up of officials from the State and Defense Departments, the CIA, and the military, who advise on foreign and security affairs.

A Uniquely Powerful Vice President

Vice President Dick Cheney, shown here with Defense Secretary Donald Rumsfeld before a White House meeting with the president in 2006, may well be the most influential vice president in American history. His views on, among other things, the war on terrorism, the conflicts in Afghanistan and Iraq, and intelligence gathering at home and abroad have shaped Bush administration foreign and national defense policies.

In 1804, the Twelfth Amendment fixed the flaw in the original Constitution under which Aaron Burr, Thomas Jefferson's running mate in 1800, had tied Jefferson in electoral votes and tried, in the House of Representatives, to grab the presidency for himself. Since then, vice presidents have been elected specifically to that office on a party ticket with their presidents. But now there is also another way to become vice president. The Twenty-Fifth Amendment (ratified in 1967) provides for succession in case of the temporary or permanent inability of a president to discharge his office. It also states that if the vice presidency becomes vacant, the president can nominate a new vice president, who takes office on confirmation by both houses of Congress. This is how Gerald Ford became vice president in 1973, when Spiro Agnew was forced to resign because of a scandal, and how Nelson Rockefeller became vice president in 1974, when Ford replaced Richard Nixon as president.

The Cabinet

The president's cabinet is not mentioned in the Constitution. No legislation designates the composition of the cabinet, its duties, or its rules of operation. Nevertheless, all presidents since George Washington have had one. It was Washington who established the practice of meeting with his top executive officials as a group to discuss policy matters. Later presidents continued the practice, some meeting with the cabinet as often as twice a week, and others paying it less attention or none at all. Today, the cabinet usually consists of the heads of the major executive departments, plus the vice president, the director of the CIA, and whichever other officials the president deems appropriate.

Rarely, if ever, though, have presidents actually relied on the cabinet as a decision-making body. Presidents know that they alone will be held responsible for decisions, and they alone keep the power to make them. According to legend, when Abraham Lincoln once disagreed with the entire cabinet, he declared, "Eight votes for and one against; the nays have it!"

Most recent presidents have convened the cabinet infrequently and have done serious business with it only rarely. Ronald Reagan held only a few cabinet meetings each year, and those were so dull and unimportant that Reagan was said to doze off from time to time. Bill Clinton, with his "policy wonk" mastery of details, thoroughly dominated cabinet discussions.

Clinton Meets with His Cabinet

Unlike the situation in parliamentary democracies, the cabinet has no formal decision-making powers. Indeed, presidents rarely consult with the cabinet about domestic and foreign policies, although they consult with individual members of the cabinet as the need arises. Here, President Bill Clinton meets with his cabinet in early 1996.

One reason for the weakness of the cabinet, especially in recent years, is simply that government has grown large and specialized. Most department heads are experts in their own areas, with little to contribute elsewhere. It could be a waste of everyone's time to engage the secretary of housing and urban development in discussions of military strategy. Another reason is that cabinet members occupy an ambiguous position: They are advisers to the president but also represent their own constituencies, including the permanent civil servants in their departments and the organized interests that their departments serve. They may have substantial political stature of their own, somewhat independent of the president's.

The President and the Bureaucracy

Many people assume that the president, because he is the chief executive of the United States, has firm control over the federal bureaucracy, the system of departments and agencies that make up the executive branch of the federal government (and which will be discussed in more detail in the next chapter). They assume that he can simply order departments and agencies to do something and they will do it. This is very rarely the case.[19]

Sometimes presidents get federal bureaucrats to act by issuing **executive orders**—formal directives to executive branch departments and agencies that have the force of law. The legitimacy of such orders are based on the constitutional position of the president as chief executive and commander-in-chief, sometimes on discretionary authority granted to the president by Congress in statutes, and often on precedents set by past presidents. Executive orders are not only about minor administrative matters; many have been issued by presidents to institute important federal policies and programs.[20] For example, George Washington issued the very first executive order, declaring U.S. neutrality in the war between Great Britain and France and ordering all diplomatic and military personnel to act accordingly. Later, Franklin Roosevelt ordered the internment of Japanese Americans during

executive order

A rule or regulation issued by the president that has the force of law, based either on the constitutional powers of the presidency or on congressional statutes.

With the Stroke of a Pen: The Executive Order over Time

World War II. President George W. Bush issued executive orders to, among other things, establish the White House Office of Faith-Based and Community Initiatives, promulgate new rules on airline passenger and baggage screening after the 9/11 attacks on the United States, and restrict stem cell research supported by federal funds.[21]

In the day-to-day operation of government, direct command is seldom feasible, however. Too much is going on. Presidents cannot keep personal track of each one of the millions of government officials and employees. The president can only issue general guidelines and pass them down the chain of subordinates, hoping that his wishes will be followed faithfully. But lower-level officials, protected by civil service status from being fired, may have their own interests, their own institutional norms and practices, that lead them to do something different. President Kennedy was painfully reminded of this during the Cuban Missile Crisis of 1962, when Soviet Premier Khrushchev demanded that U.S. missiles be removed from Turkey in return for the removal of Soviet missiles from Cuba: Kennedy was surprised to learn that the missiles had not already been taken out of Turkey, for he had ordered them removed a year earlier. The people responsible for carrying out this directive had not followed through.[22]

To a large extent, a president must *persuade* other executive branch officials to do things. He must bargain, compromise, and convince others that what he wants is in the country's best interest and in their own interest as well. Neustadt put it strongly: "Presidential power is the power to persuade."[23]

Of course, presidents can do many things besides persuade: appoint top officials who share the president's goals; put White House observers in second-level department positions; reshuffle, reorganize, or even—with the consent of Congress—abolish agencies that are not responsive; influence agency budgets and programs through OMB review; and stimulate pressure on departments by Congress and the public.

Worrisome Days

Military conflict between the Soviet Union and the United States was barely avoided during the Cuban Missile Crisis in early October 1962. Attempts by the U.S.S.R. to ship offensive missiles into Cuba and U.S. military inaction on removing from Turkey missiles aimed at the Soviet Union, as earlier promised, fed the crisis atmosphere. Here, President John F. Kennedy consults with his brother, close confidant, and Attorney General Robert Kennedy about how to proceed.

Still, the president's ability to gain bureaucratic acquiescence is limited. The federal bureaucracy is not merely a creature of the president but is itself a partly independent governmental actor. It is also subject to influences from the political linkage level—especially by public opinion and organized interests, often working through Congress. Congress, after all, appropriates the money. This constrains what presidents can do and helps ensure that the executive branch will respond to broad forces in society rather than simply to the wishes of one leader. We will examine these issues in more detail in Chapter 13 on Bureaucracy.

The President and Congress: Perpetual Tug-of-War

The president and Congress are often at odds. This is a *structural* fact of American politics, deliberately intended by the authors of the Constitution.[24]

Conflict by Constitutional Design: How Exceptional?

The Founders created a system of separation of powers and checks and balances between Congress and the president, setting "ambition to counter ambition" in order to prevent tyranny. Because virtually all constitutional powers are shared, there is a potential for conflict over virtually all aspects of government policy. We saw in Chapter 2 that our system is quite exceptional in this regard. In parliamentary systems such as Great Britain, Germany, Sweden, and Japan, there is no separation of powers between the executive and legislative branches. Recall that in such systems the prime minister and cabinet—who together make up the government, what we would call the executive branch—are themselves parliamentarians selected by the majority party or a majority coalition of parties in parliament. The executive and legislative functions thus are fused in such systems, not separated. The government—the prime minister and the cabinet—serves at the behest and will of parliament and can be dissolved by it. So checks and balances between the executive and legislative powers do not exist because the executive and the legislative are one and the same. In other presidential-congressional systems where separation of powers and checks and balances exist in theory—as in many Latin American countries, such as Argentina and Mexico—presidents have strong decree powers that allow them to bypass many of the checks from the legislative branch that exist on paper. Not so in the United States; separated powers and mutual checks are real and consequential for what government does.

Shared Powers Under the Constitution, presidents may propose legislation and can sign or veto bills passed by Congress, but both houses of Congress must pass any laws and can (and sometimes do) override presidential vetoes. Presidents can appoint ambassadors and high officials and make treaties with foreign countries, but the Senate must approve them. Presidents nominate federal judges, including U.S. Supreme Court justices, but the Senate must approve the nominations. Presidents administer the executive branch, but Congress appropriates funds for it to operate, writes the legislation that defines what it is to do, and oversees its activities.

Presidents cannot always count on the members of Congress to agree with them. The potential conflict written into the Constitution becomes real because

SIMULATION

You Are Appointing a Supreme Court Justice

divided government
Control of the executive and
the legislative branches by
different political parties.

the president and Congress often disagree about national goals, especially when there is **divided government,** that is, when the president and the majority in the House and/or the Senate belong to different parties. It is not uncommon, however, for presidents to clash with members of Congress even if they are of the same party. George W. Bush ran into trouble with co-partisans on a number of issues during his second term: the NSA's domestic surveillance program, the nomination of Harriett Miers to the Supreme Court (she later withdrew), and the port operations contract to a company owned by the government of Dubai.

Separate Elections   In other countries' parliamentary systems, the national legislatures choose the chief executives so that unified party control is ensured. But in the United States, there are separate elections for the president and the members of Congress. Moreover, our elections do not all come at the same time. In presidential election years, two-thirds of the senators do not have to run and are insulated from new political forces that may affect the choice of a president. In nonpresidential, "off" years, all members of the House and one-third of the senators face the voters, who sometimes elect a Congress with views quite different from those of the president chosen two years earlier. In 1986, for example, halfway through Reagan's second term, the Democrats recaptured control of the Senate and caused Reagan great difficulty with Supreme Court appointments and other matters. The Republicans did the same thing to Clinton in 1994 after they gained control of Congress.

Outcomes   In all these ways, our constitutional structure ensures that what the president can do is limited and influenced by Congress, which in turn reflects various political forces that may differ from those that affect the president. At its most extreme, Congress may even be controlled by the opposing party. This divided government situation always constrains what presidents can do and may sometimes lead to a condition called "gridlock" in which a president and Congress are locked in battle, neither able to make much headway. This is hardly surprising; a president is not only the chief executive of the United States but the leader of his party, so members of the opposition are not inclined to give him what he wants on the chance that it will benefit his election prospects or those of his party in Congress.

What Makes a President Successful with Congress?

A number of political scientists have studied presidents' successes and failures in getting measures that they favor enacted into law by Congress and have suggested reasons some presidents on some issues do much better than others.[25]

**Presidential Success in Polls
and Congress**

Party and Ideology   The most important factor is a simple one: When the president's party controls both houses of Congress, he is much more likely than at other times to find that he gets his way in terms of legislation, approval of his appointments, and more gentle handling of executive branch problems by congressional oversight committees.[26] The president's success under this condition of unified control does not come from the president ordering party members around. Rather, the president and the members of his party in Congress tend to be like-minded on a wide range of issues, sharing values and policy preferences and a common interest in reelection. For these reasons, members of Congress tend to go along most of the time with a president of their own party.[27]

Breakfast at Camp David

Presidential success with Congress often depends on building a consultative relationship. Here, President George W. Bush meets with Republican House and Senate leaders over breakfast at Camp David to talk about the legislative agenda for the upcoming session of Congress.

In less partisan times, when parties were not very cohesive internally, a president's success in Congress required that his party have very large majorities in the House and Senate—much like Calvin Coolidge could count on in the 1920s, Franklin Roosevelt in the 1930s, and Lyndon Johnson in the 1960s—because some members of the president's party were as likely to vote with the opposition as with members of the president's party. Liberal Republicans, for example, often supported the Democratic position, while conservative Democrats often voted with Republicans in the past. So a president needed as many representatives and senators from his party as he could get to increase his odds of success. Recently, however, Republicans have shown that unified party control in support of the president is possible even with slim majorities, so long as party members act cohesively. One reason President George W. Bush enjoyed such success in Congress in 2003 and 2004 was the fact that the majority Republicans stuck together, with very few defections in their ranks in either the House or the Senate. (The "Using the Framework" feature shows, however, that the president does not always get his way even under the most favorable circumstances.)

Foreign Policy and National Security Issues   Presidents tend to do better with Congress on foreign policy issues than on domestic ones, mainly because Americans want to appear united when dealing with other countries and because members' constituents pay less attention to events abroad than to what is going on in the United States. Political scientist Aaron Wildavsky went so far as to refer to "two presidencies," domestic and foreign, with the latter presidency much more dominant. Wildavsky found, for example, that from 1948 to 1964, 59 percent of presidents' proposals on foreign policy were passed, but only 40 percent of their domestic proposals.[28]

This difference between domestic and foreign policy success by the president has decreased since the Vietnam War, but it remains significant. Although there was significant dissent, Congress voted in January 1991, despite many misgivings, to authorize President George H. W. Bush to use force against Iraq, once again illustrating presidential primacy in foreign

Using the Framework

Private Accounts in Social Security

Why did President Bush fail to get his way with Congress on Social Security reform?

Background: President George W. Bush tried for a very long time to convince Congress to add voluntary private accounts to the Social Security system. The idea was that a portion of the payroll tax paid into Social Security would be turned over to individuals to invest on their own. He claimed that such private accounts would bring bigger returns for seniors and ease long-term fiscal problems in the federal retirement system. Though he featured private accounts in his State of the Union address on February 2, 2005, and launched a 60-day, 60-stop campaign-style national tour to push his idea, it went nowhere in Congress, though Republicans controlled both the House and Senate. How could a president with such a good track record on many important pieces of legislation fail to achieve one of his most cherished legislative objectives? We can understand what happened—or in this case, what failed to happen—by looking at how structural, political linkage, and governmental factors affected congressional behavior.

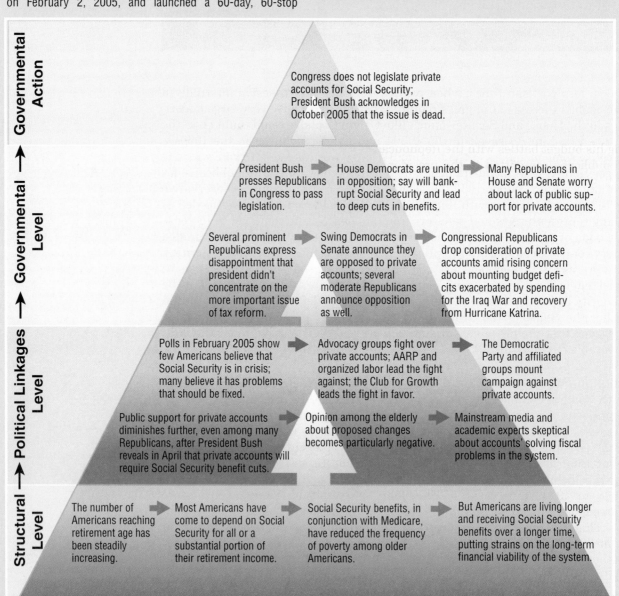

Governmental Action

Congress does not legislate private accounts for Social Security; President Bush acknowledges in October 2005 that the issue is dead.

Governmental Level

President Bush presses Republicans in Congress to pass legislation.

House Democrats are united in opposition; say will bankrupt Social Security and lead to deep cuts in benefits.

Many Republicans in House and Senate worry about lack of public support for private accounts.

Several prominent Republicans express disappointment that president didn't concentrate on the more important issue of tax reform.

Swing Democrats in Senate announce they are opposed to private accounts; several moderate Republicans announce opposition as well.

Congressional Republicans drop consideration of private accounts amid rising concern about mounting budget deficits exacerbated by spending for the Iraq War and recovery from Hurricane Katrina.

Political Linkages Level

Polls in February 2005 show few Americans believe that Social Security is in crisis; many believe it has problems that should be fixed.

Advocacy groups fight over private accounts; AARP and organized labor lead the fight against; the Club for Growth leads the fight in favor.

The Democratic Party and affiliated groups mount campaign against private accounts.

Public support for private accounts diminishes further, even among many Republicans, after President Bush reveals in April that private accounts will require Social Security benefit cuts.

Opinion among the elderly about proposed changes becomes particularly negative.

Mainstream media and academic experts skeptical about accounts' solving fiscal problems in the system.

Structural Level

The number of Americans reaching retirement age has been steadily increasing.

Most Americans have come to depend on Social Security for all or a substantial portion of their retirement income.

Social Security benefits, in conjunction with Medicare, have reduced the frequency of poverty among older Americans.

But Americans are living longer and receiving Social Security benefits over a longer time, putting strains on the long-term financial viability of the system.

affairs. Congress eventually supported Clinton's decision to send U.S. forces to Haiti, Bosnia, and Kosovo as part of multinational peacekeeping operations, despite considerable initial grumbling. The generalization about presidents having an easier time with Congress on foreign policy issues than on domestic ones does not hold, however, when foreign policy concerns trade and other global economic issues that directly affect constituents. Nor does it hold when foreign policy and military action goes wrong. In 2005 and 2006, as news of prisoner abuse and secret prisons for suspected terrorism detainees held by the United States began to trouble increasing numbers of Americans and prompt criticism from friendly governments, Congress passed laws outlawing harsh and inhumane treatment and requiring periodic reports from the administration on such prisons and prisoners.

In a national defense crisis, of course, presidents almost always get their way. After the attack on Pearl Harbor, Congress swiftly approved bills on military mobilization submitted by Franklin Roosevelt. After Nine-Eleven, Congress quickly approved the USA Patriot Act on homeland security and passed emergency military budget supplements as the president requested.

Vetoes   When the issue is a presidential veto of legislation, the president is again very likely to prevail. Vetoes have not been used often, except by certain "veto-happy" presidents, such as Franklin Roosevelt, Truman, and Ford. But when vetoes have been used, they have seldom been overridden—only 5 percent of the time for Truman and only 1.5 percent for Roosevelt. Bill Clinton did not use the veto at all during his first two years in office, when he had a Democratic majority in Congress, but then used it 11 times in 1995 alone during his budget battles with the Republican-controlled 104th Congress. Because Republicans committed to the president's agenda controlled the House from 2001 through 2006 and the Senate between 2003 and 2006, George W. Bush did not resort to the veto at all during this period.

Popularity   Most scholars and observers of Washington politics, as well as elected officials and political operatives, agree that presidential effectiveness with Congress is significantly affected by how popular a president is with the American people.[29] The reasons are not hard to fathom. Voting against proposals from a very popular president may encourage quality challengers in the next election, for example, or slow the flow of campaign funds to one's war chest, whether the president is of one's party or not. Voting with a popular president, on the other hand, can offer protective cover for a member of Congress who favors the proposal but whose constituents may not ("This is a vote for the president.").[30] When a president's popular approval collapses—as George W. Bush's did in 2006—even members of his own party are loath to follow executive leadership. Bush was unable to win his own party's approval in Congress, for example, for policies he favored on immigration and Social Security reform.

The President and the People: An Evolving Relationship

The complicated relationships among the president, the executive branch as a whole, and Congress also interact with public opinion, the political parties, and organized interests to shape the presidency. Particularly important in this interaction is the special relationship between the president and the general public, which has evolved over many years to make the presidency a more democratic office. Let's look at several aspects of this relationship.

Getting Closer to the People

The Founders thought of the president as an elite leader, relatively distant from the people, interacting with Congress often but with the people only rarely. Most nineteenth-century presidents and presidential candidates thought the same. They seldom made speeches directly to the public, for example, generally averaging no more than 10 such speeches per year.[31] In the earliest years of the American Republic, presidents were not even chosen directly by the voters but by electors chosen by state legislators or, in case no one got an electoral college majority, by the House of Representatives. The Constitution thus envisioned very indirect democratic control of the presidency.

As we have also seen, however, this system quickly evolved into one in which the people played a more direct part. The two-party system developed, with parties nominating candidates and running pledged electors and the state legislators allowing ordinary citizens to vote on the electors. Presidential candidates began to win clear-cut victories in the electoral college, taking the House of Representatives out of the process. (The 2000 election was the first since the election of 1888, of course, in which the electoral college vote winner—George W. Bush—lost the national popular vote.) Voting rights were broadened as well. Property and religious qualifications were dropped early in the nineteenth century. Later, slaves were freed and given the right to vote; still later, women, Native Americans, and 18-year-olds won the franchise.

By the beginning of the twentieth century, presidents began to speak directly to the public. Theodore Roosevelt embarked on a series of speech-making tours in order to win passage of legislation to regulate the railroads. Woodrow Wilson made appeals to the public a central part of his presidency, articulating a new theory of the office that highlighted the close connections between the president and the public. Wilson saw the desires of the public as the wellspring of democratic government: "As is the majority, so ought the government to be."[32] He argued that presidents are unique because only they are chosen by the entire nation. Presidents, he said, should help educate the citizens about government, interpret their true will, and faithfully respond to it.

Selling His Program

Presidents and their communications staffs try to control the way the news media report on presidential initiatives, whether it be through press releases, website postings, or visual presentations for television. Here, President Bush heralds his competitive initative in an appearance in 2006.

Wilson's theory of the presidency has been followed more and more fully in twentieth-century thought and practice. All presidents, especially since Franklin Roosevelt, have attempted to both shape and respond to public opinion; all, to one degree or another, have attempted to speak directly to the people about policy.[33]

More and more frequently, presidents go public, using television to bypass the print media and speak to the public directly about policy. They have held fewer news conferences with White House correspondents (where awkward questions cannot be excluded).[34] Richard Nixon pioneered prime-time television addresses, at which Ronald Reagan later excelled. Bill Clinton was more interactive with citizens, appearing on radio and TV talk shows and holding informal but televised "town hall meetings." George W. Bush likes to appear before carefully screened audiences of supporters, whether pushing for tax cuts, changes in Social Security, or support for his policies in Iraq.

Leading Public Opinion

Especially since the rise of television, modern presidents have enhanced their power to shape public opinion. Some studies have indicated that when a popular president takes a stand in favor of a particular policy, the public's support for that policy tends to rise. A determined president, delivering many speeches and messages over a period of several weeks or months, may be able to gain 5 to 10 percentage points in support of that policy in the polls, usually on issues where the public's views have not yet crystallized.[35] But there are many cases where presidents have tried but failed to move public opinion in a favorable direction, despite strong efforts to build public support for favored programs. Bill Clinton's plan for a national health insurance system actually lost support the more he campaigned for it in 1993 and 1994. George W. Bush failed to convince the public to sustain support for the occupation and transformation of Iraq.

The power to lead the public, though not as likely to happen as often believed, also implies a power to *manipulate* public opinion if a president is so inclined—that is, to deceive or mislead the public so that it will approve policies that it might oppose if it were fully informed.[36] It is useful to remember that every modern White House has had communications specialists adept at getting out the administration's views, whether through formal channels—such as press releases, the daily briefing for reporters, and materials posted on the White House website—or informal ones, including leaks to favored journalists and in-house-written but anonymous news stories and commentaries for use in newspapers, television news broadcasts, and weblogs.[37] Especially in foreign affairs, presidents can sometimes control what information the public gets, at least in the short run.

Champions of energetic presidential leadership must face the possibility that that leadership will go wrong and result in demagoguery or manipulation. The dilemma cannot be resolved. The power to do good is the power to do evil as well. But many safeguards exist, including the capacity of the public to judge character when it is choosing a president, as well as the ability of other national leaders to counteract a deceitful president. Johnson and Nixon learned this bitter lesson—the former declined to run for a second term; the latter resigned.

Responding to the Public

In any case, the relationship between presidents and the public is very much a two-way street. Besides trying to lead the people, presidents definitely tend to respond to public opinion. Electoral competition produces presidents who tend to share the public's policy preferences. Moreover, most presidents want to be reelected or to win a favorable place in history, and they know that they are unlikely to do so if they defy public opinion on many major issues. Usually, they try to anticipate what the public will want in order to win electoral reward and avoid electoral punishment.

What presidents *want* to do so often resembles what the public wants—that is one reason they were elected in the first place—that there is no conflict to observe. Only occasionally does a modern president get so badly out of touch with the public that the full power of public opinion is revealed. More often, in day-to-day politics, it simply turns out that what the president does is largely in harmony with what the general public wants. As a general matter, when polls show that public opinion has changed, presidents have tended to shift policy in the same direction.[38]

There is plenty of evidence that presidents pay attention to what the public is thinking. At least since the Kennedy administration, presidents and their staffs have carefully read the available public opinion surveys and now have full-blown polling operations of their own.[39] President Clinton employed several of the best pollsters in the business—including Stanley Greenberg (the author's brother)—to chart his electoral campaigns and legislative agenda. Although such polling is often deplored, it helps presidents choose policies that the American public favors and change or discard those that are unpopular.

This is not to say that presidents follow what the public wants all the time. President Reagan, for example, cut social programs during the 1980s despite strong evidence that the public was opposed to cuts. Bill Clinton pushed through the NAFTA treaty in 1993 despite majority public opinion against it. It seems that presidents, although sensitive to public opinion most of the time, sometimes push for unpopular policies they believe to be in the public interest, perhaps expecting that the public will eventually come around.

FIGURE 12.1 • Trends in Presidential Popularity, 1946–2006

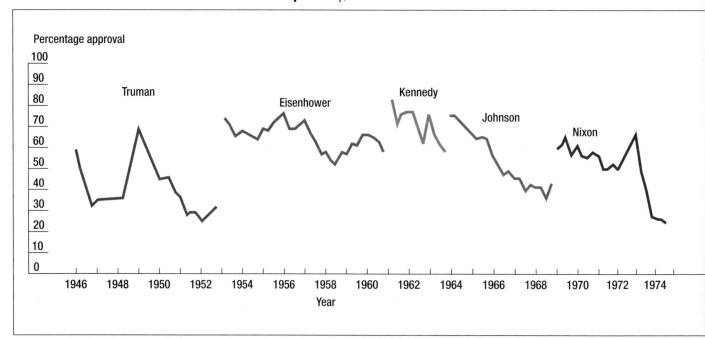

Popularity ratings of presidents rise and fall in response to political, social, and economic events.

Source: Gallup surveys (graph based on average approval for each year; 2006 is through June 2006).

Keeping in Touch with the Public

On his way to a press conference with his aides, President Bill Clinton confers with pollster Stanley Greenberg on how the public feels about a range of issues before the government. Like Clinton, all modern presidents have tried to stay in touch with public opinion using professional pollsters.

Presidential Popularity

The public also influences presidents through its judgments about presidential performance: that is, through **presidential popularity** or unpopularity. Since the 1930s, Gallup and other poll takers have regularly asked Americans whether they approve or disapprove of "the president's handling of the job." The percentage of people who approve varies from month to month and year to year, and as time passes, these varying percentages can be graphed in a sort of fever chart of how the public has thought the president was doing (see Figure 12.1).

presidential popularity

The percentage of Americans who approve a president's handling of his job.

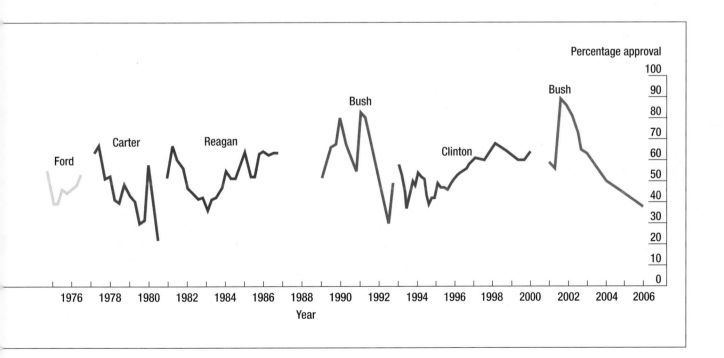

Using the Democracy Standard

Are Presidents responsive to the people?

PROPOSITION: **The presidency has evolved into a highly democratic institution that is responsive to the American people.**

AGREE   The framers did not conceive of the office in very democratic terms, but it has become the most democratic institution in the American federal system. It is, after all, the only nationally elected office. Members of the Supreme Court are not elected by the people, for example, and members of the House and Senate, although elected by the people, represent only congressional districts and states, not the entire nation. Being elected by the whole people, even though these votes are filtered through the Electoral College, it is only the president who can claim a national mandate for his programs and actions. Thus, it is only the president who can overcome the inherent stasis of the constitutional system and move the government to action in the interests of and in response to the American people as a whole.

Although presidents often claim mandates from the people, they are more likely to lead and shape public opinion than to respond to it, especially in the area of foreign and military affairs, so the institution cannot be said to be democratic. For example, Lyndon Johnson first got his way in escalating the war in Vietnam because of the inaccurate information that was released on the Gulf of Tonkin incident. President George W. Bush gained support for the invasion of Iraq because of his warnings about Saddam Hussein's weapons of mass destruction. Presidents can pretty much go their own way in foreign policy, knowing that the people will eventually follow their lead. Because elections happen only every four years, moreover, and assuming that the public has a short memory, presidents have plenty of time to follow their own agendas early in their term without regard to the public. Because presidents can only serve two terms, then, there is no compelling reason they need to pay close attention to the public during their second term.   **DISAGREE**

CONSIDER   If you believe that the United States ought to be as democratic as possible, then you will be heartened by the evidence suggesting that modern presidents are highly responsive to the wishes of the public. If you believe, as the framers did, that political decision makers ought to be insulated from direct pressures from the public, then you will be discouraged by such evidence.

• What about your own sense of presidential responsiveness to public opinion? • Thinking about recent presidents, to what extent did they seem to follow public opinion? • To what extent did they seem to ignore public opinion? • And, to what extent did they seem to be shaping—even manipulating—public opinion? • How about your own stand on important issues? • Have recent presidents acted in ways that support your preferences? • Or have they generally acted contrary to your positions on the issues?

A number of factors seem to be especially important in determining presidential popularity, including the stage in the president's term of office, the state of the economy, and foreign policy crises.[40]

Historically, except for the two Bushes–the 41st president and the 43rd—most presidents have begun their terms of office with a majority of Americans—usually 60 percent or more—approving of how they are handling their job. Most presidents have tended to lose popularity as time passes. But this loss of popularity does not represent an inexorable working of time; Eisenhower, Reagan, and Clinton actually gained popularity during their second terms. Those who lose popularity do so in response to bad news. Good news generally makes presidents more popular.[41]

One of the most serious kinds of bad news involves economic recession. When the economy goes sour, fewer Americans approve of the president. This happened to George H. W. Bush in mid-1991, as the economy faltered. On the other hand, the spectacular performance of the American economy in the mid- and late-1990s greatly benefited Bill Clinton, whose historically high approval numbers were sustained even as Congress was attempting to remove him from office.

Successful military actions tend to add to presidential popularity, as Ronald Reagan happily discovered after the U.S. invasion of Grenada in 1982. The senior Bush's approval rating soared on the successful conclusion of the war with Iraq, while the junior Bush's success in Afghanistan sustained his high popularity. Conversely, an unsuccessful war is bad news for a president, especially a limited war that drags on with high casualty rates, such as the Korean War (which detracted from Truman's already low popularity in 1950 and 1951) or the Vietnam War. Rising casualties in Iraq and news of prisoner abuse steadily eroded George W. Bush's public approval after 2003.

Rate the Presidents

Popular Support and the Transformation of the Presidency

When considering the role of the chief executive, the framers never intended that it be a democratic office. In creating the electoral college, for example, they imagined an independent body whose members (or electors) would be chosen by state legislatures rather than the people, and who would select the president from among the nation's leading citizens, free from the pressures of public opinion. Because a president chosen in such a manner would not be beholden to the people for his election or reelection, he would not be overly concerned with or unduly influenced by the views of the mass public.

In addition, when designating the powers and responsibilities of the president in Article II of the Constitution, the framers evidently envisioned an office somewhat detached from national policymaking, something like a constitutional monarchy, in which the officeholder would symbolize the nation but not do much in the way of running it. Although they gave the president important powers for conducting foreign affairs and defending the nation against civil unrest and invasion by foreign powers, they placed most national policymaking powers in the legislative branch.

As we have described at various places in this chapter, the presidency has become a much more powerful office than the framers had envisioned—and a much more popular one. Because the president is—along with his vice president—the only nationally elected official in our government, holders of the office are prone to claim the mandate of the people when governing, and the American people are prone, for their part, to see the president as the center of governance and the locus for their hopes and aspirations for the nation. Presidents have used these ties to the people as the foundation for expanding presidential powers in the course of responding to national problems and emergencies.

Summary

The American presidency began small; only a few nineteenth-century presidents (among them Jefferson, Jackson, Polk, and Lincoln) made much of a mark. In the twentieth century, however, as a result of industrialization, two world wars and the Cold War, and the Great Depression, presidential powers and resources expanded greatly. The presidency attained much of its modern shape under Franklin Roosevelt. Today, presidents play important roles in fashioning and carrying out the domestic and foreign policies of the United States and, because of the constitutional designation of the president as commander-in-chief, are responsible for the deployment and use of American troops abroad.

Presidents have varied in personality and style, with significant consequences. Despite the enormous resources and large staffs available to presidents, they are constrained in what they can do, especially concerning domestic policy. Presidents cannot always control their own executive branch. They engage in tugs-of-war with Congress, pushing their programs with varying success, depending on their party's strength in the legislature, their popularity and legislative skills, and the nature of the issue.

The presidency has become a far more democratic office than the framers envisioned. Not only do Americans play a more important role in the election of the president than the framers intended, but research shows that presidents listen to public opinion and respond to it most of the time, though they sometimes act without regard to it and even, on occasion, try to manipulate it.

mypoliscilab
Where participation leads to action!

Web Exploration
Impeachment

ISSUE: Although rarely used, Congress's ultimate weapon in its perpetual struggle with the president is its power to impeach the president and remove him from office.

SITE: Access the Jurist website at the University of Pittsburgh Law School in MyPoliSciLab at **www.mypoliscilab.com.** Go to the "Web Explorations" section for Chapter 12 and open "impeachment." Scroll down to "Impeachments in History"

and the "Clinton Controversy" and select "Proposed Articles of Impeachment." Also go to the "Nixon Watergate" section of the "Web Explorations" and read about the Nixon impeachment. Compare the articles of impeachment brought against each president.

WHAT YOU'VE LEARNED: How serious do you judge the accusations to be against each president? Did Nixon and/or Clinton, in your view, violate their oaths of office? Had you been a senator at the time, would you have voted for removal of the president from office? Why?

HINT: Pay special attention to the "obstruction of justice" charges against the two presidents, and judge their relative seriousness.

Internet Sources

The Center for the Study of the Presidency
www.thepresidency.org

Access to research on the presidency sponsored by the Center for the Study of the Presidency.

U.S. Government Information/Executive Orders
**http://usgovinfo.about.com/library/weekly/
aa121897.htm**

Information about presidential executive orders, from George Washington to George W. Bush.

Miller Center of Public Affair's "American Presidency" website
www.americanpresident.org

A site full of historical documents and description of how the role of the president has changed.

Potus
www.potus.com

Biographies and other information about American presidents.

National Archives Presidents Site
**www.archives.gov/presidential_libraries/addresses/
addresses.html**

Access to presidential addresses, libraries, and other information about the office.

Roper Center
www.lib.uconn.edu/RoperCenter/

Reports on all major presidential job performance and popularity polls.

Watergate Site
**www.washingtonpost.com/
wp-srv/national/longterm/watergate/front.htm**

Complete information on the Watergate affair: background, congressional testimony, official statements, press coverage, speeches, court rulings, biographies of the leading players, and more.

White House Home Page
www.whitehouse.gov/

Information on the first family, recent presidential addresses and orders, text from news conferences, official presidential documents, and ways to contact the White House.

Suggestions for Further Reading

Cronin, Thomas E., and Michael A. Genovese. *The Paradoxes of the American Presidency.* New York: Oxford University Press, 2004.

Examines the implications of our often conflicting and unrealistic expectations about the office of president.

Edwards III, George C., and Stephen J. Wayne. *Presidential Leadership: Politics and Policy Making.* Belmont, CA: Thomson Wadsworth, 2006.

A comprehensive textbook on the American presidency by two of the leading scholars of the office.

Howell, William G. *Power Without Persuasion: The Politics of Direct Presidential Action.* Princeton, NJ: Princeton University Press, 2003.

Rejecting the common view among political scientists that presidential power is based primarily on the president's ability to persuade, Howell suggests instead that presidents have many tools for taking unilateral action to get their way.

Morris, Edmund. *Theodore Rex.* New York: Random House, 2001.

A fascinating account of the presidency of Theodore Roosevelt and how the intersection of his personality with a particular moment in American history helped transform the presidential office.

Pfiffner, James, and Roger H. Davidson, eds. *Understanding the Presidency,* 3rd ed. New York: Longman Publishers, 2004.

A comprehensive anthology of recent scholarship on all aspects of the presidency and its place in the American political system.

Yoo, John. *The Powers of War and Peace: The Constitution and Foreign Affairs After 9/11.* Chicago: University of Chicago Press, 2005.

An argument for expansive presidential powers in the post-9/11 world by one of the architects of Bush administration policies on the treatment of detainees during war.

The Return of Big Government After 9/11

President George W. Bush came to office imbued with a conservative philosophy, committed to reducing the size, reach, and cost of the federal government. Although he often talked of "compassionate conservatism" during the 2000 election campaign—which implied to many people that the federal government would need to do more in the future—he simultaneously promised to cut taxes, reduce the size and cost of government in Washington, cut back intrusive regulations, and return more responsibilities to the states. Echoing the words of President Ronald Reagan, Bush told a group of California Republicans during the campaign that "You can't be for big government and big bureaucracy and still be for the little guy."[1]

Rather than shrinking, however, during Bush's watch the federal government grew in important ways: in the number of civilian employees (more than 100,000 added between 2000 and 2006), the number of military personnel in active service, the size of the budget, and the degree of its intrusiveness in everyday life. The main reason for this dramatic turnabout is fairly straightforward: the attack on the United States on September 11, 2001, and the particular strategies President Bush settled on to respond to them and prevent future attacks.

The president's response to Nine-Eleven included both domestic and foreign policies; each contributed to the growth of the federal government's size, cost, and reach. On the domestic protection front, President Bush supported two major changes in Congress. First, although initially reluctant to federalize this function, he strongly supported the creation of the Transportation Security Administration to take over all baggage and passenger screening at U.S. airports. This agency now employs approximately 45,000 screeners. Second, he agreed to the creation of the Department of Homeland Security, the largest reorganization of the federal government in more than half a century. The new department brought together two dozen existing federal agencies, and employs roughly 146,000 government employees, making it the third-largest Cabinet department.

The mandate of the new department is sweeping: the oversight and coordination of virtually all agencies responsible for homeland security, including border and transportation security, emergency preparedness and response, national communications and infrastructure protection, and coordination of intelligence. To meet these goals, the new department is authorized, among other things, to collect more information than in the past about people living in or traveling to the United States, impose tighter rules on transportation and shipping, and more intensely regulate the flow of people across the nation's borders. To head the new department, the president appointed Tom Ridge, the former

governor of Pennsylvania. He was followed in early 2005 by former federal judge Michael Chertoff.

President Bush also supported Attorney General John Ashcroft's aggressive use of the Department of Justice for counterterrorism, an effort carried on by Attorney General Alberto Gonzales after Ashcroft's resignation in early 2005. Bolstered by the authority granted to the Justice Department by the USA Patriot Act and several presidential directives, the Justice Department broadly expanded its use of wire-taps and checks of e-mail communications, detained suspected terrorists and terrorist supporters, registered and questioned men from Middle Eastern and Muslim countries, monitored library checkouts for suspicious material, and issued scores of federal indictments for terrorism-related activities (see Chapter 15 for more details on these activities). In the end, the Justice Department has been considerably more active than recent Justice Departments in investigating, indicting, detaining, and prosecuting citizens and noncitizens alike. Needless to say, as the Justice Department's responsibilities expanded, so did its budget and the number of its employees.

President Bush also initiated a number of policies that required a dramatic increase in the budget of the Department of Defense, a slight increase in the size of the active duty armed forces (although not big enough for critics of the administration, who believed that the United States's new commitments and responsibilities around the world required a much larger military), a very large mobilization of national guard and reserve units, and accelerated efforts to beef up the combat readiness and logistical support for U.S. military forces. The first policy was to topple the Taliban regime in Afghanistan and go after the Al Qaeda terrorist organization rooted in that country. The second policy was to mount a series of small military operations to root out terrorist organizations around the world, including actions in Yemen, the Philippines, and Somalia. The third policy was the war in Iraq, waged—in the president's view—to rid the world of one leader of the "axis of evil," countries he believed capable and willing to supply weapons of mass destruction to terrorist organizations (no such weapons were found after U.S. forces occupied Iraq).

Nine-Eleven and the war on terrorism contributed greatly, then, to the growth in the size, cost, and scope of responsibilities of the federal bureaucracy. Although somewhat surprising that this growth occurred during the presidency of an avowed small-government conservative, the general pattern is consistent with the history of growth of the executive branch of the federal government. When problems appear that seem solvable only at the national level—be they external security threats, financial crises, racial conflict, or environmental deterioration—the American public and its political leaders have repeatedly turned to the national government for solutions, for it is primarily the government in Washington that has the ability to mobilize and coordinate the vast human and material resources to tackle such big problems. (As citizens and leaders worry, for example, about a possible avian flu pandemic, they have turned to the president and the executive branch to make the necessary preparations for protecting the public.) Invariably, the result grants more power to the federal government, increases the cost of government, and expands the size of the bureaucratic machinery in the executive branch. This chapter will examine the federal bureaucracy—its history, its form, and how it works with other government institutions and actors. ■

Thinking Critically About This Chapter

This chapter is about the federal bureaucracy—the executive branch of the federal government responsible for carrying out policies fashioned by Congress, the federal courts, and the president—how it is organized, what it does, and what effects its actions have on public policies and American democracy.

 Using the Framework You will see in this chapter how the federal bureaucracy has grown over the years, primarily as a result of structural transformations in the economy and international position of the United States, but also because of the influence of political linkage level actors and institutions, including voters, public opinion, and interest groups. Primary responsibility for many of the enduring features of the federal bureaucracy will be shown to be associated with our political culture and the Constitution.

 Using the Democracy Standard You will see in this chapter that the federal bureaucracy in general, despite much speculation to the contrary, is fairly responsive to the American people, reacting in the long run to pressures brought to bear on it by the elected branches, the president, and Congress. On the other hand, bureaucrats in specific agencies, in specific circumstances, can be relatively immune from public opinion, at least in the short and medium run. You will be asked to think about what this means in terms of our democratic evaluative standard.

The American Bureaucracy: How Exceptional?

federal bureaucracy
The totality of the departments and agencies of the executive branch of the national government.

The **federal bureaucracy** in America is different from bureaucracies in other democratic nations. Structural influences such as the American political culture and the constitutional rules of the game have a great deal to do with these differences.

Hostile Political Culture

Americans generally do not trust their government and government leaders (see Chapter 4's section on political culture), nor do they have much confidence that government can accomplish most of the tasks assigned to it. They believe, on the whole, that the private sector can usually do a better job and, most of the time, want responsibilities lodged there rather than with government. At the same time, when difficulties or emergencies occur—whether economic depression, natural disasters, or terrorist attacks—they want the federal government to be ready and able to respond.

This generally hostile environment influences the American bureaucracy in several important ways that, paradoxically, make it more difficult for it to respond when needed. For one thing, our public bureaucracy is surrounded by more legal restrictions and is subject to more intense legislative oversight than bureaucracies in other countries. Because **civil servants** have so little prestige, moreover, many of the most talented people in our society do not aspire to work in government. In many other democratic countries, by way of contrast, civil service is highly respected and attracts talented people. In France, Britain, and Germany, for example, the higher **civil service** positions are filled by the top graduates of the countries' elite universities, on the basis of rigorous examinations, and are accorded enormous prestige. Not surprisingly, given the elite educations that are required for these posts and the prestige accorded to civil servants, people of decidedly upper-class and aristocratic backgrounds fill the top civil service posts in France, Great Britain, and Germany; in the United States, the civil service looks much more like the general American population in terms of family background, race, gender, and the like.[2] Finally, the highest policymaking positions in the U.S. executive branch are closed to civil servants; they are reserved for presidential political appointees. This is not true in other democracies.

Incoherent Organization

Our **bureaucracy** is an organizational hodgepodge. It does not take the standard pyramidal form, as bureaucracies elsewhere do. There are few clear lines

civil servants

Government workers employed under the merit system; not political appointees.

civil service

Federal government jobs held by civilian employees, excluding political appointees.

bureaucracy

A large, complex organization characterized by a hierarchical set of offices, each with a specific task, controlled through a clear chain of command, and where appointment and advancement of personnel is based on merit.

Elites in Training

In some democratic societies such as Japan, Great Britain, and France, the upper reaches of the civil service are staffed by people from upper-class backgrounds, schooled in the nation's most prestigious academic institutions, side-by-side with people who will run their nation's top business corporations. This photo shows students at one of these institutions, France's L'Ecole Nationale D'Administration in Strasbourg.

of control, responsibility, or accountability. Some executive branch units have no relationship at all to other agencies and departments. As one of the leading students of the federal bureaucracy once put it, other societies have "a more orderly and symmetrical, a more prudent, a more cohesive and more powerful bureaucracy," whereas we have "a more internally competitive, a more experimental, a noisier and less coherent, a less powerful bureaucracy."[3] Our bureaucracy was built piece by piece over the years in a political system without a strong central government. Bureaucracies in other democratic nations were often created at a single point in time, by powerful political leaders, such as Frederick the Great in Prussia and Napoleon in France.[4]

Comparing Bureaucracies

Divided Control

Adding to the organizational incoherence of our federal bureaucracy is the fact that it has two bosses—the president and Congress—who are constantly vying with one another for control. In addition, the federal courts keep an eye on it. This situation is created by the separation of powers and checks and balances in our Constitution, which give each branch a role in the principal activities and responsibilities of the other branches.[5] No other democratic nation has opted for this arrangement. Civil servants in parliamentary democracies are accountable to a single boss, a cabinet minister appointed by the prime minister.

How the Executive Branch Is Organized

The Constitution neither specifies the number and kinds of departments to be established nor describes other bureaucratic agencies. The framers apparently wanted to leave these questions to the wisdom of Congress and the president. Over the years, a large and complex bureaucracy was created to meet a wide range of needs. The most immediate reasons behind the transformation of the federal government's role and the growth of the bureaucracy have been political linkage sector pressures—from public opinion, voters, parties, interest groups, and social movements—on government decision makers. The more fundamental reasons have been changes in such structural level factors as the U.S. economy, the nation's population, and the role of the United States in the world, including involvement in war. In Chapter 3, we examined how these things transformed the role and responsibilities of the federal government over the course of American history. The general picture has been one of growth in the government's size and responsibilities. (However, determining just how big the government has grown depends on what measures one uses as we show in the "By the Numbers" feature.)

The executive branch is made up of several kinds of administrative units, which make the federal bureaucracy a very complicated entity:

- The most familiar are *departments,* which are headed by cabinet-level secretaries, appointed by the president and approved by the Senate. Departments are meant to carry out the most essential government functions, as suggested by the first three to be established—War, State, and Treasury. Departments vary greatly in size and internal organization. The Department of Agriculture, for example, has almost 50 offices and bureaus, whereas the Department of Housing and Urban Development has only a few operating agencies. And they range in size from the Department of Defense, with almost 700,000 employees (civilian) in 2005, to the Department of Education, with about 4,500 employees. Over the years, departments (and employees) were added as the need arose, as powerful groups demanded them, or as presidents and members of Congress wished to signal a new national need or to cement political alliances with important constituencies (see Chapter 3 for a discussion of the expansion of the federal government). The timeline in Figure 13.1 shows (see pages 390–391) when each department was established. As you saw in the chapter-opening story, the newest department, Homeland Security, was created in the wake of terrorist attacks on the United States to take on the important role of coordinating anti-terrorism activities on the homefront.

Department of Homeland Security

- Subdivisions within cabinet departments are *bureaus* and *agencies*. Departmental bureaus and agencies are not only numerous but varied in their relative autonomy. In some departments, such as the Department of Defense, bureaus and agencies are closely controlled by the department leadership, and the entire department works very much like a textbook hierarchical model. In other cases, where the bureaus or agencies have fashioned their own relationships with interest groups and powerful congressional committees, the departments are little more than holding companies for powerful bureaucratic subunits.[6] During the long reign of J. Edgar Hoover, for example, the FBI did virtually as it pleased, even though it was (and remains) a unit within the Justice Department. The Federal Emergency Management Agency (FEMA), while theoretically under the umbrella of Homeland Security, exercised considerable independence from departmental leaders until its poor performance in the wake of the Hurricane Katrina disaster forced changes.[7] Some departments have so many diverse responsibilities that central coordination is almost impossible to achieve. The Department of Homeland Security, for example, has bureaus and agencies responsible for border control, immigration and citizenship, disaster relief and recovery, transportation security, and emergency preparedness against terrorist use of nuclear, biological, and other weapons. It also houses the U.S. Secret Service, for protection of the president and other high public officials, and the U.S. Coast Guard, for protection and assistance for public and private maritime activities.

- *Independent executive agencies* report directly to the president rather than to a department- or cabinet-level secretary. They are usually created to give greater control to the president in carrying out some executive function or to highlight some particular public problem or issue that policymakers wish to address. The Environmental Protection Agency was given independent status to focus government and public attention on environmental issues and to give the federal government more flexibility in solving environmental problems.

- *Government corporations* are agencies that operate very much like private companies. They can sell stock, retain and reinvest earnings, and borrow money, for instance. They are usually created to perform some crucial economic activity that private investors are unwilling or unable to perform. The Tennessee Valley Authority, for example, was created during the Great Depression to bring electricity to most of the upper South; today it provides about 6 percent of all U.S. electrical power. The U.S. Postal Service was transformed from an executive department to a government corporation in 1970 in the hope of increasing efficiency.

Evolution of the Federal Bureaucracy

- *Quasi-governmental organizations* are hybrids of public and private organizations. They allow the federal government to be involved in a particular area of activity without directly controlling it. They are

By the Numbers

How big is the federal government? Did it really shrink in the 1980s and 1990s, as some people say?

When Bill Clinton proclaimed in 1996 that "the era of big government is over," he was sharing a vision of government espoused by his two conservative predecessors: Ronald Reagan and George H. W. Bush. The notion that the government in Washington is too big and ought to be cut down to size is a recurring theme in American political discourse. Recently, the call to "downsize" or "right size" government has taken an especially strong turn, with recent presidents committed to this vision of a "leaner" and theoretically more efficient government.

What should we make of all these calls to downsize? Just how big is government?

Why It Matters: A significant number of Americans want a smaller government that does less; a significant number of Americans want a bigger government that does more. Whichever camp you fall into, it makes sense that we have accurate measures of what is actually going on.

Calculating the Size of the Federal Government: In addition to using the size of the federal budget as a measure of the size of government—we do this in Chapter 17—it is fairly common among academics, journalists, and politicians to use the number of federal employees as a simple, straightforward measure. Using this metric, the size of the

government in Washington is not only relatively small at roughly 1.8 million employees out of a total of 138 million civilian employees in 2003, but shrinking.

Criticism of the Measure of Government Size: Critics point out that the number of federal civilian employees measures only a portion of the total number of employees who produce goods and services for the federal government. The following, they say, should be included (all figures are for 1996, based on research by Paul Light, and are the most recent on the subject; the growth after 2001 is not included):

- Employees who work in government contract-created jobs, such as employees working for defense contractors on federal projects (5.6 million).
- Employees who work in government grant-created jobs, such as employees working on federally funded road construction grants or on federally funded university research projects (2.4 million).
- Employees hired by state and local governments to meet federal mandates in areas such as child health and nutrition, safe schools, and pollution control (4.6 million).
- U.S. Postal workers, who are not counted as federal civilian employees (0.8 million) because they work for a government corporation.

distinguished from government corporations by the fact that a portion of the boards of directors are appointed by the private sector. The Corporation for Public Broadcasting fits into this category, as does the Federal Reserve Board, responsible for setting the nation's monetary policy (see Chapter 17 for more on the "Fed").

- *Independent regulatory commissions,* such as the Securities and Exchange Commission and the Consumer Product Safety Commission, are responsible for regulating sectors of the economy in which it is judged that the free market does not work properly to protect the public interest. The commissions are "independent" in the sense that they stand outside the departmental structure and are protected against direct presidential or congressional control. A commission is run by commissioners with

- Uniformed military personnel (1.4 million).

Adding these categories together gives a total of direct and indirect federal government employment of almost 17 million people in 1996, almost as many as worked in the American manufacturing sector.

How about the question of whether government is shrinking? The following graph shows what is happening. (Unfortunately, there is no information available for "mandate-created jobs" prior to 1996, so it cannot be included in the chart.)

The picture is pretty clear: Although the overall size of government is considerably larger than it first appears using only the numbers of federal civilian employees, the size of government shrank during the period 1984 to 1996. One other fact is worth noting: Most of the shrinkage of government in this period was related to decreases in the size of the defense sector, including cuts in the number of uniformed military personnel and decreases in defense contracting to the private sector. Considering only the domestic side of the equation, the total size of the federal government actually increased by about 15 percent between 1984 and 1996.

What to Watch For: Numbers that are reported by government, journalists, and academics about government may often be correct, yet incomplete. Always try to expand your search to include multiple measures of the phenomenon or institution you are trying to understand.

What Do You Think?   In formulating an opinion about the appropriate size for government, consider what responsibilities and tasks should be the responsibility of the federal government. Are these responsibilities and tasks being accomplished to your satisfaction? Are there too many people working either directly or indirectly for the federal government in terms of the responsibilities and tasks? Too few? Or just about the right number?

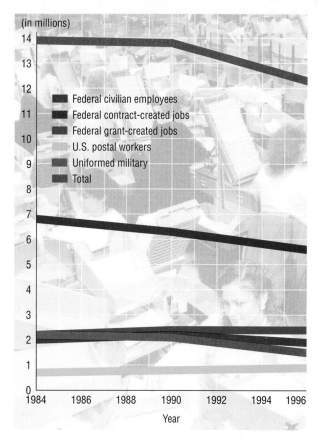

Federal Government Jobs

Source: Paul C. Light, *The True Size of Government* (Washington, D.C.: The Brookings Institution, 1999).

long, overlapping terms, and many require a balance between Republicans and Democrats.

- *Foundations* are units that are separated from the rest of government to protect them from political interference with science and the arts. Most prominent are the foundations for the Arts and for the Humanities and the National Science Foundation. Over the years, members of Congress and presidential administrations have tried on various occasions to redirect the activities of these foundations—for example, to deny grants for the support of controversial art projects or for certain areas of scientific inquiry—but such efforts, while not unimportant, have not undermined the autonomy of government foundations to the extent many critics have feared.

FIGURE 13.1 • Timeline: Creation of Executive Branch Departments and Selected Agencies, Independent Commissions, and Corporations

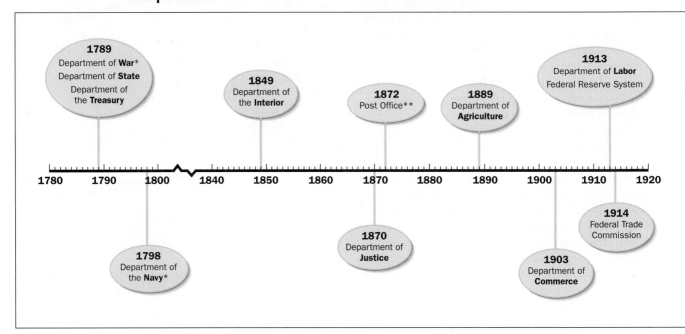

*Became part of newly formed Department of Defense in 1947.
**Transformed into U.S. Postal Service, an independent agency in 1970.
***Later split into Department of Education and Department of Health and Human Services.

What Do Bureaucrats Do?

bureaucrat

A person who works in a bureaucratic organization.

Bureaucrats engage in a wide range of activities that are relevant to the quality of democracy in the United States and affect how laws and regulations work. Let's look at the more prominent and significant of these activities.

Executing the Law

The term *executive branch* suggests the branch of the federal government that executes or carries out the law. The framers of the Constitution assumed that Congress would be the principal national policymaker and stipulated that the president and his appointees to administrative positions in the executive branch "shall take care that the laws be faithfully executed" (Article II, Section 2). For the most part, this responsibility is carried out routinely; mail is delivered, troops are trained, Social Security checks are mailed on time; and foreign intelligence is collected.

Sometimes, executing the law is not so easy, however, because it is not always clear what the law means. Often (all too often, according to some critics[8]), Congress passes laws that are vague about goals and short on procedural guidelines. It may do so because its members believe that something should be done about a particular social problem but are unclear on specifics about how to solve it or disagree among themselves. The Office of Economic Opportunity, for example, was created in 1965 as part of Lyndon Johnson's War on Poverty, with a

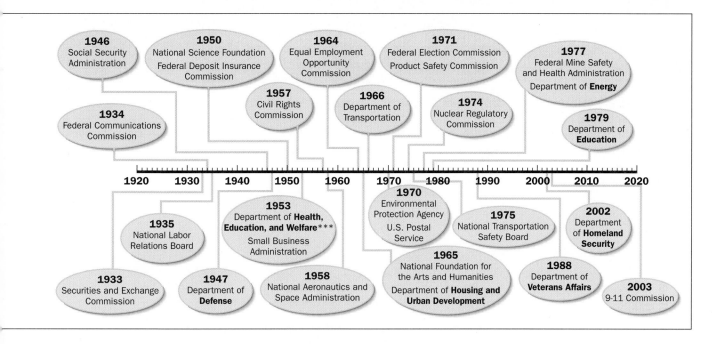

mandate to "eliminate poverty," but it received virtually no guidance about what time frame was contemplated or what specific things it ought to do. The Department of Homeland Security makes its own determinations about how to distribute its grants to urban areas for security upgrades. Vaguely written statutes and directives, then, leave a great deal of discretion to bureaucrats.

Regulating (Rule-Making)

Congress often gives bureaucratic agencies the power to write specific rules. Because of the complexity of the problems that government must face, Congress tends to create agencies and to specify the job or mission that it wants done and then charges the agency with using its expertise to do the job. Congress created the Environmental Protection Agency (EPA), for instance, and gave it a mission—to help coordinate the cleanup of the nation's air and water—but it left to the EPA the power to set the specific standards that communities and businesses must meet. The standards set by the EPA have the force of law unless they are rescinded by Congress or overruled by the courts. The Food and Drug Administration (FDA) writes rules about the introduction of new drugs that researchers and pharmaceutical companies are obliged to follow. (See the "Using the Framework" feature for more on the FDA.)

Some critics believe that Congress delegates entirely too much lawmaking to the executive branch, but it is difficult to see what alternative Congress has. It cannot micromanage every issue. And in the end, Congress retains control; it can change the rules written by bureaucrats if they drift too far from congressional intent or constituent desires.

Other critics simply believe that there are too many rules and regulations. When candidates promise to "get government off our backs," the reference is to the purported burdens of regulation. Several attempts have been

SIMULATION

You Are a Federal Administrator

Using the Framework

The FDA Rules on Genetically Engineered Food

How can unelected bureaucrats make important rulings that affect peoples lives?

Background: One of the emerging conflicts that will be playing itself out over the next few years, both in the United States and in the global economy, concerns the safety of genetically engineered food and the rules that will apply for protecting the public from its possible harmful effects. In the United States, unless Congress chooses to act in its own right, the rules will be made by the Food and Drug Administration. We can better understand why the FDA can make rules on genetically engineered foods by using a broad perspective that takes into account structural, political linkage, and governmental level factors.

Governmental Action

The FDA issued rules in 2000 specifying how genetically engineered food is to be tested for safety and wholesomeness and requiring packaging to carry a warning label for consumers.

Governmental Level

The FDA scientific staff pressed the FDA's leadership to become active in this area of rulemaking. ➡ The FDA leadership, attentive to the growing interest in rules to regulate in the area of genetically engineered food, held a series of hearings on the subject in 1999. ➡ Congress created the Food and Drug Administration, defined its overall mission, but left room for the FDA to make rules in its areas of responsibility.

The Court has allowed bureaucratic agencies to make rules within the boundaries set by Congress. ➡ No laws specifically addressing genetically engineered food have been enacted, leaving rulemaking in this area to the FDA.

Political Linkages Level

Public opinion polls show that some Americans are beginning to worry about genetically engineered food and want some action. ➡ Interest groups, for and against genetically engineered food, have pressed their positions on public officials, using both "inside" and "outside" forms of lobbying.

Structural Level

The Constitution says little about the organization and operations of the Executive Branch and leaves the details to be filled in by Congress. ➡ Scientific researchers have made dramatic breakthroughs in plant and animal genetics, causing some segments of society to call for regulations. ➡ Global agribusiness corporations are always looking for the most efficient forms of production, and genetically engineered products help them do this.

made to roll back executive branch rule-making. Under Ronald Reagan, required **cost-benefit analysis** was introduced as a way to slow the rule-making process, for example, and the result was a decline in the number of rules promulgated during his presidency. After a period of a growth in federal regulations during the presidencies of George H. W. Bush and Bill Clinton, the second President Bush managed to cap further growth, consistent with his conservative philosophy (see Figure 13.2).

cost-benefit analysis
A method of evaluating rules and regulations by weighing their potential costs against their potential benefits to society.

Adjudicating

Congress has given some executive branch agencies the power to conduct quasi-judicial proceedings in which disputes are resolved. Much as in a court of law, the decisions of an administrative law judge have the force of law, unless appealed to a higher panel. The National Labor Relations Board, for instance, adjudicates disputes between labor and management on matters concerning federal labor laws. Disputes may involve claims of unfair labor practices, for example—firing a labor organizer falls into this category—or

FIGURE 13.2 • Growth in Federal Agency Rules and Regulations

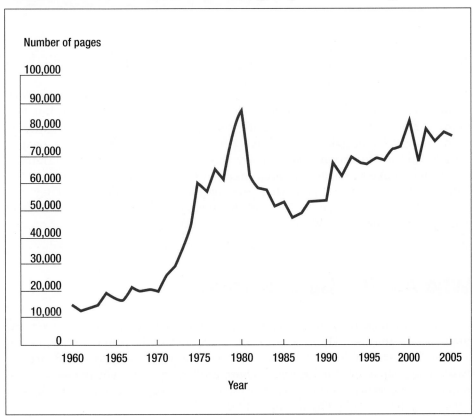

This graph shows the annual number of pages in the *Federal Register,* which is published daily and contains all new rules and changes to existing rules proposed by each and every executive branch agency. While not perfect, tracking its growth is an interesting way, widely used by scholars and journalists, to chart the course and scale of bureaucratic regulation in the United States. The graph shows the dramatic rise in regulations during the 1970s, the decline during the Reagan years, the slow increase in rule writing during the first Bush and Clinton presidencies, and a leveling out during George W. Bush's tenure in office.

Monitoring Dangerous Chemicals

Congress identifies tasks and creates agencies to complete them using their own expertise. For example, the Environmental Protection Agency was created by Congress to clean up and prevent pollution in the nation's air and water; the EPA creates and implements environmental standards without much direct congressional involvement. Here, an EPA inspector examines toxic chemical storage barrels for possible leaks.

SIMULATION

You Are the President of MEDICORP

disagreements about whether proper procedures were followed in filing for a union certification election.

It is quite clear that bureaucrats exercise a great deal of discretion. They do not simply follow a set of orders from Congress or the president, but find many opportunities to exercise their own judgment. Because bureaucrats make important decisions that have consequences for many other people, groups, and organizations, we can say that they are policymakers. And, because they make the overwhelming majority of public policy decisions in the United States,[9] we can say they are important policymakers. They are *unelected* policymakers, however, and this fact should immediately alert us to some potential problems with regard to the practice of democracy.

Who Are the Bureaucrats?

PARTICIPATION

Who Wants to Be a Bureaucrat?

Because bureaucrats exercise substantial discretion as policymakers, we want to know who they are. How representative are they of the American people? In a democracy, we would probably want to see a pretty close correspondence between the people and bureaucrats. There are several different personnel systems in the executive branch: career civil service, separate merit services in specific agencies, and political appointees.

The Merit Services

Merit services choose employees on the basis of examinations, educational credentials, and demonstrable skills. These services have evolved in size and complexity, in tandem with the federal bureaucracy, and are of three general types.

Competitive Civil Service   From the election of Andrew Jackson in 1828 until the late nineteenth century, the executive branch was staffed through what is commonly called the **spoils system.** It was generally accepted that the "spoils of victory" belonged to the winning party. Winners were expected to clear out people who were loyal to the previous administration and to replace them with their own people. Also known as **patronage,** this system of appointment caused no great alarm in the beginning because of the small and relatively unimportant role of the federal government in American society. The shortcomings of the War Department and other bureaucratic agencies during the Civil War, however, convinced many people that reform of the federal personnel system was required. Rampant corruption and favoritism in the government service during the years after the Civil War gave an additional boost to the reform effort, as did the realization that the growing role of the federal government required more skilled and less partisan personnel. The final catalyst for change was the assassination in 1881 of President James Garfield by a person who, it is said, badly wanted a government job but could not get one.

The Civil Service Act of 1883, also known as the Pendleton Act, created a bipartisan Civil Service Commission to oversee a system of appointments to certain executive branch posts on the basis of merit. Competitive examinations were to be used to determine merit. In the beginning, the competitive civil service system included only about 10 percent of federal positions. Congress gradually extended the reach of the career civil service; today, it covers about 60 percent of federal employees. In 1978, Congress abolished the Civil Service Commission and replaced it with two separate agencies, the Office of Personnel Management (OPM) and the Merit Systems Protection Board. The former administers the civil service laws, advertises positions, writes examinations, and acts as a clearinghouse for agencies that are looking for workers. The latter settles disputes concerning employee rights and obligations, hears employee grievances, and orders corrective action when needed.

The civil service system took an important hit when President Bush convinced Congress that the normal civil service rules would not apply in the newly created Department of Homeland Security. The president claimed that the new department needed greater flexibility in hiring and firing employees and assigning jobs, in establishing a system of pay-for-performance, and in limiting labor union bargaining rights over working conditions if it was to do the best job possible in defending the nation against terrorism. Critics claimed that this move was but the first step in rolling back other civil service pay and personnel procedures across the entire federal bureaucracy.[10]

Agency Merit Services   Many federal agencies require personnel with particular kinds of training and experience appropriate to their special missions. For such agencies, Congress has established separate merit systems administered by each agency itself. The Public Health Service, for instance, recruits its own doctors. The Department of State has its own examinations and procedures for recruiting foreign service officers. The National Aeronautics and Space Administration (NASA) recruits scientists and engineers without the help of the Office of Personnel Management. About 35 percent of all federal civilian employees fall under these agency-specific merit systems.

Excepted Authorities   There are other variations on how civil servants are hired.[11] Schedule A allows various departments and agencies to hire attorneys and accountants who are tested and certified by professional associations. Schedule B appointments are used to hire people with skills that are needed and in short supply, as determined by the agencies themselves, in consultation

spoils system

The practice of distributing government offices and contracts to the supporters of the winning party; also called *patronage.*

patronage

The practice of distributing government offices and contracts to the supporters of the winning party; also called the *spoils system.*

Merit System

with the OPM. Schedule C is used to hire people in what are called "policy-sensitive" positions, such as personal assistants and drivers. Other excepted authorities allow hiring for short assignments in areas of special service to the country, such as the Peace Corps.

Senior Executive Service   Created in 1978, these 9,000 or so positions were meant to be a sort of super–civil service, somewhat akin to the top civil service posts in France filled by *grand ecoles* graduates, requiring high levels of education and skills. Individuals in these positions are granted broad responsibilities and autonomy, with promotions, salary increases, and termination determined by rigorous performance reviews. The original idea was that they would serve as a corps of highly skilled people who could be deployed to various agencies as need appeared for their services, serving as a bridge between political appointees at the tops of the agencies and the career civil service. Things have not worked out that way, however; members of the senior executive service have not been entirely trusted by political appointees, and most have stayed put within their agencies throughout their careers.[12]

How Different Are Civil Servants?   Civil servants are similar to other Americans.[13] Their educational levels and regional origins are close to those of other Americans, for example, although they tend to be a little bit older and a little better paid (higher-level civil servants still seriously lag behind their counterparts in the private sector), and they have better job security. Civil servants' political beliefs and opinions also are pretty close to those of the general American public, although they tend to favor the Democrats a bit more than the general public and are slightly more liberal on social issues than the national average.[14] Women and minorities are very well represented (the latter are actually overrepresented), with women holding 44 percent of all nonpostal jobs and racial and ethnic minorities 31 percent.[15] It is worth noting, however, that women and minorities are overrepresented in the very lowest civil service grades and are underrepresented in the highest. They also are far less evident in the special-agency merit systems (such as the Foreign Service and the FBI) and in the professional categories (scientists at the National Institutes of Health; doctors in the Public Health Service).[16]

Political Appointees

The highest policymaking positions in the federal bureaucracy (e.g., department secretaries, assistants to the president, leading officials in the agencies), about 3,000 in number, enter government service not by way of competitive merit examinations but by presidential appointment. About 500 of them require Senate confirmation. These patronage positions, in theory at least, allow the president to translate his electoral mandate into public policy by permitting him to put his people in place in key policymaking jobs. Top appointees who have the confidence of the president tend to become important policymakers and public figures in their own right. Defense Secretary Donald Rumsfeld, for example, exercised broad discretion in strategic and tactical decision making in the wars in Afghanistan and Iraq until he resigned in 2006.

Most presidents use patronage not only to build support for their programs but also to firm up their political coalition by being sensitive to the needs of important party factions and interest groups. Ronald Reagan used his appointments to advance a conservative agenda for America and made conser-

Madame Secretary

Long-time confidant Condoleezza Rice helped George W. Bush shape his foreign and national defense policies, first as his National Security Adviser, then as his Secretary of State. Here, Secretary Rice meets with German Chancellor Angela Merkel in Berlin in 2005.

vative beliefs a prerequisite for high bureaucratic appointments.[17] President Clinton, by contrast, promised to make government "look more like America" and did so by appointing many women and minorities to top posts in his administration.

Presidents also reserve important appointments for people they trust and who bring expertise and experience. John F. Kennedy appointed his brother and political confidant Bobby to the post of attorney general. George W. Bush has been particularly eager and successful in filling both cabinet posts and his inner circle with people with much experience in the upper reaches of the federal government, including several who had served in his father's administration; namely, Donald Rumsfeld (secretary of defense), Colin Powell (secretary of state in his first administration), and Condoleezza Rice, his first national security adviser and second secretary of state.

Presidents also want to find places for appointments for people who played important roles in their election, whether or not they possess the requisite skills for the job.[18] The idea is to give the less skilled positions where they will be out of harm's way, in places not critical to advancing the president's agenda. In Republican administrations, political cronies are likely to end up in Housing and Urban Development, although the inexperienced Michael Brown was made head of FEMA for no apparent reason, with disastrous results for New Orleans and the Gulf Coast following Katrina. Democratic administrations tend to use the Department of Commerce and the Small Business Administration to reward their campaign workers and contributors.

Top political appointees do not last very long on the job. On average, they stay in office only 22 months; political scientist Hugh Heclo called them "birds of passage."[19] They leave for many reasons. Most are accomplished people from the private sector who see government service as only a short-term commitment. Most make financial sacrifices to become top bureaucratic officials. Many don't find the public notoriety appealing. Some find themselves the target of partisan campaigns that later prove groundless but leave them with damaged reputations. Finally, many become frustrated by how difficult it is to change and implement public policy.

Political and Governmental Influences on Bureaucratic Behavior

Rather than there being a single chain of command with clear lines of authority, the bureaucracy in general (and bureaucrats in particular) must heed several important voices, among the most important of them, the public (including interest groups), the press, the president, Congress, and the courts. Figure 13.3 gives an overview of these several influences on bureaucratic behavior.

The Public and the Press

Most Americans pay little attention to bureaucratic agencies as such. The public focuses mainly on the *content* of public policies rather than on the bureaucratic agencies or the bureaucrats who carry them out. Americans have opinions about Social Security—level of benefits, eligibility, taxes, and so on—but do not concern themselves much with the Social Security Administration per se. In general, then, the public does not directly know or think much about bureaucratic agencies.

There are exceptions to this generalization, however. Some agencies are constantly in the public eye and occasion the development of opinions. Because taxes are a constant irritant for most people, Americans tend to have opinions about the Internal Revenue Service. Foul-ups can often focus public attention on an agency, as well. Thus, the Securities and Exchange Commission came to public attention in the aftermath of the collapse of Enron and Arthur Andersen because of its lax enforcement of accounting practices. The FBI and the CIA came

FIGURE 13.3 • Popular Control of the Bureaucracy: Imperfect Popular Sovereignty

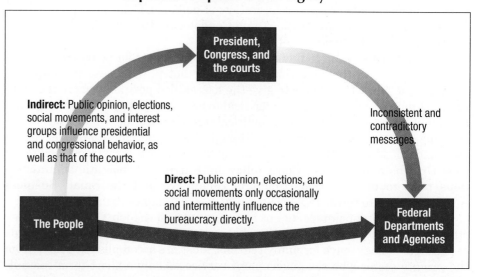

Popular control of the federal bureaucracy is complex, indirect, and only partially effective. The public does not elect government bureaucrats, and public opinion has little direct effect on their behavior. However, members of Congress and the president, all of whom are answerable to the electorate and attentive to public opinion, exercise an important influence on bureaucratic behavior. So, too, do federal judges. Because elected officials and judges often send mixed signals, however, some of the effectiveness of such controls is diminished.

For the most part, regulatory agencies go about their business without much public attention. Occasionally, however, people become sufficiently concerned about regulatory agency actions or lack of action that they find ways to express their views. Here, a demonstrator concerned about (in her view) the unsuitability of programming on network television shows her displeasure outside a meeting of the Federal Communications Commission.

under fire in 2005 for intelligence failures relating to Nine-Eleven and Iraq's purported weapons of mass destruction. Later in the same year, the Army Corps of Engineers and FEMA were strongly criticized during and after the Hurricane Katrina disaster, the first for its failed levee system in and around New Orleans, the second for its painfully slow and incomplete rescue and recovery operations.

Hurricane Katrina and New Orleans

Needless to say, bureaucratic failures are pointed out to the public by the various news media and information sources described in Chapter 6. Scandals and disasters, we learned, are particularly attractive to the news media, so information about them gets to the public in short order through a variety of outlets, from television news broadcasts to weblogs. The news media are also more likely to report goings-on in bureaucratic agencies when there is controversy—for example, the debate over the Justice Department's use of the USA Patriot Act to conduct surveillance on American citizens. The news media are less likely, perhaps, to report on the routine activities of reasonably effective agencies, whether the U.S. Passport Office in the Department of State or the National Archives.

Interest Groups

Because bureaucratic agencies make important decisions that affect many people, interest and advocacy groups pay lots of attention to what they do, and use a variety of lobbying tools (see Chapter 7) to influence these decisions. Groups lobby Congress, for example, to shape the missions of executive branch departments and agencies, as environmental organizations did to give the EPA authority over development in wetland areas. Groups also lobby bureaucratic agencies directly, as when they appear before them to offer testimony on proposed rules. (Public comment is required in many agencies before binding rules can be issued.) Although various environmental, labor, and consumer advocacy associations regularly offer formal comment on rules, this process is dominated by associations that represent business and the professions who often get their way.[20] It is hardly surprising, then, to learn that livestock producers for years were able to prevent the Department of Agriculture from imposing stringent rules for tracking cattle products as they made their way from the ranch to the dinner table, something that came to light only after "mad cow" disease was discovered in several cows in the United States in 2003 and 2005.

The President

Being the nation's chief executive, the president is the formal head of the executive branch. But as we saw in Chapter 12, the president's ability to control the executive branch is limited. Virtually every modern president has been perplexed by the discovery that he cannot assume that bureaucrats will do what he wants them to do.[21]

Richard Nixon was so frustrated by his inability to move the federal bureaucracy that he came to think of it as an alien institution filled with Democratic party enemies. His strategy was to intimidate bureaucrats or bypass them. He created the notorious "plumbers" unit in the White House to act as his personal domestic surveillance and espionage unit. Revelation of its activities was one of the factors leading the House Judiciary Committee to recommend approval of three articles of impeachment in the Watergate scandal.

Why Presidents Are Often Stymied by the Bureaucracy   The sheer size and complexity of the executive branch is one reason presidents are frustrated by it. There is so much going on, in so many agencies, involving the activity of tens of thousands of people, that simply keeping abreast of it all is no easy task. Moreover, because of civil service regulations, presidents have no say about the tenure or salary of most bureaucrats. When presidents want something to happen, they are unlikely to get instantaneous acquiescence from bureaucrats, who do not fear them as they would fear a private employer. Presidents also find that they are not the only ones trying to control the actions of bureaucrats; they must always share executive functions with Congress and sometimes with the courts. Finally, bureaucratic agencies are heavily insulated against presidential efforts to control them because of agency alliances with powerful interest groups.

Tools of Presidential Leadership   Presidents are not entirely helpless, of course. They have a number of ways to encourage bureaucratic compliance.[22] Occasionally, because of a crisis or a widely shared national commitment, decisive bureaucratic action is possible, as during Roosevelt's New Deal era, Lyndon Johnson's first years as president, Ronald Reagan's first administration, and George W. Bush's war on terrorism.

Even during ordinary times, however, the president is not helpless. First, although it is difficult to measure precisely, the president's prestige as our only nationally elected political leader makes his wishes hard to ignore. When Teddy Roosevelt called the presidency a "bully pulpit," he meant that only the president can speak for the nation, set the tone for the government, and call the American people to some great national purpose. A popular president, willing and able to play this role, is hard to resist. Bureaucrats are citizens and respond like other Americans to presidential leadership. When a president chooses to become directly involved in some bureaucratic matter—for example, with a phone call to a reluctant agency head or a comment about some bureaucratic shortcoming during a press conference—most bureaucrats respond. Research done over many years in many agencies demonstrates, in fact, that career civil servants will generally go along with the president, whether Republican or Democrat, conservative or liberal.[23]

The power of appointment is also an important tool of presidential leadership. If a president is very careful to fill the top administrative posts with people who support him and his programs, he greatly increases his ability to have his way. Although the Senate must advise on and consent to many of his choices, it rarely interferes, recognizing, perhaps, that a coherent administration requires that a president have his own people in place.

The president's power as chief budget officer of the federal government is also a formidable tool of the administration. No agency of the federal bureaucracy, for instance, can make its own budget request directly to Congress; its budget must be submitted to Congress as part of the president's overall budget for the U.S. government. The president's main budgetary instrument, the Office of Management and Budget, also has the statutory authority to block proposed legislation coming from any executive branch agency if it deems it contrary to the president's budget or program.

Congress

Congress also exercises considerable influence over the federal bureaucracy by legislating agency organization and mission, confirming presidential appointments, controlling the agency budget, holding oversight hearings, and using inspectors general.

Legislating Agency Organization and Mission The president and Congress share control over the executive branch. The congressional tools of control, in fact, are at least as formidable as those of the president.[24] Congress legislates the mission of bureaucratic agencies and the details of their organization and can change either one, and alter agency policy as well. In 1999, for example, Congress passed a bill requiring the Census Bureau to do the 2000 census by direct count, disallowing the use of statistical sampling, which the technical staff at the Bureau wanted to use. Congress also can and does create new departments, such as the Department of Homeland Security. The new department was created by Congress in 2002 after members of both parties in the House and Senate determined that the president's approach—an Office of Homeland Security in the White House Office—would not have the necessary authority and resources to coordinate the government's antiterrorism activities. After initial resistance, the president agreed and signed legislation creating the new cabinet-level department.

Confirming Presidential Appointments Top-level executive branch posts are filled through presidential nomination and Senate confirmation. Although the Senate almost always approves presidential nominations to these posts, it will sometimes use the "advice and consent" process to shape policies in bureaucratic departments and agencies. It occasionally turns down presidential nominations, as it did in the case of George H. W. Bush's nominee for the post of defense secretary, John Tower. At other times, it can simply draw out and delay the process in a bid to gain concessions from the president and the nominee on future policies. Former Senate Foreign Relations Committee Chairman Jesse Helms was a master at this, for example, gaining concessions on policies concerning Cuba, foreign aid, and funding for international population control agencies. Defeat of nominees and long delays are most likely to happen during periods of divided government[25] or when the

Viewing the Damage

Although nominally under the control of the president, most bureaucratic agencies, including the Department of Homeland Security and the Federal Emergency Management Agency (FEMA), must answer to Congress as well. Here, Homeland Security Committee chairperson Susan Collins reviews Homeland Security and FEMA preparation and response to Hurricane Katrina while on a tour of devastated areas with Governor Kathleen Blanco of Louisiana and members of her Senate committee.

parties are closely divided and highly partisan, which is the case today. Democrats managed to hold up several presidential nominations in late 2005 and early 2006 for top positions at FEMA, questioning the backgrounds and qualifications in disaster relief and recovery of several of the president's nominees, given the nation's unfortunate experience with FEMA's then-director Michael Brown during the Hurricane Katrina disaster.

Controlling the Agency Budget   Congress can also use its control over agency budgets to influence agency behavior. (One common result is seemingly irrational distribution of agency funds as you can see in the "Mapping American Politics" feature.) In theory, Congress uses the budget process to assess the performance of each agency each year, closely scrutinizing its activities before determining its next **appropriation,** the legal authority for the agency to spend money. Congress has neither the time nor the resources actually to do such a thing and usually gives each agency some small increment over what it had in the previous year.[26] Of course, if a particular agency displeases Congress, its budget may be cut; if a new set of responsibilities is given to an agency, its budget is usually increased. Sometimes these agency budget actions are taken with the full concurrence of the president; often they are not. Congress sometimes lends a sympathetic ear and increases the budgets of agencies that are not favored by the president. In the 1980s, Congress consistently gave more money than President Reagan wanted given to the EPA, the National Institutes of Health, and the National Science Foundation.

Holding Oversight Hearings   Oversight hearings are an important instrument for gathering information about the policies and performance of executive branch departments and agencies and a handy forum for conveying the views of the members of Congress to bureaucrats. There is a great deal of evidence that agency heads listen when the message is delivered clearly.[27] For example, after the Senate Finance Committee held hearings on Internal Revenue Service harassment of taxpayers in 1999, the head of the IRS responded

appropriation

Legal authority for a federal agency to spend money from the U.S. Treasury.

by apologizing to taxpayers and promising changes in his agency's behavior and policies. The SEC took a tougher line on accounting practices in public corporations after its leaders underwent hours of congressional grilling in the aftermath of the collapse of Enron and WorldCom in 2002.

Congress does not always speak with a single voice, however. Congress is a highly fragmented and decentralized institution, and its power is dispersed among scores of subcommittees. Often the activities of a particular bureaucratic agency are the province of more than a single committee or subcommittee, and the probability of receiving mixed signals from them is very high. A skilled administrator can often play these competing forces off of each other and gain a degree of autonomy for his or her agency.

Using Inspectors General   Starting in 1978, Congress has established the office of inspector general in nearly every executive branch department and agency. These inspectors general report directly to Congress and are charged with keeping an eye out for waste, fraud, and bureaucratic abuses of power. The inspectors general in the Department of Education, for example, recently reported widespread fraud in several department grant and loan programs. Inspectors general issue periodic formal reports to the relevant congressional committees and many meet with congressional staffers on a regular basis, giving Congress a good handle on what is going on in the bureaucracy.

The Courts

In our system of separation of powers and checks and balances, the federal judiciary also has a say in what bureaucratic agencies do. It does so in a less direct manner than the president and Congress, to be sure, because the judiciary must wait for cases to reach it and cannot initiate action on its own (see Chapter 14 for more details). Nevertheless, the courts affect federal agencies on a wide range of issues. For example, executive branch agencies cannot violate the constitutional protections afforded to citizens by the Bill of Rights, so citizens who feel their rights have been violated have turned to the courts for relief on a variety of issues, including illegal searches, detentions without trials, denial of access to an attorney, and harsh treatment by federal authorities. Executive branch agencies are also obligated to treat citizens equally, that is, on a nondiscriminatory basis, and turn to the courts for relief when they feel that discriminatory practices have occurred. The Small Business Administration cannot deny loans to women or racial minorities, for example, nor can federal highway funds be denied to minority contractors. The role of the courts in constraining and monitoring federal authorities on issues related to individual rights and equal protection is covered in detail in Chapters 15 and 16.

The Administrative Procedure Act of 1946, amended several times since, sets out a set of procedures on how executive branch agencies must make their decisions.[28] Basically, the Act attempts to make sure that agencies are bound by the due process guarantees in the Fifth and Fourteenth Amendments, which means, in the end, that they cannot act capriciously or arbitrarily when carrying out their missions, whether distributing benefits, overseeing federal programs, enforcing regulations, or formulating new regulatory rules. The amended Act requires, among other things, that agencies give adequate notice of their actions, solicit comments from all interested parties, and act without bias or favoritism. Citizens, advocacy groups, and interest groups pay attention to decisions and rules from agencies that directly affect them, and it is quite common for them to turn to the courts when they feel that agencies have acted improperly. Thus, the FCC's decision to allow more cross-media ownership by

Mapping American Politics

Tracking where Homeland Security dollars end up

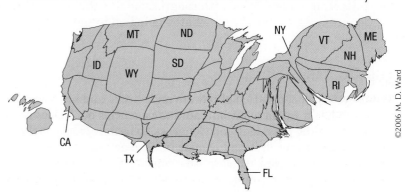

Introduction: The Department of Homeland Security (DHS) was established in 2002 to coordinate federal, state, and local efforts to defend the nation against terrorist attacks and deal with their aftermath and recovery. The establishment of the new executive branch department was triggered, of course, by the 9/11 terrorist attacks on the World Trade Center in New York City and on the Pentagon near Washington, D.C. The terrorists selected targets that were not only of great symbolic importance—the plane that crashed in Pennsylvania seems to have been headed toward a major target in the nation's capital as well—but critical to the operations of American government and economy. One would assume, then, that the Department of Homeland Security would distribute its funds to states

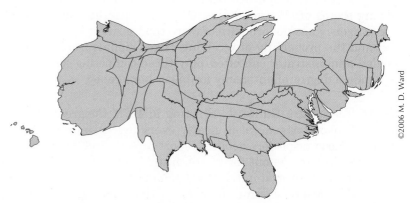

Gross State Products: States Drawn to Size of Their Economy

©2006 M. D. Ward

Homeland Security Department: Spending Per Capita by State

©2006 M. D. Ward

large corporations was challenged in federal court in 2005 by a coalition of consumer and industry groups.

Reforming the Federal Bureaucracy

VIDEO ROUNDTABLE

Bureaucratic Reform

How can we improve the federal bureaucracy? The answer depends on what a person thinks is wrong with it and what needs improving. Let's look at some possibilities.

Scaling Back Its Size

If the problem with the federal bureaucracy is perceived to be its size, there are two ways to trim government activities: slimming them down and transferring control of their activities away from the government.

and communities in some rough proportion to their vulnerability to attack and their centrality to the health and survival of the nation. In fact, as with other executive agencies, the distribution depends not just on assessments by professionals and leaders at Homeland Security, but also on the wishes of representatives and senators ever anxious to bring federal dollars to their districts and states. But just how far does DHS spending deviate from the nation's security and recovery needs?

Mapping Importance and Spending:
There is no commonly agreed upon metric to say how important different targets might be for potential terrorists, no sure way to gauge symbolic importance and economic impact. As a rough measure, we use the total size of each state's economy, shown in the cartogram on the top. This assumes that the size of a state's economy indicates its importance in the overall economic life of the nation and that serious damage to targets in the most economically important states would have the most negative effects on the entire country. The cartogram on the bottom shows states drawn in terms of per-capita DHS spending. If spending were going to where it was needed, and if the size of a state's economy is a reasonable indicator of its importance as a possible terrorist attack, the two cartograms should look very similar. It is clear that they do not. Note how much money goes to less economically important states, including Idaho, Wyoming, the Dakotas, New Hampshire, Vermont, Rhode Island, and Maine. Note, as well, how little goes to California, Texas, New York, and Florida.

What Do You Think?
How do you assess DHS spending in terms of national needs? Do you think one would see a better match between the two if we had some better measure of a state or city's symbolic and economic importance than we used here, the total size of a state's economy? Finally, if you believe there is a serious and troubling mismatch between needs and spending, how do you think we might improve matters? Should the influence of individual members of Congress on how executive departments and agencies spend their appropriated budget be diminished perhaps?

Map note: Alaska is not shown, although information about Alaska is included in calculations where relevant, and Hawaii is moved closer to the mainland.

Sources (gross state product for 2004): Bureau of Economic Analysis (**www.bea.gov/bea/regional/data.htm**); the U.S. Bureau of the Census, *Statistical Abstract of the United States, 2006,* Table 17.

Source (for HSD spending in 2004): V. de Rugy, "What Does Homeland Security Spending Buy?" (Washington, D.C.: The American Enterprise Institute, 2005).

Cutting the Fat For observers who worry that the federal bureaucracy is simply too big and costly, the preferred strategy is what might be called the "meat ax" approach. Virtually every candidate seeking office promises to "cut the fat" if elected. Bill Clinton made such a promise during the 1992 presidential campaign, and he carried through after his election. In the early weeks of his administration, he ordered that 100,000 federal jobs be eliminated within four years, that freezes be placed on the salaries of government workers, that cost-of-living pay adjustments be reduced, and that the use of government vehicles and planes be sharply restricted. To some extent this effort to cut the size and cost of the bureaucracy has worked; the number of federal employees decreased throughout the 1990s, and, while their number increased after 9/11, the increase was less than might have been expected given the wide range of new activities the government is engaged in related to homeland security. One way this has happened, of course, is that the federal government has off-loaded many of its activities to the states—the No Child Left Behind testing requirements, for example—which have been forced to hire more people.

privatization

The process of turning over certain government functions to the private sector.

The Changing Face of the Federal Bureaucracy

Privatizing   A much discussed strategy for scaling back the federal bureaucracy is to contract out some of its functions and responsibilities to the private sector.[29] This **privatization** approach is based on two beliefs:

- Private business can almost always do things better than government.
- Competitive pressure from the private sector will force government agencies to be more efficient.

Privatization has actually been happening for many years. For example, the defense department does not produce its own weapons systems but uses an elaborate contracting system to design, build, and purchase fighter planes, submarines, and missiles from private corporations. In Iraq, moreover, the defense department depends on private contractors, including companies such as Halliburton and its subsidiary Kellogg Brown and Root, to feed and house soldiers, fight oil field fires and rebuild oil pipelines, build telephone networks, maintain the military's high-tech weapons, make gasoline deliveries to Iraqi consumers, train local police, protect dignitaries, and more. The Corps of Engineers uses private contractors to build and maintain levees and clear waterways. NASA uses private contractors to build and maintain the space shuttle. Some agencies use private companies to manage their payroll systems and run their food services. While it is evident to all observers that the contracting out has been expanding dramatically, the exact number of people working on a contract basis for the federal government is hard to determine.[30]

Advocates of privatizing simply want to expand the process, turning over to private companies functions such as the postal system, the federal prisons, and air traffic control. Critics worry that privatizing government carries significant costs.[31]

- Some matters seem so central to the national security and well-being that citizens and officials are unwilling to risk that the private sector will necessarily do the job well or at all. A good recent example is the transfer of the responsibility for screening airline passengers and bag-

Private Contractors at War

Many traditional government responsibilities have been turned over to the private sector in recent years. In Iraq, private contractors do everything from running oil operations to supplying food and lodging for coalition troops and providing armed protection for coalition and Iraqi officials. These private contractors are seen in action in Iraq in 2004.

gage from private companies to a new government agency, the Transportation Security Administration.

- Private business firms might not be willing to provide services if they do not generate a profit. Delivering mail to remote locations is something that the Postal Service does, for instance, but that a private company might decide not to do.

- A private business under government contract is several steps removed from political control, and the normal instruments of democratic accountability, however imperfect, might not be as effective in controlling private business as they are in controlling government agencies. The voice of the public, expressed in public opinion polls or elections, might not be heard with much clarity by private companies, particularly if they are the only supplier of some essential service.

- Private contractors may not be bound by many of the regulations and statutes that apply to other executive branch employees. For example, the military apparently has depended a great deal on private contractors to interrogate detainees in Afghanistan, Iraq, and Guantanamo Bay, believing, perhaps, that contractors could use methods not sanctioned for use by active service military personnel.

Reinventing Government

If the problem with the federal bureaucracy is perceived to be the inefficiencies of its operations and excessive **red tape,** then the key to reform might be to reinvent governmental bureaucracy along businesslike lines. President Clinton turned over the responsibility for "reinventing government" to Vice President Al Gore at the beginning of his administration. The term "reinventing government" comes from a popular and influential book by that name written by David Osborne and Ted Gaebler,[32] although the ideas for these reforms come from advocates of what is called "the new public management."[33] "Reinventing" advocates propose transforming the federal bureaucracy not only by cutting the fat and privatizing (as discussed in the preceding section), but also by introducing business principles into the executive branch. They believe that government agencies will provide better public services if they are run like private businesses: using pay-for-performance to determine salaries, for example, or focusing more on customer needs. Most observers are not impressed so far by either the scale or effectiveness of efforts to make government more "business-like."[34]

red tape
Overbearing bureaucratic rules and procedures.

Protecting Against Bureaucratic Abuses of Power

Many people believe that the problem with a bureaucracy of the size, shape, and power of our present one is that it is potentially unresponsive to the public and a dangerous threat to individual liberty. The preferred solution has been closer control over the bureaucracy by elected political bodies and by clear legislative constraints. Accordingly, many legislative enactments have tried to keep bureaucratic activity within narrow boundaries. The Freedom of Information Act of 1966 was designed to enhance the ability of the press and private citizens to obtain information about bureaucratic policies and activities. The Ethics in Government Act of 1978 strengthened requirements of financial disclosure by officials and prohibitions against conflicts of interest. Some reformers would like to see greater protection provided for **whistle-blowers**—

whistle-blowers
People who bring official misconduct in their agencies to public attention.

Using the Democracy Standard

Does the federal bureaucracy advance or retard democracy in the United States?

PROPOSITION: The federal bureaucracy is inherently undemocratic because it is filled with unelected people who make important government decisions that affect the lives of Americans.

AGREE The bureaucracy is out of control. Although the number of federal civil servants is not much different from what it was 10 or 15 years ago, the federal government and its unelected bureaucrats seem to be intruding further and further into our lives. Career civil servants at the Environmental Protection Agency issue rules on how farmers can use wetlands and on which animal species are endangered and protected from hunters. Employees of the Bureau of Land Management make rules for grazing on public lands that ranchers must follow. And the people who work for the new Department of Homeland Security, in the name of protecting us against terrorism, are gathering information about our private lives and living habits and are making travel inconvenient and unpleasant.

DISAGREE Civil servants are merely carrying out the missions defined for them by elected public officials, namely, Congress and the president. And, since they are especially sensitive to the wishes of the public because of their desire to be effective and to be reelected, the president and members of Congress pay close attention to what civil servants in the bureaucratic agencies are doing and intervene to force changes in bureaucratic behavior when civil servants go astray and act contrary to the public interest and the wishes of the public. A further safeguard against civil servants running amok is the fact that we have a pretty representative federal bureaucracy; civil servants are pretty much like other Americans and have similar concerns, interests, and values.

CONSIDER It is certainly the case that members of the federal bureaucracy make important decisions and that they exercise considerable discretion when carrying out the missions defined by Congress and the president.

• To what extent do you believe this to be problematic for democracy in the United States today?   • Are you confident that the president and Congress practice enough oversight to ensure that bureaucrats conform to the general wishes of the public when they issue rules or make other important decisions?   • Are you reassured that civil servants who work for the federal government are enough like the rest of us that we can trust them to make rulings and decisions that fit our interests and values?   • If not, what do you think we can do to keep bureaucrats responsive and responsible to the American people?

bureaucrats who report corruption, financial mismanagement, abuses of power, or other official malfeasance.

Increasing Presidential Control

One suggestion for reform of the federal bureaucracy is to have it more closely controlled by elected representatives of the people. This suggestion follows directly from the principle of popular sovereignty, which requires that the elected representatives of the people closely control the bureaucracy. Popular sovereignty implies that administrative discretion should be narrowed as much as possible and that elected officials should communicate clear directions and unambiguous policies to bureaucratic agencies. (Note that this goal is very different from the one envisioned by the advocates of privatization and reinventing government.) Some advocates of popular sovereignty have argued that the president is the only public official who has an interest in seeing that the bureaucracy *as a whole* is well run and coherently organized. Accordingly, one suggestion for reform is to increase the powers of the president so that he can be the chief executive, in fact and not just in name.[35]

Summary

The executive branch has grown in size and responsibility. This growth is a consequence of a transformation in the conception of the proper role of government because of structural changes in the economy and society. Although *bureaucracy* is not a popular concept in the American political tradition, we have created a sizable one. The reason is partly that bureaucratic organizations have certain strengths that make them attractive for accomplishing large-scale tasks.

Bureaucrats are involved in three major kinds of activities: executing the law, regulating, and adjudicating disputes. In each of these, they exercise a great deal of discretion. Because they are unelected policymakers, democratic theory demands that we be concerned about who the bureaucrats are. In the merit services, they are very much like other Americans in terms of background and attitudes. Political appointees, however, the most important bureaucratic decision makers, are very different from their fellow citizens.

Several political and governmental actors and institutions affect bureaucratic behavior, including the president, Congress, and the courts as well as public opinion and interest groups. Bureaucratic pathologies, while real, are either exaggerated or the result of forces outside the bureaucracy itself: the constitutional rules and the struggle between the president and Congress. Proposals to reform the executive branch are related to what reformers believe is wrong with the federal bureaucracy. Those who worry most about size and inefficiency propose budget and personnel cuts, privatization, and the introduction of business principles into government. Those who want to make democracy more of a reality propose giving more control over the bureaucracy to the president and diminishing the role of interest groups.

mypoliscilab
Where participation leads to action!

Web Exploration
Who Are the Bureaucrats?

ISSUE: Although women are well represented in the federal bureaucracy, their presence in the upper-most, politically appointed, decision-making positions in the Executive Branch may be less than equitable. Or, they may be well represented in decision-making positions in some agencies and not others.

SITE: Access the Plumbook, which lists all federal politically appointed offices, in MyPoliSciLab at **www.mypoliscilab.com.** Go to the "Web Explorations" section for Chapter 13. Select "Who are the bureaucrats?" and then open "how representative?" Select three Executive Branch Depart-ments and review the names of the people who hold top offices in the Departments.

WHAT YOU'VE LEARNED: How well are women represented in the Executive Branch departments you selected? If women are better represented in some as compared with others, why do you think that is the case?

HINT: Because women professionals in American society are most heavily represented in education, welfare, the health professions, and in the law, the Departments with their principal missions in these areas are likely to have the most women available for appointment.

Internet Sources

The Federal Register
www.archives.gov/federal_register
   All rules issued by federal agencies can be found here.

Fedworld
www.fedworld.gov/
   The gateway to the federal government's numerous web-sites and Gophers; connections to virtually every federal department, bureau, commission, and foundation, as well as access to government statistics and reports.

The President's cabinet
www.whitehouse.gov/government/cabinet.html
   A site listing all cabinet members, as well as links to each department's website.

Office of Personnel Management
www.opm.gov/
   The best site to find statistics and other information about federal government employees.

Yahoo: Executive Branch
http://dir.yahoo.com/Government/U_S__Government/Executive_Branch/
   Similar to Fedworld; which one to use depends on personal taste.

Suggestions for Further Reading

Aberbach, Joel D., and Mark A. Peterson, eds., *The Executive Branch* (New York: Oxford University Press, 2005).
   A highly accessible collection of essays on diverse aspects of the federal executive branch by leading scholars and practitioners.

Goodsell, Charles T. *The Case for Bureaucracy,* 4th ed. Washington, D.C.: CQ Press, 2003.
   A well-written polemic that suggests that most criticisms of bureaucracy are not well-founded.

Kerwin, Cornelius M. *Rulemaking: How Government Agencies Write Law and Make Policy.* Washington, DC: CQ Press, 2003.
   A comprehensive treatment of rule-making by executive branch agencies.

The 9/11 Commision Report: Final Report of the National Commission on Terrorist Attacks Upon the United States. New York: W. W. Norton, 2004.
   An exhaustive study of how 9/11 happened and a set of recommendations—including reorganization of the executive branch—for better homeland defense and security.

Sobel, Robert, and David B. Sicilia. eds. *The U.S. Executive Branch: A Biographical Directory of Heads of State and Cabinet Officers.* Westport, CT: Greenwood Press, 2003.
   Biographical sketches of heads of cabinet departments from the beginning of the republic to today.

Stone, Bob, and Tom Peters. *Confessions of a Civil Servant: Lessons in Changing American Government and the Military.* Lanham, MD: Rowman & Littlefield Publishers, 2003.
   An inside look at the accomplishments and failures of the reinventing government movement.

Washington Monthly.
   Washington's leading journal of "bureaucracy bashing"; filled with outrageous and (sometimes) illuminating stories.

CHAPTER **14**

The Courts

The Battle for the Courts

Tension filled the hearing room as Samuel Alito, President Bush's nominee for a position on the U.S. Supreme Court, began testifying before the Senate Judiciary Committee on January 9, 2006. Knowing that federal courts were deciding cases having to do with the most contentious issues of the day—including presidential powers in times of war, affirmative action, gay rights, the relationship between church and state, the role of the federal government in relationship to the states, and more—Republican and Democratic partisans and conservative and liberal advocacy groups were mobilized to contest Alito's nomination. Lurking in the background was the issue of the judicial filibuster. Republicans believed the filibuster (see Chapter 11 for more on the filibuster and cloture) could not be properly used when the Senate was exercising its constitutional duty to "advice and consent" on judicial nominations. Most Democrats believed it was the only way to prevent the accession of judges to the federal bench who would threaten hard-won rights and protections, particularly a woman's right to terminate her pregnancy. Would the Democrats use it to block Alito? If they did, would Republicans ban the practice, using their majority in the Senate to redefine the chamber's rules?

Partisan tensions over the judicial filibuster had been festering for years. Things first came to a head on November 14, 2003, when, after 40 hours of continuous debate, Republicans fell 7 votes short of the 60 votes needed to end Democratic filibusters blocking Senate votes on several very conservative Bush federal judicial nominees: Carolyn Kuhl to the Ninth Circuit Court of Appeals, Priscilla Owen for the Fifth Circuit, and Janice Rogers Brown to the federal appeals court for the District of Columbia circuit. Republicans were furious. Senate Judiciary Chairman Orrin Hatch (R–UT) fumed, "This is petty politics . . . cheap politics . . . and can lead to more partisan division in the Senate." Senate Majority Leader Bill Frist (R–TN) called this use of the filibuster "intolerable." President Bush issued a statement after the vote that "the Democrats' obstructionist tactics are shameful, unfair, and . . . all too common."[1]

Democrats were not impressed, pointing out that Republicans had blocked many Clinton nominees during the 1990s but had not needed the filibuster because, as the majority, they could stop nominations in committee, never allowing them to reach the floor of the Senate. As chair of the Judiciary Committee during the Clinton years, the very same Orrin Hatch who insisted in 2003 that every nominee was entitled to an "up or down" vote refused to hold hearings for several Clinton nominees, delayed hearings for others for up to 18 months (causing several to withdraw), and engineered negative votes on his committee for still others.

The issue was revived when President Bush renominated Priscilla Owen in early 2005. When Democrats announced they would again use the filibuster to block the nomination, Majority Leader Frist warned that he would ask the presiding officer of the Senate—Vice President Richard Cheney—to disallow it. If Democrats appealed, Republicans would approve the ruling by a simple majority vote—a filibuster cannot be used on issues related to rulings by the presiding officer—which they could easily muster. Democrats warned that if this so-called nuclear option was imposed by Republicans, they would tie up the business of the Senate for the foreseeable future, something they could easily do, given that much of the Senate's business is done through unanimous consent (requiring roll call votes on all routine business would slow action in the Senate to a crawl). Partisans on both sides in the Senate and the country were itching for a fight on this issue because they believed the stakes had never been higher. A train-wreck loomed.

Into the fray stepped the so-called gang of 14, a group of Republican and Democratic moderates who worked out a compromise in May 2005. Wielding enormous power because their 14 votes would be decisive on any vote related to this issue, whether on a cloture vote to end a filibuster or a vote on rulings from the presiding officer, they agreed that the judicial filibuster could be used only in undefined "extraordinary circumstances." Under the agreement, the Senate confirmed the long-delayed nominations of Priscilla Owen, Janice Rogers Brown, and another nominee, but took no action on two other nominees who presumably fit the "extraordinary circumstances" requirement that would allow Democrats to use the filibuster.

Most observers believed that the agreement was just a temporary truce that might break down at any time, especially when it came to nominations to the Supreme Court. The agreement held when John Roberts was nominated for the post of Chief Justice after the death of Chief Justice William Rehnquist in late 2005, perhaps because he was a conservative jurist replacing the conservative Rehnquist (the widespread respect and support he enjoyed in Congress and the legal community, and his winning personality, didn't hurt his cause either). Conservative judge Samuel Alito was another matter because President Bush nominated him to replace the retiring Sandra Day O'Connor, a relatively moderate voice and swing vote on the Court who played an important role in protecting abortion rights and affirming the use, under certain circumstances, of affirmative action in higher education admissions. In the end, however, the Democrats were unable to mount much of a challenge to Alito, and calls for a filibuster by a few Democratic senators (including John Kerry) failed to gain traction. His nomination was confirmed on January 31, 2006.

In the system of separated powers and federalism created by the framers, the judicial branch, most especially the Supreme Court, assesses, in cases that come before it, the legitimacy of actions taken by the other two branches and by the states in light of the Constitution. Although the Supreme Court does not legislate or regulate on its own, its decisions strongly influence the overall shape of federal and state policies in a number of important areas. As such, the Supreme Court is a key national policymaker. The fact that an unelected Supreme Court makes important decisions about public policies raises fundamental questions about the degree to which popular sovereignty and majority rule prevail in our system. ∎

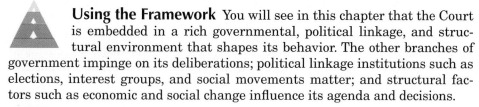

Thinking Critically About This Chapter

Using the Framework You will see in this chapter that the Court is embedded in a rich governmental, political linkage, and structural environment that shapes its behavior. The other branches of government impinge on its deliberations; political linkage institutions such as elections, interest groups, and social movements matter; and structural factors such as economic and social change influence its agenda and decisions.

Using the Democracy Standard You will see in this chapter that an unelected Court makes important decisions about public policies, raising fundamental questions about the degree to which popular sovereignty and majority rule prevail in our system. You will also see that the Court often turns its attention to cases that involve issues of political equality and liberty, so essential to the existence of a healthy representative democracy.

The Structural Context of Court Behavior

The judicial Power of the United States shall be vested in one supreme Court, and in such inferior Courts as the Congress may from time to time ordain and establish.
—U.S. CONSTITUTION, ARTICLE III, SECTION 1

We are under a Constitution, but the Constitution is what the judges say it is, and the judiciary is the safeguard of our liberty and our property under the Constitution.
—CHIEF JUSTICE CHARLES EVANS HUGHES (1907)

Constitutional Powers

The Constitution speaks only briefly about the judicial branch and doesn't provide much guidance about what it is supposed to do or how it is supposed to go about its job. The document says little about the powers of the judicial branch in relationship to the other two federal branches or about its responsibilities in the area of constitutional interpretation. Article III is considerably shorter than Articles I and II, which focus on Congress and the president. It creates a federal judicial branch, it creates the office of "chief justice of the United States," it states that judges shall serve life terms, it specifies the categories of cases the Court may or must hear (to be explained later), and it grants Congress the power to create additional federal courts as needed. Article III of the Constitution is virtually devoid of detail.

The Power of Judicial Review

judicial review

The power of the Supreme Court to declare actions of the other branches and levels of government unconstitutional.

Extremely interesting is the Constitution's silence about **judicial review,** the power of the Supreme Court to declare state and federal laws and actions null and void when they conflict with the Constitution. Debate has raged for many years over the question of whether the framers intended that the Court should have this power.[2]

The framers surely believed that the Constitution ought to prevail when other laws were in conflict with it. But did they expect the Supreme Court to make the decisions in this matter? Jefferson and Madison thought that Congress and the president were capable of rendering their own judgments about the constitutionality of their actions. Alexander Hamilton, however, believed that the power of judicial review was inherent in the notion of the separation of powers and was essential to balanced government. As he put it in *The Federalist,* No. 78 (see the Appendix), the very purpose of constitutions is to place limitations on the powers of government, and it is only the Court that can ensure such limits in the United States. The legislative branch, in particular, is unlikely to restrain itself without the helping hand of the judiciary.

Advocates of Judicial Review

Although the Constitution is silent on the issue of judicial review, most of the Founders probably agreed with Alexander Hamilton (left), who argued that the Supreme Court's power to interpret the Constitution and declare state and federal laws and actions unconstitutional is inherent in the notion of the separation of powers. However, it was not until the Supreme Court's 1803 *Marbury* v. *Madison* decision that Chief Justice John Marshall (right) affirmed the Court's power of judicial review.

Hamilton's view was undoubtedly the prevailing one among the framers. They were firm believers, for instance, in the idea that there was a "higher law" to which governments and nations must conform. Their enthusiasm for written constitutions was based on their belief that governments must be limited in what they could do in the service of some higher or more fundamental law, such as that pertaining to individual rights. The attitudes of the time, then, strongly supported the idea that judges, conversant with the legal tradition and free from popular pressures, were best able to decide when statutory and administrative law were in conflict with fundamental law.[3]

Marbury v. *Madison*   Chief Justice John Marshall boldly claimed the power of judicial review for the U.S. Supreme Court in the case of *Marbury* v. *Madison* in 1803.[4] The case began with a flurry of judicial appointments by President John Adams in the final days of his presidency, after his Federalist party had suffered a resounding defeat in the election of 1800. The apparent aim of these so-called midnight appointments was to establish the federal courts as an outpost of Federalist party power (federal judges are appointed for life) in the midst of Jeffersonian control of the presidency and the Congress.

Judicial Review

William Marbury was one of the midnight appointments, but he was less lucky than most. His commission was signed and sealed, but it had not been delivered to him before the new administration took office. Jefferson, knowing what Adams and the Federalists were up to, ordered Secretary of State James Madison not to deliver the commission. Marbury sued Madison, claiming that the secretary of state was obligated to deliver the commission, and he asked the Supreme Court to issue a **writ of mandamus** to force Madison to do so.

writ of mandamus
A court order that forces an official to act.

Marshall faced a quandary. If the Court decided in favor of Marbury, Madison would almost surely refuse to obey, opening the Court to ridicule for its weakness. The fact that Marshall was a prominent Federalist political figure might even provoke the Jeffersonians to take more extreme measures against the Court. But if the Court ruled in favor of Madison, it would suggest that an executive official could defy without penalty the clear provisions of the law.

Marshall's solution was worthy of Solomon. The Court ruled that William Marbury was entitled to his commission and that James Madison had broken the law in failing to deliver it. By this ruling, the Court rebuked Madison. However, the Court said it could not compel Madison to comply with the law because the section of the Judiciary Act of 1789 that granted the Court the power to issue writs of mandamus was unconstitutional. It was unconstitutional, he said, because it expanded the **original jurisdiction** of the Supreme Court as defined in Article III, which could not be done except by constitutional amendment.

original jurisdiction
The authority of a court to be the first to hear a particular kind of case.

On the surface, the decision was an act of great modesty. It suggested that the Court could not force the action of an executive branch official. It suggested that Congress had erred in the Judiciary Act of 1789 by trying to give the Supreme Court too much power. Beneath the surface, however, was a less modest act: the claim that judicial review was the province of the judicial branch alone. In Marshall's words in his written opinion, "It is emphatically the province and duty of the judicial department to say what the law is." In making this claim, he was following closely Hamilton's argument in *The Federalist,* No. 78.

Until quite recently, the Supreme Court used the power of judicial review with great restraint, perhaps recognizing that its regular use would invite retaliation by the other branches. Judicial review of a congressional act was not exercised again until 54 years after *Marbury* and was used to declare acts of Congress unconstitutional only about 150 times since then until the late 1990s. However, the Court has been much less constrained about overruling the laws of the states and localities; it has done so more than 1,000 times.

In the past few years, the Court has been much more inclined to review and overturn congressional actions, especially in cases involving federalism and the powers of Congress under the commerce clause (see Chapter 3), trimming back the power of the federal government relative to the states. Indeed, it has been invalidating congressional actions at a rate double that of the Warren Court of the 1960s, considered by many to be the most "activist" Court since the early 1930s.[5]

Comparing Judiciaries

How Exceptional?   For a very long time, judicial review was largely an American phenomenon, but this has changed dramatically over the past several decades. A written constitution to which legislative laws are subordinate and an independent judiciary empowered to rule on the validity of such laws relative to the constitution, particularly in the area of individual rights, were slow in coming in many other democracies, but have now been widely adopted.[6] For example, the defeated Axis powers in World War II each adopted written constitutions and constitutional courts with the power of judicial review, Japan in 1946, Italy in 1948 and 1956, and Germany in 1949. France established a constitutional council in 1958. New democratic constitutions incorporating judicial review were adopted in Greece, Spain, and Portugal in the 1970s; in several Latin American countries in the late 1980s and early 1990s (Nicaragua, Brazil, Columbia, Mexico, and Peru); in South Africa in 1995; as well as in several former communist countries in eastern and central Europe (including the Czech Republic, Hungary, and Slovakia). Sweden formally incorporated judicial review in 1979. Canada passed a Charter of Rights and Freedoms in 1982, with provisions for the establishment of judicial review to protect them. New Zealand did the same in 1990.[7] And this is but the tip of the iceberg. In fact, as one legal scholar has put it, "What was once a unique feature of the American governmental system has become an aspect of constitutional governance almost everywhere in the democratic world."[8]

This is not to say that judicial review is done exactly the same way as in the United States. In most places, especially in Europe, the power of judicial review is lodged in a single constitutional court. It and only it is empowered to render judgments about the constitutionality of laws. In the United States—and in several other countries sharing a common law tradition, such as Ireland, India, New Zealand, Australia, and Canada—all courts are empowered to render such judgments. The power of judicial review is widely distributed here; any state or federal court can rule on the constitutionality of state and federal laws.[9] Ultimately, of course, in the United States, it is the Supreme Court that takes final responsibility for judging the constitutionality of laws, if it so chooses.

Judicial Review and Democracy   Judicial review involves the right of a body shielded from direct accountability to the people—federal judges are appointed, not elected, and serve for life (barring impeachment for unseemly, unethical, or illegal behavior)—to set aside the actions of government bodies whose members are directly elected. Some observers believe that this is the only way to protect the rights of political and racial minorities, to check the potential excesses of the other two government branches and the states, and to preserve the rules of the democratic process. Others believe that judicial review has no place in a democratic society. One prominent democratic theorist has described the issue this way:

> *But the authority of a high court to declare unconstitutional legislation that has been properly enacted by the coordinate constitutional bodies— . . . in our system, the Congress and the president—is far more controversial . . . The contradiction*

*remains between imbuing an unelected body—or in the American case, five out of
nine justices on the Supreme Court—with the power to make policy decisions that
affect the lives and welfare of millions of Americans. How, if at all, can judicial review be justified in a democratic order?*[10]

We come back to this issue later in this chapter.

The U.S. Court System: Organization and Jurisdiction

Our country has one judicial system for the national government (the federal
courts) and another in each of the states. In each state, courts adjudicate cases
on the basis of the state's own constitution, statutes, and administrative
rules.[11] In total, the great bulk of laws, legal disputes, and court decisions
(roughly 99 percent) are located in the states. Most important political and
constitutional issues, however, eventually reach the federal courts. In this
chapter, our focus is on these federal courts. In the following sections, we'll look
at the source of the federal court's power and the organization of its system.

Constitutional Provisions

The only court specifically mentioned in the Constitution's Article III is the
U.S. Supreme Court. The framers left to Congress the tasks of designing the
details of the Supreme Court and establishing "such inferior courts as the
Congress may from time to time ordain and establish." Beginning with the
Judiciary Act of 1789, Congress has periodically reorganized the federal court
system. The end result is a three-tiered pyramidal system (see Figure 14.1),
with a handful of off-shoots. At the bottom are 94 U.S. federal district courts,
with at least one district in each state. In the middle are 13 courts of appeal.
At the top of the pyramid is the Supreme Court. These courts are called
constitutional courts because they were created by Congress under Article
III, which discusses the judicial branch. Congress has also created a number of
courts to adjudicate cases in highly specialized areas of concern, such as taxes,
patents, and maritime law. These were established under Article I, which specifies the duties and powers of Congress, and are called **legislative courts.**

    Article III does not offer many guidelines for the federal court system, but
the few requirements that are stated are very important. The Constitution requires, for instance, that federal judges serve "during good behavior," which
means, in practice, until they retire or die in office, as Chief Justice William
Rehnquist did in 2005 at the age of 81. Because impeachment by Congress is the
only way to remove federal judges, the decision about who will be a judge is an
important one. Article III also states that Congress cannot reduce the salaries of
judges once they are in office. This provision was designed to maintain the independence of the judiciary by protecting it from legislative intimidation.

    Article III also specifies the subject matter of cases that are solely the
province of the federal courts:

- The Constitution (e.g., disputes involving the First Amendment or the commerce clause).
- Federal statutes and treaties (including disputes involving ambassadors and other diplomats).

constitutional courts
Federal courts created by
Congress under the authority
of Article III of the
Constitution.

legislative courts
Highly specialized federal
courts created by Congress
under the authority of Article
I of the Constitution.

FIGURE 14.1 • The U.S. Federal Court System

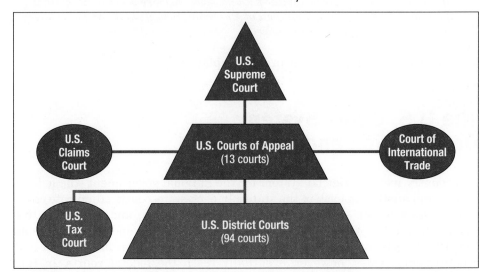

The federal court system is a three-tiered pyramidal system, with the Supreme Court at the top. Below it are 13 federal courts of appeal and 94 district courts, with at least one district in each state. Additional courts exist to hear cases in highly specialized areas, such as taxes, international trade, and financial claims against the U.S. government.

Source: Administrative Office of the U.S. Courts.

- Admiralty and maritime issues (disputes involving shipping and commerce on the high seas).
- Controversies in which the U.S. government is a party.
- Disputes between the states.
- Disputes between a state and a citizen of another state.
- Disputes between a state (or citizen of a state) and foreign states or citizens.

Popular Election of Judges

grand juries

Groups of citizens who decide whether there is sufficient evidence to bring an indictment against accused persons.

petit (trial) juries

Juries that hear evidence and sit in judgment on charges brought in civil or criminal cases.

Federal District Courts

Most cases in the federal court system are first heard in one of the 94 district courts. District courts are courts of original jurisdiction, that is, courts where cases are first heard; they do not hear appeals from other courts. They are also trial courts; some use juries—either **grand juries,** which bring indictments, or **petit (trial) juries,** which decide cases—and in some, cases are heard only by a judge.

Most of the business of the federal courts takes place at this level. In 2005, about 323,000 cases were filed; roughly 78 percent of them were civil cases, and 22 percent were criminal cases. Civil cases include everything from antitrust cases brought by the federal government (as in the Justice Department's successful action against Microsoft in 2000) to commercial and contract disputes between citizens (or businesses) of two or more states. Criminal cases include violations of federal criminal laws, such as bank robbery, interstate drug trafficking, and kidnapping.

Most civil and criminal cases are concluded at this level. In a relatively small number of disputes, however, one of the parties to the case may feel that a mistake has been made in trial procedure or in the law that was brought to bear in the trial, or one of the parties may feel that a legal or constitutional issue is at stake that was not taken into account at the trial stage or was wrongly interpreted. In such cases, one of the parties may appeal to a higher court—a Court of Appeals.

Case Overload

U.S. Courts of Appeal

The United States is divided into 12 geographic **circuit courts** (see the map in Figure 14.2) that hear appeals from federal district courts. The one for Washington, D.C., not only hears appeals from the federal district court there but is charged with hearing cases arising from rule-making by federal agencies. There is also a 13th circuit court, called the U.S. Court of Appeals for the Federal Circuit, located in Washington, D.C., that hears cases from all over the nation on patents and government contracts. In 2005, more than 68,000 cases were filed in the federal appeals courts, although only about 8,600 reached the formal hearing stage (most of these end in negotiated settlements without going to trial). Cases cannot originate in these courts but must come to them from district courts. Because they exist only to hear appeals, they are referred to as **appellate courts.** New factual evidence cannot be introduced before

circuit courts

The 12 geographical jurisdictions and one special court that hear appeals from the federal district courts.

appellate courts

Courts that hear cases on appeal from other courts.

FIGURE 14.2 • U.S. Federal Circuit Courts

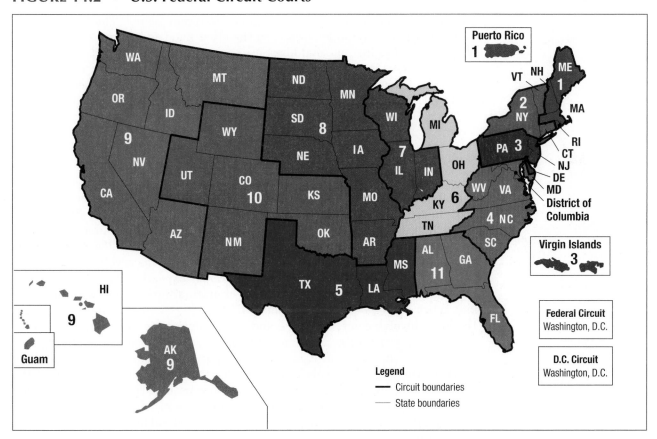

The United States is divided into 12 geographic regions (including the D.C. Circuit Court), each housing a federal circuit court of appeals. One additional circuit court of appeal, the Federal Circuit Court, is located in Washington, D.C.

Source: Administrative Office of the U.S. Courts.

briefs

Documents setting out the arguments in legal cases, prepared by attorneys and presented to courts.

opinion

The explanation of the majority's reasoning that accompanies a court decision.

precedents

Rulings by courts that guide judicial reasoning in subsequent cases.

stare decisis

The legal doctrine that says precedent should guide judicial decision making.

You Are a Young Lawyer

such courts; no witnesses are called or cross-examined. At the appellate level, lawyers do not examine witnesses or introduce new evidence; instead, they submit **briefs,** which set out the legal issues at stake. Judges usually convene as panels of three (on important cases, there are more—sometimes seven members) to hear oral arguments from the lawyers on each side of the case and to cross-examine them on points of law. Weeks or even months later, after considerable study, writing, and discussion among the judges, the panel issues a ruling. In important cases, the ruling is usually accompanied by an **opinion** that sets forth the majority side's reasoning for the decision.

Once appellate decisions are published, they become **precedents** that guide the decisions of other judges in the same circuit. Although judges do not slavishly follow precedents, they tend to move away from them only when necessary and only in very small steps. This doctrine of closely following precedents as the basis for legal reasoning is known as **stare decisis.**

It is important to know that the decisions of the 12 geographic circuit courts determine the meaning of laws for the people who live in the states covered by each circuit. They have become more important as they have ruled on more cases—more than 60,000 in 2005—without review by the Supreme Court, which decides fewer than 100 cases each year.

Sometimes particular circuits play a particularly important role in changing constitutional interpretation. Currently, the Fourth Circuit Court, based in Richmond, Virginia, has been a leader in the trend toward reasserting the power of the states in the federal system, a view that the Supreme Court, the highest court in the land, has found to be congenial in recent years.[12] The Ninth Circuit Court, which sits in San Francisco, on the other hand, is known to be especially liberal on civil rights and civil liberties cases. Although it has had several of its rulings reversed in recent years by the more conservative U.S. Supreme Court, the Ninth Circuit's rulings, nevertheless, cover over 56 million people in the western United States, roughly 20 percent of the American population.

The Supreme Court

Congress decides how many judges sit on the Supreme Court. The first Court had six members. The Federalists, however, reduced the number to five in 1801 to prevent newly elected president Thomas Jefferson from filling a vacancy. In 1869, Congress set the number at its present nine members (eight associate justices and the chief justice). It has remained this way ever since, weathering the failed effort by President Franklin Roosevelt to "pack" the Court with more politically congenial justices by expanding its size to 15.

The Supreme Court is both a court of original jurisdiction and an appellate court. That is, some cases must first be heard in the Supreme Court. Disputes involving ambassadors and other diplomatic personnel, or one or more states, start in the Supreme Court rather than in some other court.

The Supreme Court also, in its most important role, serves as an appellate court for the federal appeals courts and for the highest courts of each of the states. Cases in which a state or federal law has been declared unconstitutional can be heard by the Supreme Court, as can cases in which the highest state court has denied a claim that a state law violates federal law or the Constitution (see Figure 14.3).

Congress determines much of the appellate jurisdiction of the Court. In 1869, following the Civil War, a Congress controlled by radical Republicans removed the Court's power to review cases falling under the Reconstruction program for the South. Responding to a plea from Chief Justice Rehnquist to

FIGURE 14.3 • How Cases Get to the Supreme Court

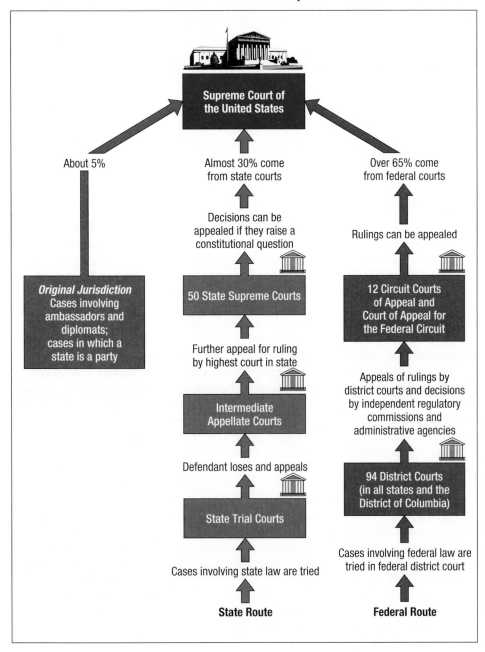

The vast majority of cases that reach the Supreme Court come to it from the federal court system. Most of the others come on appeal from the highest state courts. A handful originate in the Supreme Court itself.

Source: Adapted from David O'Brien, *Storm Center: The Supreme Court in American Politics,* 7th ed. (New York: Norton, 2005).

lighten the Court's caseload, Congress dropped the requirement that the Supreme Court *must* hear cases in which a state court declares a federal statute unconstitutional. It can choose, but is not obligated, to do so.

Because it is the highest appellate court in the federal court system, the decisions and opinions of the Supreme Court become the main precedents on federal and constitutional questions for courts at all other levels of jurisdiction. It is for this reason that Supreme Court decisions receive so much attention from other political actors, the media, and the public.

Appointment to the Federal Bench

Selecting Federal Judges

Because federal judges are appointed for life and make important decisions, it matters in a democratic society who they are and how they get to the bench. If they are isolated from popular influence, democracy is at risk. If they are too responsive, they ignore their judicial role.

Who Are the Appointees?

The Constitution offers no advice on what qualifications a federal judge should have. By custom and tradition, appointees to the federal bench must be lawyers, but until quite recently, they did not have to have judicial experience. Indeed, almost one-half of all Supreme Court justices during the twentieth century had no prior experience as judges. Among the ranks of the "inexperienced" are some of the most prominent and influential justices in our history, including John Marshall, Louis Brandeis, Harlan Stone, Charles Evans Hughes, Felix Frankfurter, and Earl Warren.[13] Former Chief Justice William Rehnquist also came to the bench without judicial experience.

As the federal courts—particularly the circuit courts and the Supreme Court—have become more important in determining American public policies, and as partisan and ideological conflicts have become more pronounced in the country, having judicial experience has become more important in the nomination and confirmation process. Because the stakes seem so high to many people—whether *Roe* v. *Wade* (1973) will be overturned, let us say, or what constitutional limits can be placed on the president during a war—they want to know the judicial philosophy and general outlook of the people who will become Supreme Court and appeals court judges. One way to know this is to examine the rulings and written opinions of nominees who have been judges. The new, though unwritten, rules about prior judicial experience became apparent in the firestorm that erupted within Republican and conservative circles after President Bush nominated Harriet Miers in late 2005 to fill the O'Connor vacancy. Many people who were normally Bush supporters were upset by the fact that Miers was an unknown in terms of constitutional law, having never served as a judge. They could not be sure they could trust her on the central issues of the day. They were much more comfortable with Bush nominees John Roberts and Samuel Alito, who had established extensive conservative records on the federal bench.

Chief Justice John Roberts

Like most lawyers, federal judges tend to come from privileged backgrounds. Moreover, federal judges, and particularly Supreme Court justices, come from the most elite parts of the legal profession. For the most part, they have been white male Protestants from upper-income or upper-middle-class backgrounds, who attended the most selective and expensive undergraduate and graduate institutions.[14] The current Supreme Court is much more diverse in terms of religion—two current members, Ginsburg and Breyer, are Jewish and five, Scalia, Thomas, Kennedy, Roberts, and Alito, are Catholic—although not as diverse in terms of race and gender. On the current Supreme Court, there is one African American (Clarence Thomas) and one woman (Ruth Bader Ginsburg). The racial and gender representativeness of judicial appointees at the circuit and district court levels is better, and improving rapidly, but it is still a long way from reflecting the composition of the legal profession, much less the American people as a whole.

The Appointment Process

Federal judges assume office after they have been nominated by the president and confirmed by the Senate. Presidents pay special attention to judicial appointments, because they are a way for presidents to affect public policy long after they leave office.

Presidents take many things into consideration besides merit. No president wants a nomination rejected by the Senate, for example, so he and his advisers consult with key senators, especially those on the Judiciary Committee, before nominations are forwarded. Nominations for district court judgeships are subject to what is called **senatorial courtesy,** the right of the senior senator from the president's party in the state where the district court is located to approve the nominee. Senatorial courtesy does not operate, however, in appointments to the circuit courts, whose jurisdictions span more than a single state, or to the Supreme Court, whose jurisdiction is the entire nation. Nevertheless, presidents must be extremely attentive to the views of key senators.

On occasion, despite presidential efforts to placate it, the Senate has refused to give its consent. Of the 143 nominees for the Supreme Court since the founding of the Republic, the Senate has refused to approve 28 of them, although only 5 after 1900. Rejection of nominees has usually happened when the president was weak or when the other party was in control of the Senate. The defeat of Ronald Reagan's nominee, Robert Bork, was the product of deep ideological differences between a Republican president and a Democratic-controlled Senate. There have also been several near defeats. G. H. W. Bush's nominee, Clarence Thomas, was confirmed by a margin of only four votes after questions were raised about his legal qualifications and about sexual harassment charges brought by law professor Anita Hill.

As the chapter-opening story shows, Senate confirmation of judicial nominees, especially for the federal appeals court and the Supreme Court, have become very contentious. Battles over presidential judicial nominees raged during the Clinton presidency and during the Bush presidency, culminating in the Democrats' use of the filibuster on several judicial nominations, Republican threats to use the nuclear option to end judicial filibusters, and the fight in the Senate and among advocacy groups over the nomination of Samuel Alito in early 2006.

Although presidents must be concerned about the merit of their candidates and their acceptability to the Senate, they also try by their appointments to make their mark on the future. Presidents go about this in different ways.

For the most part, presidents are interested in nominating judges who share their ideological and program commitments. John Adams nominated John Marshall and a number of other judges to protect Federalist principles during the ascendancy of the Jeffersonians. Franklin Roosevelt tried to fill the courts with judges who favored the New Deal. Ronald Reagan favored conservatives who were committed to rolling back affirmative action and other civil rights claims, abortion rights, protections for criminal defendants, and broad claims of **standing** in environmental cases. Both George H. W. Bush and his son George W. Bush carried on the Reagan tradition of nominating conservative judges to the federal courts.

Bill Clinton, eager to avoid a bitter ideological fight in the Senate, where he was trying to forge a bipartisan coalition to support the North American

---

senatorial courtesy

The tradition that judicial nominations for federal district court appointments be cleared by the senior senator of the president's party from the relevant state.

standing

Authority to bring legal action because one is directly affected by the issues at hand.

Judge Roberts Makes the Rounds

Like most recent nominees for the Supreme Court, John Roberts had extensive federal judicial experience before his elevation to the high court in 2005. Here then–Senate Majority Leader Bill Frist (R–TN) welcomes him to the Senate for consultations prior to Roberts' confirmation hearings.

Free Trade Agreement and a national crime bill, nominated two judges with reputations as moderates for the High Court—Ruth Bader Ginsburg and Stephen Breyer—in the first years of his administration. The Ginsburg nomination was also indicative of Clinton's apparent commitment to diversifying the federal court system. More than one-half of federal court nominees during his presidency were women and minorities.

Presidents are often disappointed in how their nominees behave once they reach the Court. Dwight Eisenhower was dumbfounded when his friend and nominee, Earl Warren, led the Court in a liberal direction by transforming constitutional law regarding civil rights and criminal procedure. Richard Nixon was stunned when Chief Justice Warren Burger voted with a unanimous Court to override the president's claim of **executive privilege** and forced him to give up the documents that would seal his fate in the Watergate affair. He and other Court observers were also surprised by the odyssey of his nominee Harry Blackmun, who, despite a conservative judicial record before joining the Court, had become one of its most liberal justices by the time of his retirement in 1994. The elder George Bush no doubt was surprised when his nominee, David Souter, refused to vote for the overturn of *Roe* in *Planned Parenthood* v. *Casey* (1992). Despite these dramatic examples, the past political and ideological positions of federal court nominees are a fairly reliable guide to their later behavior on the bench.[15]

executive privilege
A presidential claim that certain communications with subordinates may be withheld from Congress and the courts.

The Supreme Court in Action

The Supreme Court meets from the first Monday in October until late June or early July, depending on the press of business. Let's see how it goes about deciding cases.[16]

Norms of Operation

A set of unwritten but clearly understood rules of behavior—called *norms*—shapes how the Court does things. One norm is *secrecy,* which keeps the conflicts between justices out of the public eye and elevates the stature of the Court as an institution. Justices do not grant interviews very often. Reporters are not allowed to stalk the corridors for a story. Law clerks are expected to keep all memos, draft opinions, and conversations with the justices they work for confidential. Justices are not commonly seen on the frantic Washington, D.C., cocktail party circuit. When meeting in conference to argue and decide cases, the justices meet alone, without secretaries or clerks. Breaches of secrecy have occurred only occasionally. As a result, we know less about the inner workings of the Court than about any other branch of government.

Seniority is another important norm. Seniority determines the assignment of office space, the seating arrangements in open court (the most junior are at the ends), and the order of speaking in conference (the chief justice, then the most senior, and so on down the line). Speaking first allows the senior members to set the tone for discussion.

Finally, the justices are expected to stick closely to *precedent* when they decide cases. When the Court departs from a precedent, it is essentially overruling its own past actions, exercising judicial review of itself. In most cases, departures from precedent come in only very small steps over many years. For example, several decisions chipped away at the **separate but equal doctrine** of *Plessy* v. *Ferguson* (1896) before it was decisively reversed in *Brown* v. *Board of Education of Topeka* (1954).

Some legal theorists, both conservative and liberal, have begun to talk of superprecedents, or super–*stare decisis* landmark rulings, that have been reaffirmed by the Court over the course of many years and whose reasoning has become part of the fabric of American law, making them especially difficult to reverse. Senator Arlen Specter, chair of the Senate Judicial Committee, asked Chief Justice nominee John Roberts during his confirmation hearings in 2005 where he stood on this issue. While Roberts agreed that such fundamental rulings exist, he was unwilling to say whether *Roe* v. *Wade* (1973) was one of them, leaving observers unsure how he would eventually stand on the abortion issue. Other legal thinkers and jurists, however, are not impressed with this idea of superprecedents; cases that are wrongly decided, they say, should not be protected against reversal, no matter how many times they have been affirmed in the past by the Court.[17]

separate but equal doctrine

The principle articulated in *Plessy* v. *Ferguson* (1896) that laws prescribing *separate* public facilities and services for nonwhite Americans are permissible if the facilities and services are *equal* to those provided for whites.

Controlling the Agenda

The Court has a number of screening mechanisms to control what cases it will hear so that it can focus on cases that involve important federal or constitutional questions.[18]

Several technical rules help keep the numbers down. Cases must be *real* and *adverse;* that is, they must involve a real dispute between two parties. The disputants in a case must have *standing;* that is, they must have a real and direct interest in the issues that are raised. The Court sometimes changes the definition of *standing* to make access for **plaintiffs** easier or more difficult. The Warren Court (1956–1969) favored an expansive definition; the Rehnquist Court (1986–2005), a restricted one. Cases must also be *ripe;* that is, all other avenues of appeal must have been exhausted, and the injury must already have taken place (the Court will not accept hypothetical cases). Appeals must

plaintiff

One who brings suit in a court.

in forma pauperis

Describing a process by which indigents may file a suit with the Supreme Court free of charge.

writ of certiorari

An announcement that the Supreme Court will hear a case on appeal from a lower court; its issuance requires the vote of four of the nine justices.

rule of four

An *unwritten* practice that requires at least four justices of the Supreme Court to agree that a case warrants review by the Court before it will hear the case.

amicus curiae

Latin for "a friend of the court"; describes a brief in which individuals not party to a suit may have their views heard.

also be filed within a specified time limit, the paperwork must be correct and complete, and a filing fee of $200 must be paid. The fee may be waived if a petitioner is poor and files an affidavit **in forma pauperis** ("in the manner of a pauper"). One of the most famous cases in American history, *Gideon* v. *Wainwright* (1963), which established the right of all defendants to have lawyers in criminal cases, was submitted in forma pauperis on a few pieces of lined paper by a Florida State Penitentiary inmate named Clarence Earl Gideon. The Rehnquist Court was less friendly to indigent petitions than previous Courts and took several steps to cut down what the Chief Justice called "frivolous" suits by "jailhouse lawyers."

The most powerful tool that the Court has for controlling its own agenda is the power to grant or not to grant a **writ of certiorari.** A grant of "cert" is a decision of the Court that an appellate case raises an important federal or constitutional issue that it is prepared to consider.[19] Under the **rule of four,** petitions are granted cert if at least four justices vote in favor. There are several reasons a petition may not command four votes, even if the case involves important constitutional issues: It may involve a particularly controversial issue that the Court would like to avoid, or the Court may not yet have developed a solid majority and may wish to avoid a split decision. Few petitions survive all of these hurdles. Of the almost 8,000 cases that are filed in each session, the Court grants cert for less than 100 (this number varies a bit year to year). In cases denied cert, the decision of the federal appeals court or the highest state court stands.

Deciding how freely to grant cert is a tricky business for the Court. Granted too often, it threatens to inundate the Court with cases. Granted too sparingly, it leaves in place the decisions of 13 different federal appeals courts on substantial federal and constitutional questions, as well as the decisions of state supreme courts, which often leads to inconsistent constitutional interpretations across the country. Because the Court now typically hears oral arguments for only about 80 cases a year—compared with roughly 150 in the 1970s and 1980s—more influence than ever is being exercised by the 13 federal circuit courts. For many important cases, the federal circuit courts have become the judicial forum of last resort.

Deciding Cases

Almost all cases granted cert are scheduled for oral argument (about 20 are decided without oral argument). Lawyers on each side are alerted to the key issues that the justices wish to consider, and new briefs are invited. Briefs are also submitted on most important cases by other parties who may be interested in the disputes. These "friend of the court," or **amicus curiae,** briefs may be submitted by individuals, interest groups, or some agency of the federal government, including the Justice Department or even the president.

Each case is argued for one hour, with 30 minutes given to each side in the dispute. Oral argument is not so much a presentation of arguments, however, as it is a give-and-take between the lawyers and the justices and among the justices themselves. When the federal government is a party to the case, the solicitor general or one of his or her deputies presents the oral arguments. Some justices—Antonin Scalia, for instance—are famous for their close grilling of lawyers. Ruth Bader Ginsburg often asks that lawyers skip abstract legal fine points and put the issues in terms of their effect on ordinary people.

After hearing oral arguments and reading the briefs in the case, the justices meet in conference to reach a decision. The custom is for each justice to state his or her position, starting with the chief justice and moving through the ranks in order of seniority. Chief justices of great stature and intellect, such as John Marshall and Charles Evans Hughes, used the opportunity to speak first as a way of structuring the case and of swaying votes. Those who did not command much respect from the other justices (e.g., Warren Burger) were less able to shape the decision process.

Political scientists have tried to determine what factors are most important in predicting how the justices will vote.[20] One approach looks at the ideological predilections of the justices and manages to explain a great deal about their voting behavior that way.[21] Another approach focuses on the diaries and personal papers of retired justices and shows that a great deal of negotiating and "horse trading" goes on, with justices trading votes on different cases and joining opinions they do not like so that they can have a hand in modifying them.[22] Another approach tries to link voting behavior to social background, types of previous judicial experience, and the political environment of family upbringing.[23] Still another believes that justices vote strategically, departing from their own policy preferences when they believe a particular decision will enhance the influence of the Court in the federal government and American society.[24] None of these approaches has been totally successful because much of what the Court does in conference is secret and can be only imperfectly reconstructed.

About all that one can say is that the justices tend to form relatively stable voting blocs over time.[25] For example, during the 1990s and early 2000s, the Rehnquist Court, on many cases involving federalism and the rights of criminal defendants, divided into two blocs, a five-member conservative one (Justices Scalia, Thomas, Rehnquist, Kennedy, and O'Connor) and a four-member liberal one (Justices Stevens, Breyer, Ginsburg, and Souter).

The vote in conference is not final, however. As Justice John Harlan once explained, "The books on voting are never closed until the decision finally comes down."[26] The justices have an opportunity to change their votes in response to the opinion supporting the majority decision. An opinion is a statement of the

TIMELINE

The Chief Justice of the Supreme Court

Oral Argument

Each side in a case before the Supreme Court is generally granted 30 minutes to argue its position. Most of the 30 minutes is taken up, however, by questions the justices pose to the lead attorneys. Photography is not allowed in the Supreme Court building, so the media depend on artists' renderings of oral argument before the Court, as in this session in 2004 concerning the president's ability to hold American citizens as enemy combatants.

opinion of the Court

The majority opinion that accompanies a Supreme Court decision.

concurring opinion

The opinion of one or more judges who vote with the majority on a case but wish to set out different reasons for their decision.

dissenting opinion

The opinion of the judge or judges who are in the minority on a particular case before the Supreme Court.

SIMULATION

You Are a Clerk to Supreme Court Justice Judith Gray

legal reasoning that supports the decision of the Court. There are three kinds of opinions. The **opinion of the Court** is the written opinion of the majority. A **concurring opinion** is the opinion of a justice who supports the majority decision but has different legal reasons for doing so. A **dissenting opinion** presents the reasoning of the minority. Dissenting opinions sometimes become the basis for future Court majorities.

If he or she votes with the majority in conference, the chief justice assigns the writing of the opinion. He or she can assign it to any justice in the majority, often to him- or herself. Some jurists and scholars believe that this power to assign is the most important role of the chief justice, and it is guarded jealously. Warren Burger was so eager to play a role in opinion assignments that, much to the distress of his colleagues, he would often delay announcing his vote so that he could place himself with the majority. Justice William Douglas angrily charged that Burger voted with the majority in *Roe* only so that he could assign the case to a justice who was closer to the minority view.[27] If the chief justice's opinion is with the minority, the opinion is assigned by the most senior member of the majority.

The justice assigned to write the opinion does not work in isolation. He or she is assisted not only by law clerks but also by other justices, who helpfully provide memoranda suggesting wording and reasoning. Justices also consider the legal reasoning presented to the Court in amicus curiae briefs.[28] Most opinions go through numerous revisions and are subject to a considerable amount of bargaining among the justices.

Demanding Judicial Support for Affirmative Action

Most major policy and political disputes in the United States eventually make their way to the Supreme Court, so demonstrations at the Supreme Court are common. Here, demonstrators in 2003 demand that the Court affirm the principle of affirmative action in a set of cases involving the University of Michigan's undergraduate and law school admissions policies. In a landmark decision issued that same year, the Court ruled that affirmative action in higher education admissions was permissible, but only if race was not used in a mechanical manner in the admissions decision, but as one among many factors in a holistic consideration of the applicant's file.

Only when an opinion is completed is a final vote taken in conference. The justices are free to change their earlier votes: They may join the majority if they are now persuaded by its reasoning, or a concurring opinion may be so compelling that the majority may decide to replace the original majority opinion with it.

The Supreme Court as a National Policymaker

People often say that the Court should settle disputes and not make policy. But because the disputes it settles involve contentious public issues (such as abortion rights and affirmative action) and fundamental questions about the meaning of our constitutional rules (such as the extent of presidential powers in wartime), the Court cannot help but make public policy.

Judges and Politics

It seems likely that the Court recognizes and cultivates its policymaking role. In the main, the Court does not see itself as a court of last resort, simply righting routine errors in the lower courts or settling minor private disputes. It sees itself, instead, as the "highest judicial tribunal for settling policy conflicts" and constitutional issues and chooses its cases accordingly.[29] The fact that decisions are not simply handed down but come with an opinion attached for the purpose of guiding the actions of other courts, litigants, and public officials is another demonstration that the Court recognizes its policymaking role. Let's look at judicial policymaking—which takes the form of the Court's constitutional interpretations as revealed in its decisions—and see how it has evolved over time.

Structural Change and Constitutional Interpretation

Scholars generally identify three periods in the history of constitutional interpretation by the Supreme Court in the United States, one stretching from the early 1800s to the Civil War, the next from the end of the Civil War to the Great Depression, and the last from World War II to the present.[30] We would add a fourth, covering the years from 1991 to the present (see Figure 14.4). We will see how changes in constitutional law have been influenced by structural factors, particularly economic change.

Period 1: National Power and Property Rights
We saw in Chapter 4 that the United States experienced significant growth and change during the first 75 years of its existence. This growth was accompanied by changes in constitutional law. Chief Justice John Marshall, who presided over the Supreme Court from 1801 to 1835, was the key judicial figure during this important period in our history.[31] Marshall was a follower of the doctrines of Alexander Hamilton, who believed that American greatness depended on a strong national government, a partnership between government and business in which industry and commerce were encouraged, and a national market economy free of the regulatory restraints of state and local governments. In a string of opinions that have shaped the fundamentals of American constitutional law—especially important are *Fletcher* v. *Peck* (1810), *Dartmouth College* v. *Woodward* (1819), *McCulloch* v. *Maryland* (1819), and *Gibbons* v. *Ogden* (1824), discussed elsewhere in this text—Marshall interpreted the Constitution to mean "maximum protection to property rights and maximum support for the idea of nationalism."[32]

FIGURE 14.4 ● **Timeline: Chief Justices of The Supreme Court
1789–2007**

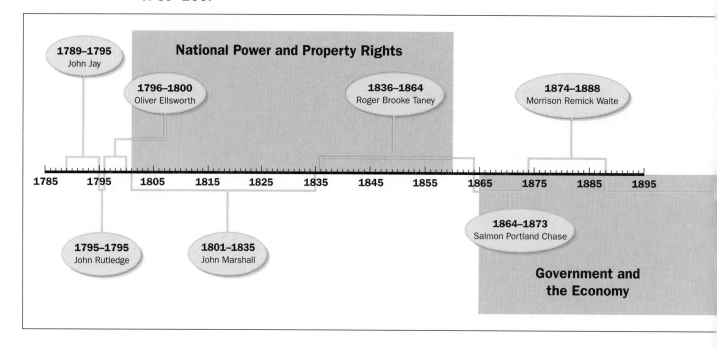

Period 2: Government and the Economy The Civil War and the Industrial Revolution triggered the development of a mass-production industrial economy dominated by the business corporation. Determining the role to be played by government in such an economy was a central theme of American political life in the late nineteenth and early twentieth centuries. The courts were involved deeply in this rethinking. At the beginning of this period, the Supreme Court took the position that the corporation was to be protected against regulation by both the state and federal governments; by the end, it was more sympathetic to the desire of the people and the political branches for the expansion of government regulation and management of the economy during the crisis of the Great Depression.

The main protection for the corporation against this regulation came from the Fourteenth Amendment. This amendment was passed in the wake of the Civil War to guarantee the citizenship rights of freed slaves. The operative phrase was from Section 1: "nor shall any state deprive any person of life, liberty, or property without due process of law"—on its face, hardly relevant to the world of the corporation. But in one of the great ironies of American history, the Court took up this expanded federal power over the states to protect rights and translated it to mean that corporations (considered "persons" under the law) and other forms of business should have increased protection from state regulation.

This reading of **laissez-faire** economic theory into constitutional law made the Supreme Court the principal ally of business in the late nineteenth and early twentieth centuries.[33] Keeping the government out of the economy in general, the Court overturned efforts by both the state and federal governments to provide welfare for the poor; to regulate manufacturing monopolies; to initiate an income tax; to regulate interstate railroad rates; to provide scholarships to students; to regulate wages, hours, and working conditions; and to protect consumers against unsafe or unhealthy products.

laissez-faire

The political-economic doctrine that holds that government ought not interfere with the operations of the free market.

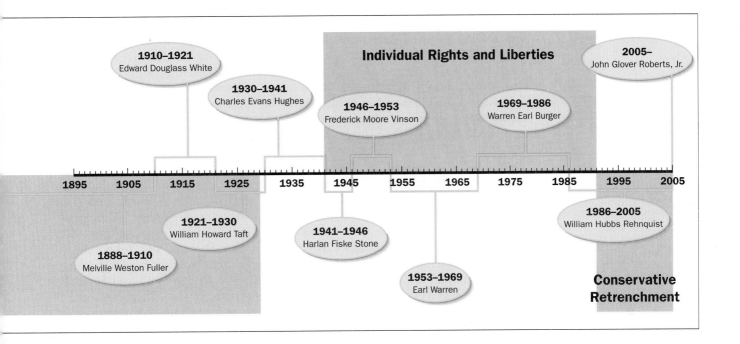

The Court also supported the use of judicial injunctions to halt strikes by labor unions.

The business–Supreme Court alliance lasted until the Great Depression. Roosevelt's New Deal reflected a new national consensus on the need for a greatly expanded federal government with a new set of responsibilities: to manage the economy; to provide a safety net for the poor, the unemployed, and the elderly; to protect workers' rights to form labor unions; and to regulate business in the public interest. The Supreme Court, however, filled with justices born in the nineteenth century and committed to the unshakable link between the Constitution and laissez-faire economic doctrine, was opposed to the national consensus and in 1935 and 1936 declared unconstitutional several laws that were part of the foundation of the New Deal. In an extraordinary turn of events, however, the Supreme Court reversed itself in 1937, finding the Social Security Act, the Labor Relations Act, and state minimum wage laws acceptable. It is not entirely clear why the so-called switch-in-time-that-saved-nine occurred, but surely Roosevelt's landslide reelection in 1936, the heightening of public hostility toward the Court, and Roosevelt's plan to "pack the Court" all played a role. Whatever the reason, the Court abandoned its effort to prevent the government from playing a central role in the management of the economy and the regulation of business, and it came to defer to the political linkage branches of government on such issues by the end of the 1930s. In doing so, it brought another constitutional era to a close.

Period 3: Individual Rights and Liberties   Three fundamental issues of American constitutional law—the relationship of the states to the nation, the nature and extent of private property rights, and the role of government in the management of the economy—were essentially settled by the time World War II broke out. From then until the mid- to late 1980s, the Court turned its main attention to the relationship between the individual and government.[34]

Most of this story is told in Chapters 15 and 16 on civil rights and civil liberties. For now, it is sufficient to point out that the Court, especially during the tenure of Chief Justice Earl Warren, decided cases that expanded protections for free expression and association, religious expression, fair trials, and civil rights for minorities. In another series of cases dealing with the apportionment of electoral districts, the Court declared for political equality, based on the principle of "one person, one vote." In many of its landmark decisions, the Court applied the Bill of Rights to the states. Although the Court's record was not without blemishes during and after World War II—see the "Using the Framework" feature on *Korematsu* v. *United States* (1944)—it made significant strides in expanding the realm of individual freedom.

Period 4: Conservative Retrenchment A new conservative majority emerged on the Supreme Court in the early 1990s, fashioned by the judicial nominations of Presidents Ronald Reagan and George H. W. Bush, and the patient efforts of conservative Chief Justice William Rehnquist. This new majority—with O'Connor and Kennedy usually, but not always, joining the three most consistently conservative justices, Scalia, Thomas, and Rehnquist—moved the Court to reconsider many of its long-established doctrines in the areas of rights and liberties (to be discussed further in Chapters 15 and 16) and the relationship between the national and state governments. Its reconsideration of federalism in favor of "states rights" was particularly noteworthy (see Chapter 3).

In a string of landmark cases, the Court curtailed national authority in favor of the states, overturning several federal statutes that were based, in its view, on an overly expansive reading by Congress of its powers under the interstate commerce clause. In 1995, for example, the Court overturned a federal statute that banned guns from the area immediately around public schools, saying that the statute were unrelated to interstate commerce. Using the same reasoning, it overturned legislation requiring background checks for gun buyers. In 2000 the Court used such reasoning to strike down parts of the Violence Against Women Act and the federal law barring age discrimination in employment.

The conservative majority on the Court also became fond of the notion of "state sovereign immunity," an idea they drew from the Eleventh Amendment, which suggests that the states enjoy a broad area of immunity from national government interference. Using this doctrine, the Court ruled in 2001 that states are immune from suits brought by state employees under the Americans with Disabilities Act. Dissenters on the Court expressed concern that this would spell trouble for many federal civil rights laws. The Court ruled in another case in 2002 that states are shielded from rulings by federal agencies acting on complaints from private individuals, a determination that may decrease the powers of agencies such as the Environmental Protection Agency.

Between 2002 and 2005, however, the Supreme Court became more moderate in a significant number of areas—especially on affirmative action, gay rights, the right of individuals to sue states for violations of federal civil rights laws, and the rights of terrorism detainees (see the discussion of these issues in Chapters 15 and 16)—with the now-retired Sandra Day O'Connor casting the decisive swing vote in many cases. Although O'Connor most often voted with the conservatives during her years on the Court—note especially her vote with the majority in 2000 in *Bush* v. *Gore* that settled the disputed vote in Florida in favor of Bush and determined the outcome of the presidential election—she surprised many people in 2003 when she joined the majority in the Michigan Law School case that upheld the use of race in law school admissions, the Texas case

Using the Framework

The Court Allows the Internment of Japanese Americans

If the Supreme Court exists to protect individual rights, why did it allow the military to keep Japanese Americans in internment camps during World War II?

Background: On the advice of the U.S. military, President Franklin Roosevelt signed a series of executive orders in early 1942 authorizing the relocation of 112,000 Japanese Americans living on the West Coast, 70,000 of whom were citizens, into internment camps. In 1944, the Supreme Court in *Korematsu* v. *United States* upheld the legality of the exclusion and confinement orders. Constitutional scholar Edward Corwin described the internment and the Court's action as "the most drastic invasion of the rights of citizens of the United States by their own government" in modern American history. Taking a broad overview of structural, political linkage, and governmental factors that influenced the Supreme Court's decision will help explain this situation.

Governmental Action

The Supreme Court announces its decision allowing the internment of Japanese Americans in *Korematsu* v. *United States* (1944).

Governmental Level

President Franklin Roosevelt, troubled by the action, but fully aware of the feelings of the public and the wishes of military leaders in wartime, signed the necessary executive orders.

The Supreme Court, unwilling to act against opinion of military leaders that Japanese Americans living on the West Coast posed a national security threat, supported the exclusion order in a case brought by Fred Korematsu.

Military authorities believed that Japanese Americans living on the West Coast posed a national security threat to the United States; asked the President to authorize curfews, relocation, and confinement.

Congress passed supporting legislation making relocation and internment possible.

Political Linkages Level

Anti-Japanese attitudes were widespread among the public, particularly in the West Coast states, who feared a Japanese invasion.

Public opinion strongly supported the war against Japan and whatever military policies were necessary to win it.

The media whipped up hysteria about a possible Japanese invasion.

Structural Level

Japanese immigrants to the United States in the late nineteenth and early twentieth centuries settled mainly in the West Coast states.

The Japanese attack on Pearl Harbor on December 7, 1941, plunged the United States into World War II and helped inflame negative attitudes toward Americans of Japanese descent.

The Constitution vests enormous powers in the president as commander-in-chief during wartime.

Deciding the 2000 Presidential Election

The outcome of the closely fought 2000 presidential election was not finally decided until the Supreme Court stopped the recount in Florida, giving the state's electoral votes to George W. Bush. Here, passionate supporters of Bush and Al Gore demonstrate in front of the Supreme Court building while awaiting its decision.

that banned states from forbidding private gay sexual behavior, and the challenge to the constitutionality of the McCain-Feingold Campaign Finance Reform law, which was rejected. In 2004 she wrote the majority opinion in the decision on the rights of citizens held as enemy combatants, pointing out that "a state of war is not a blank check for the president when it comes to the rights of the nation's citizens."[35] Some veteran Court observers suggested that O'Connor's emergence during this period made her the most important person on the Rehnquist Court in the 2000s, noting that legal briefs submitted to the Court and oral arguments before the justices were, more often than not, directed to her concerns and favored legal doctrines.[36] Her importance as the swing vote moving the Court in a less conservative direction is why the confirmation hearings for the strongly conservative Samuel Alito in 2006, nominated by President Bush to replace O'Connor, were so contentious. Conservative hopes and liberal fears were vindicated in 2006 when Alito voted with the Court majority giving police greater power to execute a search warrant without "knocking and announcing," and approving Arizona's strict insanity tests under which a schizophrenic teen was convicted of shooting a police officer.

The Debate Over Judicial Activism

Has the Court become too involved in national policymaking? Many people think so; others think not. Let us examine several of the ways in which what is called **judicial activism** is expressed.

judicial activism

Actions by the courts that go beyond the strict role of the judiciary as interpreter of the law and adjudicator of disputes.

Judicial Review We have already seen how the Court under John Marshall's leadership claimed the right of judicial review in the case of *Marbury* v. *Madison* (1803). Still, the power was not exercised by the Court to any great extent until the late nineteenth century. The use of judicial review increased during the twentieth century, however, with most of the Court's adverse attention being paid to the states. As described earlier, however, the Rehnquist Court was fairly aggressive in overturning federal statutes, averaging almost six per term in the years from 1994 to 2005, compared with one every two years from the end of the Civil War to the early 1990s.[37] Oddly, given the tendency of conservative activists and organizations to be the most vociferously concerned about an overly activist judiciary, it was the most conservative members of the Court who most frequently voted to overturn congressional statutes during these years.[38] These trends in the use of judicial review suggest that the Court has become more willing to monitor the activities of other governmental entities.

Reversing the Decisions of Past Supreme Courts Despite the norm of precedent that guides judicial decision making, the Warren, Burger, and Rehnquist Courts overturned a number of previous Court decisions. The most dramatic instance was the reversal by the Warren Court of *Plessy* v. *Ferguson* (1896), which had endorsed legal segregation in the South, by *Brown* v. *Board of Education* (1954), which removed segregation's legal underpinnings. The Rehnquist Court overturned a number of previous Court decisions that had expanded the rights of criminal defendants and that had supported the extension of federal government power, reviewed earlier. To be sure, the Court is reluctant to overturn so-called superprecedents—though it did so in the *Brown* decision— but it can do so if it so chooses. Sensing that the new Roberts Court might want to reconsider *Roe,* abortion opponents persuaded the South Dakota legislature and governor to pass a law in 2006 that for all intents and purposes bans abortion in the state, knowing full well that pro-choice forces would ultimately be forced to challenge its constitutionality in the courts.

Deciding "Political" Issues Critics claim that the Court is taking on too many matters that are best left to the elected branches of government. An often-cited example is the Court's willingness to become increasingly involved in the process of drawing congressional electoral district boundaries in the states. Defenders of the Court argue that when such basic constitutional rights as equality of citizenship are at peril, the Court is obligated to protect these rights, no matter what other government bodies may choose to do. The Court's intervention in the 2000 presidential election generated widespread criticism for its meddling in politics, though its many defenders insist that the Court's decision in *Bush* v. *Gore* saved the nation from a constitutional crisis.

Remedies The most criticized aspect of judicial activism is the tendency for federal judges to impose broad remedies on states and localities. A **remedy** is what a court determines must be done to rectify a wrong. Since the 1960s, the Court has been more willing than in the past to impose remedies that require other governmental bodies to take action. Some of the most controversial of these remedies include court orders requiring states to build more prison space and mandating that school districts bus students to achieve racial balance. Such remedies often require that governments spend public funds for things they do not necessarily want to do. Critics claim that the federal judiciary's legitimate role is to prevent government actions that threaten rights and liberties, not to compel government to take action to meet some policy goal.

Original Intent Much of the debate about the role of the Court centers on the issue of the original intent of the framers. Advocates of **original intent** believe that the Court must be guided by the original intent of the framers

PARTICIPATION

The Courts and School Vouchers

remedy

An action that a court determines must be taken to rectify a wrong.

original intent

The doctrine that the courts must interpret the Constitution in ways consistent with the intentions of the framers rather than in light of contemporary conditions and needs.

Tight Quarters

Federal courts often require that states "remedy" a situation found to be in violation of federal standards or constitutional protections. A good example is prison overcrowding, shown here in an Alabama state prison in 1982. For many years, the courts have insisted that the states do something to end the problem, even if it means spending additional state monies.

strict construction

The doctrine that the provisions of the Constitution have a clear meaning and that judges must stick closely to this meaning when rendering decisions.

and the exact words found in the Constitution, using **strict construction** as a way to stay close to its true meaning. Originalists believe that the expansion of rights that has occurred since the mid-1960s—such as the new right to privacy that formed the basis of the *Roe* v. *Wade* decision and rights for criminal defendants—is illegitimate, having no foundation in the framers' intentions or the text of the Constitution. Justices Antonin Scalia and Clarence Thomas are the strongest originalists on today's Court.

Opponents of original intent and strict construction believe that the intentions of the framers are not only impossible to determine but also unduly constricting. In this view, jurists must try to reconcile the fundamental principles of the Constitution with changing conditions in the United States and the democratic aspirations of the American people.

Clearly, the modern Supreme Court is more activist than it was in the past; most justices today hold a more expansive view of the role of the Court in forging national policy than did their predecessors. And because the Court is likely to remain activist under Chief Justice John Roberts, the debate about judicial activism is likely to remain important in American politics.

Outside Influences on the Court

The courts make public policy and will continue to do so, but they do not do so in splendid isolation; many other governmental and political linkage actors and institutions influence what they do. Recall that the influence of structural factors has already been examined at several places in this chapter.

Governmental Influences

The Supreme Court must coexist with other governmental bodies that have their own powers, interests, constituencies, and visions of the public good. Recognizing this, the Court usually tries to stay somewhere near the boundaries of what is acceptable to other political actors. Being without "purse or sword," as Hamilton put it in *The Federalist,* No. 78, the Court cannot force others to obey its decisions. It can only hope that respect for the law and the Court will cause government officials to do what it has mandated in a decision. If the Court fails to gain voluntary compliance, it risks a serious erosion of its influence, for it then appears weak and ineffectual.

The President   The president, as chief executive, is supposed to carry out the Court's decrees. However, presidents who have opposed particular decisions or been lukewarm to them have dragged their feet, as President Eisenhower did on school desegregation after the Court's *Brown* decision.

The president has constitutional powers that give him some degree of influence over the Court. In addition to the Court's dependence on the president to carry out its decisions (when the parties to a dispute do not do it voluntarily), for example, the president influences the direction of the Court by his power to nominate judges when there are vacancies. He can also file suits through the Justice Department or introduce legislation to alter the Court's organization or jurisdiction (as Franklin Roosevelt did with his Court-packing proposal).

Congress   Although Congress can alter the size, organization, and appellate jurisdiction of the federal courts, it rarely does so.[39] The size of the Court, for example, has not changed since 1860. Nor, since that time, has Congress changed its jurisdiction as a reaction to its decisions, despite the introduction of many bills over the years to do so. In 2003, for example, a bill was introduced by Republicans in the House to take away the Court's jurisdiction to hear cases challenging the inclusion of the phrase "under God" in the Pledge of Allegiance. In 2004 a resolution was introduced in the House decrying the citation of the opinions of foreign and international courts and international law in U.S. judicial pronouncements—something Justice Kennedy had done in his majority opinion in a case overturning the state of Texas's antisodomy statute in *Lawrence* v. *Texas* (2003)—and threatening impeachment for any federal judge doing so. Although these and a dozen or so other bills and resolutions failed to pass Congress, they were enough to earn a strong rebuke from Chief Justice Rehnquist in his 2004 annual report on the federal courts, who worried about these legislative threats to judicial independence.[40] Congress is more likely to bring pressure to bear on the courts by being unsympathetic to pleas from the justices for pay increases or for a suitable budget for clerks or office space. The Senate also plays a role in the appointment process, as we have learned, and can convey its views to the Court during the course of confirmation hearings. Finally, Congress can change statutes or pass new laws that specifically challenge Supreme Court decisions, as it did when it legislated the Civil Rights Act of 1991 to make it easier for people to file employment discrimination suits.[41]

Political Linkage Influences

The Supreme Court is influenced not only by other government officials and institutions but also by what we have termed political linkage factors.

Groups and Movements   Interest groups, social movements, and the public not only influence the Court indirectly through the president and Congress but often do so directly. An important political tactic of interest groups and social movements is the **test case.** A test case is an action brought by a group that is

test case
A case brought to force a ruling on the constitutionality of some law or executive action.

Civil Rights Champion

Social movements use test cases to challenge the constitutionality of laws and government actions. After a long search, NAACP attorney Thurgood Marshall—shown here in front of the Supreme Court, where he would later sit as a justice—selected Linda Brown, a fifth-grader from Topeka, Kansas, who was not permitted to attend the school closest to her house because it was reserved for whites, as the principal plaintiff in *Brown v. Board of Education of Topeka,* the historic case that successfully challenged school segregation.

designed to challenge the constitutionality of a law or an action by government. Groups wishing to force a court determination on an issue that is important to them will try to find a plaintiff on whose behalf they can bring a suit. When Thurgood Marshall was chief counsel for the NAACP in the 1950s, he spent a long time searching for the right plaintiff to bring a suit that would drive the last nail into the coffin of the *Plessy* separate-but-equal doctrine that was the legal basis for southern segregation. He settled on a fifth-grade girl named Linda Brown who was attending a segregated school in Topeka, Kansas. Several years later, he won the landmark case *Brown v. Board of Education of Topeka* (1954).

Many test cases take the form of **class action suits.** These are suits brought by an individual on behalf of a class of people who are in a similar situation. A suit to prevent the dumping of toxic wastes in public waterways, for example, may be brought by an individual in the name of all the people living in the area who are adversely affected by the resulting pollution. Class action suits were invited by the Warren Court's expansion of the definition of standing in the 1960s. The Rehnquist Court later narrowed the definition of *standing,* making it harder to bring class action suits.

Interest groups often get involved in suits brought by others by filing amicus curiae briefs. Pro-abortion and anti-abortion groups submitted 78 such briefs in *Webster* v. *Reproductive Health Services* (1989), a decision that allowed states to regulate and limit abortion availability.[42] These briefs set out the group's position on the constitutional issues or talk about some of the most important consequences of deciding the case one way or the other. In a sense, this activity is a form of lobbying. Some scholars believe that the Court finds such briefs to be a way to keep track of public and group opinion on the issues before it, which is helpful to its work.[43]

Leaders The Supreme Court does not usually stray very far from the opinions of public and private sector leaders when a consensus exists among them.[44]

class action suit
A suit brought on behalf of a group of people who are in a situation similar to that of the plaintiffs.

Using the Democracy Standard

Does the Supreme Court advance or retard democracy in the United States?

PROPOSITION: **The framers intended that the Supreme Court be a nondemocratic institution, and it ought to stay that way. It has served us well throughout our history.**

AGREE   For a representative democracy to function at all, there must be a referee that stands above the fray, free from the pressure of other elected officials and the public, preserving the rules, overseeing the orderly changing of some rules when the situation demands it, protecting minorities against the potentially tyrannical behavior of the majority, and protecting individuals in the exercise of their constitutionally guaranteed rights. The Supreme Court has done a pretty good job carrying out these responsibilities throughout our history. For example, the Court has been an important factor in the spread and protection of free speech and freedom of the press in the United States, and eventually became a force for ensuring that African Americans would be treated as equal citizens.

A representative democracy cannot remain democratic if   **DISAGREE**   one of its core government institutions, with the power to make binding decisions for the nation as a whole, is neither responsible nor responsive to the people. At some point, the Supreme Court cannot avoid going its own way, sometimes legitimately so—for example, when it has protected the constitutional rights of unpopular individuals and minority groups—and sometimes illegitimately—for example, when it has served as a bulwark against efforts by the people to regulate powerful economic institutions. Especially egregious was the Court's intervention in the 2000 election contest in Florida which decided the outcome of the 2000 presidential election.

CONSIDER   Over the years, public opinion pollsters have consistently reported that Supreme Court justices, along with military leaders, are the most respected officials in the American government—regularly outpacing presidents and members of Congress—and in American society—higher in the esteem of the public than religious, corporate, labor, or educational leaders. Supreme Court justices are held in such regard even though they are not elected by the people, they deliberate cases out of public view, and make decisions that are sometimes abstract and complex.

• How would you explain this? • Do you believe the Court has such a high standing with the public because most people don't know much about it and don't see it in operation, with its inevitable disputes among the justices, compromises on decisions, and careful crafting of opinions to gain widespread acceptance—that is, playing politics? • Or is the Court's high standing a product of the valuable role it plays in American democracy, acting as a referee on the rules and settling disputes among contending groups? • How about you? • How would you rate the Supreme Court compared to other governmental and societal institutions and organizations? • Why do you feel this way?

Social and economic leaders use their influence in a number of ways. As we learned in earlier chapters, their influence is substantial in the media, the interest group system, party politics, and elections at all levels. It follows, then, that elites play a substantial role in the thinking of presidents and the members of Congress as they, in turn, deal with the Court. In addition to this powerful but indirect influence, the Court is also shaped by developments on issues and doctrine within the legal profession as these are expressed by bar associations, law journals, and law schools. To take but one example, Justice O'Connor, in her opinion in the 2004 Michigan Law School affirmative action case, justified her vote by pointing out that the use of race as one criterion among many in law school admission decisions was now widely accepted in the university and legal communities, as was the legitimacy of the goal of "diversity" in higher education.

Public Opinion   We might think that the Supreme Court is immune from public opinion, since the justices are appointed for life and do not need to face the electorate. There is reason to believe, however, that what the Court does and what the public wants—at least as expressed in public opinion polls—are highly correlated; a substantial body of research shows that Court rulings and public opinion are consistent with one another about two-thirds of the time, about the same as level of consistency with the public as the president and Congress.[45] There does not seem to be a yawning gap, then, between the public and the Supreme Court. We cannot say for sure, however, that public opinion causes the Court to act in particular ways when making decisions.[46] Indeed, it is just as likely that third factors—such as major events, political developments, and cultural changes conveyed in the media—shape the perceptions of judges and citizens alike. Nevertheless, the close association between Court decisions and public opinion is good news in a society that aspires to be democratic.

Having said that, it also is important to point out that there have been times during our history when the Court was so influenced by other political actors that it set aside, if only for a short while, its responsibility to protect the rights and liberties of all citizens. Although the Court has played an important role in advancing rights and liberties in the United States (see Chapters 15 and 16), it has not been entirely immune from pressure brought to bear by the public, other government officials, and private-sector leaders, to punish suspect groups. For example, the Court went along with local, state, and federal actions to punish dissident voices during the McCarthy era's anti-Communist hysteria of the 1950s. It also approved the forced relocation and internment of Japanese Americans during World War II, as discussed earlier in the "Using the Framework" feature.

Summary

Article III of the Constitution is vague about the powers and responsibilities of the U.S. Supreme Court. Especially noteworthy is the Constitution's silence on the Court's most important power, judicial review. Nevertheless, the Court has fashioned a powerful position for itself in American politics, coequal with the executive and legislative branches.

The federal court system is made up of three parts. At the bottom are 94 federal district courts, in which most cases originate. In the middle are 13 appeals courts. At the top is the Supreme Court, with both original and appellate jurisdiction.

The Supreme Court operates on the basis of several widely shared norms: secrecy, seniority, and adherence to precedent. The Court controls its agenda by granting or not granting a writ of certiorari to cases filed with it. Cases before the Court wend their way through the process in the following way: submission of briefs, oral argument, initial consideration in conference, opinion writing, and final conference consideration by the justices. Published opinions serve as precedents for other federal courts and future Supreme Court decisions.

The Supreme Court is a national policymaker of considerable importance. Its unelected, life-tenured justices cannot, however, do anything they please, because the Court is significantly influenced by other political linkage and governmental factors. As a result, Court decisions rarely drift very far from public and elite opinion.

Constitutional interpretation by the Supreme Court, heavily influenced by structural changes in American history, has progressed through four stages. In the first, the Court helped settle the question of the nature of the federal union. In the second, it helped define the role of the government in a free enterprise economy. In the third, the Court focused on issues of civil liberties and civil rights. In the fourth, the Court took a more conservative turn in areas such as federalism, where it tended to support states rights over federal authority, and the rights of the accused, which it scaled back.

The decisions of the Court are influenced by structural, political linkage, and governmental factors. The president and Congress are especially important in this regard, but so too are interest groups and public and elite opinion.

mypoliscilab
Where participation leads to action!

Web Exploration
Who Is Appointed to the Supreme Court?

ISSUE: Appointees to the Supreme Court come from a very select group of Americans, not at all representative of the general population either in terms of demographic background or achievement and training.

SITE: Access the Cornell Law School home page in MyPoliSciLab at **www.mypoliscilab.com.** Go to the "Web Explorations" section for Chapter 14 and open "who is appointed . . . ," then open "biographies." Read the short biographies of each of the present members of the Supreme Court.

WHAT YOU'VE LEARNED: What kinds of people become justices? What can you say about their occupational and educational backgrounds and their other experiences?

HINT: Not surprisingly, they are all lawyers and have served as judges. Some have experience in politics and public service as well.

Internet Sources

Federal Courts Home Page
www.uscourts.gov
Information and statistics about the activities of U.S. District Courts, Circuit Courts of Appeal, and the Supreme Court.

Find Law.com
www.findlaw.com
A treasure trove of links to information about the nation's courts and the legal profession.

Legal Information Institute, Cornell University Law School
www.law.cornell.edu
The gateway to a world of information and links to associated law and court sites on the Web. Among its sections you will find the following: the Supreme Court Calendar; Biographies and Opinions of the Justices; Directories of law firms, law schools, and legal associations; Constitutions and Codes, including U.S. statutes, regulations, and judicial rules of procedure; www.nytimes.com/pages/politics/politicsspecial1/ index.html and Court opinions, including those of state supreme courts.

The Oyez Project
www.oyez.org/oyez/frontpage
A website that archives multimedia material concerning the United States Supreme Court (including recordings of oral arguments).

Certiorari Grants at Duke Law
**www.law.duke.edu/publiclaw/supremecourtonline/
certgrants/**
> *A website describing all recent cases that were granted a
> writ of certiorari and links to opinions for those cases
> that have been decided.*

Senate Judiciary Committee
www.senate.gov/~judiciary/nominations.cfm
> *Track the status of federal judicial nominations and con-
> firmations.*

The Supreme Court
www.supremecourtus.gov/
> *The official website of the Supreme Court with a wealth
> of information about the Court's docket and decisions.*

Suggestions for Further Reading

Ackerman, Bruce. *We the People: Transformations.*
Cambridge, MA: Harvard University Press, 2000.
> *A compelling interpretation of American constitutional
> history in which popular pressures are the prime cause
> for major transformations in the U.S. Supreme Court's
> approach to major issues.*

Barnett, Randy E. *Restoring the Lost Constitution: The
Presumption of Liberty.* Princeton, NJ: Princeton University
Press, 2003.
> *A conservative case for understanding the Constitution
> as a legal framework for the protection of individual
> rights.*

Breyer, Stephen. *Active Liberty: Interpreting Our
Democratic Constitution.* New York: Knopf, 2005.
> *The Justice's attempt to define a coherent doctrine of a
> "Living Constitution."*

McCloskey, Robert G. *The American Supreme Court,* 4th ed.
Chicago: University of Chicago Press, 2005.
> *First published 40 years ago, and revised for the 2005
> edition by noted legal scholar Sanford Levinson, this re-
> mains the classic interpretation of the Supreme Court's
> role in shaping the meaning of the Constitution.*

O'Brien, David M. *Storm Center: The Supreme Court in
American Politics,* 7th ed. New York: W. W. Norton, 2005.
> *The leading textbook on the Court and how it operates.*

O'Connor, Sandra Day. *The Majesty of the Law: Reflections
of a Supreme Court Justice.* New York: Random House,
2003.
> *Reflections on the law and the Supreme Court by the
> now-retired jurist.*

Randall, Richard S. *American Constitutional Development.*
New York: Longman Publishers, 2002.
> *A constitutional law textbook with Supreme Court cases
> and commentary.*

Schwartz, Bernard. *Decision: How the Supreme Court
Decides Cases.* New York: Oxford University Press, 2005.
> *A revealing behind-the-scenes look at how the Supreme
> Court considers and decides the cases before it.*

PART 5   What Government Does

Parts 2 and 3 of this book examined the structural and political linkage influences on government institutions and public officials. Part 4 examined government institutions and public officials. This part examines what government does and how effective it is in tackling the most important problems facing the United States.

As such, this part represents a kind of summing up; it examines how effectively our political and governmental institutions operate to fulfill the needs and expectations of the American people. These chapters also address the democracy theme, asking whether public policies are the outcome of a democratic process and whether policies improve the health and vitality of democracy in the United States.

Chapters 15 and 16 look at the status of civil liberties and civil rights in the United States, with special attention paid to the decisions of the Supreme Court concerning our most cherished rights and liberties. Chapter 17 examines domestic policies, with particular attention given to patterns of government spending, the tax system, regulation of the economy, and social welfare. Chapter 18 looks at American foreign and national defense policies.

CHAPTER 15

Freedom: The Struggle for Civil Liberties

IN THIS CHAPTER

- Why liberty is so important in a democracy

- How liberties were gradually applied to the states by the Supreme Court

- How the Supreme Court's interpretation of the meaning of liberties has changed

- How the struggle for democracy has increased the enjoyment of liberties in the United States

- How the war on terrorism may affect civil liberties

Campus Speech Codes and Free Speech

- Campus newspapers across the nation refused to accept a paid advertisement from conservative activist David Horowitz in which he opposed reparations for slavery. Many of the handful of newspapers that ran the ad "Ten Reasons Why Reparations for Slavery is a Bad Idea—and Racist Too" faced angry demonstrations, vandalism of their offices, and theft of the papers containing the offending ads.
- During a class at the University of Michigan, a student argued that homosexuality could be treated with psychotherapy. He was accused of violating a campus rule against victimizing people on the basis of their sexual orientation.
- At Southern Methodist University, a student was sentenced to work for 30 hours with minority organizations because, among other things, he sang "We Shall Overcome" in a sarcastic manner.[1]
- According to the University of Montana's harassment policy, if a woman "feels" she has been mistreated, that alone proves mistreatment.
- Top officials at the University of Texas, Austin, denounced as abhorrent the statement of law school professor Lino Graglia that black and Hispanic students were not competitive with whites in law school because most of them come from cultures that do not encourage academic achievement or that look upon academic failure as a disgrace. Although Rev. Jesse Jackson joined hundreds of students and faculty members calling for Graglia's dismissal, civil libertarians came to his defense on the grounds of the professor's free speech rights under the Constitution.
- At San Diego State University a student was admonished by school administrators and warned that he might be expelled for getting into a heated argument with four Arab students he encountered in the school's library who had been quietly celebrating the September 11 attacks on the World Trade Center.
- In 2002, a student at California Poly posted fliers for a talk by black conservative C. Mason Weaver, who believes that government assistance programs keep African Americans locked in dependence and poverty. The student was accused by several other students of racial insensitivity, brought before a campus disciplinary board, and found guilty of "disruption" for posting the lecture announcement.
- Stanford University enacted a speech code in 1990 that prohibits "personal vilification of students on the basis of their sex, race, color, handi-

cap, religion, sexual orientation, or national and ethnic origin." The code was strongly opposed by Stanford's eminent constitutional scholar Gerald Gunther, who claimed that hate speech should not be banned but vigorously rejected "with more speech, with better speech, with repudiation and contempt." In 1995, the California Supreme Court agreed with Gunther's position, saying that the Stanford code unconstitutionally restricts free speech rights under the First Amendment to the Constitution.[2]

The college campus has become one of the most visible battlegrounds in the continuing struggle over the meaning of free speech in the United States, as traditional notions of liberty come into conflict with newer notions of equal citizenship (or civil rights, to be discussed in the next chapter). Campus speech codes have been instituted at many colleges and universities across the country in an effort to rid campuses of speech that may offend women and members of various minority groups. Many civil libertarians, like Gerald Gunther, although protective of the rights of minority students to have a supportive learning environment, have fought hard against such codes in the service of free speech and a free society. By and large, the courts have sided with the civil libertarians, as in the Stanford case. ■

Thinking Critically About This Chapter

Using the Framework You will see in this chapter how structural, political linkage, and governmental factors influence the meaning and practice of civic freedoms. Although the decisions of the Supreme Court are particularly important in determining the status of civil liberties at any particular moment in American history, you will learn how they are also the product of influences from a wide range of actors, institutions, and social processes.

Using the Democracy Standard You will see in this chapter how the expansion of the enjoyment of civil liberties in the United States has been a product of the struggle for democracy and how civil liberties are fundamental to the democratic process itself.

Civil Liberties in the Constitution

civil liberties
Freedoms found primarily in the Bill of Rights that are protected from government interference.

We saw in Chapter 2 that the framers were particularly concerned about establishing a society in which liberty might flourish. While government was necessary to protect liberty from the threat of anarchy, the framers believed that government might threaten liberty if it became too powerful. **Civil liberties** are freedoms protected by constitutional provisions, laws, and practices from certain types of government interference. As embodied in the Bill of Rights, civil liberties are protected by prohibitions against government actions that threaten the enjoyment of freedom. These liberties fall into two major groups: first, those associated with freedoms of expression, belief, and association; and second, those involving protections for people accused of committing a crime.

In the Preamble to the Constitution, the framers wrote that they aimed to "secure the Blessings of Liberty to ourselves and our Posterity." But in the original Constitution, they protected few liberties from the national government they were creating and almost none from state governments. To safeguard against tyranny, the framers preferred to give the national government little power with which to attack individual liberties. Rather than listing specific prohibitions against certain kinds of actions, then, they believed that a republican constitutional design that fragmented government power and that included separation of powers, checks and balances, and federalism would best protect liberty. Still, the framers singled out certain freedoms as too crucial to be left unmentioned. For example, the Constitution prohibits Congress and the states from suspending the writ of **habeas corpus,** except when public safety demands it because of rebellion or invasion, and from passing **bills of attainder** or **ex post facto laws** (see Table 15.1 for an enumeration).

habeas corpus
The legal doctrine that a person who is arrested must have a timely hearing before a judge.

bill of attainder
A governmental decree that a person is guilty of a crime that carries the death penalty, rendered without benefit of a trial.

ex post facto law
A law that retroactively declares some action illegal.

As we saw in Chapter 2, many citizens found the proposed Constitution too stingy in its listing of liberties, so that the Federalists were led to promise a "bill of rights" as a condition for passing the Constitution. The Bill of Rights was passed by the 1st Congress in 1789 and was ratified by the required number of states by 1791. Passage of the Bill of Rights made the constitution more democratic by specifying protections of political liberty and by guaranteeing a context of free political expression that makes popular sovereignty possible.

TABLE 15.1 • Civil Liberties in the U.S. Constitution

The exact meaning and extent of civil liberties in the Constitution are matters of debate, but here are some freedoms spelled out in the text of the Constitution and its amendments or clarified by early court decisions.

Constitution

Article I, Section 9
Congress may not suspend a writ of habeas corpus.
Congress may not pass bills of attainder or ex post facto laws.

Article I, Section 10
States may not pass bills of attainder or ex post facto laws.
States may not impair obligation of contracts.

Article III, Section 2
Criminal trials in national courts must be jury trials in the state in which the defendant is
    alleged to have committed the crime.

Article III, Section 3
No one may be convicted of treason unless there is a confession in open court or
    testimony of two witnesses to the same overt act.

Article IV, Section 2
Citizens of each state are entitled to all privileges and immunities of citizens in the
    several states.

The Bill of Rights

First Amendment
Congress may not make any law with respect to the establishment of religion.
Congress may not abridge the free exercise of religion.
Congress may not abridge freedom of speech or of the press.
Congress may not abridge the right to assemble or to petition the government.

Second Amendment
Congress may not infringe the right to keep and bear arms.

Third Amendment
Congress may not station soldiers in houses against the owner's will, except in
    times of war.

Fourth Amendment
Citizens are to be free from unreasonable searches and seizures.
Federal courts may issue search warrants based only on probable cause and specifically
    describing the objects of search.

Fifth Amendment
Citizens are protected against double jeopardy (being prosecuted more than once for
    the same crime) and self-incrimination.
Citizens are guaranteed against deprivation of life, liberty, or property without due
    process of law.
Citizens are guaranteed just compensation for public use of their private property.

Sixth Amendment
Citizens have the right to a speedy and public trial before an impartial jury.
Citizens have the right to face their accuser and to cross-examine witnesses.

Eighth Amendment
Excessive bail and fines are prohibited.
Cruel and unusual punishments are prohibited.

Reading the Constitution and its amendments, however, reveals how few of our most cherished liberties are to be found in this document. Decisions by government officials and changes brought about by political leaders, interest groups, social movements, and individuals remade the Constitution in the long run; hence many of the freedoms we expect today are not specifically mentioned there. Some extensions of protected liberties were introduced by judges and other officials. Others have evolved as the culture has grown to accept novel and even once-threatening ideas. Still other liberties have secured a place in the Republic through partisan and ideological combat. The key to understanding civil liberties in the United States is to follow their evolution over the course of the nation's history.

Rights and Liberties in the Nineteenth Century

During the nineteenth century, the range of protected civil liberties in the United States was somewhat different from their range today. Especially noteworthy were the special place of **economic liberty** and the understanding that the Bill of Rights did not apply to state governments.

economic liberty

The right to own and use property free from excessive government interference.

Economic Liberty in the Early Republic

Liberty may be understood as protection against government interference in certain kinds of private activities. Among the few such protections mentioned in the original Constitution was one that concerned the use and enjoyment of private property, stated most directly in the Constitution in the language of contracts (i.e., the freedom to enter into binding private agreements about many things, including the use of one's property): "No State shall . . . pass any . . . Law impairing the Obligation of Contracts" (Article I, Section 10).[3] The framers protected private property in a number of other constitutional provisions as well, including provisions that created a system for recognizing intellectual property (patents and copyrights) and for safeguarding property in the form of slaves by requiring Americans to return runaway slaves to their owners (see Chapter 2). The "full faith and credit" clause (Article IV, Section 1), moreover, obligated each state to recognize contracts and other legal obligations entered into by its citizens with citizens or legal bodies in other states. The so-called takings clause of the Fifth Amendment—ratified in 1791 with other amendments that constitute the Bill of Rights—declares that "private property [shall not] be taken for public use, without just compensation." The importance of property rights as a fundamental liberty in the body of the Constitution and its Amendments was reinforced by more than a century of judicial interpretation.[4]

The Marshall Court (1801–1835) Although the Supreme Court ruled (in *Barron* v. *Baltimore,* 1833) that the Bill of Rights did not apply to the states, it ruled on several occasions that the **contract clause** in the Constitution directly applied against unwarranted state action. In the hands of Chief Justice John Marshall, the clause became an important defense of property rights against interference by the states. In *Fletcher* v. *Peck* (1810), for example, the Marshall Court upheld a sale of public land, even though almost all of the legislators who had voted for the land sale had been bribed by the prospective purchasers. Chief Justice Marshall wrote in his majority opinion that even a

contract clause

The portion of Article I, Section 10, of the Constitution that prohibits states from passing any law "impairing the obligations of contracts."

fraudulent sale created a contract among private individuals that the state could not void. In *Dartmouth College* v. *Woodward* (1819), Marshall argued in his majority opinion that New Hampshire could not modify the charter of Dartmouth College because the original charter constituted a binding contract, the terms of which could not be changed without impairing the obligations in the original contract. The framers' attempt to protect the contractual agreements of private parties ballooned in the hands of the Marshall Court to bar virtually any and all changes by the states of established property relations.[5] This expansion of property rights protections under the contract clause made it very difficult for states to regulate business activities because any such regulation could be interpreted as interfering with those binding contracts by which businesses were established and operated.

The Taney Court (1836–1864)   Under the leadership of Chief Justice Roger Taney, the Court began to make a distinction between private property used in ways that encouraged economic growth and private property used for simple enjoyment. In landmark cases, the Taney Court issued rulings favoring the former when the two concepts of property conflicted.[6] In his opinion in *Charles River Bridge* v. *Warren Bridge* (1837), Chief Justice Taney argued in his majority opinion that Massachusetts, in chartering the Charles River Bridge, had not agreed to create a monopoly that closed off competitors. He ruled that Massachusetts could charter the rival Warren River Bridge because the states should encourage economic competition and technological advances. It did not matter that as a result the stockholders in the Charles River Bridge would lose money. Taney argued that the "creative destruction" of established but idle property in a dynamic market economy is the price of economic and social progress.

The Court's defense of property rights was especially and tragically strong when it came to slavery. Until the Civil War, courts in the North and the South consistently upheld the right of slaveholders to recapture fugitive slaves. In his opinion in *Dred Scott* v. *Sandford* (1857)—a case that helped bring on the Civil War—Chief Justice Taney claimed that slaves were not cit-

Slaves Toiling in the Cotton Fields

Prior to passage of the Thirteenth and Fourteenth Amendments after the Civil War, African American slaves were considered to be nothing more or less than the private property of their owners. This legal definition of their status was confirmed by the Supreme Court on several occasions.

izens who possessed rights but simply private property belonging to their owners, no different from land or tools.

Economic Liberty After the Civil War

The Fourteenth Amendment, passed after the Civil War, was designed to guarantee the citizenship rights of the newly freed slaves. It included a clause—the **due process clause**—stating that no state "may deprive a person of life, liberty, or property, without due process of law." Strangely, the Supreme Court in the late nineteenth century interpreted this clause as a protection for businesses against the regulatory efforts of the states.

The Court's most famous decision in this regard was *Lochner* v. *New York* (1905). Lochner ran a bakery in Utica, New York. He was convicted of requiring an employee to work more than 60 hours per week, contrary to a New York state maximum-hours statute. But Justice Rufus Peckham wrote for a 5–4 Supreme Court majority that the right of employer and employee to negotiate hours of work was part of the "liberty" of which, under the Fourteenth Amendment, no person could be deprived without due process of law. In other words, New York State had no right to regulate the hours of labor.

The nineteenth century was an era in which the rights of property were expanded, refined, and altered to become consistent with an emerging, dynamic industrial economy. The twentieth century would bring new approaches to property rights and to political liberties in general. These new approaches would be triggered by structural transformations in the economy and culture, the efforts of new political groups and movements, and the actions of government officials, all of which we will examine in greater detail.

Nationalization of the Bill of Rights

Americans rightly understand the Bill of Rights to be a foundation of American freedom. Until the twentieth century, however, the protections of the Bill of Rights did not apply to the states, only to the national government. The Supreme Court only gradually applied the Bill of Rights to the states through a process known as **selective incorporation.**

The framers were worried more about national government intrusions on individual freedom than about state government intrusions. Most of the states, after all, had bills of rights in their own constitutions, and, being closer to the people, state governments would be less likely to intrude on the people's freedom, or so the framers believed. This reading of the Bill of Rights as a prohibition of certain actions by the national government seems explicit in the language of many of the first 10 amendments. The first, for instance, starts with the words "*Congress shall make no law. . . .*" This understanding of the Bill of Rights as a set of prohibitions against certain actions by the national government and not the states was confirmed by John Marshall in *Barron* v. *Baltimore* (1833). It is apparent that the majority in Congress wanted to change the reach of the Bill of Rights, extending it to the states, however, when it approved the Fourteenth Amendment after the Civil War. Three clauses in this amendment specify that the states cannot violate the rights and liberties of the people living in them:

- The first specifies that all persons born or naturalized in the United States are citizens of both the United States and the states in which they reside.

due process clause
The section of the Fourteenth Amendment that prohibits states from depriving anyone of life, liberty, or property "without due process of law," a guarantee against arbitrary or unfair government action.

selective incorporation
The gradual and piecemeal incorporation of the protections of the Bill of Rights by the U.S. Supreme Court.

- The **privileges and immunities clause** specifies that no *state* "shall make or enforce any law which shall abridge the privileges or immunities of citizens of the United States."

- The due process clause specifies that no *state* shall "deprive any person of life, liberty, or property, without due process of law."

Although Congress wrote the Fourteenth Amendment to guarantee that states would protect all of U.S. citizens' rights and liberties, including those found in the Bill of Rights, the Supreme Court was very slow in **nationalizing** or **incorporating** the Bill of Rights, making it binding on the state governments. Indeed, the Supreme Court has not yet fully incorporated or nationalized the Bill of Rights. Rather, it has practiced selective incorporation, only slowly adding, step by step, even traditional civil liberties to the constitutional obligations of the states.

How does the Supreme Court decide whether to incorporate some portion of the Bill of Rights? That is, what standard does the Court use to protect a liberty specified in the Bill of Rights from violation by a state government? The answer is quite simple and is spelled out, strange as it may seem, in footnote 4 of the opinion of the Court in *United States* v. *Carolene Products Company* (1938), written by Justice Harlan Fiske Stone, where he set out the legal standards the Court had been using in this area of constitutional interpretation, which he hoped and expected future justices would follow. Stone suggested in his footnote that most legislative enactments by states would fall under what he called **ordinary scrutiny,** meaning that the Court would assume, unless convinced otherwise, that its actions were constitutional. However, the footnote declares, three types of state actions would automatically be presumed unconstitutional, the burden being on the states to prove otherwise. When state actions are presumed to be unconstitutional, the Court is said to be exercising **strict scrutiny.** The three types of suspect state actions that bring strict scrutiny seem to do the following:

- Contradict specific prohibitions in the Constitution, including those of the Bill of Rights.

privileges and immunities clause

The portion of Article IV, Section 2, of the Constitution that states that citizens from out of state have the same legal rights as local citizens in any state.

nationalizing

The process by which provisions of the Bill of Rights become incorporated. See *incorporation.*

incorporation

The process by which the Supreme Court has made most of the provisions of the Bill of Rights binding on the states. See *nationalizing.*

ordinary scrutiny

The assumption that the actions of elected bodies and officials are legal under the Constitution.

strict scrutiny

The assumption that actions by elected bodies or officials violate constitutional rights.

Gun Sale

Whereas the Second Amendment makes it difficult for Congress to pass laws restricting the sale and use of firearms, states can do so more easily because the Second Amendment has not yet been incorporated by the Supreme Court.

VIDEO DEBATE

Gun Control

- Restrict the democratic process.
- Discriminate against racial, ethnic, or religious minorities.

The first of these is the subject matter of this chapter. The second has been addressed at several points in the text. The third is the subject of Chapter 16. In the remainder of this chapter, we focus on specific civil liberties, clarifying their present status in both constitutional law and political practice.

Freedom of Speech

Congress shall make no Law . . . abridging the freedom of speech.
—First Amendment to the U.S. Constitution

What Speech Is Protected by the Constitution?

Speech can take many forms. The Court has had to consider which forms of speech are protected under the Constitution.

Political Speech   For many people, the right to speak one's mind is the first principle of a free and democratic society. Democratic theorists have argued, by and large, that a democratic society is based not only on popular sovereignty, but on the existence of a range of freedoms that allow free and open conversations among the people about the kind of government that is best for them and the sorts of public policies they consider most appropriate. Central among these freedoms, as we discussed in Chapter 1, is speech, the idea being that public conversations about government and politics depend on the ability and willingness of people to express their views, even if it means saying unpopular, even inflammatory, things in an open "marketplace of ideas," as Justice Oliver Wendell Holmes put it in his famous and influential dissenting opinion in *Abrams* v. *United States* (1919).

FIGURE 15.1 • Timeline: Milestones in Free Expression (Speech and Free Press)

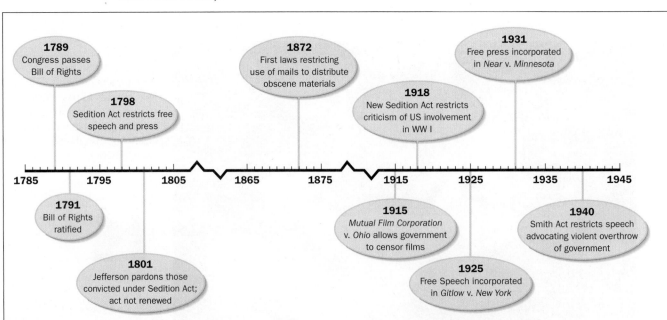

Source: Pearson Education, publishing as Infoplease.com.

Given the centrality of free speech to democracy, it is perhaps odd that free speech was not incorporated (made applicable to state governments) by the Supreme Court until 1925 in *Gitlow* v. *New York* (1925). Benjamin Gitlow had published *The Left Wing Manifesto,* which embraced a militant, revolutionary socialism to mobilize the proletariat to destroy the existing order in favor of communism. Gitlow did not advocate specific action to break the law, but he was nonetheless convicted of a felony under the New York Criminal Anarchy Law (1902).

The Supreme Court majority held that New York State was bound by the First Amendment—thus incorporating the First Amendment, making it binding on all states—but then argued that even the First Amendment did not prohibit New York from incarcerating Gitlow for his publishing and distributing his pamphlet because it represented a danger to peace and order for which, said Justice Edward Sanford, "A single revolutionary spark may kindle a fire that, smoldering for a time, may burst into a sweeping and destructive conflagration. It cannot be said that the State is acting . . . unreasonably when . . . it seeks to extinguish the spark without waiting until it has enkindled the flame or blazed into the conflagration." In his famous dissent, Justice Oliver Wendell Holmes said, "Every idea is an incitement . . . Eloquence may set fire to reason. But whatever may be thought of the redundant discourse before us, it had no chance of starting a present conflagration."

Freedom of speech has grown in the ensuing years so that far more speech is protected than is not (see Figure 15.1). In general, no U.S. government today—whether federal, state, or local—may regulate or interfere with the content of speech without a compelling reason. For a reason to be compelling, a government must show that the speech poses a "clear and present danger"—the standard formulated by Holmes in *Schenck* v. *United States* (1919)—that it has a duty to prevent. The danger, moreover, must be very substantial, and the relationship between the speech and the danger must be direct, such as falsely yelling "Fire!" in a crowded theater. The danger must also be so immediate that the people responsible for maintaining order cannot afford to tolerate the

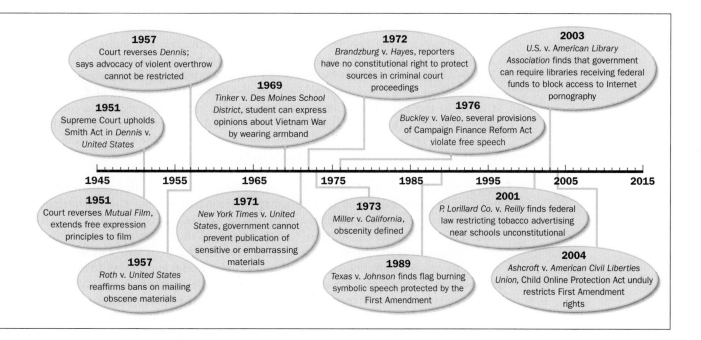

speech. As the Court put it in *Brandenburg* v. *Ohio* (1969), in a case involving an appeal of the conviction of a leader of the Ku Klux Klan under Ohio's criminal syndicalism law, ". . . the constitutional guarantees of free speech . . . do not permit a State to forbid or proscribe advocacy of the use of force or of law violation except where such advocacy is directed to incitement or producing imminent lawless action and is likely to incite or produce such action." Abstract advocacy of ideas, even ideas considered dangerous by police, politicians, or popular majorities, is protected unless it meets both conditions.

Not all political speech is protected against government restriction. The Supreme Court has allowed governments to restrain and punish speakers whose words can be shown to lead or to have led directly to acts of violence or vandalism, interfered with the constitutional rights of others (e.g., blocking access to an abortion clinic), disrupted a legitimate government function (e.g., a sit-in demonstration in the House chambers), talked to others of information contained in classified documents, or trespassed on private or public property, whether peoples' businesses and homes or at a secured defense installation. The Court has also allowed some restrictions on speech during time of war. But over the years, the Court has been careful to keep the leash tight on government officials who have tried to quiet the voice of citizens. Any attempt to restrict political speech must be content neutral (i.e., it can't favor some views over others), serve a legitimate government purpose, be narrowly tailored to address a specific problem (i.e., it cannot be vague), and not have a chilling effect on other people's willingness to exercise their free speech rights. All in all, then, freedom of speech has gained powerful legal foundations over the years and is an important component of democracy in the United States.[7]

Hate Speech

Actions and Symbolic Speech   Difficult questions about free expression persist, of course. Speech mixed with *conduct* may be restricted if the restrictions are narrowly and carefully tailored to curb the conduct while leaving the speech unmolested. Symbolic expressions (such as wearing armbands or picketing) may also receive less protection from the Court. The use of profanity or words that are likely to cause violence ("fighting words") may be regulated in some cases, as may symbolic actions that prevent others from carrying out legitimate activities. Still, freedom of speech throughout the United States has grown to the point at which contenders wrestle with relatively peripheral issues, leaving a large sphere of expressive freedom. *Texas* v. *Johnson* (1989) shows just how far the protection of free speech has expanded. In this case, Gregory Johnson challenged a Texas state law against flag desecration under which he had been convicted for burning an American flag as part of a demonstration at the 1984 Republican convention. Although dominated by a conservative majority, the Rehnquist Court overturned the Texas law, saying that flag burning falls under the free expression protections of the Constitution unless imminent incitement or violence is likely.

Suppression of Free Expression   A major exception to the expansion of freedom of expression has been the periodic concern among the authorities about internal security and national defense.[8] Fearing a rise of radicalism inflamed by the French Revolution, Congress passed the Sedition Act of 1798 to forbid criticism of the government and its leaders. The Civil War saw some restrictions on speech by the states, although the national government remained surprisingly lenient on this score (the Lincoln administration did, however, jail some rebel sympathizers without trial and used military tribunals to try civilians accused of actively helping the southern cause). Censorship of dissent

Burning the Flag

Can state legislatures or Congress pass laws prohibiting flag burning? Although many Americans are infuriated by flag burning and want the practice banned, the Supreme Court has ruled that such laws violate freedom of expression. The only alternative for people who feel strongly about this issue is to amend the Constitution to protect the flag, but proposed amendments have not so far gained sufficient support in Congress.

and protests occurred during and after World War I; 32 states enacted laws to suppress dangerous ideas and talk, and local, state, and national officials led raids on the offices of "radicals." Hoping to become president, Attorney General A. Mitchell Palmer conducted raids on the headquarters of suspect organizations in 1919 and 1920, sending the young J. Edgar Hoover out to collect information on suspected anarchists and communists.

A similar period of hysteria followed World War II. Its foundations were laid when the Democrat-controlled House of Representatives created the House Committee on Un-American Affairs (generally referred to as the HUAC). When the Republicans won control of the Congress in 1952, they professed to see security risks in the Truman administration, labor unions, and Hollywood. Soon Democrats and Republicans alike were exploiting the "Red scare" for political gain. The greatest gain (and, subsequently, the hardest fall) was for Senator Joseph McCarthy (R–WI). McCarthy brandished lists of purported communists and denounced all who opposed him as traitors.[9]

Many civil libertarians also worry about the possible chilling effect on free speech and privacy violations of new laws passed to fight the so-called war on terrorism. Most important is the USA Patriot Act—passed in 2001 and renewed in 2006 with a few small changes to allow for a little more judicial oversight—granting the federal government access to Americans' private and business records. Revelations that the FBI and the NSA had been conducting secret and warrantless searches of phone conversations (land lines and cell phones), financial transactions, and Internet communications ever since 9/11 led to intense press scrutiny, public condemnation, and congressional probes in early 2006, but the opposition was unable to block renewal of the Patriot Act.

VIDEO
ROUNDTABLE

Political Correctness

Freedom of the Press

> *Congress shall make no law . . . abridging the freedom . . . of the press.*
> —First Amendment to the U.S. Constitution

In an aside in the opinion of the Court in *Gitlow* v. *New York* (1925), the Supreme Court included freedom of the press as a freedom guaranteed against state interference by the Fourteenth Amendment. Incorporation of this aspect of the Bill of Rights seems reasonable in light of the importance of the free flow of information in a society that aspires to freedom and democracy. In *Near* v. *Minnesota* (1931), the Court made good on the promise of *Gitlow* by invalidating the Minnesota Public Nuisance Law as a violation of freedom of the press.[10] Jay Near published the *Saturday Press,* a scandal sheet that attacked local crime, public officials, and a few other groups that he disliked: Jews, Catholics, blacks, and unions, for example. Near and his associates were ordered by a state court not to publish, sell, or possess the *Saturday Press*. This sort of state action is called **prior restraint** because it prevents publication before it has occurred. Freedom of the press is not necessarily infringed if publishers are sued or punished for harming others after they have published, but Minnesota was trying to keep Near and his associates from publishing in the future.

Prior Restraint   The prohibition of prior restraint on publication remains the core of freedom of the press. Freedom of the press and freedom of speech tend to be considered together as freedom of expression, so the general principles applicable to free speech apply to freedom of the press as well. Thus, the Court will allow the repression of publication only if the state can show some "clear and present danger" that publication poses, similar to its position on free speech. In *New York Times* v. *United States* (1971), the Court ruled that the U.S. government could not prevent newspapers from publishing portions of the Pentagon Papers, secret government documents revealing the sordid story of how the United States had become involved in the Vietnam War. A major expansion of freedom of the press in *New York Times* v. *Sullivan* (1964) protects newspapers against punishment for trivial or incidental errors when they are reporting on public persons. This limits the use or threat of libel prosecutions by officials because officials can recover damages only by showing that the medium has purposely reported untruths or has made no effort to find out if what is being reported is true.

prior restraint
The government's power to prevent publication, as opposed to punishment afterward.

Civil Liberties and National Security

Reporting on the War

Graphic reporting on the Vietnam War, such as this image from the Central Highlands of Vietnam during a battle with Viet Cong troops, helped turn public opinion against U.S. involvement there. The Johnson and Nixon administrations tried to rein in the press but had little luck doing so.

Protecting Sources   Many reporters and executives in news organizations believe that reporters must be able to protect their sources if they are to have access to insider information that the public needs to know. Without protection of sources, newspeople suggest, the stream of information that the public requires in a democracy will flow more slowly. This is the argument that *New York Times* reporter Judith Miller made when she went to jail for 85 days in 2005 for refusing to testify about her source in the administration who had revealed the identity of CIA operative Judith Plame, the wife of a vocal critic of President Bush's reasons for going to war in Iraq. Although most states have shield laws allowing reporters to protect their sources, there is no such federal law, and the Supreme Court has rejected the argument that constitutional doctrines on freedom of the press give reporters immunity from testifying when they have been issued a subpoena by a court (see *Branzburg* v. *Hayes,* 1972).

SIMULATION

Balancing Liberty and Security at a Time of War

Offensive Media   *Pornography* is a nonlegal term for offensive sexual materials: the legal term is **obscenity.** Although the courts have held that *obscenity* is unprotected by the First Amendment, the definition of obscenity has provoked constitutional struggles for half a century. Early disputes concerned the importation and mailing of works that we regard today as classics: James Joyce's *Ulysses* and D. H. Lawrence's *Lady Chatterley's Lover,* for example.[11] Although the justices admitted that principled distinctions sometimes eluded them (Justice Potter Stewart once said that he did not know how to define hard-core pornography but that he knew it when he saw it), a reasonably clear three-part test emerged from *Miller* v. *California* (1973):

obscenity

As defined by the Supreme Court, the representation of sexually explicit material in a manner that violates community standards and is without redeeming social importance or value.

1. The average person, applying contemporary community standards, must find that the work as a whole appeals to the prurient interest (lust).

2. The state law must specifically define what depictions of sexual conduct are obscene.

3. The work as a whole must lack serious literary, artistic, political, or scientific value.

If the work survives even one part of this test, it is not legally obscene and is protected by the First Amendment. Community standards, applied by juries, are used to judge whether the work appeals to lust and whether the work is clearly offensive. However, literary, artistic, political, and scientific value (called the *LAPS test,* after the first letter of each of the four values) is *not* judged by community standards but by the jury's assessment of the testimony of expert witnesses. If, and only if, all three standards are met, the Supreme Court will allow local committees to regulate the sale of obscene materials. Because these tests are not easily met in practice, the *Miller* ruling has done little to stem the tide of sexually explicit material in American popular culture.[12] The Court has ruled, however, in *New York* v. *Ferber* (1982) that states can prohibit the production, distribution, and sale of child pornography.

Recently, many Americans have begun to worry about the availability to minors of sexually offensive material on the Internet. Responding to this concern, Congress and President Clinton cooperated in 1996 to pass the Communications Decency Act, which made it a crime to transmit over the Internet or to allow the transmission of indecent materials to which minors might have access. The Supreme Court, in *Reno, Attorney General of the United States* v. *American Civil Liberties Union* (1997), ruled unanimously that the legislation was an unconstitutional violation of the First Amendment, being overly broad and vague and violative of the free speech rights of adults to receive and

Controversial Art

The distinction between art and obscenity can be very difficult to establish, and battles over the banning of controversial works, such as Robert Mapplethorpe's homoerotic photographs, are quite common in American communities.

send information (the Court reaffirmed this ruling in 2004). The strong and un-ambiguous words of the opinion of the Court make it clear that government ef-forts to regulate the content of the Internet will not get very far. It may well be the case, however, that Internet-filtering software that allows parents to keep objectionable material from their children will accomplish the same end as gov-ernment regulation without danger of violating the Constitution.

Free Exercise of Religion

> *Congress shall make no law . . . prohibiting the free exercise [of religion].*
> —First Amendment to the U.S. Constitution

For much of our history, Congress did not impede the exercise of religion be-cause it did not legislate much on the subject. Because the states were not cov-ered by the First Amendment, the free exercise of religion was protected by state constitutions or not at all. The Supreme Court was content to defer to the states on issues of religious freedom.

As late as 1940, in *Minersville School District* v. *Gobitis,* the Supreme Court upheld the expulsion of two schoolchildren who refused to salute the flag because it violated their faith as Jehovah's Witnesses. Justice Harlan Stone wrote a stinging dissent:

> *The Constitution expresses more than the conviction of the people that demo-cratic processes must be preserved at all costs. It is also an expression of faith and a command that freedom of mind and spirit must be preserved, which gov-ernment must obey, if it is to adhere to that justice and moderation without which no free government can exist.*

Stone's dissent, as well as a series of decisions deferring to state restrictions on Jehovah's Witnesses in 1941 and 1942, eventually moved other justices to Stone's side. In *West Virginia* v. *Barnette* (1943), the Court reversed *Gobitis* and firmly established free exercise of religion as protected against the states.

The core of the nationalized **free exercise clause** today is that govern-ment may not interfere with religious *beliefs.* This is one of the few absolutes in U.S. constitutional law. Religious *actions,* however, are not absolutely protected. The Court has upheld state laws, for instance, outlawing the use of peyote (an illegal hallucinogen) in Native American religious ceremonies (*Employment*

free exercise clause

That portion of the First Amendment to the Constitution that prohibits Congress from impeding reli-gious observance or imping-ing upon religious beliefs.

Division v. *Smith,* 1990). Congress and President Clinton tried to overturn this decision with the Religious Freedom Restoration Act in 1993, but the Act was declared unconstitutional in *City of Boerne* v. *Flores* (1997) because the act, in view of the Court majority, unduly extended national government power over the states. By and large, then, people are free in the United States to believe what they want to believe religiously, and to worship as they wish unless worship practices violate general statutes that serve some compelling public purpose, such as state and federal drug laws or local public health ordinances (which in most locales do not permit such religious practices as animal sacrifice).

Establishment of Religion

Congress shall make no law respecting an establishment of religion.
—First Amendment to the U.S. Constitution

Freedom of conscience requires that government not favor one religion over another by granting it special favors, privileges, or status. It requires, in Jefferson's famous terms, "a wall of separation between church and state." Nevertheless, incorporation of the **establishment clause** proved to be a particularly messy matter. In *Everson* v. *Board of Education* (1947), Justice Hugo Black for the Supreme Court determined that no state could use revenues to support an institution that taught religion, thus incorporating the First Amendment ban into the Fourteenth Amendment. But the majority in that case upheld the New Jersey program that reimbursed parents for bus transportation to parochial schools. A year later, Justice Black wrote another opinion incorporating the establishment clause in *McCollum* v. *Board of Education* (1948). This time, a program for teaching religion in public schools was found unconstitutional. In *Zorach* v. *Clauson* (1952), however, the Court upheld a similar program in New York State that let students leave school premises early for religious instruction. The establishment clause had been incorporated, but the justices were having a difficult time determining what "separation of church and state" meant in practice.

establishment clause
The part of the First Amendment to the Constitution that prohibits Congress from establishing an official religion; the basis for the doctrine of the separation of church and state.

The *Lemon* Test   The Warren Court (1953–1969) brought together a solid church–state separationist contingent whose decisions the early Burger Court (1969–1973) distilled into the major doctrine of the establishment clause: the "*Lemon* test." In *Lemon* v. *Kurtzman* (1971), Chief Justice Warren Burger specified three conditions that every law must meet to avoid "establishing" religion:

1. The law must have a secular *purpose*. That secular purpose need not be the only or primary purpose behind the law. The Court requires merely some plausible nonreligious reason for the law.

2. The *primary effect* of the law must be neither to advance nor to retard religion. The Court will assess the probable effect of a governmental action for religious neutrality.

3. Government must never foster *excessive entanglements* between the state and religion.

While lawyers and judges frequently disagree about each of the three "prongs" of the *Lemon* test, the test has erected substantial walls that bar mixing church and state. The Rehnquist Court took many of the bricks out of the walls, however. In *Rosenberger* v. *University of Virginia* (1995), it ruled that the university (a state-supported institution) must provide the same financial

Feeding the Hungry

President Bush and many conservative religious leaders believe that social services are best delivered by faith-based organizations and that federal monies should be funneled to these organizations to help them do so. Here, volunteers at the Amen Place soup kitchen at the St. Casimir Catholic Church rest for a few minutes after preparing Thanksgiving dinner for the needy.

subsidy to a student religious publication that it provides to other student publications. In 2002, in *Zelman* v. *Simmons-Harris,* decided by a 5–4 vote, the Court approved Cleveland's program of school vouchers that provides public money to parents who want to send their children to private schools, whether secular or religious. The Court majority based its ruling on the fact that public monies do not go directly to religious schools in the Cleveland program but rather to parents who are free to choose their children's school(s). In other cases, the Rehnquist Court ruled that public monies can go to parochial schools if they are for programs that are similar to ones in public schools and not used to advance religious instruction. This would include things such as funds to purchase science books or support drug education programs.[13] However, the Rehnquist Court was unwilling to depart too far from the principle of separation of church and state; in 2004, for example, the Court ruled that the state of Washington had done no constitutional harm when it denied a state-funded scholarship to a student studying for the ministry.

With regard to religious displays in courthouses and other public buildings, the Rehnquist Court seemingly adopted Justice Sandra Day O'Connor's somewhat vague proposition that the establishment clause does not forbid religious displays in courthouses and other public buildings unless a "reasonable observer would view them as endorsing religious beliefs or practices."[14] The Court seems to have decided that it will need to look at such things as religious displays—lights, manger scenes, and the like—at public buildings on a case-by-case basis. In 2005, it ruled in one instance that hanging framed copies of the Ten Commandments in a courthouse in Kentucky went too far in promoting a particular set of religious beliefs (*McCreary County, Kentucky, et al.* v. *ACLU).* As Justice David Souter put it in his majority opinion, "The reasonable observer could only think that the counties meant to emphasize and celebrate the religious message . . . The display's unstinting focus was on religious passages [posted with the Commandments], showed that the counties posted the Commandments precisely because of their sectarian content." In another ruling handed down the same day *(Van Orden* v. *Perry),* the Court allowed a display of a six-foot-high monument of the Ten Commandments in

Church–State Controversy

The church–state separation issue continues to generate controversy in American politics. Here religious protestors in 2004 object to the ruling of the Eleventh Circuit Court upholding a federal district court's decree ordering the removal of a large and prominently display of the Ten Commandments from the Alabama state court house. After he refused to comply with the ruling to remove the display he had placed at the court house, Alabama Supreme Court Justice Roy Moore was removed from his position by Alabama's Court of the Judiciary.

front of the state capitol in Austin because it was one of 40 monuments and historical markers that, in the words of Justice Stephen Breyer, ". . . served a mixed but primarily nonreligious purpose."

Waiting in the wings are a range of issues involving the separation of church and state that the Court will eventually consider, given the number of cases that are working their way up from state courts and federal district courts. These include the legitimacy of the words "one nation under God" in the Pledge of Allegiance, the acceptability of the nondenominational prayers that open the daily sessions in Congress, and more. The point here is fairly straightforward: The debate over where to draw the line that separates church and state is a continuing one in America and is unlikely to ever be resolved once and for all.

Religion in Public Schools   One of the most controversial aspects of constitutional law regarding the establishment of religion concerns school prayer. Although a majority of Americans support allowing a nondenominational prayer or a period of silent prayer in the schools, the Court has consistently ruled against such practices since the early 1960s, perhaps believing that children in school settings, as opposed to adults in other areas of life, are more likely to feel pressure from those conveying religious messages. In *Engel* v. *Vitale* (1962), the Court ordered the state of New York to suspend its requirement that all students in public schools recite a nondenominational prayer at the start of each school day. In *Stone* v. *Graham* (1980), the Court ruled against posting the Ten Commandments in public school classrooms. In *Lee* v. *Weisman* (1992), it ruled against allowing school-sponsored prayer at graduation ceremonies. In *Santa Fe Independent School District* v. *Doe* (2000), the Court ruled that student-led prayers at school-sponsored events such as football games are not constitutionally permissible because they have the "improper effect of coercing those present to participate in an act of religious worship." In these and other cases the Court has consistently ruled against officially sponsored prayer in public schools as a violation of the separation of church and state.

Returning prayer to the public schools and making schools less secular are very high on the agenda of religious conservatives. Bills supporting voluntary classroom prayer (such as a moment of silent contemplation) are constantly being introduced into Congress and state legislatures, with little success so far. Christian conservatives have also tried without success to pass a school prayer constitutional amendment. In several very religious communities, school officials have simply ignored the Supreme Court and continue to allow prayer in public classrooms.

An important battle about religion in the schools concerns attempts by some committed believers to either exclude Darwinian evolutionary biology from the school curriculum or to balance it with alternative interpretations such as "creationism" (the idea that God created the earth as described in the bible) or "intelligent design" (the idea that the natural world is so complex that it could not have evolved as scientists propose, advocated by the Discovery Institute in Seattle). Because courts at all levels have rejected the teaching of "creationism" as an improper intrusion of religion into public education, many religious activists have pushed "intelligent design" as an alternative approach that might pass court muster. The Dover, Pennsylvania, school board tried this strategy but lost in federal court. As Judge John Jones put it in his opinion in *Kitzmiller* v. *Dover Area School District* (2005), ". . . we conclude that the religious nature of ID [intelligent design] would be readily apparent to an objective observer, adult, or child. . . . The overwhelming evidence at trial established that ID is a religious view, a mere relabeling of creationism, and not a scientific theory."

With no sign that the tide of religious feeling is about to recede in the United States, debates over school prayer, religious displays in school, and the teaching of evolution will continue for the foreseeable future. The main reason these issues will linger is that neither the courts nor the American people are entirely certain where the line between church and state should be drawn.

Privacy

The freedoms addressed so far—speech, press, and religion—are explicitly mentioned in the Bill of Rights. The freedom to be left alone in our private lives—what is usually referred to as the *right to privacy*—is nowhere mentioned. Nevertheless, most Americans consider the right to privacy one of our most precious freedoms; most believe we ought to be spared wiretapping, e-mail snooping, and the regulation of consensual sexual activities in our own homes, for instance. Many (though not all) constitutional scholars believe, moreover, that a right to privacy is *inherent* (there, but not explicitly stated) in the Bill of Rights; note the prohibitions against illegal searches and seizures and against quartering of troops in our homes, as well as the right to free expression and conscience. Such scholars also point to the Ninth Amendment as evidence that the framers believed in the existence of liberties not specifically mentioned in the Bill of Rights: "The enumeration in the Constitution of certain rights, shall not be construed to deny or disparage others retained by the people." The Supreme Court agreed with this position in *Griswold* v. *Connecticut* (1965), in which it ruled that a constitutional right to privacy exists when it struck down laws making birth control illegal.

Most jurists and legal scholars have come to accept that a fundamental right to privacy exists. This was affirmed by conservative Supreme Court nominees John Roberts (in late 2005) and Samuel Alito (in early 2006) during their confirmation hearings in the Senate. Where disagreements occur is the nature and scope of private acts that are free from government intrusion. How far should privacy be protected, for example, on matters such as abortion, gay and lesbian rights, the right to die, and the security of interpersonal communications during wartime? Controversies exist on each of these matters.

Griswold's right to privacy doctrine later became an important precedent in *Roe* v. *Wade* (1973), in which the Court ruled in favor of a woman's right to terminate her pregnancy. Privacy in intimate sexual matters was an important component in the Court's decision in *Lawrence* v. *Texas* (2003) that state antisodomy laws prohibiting consensual gay and lesbian sexual relations are unconstitutional. "Private lives in matters pertaining to sex," declared Justice Anthony Kennedy in his majority opinion, are a protected liberty.

It is relatively unclear yet whether the courts will support a privacy-based "right to die." So far the Supreme Court has refused to endorse or reject the existence of such a right. The status of this potential right was at the heart of the notorious Terri Schiavo case in Florida. Had Ms. Schiavo made it clear before the heart attack with extensive brain damage that put her first into a coma and then into a "persistent vegetative state" that she would not want to be sustained in such a situation, as her husband insisted? Or would she have wanted to be sustained on a feeding tube, as her parents insisted? The Florida courts ruled on several occasions that her feeding tube could be removed. A law passed in record time by Congress and signed by President Bush in 2005 insisted that the federal courts take up jurisdiction in the case. Both federal district and circuit courts supported the position of the Florida Supreme Court.

In 2004, the Ninth Circuit Court of Appeals upheld Oregon's assisted suicide law (called the Death with Dignity Act) passed by voters in 1994. In its opinion the justices strongly criticized Attorney General John Ashcroft's announcement that any doctor prescribing drugs that are used by patients to end their lives would be subject to prosecution under the federal Controlled Substances Act, saying that his action "far exceeds the scope of his authority under federal law." The Supreme Court upheld the ruling of the Ninth Circuit in 2006 in *Gonzales* v. *Oregon.* Interestingly, the ruling was based on very narrow grounds—whether the Attorney General could prosecute doctors for prescribing end-of-life drugs—but did not consider whether doctor-assisted suicide was a protected privacy-based right. The Court's ruling leaves the matter, at least for the time being, in the hands of the states, unless Congress chooses to legislate on the issue.

Finally, there are issues relating to government intrusion on private communications. News in late 2005 about the government's extensive surveillance operations targeting American citizens in the name of the war on terrorism— whether in a fashion authorized by the USA Patriot Act or in secret, warrantless phone and Internet searches by the NSA—created a firestorm of criticism about possible violation of fundamental American liberties. We will look at this in more detail later in this chapter.

PARTICIPATION

Civil Liberties in Today's World: Privacy and the Rights of the Accused

So, a right to privacy is well established in principle. Disagreements continue to exist, however, on what this means in practice.

Rights of the Accused

Rights of the Accused

Five of the 10 amendments that make up the Bill of Rights concern protections for individuals suspected, accused, or convicted of a crime, suggesting that the framers were deeply concerned about this aspect of freedom. Most Americans today treasure the constitutional rights and liberties that protect innocent individuals—what are generally termed due process protections—from wrongful prosecution and imprisonment. But most Americans also want to control crime as much as possible. Balancing the two sentiments is not easy.

Unreasonable Searches and Seizures The Fourth Amendment secures the right of all persons against unreasonable searches and seizures and allows the granting of search warrants only if the police can specify evidence of serious lawbreaking that they reasonably expect to find. Until the Warren Court compelled the states to abide by the Fourth Amendment in 1961, they had frequently used searches and seizures that the federal courts would consider "unreasonable" in an effort to control crime. In *Mapp* v. *Ohio* (1961), the Supreme Court enunciated that the **exclusionary rule** to prevent the police and prosecutors from using evidence that had been gained through warrantless and unreasonable searches to convict people must be followed by the states. A majority of the justices believed that the threat of perpetrators' being freed in cases where unreasonable searches had been conducted eventually would force the police to play by the constitutional rules while conducting their investigations.

> **exclusionary rule**
>
> A standard promulgated by the Supreme Court that prevents police and prosecutors from using evidence against a defendant that was obtained in an illegal search.

The Warren Court (1953–1969) demanded that the police get warrants whenever the person to be subjected to a search had a "reasonable expectation of privacy."[15] The Burger Court (1969–1986) limited the places in which privacy could be reasonably expected, allowing searches of moving cars stopped even for routine traffic infractions and of garbage cans set out for collection. The Burger Court authorized a "good faith" exception to the exclusionary rule, under which prosecutors may introduce evidence obtained illegally if they can show that the police had relied on a warrant that appeared valid but later proved to be invalid.[16] The Court allowed another exception for illegally gathered evidence that

You Have the Right to Remain Silent . . .

The right to due process when accused of a federal crime was part of the Constitution from the outset, but it was the Supreme Court's *Miranda* decision in 1966 that required law enforcement officials in states and localities to inform the accused of their rights at the time of arrest.

would have been discovered eventually without the illegal search.[17] The Rehnquist Court went well beyond these exceptions. In *Murray* v. *United States* (1988), it allowed prosecutors to use products of illegal searches if other evidence unrelated to the illegal evidence would have justified a search warrant. The combination of "good faith," "inevitable discovery," and "retroactive probable cause" considerably narrowed the exclusionary rule. The Rehnquist Court (1986–2005) further narrowed the exclusionary rule when it held in *Wyoming* v. *Houghton* (1999) that police who have **probable cause** to search an automobile for illegal substances may also search personal possessions (in this case, a purse) of passengers in the car. In *Wilson* v. *Arkansas* (2006), the Roberts Court ruled that police need not knock or announce their presence when entering a house with a search warrant.

However, the Court has stopped short of taking the exclusionary rule back to pre-Warren Court days. It ruled, for example, that police could not search every driver or car involved in petty traffic offenses. Thus, a bag of marijuana discovered in a search incident to a speeding ticket in *Knowles* v. *Iowa* (1998) was excluded as the product of an illegal search. Moreover, the Court ruled in *Kyllo* v. *United States* (2001) that police could not use high-technology thermal devices to search through the walls of a house to check for the presence of high-intensity lights used for growing marijuana. Justice Scalia was especially incensed, saying in his opinion that to allow such searches "would leave the homeowner at the mercy of advancing technology. . . . "

Self-Incrimination   The Warren Court was instrumental in incorporating Fifth Amendment protections against self-incrimination. It determined, for example, that the privilege not to be forced to incriminate oneself was useless at trial if the police coerced confessions long before the trial took place. To forestall "third-degree" tactics in the station house, the Court detailed a stringent set of procedural guarantees: the famous rights established in *Miranda* v. *Arizona* (1966). Once detained by authorities, all persons had to be informed of their rights to remain silent and to consult with an attorney. Although the Burger Court upheld *Miranda,* it allowed exceptions: It allowed the use of information obtained without "Mirandizing" suspects if the suspects took the stand in their own defense. It also allowed the use of information obtained without *Miranda* warnings if some immediate threat to public safety had justified immediate questioning and postponing warnings.[18] The Rehnquist Court went beyond these exceptions when it held that a coerced confession may be "harmless error" that does not constitute self-incrimination.[19] The main principle of the Miranda decision was upheld by the Rehnquist Court, however, in *Dickerson* v. *United States* (2000) and reaffirmed in three 2004 decisions.

The Right to Counsel   The Sixth Amendment's right to counsel was incorporated in two landmark cases. In *Powell* v. *Alabama* (1932)—the famed Scottsboro Boys prosecution—the Court ruled that legal counsel must be supplied to all indigent defendants accused of a **capital crime** (any crime in which the death penalty can be imposed). Before this decision, many poor people in the southern states, especially African Americans, had been tried for and convicted of capital crimes without the benefit of an attorney. Thirty-one years later, in *Gideon* v. *Wainwright* (1963), the Court ruled that defendants accused of any felony in state jurisdictions are entitled to a lawyer and that the states must supply a lawyer when a defendant cannot afford to do so. Justice Black wrote the following for a unanimous Court:

probable cause

Legal doctrine that refers to a reasonable belief that a crime has been committed.

SIMULATION

You Are a Police Officer

capital crime

Any crime for which death is a possible penalty.

Gideon's Petition

Before Clarence Gideon won his case before the Supreme Court in 1963, states did not have to provide attorneys for people accused of a felony. Gideon wrote his appeal letter—shown here—from his prison cell in Florida. The Court agreed with Gideon, incorporating this part of the Sixth Amendment.

> *Not only . . . precedents but also reason and reflection require us to recognize that in our adversary system of criminal justice, any person hauled into court, who is too poor to hire a lawyer, cannot be assured of a fair trial unless counsel is provided for him. This seems to be an obvious truth.*

By incorporating the Sixth Amendment's guarantee of legal counsel, the Court has ensured that every criminal defendant in the United States can, at least in theory, mount a defense regardless of socioeconomic status.

Capital Punishment   The Burger Court examined capital punishment in the states under the Eighth Amendment's prohibition of "cruel and unusual punishment." In *Furman* v. *Georgia* (1972), a split Court found that the death penalty, as used in the states, constituted "cruel and unusual punishment." Responding to the Court's criticisms, Congress and 35 states passed new authorizations of the death penalty aimed at making the imposition of capital punishment more consistent and less capricious and arbitrary. The Burger Court held in *Gregg* v. *Georgia* (1976), after states had changed their sentencing procedures, that capital punishment was not inherently cruel or unusual so long as procedures were nonarbitrary and nondiscriminatory. However, the Court tended to create an "obstacle course" of standards that the states had to meet if they wanted to use the death penalty. Basically, the Court insisted that defendants be given every opportunity to show mitigating circumstances so that as few convicts as possible would be killed.

The Rehnquist Court at first expedited the use of the death penalty. (Some of the reasons are examined in the "Using the Framework" feature.) In *McCleskey* v. *Kemp* (1987), the Court said that statistical evidence that blacks who kill whites are four times more likely to be sentenced to death than whites who kill blacks is not sufficient to prove racism in death penalty cases; individual defendants, it ruled, must show that racism played a role in their specific cases. In *Penry* v. *Lynaugh* (1989), the Court allowed the execution of a convicted murderer who had the intelligence of a seven-year-old. In *Stanford* v. *Kentucky* (1989), it allowed the execution of a minor who had been convicted of murder. The Rehnquist Court also limited avenues of appeal and delay in death penalty cases. In *McCleskey* v. *Zant* (1991), it made delays much less likely by eliminating many means of challenging capital convictions. In *Keeney* v. *Tamayo-Reyes* (1992), the Court limited the right of "death row" inmates convicted in state courts to appeal to the Supreme Court.

From the middle of the 1960s to the late 1990s, political leaders and public opinion strongly supported the use of the death penalty. In this environment, the Court removed most of the obstacles to its use. It is hardly surprising, then, that the number of people executed in the United States in 1999 reached its highest level (98) since 1976, when the Court reinstated the death penalty, with Texas accounting for more than one-third of the total[20] (see Figure 15.2).

Although still strongly in favor of capital punishment in principle, the public and many elected officials and judges seem to be having second thoughts about how fairly it is used in practice. Most of the rethinking about the death penalty is based on rising concerns about executing the mentally retarded, the quality of legal defense for those accused of murder, the fairness of the system toward racial minorities, and the desire to see a wider use of DNA evidence where relevant. The exoneration of several death row inmates by the use of DNA evidence in the early 2000s, as well as a long-term drop in the

FIGURE 15.2 • Executions in the United States, 1977–2005

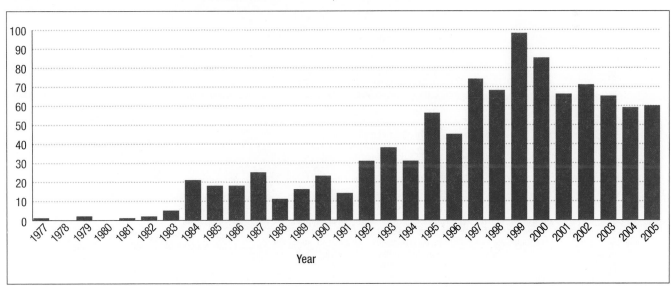

Fueled by fear of violent crime, executions in the United States increased dramatically from the early 1980s to the late 1990s but declined significantly after that as public concerns rose about how fairly the death penalty is used.

Source: Bureau of Justice Statistics, "Capital Punishment 2006."

Using the Framework

The Death Penalty

Why did executions in the United States peak in the 1990s, then decline?

Background: Between the reinstatement of the death penalty by the Supreme Court in 1976 and the end of 2001, 737 inmates were executed in the United States. Of that total, 619 (84 percent) took place in the 1990s. In 1999, 98 executions were carried out, the highest total since 1951, with Texas, Virginia, and Florida leading the way. Recently, however, the number of executions has declined. We can understand better why this is so by looking broadly at how structural, political linkage, and governmental factors have influenced the death penalty issue.

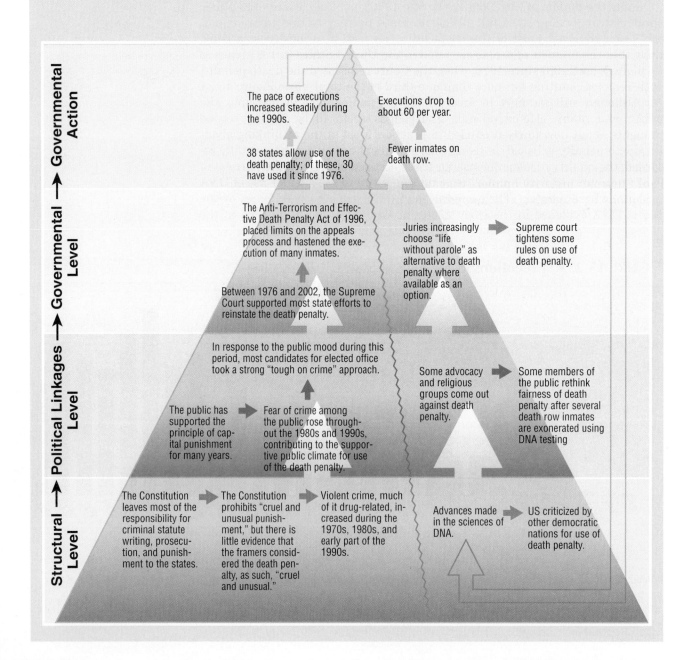

Governmental Action

The pace of executions increased steadily during the 1990s.

Executions drop to about 60 per year.

38 states allow use of the death penalty; of these, 30 have used it since 1976.

Fewer inmates on death row.

Governmental Level

The Anti-Terrorism and Effective Death Penalty Act of 1996, placed limits on the appeals process and hastened the execution of many inmates.

Juries increasingly choose "life without parole" as alternative to death penalty where available as an option.

Supreme court tightens some rules on use of death penalty.

Between 1976 and 2002, the Supreme Court supported most state efforts to reinstate the death penalty.

Political Linkages Level

In response to the public mood during this period, most candidates for elected office took a strong "tough on crime" approach.

The public has supported the principle of capital punishment for many years.

Fear of crime among the public rose throughout the 1980s and 1990s, contributing to the supportive public climate for use of the death penalty.

Some advocacy and religious groups come out against death penalty.

Some members of the public rethink fairness of death penalty after several death row inmates are exonerated using DNA testing

Structural Level

The Constitution leaves most of the responsibility for criminal statute writing, prosecution, and punishment to the states.

The Constitution prohibits "cruel and unusual punishment," but there is little evidence that the framers considered the death penalty, as such, "cruel and unusual."

Violent crime, much of it drug-related, increased during the 1970s, 1980s, and early part of the 1990s.

Advances made in the sciences of DNA.

US criticized by other democratic nations for use of death penalty.

violent crime rate in the United States, have also had an effect on public opinion. A majority of Americans still favor the death penalty, but many say they are worried about how fairly it is used and say they support life sentences without the possibility of parole as an alternative to the death penalty in capital cases. President George W. Bush asked Congress to look at this alternative to the death penalty in federal cases in his 2005 State of the Union message. (See the "Mapping American Politics" feature for a consideration of how the death penalty sentencing is related to the incidence of violent crime).

Concerns about fairness led several governors in the early and mid-2000s to impose moratoriums on the use of the death penalty, including Governor George Ryan of Illinois and Governor Parris Blendening of Maryland. In 2003 Ryan, reacting to research by Northwestern University students that exonerated 19 inmates on Illinois's death row and to the findings of a commission appointed to study the fairness of trials and sentencing procedures in capital cases, commuted the sentences of all death row inmates in Illinois. For its part, the New York state legislature refused to reinstate the death penalty after the state's highest court ruled that its existing law was unconstitutional. By 2005, 28 of 37 death penalty states, including Texas, had legislated life without parole as a sentence that juries might consider in capital cases, and most of them had legislated or were considering legislation that would require DNA testing in such cases. In 2006, the New Jersey legislature imposed a moratorium on executions.

Much to the surprise of seasoned observers, the Rehnquist Court began in 2002 to pull back from its unstinting support for the death penalty. In *Atkins* v. *Virginia* (2002), the Court followed the lead of 18 states in banning the use of the death penalty for mentally retarded defendants, saying, in Justice John Paul Stevens's majority opinion, that "a national consensus now rejects such executions as excessive and inappropriate"and that "society views mentally retarded offenders as categorically less culpable than the average criminal." In *Ring* v. *Arizona* (2002), the Court overruled the death sentences of more than 160 convicted killers, declaring that only juries, and not judges, can decide on the use of the death penalty for those convicted of capital crimes. In 2005, the Supreme Court struck down death penalty convictions in cases in which it was convinced that a defendant had inadequate legal defense, another in which a defendant was brought to a death penalty sentencing hearing in shackles (terming it "inherently prejudicial"), and yet another in which the defendant was under the age of 18. It also rebuked the Fifth Circuit Court of Appeals for failing to follow an earlier Supreme Court ruling that had advised the Fifth Circuit to rethink the fairness of the death penalty in a case from Texas in which it was shown that the prosecutor had systematically excluded African Americans from a jury that had convicted and sentenced an African American man. It eventually ordered a new trial.[21] And, in 2006, the Roberts Court ruled unanimously that states cannot deny the introduction of evidence in capital cases that suggests a person other than the defendant had committed the crime.

Of course, the main evidence supporting the proposition that beliefs about the death penalty are changing among the public (whose members make up juries), lawyers (whether prosecutors or defense attorneys), and judges is that the number of executions each year in the United States has been falling from its high point in 1999 (see Figure 15.2). And the numbers will decline further, because fewer death penalty sentences are being imposed; in 2005 there were only 96 such sentences handed out in state and federal jurisdictions across the country, down dramatically from 296 in 1999.[22] By the end of 2003, federal prosecutors were reporting they were having trouble convincing juries to impose the death penalty at all; in federal capital trials, Bush administration

Mapping American Politics

Violent crime and the death penalty

Introduction: It is well known that the United States has more prisoners on death row and executes more prisoners annually than any other rich democratic country. However, the use of the death penalty is not distributed uniformly across the United States. State-by-state variations are extraordinarily high. Why this is the case is not entirely obvious. One reason could be that the frequency of violent crime—including murder—varies substantially among the states. Or it could be that violent crime does not vary very much, but that the responses to it by the public, prosecutors, and juries vary a great deal. Some states, that is to say, may be more inclined than others to use the ultimate penalty in response to crime. We examine the two explanations in these cartograms.

States Sized by Violent Crime Rate per 100,000 People

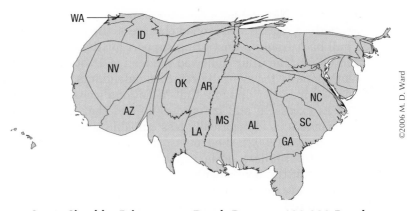

States Sized by Prisoners on Death Row per 100,000 People

©2006 M. D. Ward

prosecutors' death penalty success rate was only about 15 percent from 2001 through 2003, compared with about 50 percent from 1988 through 2000.[23]

Capital Punishment Elsewhere: How Exceptional? With the exception of Japan, the United States is the only rich democratic country that uses capital punishment. Over the course of the past three decades, first the rich democracies, then many other nations, either banned the death penalty outright or stopped using it even when it remained on the books. The total number of nations that have either banned capital punishment or not used it in more than 10 years reached 120 in 2004. Turkey, to take one example, last executed someone in 1984 and has since banned the death penalty as part of a set of conditions for eventually joining the European Union. India began legislative deliberations in 2005 to eliminate capital punishment from its criminal law. In 2006, 76 nations retained and used the death penalty for certain crimes—usually murder, terrorism, or war crimes, although Saudi Arabia and

Comparing Civil Liberties

Crime and Punishment Maps: The cartogram on the top shows the rate of violent crime for each state per 100,000 people. States are expanded or diminished in size by their rate of violent crime. If the violent crime rates were relatively uniform across the country, the cartogram would appear undistorted, similar to a standard map. We can see that the first cartogram is only slightly distorted. To be sure, Oklahoma, Louisiana, Florida, South Carolina, Tennessee, Maryland, and Delaware are enlarged a bit because they suffer from more violent crime than other states, and California, Texas, and New York are smaller because their crime rates are lower than those of other states. Nevertheless, the variation among the states is not great. In the second cartogram, in contrast, each state is expanded or diminished by how many prisoners it has on death row per 100,000 people (the number of annual executions in the United States is not high enough to allow for statistical analysis of the sort being used here). This cartogram suggests that the imposition of capital sentences has little to do with levels of violent crime and much more to do with state-by-state differences in political cultures, legal codes, prosecutorial practices, and jury behaviors. States that are especially prone to impose death penalty sentences include most states of the Deep South (Louisiana, Mississippi, Arkansas, Alabama, North Carolina, South Carolina, and Georgia), as well as Idaho, Arizona, Nevada, and Oklahoma. The New England states practically disappear (their death row inmate populations per 100,000 are extremely low), and Washington and California are quite small as well. Surprisingly, while it annually leads the nation in executions, Texas has a lower-than-average death row inmate population, relative to the size of its population.

What Do You Think? Should the penalty for a crime in one state be different from that in another state? Should there be federal statutes or guidelines that ensure national uniformity in sentencing for felony crimes, including the imposition of the death penalty? Or should the people in each state be free, as they are now, to treat crime in a way that seems most appropriate to them? How about your state? Does it have a relatively high death row population or a low one? Why do you think that might be the case?

Source: U.S. Bureau of the Census, *Statistical Abstract of the United States, 2006,* Table 295 (violent crime), Tables 17 and 337 (death row prisoners).

Singapore, among others, have executed people for drug offenses—with China leading the way, followed closely, on a per-capita basis by Iran, Kuwait, and Saudi Arabia. In total numbers, China executed about 3,400 people in 2004, compared with 59 in the United States.[24]

Civil Liberties and the Fight Against Terrorism

Because involvement in war raises public and governmental concerns about public safety and national security and tends to encourage patriotic sentiments and feelings of national unity, wars have almost always led to some restrictions on civil liberties in democratic countries, including the United

States, particularly for those who vocally dissent from the war effort and those who seem to be associated with the enemy in one way or another.[25] Note, for example, the Sedition Act of 1798, which made criticism of government officials and their policies off limits, the use of military tribunals for civilians during the Civil War, the Red Scare following World War I, the forced internment of Japanese Americans during World War II, and the McCarthy anticommunist hysteria in the early years of the Cold War with the Soviet Union.[26]

What President Bush has called the war on terrorism abroad and its domestic manifestation—homeland security—have generated significant restrictions on civil liberties.

The Patriot Act

- The USA Patriot Act, passed soon after the 9/11 attacks on the United States, gave the federal government expanded powers to use wiretapping and electronic surveillance, impose stricter penalties for harboring or financing terrorists, monitor the bank accounts and e-mail of suspect individuals and organizations, turn away from our borders anyone who endorses terrorism, and detain any noncitizens living in the United States whom the attorney general deemed to be a threat to national security.

- The USA Patriot Act and administration guidelines expanded the use of a little-known and little-used law created in the 1970s to give the FBI secret access to customer, telephone, and financial records of U.S. citizens. About 30,000 "national security letters" demanding such access are issued annually. Under terms of the law, people are given no notice of the request, firms are obligated to comply, and no one is permitted to make public the fact that such requests have been made. Issuance of these letters requires approval by the Office of Intelligence Policy and Review in the Justice Department; there is no judicial oversight.[27]

- President Bush, claiming authority as commander-in-chief and with a legislative mandate from Congress "to use all necessary and appropriate force . . . against nations, organizations, or persons" associated with the 9/11 attacks on the United States,[28] issued executive orders authorizing the use of military tribunals to try any noncitizen, whether arrested here or abroad, suspected of being tied directly or indirectly to acts of terrorism against the United States. The president also ordered the detention of more than 1,200 people for questioning, the questioning of more than 5,000 noncitizens of Middle Eastern and/or Muslim origins about terrorism, the tightening of visa restrictions on people from the Middle East and Muslim countries, and the surveillance of conversations between some suspected terrorists and their attorneys. The president also authorized the indefinite detention of American citizens discovered to have been fighting against U.S. troops in Afghanistan or aiding Al Qaeda, designating them "enemy combatants." Finally, the Bush administration instituted secret deportation hearings for detainees held on immigration violations and indefinite detention for people designated "material witnesses" in terrorism cases.

- President Bush authorized a vast eavesdropping and data-mining operation by the National Security Agency on the electronic and wire communications of American citizens. Under terms of the Foreign Intelligence Surveillance Act, NSA eavesdropping on American citizens requires a warrant granted by a special court. When it was revealed in late 2005 that the NSA had been doing this without warrants, the president claimed he had the power to do so as the commander-in-chief charged with protecting the country and by congressional post-9/11 legislation cited in the previous paragraph. The president also authorized

Post–9/11 Scrutiny

Pakistani and Saudi men and their families line up at a Los Angeles federal building in late 2002 to verify their legal status in the United States under the National Security Entry-Exit Registration System. This program to increase surveillance of men from selected Muslim countries was instituted in the wake of Nine-Eleven. The program was eventually terminated after criticism mounted from civil liberties advocates and Muslim organizations in the United States and the governments of several Muslim countries.

searches by the Central Intelligence Agency and the Department of the Treasury of international banking transactions to trace potential terrorist financial networks.

While Americans supported most of these homeland security measures in the immediate aftermath of the September 11, 2001, attacks on the United States—polls showed, for example, that strong majorities favored the use of military tribunals, detention of terrorism suspects, restrictions on immigration from the Middle East and other Muslim countries, greater use of electronic surveillance, and more in late 2001[29]—civil libertarians have won some notable victories in the courts and at other levels of government. Between 2002 and 2005, for example, 399 towns and cities and seven state legislatures passed resolutions demanding the termination of the USA Patriot Act. Concerns about specific provisions of the act have been raised by a wide range of organizations, including a number of conservative libertarian organizations (such as the American Conservative Union) and public figures (such as former congressman Bob Barr and columnist William Safire), the American Library Association, the U.S. Chamber of Commerce, the National Association of Manufacturers, and the National Association of Realtors. (Business opposition comes from worries about access to firms' proprietary information, the privacy of customers and suppliers, and paperwork burdens.)[30]

The effort by President Bush to convince Congress to renew the USA Patriot Act—the act was set to expire at the end of 2005, presumably because legislators were uneasy about its long-term civil liberties implications—led to a furious debate battle in the Congress in early 2006, many of whose members were deeply concerned about the NSA's surveillance program and the FBI's use of national security letters. Not surprisingly, the strongest critics were Democrats, but a number of Republicans also wanted sections of the act amended in a way that would better safeguard the liberties of American citizens. The USA Patriot Act was renewed in March 2006, however, with only minor changes in its original provisions. For example, searches of library and bookstore records now require judicial approval. Also, businesses and individuals now can challenge the gag order surrounding government subpoenas to

Using the Democracy Standard

Are civil liberties strong enough in the United States to sustain democracy?

PROPOSITION: **One reason that democracy is alive and well in the United States is that civil liberties are so well developed and protected.**

AGREE   Citizens of the United States live in the freest political society in the world. Powerful constraints prevent government from intruding upon people's ability to believe what they want and to exercise their rights of free expression, association, and petition. Although government has violated several of these rights in the past, political practices and Supreme Court decisions have greatly expanded the domain of political freedom in the current era and made violation of basic civil liberties unlikely in the future. For example, even as the United States fights a war on terrorism and tries to ensure homeland security, the strong tradition of support among elites and the public for civil liberties, and the vigilance of the judiciary, have blocked government officials from going too far in restricting freedom in the name of security.

DISAGREE   This claim cannot be supported for two reasons. First, although freedom exists in theory in the United States, not all people have the capacities and resources to use their liberties effectively. All Americans may enjoy freedom of expression as a formal right, for example, but only a handful can make their voices heard in an effective way. Thus, only a privileged few can make significant campaign contributions; form political lobbying organizations; and run ads for their favorite candidates, parties, and issues. Second, we are in the middle of a war, and we know that civil liberties and war have never comfortably coexisted in the United States. So we cannot be certain that civil liberties are not being sacrificed for a greater sense of security in a world where terrorists can strike at any time.

CONSIDER   It is important to recognize that the freedoms of speech, association, press, conscience, and religion are far more extensively developed and protected in the United States today than in the past. But we cannot evade the two issues raised in the "disagree" position: the uneven capacity to make use of the available freedoms and the new threat to traditional civil liberties posed by the war on terrorism and homeland security.

• How do you feel about these two "flies in the ointment," as it were?   • Can all Americans avail themselves of the opportunities provided by their civil liberties?   • Or are they, in reality, rights whose advantages are useful only to the more educated and economically privileged?   • Likewise, do you believe that the war on terrorism and homeland security threaten our freedom?   • Or, do you think that this threat has been exaggerated by civil libertarians?

search their records, although only after waiting a year. And, they are no longer required to tell the government the name of their lawyer. That the USA Patriot Act was renewed with so few changes is probably testament to the public's strong support for government actions that prevent terrorist attacks. By a two-to-one margin Americans say they are more concerned that the government has not gone far enough in protecting the country as compared with not going far enough to protect civil liberties.[31]

The courts have begun to look at the issue of the proper balance between security and civil liberties at a time when people feel legitimately threatened by terrorism. For example, the Sixth Circuit Court ruled in 2002 that the government could not hold deportation hearings for Middle Eastern men behind closed doors. Additionally, two federal appeals courts separately ruled in late 2003 that American citizens arrested on U.S. soil could not be held indefinitely simply by designating them "enemy combatants." In a stunning blow to the Bush administration's claim of extraordinary executive power in wartime, the Supreme Court ruled in 2004 (*Hamdi* v. *Rumsfeld*) that both foreigners and American citizens detained as "enemy combatants" have a right to contest the basis of their detentions. In her opinion in the case, Justice Sandra Day O'Connor reminded everyone, "We have long since made clear that a state of war is not a blank check for the president when it comes to the rights of the nation's citizens." And, in 2006, the Roberts Court ruled that all detainees held at Guantanamo Bay and elsewhere are entitled to protections guaranteed under the Geneva Convention. (In response, the White House asked Congress to agree to new guidelines to cover such detainees.)

The direction that civil liberties will take as a result of the war on terrorism is hard to predict. All we can say with any degree of certainty at this point is that some restrictions will exist for the duration of the war on terrorism and that the severity of these restrictions will be directly related to the degree to which the American people feel afraid that further attacks will occur, and their judgment about how much freedom they are willing to trade for security.

Summary

The formal foundation of American liberties is found in the Constitution and its amendments, particularly the Bill of Rights and the Fourteenth Amendment, but their actual enjoyment depends on the actions of courts, the behavior of government officials, and the struggle for democracy. American history has witnessed an expansion of the boundaries of liberties, especially during the twentieth century, although much remains to be done.

During the nineteenth century, the Supreme Court concerned itself mainly with rights to property. Somewhat belatedly, it nationalized the constitutional protection of civil liberties (i.e., made them applicable to the states) by using the Fourteenth Amendment as its main instrument. The familiar liberties of expression, association, press, and religion, as well as certain due process protections for the accused, were gradually incorporated and guaranteed throughout the nation. The expansion of the rights of the accused was always a hotly disputed political issue, and the conservative orientation of the Rehnquist Court resulted in the reversal of many of the due process innovations of the Warren and Burger Courts.

The fight against terrorism has resulted in restrictions on the civil liberties of noncitizens living in the United States. How long these restrictions remain in place will depend on the severity and duration of the war on terrorism.

Web Exploration
Disputes About Religious Freedom

ISSUE: Americans continue to disagree with one another about the meaning of religious freedom.

SITE: Access the Christian Coalition and Americans United for the Separation of Church and State in MyPoliSciLab at **www.mypoliscilab.com.** Go to the "Web Explorations" section for Chapter 15. Select "Disputes About . . . ," then "religious freedom." Examine the "press room" section of both organizations.

WHAT YOU'VE LEARNED: Compare which issues each organization focuses on and how the issues are treated by each. Which site is closer to reflecting your own understanding of religious freedom? Do you believe there is common ground upon which the two groups might meet, or do you believe that the differences in view are irreconcilable?

HINT: Your views on religious freedom probably depend not only on your specific religious views but also on your support for the doctrine of "separation of church and state."

Internet Sources

The American Civil Liberties Union
www.aclu.org
   Website of the long-time defender of civil liberties in the United States.

Bureau of Justice Statistics
www.ojp.usdoj.gov/bjs/
   Official statistics on crimes, trials, incarceration rates, executions are available at this site.

The Cato Institute
www.cato.org
   A comprehensive site covering civil liberties issues from the conservative libertarian point of view.

The Death Penalty Information Center
www.deathpenaltyinfo.org
   Up-to-date information on the status of the death penalty in the United States and other nations around the world.

Findlaw Supreme Court Opinions
www.findlaw.com/casecode/supreme.html
   Find historical and contemporary Supreme Court decisions and opinions on civil liberties at this site.

First Amendment Cyber-Tribune
http://w3.trib.com/FACT/index.html
   This comprehensive site is an outstanding gateway to information on the First Amendment freedoms discussed in this chapter and provides links for each freedom to background documents, court cases, breaking news, op-ed pieces, bibliographies, First Amendment websites, civil liberties organizations, and even an online question-and-answer section.

Suggestions for Further Reading

Abraham, Henry J., and Barbara A. Perry. *Freedom and the Court,* 8th ed. Lawrence, KS: University of Kansas Press, 2003.
   A trusted introduction to the study of civil rights and liberties for more than 30 years.

Downs, Donald Alexander. *Restoring Free Speech and Liberty on Campus.* New York: Cambridge University Press, 2005.
   A passionate and detailed defense of free speech on campus in the face of campus speech codes.

Epstein, Lee, and Thomas G. Walker. *Constitutional Law for a Changing America.* Washington, D.C.: CQ Press, 2005.
   Shows what aspects of constitutional law have changed over the years, and why.

Fallon, Richard. *The Dynamic Constitution: An Introduction to American Constitutional Law.* New York: Cambridge University Press, 2004.
   An accessible introduction to all aspects of American constitutional law.

Fisher, Louis. *American Constitutional Law: Constitutional Rights,* 6th ed. Durham, NC: Carolina Academic Press, 2005.
   A comprehensive discussion of the issues and controversies that have surrounded the Bill of Rights since the founding of the United States.

Hymann, Philip B. *Terrorism, Freedom, and Security.* Cambridge, MA: MIT Press, 2004.
   A balanced look at the tension between national security and civil liberties in the face of credible terrorist threats.

Stone, Geoffrey R. *Perilous Times: Free Speech in Wartime.* New York: W.W. Norton, 2004.
   A history of the tension between free speech and national security during American conflicts.

Zimring, Franklin. *The Contradictions of American Capital Punishment.* New York: Oxford University Press, 2003.
   Examines the question of why Americans so strongly support the death penalty compared with people in other rich democracies.

CHAPTER 16

Civil Rights: The Struggle for Political Equality

IN THIS CHAPTER

- Why civil rights are important in a democracy

- Civil rights in the Constitution

- How civil rights protections expanded

- The present status of civil rights protections for racial minorities, women, and gays and lesbians

The Return of Segregated Schools

"I don't know why they left," said one fourth-grader at Reid Park Elementary School in Charlotte, North Carolina. "Maybe they didn't like it here."[1] She was referring to the virtual disappearance of white children at her school where, only one year earlier, about one-third of her schoolmates had been white. What was happening at Reid Park Elementary was happening all over the South at the turn of the new century. Fifty years after the Supreme Court had ruled in *Brown* v. *Board of Education* (1954) that "separate but equal" was unconstitutional, schools were becoming more segregated. By 2001, only 30 percent of black children in the South were in schools that were majority white, a decrease from 44 percent as recently as 1988; by 2001, about one-third of black children were in schools that were almost 100 percent black.[2]

For those Americans committed to a racially integrated society, there was much to be proud of in the record of desegregation of public education in the United States after the *Brown* decision, especially in the South where school segregation was official policy from the early twentieth century until the Court's 1954 decision. After a slow start for a few years following *Brown,* school integration took off in the mid-1960s and gained steadily until it reached its peak in the late 1980s. By 1988, only one in four black children were in schools that were 90 to 100 percent black, a far cry from the pre-*Brown* years when virtually all black children were in such schools. During the 1990s, however, the trend reversed all over the South, with more black children going to school where there were few whites or none at all and where white children had less contact with African American children than in many years.[3] (It is worth pointing out, however, that despite the reversal in integration trends in the region, the school integration record of the South remains better than that of any other region of the country; in the Northeast, for example, more than one-half of all African American children are in schools that are 90 to 100 percent black, closely followed by the states in the Midwest. In addition, black children are least exposed to white children in public schools in New York, Illinois, Michigan, California, Maryland, and New Jersey and are most exposed to their white counterparts in the South and the border states.[4])

So why did the trend in the South toward a more integrated public school system first level off, then recede during the 1990s? The answer is fairly straightforward: The federal courts, following the lead of the Supreme

Court in *Dowell* v. *Oklahoma City* (1991)—which ruled that school districts that had made lengthy good-faith efforts to end the effects of previously legal school segregation in their jurisdictions had fulfilled their constitutional obligations for equal protection of the races in education—began to lift court-ordered desegregation plans that required busing and other methods to integrate schools across local jurisdictions. About 40 school districts over the past 10 years have been relieved of such orders, and it is precisely in these districts where the reversal in school integration trends are most evident.

But that still leaves the question of why lifting federal court orders would lead to such a development. Again, the answer is fairly straightforward: When most whites and most blacks live in racially homogeneous neighborhoods—as they do because of white flight to the suburbs and the existence of informally segregated housing markets—local neighborhood schools, absent busing or other student assignment strategies designed to foster integration, will also be racially homogeneous.

It remains to be seen what the outcomes of these changes will be. Many whites and African Americans believe that integrated schooling, whether achieved voluntarily or under court order, is important for children's educational achievement and for teaching tolerance in a racially diverse society. However, other whites and African Americans believe that integration by itself does little to increase academic achievement, and that court-ordered busing mainly leads to intergroup tensions and wasted tax money. Many African

Americans who think this way are becoming attracted to the idea of school vouchers that allow children to use public funds to go to either a public or private school as a way to improve schools in predominantly black neighborhoods. The thinking here is that competition for students among schools will force them to offer a better educational product.

Civil rights are government guarantees of equality for people in the United States regarding judicial proceedings, the exercise of political rights, treatment by public officials, and access to and enjoyment of the benefits of government programs. (The terms *equal citizenship* and *civil rights* often are used interchangeably.) The expansion of civil rights protections for African Americans, as well as for other racial, ethnic, and religious minorities, and for women is one of the great achievements of American history. However, it did not come easily or quickly; it took the struggle of millions of Americans to force change from political leaders and government institutions. The result has been a significant democratization of the republican constitutional system of the framers. As this opening story suggests, however, the expansion of civil rights protection in the United States is neither complete nor free of problems and controversy. ■

Thinking Critically About This Chapter

 Using the Framework In this chapter, you will see that the meaning of civil rights has changed over the course of American history, and you will learn how structural, political linkage, and governmental factors, taken together, explain that change.

 Using the Democracy Standard In this chapter, you will learn how civil rights is at the very center of our understanding of democracy in the United States. You will see how the struggle for democracy helped expand civil rights protections. You also will see how the expansion of civil rights has enhanced formal political equality in the United States, one of the basic foundations of a democratic political order.

Civil Rights Before the Twentieth Century

Civil rights for women and racial minorities was a comparatively late development in the United States, and most major advances were not evident until well into the twentieth century. In this section, we look at the period before the expansion of civil rights.

civil rights

Guarantees of equal treatment by government officials regarding political rights, the judicial system, and public programs.

Equality

An Initial Absence of Civil Rights

Neither the original Constitution nor the Bill of Rights said anything about equality beyond insisting that all Americans are equally entitled to due process in the courts.[5] Indeed, the word *equality* does not appear in the Constitution at all. Nor did state constitutions offer much in the way of guaranteeing equality other than equality before the law. Americans in the late eighteenth and early nineteenth centuries seemed more interested in protecting individuals against government (see Chapter 15) than in guaranteeing certain political rights through government.[6] For most racial or ethnic minorities and women, equality eluded constitutional protection until the twentieth century, although the groundwork was laid earlier.

The inequality of African Americans and women before the Civil War is quite striking. In the South, African Americans lived in slavery, with no rights at all. Outside the South, although a few states allowed African Americans to vote, the number of states doing so actually declined as the Civil War approached, even as universal white male suffrage was spreading. In many places outside the slave South, African Americans were denied entry into certain occupations, required to post bonds guaranteeing their good behavior, denied the right to sit on juries, and occasionally threatened and harassed by mobs when they tried to vote or to petition the government. Chief Justice Roger Taney, in *Dred Scott* v. *Sandford* (1857), went so far as to claim that the Founders believed that blacks had no rights that whites or government were bound to honor or respect. As for women, no state allowed them to vote, few allowed them to sit on juries, and a handful even denied them the right to own property or enter into contracts.

Many African Americans and women refused to play a passive political role, however, even though the pre–Civil War period was not conducive to their participation in politics. African Americans, for instance, voted in elections where they were allowed, helped organize the Underground Railroad to smuggle slaves out of the South, and were prominent in the abolitionist movement against slavery. Both black and white women played an important role in the abolitionist movement—the antislavery speaking tours of Angelina and Sarah Grimké caused something of a scandal in the 1840s when women's participation in public affairs was considered improper—and a few began to write extensively on the need for women's emancipation and legal and political equality. In 1848, Elizabeth Cady Stanton issued her call for a convention on women's rights to be held at the village of Seneca Falls, New York. The Declaration of Sentiments and Resolutions issued by the delegates to the convention stands as one of the landmarks in women's struggle for political equality in the United States:

> *All men and women are created equal . . . but the history of mankind is a history of repeated injuries and usurpations on the part of man toward woman, having in direct object the establishment of a direct tyranny over her. . . . [We demand] that women have immediate admission to all the rights and privileges which belong to them as citizens of the United States.*

Advocating for Women's Rights

In 1848, Elizabeth Cady Stanton helped organize the Seneca Falls Convention on women's rights. The resulting Declaration of Sentiments and Resolutions was patterned after the Declaration of Independence, stating that "all men and women are created equal," and included a list of the injustices of men against women. Stanton remained an activist for many years, helping to found the National Women's Suffrage Association in 1869 to press for the vote for women, and became the first president of the National American Woman Suffrage Association in 1890.

The Civil War Amendments

After the Civil War, the Thirteenth Amendment to the Constitution outlawed slavery throughout the United States, settling the most divisive issue of the nineteenth century. The Fourteenth Amendment reversed *Dred Scott* by making all people who are born or naturalized in the United States, black or white, citizens both of the United States and of the states in which they reside. To secure the rights and liberties of recently freed slaves, Article I of the amendment further provided that "no State shall make or enforce any law which shall abridge the privileges or immunities of citizens of the United States" (the *privileges and immunities clause*); "nor shall any State deprive any person of life, liberty, or property, without due process of law" (the *due process clause*); "nor deny to any person within its jurisdiction the equal protection of the laws" (the *equal protection clause*). The Fifteenth Amendment guaranteed African American men the right to vote. Imposing as this constitutional language sounds, the Supreme Court would soon transform it into a protection for property rights, but not for African Americans or women.

Undermining the Civil War Amendments   The privileges and immunities clause was rendered virtually meaningless by the *Slaughterhouse Cases* (1873). Writing for the Court, Justice Samuel Miller found that the clause protected only the rights of people as citizens of the United States and were not obligations of state governments. In these cases, the Court denied citizens protection against abuses by state governments, including African Americans disfranchised by state actions. Within five years of its passage, then, the Fourteenth Amendment had been seriously compromised by the Court, which foiled an attempt by the post–Civil War Radical Republican Congress to amend the Constitution in favor of equality.

The equal protection clause survived the *Slaughterhouse Cases* but soon lost all practical meaning. First, the Court said that the Fourteenth Amendment gave Congress no power to prohibit discrimination unless it was practiced by state government. "Equal protection of the laws" did not, therefore, preclude race discrimination by private owners or managers of restaurants, theaters, hotels, and other public accommodations, the Court said in the *Civil Rights Cases* (1883). Then the Court made even state-sponsored discrimination constitutional in *Plessy* v. *Ferguson* (1896). The Court said that the states could separate the races in intrastate railways if they provided "equal" facilities for the races. This doctrine of "separate but equal" would provide the legal foundation for **Jim Crow** segregation in the South and would remain in force until it was overturned in *Brown* v. *Board of Education of Topeka* more than half a century later. The Fifteenth Amendment's voting guarantees were also rendered ineffectual—this time by a variety of devices invented to prevent African Americans from voting in the former states of the Confederacy. The **poll tax** was a tax required of all voters in many states, and it kept many African Americans away from the polls, given their desperate economic situation in the South in the late nineteenth and early twentieth centuries. Several states required voters to pass a **literacy test** devised and administered by local officials (see Table 16.1). The evaluation of test results was entirely up to local officials, who rarely passed blacks, even those with a college education or a Ph.D. degree. If white voters failed the literacy test, many states allowed them to vote anyway under the **grandfather clause,** which provided that anyone whose ancestors had voted prior to 1867 could vote as well. Since the ancestors of African Americans in the South had been slaves, the grandfather clause was no help to them at all. Several states instituted **white primaries**

Jim Crow
Popular term for the system of legal racial segregation that existed in the American South until the middle of the twentieth century.

poll tax
A tax to be paid as a condition of voting; used in the South to keep African Americans away from the polls.

literacy test
A device used by the southern states to prevent African Americans from voting before the passage of the Voting Rights Act of 1965, which banned its use; usually involved interpretation of a section of a state's constitution.

grandfather clause
A device that allowed whites who had failed the literacy test to vote anyway by extending the franchise to anyone whose ancestors had voted prior to 1867.

white primaries
Primary elections open only to whites.

TABLE 16.1 • Selected Items from the Alabama Literacy Test

These 10 questions are part of the 68-question Alabama Literacy Test used to decide on the eligibility of voters in that state. The test and others like it were declared illegal by the 1965 Voting Rights Act. Most white voters who were unable to pass this or similar tests in the states of the Deep South were protected by a "grandfather clause" allowing people to vote whose grandfathers had done so.

1. A person appointed to the U.S. Supreme Court is appointed for a term of _____.

2. If a person is indicted for a crime, name two rights which he has.

3. Cases tried before a court of law are of what two types: civil and _____.

4. If no candidate for president receives a majority of the electoral vote, who decides who will become president?

5. If no person receives a majority of the electoral vote, the vice president is chosen by the Senate. True or False?

6. If an effort to impeach the President of the United States is made, who presides at the trial?

7. If the two houses of Congress do not agree to adjournment, who sets the time?

8. A president elected in November takes office the following year on what date?

9. Of the original thirteen states, the one with the largest representation in the first Congress was _____.

10. The Constitution limits the size of the District of Columbia to _____.

Answers: (1) good behavior, life; (2) jury trial, protection against self incrimination, right to counsel, speedy trial, protection against excessive bail; (3) criminal; (4) the House of Representatives; (5) true; (6) though not stipulated in the Constitution, the House has always turned to its Judiciary Committee to manage the impeachment process; (7) the president; (8) January 20; (9) Virginia; (10) not to exceed 10 miles square.

that excluded African Americans from the process of nominating candidates for local, state, and national offices. The states based these primaries on the argument that political parties were private clubs that could define their own membership requirements, including skin color. For those African Americans who might try to vote anyway in the face of the poll tax, the literacy test, and the white primary, there was always the use of terror as a deterrent: Night riding, bombings, and lynchings were used with regularity, especially during times when blacks showed signs of assertiveness.

The statutory devices for keeping African Americans away from the polls were consistently supported by state and federal courts until well into the twentieth century. Terror as a means of preventing voting remained a factor until the 1960s, when the civil rights movement and federal intervention finally put an end to it

Women and the Fifteenth Amendment   Politically active women were stung by their exclusion from the Fifteenth Amendment's extension of the right to vote, as the amendment said only that no state could exclude people on the grounds of "race, color, or previous condition of servitude." Thus, they quickly turned their attention to winning the vote for women. Once the Supreme Court had decided, in *Minor* v. *Happersett* (1874), that women's suffrage was not a right inherent in the national citizenship guarantees of the Fourteenth Amendment, women abandoned legal challenges and turned to more direct forms of political agitation: petitions, marches, and protests. After many years of struggle, the efforts of the women's suffrage movement bore fruit in the Nineteenth Amendment, ratified in 1920: "The right of citizens of the United States to vote shall not be denied or abridged by the United States or by any State on account of sex."

The Contemporary Status of Civil Rights for Racial Minorities

We saw in Chapter 15 how the Supreme Court, using the guidelines written by Justice Harlan Fiske Stone in *United States* v. *Carolene Products Company* (1938), gradually extended the protections of the Bill of Rights to the states, based on the Fourteenth Amendment. Recall that among the actions by the states that would trigger **strict scrutiny** under the *Carolene* guidelines were those that either "restricted the democratic process" or "discriminated against racial, ethnic, or religious minorities." This reading of the Fourteenth Amendment, particularly the equal protection clause, lent judicial support to the gradual advance of civil rights guarantees for African Americans and other minorities and eventually (although less so) for women. In the following sections, we look at the extension of the civil rights of racial minorities, women, and other groups. Here we concentrate mainly (although not exclusively) on Supreme Court decisions,[7] the actions of other branches of government regarding civil rights, and the political standing of these groups (see Chapter 8 for more information on the civil rights, women's, and other social movements that were instrumental in expanding civil rights in the United States).

Two basic issues have dominated the story of the extension of civil rights for African Americans since the mid-1960s:

- The ending of legally sanctioned discrimination, separation, and exclusion from citizenship.
- The debate over what actions to take to remedy the past wrongs done to African Americans.

We examine both in this section.

Ending Government-Sponsored Separation and Discrimination

We reviewed earlier how the Constitution was long interpreted to condone slavery and segregation. In the twentieth century, however, the legal and political battles waged by the civil rights movement eventually pushed the Supreme Court, the president, and Congress to take seriously the equal protection clause of the Fourteenth Amendment.

In 1944, amid World War II (a war aimed in great part at bringing down the racist regime of Adolf Hitler) and the NAACP's campaign to rid the nation of segregation, the Supreme Court finally declared that race was a **suspect classification** that demanded strict judicial scrutiny. This meant that any state or national enactment using racial criteria was presumed to be unconstitutional.

Pressed by the legal efforts of the NAACP, the Court gradually chipped away at *Plessy* and the edifice of segregation. In *Smith* v. *Allwright* (1944), the Court declared that the practice of excluding nonwhites from political-party primary elections was unconstitutional. Then the Court ruled that the states'

strict scrutiny
The assumption that actions by elected bodies or officials violate constitutional rights.

The Struggle for Equal Protection

suspect classification
The invidious, arbitrary, or irrational designation of a group for special treatment by government.

Grudging Integration

The erosion of official segregation in education came slowly and reluctantly in many parts of the nation. When ordered by a federal court in 1948 to admit a qualified black applicant, the University of Oklahoma law school did so but forced the lone student to sit separated from other students.

practice of providing separate all-white and all-black law schools was unacceptable. Many of the key cases before the Supreme Court that eroded the official structure of segregation were argued by Thurgood Marshall—later a justice of the Supreme Court—for the NAACP.[8]

The great legal breakthrough for racial equality came in *Brown* v. *Board of Education of Topeka* (1954), also argued by Thurgood Marshall, in which a unanimous Court declared that "separate but equal" was inherently contradictory and that segregation was constitutionally unacceptable in public schools because it violated guarantees of equal protection. Chief Justice Earl Warren, speaking for a unanimous Court, said that education was "perhaps the most important function of state and local governments" and that segregation in education communicated the message that blacks were inferior and deserving of unequal treatment. "In the field of education [in Warren's words] the doctrine of 'separate but equal' has no place."[9] *Brown* was a constitutional revolution, destined to transform racial relations law and practices in the United States.[10]

The white South did not react violently at first, but it did not desegregate either. Once recognition spread that the Court was going to enforce civil rights, however, massive resistance to racial integration gripped the South. This resistance was what Dr. Martin Luther King, Jr., and others had to work (and die) to overcome. The Court—even with many follow-up cases—was able to accomplish little before the president and Congress backed up the justices with the 1964 Civil Rights Act and the 1965 Voting Rights Act. The civil rights movement and supportive changes in American public opinion in favor of protections for blacks helped spur these legislative and judicial actions.

The drive to protect the rights of racial minorities has occupied the nation ever since. The main legal doctrine on racial discrimination is straightforward:

The March on Washington

Dr. Martin Luther King, Jr., waves to a crowd of an estimated half million people at the March on Washington at the Lincoln Memorial after delivering his "I Have a Dream" speech on August 28, 1963. This event, one of the high points of the civil rights movement, helped convince Congress to pass the Civil Rights Act of 1964.

Any use of race in law or government regulations to discriminate will trigger strict scrutiny (a presumption of unconstitutionality) by the courts. Recall from our earlier discussion that a state or the federal government can defend its acts under strict scrutiny only if it can produce a *compelling* government interest for which the act in question is a *necessary* means. Almost no law survives this challenge; laws that discriminate on the basis of race are dead from the moment of passage. In *Loving* v. *Virginia* (1967), for example, the Court ruled that Virginia's law against interracial marriage served no compelling government purpose that would justify unequal treatment of the races. Needless to say, other racial minority groups in addition to African Americans—Hispanics, Asian Americans, and Native Americans—have benefited from the constitutional revolution that has occurred.[11]

To say that racial discrimination in the law is no longer constitutionally acceptable does not mean that discrimination against racial minorities has disappeared from the United States. More than one-third of African Americans and more than one in five Latino and Asian men report they have experienced job discrimination in 2001. Overwhelming majorities of African Americans, Latinos, and Asians said they had been subject to poor service in stores and restaurants because of their race and had had disparaging remarks directed at them.[12] Sixty-six percent of African American men in 2003 and 39 percent of Hispanic men said they had experienced discrimination from government and/or employers during the past year.[13] Sixty-one percent of African Americans reported in 2006 that there had been no real progress for blacks in recent years (only 31 percent of whites agreed).[14] All minorities reported bad experiences with racial profiling by police. In the 2001 poll, for example, 52 percent of black men and 25 percent of Latino and Asian men claimed to have been stopped by police for no apparent reason. A 2004 report from Amnesty International confirmed these numbers.[15] Although various police departments have taken steps to stop these practices, the courts have never defined racial profiling as suspect, especially if some important law enforcement need is being met by it.

Race and the Death Penalty

Affirmative Action

It is now widely accepted that the Constitution protects racial minorities against any discrimination or disadvantage that is sanctioned or protected by law or government action. The issues are not as clear-cut, however, in the area of government actions that *favor* racial minorities (and women) in **affirmative action** programs designed to rectify past wrongs.[16]

Origins of Affirmative Action

The main goal of the civil rights movement of the 1950s and 1960s was to remove barriers to equal citizenship for black Americans. This goal was largely accomplished in the federal courts by passage of the 1964 Civil Rights Act and the Voting Rights Act of 1965 and by broad changes in public attitudes about race. But even with these important changes, the economic and social situations of African Americans did not seem to be improving much. It seemed to an increasing number of people that ending discrimination was a start, but that more proactive government actions would be required if African Americans were to escape the conditions that years of discrimination had put them in. President Lyndon Johnson, Robert Kennedy, and Martin Luther King, Jr., among others, eventually came to believe that the advancement of black Americans could happen only if there was a broad societal effort to eradicate poverty by equipping the poor, black and white, with the tools for success. This led to the founding of the Johnson administration's Great Society and War on Poverty and programs such as Head Start.

After Martin Luther King's assassination, however, and the urban riots that followed, many people in government, the media, higher education, and the major foundations began to support the notion that progress for African Americans would happen only if government encouraged racial preferences in hiring, contracts, and college admissions. Somewhat surprisingly, it was Richard Nixon, not generally thought of as a booster of civil rights, who took the most important step, requiring in his 1969 Philadelphia Plan that construction companies with federal contracts and the associated construction trade unions hire enough blacks and other minorities to achieve "racial balance" (a proportion roughly equal to the racial balance in the community).

Although initially skeptical of racial preferences, Justices William Brennan, Byron White, Thurgood Marshall, and Harry Blackmun supported temporary programs to remedy the effects of past discrimination. Joined by Justice Lewis Powell, they formed the majority in *Regents* v. *Bakke* (1978), in which the Court authorized a compromise on affirmative action programs. The Constitution and federal law prohibited employers and admissions committees from using strictly racial quotas, the Court said, but it saw no problem with the use of race as one factor among several in hiring or admissions.

Since *Bakke,* government and higher education racial preference programs have become relatively permanent rather than temporary, and their aim has shifted from providing remedies for past discrimination to enhancing diversity. The proliferation of diversity programs, diversity training, and diversity offices has become commonplace in colleges and universities, in government, and in the corporate world.

Why Affirmative Action?

For the most part, according to proponents, affirmative action programs that promote diversity are needed for the following reasons:

- The effects of past discrimination disadvantage, to one degree or another, all members of discriminated-against groups, so simply removing barriers to advancement is insufficient. The proper remedy is to prefer members of such groups in hiring, contracts, and education until such time as they reach parity with the majority.

- In a diverse society such as the United States, tolerance and a sense of community can develop only if we work together in educational, workplace, and government institutions that are diverse.

- People from disadvantaged and discriminated-against groups will improve themselves only if they have experience with successful role models in important institutions.

Critics of affirmative action are not convinced by these arguments. They believe the following to be true:

- Affirmative action violates one of the most basic American principles: that people be judged, rewarded, and punished as individuals, not because they are members of one group or another.

- Affirmative action benefits those within each preferred group who are already advantaged and need little help. Thus, the main beneficiaries of affirmative action in higher education have been middle-class African Americans, not the poor.

- Affirmative action seeks to remedy the effects of past discrimination by discriminating against others today—most notably, white males—simply because they belong to nonpreferred groups.

- Affirmative action increases intergroup and interracial tension by heightening the saliency of group membership. That is, social friction is increased by encouraging people to think of themselves and others as members of groups and to seek group advantages in a zero-sum game in which one group's gain is another group's loss.

Public Opinion on Affirmative Action In survey after survey, a vast majority of Americans say they approve of the diversity goals of affirmative action—

VIDEO DEBATE

Affirmative Action

Sharing the Danger

For many years, fire departments in all parts of the country were strictly segregated, with most firefighter spots going to white males as a matter of policy. In such situations, the Court has allowed the use of affirmative action to redress past discriminatory practices. These firefighters have just finished putting out a fire in Chapel Oaks, Maryland.

special programs to help those who have been discriminated against get ahead; outreach programs to hire minority workers and find minority students—but disapprove of racial preferences in hiring, awarding of government contracts, and admission to colleges.[17] Most polling organizations show the following pattern: When asked whether they generally support affirmative action, about 60 to 65 percent of Americans say they approve;[18] when the survey asks whether they favor affirmative action programs that involve preferential treatment or "set-asides" for racial minorities and women, support erodes dramatically, to no more than 40 percent.[19] Not surprisingly, perhaps, racial differences on the issue of preferential treatment are wide; in 2003, 55 percent of African Americans supported affirmative action programs that involved preferential treatment, whereas only 24 percent of whites did.[20]

American discomfort with affirmative action programs can perhaps be best seen in actions in several of the states. For example, referenda banning affirmative action in any state and local government activity were passed in California (1996) and Washington (1997)—two very liberal states—and other states have severely restricted affirmative action by executive order of their governors.[21]

The Supreme Court on Affirmative Action

The Supreme Court has been grappling for years with the issue of which forms of affirmative action, if any, are constitutionally permissible. Recall that the prevailing constitutional doctrine on matters of race holds that any mention of race in a government statute, ordinance, or rule is subject to strict scrutiny—that is, unconstitutional—unless the government can show some compelling and necessary reason for it. Historically, of course, there is good reason for the Court to take this position, given the fact that laws mentioning race were usually designed to deny equal protection to African Americans and other racial minorities. But what about government actions meant to compensate African Americans and others for past discriminatory actions?

Since the mid-1980s, the Supreme Court has been moving toward the position that laws and other government actions that are not colorblind should be subject to strict scrutiny. In *Wygant* v. *Jackson Board of Education* (1986) and *Richmond* v. *Croson Co.* (1989), the Supreme Court said that programs that narrowly redress specific violations will be upheld as constitutional but that broader affirmative action programs that address society's racism will be struck down. In *Adarand Constructors* v. *Peña* (1995), the Court ruled by a 5–4 majority that the federal government must abide by the strict standards for affirmative action programs imposed on the states in the *Richmond* case and could not award contracts using race as the main criterion. In *Miller* v. *Johnson* (1995), the Court ruled, again by a 5–4 majority, that race could not be used as the basis for drawing House district lines in an effort to increase the number of racial minority members in Congress.[22] In 1997, the Court refused to overturn a ruling of the Ninth Circuit Court that California's anti–affirmative action Proposition 209 was constitutionally permissible. In 2001, the Court let stand a decision by the Eleventh U.S. Circuit Court of Appeals that disallowed a Fulton County, Georgia, program setting annual goals for awarding county contracts to blacks, Hispanics, Asians, Native Americans, and women.

Given these decisions, civil rights organizations were braced for a decision by the Supreme Court that would render affirmative action admissions policies unconstitutional once and for all. When the Court agreed to hear two admissions cases involving the University of Michigan—one involving its undergraduate program, the other its law school—liberals dreaded the outcome, while conservatives could hardly wait for the ruling. The Court stunned virtually every political observer when it ruled by a 5–4 vote in late June 2003 that universities could take race into consideration when considering applications for admission, so long as the consideration of race was not done in a mechanically quantitative manner or used as part of a racial and ethnic quota system, reaffirming, as it were, its position in the 1978 *Bakke* decision. (See the "Using the Framework" feature for more on why this happened.) In its twin decisions, the Court rejected the University of Michigan's undergraduate admissions affirmative action program—because it automatically assigned extra points to each minority applicant—but accepted the law school's—whose admissions process uses race as but one among several factors in a wholistic examination of each applicant's file. What surprised observers the most, perhaps, was not the decision itself, but the broad language that Justice Sandra Day O'Connor used in her majority opinion, in which she stressed that achieving diversity in universities, and especially in its elite law schools, was indeed a compelling reason for not applying strict scrutiny by the Court:

> *In order to cultivate a set of leaders with legitimacy in the eyes of the citizenry, it is necessary that the path to leadership be visibly open to the talented and qualified individuals of every race and ethnicity . . . Access to legal education (and thus the legal profession) must be inclusive of talented and qualified individuals of every race and ethnicity so that all members of our heterogeneous society may participate in the educational institutions that provide the training and education necessary to succeed in America. . . . Cross-racial understanding helps to break down racial stereotypes and better prepares graduates for the working world . . . The law school's educational judgment that such diversity is essential to its educational mission is one to which we defer.*[23]

After the University of Michigan cases, here is where affirmative action stands under federal constitutional law at the present time:

- Any program by a government entity that uses race to define who receives or does not receive benefits is subject to strict scrutiny—that is, considered unconstitutional unless compelling and necessary reasons for the program are proved. This holds whether or not such programs are designed to discriminate against or favor racial minorities.

- With respect to the award of government contracts and government hiring—whether federal, state, or local—affirmative action programs are acceptable only if they are narrowly tailored to rectify past discriminatory actions by that particular government agency. In the view of the Court, rectifying past racist actions by a particular government agency is a compelling reason. Such programs, however, must be temporary efforts to transcend past practices and not a permanent feature of hiring and contracting. Affirmative action in hiring and contracting is not valid if it is designed simply to increase diversity or to decrease racism in society.

- With respect to admission to educational institutions—into undergraduate and graduate programs, law schools, and medical schools—actions to rectify past discriminatory admissions policies by a particular higher education institution are compelling and necessary, and are permitted.

- With respect to higher education admissions, the goal of achieving a diverse student body is a compelling reason to have affirmative action programs. However, race can only be used if it is one among several factors considered in a wholistic consideration of each applicant's file; formulas in which students of a particular race or ethnicity automatically receive a set number of points are not permissible.

Using the Framework

Affirmative Action

Why has the Supreme Court narrowed the scope of affirmative action programs?

Background: During the 1990s, the Supreme Court rendered a number of decisions that narrowed the use of racial preferences in the areas of government hiring and contracting, congressional redistricting, and university admissions. It therefore came as a great surprise to both proponents and critics of affirmative action when the Supreme Court ruled by a 5–4 vote in a pair of cases involving the University of Michigan in 2003 that affirmative action of a certain kind—one that uses race as only one among several factors in a wholistic consideration of each individual's file—is permissible in university admissions. The ruling was made possible by the emergence in the late 1990s of a new Court majority on certain issues led by Sandra Day O'Connor.

Governmental Action

In an exception to the Court's general drift, it rules in 2003 that the use of race in university admissions is permissible if it is not used as part of a mechanical, quantitative formula.

The Supreme Court rejects diversity as a compelling state interest in programs involving government jobs and contracting, and in congressional districting. It also refuses to hear cases from the circuit courts that reject affirmative action in university admissions programs, letting the decisions stand.

Governmental Level

Republican presidents Reagan and Bush nominated conservatives to the Court. ➡ The Senate approved the nominees. ➡ A narrow but firm conservative majority under the leadership of Chief Justice William Rehnquist controlled the Court on many issues during the early 1990s.

A new majority led by Sandra Day O'Connor appeared on a number of issues in the late 1990s. Briefs from elite universities, major corporations, and former top military officials convinced her that affirmative action to increase diversity is sometimes a compelling goal in important institutions.

Political Linkages Level

The Christian conservative movement and other conservative organizations—who are against affirmative action—gained political influence in the 1980s. ➡ Republicans, whose platform rejects affirmative action, reached parity with Democrats in national elections. ➡ Republicans won control of the Senate from 1981–1986 and from 1995 to 2000.

The political influence of civil rights organizations declined in the 1980s and 1990s. ➡ The majority white population reported in polls that it believed the goals of the civil rights movement have been met. ➡ A substantial majority of Americans reported support for nondiscrimination laws but distaste for laws that give minorities and women special advantages in college admissions, jobs, and government contracts.

Structural Level

The Fourteenth Amendment's promise of "equal protection of the laws" bars government discrimination against groups of citizens but is unclear about the need for remedies for past discrimination. ➡ The political culture honors individual rather than group rights and responsibilities. ➡ The white middle and working classes suffered economic reverses during the 1980s and early 1990s, creating a climate that was generally hostile to affirmative action programs.

Affirmative action programs in the United States have been designed to help not only African Americans, of course, but other racial and ethnic minorities as well, including Hispanics, Asian Americans, and Native Americans. Most of the programs also include women as beneficiaries. The present Supreme Court guidelines on affirmative action described here apply to all of these groups, not only African Americans.

The Contemporary Status of Civil Rights for Women

As the civil rights movement helped put the issue of equality for African Americans on the nation's political agenda, so did several women's rights movements advance civil rights protections for women. The struggle for women's suffrage, for example, was long and hard, finally succeeding in 1920. Fifty years later, the women's movement of the 1970s and 1980s helped win civil rights protections for women and broaden the participation of women in all aspects of American society, economy, and politics. Although the movement did not win one of its main objectives—passage of the Equal Rights Amendment (ERA) to the U.S. Constitution—the broad advance of women in gaining equal treatment and respect on virtually all fronts in the United States attests to its overall effectiveness.[24] Issues such as pay equity, family leave, sexual harassment, and attention to women's health problems in medical research are now a part of the American political agenda. Women have made important gains economically and are becoming more numerous in the professions, corporate managerial offices (although there is some evidence that a glass ceiling remains), and political office.

Comparing Civil Rights

U.S. Women Win It All

Title IX had the effect of increasing funding for women's sports in American colleges and universities and encouraging more women to participate in sports. One result was a dramatic improvement in the quality of America's national teams. Here, members of the U.S. Women's Soccer Team celebrate their victory in the Women's World Cup in 1999.

In terms of constitutional law, however, the expansion of civil rights protections for women has taken a path that differs decidedly from that for African Americans.[25]

Intermediate Scrutiny

By 1976 the proposed Equal Rights Amendment (ERA) to the Constitution to guarantee full legal equality for women had stalled, falling short of the required three-fourths of the states. Moreover, the Supreme Court did not have the necessary votes for a strict scrutiny interpretation of gender classification. There was support, however, for the new doctrine that came to be called **intermediate scrutiny.** In *Craig* v. *Boren* (1976), six justices supported Justice William Brennan's compromise, which created a more rigorous scrutiny of gender as a *somewhat* suspect classification. In the view of the justices, the use of strict scrutiny would endanger traditional sex roles, while the use of ordinary scrutiny would allow blatant sex discrimination to survive. The Burger Court defined a test that it believed to be "just right." Under intermediate scrutiny, government enactments that relied on gender would be constitutional if the use of gender were *substantially related* to an *important objective.* Intermediate scrutiny defines a legal test, then, somewhere between strict and lax. The test in *Craig* was reaffirmed in *United States* v. *Virginia* (1996). Thus, for example, certain laws protecting pregnant women from dangerous chemicals in the workplace have passed this test. The improvement of women's rights under the doctrine of intermediate scrutiny is less than what many in the women's movement wanted.

Thus, women's rights have not followed the path of other rights and liberties. The nation has not restructured civil rights for women based on an expansive reading of the equal protection clause of the Fourteenth Amendment by the courts. Rather, advances have come by virtue of changing societal attitudes about the role of women in society, increased involvement of women in politics (see Figure 16.1), and new statutes designed to equalize women's opportunities. In the private sector, women have made important advances in the corporate world and in the professions. In the public sector, more and more women hold important elected and appointed positions in all levels of government and serve in all branches of the armed services. Women also have successfully pushed for laws that compensate for past injustices. One example of such a law is Title IX of the Civil Rights Act of 1964, which prohibits discrimination against women at federally funded institutions, including universities. Title IX is generally credited with enhancing funding for women's sports programs in colleges and dramatically improving the quality of women's athletics in the United States.

Abortion Rights

One of the most controversial decisions of the Burger Court was *Roe* v. *Wade* (1973). Two recent graduates of the University of Texas Law School, Linda Coffee and Sarah Weddington, were looking for a client who would challenge a Texas statute that prohibited physicians from performing abortions except to save the life of the pregnant woman.[26] They found a client in Norma "Pixie" McCorvey, a 21-year-old divorcee who had already given birth to a child. McCorvey claimed that she had been gang raped, but her attorneys doubted her story. They argued instead for a general constitutional right to decide not to complete a pregnancy.

FIGURE 16.1 • Percentage of Elective Offices Held by Women, 1979–2006

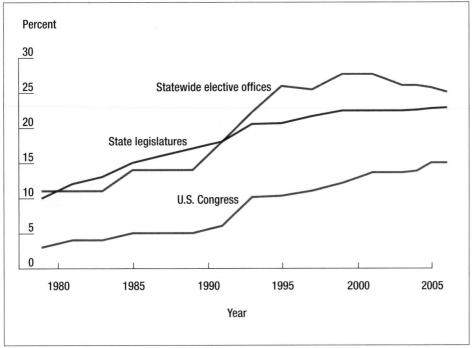

Although accounting for more than one-half the American population, women hold a much smaller proportion of elected federal, state, and local offices across the nation than men. However, the percentage of offices held by women has been increasing steadily since the 1970s. Given rising education and incomes among women, as well as changing social attitudes toward women's role in society, the proportion of elected offices held by women is likely to continue to increase.

Source: Center for American Women and Politics (January 2006).

For women's rights activists Coffee and Weddington, the federal courts offered an alternative to the Texas legislature. The case transformed abortion from a legislative issue into a constitutional issue, from a matter of policy into a matter of rights. Eleven states had reformed their statutes to allow women to have abortions when the woman's health, fetal abnormalities, or rape or incest were involved. Four more states (Alaska, Hawaii, Washington, and New York) went further and repealed prohibitions of abortion. In most state legislatures, however, progress was slow or nonexistent.

The litigation over abortion reflected changes in public opinion, pressure by interest groups, and persisting inequities against women. Disapproval of abortion decreased and discussion of abortion increased during the 1960s, even among Roman Catholics.[27] Numerous groups worked to reform or to eliminate abortion laws before *Roe* was decided.[28] The pro-choice team benefited from 42 amicus curiae briefs. The medical profession, which had been instrumental in making abortion a crime in the nineteenth century,[29] supported reform in the 1960s.

Justice Harry Blackmun's opinion for the majority prohibited the states from interfering with a woman's decision to have an abortion in the first two trimesters of her pregnancy and prohibited any state actions in the third trimester that might threaten the life or health of the mother. He based his

Demanding Equality

The women's movement helped raise Americans' awareness of the issue of equality for women, pressing not only for their right to choose to terminate a pregnancy, but for greater access to political power and job opportunities. Here, a demonstrator in New York dramatically expresses the case for equality.

VIDEO DEBATE

Abortion

opinion on the right to privacy, first given constitutional protection in *Griswold* v. *Connecticut* (1965), even though no such right is mentioned in the Constitution.

The Court's decision hardly resolved matters. Anti-abortion groups, energized by the repeal of abortion laws, struck back after *Roe*. Single-issue, anti-abortion politics surfaced in the 1976 and subsequent elections and became an important factor in the emergence of a conservative movement in American politics and the rising political power of the Republican Party. In this environment, and with the appointment of several Supreme Court justices concerned about the sweeping character of the *Roe* ruling, many states began to place restrictions on abortion, ranging from parental notification to waiting periods, counseling about alternatives to abortion, and prohibitions on the use of public money for the procedure. In *Webster* v. *Reproductive Health Services* (1989), the Court seemed to invite these restrictions. A few years later, however, in *Planned Parenthood* v. *Casey* (1992), the Court ruled that these restrictions cannot go so far as to make abortion impossible to obtain. In the words of Justice Sandra Day O'Connor, while some restrictions are acceptable, none could "place an undue burden" on a woman's fundamental right to terminate a pregnancy. Furthermore, the Court has ruled in a number of cases since *Casey,* most recently in 2006, that state and federal laws and regulations restricting abortions must always contain exceptions for situations in which the life or health of the mother is at risk.

Many abortion opponents, however, now believe that a direct challenge to *Roe* might be successful given the addition of two more conservatives to the Court (Roberts in 2005 and Alito in 2006). This apparently was the reason South Dakota passed a law in 2006 that banned abortions in the state. Republican legislators and Governor Michael Rounds said they hoped and expected that the constitutionality of the new statute would be tested in the courts by pro-choice groups. Their hopes were dashed by South Dakota voters who supported a ballot initiative in 2006 rejecting the statute.

Sexual Harassment

Another issue of concern to many women (and many men) is sexual harassment in the workplace. One poll reported that 21 percent of women say they have experienced sexual harassment at work.[30] Many have filed complaints with the Equal Employment Opportunity Commission (EEOC), which reported that almost 13,000 complaints for sexual harassment were filed with the agency in 2005.

People disagree, of course, about what kinds of behavior constitute sexual harassment, although the courts, regulatory agencies, and legislative bodies are gradually defining the law in this area. In 1980, the EEOC ruled that making sexual activity a condition of employment or promotion violates the 1964 Civil Rights Act, a ruling upheld by the Supreme Court. The EEOC also ruled that creating "an intimidating, hostile, or offensive working environment" is contrary to the law. The U.S. Supreme Court took a major step in defining sexual harassment when it ruled unanimously, in *Harris* v. *Forklift Systems, Inc.* (1993), that workers do not have to prove that offensive actions make them unable to do their jobs or cause them psychological harm, only that the work environment is hostile or abusive. In a pair of rulings in June 1998, the Court broadened the definition of sexual harassment by saying that companies were liable for the behavior of supervisors even if top managers were unaware of harassing behavior. However, companies were offered a measure of protection by the Court when it ruled that companies with solid and well-communicated harassment policies could not be held liable if victims failed to report harassment in a reasonable period of time.

An increase in public awareness about sexual harassment has triggered an increase in lawmaking by state legislatures to erase sexual harassment in the workplace. Many private companies have also begun to specify appropriate behavior on the job for their employees.

Broadening the Civil Rights Umbrella

The expansion of civil rights protections for women and racial minorities encouraged other groups to press for expanded rights protections.

The Elderly and the Disabled

Interest groups for the elderly have pressed for laws barring age discrimination and have enjoyed some success in recent years. Several federal and state laws, for instance, now bar mandatory retirement. And, the Age Discrimination in Employment Act passed in 1967 prohibits employers from discriminating against employees over the age of 40 in pay, benefits, promotions, and working conditions. The courts have also begun to strike down hiring practices based on age unless a compelling reason for such age requirements can be demonstrated. But problems persist; downsizing companies often lay off older workers first because the pay and benefits of older workers are almost always higher than those of younger workers.

Disabled Americans have also pushed for civil rights and other protections and have won some notable victories, including passage of the Americans with Disabilities Act of 1990. The act prohibits employment discrimination against the disabled and requires that reasonable efforts be made to make places of

Better Access

Since passage of the Americans with Disabilities Act in 1990, increasing numbers of public and private buildings have become more accessible to people in wheelchairs. In spite of the Act, accessibility for the disabled to public and private buildings remains less than many of its proponents had hoped when it was first signed into law.

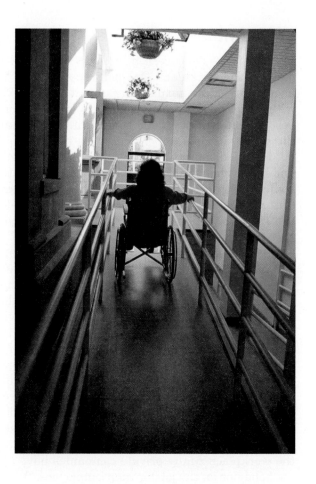

You Are the Mayor

employment and public facilities (such as concert halls, restaurants, retail shops, schools, and government offices) accessible to them. The proliferation of wheelchair ramps and wheelchair-accessible toilet facilities is a sign that the legislation is having an important effect. Several advocates for the disabled, however, claim that the act depends too much on voluntary compliance.

In 2001, the Supreme Court dramatically narrowed the reach of the Disabilities act, saying that state employees could not sue states for damages arising from violations of the act, as provided for in the legislation. Advocates for the rights of the disabled worried that this judicial ruling expanding the scope of state immunity from congressional actions means that other sections of the Disabilities Act are doomed, including the requirement that state governments make their services and offices accessible to people with disabilities. Others worried that a wide range of civil rights laws that require nondiscriminatory behavior by state agencies—schools and hospitals, for example—may be at risk, as well, because the basis of the Court's decision was that Congress had gone beyond its authority in telling the states what to do under the interstate commerce clause.[31] If the states are immune from the requirements of the Americans with Disabilities Act, the reasoning goes, why should it not be immune from the provisions of other civil rights laws passed by Congress? In *Tennessee* v. *Lane* (2004), the Court ruled that the disabled could sue a state for money damages in federal court if the state fails to make its courts fully accessible. The Supreme Court was silent, however, on whether this right to sue extends to other areas in which states have not fully complied with other federal civil rights requirements, so the issue still remains unsettled.

Gays and Lesbians

The gay and lesbian civil rights movement began in earnest following the 1969 "Stonewall rebellion"—three days of rioting set off by police harassment of the patrons of a popular gay bar in Greenwich Village in New York. The movement picked up steam as the gay community reacted to the powerful inroads of AIDS and in response to the Supreme Court's decision in *Bowers* v. *Hardwick* (1986) upholding Georgia's ban against homosexual sexual relations. The movement was also inspired by and borrowed many of the tactics of the civil rights and women's movements. The goal was to gain the same civil rights protections under the law enjoyed by African Americans and other minority groups and to gain respect from the public. The tactics have ranged from patient lobbying and voting to mass demonstrations and deliberately shocking actions by groups such as ACT-UP. While some important gains have been made by the gay and lesbian movement, its open advocacy for civil rights for homosexuals has suffered strong counterattacks by groups strongly opposed to its objectives, such as the Christian Coalition and Focus on the Family.

Gays and lesbians have moved toward equal treatment in a variety of settings in the private sector. Gains in the areas of high culture and mass entertainment have been important. Sympathetic gay and lesbian characters appear regularly on network (*Will and Grace* and *The Ellen DeGeneres Show*) and cable television (*Queer Eye for the Straight Guy*), in the movies (*Brokeback Mountain*), and in plays such as *The Birdcage* and *Angels in America*.[32] Many gays and lesbians have "come out of the closet," and the number of Americans who are aware of gay and lesbian relatives, friends, and co-workers has increased. Many private corporations (including Coors and Disney), universities, labor unions, and nonprofits have instituted same-sex partner health care and retirement benefits.

Not surprisingly, given the advances they have made in the arts and mass entertainment, public attitudes about gays and lesbians are growing steadily more tolerant. Fewer Americans today than in the past think that gay and lesbian relationships are wrong. Substantial majorities, moreover, favor ending discrimination against gays and lesbians in jobs, housing, and education and favor passing hate-crime legislation. Most Americans still strongly oppose the idea of same-sex marriage,[33] although 44 percent of 18- to 29-year-olds favor it.[34]

The gay and lesbian movement's political efforts have had mixed success. In presidential politics, partial advances have been the order of the day. When Bill Clinton was a presidential candidate, for example, he promised to lift the ban on gay people in the military, but as president he was forced in 1993 to reverse course in light of the hostile reaction from Congress and the armed services. The resulting "don't ask, don't tell, don't pursue" policy satisfied very few people, and the Navy has routinely flouted the policy, as when in 1998 it dismissed a sailor it discovered to be gay by tracking down his identity on his America Online profile page. Candidates for the Democratic presidential nomination in 2004 all endorsed some form of same-sex civil unions, although none publicly supported same-sex marriage. President Bush, however, strongly opposed both **civil unions** and marriages for gays, using part of his 2004 State of the Union address to attack judges for their support of such arrangements and supporting several attempts by Republican conservatives in the Senate to pass a constitutional amendment to rectify the situation.

Civil rights for gays and lesbians has not been treated sympathetically by Congress. In 1993—responding to decisions by several major universities to bar military recruiters from campus because the military would not allow openly practicing homosexuals to serve—Congress passed the so-called

civil union

A status in which same-sex couples have the same legal rights, benefits, and protections as married couples.

Solomon Amendment, which bars federal money to colleges and universities that deny military recruiters the same campus access as other private and public employers. In 1996, Congress passed the Defense of Marriage Act, defining marriage as a union of a man and a woman and declaring that states are under no legal obligation to recognize same-sex marriages performed in other states.

The most important civil rights gains for gays and lesbians have occurred in the courts. At the state level, Vermont's high court ruled in 2003 that same-sex couples must have the same legal rights, protections, and benefits as heterosexual married couples, including matters such as joint tax returns, property ownership, insurance benefits, and medical decisions involving a spouse. In 2004, the Massachusetts high court ruled that same-sex couples have the same right to marry as heterosexual couples, citing the state constitution's provision for equal rights for all citizens (although it ruled in 2006 that same-sex couples from other states could not legally marry in Massachusetts). Gays and lesbians also won important Supreme Court cases. The Court ruled in *Romer* v. *Evans* (1996), for example, that state laws designed to deny basic civil rights to gays and lesbians are unconstitutional. In this case, the Court looked at Colorado's provision (known as Amendment 2) prohibiting local communities from passing gay antidiscrimination ordinances. In declaring the law constitutionally unacceptable because of its denial of equal protection, Justice Anthony Kennedy declared in his opinion that "a state cannot so deem a class of persons [gays and lesbians] a stranger to its laws." And, in a stunning and highly unexpected decision in 2003, the Supreme Court overturned its own *Bowers* decision from 1986 and ruled in *Lawrence* v. *Texas* that state antisodomy laws designed to make homosexual sexual relations illegal were unconstitutional. Justice Kennedy again gave the ruling a very expansive reading in his majority opinion, declaring that gay people "were entitled to freedom, dignity, and respect for their private lives."

Although gays and lesbians have won significant civil rights protections in a handful of states—Massachusetts permits same-sex marriage; California,

Brief Victory

Gay activists celebrate the decision of the state supreme court in 2004 permitting same-sex marriage in Massachusetts. The ruling not only encouraged gay activists to push for same-sex marriage in other cities and states, but sparked a powerful political response from religious conservatives across the country. On election day 2004, in fact, 11 states adopted ballot propositions banning same-sex marriage.

Using the Democracy Standard

Is equal citizenship a reality in the United States?

PROPOSITION: Civil rights were not a prominent feature of the original Constitution nor has the promise of equality been realized over the course of our history.

AGREE   There is no provision in the original Constitution ensuring equality of citizenship for women, African Americans, and Native Americans. Women were denied the vote well into the twentieth century; most African Americans were slaves until passage of the Thirteenth Amendment and were not admitted into full citizenship across the nation until at least 1965 after passage of the Civil Rights Act and the Voting Rights Act. Even today, women, racial and ethnic minorities, and gays and lesbians continue to be discriminated against in a wide range of institutions and fail to play a role in the political process commensurate with their numbers in the population. This is still a political system run by and for the benefit of white men.

DISAGREE   While it is true that the framers largely ignored the issue of equal citizenship, the story of the United States is the story of the gradual inclusion of all identifiable groups into the political process as equal citizens. To be sure, although discrimination has not been eliminated in all areas of American life, it is now no longer constitutionally possible for government and other public institutions such as universities to discriminate against women and racial and ethnic minorities. Barriers to discrimination are also falling for gays and lesbians. And, not only has government discrimination against these groups ended, but many new affirmative action programs are in place to make up for past discrimination and to increase the diversity in the country's most important institutions. As to the issue of participation and power, although it is true that levels of political participation and political power are not the same for all groups in American society, this has more to do with inequalities in the distribution of income, wealth, and education than with formal mechanisms of exclusion.

CONSIDER   Political equality is one of the three pillars of democracy, equal in importance to popular sovereignty and political liberty. Consequently, to evaluate "how democratic" we are, we need to know if equality is a goal we are about to reach, or whether it is one receding into the distance.

• What do you think? • In your view, have women, racial and ethnic minorities, and members of other historically discriminated-against groups become equal citizens? • If so, have they become equal citizens in both legal terms and political influence? • Or, on the other hand, do you believe, as some Americans do, that these groups have become more than equal to others, that government officials pay them too much heed and do too much for them at the expense of others? • If you believe this, how would you explain the influence of such groups? • Why do political leaders pay attention to their demands at all?

Civil Rights and Gay Adoption

Maine, Hawaii, Vermont, and New Jersey permit same-sex civil unions or civil partnerships with rights similar to those of married couples; and Illinois bars discrimination based on sexual orientation—11 states in 2004 and 7 more in 2006 passed ballot initiatives banning same-sex marriage (making a total of 23). As of 2006, moreover, defense-of-marriage laws in one form or another were on the books in 40 states. This state constitutional and legislative landscape no doubt reflects the general contours of public opinion. The Pew Research Center reports, for example, that 53 percent of Americans disapproved of same-sex marriage in 2005, while only 36 percent approved. However, Pew also reports that 53 percent of Americans support civil unions that provide rights and benefits for homosexual couples similar to marriage.[35]

It is evident that the struggle over gay and lesbian civil rights will remain an important part of the American political agenda for a long time to come. The eventual outcome remains very much in doubt, however. While gays and lesbians have made important advances, to be sure, many religious conservatives have been politically mobilized by the possibility that state courts and the U.S. Supreme Court might eventually sanction same-sex marriage as a basic civil right.

Summary

The Constitution and the Bill of Rights are relatively silent on equality, other than providing for equality before the law. Important advances for civil rights were the passage of the Thirteenth, Fourteenth, and Fifteenth Amendments after the Civil War. The Fourteenth Amendment, with its specification that all persons born or naturalized in the United States are citizens of both the nation and the states in which they live and that federal and state governments must provide for "equal protection of the laws," was a particularly important civil rights milestone, even though the Supreme Court was slow to act on its promise.

The Court paid little attention during the nineteenth century to the issue of equality for racial minorities and women. Under the pressure of structural changes in society, the transformation of attitudes about race and gender, and the political efforts of racial and ethnic minority group members and women of all races, the Court slowly began to pay attention by the middle of the twentieth century. Important advances toward equality have been made by both racial minorities and women. Although constitutional law now fully protects both racial minorities and women against discrimination sanctioned by law or government action, the status of affirmative action programs meant to rectify past wrongs and to compensate for institutional barriers to equality remains unsettled.

The question of whether lesbians and gay men can be discriminated against in housing, employment, and education has been largely settled, although the issues of gays and lesbians in the military and same-sex marriages remain the subject of considerable political debate.

Web Exploration
Same-Sex Marriage

ISSUE: Passions run high on the issue of same-sex marriages.

SITE: Access two sites that take contrasting positions on the issue of same-sex marriage: the Family Research Council and TurnOut. Go to MyPoliSciLab at **www.mypoliscilab.com.** Go to the "Web Explorations" section for Chapter 16, select and open "same-sex marriage." At the Family Research Council site, select "Policy Areas," then look at both "marriage and family" and "human sexuality." At the TurnOut site, select "issues," and then "the right to marry."

WHAT YOU'VE LEARNED: Compare the coverage of the issue of same-sex marriage at each site. Is each telling the full story? Are there areas of agreement between the two sides, or is the gap between them a yawning one?

HINT: On issues involving conflicts over fundamental values, agreement and compromise are often very difficult to achieve.

Internet Sources

Civil Rights Project
www.civilrightsproject.harvard.edu
Cutting-edge research on race in America.

Cornell Law Library/Civil Rights
www.law.cornell.edu
Links to the Constitution, landmark and recent Supreme Court civil rights decisions, international treaties on human rights, the Civil Rights Division of the Justice Department, and more.

Issues: Gay Rights
www.politics1.com/issues-gay.htm
Links to organizations in favor of and opposed to advancing gay and lesbian civil rights.

Martin Luther King, Jr., Home Page
www.seattletimes.com/mlk/
Created by the Seattle Times, the site includes study guides on King and the civil rights movement, interactive exercises, audios of King speeches, and links to other King and civil rights websites.

Yahoo/Civil Rights
**www.yahoo.com/Society_and_Culture/
Issues_and_Causes/Civil_Rights/**
Links to a vast compendium of information on civil rights and to organizations devoted to the protection and expansion of domestic and international rights.

Suggestions for Further Reading

Barry, Brian. *Culture and Equality.* Cambridge, MA: Harvard University Press, 2001.
An assault on multiculturalism in the name of liberal egalitarianism by a distinguished political philosopher.

Bowen, William G., and Derek C. Bok. *The Shape of the River: Long-Term Consequences of Considering Race in College and University Admissions.* Princeton, NJ: Princeton University Press, 1998.
Based on surveys of more than 60,000 white and African American students at highly selective colleges and universities, Bowen and Bok argue that affirmative action in college and university admissions has had substantial and widespread positive effects on American society.

Branch, Taylor. *At Canaan's Edge: America in the King Years, 1965–1968.* New York: Simon and Schuster, 2006.
The third volume in Taylor Branch's brilliant and award winning biographies of Martin Luther King; focuses not only on King in this volume but on the transformation of race relations and American politics during this decisive period.

Fallon, Richard H. *The Dynamic Constitution: An Introduction to Constitutional Law.* New York: Cambridge University Press, 2004.
An accessible introduction to the Supreme Court's interpretation of equal protection in the Constitution.

Gates, Henry Louis, Jr. *America Behind the Color Line.* New York: Warner Books, 2004.
An examination of the legacy of the civil rights movement for African Americans.

Gerstmann, Evan. *Same-Sex Marriage and the Constitution.* New York: Cambridge University Press, 2003.
A careful examination of the constitutional issues at the root of this contemporary controversy.

Jacobs, Lawrence and Theda Skocpol, eds. *Inequality and American Democracy: What We Know and What We Need to Learn.* New York: Russell Sage Foundation, 2005.
A report from the American Political Science Association carefully detailing the extent of inequality in the United States, including inequality among races, as well as some of its repercussions.

Katznelson, Ira. *When Affirmative Action Was White: An Untold History of Racial Inequality in Twentieth-Century America.* New York: W.W. Norton, 2005.
An eye-opening look at how a long list of federal government programs, beginning in the New Deal, favored whites over blacks.

CHAPTER 17

Domestic Policy

IN THIS CHAPTER

- How government policies affect the lives and well-being of Americans

- The federal budget, the deficit, and the national debt

- What tools government uses to manage the economy

- Why government subsidizes some business activities and regulates others

- How and why American domestic policies are different

Whatever Happened to the Budget Surplus?

When asked to comment on the dramatic downturn in the nation's budget outlook in 2003, former Congressional Budget Office Robert Reischauer invoked John Milton's epic work *Paradise Lost,* which described a dramatic fall from grace, from heaven to hell. He said, "It really has been a Miltonian experience, from the heights to the depths."[1]

Paradise Lost indeed! In early 2001, federal officials and private economists issued confident predictions that the government's budget would be in the black by more than $230 billion in 2002, and that total cumulative surpluses over a 10-year period would be about $5.6 trillion. For elected officials in Washington, the news could not have been better. As officeholders who must periodically face the voters, elected officials of both parties were delighted with the prospect of an ever-growing budget cornucopia that could be used to safeguard Social Security and Medicare, pay down the national debt, and pay for new educational and drug benefit programs—with ample room left over for tax cuts.

All this changed dramatically in 2002. The Bush White House announced that the federal budget was going to be at least $106 billion in the red for 2002 and would remain in deficit until at least 2005, perhaps longer. The Congressional Budget Office (CBO) estimated that the 10-year accumulated deficit would be $1.6 trillion. The change from an estimated surplus of $5.6 trillion to a deficit of $1.6 trillion represented the most dramatic reversal of the fiscal health of the nation in more than 50 years.

However, the worst was yet to come. By the time President Bush submitted his fiscal year 2007 budget to Congress in early February 2006, the CBO was predicting that annual budget deficits would not disappear for a long time and that the accumulated national debt would grow bigger and faster than it had forecast four years earlier. It estimated that accumulated annual deficits for the years 2006 to 2011—what would be added to the national debt—would be $1.4 trillion, not even counting additional deficits that would occur if tax breaks set to expire during this period were made permanent, as President Bush has asked Congress to do.[2]

How had things changed so dramatically in so short a time? What caused the deficits to reappear is fairly obvious, although Democrats, Republicans, economists, and budget analysts disagree about how much weight to give to each factor. First, budget estimates did not accurately predict the troubles that would visit the American economy in the early 2000s: the 2001 economic recession, the 2002 stock market collapse (the market lost almost 20 percent of its value), and 2003's jobless recovery. Taken together, these developments put a serious dent in government receipts; with individuals and companies earning less and capital gains falling, fewer taxes were flowing into the federal treasury.

Second, congressional and executive branch budget officials in early 2001 could not have foreseen the terrorist attacks on the United States and the tremendous costs that eventually would be associated with rebuilding and recovering from them, including the war against the Taliban regime in Afghanistan that had harbored the Al Qaeda leadership and enhancing homeland security. Nor could budget officials have anticipated the enormous costs associated with waging the war in Iraq, which amounted to roughly $250 billion from the invasion in 2003 through the end of 2005. Two supplementary appropriations for 2006 came to about $100 billion.[3]

Third, there is no gainsaying the effect of President Bush's three massive tax cuts—the first was for $1.35 trillion over 10 years—on the shrinking long-term surplus. While the rebates to taxpayers in 2001 and the reductions in certain taxes in 2002 probably kept the recession from becoming more serious than it was—because the returned taxes acted as an economic stimulant—budget officials were eventually forced to take account of substantially reduced federal revenues caused by tax cuts when thinking about the long-term state of the budget.

Also adding to the long-term shift from surplus to deficit was the very expensive Medicare prescription drug benefit program that was legislated in 2003 and went into effect in 2006, something government budget officials had no way of predicting when they had painted their rosy budget portrait in 2001. The CBO estimated at the time of its passage that the new program would add $534 billion in accumulated deficits over the first 10 years of its existence. To be sure, virtually everyone thought that some sort of drug benefit program was long overdue—seniors wanted it, and both Al Gore and George W. Bush had promised during the 2000 election campaign to get them this benefit if elected (although Gore and the Democrats did not like the form it eventually took). Nevertheless, the cost of the program will be considerable as it phases in over the next few years.

Annual decisions about taxes and federal government spending are among the most important decisions that presidents and members of Congress make. They determine in broad outline what activities and programs the federal government will undertake and how the government will pay for them. They affect how the national economy works and who in society will benefit or lose from government activities. Finally, budget policies are not made in a vacuum; these decisions are profoundly affected by what is going on in the nation and in the world.

In this chapter and the next, we turn our attention to an examination of a broad range of federal government activities and programs and the effect they have on the American people. Obviously, we cannot cover every policy area in the allotted space. We focus, instead, on policy areas we consider most important for ensuring the economic and social well-being of the American people and protecting their security. In Chapter 18, we look in detail at U.S. foreign and military policy. In this chapter, we look at federal domestic policies. We pay special attention to budget priorities—what activities the federal government spends money on—taxes, management of the economy, regulation, and income support and medical programs, including social insurance programs such as Social Security and Medicare, and means-tested programs such as food stamps and Medicaid. ■

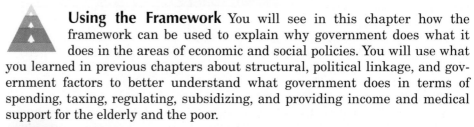

Thinking Critically About This Chapter

Using the Framework You will see in this chapter how the framework can be used to explain why government does what it does in the areas of economic and social policies. You will use what you learned in previous chapters about structural, political linkage, and government factors to better understand what government does in terms of spending, taxing, regulating, subsidizing, and providing income and medical support for the elderly and the poor.

Using the Democracy Standard In previous chapters, you used the democracy standard to examine the extent to which American political and government institutions enhanced popular sovereignty, political equality, and liberty. You will use the democracy standard in this chapter to ask whether the American people get the sorts of policies and performance they want from government.

Why So Many Government Domestic Programs?

It is hard to imagine any activity in our daily lives that is not touched in one way or another by what the government does regarding the food supply, energy, health care, transportation, education, public safety, environmental quality, and the economy. Why does it do so many things in a country long committed to the idea of limited government? One must start, of course, with the Constitution itself, which gives the federal government a number of broad areas of responsibility, including the charges that it "establish Justice, insure Domestic tranquility . . . promote the general Welfare, and secure the blessings of Liberty . . . ."

Although one must start with the Constitution, one cannot end there. While the Constitution provides broad grants of responsibility and power, it has been the American people, using the political tools available to them in a democracy—those reviewed in previous chapters, including social movements, parties and elections, public opinion, and advocacy and interest groups—who have pressed elected and unelected officials over the course of American history to institute a broad range of policies and programs to improve and protect their safety and well-being. The American people, as well as business leaders on a number of occasions (see below and Chapter 7), have asked government to do more because of profound economic and social changes that have affected their lives, often creating problems that have not been easily solved by individuals or the private market (see below and Chapter 4).

The federal government does so many things on the domestic policy front that it is impossible to do them justice in a single chapter. Rather than skip lightly over every area of government domestic activity, we concentrate in this chapter on two broad ones that are enormously consequential for Americans, namely, the economy and social welfare (broadly understood as programs that provide income support and access to medical care for the elderly, the very young, and the poor). Unfortunately, we cannot examine, except in passing, federal policies and programs in the areas of education, transportation, health, and agriculture.

Governments in all rich democracies play a substantial role in managing economic affairs and providing social welfare for their citizens. Let's see why.

Comparing Economic Policy

Managing the Economy

No government today would dare leave problems such as stagnant economic growth, unemployment, international trade imbalances, or inflation to work themselves out "naturally." Citizens and political leaders in the rich democracies have learned that free market economies, left to themselves, are subject to periodic bouts of **inflation** and unemployment, as well as occasional collapses of employment and economic output (called **depressions**). Government responsibility for the state of the national economy is now so widely accepted that national elections are often decided by the voters' judgment of how well the party in power is carrying out this responsibility. When times are good, the party or president in power is very likely to be reelected; when times are bad, those in power have an uphill battle staying in office.

inflation

A condition of rising prices and reduced purchasing power.

depression

A severe and persistent drop in economic activity.

Social Welfare

All rich democracies have programs that protect the minimum standards of living of families and individuals against loss of income due to economic instability, old age, illness and disability, and family disintegration.[4] Nations that provide such a range of programs are often called **welfare states.** All rich democracies are also social welfare states, and the reason is simple: Their citizens have demanded it. They have apparently recognized that market economies, even when working at peak efficiency, do not guarantee a minimum decency of living for all or offer protection against economic dislocations

welfare state

The set of government programs that protects the minimum standard of living of families and individuals against loss of income.

Protect Our Jobs

The government is regularly held accountable for economic hardships. Here, demonstrators in Ohio protest President George W. Bush's inability to stop the outsourcing of manufacturing jobs. Outsourcing and what to do about it was an important issue in the 2004 presidential campaign.

even for people making their best efforts.[5] The term *welfare state,* of course, is often used pejoratively in the United States to refer to hand-outs to the "undeserving poor," but students of politics and government use the term to cover a range of income maintenance, medical, and other social service programs with a broad and diverse set of beneficiaries, not just the poor. We use it in this sense in this chapter.

Economic Policy

Government economic policies have a number of objectives; all have consequences for the American people.

The Goals of Economic Policy

Although economic policy goals sometimes conflict, and involve important trade-offs,[6] they are consistently driven by five key concerns, which we will explore next.

The quintessential goal of economic policymakers is sustained economic growth—defined here as an annual increase in the **gross domestic product (GDP).** A growing economy generally means more jobs, more products, and higher incomes, so most Americans support this goal. Economic growth is also the basis for increased profits, so business tends to support it as well. For political leaders, economic growth, accompanied by rising standards of living, brings public popularity and heightened prospects for reelection, as well as more revenues for government programs.

gross domestic product (GDP)

Monetary value of all goods and services produced in a nation each year, excluding income residents earn abroad.

In addition to having economic growth, most people want to avoid inflation, a condition in which the purchasing power of money declines. With serious inflation, people's wages, salaries, savings accounts, and retirement pensions diminish in value. So, too, do the holdings of banks and the value of their loans. To nobody's surprise, political leaders seek policies that dampen inflation and provide stable prices. Their problem is that such policies often require slower economic growth, with lower wages and higher levels of unemployment, and these conditions are harmful to broad sectors of the population, usually the most vulnerable sectors.

All nations, including the United States, strive to keep their **balance of payments** in positive territory, that is, to export more manufactured goods and services—things such as insurance and banking—than they import. They do so because sustained negative trade balances lead to a decline in the value of a nation's currency in international markets, as more money leaves the country than is brought in. In this situation, businesses and consumers find that their dollars buy less, and they must either do without or borrow to make up the difference.

Most people also want to avoid what are called negative **externalities,** the bad side-effects that often accompany normal economic activity. A growing manufacturing economy, for example, often produces things such as air and water pollution, toxic wastes, and workplace injuries and health hazards. In response to these negative externalities, the public over the years has pressed the government to take compensatory action—for example, to prosecute polluters and hold them responsible for cleanups.

Finally, there is a range of economic activities that is essential for the health of the national economy but that is unlikely to be provided by private firms. Almost without exception, governments in the rich democracies, including the United States, have stepped into the breach and provided support for such vital activities and services, either by direct subsidy and tax incentives or by public ownership (although not in the United States). For example, the United States and all European countries subsidize farmers, who are vital to the nation's food supply. Also, the federal government encourages business

balance of payments
The annual difference between payments and receipts between a country and its trading partners.

externalities
The positive and negative effects of economic activities on third parties.

Farm Subsidies and Domestic Policy

Waiting to be Delivered

For a very long time now, the United States has been running very large trade deficits. Negative trade balances are especially notable with regard to petroleum, consumer electronics, and automobiles—products that the United States once exported more than it imported. Here, Toyota cars are lined up in the port of Seattle after their arrival from Japan prior to their shipment to dealerships across the country.

activity in America's inner cities by using enterprise zone tax incentives; supports the defense industry by directly purchasing weapons systems and subsidizing research; and pays for essential infrastructure such as airports, harbors, and highways.

The Tools of Macroeconomic Policy

Government actions affect (but do not solely determine) the rate of inflation, the level of unemployment, and the growth of income and output in the national economy. This always has been so. What is new since the end of World War II is that government leaders, economists, and citizens know this to be true and insist that government use whatever means it has available to ensure good economic outcomes.

macroeconomic policy
Policy that has to do with the performance of the economy as a whole.

Government efforts to encourage economic growth, low unemployment, and stable prices fall under the heading of **macroeconomic policy,** or policy that affects the performance of the economy as a whole. The main tools of macroeconomic policy are **fiscal policy** (having to do with government spending and taxes) and **monetary policy** (having to do with the supply and cost of money).

fiscal policy
Government efforts to affect overall output and incomes in the economy through spending and taxing policies.

Fiscal Policy   In theory, fiscal policy is a flexible tool for stimulating the economy when it is underperforming and for slowing down the economy when it is getting too hot—that is, growing so fast that it triggers inflation. The president and Congress can increase government spending or decrease taxes when economic stimulation is required (the argument George W. Bush made in favor of several tax cut proposals during his presidency), thus getting more money into circulation; they can cut spending or increase taxes when the economy needs a cooling-off period.

monetary policy
Government efforts to affect the supply of money and the level of interest rates in the economy.

Fiscal tools are not easy to use, however. Decisions about how much government should spend or what level and kinds of taxes ought to be levied are not made simply on the basis of their potential effects on economic stability and growth. Most of the elderly want Social Security and Medicare benefits to keep pace with inflation, for example, regardless of their effect on the overall economy.

Monetary Policy   The Federal Reserve Board (commonly known as the Fed) is responsible for monetary policy. It is made up of seven members (called governors) who serve overlapping 14-year terms and a chair who serves a renewable four-year term. Each is appointed by the president. Alan Greenspan was chair of the Federal Reserve from 1987 to 2006, when he retired and was replaced by Ben Bernanke. The Fed is closely connected with, and very solicitous of, the needs of commercial and investment bankers and generally prefers to control inflation as a first order of business to protect the value of financial assets. The Fed is relatively independent; aggressive actions by Congress or the president to pressure the Fed would surely trigger adverse reactions on Wall Street and in the financial community at home and abroad—reactions that neither the president nor Congress is eager to confront.

The Fed makes decisions that affect how much money is available to businesses and individuals from banks, savings and loans, and credit unions. The more money that is available and the lower the interest rates at which money can be borrowed, the higher overall consumer and business spending are likely to be. For example, if the Fed wants to increase total spending in the economy (called *aggregate demand*), it increases the money supply (by having

Passing the Torch at the Fed

Allan Greenspan was both admired and villified during his 18-year tenure as Chair of the Federal Reserve Board. Here, he shakes hands with President George W. Bush at the swearing-in ceremony for his successor, Ben Bernanke, in October 2006.

its *open market committee* buy back government securities from the private sector) and lowers the **discount rate,** or the cost member banks pay to borrow money from the Fed. If it wants to slow down the economy, it decreases the money supply and increases interest rates.

discount rate

The interest rate the Federal Reserve charges member banks to cover short-term loans.

The Federal Budget and Fiscal Policy

Decisions by the president and Congress on spending and taxes constitute America's fiscal policy. The spending part of this fiscal equation is defined in the budget. The federal budget has a number of interesting characteristics.[7] First, it is an executive budget, meaning that it is prepared by the president and his staff (and the Office of Management and Budget, or the OMB), considered, amended, and passed by Congress, then put into effect by the president and the executive branch. Before 1921, the budget was prepared in Congress. Second, the budget is an annual one—that is, a new one is prepared and legislated each year—although many budget experts would prefer to see biennial budgets, as is the practice in many states. Third, the budget takes the form of line items, with funds allocated for specific activities of federal programs such as salaries, supplies, travel, and the like, rather than a lump sum given to an agency or department that might be used more flexibly. From start to finish, preparation of the annual budget takes longer than a year.[8] (See Table 17.1 for a timeline of the budget process.)

Budget-making in Congress is never easy, even in the best of times—when revenues are plentiful, economic prospects are good, and Republicans and Democrats are willing to settle their differences through compromise. Absent these conditions, the processes by which 13 or 14 separate annual appropriations bills work their way through Congress and by which new tax legislation is considered can become a torturous, conflict-laden, blame-apportioning

VISUAL LITERACY

Evaluating Federal Spending and Economic Policy

TABLE 17.1 • Timeline: Fashioning the Federal Budget

February–March	After consulting with staff, the OMB, and key congressional and executive branch officials, the president formulates general budget and fiscal guidelines
Late spring	OMB issues specific budget guidelines for federal departments and agencies
August–October	Executive branch departments and agencies submit budget proposals to OMB; OMB reviews requests and asks departments and agencies, in most cases, to refashion and resubmit to keep in line with presidential guidelines
October–December	Consulting with presidential staff, as well as with the Council on Economic Advisors and Treasury officials, OMB staff and leaders formulate department and agency budgets for presidential review
Late December	With presidential feedback, OMB prepares data and final budget documents for submission to Congress
First Monday in February	President submits budget request to Congress
February 15	Deadline for Congressional Budget Office to make recommendations to House and Senate Budget Committees on the overall shape of the budget
March	Standing committees send their budget estimates to Budget Committees in each chamber
April 1	Deadline for House and Senate Budget Committees to issue budget resolution on overall spending ceilings, revenues, and fiscal outlook
April 15	House and Senate complete action on concurrent resolutions on budget; resolutions used as guidelines for committee and subcommittee actions
Mid-April–end of June	Standing committees in House and Senate consider authorizing legislation for programs where needed (appropriations cannot be made unless authorizing legislation has been adopted, sometimes annually, sometimes every few years)
	Beginning in House, appropriations committees and subcommittees consider 13 or 14 appropriations bills and mark up final bills for floor action; bills are passed on to Senate after receiving House approval
June 30	Deadline for House appropriations bills
July–September 15	Senate completes action on appropriations bills; House-Senate conference committees meet to iron out differences in bills; conference reports on appropriations bills voted on in House and Senate
September 25	Deadline for second concurrent resolution on overall budget, specifying total spending in all bills, revenues, and fiscal consequences of appropriations
July–September	President signs appropriations bills after they are passed by House and Senate
October 1	Fiscal year begins; departments and agencies operate under auspices of new budget authorities and appropriations

business, filled with anger and vituperation. In recent years, as partisanship has increased, the budget process has become particularly slow, with appropriations bills not passed by the dates specified in the rules of each house, leading either to the shutdown of the government—as happened twice during the Clinton administration—or the use of continuing resolutions to allow various government agencies to function temporarily. Needless to say, these outcomes make it exceedingly difficult for agencies to plan and execute policy on a rational and consistent basis.

Spending

The federal government spent about $2.7 trillion in 2006, almost 21 percent of GDP, up from a little more than 20 percent in 2005.[9] Figure 17.1 shows the change over time in federal outlays as a percentage of GDP. Several things are immediately apparent.

Where the Money Goes

First, the most dramatic increases in federal government spending are associated with involvement in major wars; note the big spikes in the graph for the years associated with World War I and World War II. Second, the relative spending level of the federal government increased steadily from the early 1930s to

FIGURE 17.1 • Federal Government Spending as a Percentage of GDP, 1869–2006

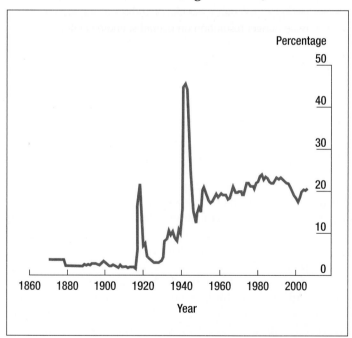

This graph shows the scale of federal government spending relative to the size of the U.S. economy. We see that the increase in the relative size of the federal government is a twentieth-century phenomenon. We also see that involvement in major wars has been an important factor in the growth in federal spending, with the major spikes coming during World Wars I and II. The permanent change in the role of the federal government in American society is also seen in the steady rise in spending triggered by the Great Depression during the 1930s. Also noteworthy was the decline of relative federal spending through the 1980s and 1990s and the recent upsurge.

Source: Office of Management and Budget, *Budget of the United States, Historical Tables, Fiscal 2007.*

the early 1980s, then leveled off and declined after that. This decrease was caused, in large part, by a substantial decrease in the relative size of the national defense budget after the end of the Cold War. Third and finally, the costs of recovery from the terrorist attacks on the United States and the subsequent wars in Afghanistan and Iraq pushed up federal spending relative to GDP once more after 2003, although not to levels characteristic of the 1970s and 1980s.

The largest portion of the federal budget—54 percent—is for mandatory spending, over which Congress and the president exercise little real control; changes in spending can occur only if Congress and the president agree to change the underlying program legislation or budget authorization bills, which is very hard to do. Mandatory expenditures are automatic, unless the program legislation is changed or language is changed in the budget authority bills, for programs such as Social Security retirement benefits or Medicare spending, which distribute benefits by formula. Medicare benefits go automatically to Americans over age 65, for example. Medicaid is distributed to the states according to a formula based on the number of poor people in each state. Expenditures on these programs happen outside the annual appropriations process and are triggered by changes in, for example, the number of elderly or poor people. Another 8 percent of the federal budget for 2006 was for payment of interest on the national debt; such payments are mandatory, as well. The upshot is that only 38 percent of the 2006 budget was discretionary, open to changes in funding through the annual appropriations process. And because the costs of mandatory programs are increasing rapidly—particularly Social Security and Medicare—elected leaders have less discretion over spending decisions.

Much of the discretionary spending budget—48 percent, in fact—was taken up by national defense in 2006, which totaled $480 billion, representing almost 18 percent of the total federal budget. Homeland security, about $32 billion in 2006, accounted for another 3 percent of discretionary spending. Taking defense, homeland security, interest on the national debt, and mandatory programs together, only about 18 percent was left in the budget in 2006 for all other federal programs and activities. Only $486 billion of the total budget of $2.67 trillion was available in 2006 for education and training, scientific and medical research, transportation, energy, agricultural research and subsidies, housing, national parks, the administration of justice, environmental protection, international affairs, the space program, public works projects, and the arts and humanities, among other things. Given increases in mandatory spending programs and the demands of the war in Iraq and homeland security, it is hardly surprising that President Bush's 2007 budget request included deep cuts in nondefense, non–homeland security discretionary programs, with the deepest cuts coming in education, job training, social services, and community development. The president also asked Congress to legislate separately to cut back on the pace of growth of Medicare.[10]

Another category of spending is off-budget supplemental appropriations, special one-time expenditures to cover emergencies. In 2006, for example, the president asked Congress for supplementary appropriations for the wars in Iraq and Afghanistan ($120 billion) and for the Hurricane Katrina disaster relief and recovery effort ($18.5 billion).[11]

Taxes

Government can spend money, of course, only if it has a stream of revenues coming in. Such revenues are raised by various kinds of taxes. Although the American system of taxation shares some features with those of other countries, it is unique in a number of ways.

First, although Americans from all walks of life report feeling squeezed by taxes, the total of all taxes levied by all government jurisdictions in the United States as a proportion of GDP is relatively low when compared with the tax bite in the other rich democracies (see Figure 17.2). And, on average, what Americans pay in taxes as a percentage of their incomes has stayed about the same for the past 25 years.[12] Second, reflecting the fact that ours is a federal system, states and localities levy their own taxes. The national government depends primarily on individual income taxes (personal and corporate) and payroll taxes to fund its activities. Other rich democracies depend more on national sales and consumption taxes. In the United States, the states get most of their revenues from sales taxes, although many have income taxes as well. Local governments depend most heavily on property taxes.

Also, the American tax system is uniquely complex. The U.S. Tax Code is a voluminous document, filled with endless exceptions to the rules and special treatment for individuals, companies, and communities, usually the product of political influence of one kind or another. Few people besides accountants and tax attorneys fully understand the Code, and their services are available mainly to those who can afford them.

Perhaps most interesting of all, although the federal income tax looks to be quite progressive—a system in which tax rates increase as income and wealth increase—in actuality it is only mildly progressive; high-income individuals pay

FIGURE 17.2 • Receipts for All Levels of Government as a Percentage of GDP in the United States and the OECD Countries, 2004

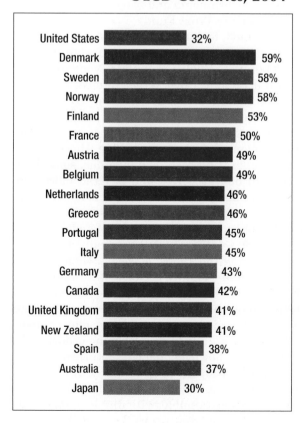

The total tax burden of the United States is lighter than that of most other rich democracies.

Source: The Organization for Economic Cooperation and Development, 2005.

only a slightly higher percentage of their income than others, after all deductions, exclusions, credits, and tax shelters are taken into account. Other federal taxes, such as Social Security and Medicare payroll taxes, and excise taxes on alcohol and cigarettes, are regressive—that is, they take a higher proportion of income in taxes from those lower in the income scale. The result is an overall federal tax system that is relatively flat, meaning that most people in the United States pay about the same percentage of their income in taxes, leaving the highly unequal income distribution of Americans relatively untouched.[13] Most analysts believe that the 2001 and 2003 tax cuts, which favored high income earners and repealed the estate tax, will eventually make the effective tax rate on the wealthy lower than that for other groups, especially if the cuts, set to expire over the next few years, are extended by Congress. President Bush has defended the cuts and pushed to make them permanent as important stimulators of economic growth and attributed to them the United States's strong economic performance after 2003.[14]

The Deficit and the National Debt

As we showed in the chapter-opening story, annual budget and the national debt are back in the news. Like any other person, organization, or institution that spends more than it makes, the federal government must borrow from others to cover the shortfall and must pay interest to those from whom it borrows. The **national debt** is the total of what the government owes in the form of Treasury bonds, bills, and notes to American citizens and institutions (financial institutions, insurance companies, corporations, etc.), foreign individuals and institutions (including foreign governments and banks), and even to itself (i.e., to units such as the Social Security Trust Fund).

Are annual deficits necessarily bad? Is having a national debt a bad thing? It depends. Economists generally agree that running a **budget deficit** in a slow economy is a good thing because it helps stimulate economic activity. They also agree that a national debt that grows larger to meet emergencies—such as waging a war—is unavoidable and that borrowing to make investments that will have positive long-term effects on society and the economy—such as building schools and roads, modernizing ports and airports, and funding research and development—is a good thing. However, going into further debt to pay current operating costs is dangerous, something akin to living on one's credit card to buy groceries and pay the mortgage. Most economists believe that running annual deficits of this sort generally drives up interest rates.

Before the 1980s, the national debt grew mainly because of deficit spending to wage war. After each war the debt, relative to GDP, gradually declined.[15] This pattern changed dramatically during the 1980s, however, when the size of annual federal budget deficits escalated—mainly because of a rapid buildup in the defense budget and big tax cuts (see Figure 17.3). The national debt as a percentage of GDP began to decline in the 1990s, however, as annual budget deficits turned into annual (and growing) surpluses caused by changes in federal fiscal policies and by the tax windfalls from a booming economy. As suggested in the chapter-opening story, however, deficits returned with a vengeance in 2002, and the budget is likely to stay in deficit for years.

While many budget and public policy experts believe that the current fiscal course of the federal government is unsustainable, with dire long-term consequences for the American people—both the liberal-leaning Brookings Institution and the conservative-leaning Heritage Foundation issued reports

SIMULATION

You Are Trying to Get a Tax Cut

national debt

The total outstanding debt of the federal government; the sum total of all annual budget deficits and surpluses.

budget deficit

The amount by which annual government expenditures exceed revenues.

TIMELINE

Growth of the Budget and Federal Spending

FIGURE 17.3 • The National Debt as a Percentage of GDP

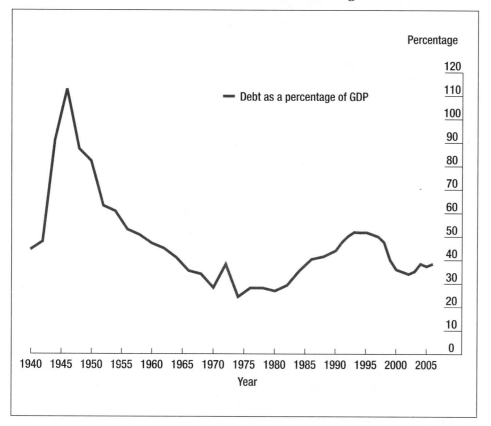

After a long period of decline, the relative national debt—that is, the size of the debt compared with the total size of the American economy (GDP)—grew dramatically during the 1980s and early 1990s, but fell after 1993. The relative size of the debt is again increasing. Even at its worst, however, the size of the relative national debt in recent decades was nowhere near the historic high point it reached during World War II.

Source: Office of Management and Budget, *Budget of the United States, Historical Tables, Fiscal 2007.*

in 2005 with identical warnings[16]—Americans have not generally listed budget deficits at or near the top of their concerns. This makes it difficult for political leaders, if they are so inclined, to call for tax increases and/or benefit cuts in popular entitlement programs to ease the problem.

Deficit Spending

Regulation

Regulation is one of the most visible and important activities of the federal government. For example, federal agencies issue rules that private businesses must follow. These rules may involve how a company treats its toxic wastes, what hiring procedures it practices, or how it reports its profits and losses.

Why Government Regulates

A free market economy, even when it is working optimally, produces a range of negative externalities that cannot be or are unlikely to be solved by private

regulations

The issuing of rules by government agencies with the aim of reducing the scale of negative externalities produced by private firms.

businesses on their own. These problems include, among others, air and water pollution, inadequate information for investors, unsafe products, unsafe and unwholesome workplaces, toxic wastes, and reckless financial practices. The American people have demonstrated on a number of occasions and consistently in public opinion surveys that they want government to do something about these problems. At various times, elected leaders have responded positively to these demands and increased regulation. As odd as it may seem, however, business leaders also have advocated government regulation to meet one problem or another. The *economic theory of regulation* holds that most regulation is caused by the political efforts of powerful businesses that turn to government for protection against competitors. This theory argues that regulation allows firms to restrict overall output, to deny entry to business competitors, and to maintain above-market prices.[17]

A History of American Regulation

A brief review of the history of regulation illustrates how the interaction of democratic and nondemocratic factors has produced today's regulatory agencies and policies.[18]

Between 1900 and World War I, laws were passed to regulate activities of powerful new corporations. These progressive era reforms were pushed by labor unions, the Populists, and middle-class Americans anxious about the conditions reported by muckraking journalists. Landmark regulatory measures included the Federal Trade Commission Act, the Meat Inspection Act, the Pure Food and Drug Act, and the Federal Reserve Act. These measures dealt with problems such as monopolies, unstable financial institutions, unwholesome products, and unsafe working conditions.

Some scholars believe, however, that large corporations were major players in the conception, formulation, and enactment of regulatory legislation.[19] Seen in this light, the Federal Reserve Act was primarily a government response to the entreaties of the American Bankers Association, which worried that financial panics would destroy its business.

Roosevelt's New Deal in the 1930s focused on speculative and unsafe practices in the banking and securities industries that had contributed to the onset of the Great Depression. The goal was to restore stability to financial markets and important industries. Legislation focused on such issues as federal bank inspection, federal deposit insurance, the prohibition of speculative investments by banks, and the creation of the Securities and Exchange Commission to regulate stock market operations. Again, the political sources of New Deal regulation were mixed. Some came from popular pressures,[20] but some also came from the business community, seeking stability in its various industries.[21]

The successes of the consumer, environmental, and civil rights movements from the late 1960s to the late 1970s resulted in a substantial increase in the federal government's regulation of business. The aim of these regulatory efforts was to protect against health and environmental hazards, to provide equal opportunity, and to allow more public access to regulatory rule-making. Under the authority of new laws, agencies such as the Environmental Protection Agency, the Equal Opportunity Employment Agency, and the Federal Drug Administration issued numerous rules that affected business operations and decisions. It was one of the only times in our history when business was almost entirely on the defensive, unable to halt the imposition of laws and regulations to which it was strongly opposed.[22]

VIDEO ROUNDTABLE

Energy Policy

Waiting for the Big One

Disappearing wetlands may have made the Gulf Coast, including this area near New Orleans, more vulnerable to major hurricanes. The devastation caused by Hurricane Katrina in 2005 may convince the public and elected leaders that new federal and state wetlands regulations should be required in the future.

By the end of the 1970s, the mood of opinion leaders both inside and outside the government had turned against regulation in the name of economic efficiency. Many blamed excessive regulation for forcing inefficient practices on American companies, contributing to sluggish economic growth, slow productivity gains, and disappointing competitiveness in the global economy. And many found fault with the government for imposing uniform national standards, strict deadlines for compliance with regulations, and detailed instructions.[23] The deregulatory mood was spurred by a business political offensive that funded think tanks, journals of opinion, foundations favorable to the business point of view, and electoral campaigns of sympathetic candidates.[24] From then until today, the watchword has been **deregulation,** the attempt to loosen the hand of government in a variety of economic sectors including banking and finance, transportation, and telecommunications.

deregulation
The process of diminishing regulatory requirements for business.

The Future of Regulation

While deregulation may mean that especially egregious, unfair, and inefficient regulations will be erased from the books, the regulatory state is likely here to stay, mainly because the public supports most existing regulatory programs, especially those aimed at environmental and consumer protection.

The regulatory state is here to stay, moreover, because economic activity and technological change bring new problems and demands for government intervention to protect the public. The ready availability of pornography on the Internet, for example, has triggered efforts by Christian conservatives and others to regulate its content. Unraveling the human genome has led to calls for regulating how this new knowledge will be used. When people become ill from tainted beef, the public demands higher standards of meat inspection and tracking. When mergers threaten competition, most consumers welcome government intervention. And when companies such as Enron collapse, taking with them the retirement savings of their employees, or when accounting firms and investment banks allow companies such as WorldCom to mislead investors, Americans demand that government protect them against similar behavior by other companies. The Sarbanes-Oxley Act of 2002, passed in response to these last developments, for example, expanded auditing and financial disclosure requirements for publicly traded companies.

Also, business itself will continue to turn to government for regulation when it suits the purpose of a particular industry. Thus, in 2004, after the discovery of mad cow disease in the United States, the National Cattlemen's Beef Association, the main trade association of the beef industry, asked political leaders to institute regulations that would restore consumer confidence in beef products and reopen foreign markets, where U.S. beef exports had been banned. Ironically, perhaps, the American Cattlemen's Association had lobbied for years against such regulation.

Social Welfare

Another important domain of domestic policy in the United States is social welfare, a broad range of programs that protects the minimum standards of living of families and individuals against some of life's unavoidable circumstances: unemployment, income loss and poverty, physical and mental illness and disability, family disintegration, and old age. Such programs account for the largest share of the annual federal budget.

social insurance

Government programs that provide services or income support in proportion to the amount of mandatory contributions made by individuals to a government trust fund.

Social welfare in the United States is provided by a complex mix of programs, but we can distinguish two basic kinds. The first is **social insurance,** made up of Social Security and Medicare, in which individuals contribute to an insurance trust fund—in reality, a set of federal government bonds—by way of a payroll tax on their earnings and receive benefits based on their lifetime contributions. The second kind is **means-tested,** meaning that benefits are distributed on the basis of need to those who can prove that their income is low enough to qualify. These programs are funded by general income tax revenues, rather than by payroll taxes. The food stamp program is an example.

means-tested

Meeting the criterion of demonstrable need.

Some social welfare programs are administered directly from Washington, while others are jointly administered by federal and state governments. Social Security is an example of a program run from the nation's capital. Payroll taxes for Social Security are levied directly on wages and salaries by the federal government, and benefit checks are issued to the elderly and the disabled by the Social Security Administration. By contrast, Medicaid is jointly funded and administered by state and federal governments. One result of such mixed programs is wide variation in benefit levels across the states.

entitlements

Government benefits that are distributed automatically to citizens who qualify on the basis of a set of guidelines set by law; for example, Americans over the age of 65 are entitled to Medicare coverage.

Some social welfare programs are **entitlement** programs; that is, payments are made automatically to people who meet certain eligibility requirements. For example, citizens whose income is under a certain level are entitled to food stamps and Medicaid. Because payments are made automatically, these expenditures are locked into the federal budget, and Congress can only tinker around the margins of the budget unless it changes the underlying statutes or passes revised program authorizations, which are hard to do.

Social Security and Medicare

The Social Security and Medicare social insurance programs that guard against loss of income due to old age, disability, and illness are the largest, most popular, and fastest growing parts of American social welfare[25] (see

Figure 17.4). Such programs account for about one-third of annual federal government expenditures. In the next sections, we'll explore both of them.

Old Age, Survivors, and Disability Insurance (OASDI)   Retirement income support under Social Security accounts for about two-thirds of the system's outlays; the other third goes to cover benefit payments for the disabled and survivors of deceased workers. The system is funded by a payroll tax on employees and employers under the Federal Insurance Contributions Act (the familiar FICA on your weekly or monthly pay stub). Because the program is paid for to a substantial degree by those who are currently working, the net effect is to redistribute income across generations.

Many Americans worry that Social Security funds will run out before they can begin collecting benefits. Presently, Social Security takes in more in payroll taxes than it pays out in benefits each year, so its trust fund shows a strong positive balance. However, because the population is aging—meaning there will be fewer working people paying taxes to pay the benefits for additional elderly recipients—a time will come when the fund will be paying out at a faster clip than it is being replenished. Especially troublesome to many is the sizable baby-boom generation, whose first members will reach retirement age in 2010. According to recent estimates by the actuary of the Social Security trust fund, the fund will not move into the red until the year 2042. The well will not run dry even then, of course; given a continued inflow of payroll taxes, the current system would be able to pay 75 percent of benefits

FIGURE 17.4 • Comparing the Size and Growth of Social Insurance and Means-Tested Programs, 2006

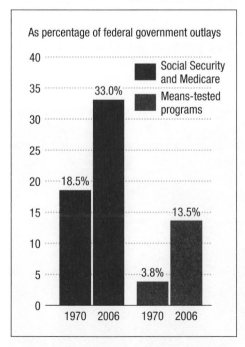

The two social insurance programs, Social Security and Medicare, receive many more federal dollars than means-tested programs, such as public assistance, food stamps, and Medicaid. Social insurance now accounts for one-third of federal government spending.

Source: Office of Management and Budget, *The Budget of the United States, 2007.*

for a very long time after that.[26] (Some scholars have suggested that these projections are based on very conservative assumptions about future economic performance, the level of immigration, and the rate of aging in the American population; their more optimistic assumptions leave Social Security with another 75 years or so before deficits appear.[27] Of course, well before then Americans could decide to solve the long-term trust fund problem by raising the payroll tax rate, raising the ceiling on taxable income subject to the payroll tax (now at $90,000), cutting back benefit levels, taxing the benefits of the wealthy, or raising the retirement age.[28] None of these changes would be politically popular, to be sure, but adapting one or more would leave years more of Social Security surpluses. Policymakers could also decide to fully or partially privatize the system, having individuals manage their own retirement accounts.[29]

Generally, Democrats think the system is in good health and requires only some tinkering to solve emerging problems. Republicans, on the other hand, believe the system is seriously flawed and that the only way to save it is with major overhauls such as individual investment accounts. President Bush tried hard in 2005 to convince the public and members of Congress to adopt a system of private accounts but, as the opening story in Chapter 7 described, the proposal never made it to the floor of either chamber.

The Evolution of Social Welfare Policy

Medicare   Since it was created in 1965, Medicare has paid for a substantial portion of the hospital and doctor bills of retirees and the disabled. Since then, it has grown into one of the largest federal programs; $338 billion was spent in 2006, more than 12 percent of the annual federal budget. The program is likely to grow quite substantially in the coming years because of the addition of a partial prescription drug benefit program in 2006. The prescription drug benefit will add about $534 billion over 10 years to Medicare expenditures, according to most estimates.

Although it may prove to be a success in the long run—it is too early to know at this writing—the prescription drug program got off to a very rough start. The program is extremely complex, with the government paying subsi-

Worried About Coverage

Michigan seniors try to figure out which of their prescription medicines are covered or not covered under the new Medicare drug plan. Many criticized the plan for its complexity and uneven coverage, although tens of millions eventually signed up.

dies to private insurance companies for offering policies to cover drug costs, each with different drug formularies, co-pays, levels of coverage, and more. Moreover, the drug benefit covers only a portion of out-of-pocket costs up to $2,250, then covers nothing until out-of-pocket costs reach $5,100, then kicks in again. Many seniors were confused by the program and not happy with the result in its first year of operation. A *Wall Street Journal*/NBC News poll reported that only 23 percent of seniors had a favorable view of the new program, while 73 percent said they found it "too complicated and confusing."[30]

Paying for Medicare is a recurring problem. Outlays have been growing at about 10 percent a year for awhile now, much faster than those for other federal programs and much faster than Medicare revenues are coming in. And waiting in the wings, again, is the baby-boom generation, which will have an enormous effect on the prescription drug program. It is no wonder, then, that the issue of controlling Medicare costs has become one of the constants of recent American politics.

Do Social Insurance Programs Work?   In an era when it is fashionable to deride the ability of government to do anything well, it is important to recognize how successful America's social insurance programs have been. There is no doubt that Social Security and Medicare work beyond the wildest dreams of their founders. Although the benefits do not allow people to live luxuriously, they provide an income floor for the retired and pay for costly medical services that, before 1965, were as likely as not to impoverish those who had serious illnesses and long hospital stays.

The effectiveness of Social Security and Medicare was shown in a 1989 Census Bureau study on the effects of government taxing and spending programs on income inequality and poverty. The principal finding was that Social Security (including Medicare) "is the Federal government's most effective weapon against poverty and reduces the inequality of Americans' income more than the tax system and more than recent social welfare [means-tested] programs."[31] In fact, Social Security and Medicare have helped reduce the elderly poverty rate from about 48 percent in the mid-1950s to about 10 percent today.[32]

Means-Tested Programs

Means-tested programs, popularly called *welfare,* account for only a small part of the annual federal budget but have attracted more popular discontent than virtually anything else government does. While Social Security and Medicare enjoy widespread support, means-tested welfare programs have long been objects of scorn.

Most Americans say they want government to help the poor,[33] but almost everyone disliked the now-defunct Aid to Families with Dependent Children (AFDC) program—not only conservatives, but liberals as well; not only average citizens, but also welfare recipients; and not only voters and political leaders, but people who work for welfare agencies. A consensus long existed that something was wrong with AFDC.[34] For most Americans, AFDC and other means-tested programs seemed to contradict such cherished cultural values as independence, hard work, stable families, and responsibility for one's own actions. Public opinion polls consistently showed that Americans believed that welfare kept people dependent; didn't do a good job of helping people stand on their own two feet; and encouraged divorce, family disintegration, and out-of-wedlock births.[35] (See the "By the Numbers" feature to learn more about the number of poor people in the United States.)

By the Numbers

How many Americans are poor?

Although the Bible says, "For you will have the poor with you always" (Matthew 26:11), it does not tell us how many of the poor will be with us at any given time.

Why It Matters: Knowing how many poor there are, and being relatively confident in the validity and reliability of that number, is extremely important for a number of reasons:

- Comparing the number who are poor in the United States over time gives us an indication of how well we are doing as a society.

- Comparing the number who are poor in the United States over time lets us know the dimensions of a serious social problem that may require government action or the mobilization of private charities, or both.

- The number of people living in poverty helps determine the size (and thus the cost) of many government programs, including food stamps, Medicaid, rent supplements, and the Earned Income Tax Credit.

Interestingly, if the numbers are to be believed, we made good progress during the 1990s—the poverty rate fell to 11.3 in 2000, its lowest point in 21 years—but increased again as the United States went through a recession and a recovery that added jobs later than usual in such recoveries. In 2004, 12.7 percent of Americans—around 37 million people—were below the poverty line, according to the Census Bureau.

The Story Behind the Poverty Measure: But what is poverty and how can we measure it? Most

would probably agree that poverty involves living in dire circumstances; that is, being poorly housed, underfed, and without adequate medical care. But we might have a harder time agreeing on the exact dividing line between adequate and inadequate living standards. To get around this, government statisticians use *income* as a proxy for calculating poverty. Rather than collect information about how people live—what their homes and apartments are like, for example—the Census Bureau collects information about how much money they earn. The assumption, of course, is that in an economy such as ours, what one earns is directly related to how one lives and consumes.

Calculating the Poverty Line: The poverty line was first calculated in 1964 by Census Bureau statisticians. They started with the Department of Agriculture's determination of what it would cost a family of four to buy enough food to survive (called the "emergency food budget"). Then, because it had been determined that the average American family in 1964 spent one-third of its after-tax income on food, the statisticians multiplied the Agricultural Department's emergency food budget figure by three to determine the official government poverty line. They then adjusted this income number for family size, creating poverty line numbers for single persons living alone, two-person families, and so on.

This 1964 baseline figure is used to the present day. Starting in 1965, and every year since then, the poverty line from the previous year is adjusted for inflation, taking into account different family sizes. The accompanying table shows the official poverty line thresholds for 2004. To be under the line is to be officially poor.

Criticisms of the Poverty Line Measure: As with most official statistics, the poverty line calculation has its critics:

The government offers several means-tested programs designed to assist low-income Americans. Let us look at the five most important ones.

Food Stamps This program, funded from the budget of the Department of Agriculture, helps poor Americans falling below a certain income line buy food

- Because the typical American household today spends a much lower proportion of its income on food than in 1964, the "emergency food budget" figure from the Agriculture Department should be multiplied not by three, as it has been since the beginning, but by five or six, to calculate the poverty threshold, say some critics. This would result in a substantial increase in the number of people officially designated as poor.

- If poverty is really about lifestyles and consumption patterns, argue conservatives, then household income calculations should include the income equivalents of noncash government benefits such as public housing, rent supplements, Medicaid support, and food stamps. Doing this would reduce the number of people officially living in poverty.

- By calculating a single, national poverty threshold, the Census Bureau fails to take into account the substantial differences in the cost of living that exist across states and communities. A family of four earning $17,000, for example, could no doubt stretch its dollars farther in rural Alabama than in San Francisco.

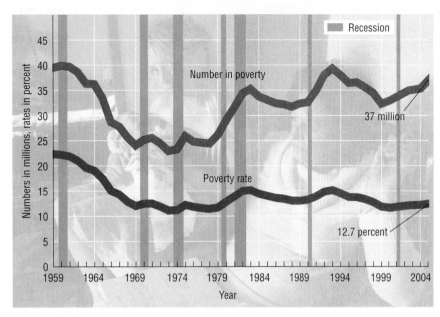

Poverty in the United States

What to Watch For: All government statistics are built on a set of assumptions, some of which are sensible and some of which defy common sense. Be aware of such assumptions when you use official statistics. Luckily, every government agency describes in detail how it collects and calculates statistics, so you can figure it out once you read the documentation.

What Do You Think? With all its problems, should we continue to depend on the Census Bureau's poverty line calculation? Do the virtues of simplicity, consistency, and comparability across the years of the present way of calculating poverty trump its several problems? Or would you rather see poverty rates calculated in some other way? What do you think should be included and excluded from such a calculation?

The Official Poverty Line in the United States in 2004

1 Person	2 People	3 People	4 People	5 People	6 People	7 People	8 People	9 or More People
$10,160	$13,078	$15,277	$20,144	$24,293	$27,941	$32,150	$35,957	$43,254

for themselves and their families. Almost 30 million people, about one-half of whom are children, received food stamps at the beginning of 2006. Food stamp benefit levels are set by the individual states under general federal guidelines, and states vary substantially in their generosity. Stamps can be used only for food; they cannot be used for alcohol, cigarettes, beauty care products, or

Giving Preschoolers a Head Start

The Head Start program for preschool poor children is one of the few means-tested programs that enjoys widespread support across the ideological and partisan spectrums. Here, children take a lunch break at a Head Start Center.

Making a Difference: Welfare Reform

gambling, despite rumors to the contrary. The program seems to have made a significant dent in the prevalence of malnutrition in the United States, even though the average benefit has never exceeded 80 cents per person per meal.[36]

Medicaid and SCHIP The federal government allocates matching funds to the states to provide medical assistance for their indigent adult citizens and children in these two rapidly growing programs (SCHIP is the acronym for the State Children's Health Insurance Program). A total of $198 billion was spent by the federal government on these programs in 2006, with much more added by the individual states. Except for having to follow the requirement to provide Medicaid and SCHIP for all public assistance recipients, the states formulate their own eligibility requirements and set their own benefit levels, meaning that variations among the states are substantial. In addition to providing medical services for the very poor, Medicaid has become increasingly used to pay for nursing home care for those who have exhausted their savings, including many people who had been long-time members of the middle class.

There is no question that Medicaid and SCHIP have been very successful in terms of allowing many poor people to gain access to needed medical services, but a number of problems continue to plague the programs. For one thing, the eligibility rules are complex and tend to exclude those who are not extremely poor, blind, disabled, or children of out-of-work parents. Indeed, only about 40 percent of the nation's officially designated poor adults are covered by Medicaid, leaving the remainder without medical benefits. Despite this, the financial costs of the programs have been rising rapidly, and a number of efforts are under way in the states and in Congress to slow down the pace of growth. In late 2005, Congress passed a bill supported by President Bush that allows the states to reconfigure and reduce benefits, charge premiums for coverage, and require co-payments for medical services.

Supplemental Security Income Created in 1974, Supplemental Security Income (SSI) is a program that provides cash benefits to the elderly, blind, and disabled poor when social insurance programs are insufficient to elevate them above the poverty line. The program is relatively small and getting smaller.

The Earned Income Tax Credit The working poor benefit greatly from a provision in the U.S. Tax Code that allows low-income individuals with at least one child to claim a credit against taxes owed or, for some, to receive a direct cash transfer from the IRS. This provision of the Tax Code benefits more than 56 million low-income Americans without much bureaucratic fuss,[37] with about three-fourths of the total going to households earning between $5,000 and $20,000.[38]

Welfare Block Grants The Temporary Assistance to Needy Families (TANF) Act, passed in 1996, replaced AFDC with an entirely new system of public assistance. (See the "Using the Framework" feature on why the change happened.) Its major features are as follows:

- The status of welfare assistance as a federal entitlement was ended. The families of poor children are no longer guaranteed assistance by the federal government.

- The design and administration of welfare programs have been turned over to the states, meaning there are 50 different welfare programs in the United States.

- States receive block grants from the federal government to help them finance the welfare systems they devise. States add their own money in varying amounts, with some states, such as New York, much more generous than others.

- States use these combined funds to give both direct cash assistance to families—usually, a monthly welfare check—and money for child care, education and training, and other services to encourage recipients to enter paid employment.

- The head of every family receiving welfare is required to work within two years of receiving benefits and is limited to a total of five years of benefits. States are allowed to impose even more stringent time requirements. States are also allowed to use their own funds (not federal block grant money) to extend the two-year and five-year limits.

- Unmarried teenage parents can receive welfare benefits only if they stay in school and live with an adult.

- States must provide Medicaid and SCHIP to all who qualify under current law.

Proponents of welfare reform believed the new welfare system would end welfare dependence, reestablish the primacy of the family in poor communities, improve the income situation of the poor as they enter the job market, and help balance the federal budget. Opponents of welfare reform believed the legislation would lead to more poverty, homelessness, and hunger—especially among children—once recipients reached their five-year time limit.

Only time will tell which of these scenarios will prevail over the long run. Here is what the research shows to date. Welfare rolls across the country have steadily diminished since the new law was passed; many people have been trained for jobs and have entered the paid workforce, and many have raised their incomes.[39] However, because pay levels for entry-level jobs are so low, only a small percentage of former welfare recipients were able to cross the official **poverty-line** threshold in the first years of the program. And, while the poverty rate decreased among former welfare recipients between 1996 and 2000, it slowly increased after that, although the percentage of those living below the poverty line remains lower than in 1996.[40]

poverty line
The federal government's calculation of the amount of income families of various sizes need to stay out of poverty.

Using the Framework

Welfare Reform

Why did our welfare system change so drastically in 1996?

Background: America's traditional welfare system, created in 1935 almost as an afterthought to Social Security, had grown to the point that it provided cash payments to families of one in nine children in the United States by 1995. Although it did not pay very much to individual families, and represented but a tiny portion of the federal government's budget, the program was never very popular with the public, grew even less popular in the 1980s and the 1990s, and was replaced by a radically new program in 1996. Examining structural, political linkage, and governmental factors that contributed to a dramatic change in welfare policy will make the story clearer.

Governmental Action

The Temporary Assistance to Needy Families Act became law in 1996.

Governmental Level

The Republican-controlled Congress delivered on its promise in the Republican Contract with America to pass a bill to radically transform welfare.

President Clinton, a believer in welfare reform (he had promised to "end welfare as we know it"), signed the bill into law near the beginning of the 1996 presidential campaign.

Political Linkages Level

The Democratic Party lost a substantial number of blue-collar, unionized workers, concerned about "wasteful spending" on welfare, from their electoral base.

Moderate Democrats of the Democratic Leadership Council (DLC) also embraced welfare reform.

Republican conservatives won control of the House and Senate in the 1994 elections.

Conservative intellectuals and think tanks attacked the AFDC welfare system during the 1980s on the grounds that it killed individual initiative and created dependency, destroyed families, and rewarded immorality.

Public opinion became more critical of welfare in the 1980s.

The Republican Party used the "welfare mess" issue with great effect in election campaigns, winning the presidency in 1980, 1984, and 1988 and the Senate for much of the 1980s.

Structural Level

The American political culture celebrates competitive individualism, small government, and self-reliance, and denigrates handouts to the "undeserving" poor.

Competitive pressures from the global economy in the 1990s pushed governments in all of the rich democracies to make their welfare states more efficient.

The fall of communism and the post–Cold War boom in the United States enhanced the attractiveness of conservative ideas in America.

Federalism allowed states to experiment with alternative modes of welfare delivery.

The American Social Welfare System: How Exceptional?

The American system of social welfare is quite exceptional compared to that found in most other rich democracies.[41] Here are the main differences.

Comparing Social Welfare Policy

- *The American system is much less costly.* Despite complaints about its overall cost, ours is among the least costly of the social welfare states.[42] Among the rich democracies, only Japan and Australia spend relatively less than we do on social welfare, and Japan is well known for the generosity of company benefits to workers. Sweden, Denmark, and Finland, on the other hand, devote fully a third of GDP to social welfare of one kind or another, compared with about 12 percent in the United States.[43] The Scandinavian countries spend only twice as much as the United States, however, if one takes into account the high taxes citizens there pay on the benefits they receive, and the American tendency to fund social welfare indirectly by widespread use of tax subsidies: the earned income tax credit, tax deductions for home mortgage interest, child care tax credits, and more.[44] But that is still a big difference.

- *The American system covers fewer people than systems in other rich democracies.* Most of western European nations blanket their entire populations with benefits. Family allowances in places such as Austria, the Netherlands, Norway, and Sweden, for instance, go to all citizens who have children. In the United States, in contrast, social welfare provision is a patchwork, and many citizens are not protected or covered at all. (To be sure, some programs work in the sense that they effectively address a given problem as you can see in the "Mapping American Politics" feature).

- *The American system favors the elderly, while others distribute benefits more evenly across age groups.* Medicare and Social Security, already the largest parts of social welfare in the United States, continue to outstrip the rate of growth of programs that benefit the nonelderly poor, especially children. In most other systems, family allowances and universal medical coverage keep benefit distributions more balanced. One result is a significant long-term decrease in the poverty rate among the elderly in the United States and an increase in the poverty rate among children.[45]

- *The American system is less redistributive.* The degree of income equality in the OECD nations (with the exception of Japan) is a function of the amount of money they spend on social welfare programs and the degree to which program coverage is universal. The United States ranks very low on both, so our social welfare state does not make much of a dent in the degree of income and wealth inequality in comparison with those of other nations.[46]

- *The American system requires less of private employers.* All western European countries require that employers help employees with their parenting obligations. For example, all require employers to offer maternity and parenting leaves (now required for workers in firms with 50 or more employees in the United States under the Family and Medical Leave Act), with pay (not required here), and all require that work schedules be adjusted for parenting needs. German mothers receive six weeks' paid leave before giving birth and eight weeks' after. Further, all western European governments mandate four to six weeks of paid vacation.

- *The American system does not include universal health coverage.* The OECD countries either provide health services directly (the National

Mapping American Politics

Childhood poverty and federal child nutrition programs

Introduction: We saw in the Chapter 13 mapping feature, where we considered spending by the Department of Homeland Security, that government spending often does not meet the purported purposes of federal programs. Many critics of government suggest that this mismatch between intentions and results is endemic, typical of an essentially ineffectual or feckless government. Are there programs that do what they set out to do? And if there are, what allows them to meet their goals? In this box we consider the child nutrition programs of the Department of Agriculture, which are intended to help poor children become more healthy and better able to take advantage of their schooling. The department administers four child nutrition programs: the National School

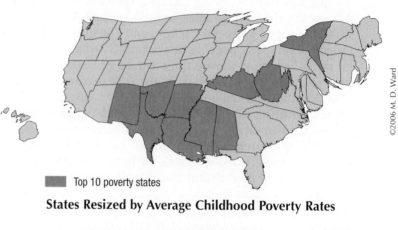

■ Top 10 poverty states

States Resized by Average Childhood Poverty Rates

©2006 M. D. Ward

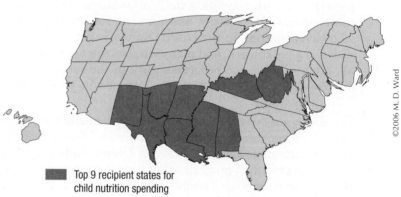

■ Top 9 recipient states for child nutrition spending

States Resized by Per-Capita Federal Child Nutrition Funds Received

©2006 M. D. Ward

Health Service in Great Britain is an example), offer universal health insurance coverage (e.g., the Canadian system), or use some combination of the two. In the United States, Medicare provides health insurance coverage for the elderly and a prescription drug benefit, Medicaid and SCHIP provides coverage for the poor, and the Veterans Administration covers costs for veterans of the military and their dependents. Other Americans must depend on private insurance, pay out-of-pocket, or do without. Almost 46 million Americans, for example, have no health insurance coverage at all.[47]

How to explain the special character of the American social welfare system? Here we identify structural and political linkage factors that influence the kind of social welfare state we have.

Constitutional Rules Federalism is one reason social welfare programs were introduced here so late. Until the 1930s, it was not clear where the main respon-

Lunch Program, the School Breakfast Program, the Child and Adult Care Food Program, and the Summer Food Service Program. If these programs are doing what they are supposed to be doing, they ought to be funneling a disproportionate share of funding to states with the most poor children.

Mapping Dollars Against Needs: The states in the top cartogram are expanded or diminished according to their average poverty rates for children under 18. States with high child poverty rates are larger than normal; states with low poverty rates are smaller than normal. The 10 states in green have the highest rates of poverty—more than 19 percent of the children under 18 living in each of these states are in poverty. The second cartogram highlights the 9 states that receive the highest per capita child nutrition program dollars (Alaska, not shown, is among the top 10). Comparing the two cartograms shows an almost exact match between needs and the flow of federal dollars. The states with the most poor children on a per-capita basis also, by and large, receive the most help from the federal government to feed these children. So it seems at least one federal program is working as advertised. And there are probably others as well.

What seems to help make this program work is that federal dollars are distributed by a formula based on child poverty rates in school districts in states across the country. Programs based on formulas of one kind or another are probably more likely than programs supported by annual appropriations to meet program goals—if the formula is designed correctly in the first place, of course—because representatives and senators are less able to intervene to support pet projects for their districts and states.

What Do You Think? Should more federal programs be based on formulas rather than annual appropriations? Do you believe they are more likely to meet program goals if taken out of the annual appropriations process? Or do you believe, as many critics do, that formulas are inflexible and can build in advantages and disadvantages for particular groups and interests?

Source: U.S. Bureau of the Census, *Statistical Abstract of the United States, 2003*. Table 699 (child poverty rates in 1999), Table 423 (federal nutrition program spending in 1999). Alaska, one of the top 10 states receiving federal nutrition dollars, is not shown.

sibility for social welfare was constitutionally lodged. In fact, it was not generally accepted that the national government had any authority at all on social welfare matters until the U.S. Supreme Court belatedly relented and accepted the New Deal. Federalism is also responsible for the incredible administrative complexity of our system and for the great unevenness in program coverage. Because of federalism, that is, our system takes into account the needs and interests of each state. The result is great variation among the states in benefits, eligibility requirements, and rules. The only large-scale programs that are universal in the European sense (uniform, comprehensive, and administered and funded by the national government) are Social Security and Medicare.

Racial Divisions It is often argued that Europe's greater propensity toward welfare states with universal coverage is a result of the ethnic and racial homogeneity in their societies when they first created them. In homogeneous societies, the argument goes, voters are willing to support generous welfare programs because recipients are believed to be very much like themselves—neighbors, down on their luck.[48]

Whether or not this argument is valid—the growing diversity within European countries, especially their large and growing Muslim populations, will eventually make it possible to test this idea—it is apparent that racial tensions influenced the shape of the American social welfare system. Some of the hostility toward AFDC, for instance, was probably related to the fact that African Americans made up a disproportionately large share of AFDC recipients (although less than a majority of all recipients), and that media stories about welfare recipients focused almost entirely on African Americans.[49]

Political Culture   Almost every aspect of the American political culture works against a generous and comprehensive social welfare system. The belief in competitive individualism is especially important. Voters who believe that people should stand on their own two feet and take responsibility for their lives are not likely to be sympathetic to appeals for helping able-bodied, working-age people.[50] Antigovernment themes in the political culture also play a role. Generous and comprehensive welfare states, such as those in Europe, are almost always large and centralized states supported by high taxes, and many Americans are deeply suspicious of politicians and centralized government, and resistant to high taxes.

Business Power   Business plays a powerful role in American politics (see Chapter 7). Almost without exception, the business community has been a voice for low taxes and limited benefits and for voluntary efforts over government responsibility. This stance is most obvious in the area of medical care. Ours is a patchwork quilt that combines social insurance for the elderly (Medicare), a means-tested program (Medicaid and SCHIP) for *some* of the poor, private insurance (Blue Cross/Blue Shield, Prudential, etc.) for many Americans, and a multitude of for-profit hospitals and nursing homes. Doctors, hospital corporations, insurance companies, and nursing home owners are major players in the American system of interest group politics, and they continuously press politicians to maintain this system of mixed government–private enterprise medical care (although some physician groups have begun to alter their views on this issue).

Weak Labor Unions   Countries where workers are organized and exercise significant political power have extensive and generous social welfare systems; countries where this is not the case have less extensive and generous social welfare systems.[51] American labor unions have never been as strong or influential as labor unions in most of the other rich democracies, partly because the proportion of American workers who belong to labor unions has always been and remains smaller than in comparable countries.

Final Thoughts on American Domestic Policies

The federal government is engaged in a wide range of programs and activities that affect the well-being of the American people, including management of the overall economy, regulation of a wide range of business activities, provision of

Using the Democracy Standard

Do Americans get the domestic policies they want from government?

PROPOSITION: **The economic and social policies that the government in Washington produces are a far cry from what the people want. Americans don't get the kinds of economic and social policies that satisfy them.**

AGREE   The discontent expressed by the public about government—it's too big, spends and taxes too much, and cannot be trusted to do the right thing—is largely related to the fact that government actions do not come close to what the public wants. Once elected, our leaders are largely unaffected by elections and focus on what special interests want, so our economic and social policies are tilted in ways that satisfy those special interests. For example, people told pollsters for years that they wanted a prescription drug benefit, but it took roughly three decades to get it. Worse yet, the final program seemed to channel most of its dollars to drug and insurance companies. Another example is a Tax Code that heavily rewards upper-income and wealthy Americans.

In broad outline, the American public gets what it wants **DISAGREE** from government in terms of economic and social policy, although, to be sure, it continues to complain about government. Even though current economic and social policies do not satisfy many conservative or liberal critics, democracy is served to the extent that policies closely match what the majority wants from government. For example, Americans want a level of government spending and taxing that is lower than that of the other rich democracies, which they get. They want a government that provides only minimal cash support and services for people who seem able but unwilling to help themselves, which they also get. In the post–Cold War arena, they want funds shifted from the defense sector to domestic needs, which elected leaders have done, until forced to change course after the September 11, 2001, attacks on the United States. The public wants a government that mostly allows the free market to operate on its own but that also pays attention to issues of consumer safety and environmental protection. Economic policies reflect these seemingly contradictory desires.

CONSIDER   The complexity and range of current economic and social welfare policies in the United States make it difficult to reach a simple verdict about how democratic public policy is in the United States.

• What overall conclusion would you make about it?   • Do the American people get what they want from government?   • How about you?   • Are you satisfied with the federal government's economic and social welfare policies?   • Which policies do you support?   • Which ones would you like to see changed?   • And, if you want things changed, do either of the two major political parties seem willing or capable of changing them?

income support and medical assistance for the elderly, and a safety net for the poor and disabled. Although not discussed in this chapter, the federal government is also engaged in programs affecting education, transportation, scientific research, agriculture, and more. Americans disagree how well the federal government carries out these activities, whether it sufficiently addresses many of the most important problems facing society, and whether it is properly financing the programs it does address. So there is much disagreement about the federal government's role. What is clear is that what the federal government does is a product of America's constitutional rules, changes in the nature of society and economy over the long course of American history, and the interplay of political forces involving a broad range of individuals, groups, and firms, as well as elected and unelected public officials.

Summary

The federal government plays an important role in national economic affairs and in providing social welfare for its citizens. Both roles arise from problems created by a dynamic free enterprise market economy and the demand by people in a democratic society that government lend a helping hand.

With respect to macroeconomic policy, the government uses both fiscal and monetary tools to try to encourage economic growth and low inflation. The annual budget fashioned by the president and Congress is the main tool of fiscal policy; decisions by the Federal Reserve Board that affect the supply of money in the economy serve as the main tool of monetary policy. Monetary policy has become increasingly important as problems in controlling the budget deficit have made fiscal policy less effective and less attractive.

The federal government also subsidizes essential infrastructure that would otherwise not be made available by private enterprise and plays an important regulatory role. The origins of the government's role may be found in market failures and diseconomies that triggered popular and business pressures on government. Despite the deregulation efforts of recent years, the regulatory responsibilities of the federal government are likely to remain substantial.

Economic policies are fashioned by the president, Congress, and the Federal Reserve Board. But others are involved as well. Interest groups play a particularly central role. Political parties are also important: Democrats and Republicans take different approaches to economic questions and support different policies when in power.

The social welfare commitment of the federal government has grown substantially since the 1930s, with the most important recent growth occurring in the social insurance programs, Social Security and Medicare. Public assistance grew more slowly and accounted for a much smaller portion of the federal government's social welfare budget. Public assistance was unpopular, however, and in 1996 it was replaced by a block grant program in which the states were given wide latitude to design their own programs.

The American welfare state is very different from others. Ours is smaller, less comprehensive, less redistributive, and more tilted toward the benefit of the elderly. Structural and political linkage factors explain most of the differences.

Web Exploration
Making It on Welfare

ISSUE: Is it possible to live a decent life under the new welfare system? Find out by preparing your own family budget and comparing it with the welfare benefits available in your state.

SITE: Access the Green Book of the House Ways and Means Committee and look at the maximum TANF family payment for your state in MyPoliSciLab at **www.mypoliscilab.com**. Go to the "Web Explorations" section for Chapter 17, select "making it on welfare," then "benefits." Select "Browse." In Section 7, look carefully at Table 7.10 on "maximum benefits" for each state.

WHAT YOU'VE LEARNED: Imagine you are a welfare recipient living in your present community. Pretend that you have two children. Prepare a monthly budget for what it would cost you to live at a minimum level of decency. Be sure to account for housing costs, including utilities, food (you will pay about half, with food stamps covering the other half), transportation (used car, with insurance and gas, or public transportation), school supplies for your children, some modest entertainment, some clothes, personal hygiene and beauty care products, and whatever else you believe to be essential. Don't worry about medical care; you'll be covered by Medicaid.

How does your budget compare with the maximum monthly benefit paid in your state? Do you believe it is possible for you and your hypothetical family to live a decent life under TANF? Is there anything you could eliminate from your budget to make it leaner?

HINT: Most students find that what they consider to be necessary for minimum decency is far above what is allowed to welfare families.

Internet Sources

American Enterprise Institute
www.aei.org
> *A prominent conservative think tank with information about social policy.*

The Brookings Institution
www.brookings.org
> *A left-of-center think tank with a wide-ranging agenda that includes many aspects of domestic policy.*

The Hoover Institution
www.hoover.org
> *A right-of-center think tank focusing on increasing freedom and improving public policy.*

Budget of the United States
www.whitehouse.gov/omb/budget/index.html
> *The budget of the United States, with numbers, documentation, and analyses.*

Electronic Policy Network
www.epn.org/
> *Reports from liberal think tanks on social welfare issues.*

Fedstats
www.fedstats.gov
> *Links to statistics and data from a broad range of federal government agencies, including those most relevant for economic and social welfare policy in the United States. These include the Federal Reserve Board, the Bureau of Labor Statistics, the Social Security Administration, the Bureau of the Census, the Bureau of Economic Analysis, and Administration for Children and Families.*

Public Agenda Online
www.publicagenda.org/
> *A nonpartisan site with comprehensive information about government policies, alternative proposals to solve societal problems, and what the public thinks about existing and alternative policies.*

Suggestions for Further Reading

Eisner, Marc Allen. *Regulatory Politics in Transition,* 2nd ed. Baltimore: Johns Hopkins University Press, 2000.
> *Argues that regulatory policies are best understood in terms of the historical periods in which they were introduced.*

Gilbert, Neil and Amitai Etzioni. *The Transformation of the Welfare State: The Silent Surrender of Public Responsibility.* New York: Oxford University Press, 2004.
> *The authors argue that changes toward the greater use of market incentives and dependence on personal responsibility are happening in all rich democracies.*

Hacker, Jacob S. *The Divided Welfare State: The Battle over Public and Private Social Benefits in the United States.* New York: Cambridge University Press, 2002.
> *Suggests that the development and form of the American welfare state is the product of the tension in the United States between values of equality and freedom.*

Howard, Christopher. *The Hidden Welfare State.* Princeton, NJ: Princeton University Press, 2001.

Argues that the American welfare state is every bit as big and comprehensive as those of western Europe, but that they take a different form: public-private partnerships, indirect subsidies and loan guarantees, and the like.

Noble, Charles. *Welfare as We Know It: A Political History of the American Welfare State.* New York: Oxford University Press, 1997.

A comprehensive, sophisticated, and lively discussion of why we have the kind of welfare state we have in the United States and why the establishment of a European-style welfare state remains out of the question here.

Page, Benjamin I., and James R. Simmons. *What Government Can Do: Dealing with Poverty and Inequality.* Chicago: University of Chicago Press, 2000.

A passionate, articulate, and empirically supported argument in favor of a larger role for government in alleviating poverty and making the United States a more equal society.

Peters, Guy B. *American Public Policy: Promise and Performance,* 6th ed. Washington, DC: CQ Press, 2004.

A comprehensive examination of the formation and content of American public policies.

Weidenbaum, Murray. *One-Armed Economist: On the Intersection of Business and Government.* Somerset, NJ: Transaction Publishers, 2004.

Former chair of the Council of Economic Advisors during the Reagan administration and a leading figure in the deregulation movement offers his insights into how economic policy is made in the United States.

CHAPTER 18

Foreign Policy and National Defense

IN THIS CHAPTER

- Why the United States is a superpower

- What new problems are emerging in the post–Cold War world

- What national security means today

- How foreign and defense policies are made

- How the political process affects foreign and defense policies

Unilateralism or Multilateralism?

In his State of the Union address on January 29, 2002, President George W. Bush announced a dramatic shift in American foreign policy. In addition to the war on terrorism, which he vowed to continue regardless of duration or cost, the president also indicated that the United States was committed to an even more ambitious foreign policy goal:

> Our . . . goal is to prevent regimes that sponsor terror from threatening America or our friends and allies with weapons of mass destruction. . . . States like these [Iraq, Iran, and North Korea], and their terrorist allies, constitute an axis of evil [emphasis added], arming to threaten the peace of the world. . . . The United States of America will not permit the world's most dangerous regimes to threaten us with the world's most destructive weapons.[1]

If these countries failed to dismantle their weapons of mass destruction programs, and if others were not prepared to help, said the president, then the United States was prepared to act militarily on its own.

Barely eight months later, in September 2002, President Bush's report to Congress, "The National Security Strategy of the United States of America," put flesh on the skeletal framework set out in his "axis of evil" speech, setting out a new grand strategy for the future. At the center of the new strategy was "preemption," the idea that in a dangerous world where terrorists and tyrants consort, and where weapons of mass destruction are increasingly likely to get into the wrong hands, the United States will reserve the right to "strike first"—that is, before it absorbs a punishing attack. In the words of the document: "We must be prepared to stop rogue states and their terrorist clients before they are able to threaten or use weapons of mass destruction against the United States and our allies and friends." And, if necessary, the document announces, we might need to act unilaterally: "The United States will constantly strive to enlist the support of the international community . . . [But] we will not hesitate to act alone . . . to exercise our right of self-defense by acting preemptively."[2]

The president also said in the strategy document that pursuing such policies required that the United States remain the preeminent military power in the world. All potential adversaries—presumably including rising powers such as China—he said, must be dissuaded "from pursuing a military build-up in hopes of surpassing, or equaling, the power of the United States." In June, in a speech at West Point, the president had put it even more bluntly: "America has, and intends to keep, military strengths beyond challenge."

Equally important, said the president in his National Security Strategy report, was his intention to fuse power

and principle, claiming that American power must be used not only to protect the United States from attack, but to spread American ideas of liberty and representative democracy, even if that caused distress among traditional allies.

Although talk of an axis of evil, preemptive military interventions, and spreading democracy generally played well in the United States, many American allies expressed alarm. None had been consulted. None thought that lumping together North Korea, Iran, and Iraq made intellectual or policy sense. None thought pressuring countries into making democratic reforms, although laudable in intention, would work. None were happy. The German Foreign Minister complained that Bush was treating the allies like mere "satellites" and warned that "success of future actions . . . will not lie in

... policies of lonely decision making"; the French Foreign Minister dismissed Bush's goals as "simplistic"; Christopher Patten, the foreign affairs minister of the European Union, worried aloud about the "absolutist" nature of the president's thinking and protested that allies were being treated as "an optional extra."[3]

The new strategic orientation of the Bush administration was put into practice in March 2003 when the president ordered U.S. armed forces to attack Iraq, remove the Saddam Hussein regime from power, and create the framework for a new Iraqi government based on representative elections. Although a significant British force joined the United States, as did very small forces from Spain, Italy, and a number of other countries, combat operations were almost entirely an American affair (the British saw significant combat around Basra and the southern provinces). Bush had tired of the U.N. weapons inspection process in Iraq, as well as the determined opposition of France, Germany, and Russia to U.S. military action, as well as China's silence. Unable to convince a majority in the U.N. Security Council to back the United States's call for the use of force, the president claimed that it was the duty of the United States to protect world peace and enforce U.N. resolutions—in this case, Resolution 1441, demanding that Iraq disarm and rid itself of weapons of mass destruction—when the United Nations was unable or unwilling to act on its own. Saying he had consulted with a number of countries in a "coalition of the willing"—30 countries, few of whom contributed combat troops or money to fund operations—Bush said in a speech on March 17, 2003, that the invasion was not only about disarming Iraq but changing the regime. Addressing himself to Iraq's citizens, he declared that "the tyrant will soon be gone. The day of your liberation is near."

Bush administration actions in Afghanistan and Iraq, the articulation of the doctrine of preemption, and assertions that a central goal of U.S. foreign and military policy was to spread liberty and democracy around the globe have triggered a debate in the United States and among our traditional allies about whether unilateralism has become the guiding principle of American foreign policy, whether this is a good thing, if it has, and whether such unilateralist policies are workable. Advocates of unilateralism argue that the United States must be engaged in the world to protect its security, its interests, and its values—it cannot be isolationist, that is to say—but it must do so on its own terms, without asking leave of international organizations or allies. To critics both here and abroad, only "multilateralism"—that is, a foreign and military policy based on consultation and cooperation with a broad range of allied countries and the United Nations—could protect the interests of both the United States and the world community.

We will have more to say about unilateralism and multilateralism in this chapter, and will point out that, in practice, the Bush administration has acted in a multilateral fashion on a number of fronts. Indeed, by early 2006, President Bush seemed to be having second thoughts about unilateralism; perhaps chastened by difficulties in Iraq, worried about nuclear weapons programs in Iran and North Korea, and surprised by the public and congressional outcry over the possibility of several American ports being run by a Dubai government-owned company, the president went on a speaking tour in March and April to stress the need for international engagement, acceptance of globalization, and cooperation with allies abroad.[4] The departure of unilateralist Defense Secretary Donald Rumsfeld in the wake of the Republican Party's stinging defeat in the 2006 congressional elections also seemed to signal that President Bush might be more open to multilateral approaches.

The debates in the United States and abroad about whether American foreign policy *is* unilateralist or multilateralist in character, and whether it *should be* unilateralist or multilateralist, will be with us for some time to come. So, too, will the debates about preemption and democracy advancement as centerpieces of U.S. doctrine. How we ultimately choose to deal with other peoples and countries as we try to protect our security, interests, and values in the world will be enormously consequential for us and for others. One can only hope that our political system operates in a fashion that allows a wide range of Americans to be engaged in the deliberations that decide the issue.   ■

Thinking Critically About This Chapter

This chapter is about American foreign and military policies, how these policies are made, and how they affect Americans and others.

Using the Framework You will see in this chapter how foreign and military policies are the product of the interaction of structural factors (such as American economic and military power, the collapse of the Soviet Union, and "globalization"), political linkage factors (such as the choices the media make about foreign news coverage, public opinion about what the U.S. role in the world ought to be, and what various interest groups want the government to do), and governmental factors (such as the objectives and actions of presidents, members of Congress, and important executive branch agencies such as the Central Intelligence Agency and the Joint Chiefs of Staff).

 Using the Democracy Standard Using the evaluative tools you learned in Chapter 1, you will see that foreign policy is not always made with the public as fully informed or as involved as they are in domestic affairs. You will see why this is so, ask whether policies would be better if they were made more democratically, and investigate how the public might play a larger role.

Foreign Policy and Democracy: A Contradiction in Terms?

Making U.S. foreign and military policy has traditionally been different from making domestic policy. For one thing, presidents and the executive branch tend to play a much more important part than they do on domestic issues, primarily because the Constitution lodges most responsibilities and powers for foreign and military affairs there rather than in Congress. Most importantly, the Constitution makes the president commander-in-chief of the nation's armed forces as well as its chief diplomat, as described in Chapter 12 on the presidency. In the perpetual tug-of-war between presidents and Congress, presidents usually prevail in the midst of diplomatic or military crises. Also, the ordinary political factors, such as public opinion and interest groups, are sometimes set aside in favor of considerations of the **national interest,** as defined by a small number of national security advisers and other executive branch officials.

national interest
What is of benefit to the nation as a whole.

Other factors also explain why ordinary citizens play a smaller role in the formation of foreign and military policy than they do in the formation of domestic policy. Public opinion, for example, is sometimes reshaped or ignored by government leaders.[5] In crisis situations, moreover, the public often "rallies 'round the flag," accepting the president's actions, at least as long as the results seem good and there is little dissent among political leaders. (When things go wrong or seem to be going wrong, however, domestic politics can return with a vengeance, as it did in the cases of both the Vietnam and Iraq wars, where public support eventually dwindled.) Also, much of foreign policy is influenced by fundamental factors such as the power and resources of the United States and its economic interests abroad.

Involvement by ordinary citizens is also diminished by the sheer complexity of international matters, their remoteness from day-to-day life, and the unpredictability of other countries' actions; all of these tend to make the public's convictions about foreign policy less certain and more subject to revision in the light of events. In military matters, the need for speed, unity, and secrecy in decision making and the concentration of authority in the executive branch mandated by the Constitution mean that the public may be excluded and that government policy sometimes shapes public opinion rather than being shaped by it.

At the same time, however, the exclusion of the public is far from total. The American public has probably always played a bigger part in the making of foreign policy than some observers have imagined, and its role has become increasingly important in such foreign policy issues as trade, immigration, global environmental protection, and corporate behavior abroad. Note, for example, the very high involvement of the public in general, and interest groups in particular (labor unions, environmental organizations, corporations, business trade associations, and the like), in the struggle over ratification of the North American Free Trade Agreement (NAFTA) and in the debate over granting China normal trade status and membership in the World Trade Organization (WTO). Public involvement was high because what was decided in these cases was certain to have important effects on jobs, wages, and environmental quality.

How Exceptional? The World's Superpower

In the autumn of 1990, the United States sent more than a half-million troops, 1,200 warplanes, and six aircraft carriers to the Persian Gulf region to roll back Iraq's invasion of Kuwait. In 1996, U.S. troops were deployed in Bosnia as part of a NATO peacekeeping operation. The warring parties signed the peace agreement in Bosnia only after the United States consented to be the guarantor of the agreement, backed by troops on the ground. In 1999, the United States supplied almost all the pilots, airplanes, ordinance, supplies, and intelligence for the NATO bombing campaign to force the Serb military out of Kosovo province. In less than three months following 9/11, American armed forces overwhelmed the Taliban and Al Qaeda in Afghanistan. In 2003, the United States invaded Iraq, and in less than four weeks had routed Iraq's regular army and its Republican Guard, gained nominal control of all its major cities, including Baghdad, and removed the Saddam Hussein regime from power. These examples reflect the status of the United States as the world's **superpower,** the only nation strong enough militarily and economically to project its power into any area of the globe. (American forces have been used abroad for many years prior to the present period, of course, as the timeline in Figure 18.1 indicates.) In this section, we will examine the foundations of this superpower status.

superpower

A nation armed with nuclear weapons and able to project force anywhere on the globe.

The American Superpower: Structural Foundations

In addition to the power of its real and potential rivals, a nation's place in the international system is largely determined by its relative economic, military, and cultural power. At the beginning of the twenty-first century, the United States enjoys advantages in all three areas. Together, they make the United States the world's only superpower, so preeminent that leaders and commentators are searching for new language to describe it. The French, for example, have started to use the term "hyperpower," while talk of a new American empire is widespread in Europe and elsewhere.[6]

From Stand-Alone to Superpower: The Evolution of Foreign Policy

Economic Power   In 2005 the United States had a population of about 296 million people—considerably fewer than China's 1.3 billion or India's roughly 1.1 billion—but enough to support the world's largest economy, with an annual gross domestic product (GDP) of more than $12.4 trillion. This was about $2.5 trillion more than the combined GDPs of France, the United Kingdom, Germany, and Japan. The United States's GDP, moreover, is about $4 trillion larger than of fast-rising China (but six times larger on a per-capita basis). The United States also ranks first in the world in total exports and imports.[7]

By all indications, the relative strength of the American economy has been increasing, even taking into consideration the 2000–2002 economic doldrums and stock market decline, with GDP growing at much faster rates in the United States than in any of the major western European nations,

FIGURE 18.1 • Timeline: Significant American Foreign Military Operations and Conflicts, Post–Civil War[*]

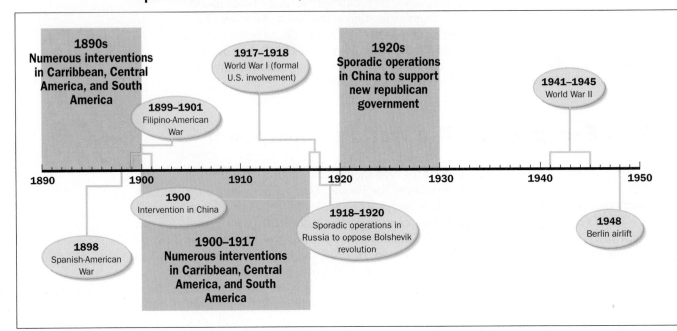

[*]Does not include foreign interventions by agencies, such as the CIA, that have not involved the armed services of the United States.

Source: In part, from Pearson Education, publishing on Infoplease.com.

Australia, New Zealand, or Japan. China is a growing economic powerhouse, to be sure, as is India, but each has a long way to go to match the size of the American economy on a per-capita basis. Throughout the 1990s especially, but also in the opening years of the twenty-first century, U.S.-headquartered companies established preeminence in the economic sectors that count the most in the new global economy: telecommunications, mass entertainment, biotechnology, software, finance, e-commerce, business services, transportation, and computer chips (see Chapter 4).

The fact that major American corporations are increasingly global affects U.S. foreign policy. For the largest of them, a substantial portion of their revenues comes from sales abroad, much of their manufacturing takes place in other countries, and many of the parts for items manufactured domestically are imported. And in industries such as oil and petrochemicals, many of the sources of raw materials are outside our borders. Because American businesses can be found almost anywhere, American national interests can be said to exist almost anywhere as well. It follows that American officials must be attentive to potential trouble spots around the globe. Today, they are especially attentive to the problem of **terrorism,** whether the threat is to government installations, such as embassies and bases, or to private American companies and their employees, thus protecting U.S. economic power.

terrorism

The use of deadly violence against civilians to further some political goal.

Military Power   This enormous economic strength enables the United States to field the most powerful armed forces in the world. The scale of military American superiority, as well as the nation's ability to deploy and use these re-

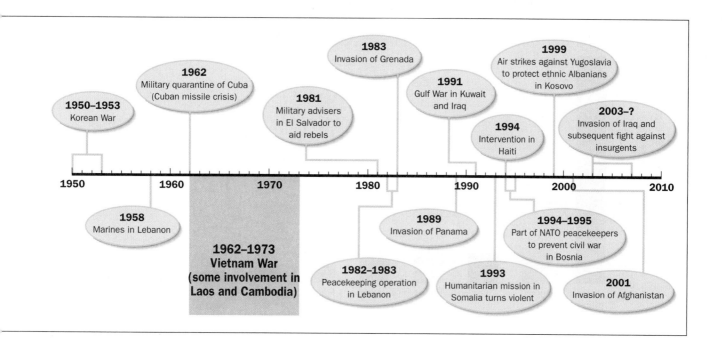

sources, is orders of magnitude beyond any existing or potential rival. Here are a few indicators of this disproportionality of U.S. military power:[8]

- In 2005, the United States's defense budget exceeded those of all other NATO countries (including the United Kingdom, France, Germany, Italy, and more), Russia, China, Japan, Saudi Arabia, and India combined (see Figure 18.2).

Evaluating Defense Spending

Microsoft in India

No matter where their head-quarters might be located, global corporations locate many of their operations across a range of countries. Here, software engineers work at a Microsoft research center in Hyderabad, India.

FIGURE 18.2 • Expenditures for National Defense, 2004 (in billions)

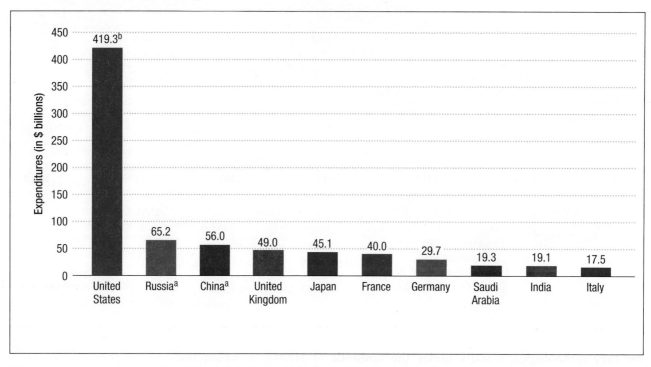

The national defense budget of the United States is orders of magnitude higher than those of friends and potential foes alike. The administration's continuing commitment to a global war on terrorism is likely to push U.S. defense spending even higher in the years ahead.

[a]2003

[b]Does not include cost of combat operations in Iraq or Afghanistan.

Source: Center for Arms Control and Non-Proliferation, 2006.

- The United States's naval power is unrivaled. It has 10 supercarrier battle groups in operation; no other country has even one supercarrier vessel, let alone full battlegroups. It has more modern submarines, moreover, than the rest of the world combined, including the stealthy Seawolf-class, nuclear-powered submarine.

- The United States's airpower is unrivaled. It has more advanced fighter aircraft and bombers, many of the stealth variety, than the rest of the world combined. Its aerial tanker fleet allows these aircraft to reach any target in the world. These aircraft also have the advantage of carrying a varied arsenal of "smart" munitions.

- The United States's ground warfare capabilities are unrivaled. While China has a large standing army, it is not as well armed as U.S. ground forces and lacks many of the logistical and technological capabilities of American forces. In addition, no other nation comes even close to matching America's armored forces, which includes approximately 9,000 M1 Abrams tanks, firing smart munitions.

- The United States's electronic warfare capabilities are unrivaled. These capabilities include, among other things, global positioning systems to guide smart weapons to their targets, self-guided anti-tank missiles that seek out enemy tanks, sophisticated jamming systems to confuse anti-aircraft guns and missiles, and underwater sensing systems to track submarines.

- The United States's strategic nuclear arsenal is unrivaled, with approximately 5,000 nuclear warheads—to be cut to roughly 2,000 by 2012—that can be delivered to their targets by strategic bombers, land-based intercontinental ballistic missiles, and submarines.

- The United States is the only country in the world with permanent and often sizeable military bases in every part of the world.[9]

Potential rivals to American military dominance have a long way to go. Russia, after the breakup of the Soviet Union left its economy and once-proud military in disarray, has renounced most foreign adventures, given up on its opposition to eastward expansion of NATO, and cut its nuclear and conventional arms under international treaties. China, on the other hand, has a fast-growing economy and millions of military personnel and is rapidly upgrading its capabilities—far beyond what is needed to simply defend itself from attack, according to many planners in the Pentagon and Congress's bipartisan U.S.–China Economic and Security Review Commission[10]—but it remains very far behind U.S. capabilities. A July 2005 Pentagon report, for example, concluded that China's ability to project conventional military force beyond its borders remains limited for the time being.[11] The richest countries of western Europe (United Kingdom, Germany, and France) together have relatively small military establishments and a relatively small number of nuclear weapons. They do, however, produce, deploy, and operate very sophisticated military technologies, usually under the umbrella of NATO, in which the United States plays the leading role.

Although powerful, the United States is not omnipotent. Its resources, for example, are not unlimited. Americans discovered this in the war with and occupation of Iraq, in which its ground forces have been stretched to the limit, requiring extended deployments of regular troops and a heavy reliance on reserve and National Guard forces. It may be the case, furthermore, that the high personnel and budget costs associated with Iraq may have reduced

The Road to Baghdad

American invasion forces took less than four weeks in 2003 to defeat Iraq's armed forces, capture its major cities, and remove the regime of Saddam Hussein from power. Here, marines battle for a key bridge leading to the center of Baghdad.

the range of options available to the Bush administration for addressing Iran and North Korea's turn toward production of nuclear weapons. Moreover, it is increasingly apparent that the nation's expansive conventional and strategic military power may not be terribly useful in the war against terrorism—a war in which the enemy is not a country, but rather loosely organized and shadowy cells that may best be uprooted by police investigations and intelligence-gathering operations in cooperation with other countries. And, America's military might has not enabled it to control events in important oil-producing nations—including Venezuela, Nigeria, and Iran—where direct intervention would surely adversely affect oil supplies and prices.

soft power
Influence in world affairs that derives from the attractiveness to others of a nation's culture, products, and way of life.

"Soft Power"   Although critics here and abroad often decry "Americanization"— by which they generally mean the spread of McDonald's, Kentucky Fried Chicken, Disney theme parks, and Hollywood movies and television sitcoms and dramas—one should not underestimate the influence of what some have called America's **soft power,** the attractiveness of its culture, ideology, and way of life for many people living in other countries. As political scientist Joseph Nye has pointed out, it is important for the U.S. position in the world that more than a half-million foreign students study in American colleges and universities; that people in other countries flock to American entertainment and cultural products; that English has become the language of the Internet, business, science, and technology; and that the openness and opportunity of American society are admired by many people around the world.[12] If this very openness and opportunity place the United States in the best position to prosper in the new global, information-based economy—which many believe to be the case—then the United States's soft power enhances its harder economic and military powers.[13]

However, a strong and growing anti-American sentiment also exists in the world. Although unfavorable views of the United States have always existed, they rose dramatically after the invasion of Iraq in the spring of 2003. Although the increase in anti-Americanism was most pronounced in the Arab and Muslim worlds, it also intensified in western Europe, Latin America, and Russia.[14] The Pew Research Center reported the following grim news in 2005, based on its annual surveys in countries around the world: ". . . anti-Americanism is deeper and broader now than at any time in modern history. It is most acute in the Muslim world, but it spans the globe—from Europe to Asia, from South America to Africa."[15] Some of these changes are shown in Figure 18.3.

How to explain these developments? Some observers suggest that the invasion of Iraq—which was opposed almost everywhere—and the long and bloody occupation there has accounted for the rise in anti-Americanism. Even in those countries allied at the time with the United States, including the United Kingdom, Italy, and Spain, public opinion was strongly against the action[16]—and has become even more pronounced over time. Some suggest that rising anti-Americanism is tied to the growing concern that the United States has become so powerful that it can act on its own in pursuit of its own interests, without consulting with other countries or the United Nations or attending to the values and wishes of others. For example, according to the Pew Research Center, 61 percent of Britons, 69 percent of Germans, 73 percent of Russians, and 84 percent of the French reported in 2005 that the United States did not take the interests of other countries into account when making foreign policy decisions.[17] Europeans seem especially alarmed by America's rejection of a multitude of international treaties and agreements and by President Bush's policy of preemption.[18] Strong American support for

VIDEO DEBATE

Americans in Iraq

FIGURE 18.3 • Favorable Views of the United States, 1999 and 2006

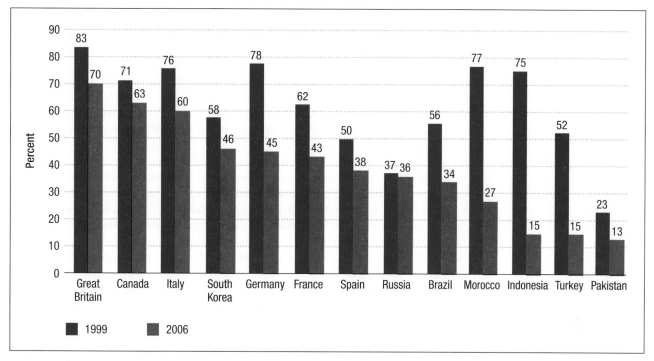

Based on its surveys in selected countries, the Pew Research Center reports that favorable views of the United States have declined, often sharply, among the world's nations. Favorable views have dropped not only in predominantly Muslim nations (Turkey and Indonesia), as might be expected, but also among traditional allies, whether these allies supported the United States in the war in Iraq (the United Kingdom, Japan, and Spain) or opposed the U.S. action there (France and Germany).

Source: "America's Image Slips, But Allies Share U.S. Concerns Over Iran, Homes," *Survey Report* (Washington, D.C: Pew Research Center for the People at the Press, June 13, 2006).

Israel has been extremely unpopular in the Muslim world, of course. It may also be the case that anti-Americanism is felt by many whose ways of life and well-being are threatened by economic and cultural globalization or who have been left behind in the global race for development—especially in the Arab world—and resent the dynamism, wealth, and power of the United States.[19] Finally, it could be that anti-Americanism exists simply because nobody likes Goliath; being the world's single superpower automatically breeds resentment.[20]

Whatever the cause, rising anti-Americanism is real, and it may be undermining some of the soft power advantages the United States has long enjoyed. This development is troubling and something that American presidents and other foreign policymakers increasingly must take into account.

The American Superpower: Strategic Alternatives

As the world's single superpower, the United States must make a number of decisions about how to use this exceptional power.

Exporting American Democracy

hegemon

Term used to refer to the dominant power during various historical periods that takes on responsibilities maintaining and protecting a regional or global system.

Goals   Like the leaders of any other country in the international system, foreign and military policymakers, most especially the president, take as one of their primary duties the defense of the nation against real or potential attacks. This goes almost without saying. Like the leaders of any other country in the international system, moreover, American leaders try to first define and then advance and protect the national interest. Components of the national interest are hard to clearly define, to be sure, and people disagree about what they might be, but at a minimum they include such things as protecting American citizens when they are living or traveling abroad and ensuring that American firms are treated fairly when operating in other countries, that vital raw materials (including oil) are available to consumers and firms, and that markets remain open to American goods and services.

But what about the goal of spreading American values? Whether rightly or wrongly, many Americans, including many political leaders, have believed that the United States has a special mission to improve the world by spreading liberty and representative democracy; many others have said that improving the world also involves spreading free enterprise and open markets. While President Bush perhaps has more clearly articulated these goals as essential elements of American foreign policy than other recent presidents, his aspirations for American foreign policy would not have been unfamiliar to Thomas Jefferson (who referred to the United States as "the empire of liberty"), Woodrow Wilson ("the world must be made safe for democracy"), Franklin Roosevelt (the "four freedoms"), or John F. Kennedy (whose inaugural address pledged to "oppose any foe to assure the survival and success of liberty"). One scholar suggests, in fact, that while President Bush's rhetoric may be different, "the U.S. quest for an international order based on freedom, self-determination, and open markets has changed astonishingly little."[21]

Finally, it has long been argued by foreign policy experts and political leaders that the dominant global power—political scientists call such countries **hegemons**[22]—must provide a range of services to the international system if the world is to enjoy any degree of stability. These include using one's power to put down states that upset the global order, protecting the international trading system, and providing economic leadership. This role was

Waiting to Vote

President Bush declared that spreading democracy was one of the main goals of his foreign policy, pointing to a newly elected government in Afghanistan installed after the American invasion in 2001 to overthrow the Taliban regime and root out Al Qaeda terrorists as an example. Under the new regime, women are allowed to vote, including these women waiting to cast their ballots in parliamentary elections in 2005.

played by the United Kingdom for much of the nineteenth century, and by France and Spain before then in the European context. The Ottoman Empire played a similar role in the sixteenth century for large swatches of the known world. Today, so the argument goes, it is the turn of the United States.[23] It must not only protect itself from attack and pursue its own interests, but use its power to prevent the outbreak of regional wars (India and Pakistan, perhaps), stop the spread of **weapons of mass destruction,** coordinate the effort to prevent pandemics, provide protection for a wide range of countries important for the world economy (e.g., European countries and Japan), and protect and maintain the international trading system (i.e., patrol key shipping lanes, provide the world's reserve currency, act as the world's banker—for the most part, through the World Bank and the International Monetary Fund), and help make and enforce trade rules.

The issue here, of course, is whether Americans and their leaders believe that U.S. foreign policy goals should include more than national defense and a strict focus on defending national interests. It is not entirely clear that either leaders or citizens generally support such goals, nor is it certain that they want to assume the responsibility for and shoulder the costs in lives and dollars of spreading American values and acting as the global hegemon.

Approaches to Using America's Power American leaders and citizens must decide not only what goals to pursue as the world's superpower, but how best to go about using power. Debate on this issue tends to be organized around two views:

- **Unilateralists** would have the United States pursue American national interests in the world on a "go it alone" basis, if necessary. While it might often act in concert with others, unilateralists would have the United States act on the international stage on its own terms, without asking the permission of others, binding itself to restrictive international agreements or following the lead of international organizations such as the United Nations. The existence of this theme in American foreign policy may explain, for example, the United States's unwillingness to sign treaties to establish an international criminal court and ban land mines. Unilateralists are also interested in using American power unilaterally, if it comes to that, to spread American values such as liberty, free enterprise, and democracy, believing these values to be universally valid and appealing. Unilateralists do not see a contradiction between power and principle. Indeed, they believe that they are inextricable.[24]

  As the chapter-opening story suggests, President George Bush has been a strong advocate of unilateralism, as have (now former) Defense Secretary Donald Rumsfeld and Vice President Richard Cheney. Both advised the president to go it alone in disarming Iraq if the United Nations failed to authorize strong measures against Saddam Hussein. Some conservative commentators have taken unilateralism to its logical end point: empire. Charles Krauthammer, Max Boot, and Robert Kaplan, among many others, have celebrated the emergence of a new and presumably benevolent American empire,[25] although the cost—in lives and treasure—of war and occupation in Iraq has dampened much of the initial enthusiasm.

- **Multilateralists** believe that American interests are compatible with the interests of others in the world and that protecting these interests requires cooperation and collaboration with other nations and

weapons of mass destruction
Nuclear, biological, or chemical weapons with the potential to cause vast harm to human populations.

Unilateralism and Multilateralism

unilateralists
Those who believe the United States should vigorously use its military and diplomatic power to pursue American national interests in the world, but on a "go it alone" basis.

multilateralists
Those who believe the United States should use its military and diplomatic power in the world in cooperation with other nations and international organizations.

global warming

The rise of mean global temperatures whether caused by human activities or naturally occurring cycles.

international organizations. Although the United States is undeniably the most powerful nation in the world, it cannot solve all important problems on its own. Problems such as **global warming,** pollution, the wider availability of the means to make weapons of mass destruction, the spread of AIDs and other infectious diseases—SARS, bird flu, and mad cow come to mind—and terrorism threaten virtually every country in the world, and solving these problems, insist multilateralists, will require broad cooperation and collaboration by many countries and international organizations. Interestingly, while much of the thrust of his foreign policy has been unilateralist in character, President Bush also moved in a multilateralist direction when needed as suggesting in the chapter-opening story.

Problems of the Post–Cold War World

Cold War

The period of tense relations between the United States and the Soviet Union from the late 1940s to the late 1980s.

Comparing Foreign and Security Policies

With the end of the **Cold War,** the main concerns of that era—the possibility of global thermonuclear war, a land war in Europe against the Soviet Union, and communist takeovers of Third World countries—have disappeared from the list of foreign policy problems that concern Americans and their leaders. But a host of problems remain. We review these in the next several sections, keeping in mind that the debate among unilateralists and multilateralists will help shape our response to each one.

Security Issues

Although the security threat represented by the Soviet Union has disappeared, many threats to American security remain.

Terrorism   The issue of terrorism moved front-and-center on the American political agenda after the September 11, 2001, attacks on the World Trade Center and the Pentagon. The retaliatory U.S. attacks on the Taliban regime and Al Qaeda in Afghanistan are likely to be but the opening rounds in a long struggle, involving a wide range of overt and covert activities, some undertaken in cooperation with others, some undertaken unilaterally, no matter who is president. At a minimum, American policymakers will try to improve intelligence gathering (sharply criticized by the 9/11 Commission in 2004), create rapid-strike armed forces to attack terrorist cells, and fashion credible policies that will make other countries less likely to offer aid and sanctuary to terrorist organizations. Their job will likely be complicated by the bitter feelings felt by many in the Arab and Muslim worlds as a result of the invasion and occupation of Iraq and American support for Israel.

axis of evil

Three countries—Iraq, Iran, and North Korea—named by President Bush in 2002 as significant threats to the security of the United States because of their purported ties to terrorism and/or weapons of mass destruction.

Weapons of Mass Destruction   As the chapter-opening story related, President Bush designated Iraq, Iran, and North Korea (the **axis of evil**) as nations both capable of creating weapons of mass destruction—chemical, biological, and/or nuclear—and using them against neighbors, American allies, or the United States. The problem of the spread and use of weapons of mass destruction, whether by axis or other so-called rogue nations, by factions within disintegrating nations, by terrorists, by nuclear scientists in places such as Pakistan seeking financial gain, is surely real, although how to go about addressing this danger is not entirely obvious. With respect to Iraq, President Bush chose direct military action, although no weapons of mass destruction were found there. With respect to North Korea and Iran, some mix of diplo-

USING ATOMIC ENERGY IS OUR CERTAIN RIGHT

Iran Defies Its Critics

President Mahmoud Ahmadinajad declared in this speech in 2006 that Iran would go ahead with nuclear energy research in the face of worldwide criticism. The worry among many is that Iran will eventually develop a weapon and make it available to other countries and to terrorist organizations.

matic pressure, multilateral, organized sanctions, International Atomic Energy Agency inspections, and threats of force have all been used, although each country seems determined to move ahead anyway. North Korea formally left the Nuclear Non-Proliferation Treaty in 2005 and tested a nuclear device in 2006. In 2006, Iran rejected British, French, German, Russian, and U.N. diplomatic efforts to slow its nuclear development.

The collapse of the centralized communist regime in the Soviet Union in the early 1990s and its break-up into several independent countries threw into question the fate of the vast Russian and former Soviet armed forces, with their millions of troops and many nuclear weapons—more than 10,000 of them. Could these weapons fall into the hands of warring ethnic factions, criminal organizations, terrorist groups, or rogue states such as Iran, creating new dangers and instability? The United States worked out agreements for drastic reductions in Russian, Ukrainian, and Kazakh nuclear weaponry. Ukraine and Kazakhstan have renounced nuclear weapons altogether, but their stockpiles of weapons remain large, and central control appears shaky. There is some evidence of Russian nuclear materials showing up on the international black market, raising dangers of **nuclear proliferation,** or the spread of nuclear weapons. A high-priority task for American foreign policy has been to prevent proliferation. However, the nuclear cooperation treaty with India that President Bush signed in early 2006 seemed to give India the go-ahead to speed up its weapons program—the new treaty allows India to import nuclear fuel and technology from abroad and keep its military facilities free from inspections—something that worries many advocates of nonproliferation in the United States and abroad.

The Middle East   The Middle East is home to some of the least developed nations in the world in terms of economic development, democracy and freedom, women's rights, and education.[26] It is also a veritable tinderbox, as evidenced by the seemingly unending conflict between Israel and the Palestinians, which stirs passions in the Arab and Muslim worlds and feeds anti-Americanism. What to do about this conflict is a matter of intense debate. Although groups such as Hamas and Hezbollah are committed to the destruction of Israel, most others support some sort of two-state solution in which Israel and Palestine live side-by-side as independent countries. The United States and the **European Union** are committed to this outcome, as is the majority of the Israeli public. A majority of the Palestinian public was presumed to favor the same solution, but the election of Hamas as the majority party in the Palestinian parliament in early 2006 raised some doubts.

SIMULATION

You Are President John F. Kennedy

nuclear proliferation
The spread of nuclear weapons to additional countries or to terrorist groups.

European Union (EU)
A common market formed by western European nations, with free trade and free population movement among them.

The Israelis seem to have come to the conclusion that no negotiating partner exists on the Palestinian side—that is to say, even before the Hamas parliamentary victory, there was no group or leader in the Palestinian Authority, in their view, either committed to a two-state solution or able to deliver on an agreement if one were to be reached—and that the best policy is to simply disengage from the Palestinians unilaterally. Israel demonstrated this by withdrawing from Gaza in 2005 under Ariel Sharon and by continuing the construction of its security wall after he was replaced as prime minister by Ehud Olmert following a disabling stroke. Meanwhile, tensions in the area remain high, with the continuation of the harsh Israeli occupation of the West Bank and attacks by various militant Palestinian factions on Israeli targets in the occupied territories and Israel itself. In the summer of 2006, moreover, Israel fought a war against the Iran-backed Hezbollah militia in Lebanon, highlighted by fierce fighting, many civilian casualties, and missiles landing in northern Israel.

As if the Israeli-Palestinian and Israel-Hezbollah-Iran conflicts were not enough to render the Arab Middle East a tinderbox, it is also a place where people are saddled with unelected and corrupt governments, near-useless educational systems, stagnant economies, and mass unemployment. And, according to some scholars, it is a place where people are deeply resentful of the non-Muslim West's economic, military, and cultural dominance of the region.[27] These circumstances inevitably feed popular discontent and threaten instability in a region that is vital to the world's energy supply, although governments in the region have managed so far to channel most popular discontent into anger against the West, the Americans, the Jews, and Israel, using the government-controlled media to do so. Needless to say, the war in Iraq has stirred the pot even further. These discontented populations, it must be said, provide many of the foot soldiers and much of the financial support for terrorism.

President Bush has made spreading democracy in the Middle East one of his highest priorities, believing that the boiling discontent in the region can only be solved by giving people a greater voice in how to run their countries. He may or may not be right in the long run. In the short run, some encourag-

South Beirut in the Aftermath

Lebanese Shiites wander around the ruins of their apartments after the U.N.–brokered cease-fire between Israel and Iran-backed Hezbollah fighters in 2006. Israelis defended the destruction in light of Hezbollah's decision to locate military bunkers and missile launchers in centers of dense civilian populations. Critics of Israel claimed it had overreacted and that its actions were disproportionate to the threat posed by Hezbollah.

ing things have happened; pressure from the administration and the example of a series of elections in Iraq, for example, seem to have convinced several governments in the region to make slight openings in the political process (in Egypt, Saudi Arabia, Lebanon, Kuwait, Bahrain, and Jordan) in 2005. With the victory of Hamas in the Palestinian elections in 2006, however, and the increasing prominence of the Muslim Brotherhood in Egypt, regimes in the region began to rethink the small democratic innovations they had instituted. For example, in early 2006 Egypt announced the suspension of promised local elections for at least two years.

The Indian Subcontinent   U.S. policymakers must also be concerned about the possible outbreak of war between India and Pakistan, each armed with nuclear weapons. The issues between the two will not be easily resolved, given the history of enmity between them, past military conflicts, and the struggle over the fate of the future of Muslim-majority Kashmir. Indeed, the two countries mobilized for war in late 2001 and 2002, and each implied that it would use nuclear weapons if necessary. The situation is complicated for the United States by the fact that Pakistan is crucial in the fight against terrorism and Al Qaeda in Afghanistan. At the same time, the United States is forming a stronger strategic alliance with India, partly as a counter to the rise of China, partly because of the increasing ties between the American and Indian economies, and partly because of sympathy with India as a target of terrorist attacks widely thought to be encouraged by Pakistan. The nuclear treaty the United States signed with India suggests, in fact, that American foreign policy has swung toward the Indian side on the subcontinent.

China   With its huge population, fast-growing economy, and modernizing military, China may pose a long-term threat to the United States. Some Americans have warned of a great "clash of civilizations" between the West and "Confucian" China.[28] Disputes over fair trade, intellectual property rights protections (on software, movies, and so on), Taiwan, treatment of Christians, and human rights periodically cloud U.S.–Chinese relations. In addition, China opposed the United States on the invasion of Iraq. But China worked with the United States on gathering intelligence about terrorism after 9/11 and supported the American resolution in the U.N. Security Council in 2006 to impose sanctions on North Korea for its test of a nuclear weapon. The United States also supported China's successful effort to join the World Trade Organization. And China and the United States have become strong trading partners, with each economy dependent on the other.

Economic and Social Issues

In addition to national security concerns, a number of other international issues have drawn the attention of American policymakers and the public.

The Global Economy   **Globalization,** or the integration of much of the world into a single market and production system, with the United States playing the leading role, has raised a number of new issues for American policymakers and American citizens to address.

globalization
The increasing worldwide integration of markets, production, and communications across national boundaries.

Trade   The United States is the world's largest trader, counting total imports and exports, and a leading player in the design and management of the global trading system. Since the end of World War II, the United States has been the

Economic Sanctions and Cuba

leading advocate of the freer and more open trading system that has evolved. In 1948 the most important trading nations adopted the **General Agreement on Tariffs and Trade (GATT),** an agreement designed to lower, then eliminate, tariffs on most traded goods and to end nontariff trade restrictions as well. Periodically, members of GATT enter into talks (called rounds) and reach new agreements designed to refine and expand the system. The Uruguay Round in 1994 agreed to replace GATT with the **World Trade Organization (WTO),** which came into being the following year. U.S. negotiators hoped that the new agreement eventually would open more markets to American agricultural products and services and halt the piracy of patented and copyrighted goods such as software and films. U.S. policymakers also negotiated the **North American Free Trade Agreement (NAFTA)** with Canada and Mexico, which was finally implemented in 1993 after a vote in Congress resolved a bitter political conflict over its implications for U.S. jobs.[29]

Most economists believe that trade is generally good for all countries involved, whether rich or poor.[30] Not everyone agrees, however. Many Americans believe that the loss of manufacturing jobs can be traced to free trade because goods manufactured abroad using cheap labor and by firms that have few labor protections or environmental requirements can enter the United States tariff-free (most economists believe the majority of manufacturing job loss can be linked to technological change and rising productivity). Organized labor passionately believes free trade costs American jobs. Others worry that a flood of cheap, yet high-quality, goods and services threatens firms that are important for the health of the American economy and point to the decline of the American auto, steel, and consumer electronics industries as examples. Still others believe that the threat of trade sanctions—a violation of free trade agreements—should be used to improve environmental standards, human rights practices, and religious toleration in other countries. Trade, then, is likely to remain an important political issue for a long time to come.

Corporations Abroad U.S.-based corporations operating abroad find themselves being scrutinized for their behavior on a variety of fronts.[31] Some ac-

Global Production and Sales

In a globalized economy, many products consumed by Americans are manufactured abroad. Here, a consumer evaluates a flat-screen television from Japan in a Costco store in California.

tivists, **nongovernmental organizations (NGO),** journalists, and members of Congress have focused the international spotlight on matters of pay and working conditions, including such issues as "sweatshop" production, child labor, the absence of labor rights in many places, and gender inequities. Others have focused on the effects of corporate production practices on local environments. Still others have focused on the purported homogenizing effects of global products on local cultures—think here of McDonald's and Hollywood—among others. Finally, organized labor, among others, has strenuously objected to the outsourcing of jobs abroad by American-based corporations, sometimes to their own subsidiaries, sometimes to subcontractors.

Intellectual Property Rights   How strongly should our foreign policy attempt to protect the intellectual property rights—patents and copyrights—of American companies and citizens? The issue is fairly straightforward when it comes to the "piracy" of movies, music tapes and CDs, and software in places such as China; Americans generally support policies that are aimed at ending these practices. Protection of patents for life-saving drugs is another matter—antimalarial and anti-AIDS medications, for example. Many Americans believe companies ought to provide such drugs at low prices or allow poor countries to find or produce generic substitutes despite the patent protections of Western pharmaceutical companies. There has been some movement on this front in the last several years. For example, the U.S. government signed an agreement in 2003 to suspend the normal trade rules of the WTO and allow the production and use of certain critical generic drugs. Global firms have lowered prices on a range of drugs—Bristol Meyers announced in 2006, for example, that it would allow companies in India and South Africa to produce generic versions of its two most powerful AIDS drugs. Assistance with AIDS drugs cannot come too soon; in 2004, 3.1 million people died of the disease, with more than 4 million more adults and children newly infected.[32]

Global Economic Instability   The United States is the leading player in the global economy and its leaders have been involved since the end of World War II in trying to ensure the health and vitality of the overall global economy. We have already discussed American efforts to stabilize and protect the global trading system, but it does much more. Most important, American leaders must be concerned with stabilizing global financial markets when necessary and in rescuing countries on the verge of economic collapse. They do so because our own economy is closely tied to the global economy. A strong American role is guaranteed by our leadership of and large financial contributions to the International Monetary Fund (charged with rectifying and preventing currency collapses) and the World Bank (charged with financing projects to assist economic development and poverty reduction). Aside from providing general leadership, the proper response to specific crises is not always clear. In 1982 and 1995, for example, the United States helped Mexico emerge from its debt crisis and financial collapse; in 2001–2002, however, it offered only modest assistance to Argentina (in the form of an IMF loan) as that country recovered from a devastating financial collapse.

Foreign Aid   The world is divided rather sharply into rich and poor nations. Rich nations, whether for humanitarian or security reasons, have given assistance to poor countries for many years in an effort to improve living standards. There have been some successes—such as the conquest of riverblindness, a disease that once affected tens of millions of Africans. But dreadful poverty persists in places such as Bangladesh and Sub-Saharan Africa. In the latter region, excepting South Africa, life expectancy has

nongovernmental organization (NGO)
A nonprofit advocacy group that tries to influence the public, national governments, and/or international organizations on issues of concern to it.

AIDS Victim

Fighting the spread of HIV-AIDS is an important goal of many governments around the world, including the United States, as well as the United Nations and a wide range of NGOs. Unfortunately, assistance will not come in time for this woman in a hospital in the Democratic Republic of the Congo.

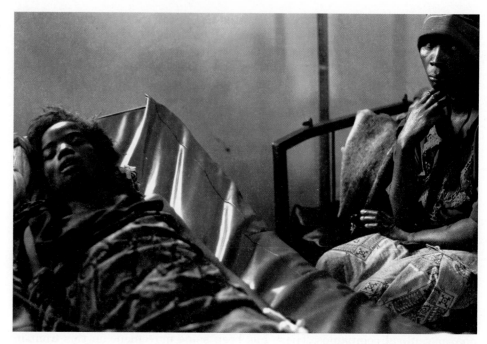

declined. Eighty-five percent of the world's 1.2 malaria deaths occurred there in 2004, as did 75 percent of the world's 3.1 million AIDS deaths. Mean household income is lower there than it was in the 1960s, and per-capita GDP has been declining.[33] Although the United States contributes to World Bank developmental loans for poor countries and has programs such as Food for Peace, the Peace Corps, and technical and educational assistance programs, our spending for foreign aid is very low. Spending for foreign aid now stands at less than 1.0 percent of the federal budget and about 0.14 percent of U.S. GDP.[34] Although we spend more dollars on foreign assistance than any other country, relative to the size of our economy we spend less than any other donor country but the Japanese (see Figure 18.4). Moreover, only about two-thirds of U.S. foreign aid goes toward economic development and humanitarian relief; the remainder is linked to promoting military and security objectives or encouraging the sale of American goods and services abroad. President Bush promised to add $5 billion over three years for economic assistance in his Millennium Challenge Account, but appropriated totals fell far short (less than $2 billion in 2006) because of deep cuts in the federal budget (see Chapter 17).

The Bush administration did take an important step forward on the aid front in 2005, however. It joined an agreement with finance ministers from the countries making up the major shareholders of the World Bank to wipe out over $55 billion in debts owed by the 18 poorest countries in the world, an action every bit as effective, perhaps, as direct cash assistance from rich countries to poor countries.

The Global Environment Increasingly, Americans realize that environmental problems cross national borders. Thus, the United States and Canada have worked out a joint approach to reduce acid rain; and the United States has signed on to agreements on the prevention and clean up of oil spills, the use of Antarctica, the protection of fish species, and the protection of the ozone layer. The United States is also a signatory to the biodiversity treaty. Global warming is a different story, however. Although the Clinton administration was in-

FIGURE 18.4 ● Foreign Aid as a Percentage of GDP, 2005

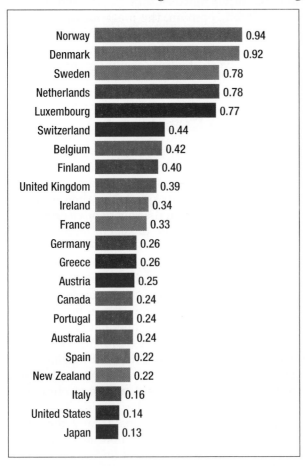

Although Americans often complain about how much aid we give to other countries, a comparison with other donor countries shows that we give very little as a percentage of GDP.

Source: Organization for Economic Cooperation and Development, 2006.

volved in hammering out the details of the Kyoto Protocol to limit greenhouse gases, Clinton never submitted the treaty to the Senate. In 2001, George W. Bush pulled out of the treaty entirely, citing his concern that strict controls on developed countries coupled with no controls on large, fast-growing economies in developing countries, such as China and India, would do irreparable harm to the American economy. Interestingly, few signatory countries have been able to meet the targets for cuts in greenhouse emissions agreed to in the Kyoto Protocol. While Germany and the United Kingdom exceeded their emissions-cut goals, most other countries, including Italy, Japan, Canada, Ireland, and Spain, experienced substantial increases in greenhouse gas emissions.[35]

Who Makes Foreign Policy?

We pointed out in Chapter 12 and at the outset of this chapter, that the president is the key player in making foreign and national security policies and is especially powerful during international crises and in times of war—recently in Afghanistan and Iraq and in the war on terrorism. But Congress has always been involved in decisions about international trade, foreign aid, military spending, immigration, and other matters that clearly and directly touch constituents' local interests. Public opinion, the mass media, the parties, and interest and advocacy groups (corporations, unions, NGOs, and religious organizations, for example) affect what both Congress and the executive branch do. (The "Using the Framework" feature examines the multiple forces that shaped U.S. policy in Kosovo.)

The President and the Executive Branch

You Are the President

Presidents rely on many people and several government agencies to help them make military and foreign policy decisions. Vice President Cheney has been very influential in the Bush administration as was former Defense Secretary Rumsfeld. Condoleezza Rice, first as national security adviser, then as secretary of state, has played a big role, too. The national security adviser plays a prominent role in every administration, advising the president on a daily basis on foreign and national security matters.[36]

The Department of State, headed by the secretary of state, is the president's chief arm for carrying out diplomatic affairs. Some secretaries of state have been extremely important in helping the president make foreign policy—Henry Kissinger in the Nixon and Ford administrations comes to mind—although others have not been among the key players in the inner circle around the president. It was widely reported, for example, that Colin Powell was less influential with President Bush, for example, than Cheney, Rumsfeld, and Rice. The department itself is organized along both functional lines—economic affairs, human rights, counterterrorism, and refugees—and geographic lines, with "country desks" devoted to each nation of the world. The State Department has 273 embassies, consulates, and missions around the world that carry out policy and advise the department on new developments. Attached to the State Department are the Arms Control and Disarmament Agency, the U.S. Information Agency, and the Agency for International

Conferring on the Invasion of Iraq

American national security policies are made by the president in consultation with close advisers and appointees, although congressional leaders often are included as well. Here, President Bush confers in early 2003 with Vice President Dick Cheney, Defense Secretary Donald Rumsfeld, Secretary of State Colin Powell, Joint Chiefs Chairman Richard Myers, and a handful of others about the invasion of Iraq.

Using the Framework

Air War in Kosovo

Why was President Clinton reluctant to use ground forces to prevent ethnic cleansing in Kosovo?

Background: Americans strongly supported the use of American ground forces in Afghanistan following the September 11, 2001, terrorist attacks on the United States, and tell pollsters they are willing to have ground forces used in a widened war against terrorism. They supported President Bush's decision to invade Iraq in 2003 because he convinced them that Iraqi weapons of mass destruction posed an imminent threat to the United States. Apparently, the American people are willing to use troops and to accept casualties when threats to the national security of the United States are clear. This has not been the case in other recent conflicts. But the long, costly, and bloody occupation of Iraq after the 2003 invasion may once again decrease Americans' willingness to put troops on the ground.

Future presidents may find it as difficult to use ground forces as Bill Clinton did in Kosovo. Announcing his plan to rely solely on an air bombing campaign to try to halt the Serb "ethnic cleansing" campaign in the Yugoslavian province of Kosovo in 1999, President Clinton renounced the use of ground combat troops. Many critics believed only troops on the ground could protect Kosovar Muslims from being forced from their homes. Air power eventually prevailed, forcing a Serb withdrawal, but it took time, and the human toll was high. Why, then, did President Clinton avoid sending ground troops? Taking a broader look at how structural, political linkage, and governmental factors affected President Clinton's decision will help explain the situation.

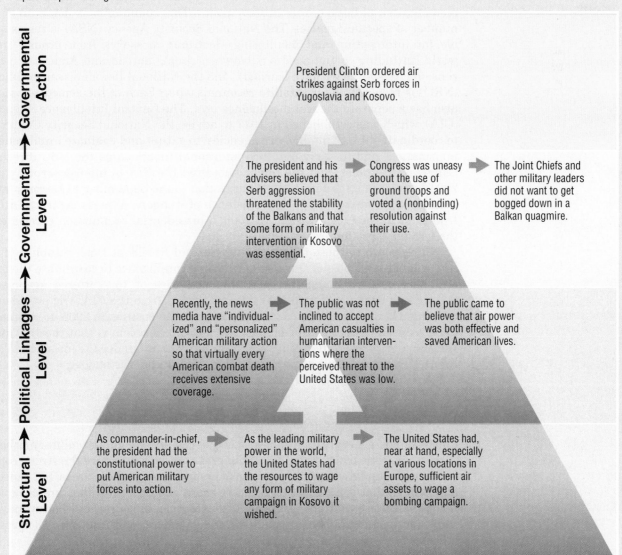

Governmental Action

President Clinton ordered air strikes against Serb forces in Yugoslavia and Kosovo.

Governmental Level

The president and his advisers believed that Serb aggression threatened the stability of the Balkans and that some form of military intervention in Kosovo was essential.

Congress was uneasy about the use of ground troops and voted a (nonbinding) resolution against their use.

The Joint Chiefs and other military leaders did not want to get bogged down in a Balkan quagmire.

Political Linkages Level

Recently, the news media have "individualized" and "personalized" American military action so that virtually every American combat death receives extensive coverage.

The public was not inclined to accept American casualties in humanitarian interventions where the perceived threat to the United States was low.

The public came to believe that air power was both effective and saved American lives.

Structural Level

As commander-in-chief, the president had the constitutional power to put American military forces into action.

As the leading military power in the world, the United States had the resources to wage any form of military campaign in Kosovo it wished.

The United States had, near at hand, especially at various locations in Europe, sufficient air assets to wage a bombing campaign.

Development, which oversees foreign economic aid. As issues of trade, U.S. corporate investment in other countries, and protection of intellectual property rights (patents and copyrights) become more important in the global economy, both the Department of Commerce, another cabinet department, and the Office of the U.S. Trade Representative, part of the Executive Office of the President, have become more important in foreign policy making.

The Department of Defense (DOD) is particularly influential in shaping foreign and military policies. The DOD is headed by a civilian secretary of defense, who has authority over the entire department and reports directly to the president. Civilian secretaries are also in charge of the Departments of the Army, Navy, and Air Force and report to the secretary of defense. Each service also has a military command structure headed by people in uniform: the army and air force chiefs of staff, the chief of naval operations, the commandant of the marine corps, and their subordinates. The uniformed chiefs of each branch serve together in the **Joint Chiefs of Staff (JCS),** headed by the chairman of the Joint Chiefs, who reports not only to the secretary of defense but also directly to the president.

Joint Chiefs of Staff (JCS)

The military officers in charge of each of the armed services.

A large intelligence community is also involved in the fashioning and implementation of foreign and military policy. This community is made up of a number of specific agencies. The National Security Agency (NSA) is responsible for intercepting and monitoring electronic messages from around the world (including communications between people abroad and American citizens on U.S. soil, as we have learned) , and the National Reconnaissance Office (NRO) is responsible for satellite reconnaissance. Each of the armed services also has a separate tactical intelligence unit. The Central Intelligence Agency (CIA), which was established in 1947 to advise the National Security Council, to coordinate all U.S. intelligence agencies, to gather and evaluate intelligence information, and to carry out such additional functions as the NSC directs. Congress, the press, and the public subjected the CIA to intense scrutiny in 2004 because of its failure to alert the nation to the September 11 terrorist attacks, and its misreading of the existence of weapons of mass destruction in Iraq prior to the U.S. invasion. In 2005, a presidential commission excoriated the CIA for these failures.

In response to these failures, Congress and President Bush established a new cabinet-level post of Director of National Intelligence to coordinate the intelligence gathering and interpretation activities of 15 scattered agencies, thus taking over some important responsibilities from the CIA. The president appointed career diplomat John Negroponte to the position in 2005. It remains to be seen how effective this change will be. One problem is that the Defense Department, whose intelligence operations do not fall under the jurisdiction of the DNI, controls about 80 percent of the U.S. intelligence budget.

Congress

Congress has generally played a less active role in foreign and military policy than in domestic policy. Members of Congress not only recognize the strong constitutional foundations of the president's preeminence in these areas, but generally believe that their constituents care more about policies that are close to home than those that are far away. The exception, of course, is when wars go badly, not meeting public expectations, as in Vietnam and Iraq; then Congress becomes more assertive.

In national defense emergencies, Congress tends to take a back seat to the president. This was the case in the immediate aftermath of the terrorist

Using the Democracy Standard

Do Americans get the foreign and national defense policies they want from government?

PROPOSITION: **Foreign and national security policymaking is not and should not be very democratic.**

AGREE   Americans care more about what is going on in the United States that affects them directly than they do about issues and developments in distant places. They also know more about what is going on in the United States—whether health care, living standards, or the environment—than they do about what is happening elsewhere, particularly in the poor countries that get very little media news coverage. Additionally, to be effective, many foreign and military policies must be made in secret, so citizens often do not have the information that is necessary to be politically effective. Given all of this, it is clear that Americans are more competent as citizens when faced with domestic matters than with military and foreign affairs. Therefore, for the most part, Americans give political, diplomatic, and military leaders a relatively free hand in making foreign and military policy, as well they should.

DISAGREE   While it is true that citizens play a smaller role in deciding foreign policies compared with domestic policies, they are not powerless. Citizens do, in fact, give their leaders a great deal of freedom in deciding what to do in foreign and military affairs, but these leaders are ultimately answerable to the people, and they know it. Presidents and members of Congress pay very close attention to public opinion and worry about the next election, so they try to be careful to avoid actions that may eventually prove unpopular. In addition, if Americans play a lesser role than required by democratic theory, it is something we ought to work on improving. If we are to be a democracy at all, citizens must be engaged in helping to decide all important policies, whether these policies are about health care or war in Iraq.

CONSIDER   It is true that Americans know less and care less about foreign affairs than they do about domestic affairs. It is also true that some secrecy is required in fashioning and conducting foreign and military policies and that speed is sometimes of the essence.

• But does this mean that ordinary Americans should have little say in what goes on in foreign and national security affairs?   • Can we really be a democracy if such an important part of public affairs is off-limits to citizens?   • What do you think?   • And, if you believe that citizens should play an important role in this area, how competent do you feel to take part?   • How well informed are you about these things?   • When you read a newspaper or watch TV news, are you more interested in stories about domestic issues or foreign affairs?   • About which do you feel more confident to offer an opinion?

attacks on the United States in 2001. No congressional leader or political party was about to take on George W. Bush's broad assertion of powers, given the crisis situation and the president's extraordinary popularity at the time. However, as reviewed earlier, as the occupation of Iraq dragged on and the president's popularity plummeted in 2005 and 2006, Congress reasserted itself, focusing most especially on the decision to invade Iraq and management by the president and his team of the aftermath.

The Constitution gives Congress the power to declare war—which it has not been asked to do since the beginning of World War II—and to decide about any spending of money. It also gives the Senate the power to approve or disapprove treaties and the appointment of ambassadors. At times, Congress has used its treaty or spending powers to challenge the president on important issues: trying to force an end to the Vietnam War, trying to gain some influence on the presidential use of American armed forces abroad (the War Powers Act of 1973 as described in Chapter 12), creating difficulties over the Panama Canal treaty and the SALT II arms control treaty, defeating the Nuclear Test Ban Treaty, resisting the Reagan administration's aid to the Nicaraguan Contras, and barely acquiescing to military and peacekeeping operations in Bosnia and Kosovo.

Congress has probably exerted its greatest foreign and military policy influence on issues that involve spending money, all of which must pass through the regular congressional appropriations process. It has tended to reduce foreign aid appropriations, for example. And military contracts are a special focus of attention because each has a great economic effect on many congressional districts and powerful interest groups.

Summary

The United States has become the world's only military superpower, with a much larger economy and much more powerful armed forces than any other nation. The United States's advantages in high-tech and smart weapons, aerial reconnaissance, and the ability to deploy large forces to world trouble-spots are particularly important.

For more than 40 years, American foreign policy was focused around the tense Cold War with the Soviet Union, competing for influence in Europe, fighting Soviet allies in Korea and Vietnam, and skirmishing over the Third World. When the Soviet Union collapsed, attention turned to other issues, including regional and ethnic conflicts, international economic competition, efforts at transition to democracy and free markets in Russia and eastern Europe, terrorism, problems of world poverty, and the global environment.

Foreign policy has traditionally been made mostly in the executive branch, where the president is assisted by a large national security bureaucracy, including the National Security Council, the Department of Defense, the Department of State, and various intelligence agencies. Congress has been little involved in crises or covert actions and has generally gone along with major decisions on defense policy; it has asserted itself chiefly on matters of foreign trade and aid, military bases, and procurement contracts. Public opinion affects policy, perhaps increasingly so, but this influence is limited by the executive branch's centralization of decision making, secrecy, and control of information. How large a part interest groups and corporations play is disputed, but it is probably substantial. Structural factors, including U.S. economic and military strength and the nature of the international system, strongly affect what policies seem feasible or desirable.

Web Exploration
What Direction for U.S. Foreign Policy?

ISSUE: Although the United States is unequaled in military and economic power, Americans are not entirely sure how they want to use that power.

SITE: Access Public Agenda Online in MyPoliSciLab at **www.mypoliscilab.com.** Go to the "Web Explorations" section for Chapter 18. Select "what direction for U.S. foreign policy," then "U.S. role." Select "America's global role" in the "issue guides" section. Then look in the section "Bills and Proposals."

WHAT YOU'VE LEARNED: See what the public thinks about the United Nations, humanitarian intervention, and foreign assistance. After looking at the poll results, would you conclude that Americans are isolationists, unilateralists, or multilateralists?

HINT: You might be surprised to learn how many Americans lean in a multilateral direction.

Internet Sources

Amnesty International
www.amnesty.org
Reports and documents from the international human rights organization.

Center for Defense Information
www.cdi.org
Analyses of the defense budget, weapons systems, and national security threats.

Defense Link
www.defenselink.mil/
The home page of the Department of Defense.

World Bank
www.worldbank.org
The website for one of the most important actors in the distribution of aid to poor countries.

The State Department
www.state.gov
The website for the department responsible for U.S. diplomacy; the site contains a wealth of information relating to countries around the world and the United States's relations with them.

The U.N. Millennium Project
www.unmillenniumproject.org
The website for the United Nations' formal effort to reduce poverty in the Third World.

International Herald Tribune Online
www.iht.com/
Complete international news with a much broader perspective than that found in most U.S. newspapers and other media outlets.

National Security Website
www.nationalsecurity.org
Essays and news about foreign and military policy, sponsored by the Heritage Foundation, from a conservative point of view.

Peacenet
www.peacenet.apc.org
A website devoted to peace, social and economic justice, and human rights; information on all of these subjects as well as links to organizations working in these fields.

Statistical Resources on the Web: Military and Defense
www.lib.umich.edu/govdocs/stats.html
A vast statistical and information compendium on military and national security issues; covers the United States and other countries.

United Nations
www.un.org
Home page of the United Nations; links to a wealth of statistics, documents and reports, U.N. departments and conferences, and information on reaching U.N. officials.

Suggestions for Further Reading

Daalder, Ivo H., and James M. Lindsay. *America Unbound: The Bush Revolution in Foreign Policy.* Washington, D.C.: Brookings Institution Press, 2003.
A balanced examination of the foreign policy innovations of President George W. Bush and how they happened.

Ferguson, Niall. *Colossus: The Price of America's Empire.* New York: Penguin Books, 2004.
The author believes that an American empire would be good for the United States and for the world but argues that it is unlikely that the United States will choose this course.

Huntington, Samuel P. *The Clash of Civilizations: Civilizations and the Remaking of World Order.* New York: Simon & Schuster, 1997.
Suggests that the post–Cold War world will be organized along the lines of competing civilizations and that one of these civilizations, Islam, presents the greatest danger to a stable world order.

Johnson, Chalmers. *The Sorrows of Empire: Militarism, Secrecy, and the End of the Republic.* New York: Metropolitan Books, 2004.

Argues that the emergence of militarism in the United States threatens American democracy and individual rights.

The National Security Strategy of the United States. Washington, D.C.: The White House, September 2006.

An utterly fascinating formulation of President Bush's strategic outlook; some parts simply extend traditional polices, while others suggest moving policies in new directions.

Nye, Joseph. *The Paradox of American Power: Why the World's Only Superpower Can't Go It Alone.* Oxford: Oxford University Press, 2002.

A passionate argument for a multilateral rather than a unilateral foreign policy.

Sen, Amartya Kumar. *Development as Freedom.* New York: Knopf, 1999.

The Nobel Prize winner in economics argues that freedom is the basis for the development of poor countries, a fact that should inform the foreign policies of the rich countries.

Veseth, Michael. *Globaloney: Unraveling the Myths of Globalization.* Lanham, MD: Rowman and Littlefield Publishers, 2005.

An entertaining and illuminating critique of the critics of globalization.

Appendix

The Declaration of Independence

When in the Course of human events, it becomes necessary for one people to dissolve the political bands which have connected them with another, and to assume among the Powers of the earth, the separate and equal station to which the Laws of Nature and of Nature's God entitle them, a decent respect to the opinions of mankind requires that they should declare the causes which impel them to the separation.

We hold these truths to be self-evident, that all men are created equal, that they are endowed by their Creator with certain unalienable Rights, that among these are Life, Liberty and the pursuit of Happiness. That to secure these rights, Governments are instituted among Men, deriving their just powers from the consent of the governed, That whenever any Form of Government becomes destructive of these ends, it is the Right of the People to alter or to abolish it, and to institute new Government, laying its foundation on such principles and organizing its powers in such form, as to them shall seem most likely to effect their Safety and Happiness. Prudence, indeed, will dictate that Governments long established should not be changed for light and transient causes; and accordingly all experience hath shown, that mankind are more disposed to suffer, while evils are sufferable, than to right themselves by abolishing the forms to which they are accustomed. But when a long train of abuses and usurpations, pursuing invariably the same Object evinces a design to reduce them under absolute Despotism, it is their right, it is their duty, to throw off such Government, and to provide new Guards for their future security.—Such has been the patient sufferance of these Colonies; and such is now the necessity which constrains them to alter their former Systems of Government. The history of the present King of Great Britain is a history of repeated injuries and usurpations, all having in direct object the establishment of an absolute Tyranny over these States. To prove this, let Facts be submitted to a candid world.

He has refused his Assent to Laws, the most wholesome and necessary for the public good.

He has forbidden his Governors to pass Laws of immediate and pressing importance, unless suspended in their operation till his Assent should be obtained; and when so suspended, he has utterly neglected to attend to them.

He has refused to pass other Laws for the accommodation of large districts of people, unless those people would relinquish the right of Representation in the Legislature, a right inestimable to them and formidable to tyrants only.

He has called together legislative bodies at places unusual, uncomfortable, and distant from the depository of their Public Records, for the sole purpose of fatiguing them into compliance with his measures.

He has dissolved Representative Houses repeatedly, for opposing with manly firmness his invasions on the rights of the people.

He has refused for a long time, after such dissolutions, to cause others to be elected; whereby the Legislative Powers, incapable of Annihilation, have returned to the People at large for their exercise; the State remaining in the mean time exposed to all the dangers of invasion from without, and convulsions within.

He has endeavoured to prevent the population of these States; for that purpose obstructing the Laws of Naturalization of Foreigners; refusing to pass others to encourage their migration hither, and raising the conditions of new Appropriations of Lands.

He has obstructed the Administration of Justice, by refusing his Assent to Laws for establishing Judiciary Powers.

He has made Judges dependent on his Will alone, for the tenure of their offices, and the amount and payment of their salaries.

He has erected a multitude of New Offices, and sent hither swarms of Officers to harass our People, and eat out their substance.

He has kept among us, in times of peace, Standing Armies without the Consent of our legislature.

He has affected to render the Military independent of and superior to the Civil Power.

He has combined with others to subject us to a jurisdiction foreign to our constitution, and unacknowledged by our laws; giving his Assent to their acts of pretended legislation:

For quartering large bodies of armed troops among us:

For protecting them, by a mock Trial, from Punishment for any Murders which they should commit on the Inhabitants of these States:

For cutting off our Trade with all parts of the world:

For imposing taxes on us without our Consent:

For depriving us in many cases, of the benefits of Trial by Jury:

For transporting us beyond Seas to be tried for pretended offences:

For abolishing the free System of English Laws in a neighbouring Province, establishing therein an Arbitrary government, and enlarging its Boundaries so as to render it at once an example and fit instrument for introducing the same absolute rule into these Colonies:

For taking away our Charters, abolishing our most valuable Laws, and altering fundamentally the Forms of our Governments:

For suspending our own Legislature, and declaring themselves invested with Power to legislate for us in all cases whatsoever.

He has abdicated Government here, by declaring us out of his Protection and waging War against us.

He has plundered our seas, ravaged our Coasts, burnt our towns, and destroyed the lives of our people.

He is at this time transporting large armies of foreign mercenaries to compleat the works of death, desolation and tyranny, already begun with circumstances of Cruelty & perfidy scarcely paralleled in the most barbarous ages, and totally unworthy the Head of a civilized nation.

He has constrained our fellow Citizens taken Captive on the high Seas to bear Arms against their Country, to become the executioners of their friends and Brethren, or to fall themselves by their Hands.

He has excited domestic insurrections amongst us, and has endeavoured to bring on the inhabitants of our frontiers, the merciless Indian Savages, whose known rule of warfare, is an undistinguished destruction of all ages, sexes and conditions.

In every stage of these Oppressions We have Petitioned for Redress in the most humble terms: Our repeated Petitions have been answered only by repeated injury. A Prince, whose character is thus marked by every act which may define a Tyrant, is unfit to be the ruler of a free People.

Nor have We been wanting in attention to our British brethren. We have warned them from time to time of attempts by their legislature to extend an unwarrantable jurisdiction over us. We have reminded them of the circumstances of our emigration and settlement here. We have appealed to their native justice and magnanimity, and we have conjured them by the ties of our common kindred to disavow these usurpations, which, would inevitably interrupt our connections and correspondence. They too have been deaf to the voice of justice and of consanguinity. We must, therefore, acquiesce in the necessity, which denounces our Separation, and hold them, as we hold the rest of mankind, Enemies in War, in Peace Friends.

We, therefore, the Representatives of the united States of America, in General Congress, Assembled, appealing to the Supreme Judge of the world for the rectitude of our intentions, do, in the Name, and by Authority of the good People of these Colonies, solemnly publish and declare, That these United Colonies are, and of Right ought to be Free and Independent States; that they are Absolved from all Allegiance to the British Crown, and that all political connection between them and the State of Great Britain, is and ought to be totally dissolved; and that as Free and Independent States, they have full Power to levy War, conclude Peace, contract Alliances, establish Commerce, and to do all other Acts and Things which Independent States may of right do. And for the support of this Declaration, with a firm reliance of the Protection of Divine Providence, we mutually pledge to each other our Lives, our Fortunes and our sacred Honor.

John Hancock,

Josiah Bartlett, Wm Whipple, Saml Adams, John Adams, Robt Treat Paine, Elbridge Gerry, Steph. Hopkins, William Ellery, Roger Sherman, Samel Huntington, Wm Williams, Oliver Wolcott, Matthew Thornton, Wm Floyd, Phil Livingston, Frans Lewis, Lewis Morris, Richd Stockton, Jno Witherspoon, Fras Hopkinson, John Hart, Abra Clark, Robt Morris, Benjamin Rush, Benja Franklin, John Morton, Geo Clymer, Jas Smith, Geo. Taylor, James Wilson, Geo. Ross, Caesar Rodney, Geo Read, Thos M:Kean, Samuel Chase, Wm Paca, Thos Stone, Charles Carroll of Carrollton, George Wythe, Richard Henry Lee, Th. Jefferson, Benja Harrison, Thos Nelson, Jr., Francis Lightfoot Lee, Carter Braxton, Wm Hooper, Joseph Hewes, John Penn, Edward Rutledge, Thos Heyward, Junr., Thomas Lynch, Junor., Arthur Middleton, Button Gwinnett, Lyman Hall, Geo Walton.

The Constitution of the United States

We the people of the United States, in Order to form a more perfect Union, establish Justice, insure domestic Tranquility, provide for the common defence, promote the general Welfare, and secure the Blessings of Liberty to ourselves and our Posterity, do ordain and establish this constitution for the United States of America.

Article I

Section 1 All legislative Powers herein granted shall be vested in a Congress of the United States, which shall consist of a Senate and House of Representatives.

Section 2 The House of Representatives shall be composed of Members chosen every second Year by the People of the several States, and the Electors in each State shall have the Qualifications requisite for Electors of the most numerous Branch of the State Legislature.

No person shall be a Representative who shall not have attained to the Age of twenty-five Years, and been seven Years a Citizen of the United States, and who shall not, when elected, be an Inhabitant of that State in which he shall be chosen.

Representatives and direct Taxes shall be apportioned among the several States which may be included within this Union, according to their respective Numbers, which shall be determined by adding to the whole Number of free Persons, including those bound to Service for a Term of Years, and excluding Indians not taxed, three fifths of all other Persons. The actual Enumeration shall be made within three Years after the first Meeting of the Congress of the United States, and within every subsequent Term of ten Years, in such Manner as they shall by Law direct. The Number of Representatives shall not exceed one for every thirty Thousand, but each State shall have at Least one Representative; and until such enumeration shall be made, the State of New Hampshire shall be entitled to chuse three, Massachusetts eight, Rhode-Island and Providence Plantations one, Connecticut five, New-York six, New Jersey four, Pennsylvania eight, Delaware one, Maryland six, Virginia ten, North Carolina five, South Carolina five, and Georgia three.

When vacancies happen in the Representation from any State, the Executive Authority thereof shall issue Writs of Election to fill such Vacancies.

The House of Representatives shall chuse their Speaker and other Officers; and shall have the sole Power of Impeachment.

Section 3 The Senate of the United States shall be composed of two Senators from each State, chosen by the Legislature thereof, for six Years; and each Senator shall have one Vote.

Immediately after they shall be assembled in Consequence of the first Election, they shall be divided as equally as may be into three Classes. The Seats of the Senators of the first Class shall be vacated at the Expiration of the second Year, of the second Class at the Expiration of the fourth Year, and of the third Class at the Expiration of the sixth Year, so that one-third may be chosen every second Year; and if Vacancies happen by Resignation, or otherwise, during the Recess of the Legislature of any State, the Executive thereof may make temporary Appointments until the next Meeting of the Legislature, which shall then fill such Vacancies.

No Person shall be a Senator who shall not have attained to the Age of thirty Years, and been nine Years a Citizen of the United States, and who shall not, when elected, be an Inhabitant of that State in which he shall be chosen.

The Vice President of the United States shall be President of the Senate, but shall have no vote, unless they be equally divided.

The Senate shall chuse their other Officers, and also a President pro tempore, in the absence of the Vice President, or when he shall exercise the Office of the President of the United States.

The Senate shall have the sole Power to try all Impeachments. When sitting for that purpose, they shall be on Oath or Affirmation. When the President of the United States is tried, the Chief Justice shall preside: And no person shall be convicted without the Concurrence of two thirds of the Members present.

Judgment in Cases of Impeachment shall not extend further than to removal from Office, and disqualification to hold and enjoy any Office of honor, Trust, or Profit under the United States: but the Party convicted shall nevertheless be liable and subject to Indictment, Trial, Judgment, and Punishment, according to Law.

Section 4 The Times, Places and Manner of holding Elections for Senators and Representatives, shall be prescribed in each state by the Legislature thereof; but the Congress may at any time by Law make or alter such Regulations, except as to the Places of Chusing Senators.

The Congress shall assemble at least once in every Year, and such Meeting shall be on the first Monday in December, unless they shall by Law appoint a different Day.

Section 5 Each House shall be the Judge of the Elections, Returns and Qualifications of its own Members, and a Majority of each shall constitute a Quorum to do Business; but a smaller number may adjourn from day to day, and may be authorized to compel the Attendance of absent Members, in such Manner, and under such Penalties, as each House may provide.

Each House may determine the Rules of its Proceedings, punish its Members for disorderly Behavior, and, with the Concurrence of two thirds, expel a Member.

Each House shall keep a Journal of its Proceedings, and from time to time publish the same, excepting such

Parts as may in their Judgment require Secrecy; and the Yeas and Nays of the Members of either House on any question shall, at the Desire of one fifth of those Present, be entered on the Journal.

Neither House, during the Session of Congress, shall, without the Consent of the other, adjourn for more than three days, nor to any other Place than that in which the two Houses shall be sitting.

Section 6 The Senators and Representatives shall receive a Compensation for their Services, to be ascertained by Law, and paid out of the Treasury of the United States. They shall in all Cases, except Treason, Felony, and Breach of the Peace, be privileged from arrest during their Attendance at the Session of their respective Houses, and in going to and returning from the same; and for any Speech or Debate in either House, they shall not be questioned in any other Place.

No Senator or Representative shall, during the Time for which he was elected, be appointed to any civil Office under the Authority of the United States, which shall have been created, or the Emoluments whereof shall have been increased, during such time; and no Person holding any Office under the United States shall be a Member of either House during his continuance in Office.

Section 7 All Bills for raising Revenue shall originate in the House of Representatives; but the Senate may propose or concur with Amendments as on other bills.

Every Bill which shall have passed the House of Representatives and the Senate, shall, before it become a Law, be presented to the President of the United States; If he approve he shall sign it, but if not he shall return it, with his Objections, to that House in which it shall have originated, who shall enter the Objections at large on their Journal, and proceed to reconsider it. If after such Reconsideration two thirds of that House shall agree to pass the bill, it shall be sent, together with the objections, to the other House, by which it shall likewise be reconsidered, and if approved by two thirds of that House, it shall become a Law. But in all such Cases the Votes of both Houses shall be determined by Yeas and Nays, and the Names of the Persons voting for and against the Bill shall be entered on the Journal of each House respectively. If any Bill shall not be returned by the President within ten Days (Sundays excepted) after it shall have been presented to him, the Same shall be a Law, in like Manner as if he had signed it, unless the Congress by their Adjournment prevent its Return, in which Case it shall not be a Law.

Every Order, Resolution, or Vote to which the Concurrence of the Senate and House of Representatives may be necessary (except on a question of Adjournment) shall be presented to the President of the United States; and before the Same shall take Effect, shall be approved by him, or being disapproved by him, shall be repassed by two thirds of the Senate and House of Representatives, according to the Rules and Limitations prescribed in the Case of a Bill.

Section 8 The Congress shall have Power

To lay and collect Taxes, Duties, Imposts and Excises, to pay the Debts and provide for the common Defence and general Welfare of the United States; but all Duties, Imposts and Excises shall be uniform throughout the United States;

To borrow money on the credit of the United States;

To regulate Commerce with foreign Nations, and among the several States, and with the Indian Tribes;

To establish a uniform Rule of Naturalization, and uniform Laws on the subject of Bankruptcies throughout the United States;

To coin Money, regulate the Value thereof, and of foreign Coin, and fix the Standard of Weights and Measures;

To provide for the Punishment of counterfeiting the Securities and current Coin of the United States;

To establish Post offices and post Roads;

To promote the Progress of Science and useful Arts, by securing for limited Times to Authors and Inventors the exclusive Right to their respective Writings and Discoveries;

To constitute Tribunals inferior to the Supreme Court;

To define and punish Piracies and Felonies committed on the high Seas, and Offences against the Law of Nations;

To declare War, grant Letters of Marque and Reprisal, and make Rules concerning Captures on Land and Water;

To raise and support Armies, but no Appropriation of Money to that Use shall be for a longer Term than two Years;

To provide and maintain a Navy;

To make Rules for the Government and Regulation of the land and naval forces;

To provide for calling forth the Militia to execute the Laws of the Union, suppress Insurrections and repel Invasions;

To provide for organizing, arming, and disciplining the Militia, and for governing such Part of them as may be employed in the Service of the United States, reserving to the States respectively, the Appointment of the Officers, and the Authority of training the Militia according to the discipline prescribed by Congress;

To exercise exclusive Legislation in all Cases whatsoever, over such District (not exceeding ten Miles square) as may, by Cession of particular States, and the acceptance of Congress, become the Seat of Government of the United States, and to exercise like Authority over all Places purchased by the Consent of the Legislature of the State in which the Same shall be, for the Erection of Forts, Magazines, Arsenals, dock-Yards, and other needful Buildings;—And

To make all Laws which shall be necessary and proper for carrying into Execution the foregoing Powers, and all other Powers vested by this Constitution in the government of the United States, or in any Department or Officer thereof.

Section 9 The Migration or Importation of such Persons as any of the States now existing shall think proper to admit, shall not be prohibited by the Congress prior to the Year one thousand eight hundred and eight, but a tax or duty may be imposed on such Importation, not exceeding ten dollars for each Person.

The privilege of the Writ of Habeas Corpus shall not be suspended, unless when in Cases of Rebellion or Invasion the public Safety may require it.

No Bill of Attainder or ex post facto Law shall be passed.

No capitation, or other direct, Tax shall be laid unless in Proportion to the Census or Enumeration herein before directed to be taken.

No Tax or Duty shall be laid on Articles exported from any State.

No Preference shall be given by any Regulation of Revenue to the Ports of one State over those of another: nor shall Vessels bound to, or from, one state, be obliged to enter, clear, or pay Duties in another.

No Money shall be drawn from the Treasury, but in Consequence of Appropriations made by Law; and a regular Statement and Account of the Receipts and Expenditures of all public Money shall be published from time to time.

No Title of Nobility shall be granted by the United States: And no Person holding any Office of Profit or Trust under them, shall, without the Consent of the Congress, accept of any present, Emolument, Office, or Title, of any kind whatever, from any King, Prince, or Foreign State.

Section 10 No state shall enter into any Treaty, Alliance, or Confederation; grant Letters of Marque and Reprisal; coin Money; emit Bills of Credit; make any Thing but gold and silver Coin a Tender in Payment of Debts; pass any Bill of Attainder, ex post facto Law, or Law impairing the Obligation of Contracts, or grant any Title of Nobility.

No State shall, without the Consent of the Congress, lay any Imposts or Duties on Imports or Exports, except what may be absolutely necessary for executing its inspection Laws: and the net Produce of all Duties and Imposts, laid by any State on Imports or Exports, shall be for the Use of the Treasury of the United States; and all such Laws shall be subject to the Revision and Control of the Congress.

No State shall, without the Consent of Congress, lay any duty of Tonnage, keep Troops, or Ships of War in time of Peace, enter into any Agreement or Compact with another State, or with a foreign Power, or engage in War, unless actually invaded, or in such imminent Danger as will not admit of delay.

Article II

Section 1 The executive Power shall be vested in a President of the United States of America. He shall hold his Office during the Term of four years, and, together with the Vice President, chosen for the same Term, be elected, as follows:

Each State shall appoint, in such Manner as the Legislature thereof may direct, a Number of Electors, equal to the whole Number of Senators and Representatives to which the State may be entitled in the Congress; but no Senator or Representative, or Person holding an Office of Trust or Profit under the United States, shall be appointed an Elector.

The Electors shall meet in their respective States, and vote by Ballot for two persons, of whom one at least shall not be an Inhabitant of the same State with themselves. And they shall make a List of all the Persons voted for, and of the Number of Votes for each; which List they shall sign and certify, and transmit sealed to the Seat of the Government of the United States, directed to the President of the Senate. The President of the Senate shall, in the Presence of the Senate and House of Representatives, open all the Certificates, and the Votes shall then be counted. The Person having the greatest Number of Votes shall be the President, if such Number be a Majority of the whole Number of Electors appointed; and if there be more than one who have such Majority, and have an equal Number of Votes, then the House of Representatives shall immediately chuse by Ballot one of them for President; and if no Person have a Majority, then from the five highest on the List the said House shall in like Manner chuse the President. But in chusing the President, the votes shall be taken by States, the Representation from each State having one Vote; a quorum for this Purpose shall consist of a Member or Members from two-thirds of the States, and a Majority of all the States shall be necessary to a Choice. In every Case, after the Choice of the President, the Person having the greatest Number of Votes of the Electors shall be the Vice President. But if there should remain two or more who have equal votes, the Senate shall chuse from them by Ballot the Vice President.

The Congress may determine the time of chusing the Electors, and the Day on which they shall give their Votes; which Day shall be the same throughout the United States.

No person except a natural-born Citizen, or a Citizen of the United States, at the time of the Adoption of this Constitution, shall be eligible to the Office of President; neither shall any Person be eligible to that Office who shall not have attained to the Age of thirty-five years, and been fourteen Years a Resident within the United States.

In Case of the Removal of the President from Office, or of his Death, Resignation, or Inability to discharge the Powers and Duties of the said Office, the same shall devolve on the Vice President, and the Congress may by Law provide for the Case of Removal, Death, Resignation, or Inability, both of the President and Vice President, declaring what Officer shall then act as President, and such Officer shall act accordingly, until the disability be removed, or a President shall be elected.

The President shall, at stated Times, receive for his Services a Compensation, which shall neither be increased nor diminished during the Period for which he shall have been elected, and he shall not receive within that Period any other Emolument from the United States, or any of them.

Before he enter on the execution of his Office, he shall take the following Oath or Affirmation:—"I do solemnly swear (or affirm) that I will faithfully execute the Office of President of the United States, and will, to the best of my Ability, preserve, protect, and defend the Constitution of the United States."

Section 2   The President shall be Commander in Chief of the Army and Navy of the United States, and of the Militia of the several States, when called into the actual Service of the United States; he may require the Opinion, in writing, of the principal Officer in each of the executive Departments, upon any subject relating to the Duties of their respective Offices, and he shall have Power to Grant Reprieves and Pardons for Offences against the United States, except in Cases of Impeachment.

He shall have Power, by and with the Advice and Consent of the Senate, to make Treaties, provided two thirds of the Senators present concur; and he shall nominate, and by and with the Advice and Consent of the Senate, shall appoint Ambassadors, other public Ministers and Consuls, Judges of the supreme Court, and all other Officers of the United States, whose Appointments are not herein otherwise provided for, and which shall be established by Law: but the Congress may by Law vest the Appointment of such inferior Officers, as they think proper, in the President alone, in the Courts of Law, or in the Heads of Departments.

The President shall have Power to fill up all Vacancies that may happen during the Recess of the Senate, by granting Commissions which shall expire at the End of their next Session.

Section 3   He shall from time to time give to the Congress Information of the State of the Union, and recommend to their Consideration such Measures as he shall judge necessary and expedient; he may, on extraordinary occasions, convene both Houses, or either of them, and in Case of Disagreement between them, with respect to the Time of Adjournment, he may adjourn them to such Time as he shall think proper; he shall receive Ambassadors and other public Ministers; he shall take Care that the Laws be faithfully executed, and shall Commission all the Officers of the United States.

Section 4   The President, Vice President and all civil Officers of the United States, shall be removed from Office on Impeachment for, and Conviction of, Treason, Bribery, or other high Crimes and Misdemeanors.

Article III

Section 1   The judicial Power of the United States, shall be vested in one supreme Court, and in such inferior Courts as the Congress may from time to time ordain and establish. The Judges, both of the supreme and inferior Courts, shall hold their Offices during good Behaviour, and shall, at stated Times, receive for their Services, a Compensation, which shall not be diminished during their Continuance in Office.

Section 2   The judicial Power shall extend to all Cases, in Law and Equity, arising under this Constitution, the Laws of the United States, and treaties made, or which shall be made, under their Authority;—to all Cases affecting ambassadors, other public ministers and consuls;—to all cases of admiralty and maritime Jurisdiction;—to Controversies to which the United States shall be a Party;—to Controversies between two or more States;—between a State and Citizens of another State;—between Citizens of different States,—between Citizens of the same State claiming Lands under Grants of different States, and between a State, or the Citizens thereof, and foreign States, Citizens or Subjects.

In all Cases affecting Ambassadors, other public Ministers and Consuls, and those in which a State shall be Party, the supreme Court shall have original Jurisdiction. In all the other Cases before mentioned, the supreme Court shall have appellate Jurisdiction, both as to Law and Fact, with such Exceptions, and under such Regulations as the Congress shall make.

The trial of all Crimes, except in Cases of Impeachment, shall be by Jury; and such Trial shall be held in the State where the said Crimes shall have been committed; but when not committed within any State, the Trial shall be at such Place or Places as the Congress may by Law have directed.

Section 3   Treason against the United States, shall consist only in levying War against them, or in adhering to their Enemies, giving them Aid and Comfort. No Person shall be convicted of Treason unless on the testimony of two Witnesses to the same overt Act, or on Confession in open Court.

The Congress shall have power to declare the Punishment of Treason, but no Attainder of Treason shall work Corruption of Blood, or Forfeiture except during the Life of the Person attained.

Article IV

Section 1   Full Faith and Credit shall be given in each State to the public Acts, Records, and judicial Proceedings of every other State. And the Congress may by general Laws prescribe the Manner in which such Acts, Records and Proceedings shall be proved, and the Effect thereof.

Section 2   The Citizens of each State shall be entitled to all Privileges and Immunities of Citizens in the several States.

A Person charged in any State with Treason, Felony, or other Crime, who shall flee from Justice, and be found in another State, shall on demand of the executive Authority of the State from which he fled, be delivered up, to be removed to the State having Jurisdiction of the crime.

No Person held to Service or Labour in one State, under the Laws thereof, escaping into another, shall, in Consequence of any Law or Regulation therein, be discharged from such Service or Labour, but shall be delivered up on Claim of the Party to whom such Service or Labour may be due.

Section 3 New States may be admitted by the Congress into this Union; but no new State shall be formed or erected within the Jurisdiction of any other State; nor any State be formed by the Junction of two or more States, or parts of States, without the Consent of the Legislatures of the States concerned as well as of the Congress.

The Congress shall have Power to dispose of and make all needful Rules and Regulations respecting the Territory or other Property belonging to the United States; and nothing in this Constitution shall be so construed as to Prejudice any Claims of the United States, or of any particular State.

Section 4 The United States shall guarantee to every State in this Union a Republican Form of Government, and shall protect each of them against Invasion; and on Application of the Legislature, or the Executive (when the Legislature cannot be convened) against domestic Violence.

Article V

The Congress, whenever two-thirds of both Houses shall deem it necessary, shall propose Amendments to this Constitution, or, on the Application of the Legislatures of two-thirds of the several States, shall call a Convention for proposing Amendments, which, in either Case, shall be valid to all Intents and Purposes, as part of this Constitution, when ratified by the Legislatures of three-fourths of the several States, or by Conventions in three-fourths thereof, as the one or the other Mode of Ratification may be proposed by the Congress; Provided that no Amendment which may be made prior to the Year One thousand eight hundred and eight shall in any Manner affect the first and fourth Clauses in the Ninth Section of the first Article; and that no State, without its Consent, shall be deprived of its equal Suffrage in the Senate.

Article VI

All Debts contracted and Engagements entered into, before the Adoption of this Constitution, shall be as valid against the United States under this Constitution, as under the Confederation.

This Constitution, and the Laws of the United States which shall be made in Pursuance thereof; and all Treaties made, or which shall be made, under the Authority of the United States, shall be the supreme Law of the Land; and the Judges in every State shall be bound thereby, any Thing in the Constitution or Laws of any State to the Contrary notwithstanding.

The Senators and Representatives before mentioned, and the Members of the several State Legislatures and all executive and judicial Officers, both of the United States and of the several States, shall be bound by Oath or Affirmation to support this Constitution; but no religious Test shall ever be required as a qualification to any Office or public Trust under the United States.

Article VII

The Ratification of the Conventions of nine States shall be sufficient for the Establishment of this Constitution between the States so ratifying the same.

Done in Convention by the Unanimous Consent of the States present the Seventeenth Day of September in the Year of our Lord one thousand seven hundred and Eighty seven, and of the Independence of the United States of America the Twelfth. In Witness whereof We have hereunto subscribed our Names.

Go. Washington, President and deputy from Virginia; Attest William Jackson, Secretary; Delaware: Geo. Read,* Gunning Bedford, Jr., John Dickinson, Richard Basset, Jaco. Broom; Maryland: James McHenry, Daniel of St. Thomas' Jenifer, Danl. Carroll; Virginia: John Blair, James Madison, Jr.; North Carolina: Wm. Blount, Richd. Dobbs Spaight, Hu Williamson; South Carolina: J. Rutledge, Charles Cotesworth Pinckney, Charles Pinckney, Pierce Butler; Georgia: William Few, Abr. Baldwin; New Hampshire: John Langdon, Nicholas Gilman; Massachusetts: Nathaniel Gorham, Rufus King; Connecticut: Wm. Saml. Johnson, Roger Sherman,* New York: Alexander Hamilton; New Jersey: Wil. Livingston, David Brearley, Wm. Paterson, Jona. Dayton; Pennsylvania: B. Franklin,* Thomas Mifflin, Robt. Morris,* Geo. Clymer,* Thos. FitzSimons, Jared Ingersoll, James Wilson, Gouv. Morris.

Articles in Addition to, and Amendment of, the Constitution of the United States of America, Proposed by Congress, and Ratified by the Legislatures of the Several States, Pursuant to the Fifth Article of the Original Constitution.

Amendment I [1791]

Congress shall make no law respecting an establishment of religion, or prohibiting the free exercise thereof; or abridging the freedom of speech, or of the press; or the right of the people peaceably to assemble, and to petition the Government for a redress of grievances.

Amendment II [1791]

A well regulated Militia, being necessary to the security of a free State, the right of the people to keep and bear Arms shall not be infringed.

Amendment III [1791]

No Soldier shall, in time of peace, be quartered in any house, without the consent of the Owner, nor in time of war, but in a manner to be prescribed by law.

Amendment IV [1791]

The right of the people to be secure in their persons, houses, papers, and effects, against unreasonable searches and seizures, shall not be violated, and no Warrants shall issue, but upon probable cause, supported by Oath or affirmation, and particularly describing the place to be searched, and the persons or things to be seized.

Amendment V [1791]

No person shall be held to answer for a capital or otherwise infamous crime, unless on a presentment or indictment of a Grand Jury, except in cases arising in the land or naval forces, or in the Militia, when in actual service in time of War or public danger; nor shall any person be subject for the same offence to be twice put in jeopardy of life or limb; nor shall be compelled in any criminal case to be a witness against himself, nor be deprived of life, liberty, or property, without due process of law; nor shall private property be taken for public use, without just compensation.

Amendment VI [1791]

In all criminal prosecutions, the accused shall enjoy the right to a speedy and public trial, by an impartial jury of the State and district wherein the crime shall have been committed, which district shall have been previously ascertained by law, and to be informed of the nature and cause of the accusation; to be confronted with the witnesses against him; to have compulsory process for obtaining witnesses in his favor, and to have the Assistance of Counsel for his defence.

Amendment VII [1791]

In suits at common law, where the value in controversy shall exceed twenty dollars, the right of trial by jury shall be preserved, and no fact tried by a jury, shall be otherwise reexamined in any Court of the United States, than according to the rules of the common law.

Amendment VIII [1791]

Excessive bail shall not be required, nor excessive fines imposed, nor cruel and unusual punishments inflicted.

Amendment IX [1791]

The enumeration in the Constitution, of certain rights, shall not be construed to deny or disparage others retained by the people.

Amendment X [1791]

The powers not delegated to the United States by the Constitution, nor prohibited by it to the States, are reserved to the States respectively, or to the people.

Amendment XI [1798]

The Judicial power of the United States shall not be construed to extend to any suit in law or equity, commenced or prosecuted against one of the United States by Citizens of another State, or by Citizens or Subjects of any Foreign State.

Amendment XII [1804]

The Electors shall meet in their respective States and vote by ballot for President and Vice President, one of whom, at least, shall not be an inhabitant of the same State with themselves; they shall name in their ballots the person voted for as President, and in distinct ballots the person voted for as Vice President, and they shall make distinct lists of all persons voted for as President, and of all persons voted for as Vice President, and of the number of votes for each, which lists they shall sign and certify, and transmit sealed to the seat of the government of the United States, directed to the President of the Senate;—The President of the Senate shall, in the presence of the Senate and House of Representatives, open all the certificates and the votes shall then be counted;—The person having the greatest number of votes for President, shall be the President, if such number be a majority of the whole number of Electors appointed; and if no person have such majority, then from the persons having the highest numbers not exceeding three on the list of those voted for as President, the House of Representatives shall choose immediately, by ballot, the President. But in choosing the President, the votes shall be taken by states, the representation from each state having one vote; a quorum for this purpose shall consist of a member or members from two-thirds of the states, and a majority of all the states shall be necessary to a choice. And if the House of Representatives shall not choose a President whenever the right of choice shall devolve upon them, before the fourth day of March next following, then the Vice President shall act as President, as in the case of the death or other constitutional disability of the President.—The person having the greatest number of votes as Vice President, shall be the Vice President, if such number be a majority of the whole number of Electors appointed, and if no person have a majority, then from the two highest numbers on the list, the Senate shall choose the Vice President; a quorum for the purpose shall consist of two-thirds of the whole number of Senators, and a majority of the whole number shall be necessary to a choice. But no person constitutionally ineligible to the office of President shall be eligible to that of Vice President of the United States.

Amendment XIII [1865]

Section 1 Neither slavery nor involuntary servitude, except as a punishment for crime whereof the party shall have been duly convicted, shall exist within the United States, or any place subject to their jurisdiction.

Section 2 Congress shall have power to enforce this article by appropriate legislation.

Amendment XIV [1868]

Section 1 All persons born or naturalized in the United States, and subject to the jurisdiction thereof, are citizens of the United States and of the State wherein they reside. No State shall make or enforce any law which shall abridge the privileges or immunities of citizens of the United States; nor shall any State deprive any person of life, liberty, or property, without due process of law; nor deny to any person within its jurisdiction the equal protection of the laws.

Section 2 Representatives shall be apportioned among the several States according to their respective numbers, counting the whole number of persons in each State, excluding Indians not taxed. But when the right to vote at any election for the choice of electors for President and Vice President of the United States, Representatives in Congress, the Executive and Judicial officers of a State, or the members of the Legislature thereof, is denied to any of the male inhabitants of such State, being twenty-one years of age, and citizens of the United States or in any way abridged, except for participation in rebellion, or other crime, the basis of representation therein shall be reduced in the proportion which the number of such male citizens shall bear to the whole number of male citizens twenty-one years of age in such State.

Section 3 No person shall be a Senator or Representative in Congress, or elector of President and Vice President, or hold any office, civil or military, under the United States, or under any State, who, having previously taken an oath, as a member of Congress, or as an officer of the United States, or as a member of any State legislature, or as an executive or judicial officer of any State, to support the Constitution of the United States, shall have engaged in insurrection or rebellion against the same, or given aid or comfort to the enemies thereof. But Congress may by a vote of two-thirds of each House, remove such disability.

Section 4 The validity of the public debt of the United States, authorized by law, including debts incurred for payment of pensions and bounties for services in suppressing insurrection or rebellion, shall not be questioned. But neither the United States nor any State shall assume or pay any debt or obligation incurred in aid of insurrection or rebellion against the United States, or any claim for the loss or emancipation of any slave; but all such debts, obligations, and claims shall be held illegal and void.

Section 5 The Congress shall have the power to enforce, by appropriate legislation, the provisions of this article.

Amendment XV [1870]

Section 1 The right of citizens of the United States to vote shall not be denied or abridged by the United States or by any State on account of race, color, or previous condition of servitude—

Section 2 The Congress shall have power to enforce this article by appropriate legislation.

Amendment XVI [1913]

The Congress shall have power to lay and collect taxes on incomes, from whatever source derived, without apportionment among the several States, and without regard to any census or enumeration.

Amendment XVII [1913]

The Senate of the United States shall be composed of two Senators from each State, elected by the people thereof, for six years; and each Senator shall have one vote. The electors in each State shall have the qualifications requisite for electors of the most numerous branch of the State legislatures.

When vacancies happen in the representation of any State in the Senate, the executive authority of such State shall issue writs of election to fill such vacancies: Provided, That the legislature of any State may empower the executive thereof to make temporary appointments until the people fill the vacancies by election as the legislature may direct. This amendment shall not be so construed as to affect the election or term of any Senator chosen before it becomes valid as part of the Constitution.

Amendment XVIII [1919]

Section 1 After one year from the ratification of this article the manufacture, sale, or transportation of intoxicating liquors within, the importation thereof into, or the exportation thereof from the United States and all territory subject to the jurisdiction thereof for beverage purposes is hereby prohibited.

Section 2 The Congress and the several States shall have concurrent power to enforce this article by appropriate legislation.

Section 3 This article shall be inoperative unless it shall have been ratified as an amendment to the Constitution by the legislatures of the several States, as provided in the Constitution, within seven years from the date of the submission hereof to the States by the Congress.

Amendment XIX [1920]

The right of citizens of the United States to vote shall not be denied or abridged by the United States or by any State on account of sex.

Congress shall have power to enforce this article by appropriate legislation.

Amendment XX [1933]

Section 1 The terms of the President and Vice President shall end at noon on the 20th day of January, and the terms of Senators and Representatives at noon on the 3d day of January, of the years in which such terms would have ended if this article had not been ratified; and the terms of their successors shall then begin.

Section 2 The Congress shall assemble at least once in every year, and such meeting shall begin at noon on the 3d day of January, unless they shall by law appoint a different day.

Section 3 If, at the time fixed for the beginning of the term of the President, the President elect shall have died, the Vice President elect shall become President. If a President shall not have been chosen before the time fixed for the beginning of his term, or if the President elect shall have failed to qualify, then the Vice President elect shall act as President until a President shall have qualified; and the Congress may by law provide for the case wherein neither a President elect nor a Vice President elect shall have qualified, declaring who shall then act as President, or the manner in which one who is to act shall be selected, and such person shall act accordingly until a President or Vice President shall have qualified.

Section 4 The Congress may by law provide for the case of the death of any of the persons from whom the House of Representatives may choose a President whenever the right of choice shall have devolved upon them, and for the case of the death of any of the persons from whom the Senate may choose a Vice President whenever the right of choice shall have devolved upon them.

Section 5 Sections 1 and 2 shall take effect on the 15th day of October following the ratification of this article.

Section 6 This article shall be inoperative unless it shall have been ratified as an amendment to the Constitution by the legislatures of three-fourths of the several States within seven years from the date of its submission.

Amendment XXI [1933]

Section 1 The eighteenth article of amendment to the Constitution of the United States is hereby repealed.

Section 2 The transportation or importation into any State, Territory, or possession of the United States for delivery or use therein of intoxicating liquors, in violation of the laws thereof, is hereby prohibited.

Section 3 This article shall be inoperative unless it shall have been ratified as an amendment to the Constitution by conventions in the several States, as provided in the Constitution, within seven years from the date of the submission hereof to the States by the Congress.

Amendment XXII [1951]

No person shall be elected to the office of the President more than twice, and no person who has held the office of President, or acted as President, for more than two years of a term to which some other person was elected President shall be elected to the office of the President more than once.

But this Article shall not apply to any person holding the office of President when this Article was proposed by the Congress, and shall not prevent any person who may be holding the office of President or acting as President, during the term within which this Article becomes operative from holding the office of President or acting as President during the remainder of such term.

Amendment XXIII [1961]

Section 1 The District constituting the seat of Government of the United States shall appoint in such manner as the Congress may direct:

A number of electors of President and Vice President equal to the whole number of Senators and Representatives in Congress to which the District would be entitled if it were a State, but in no event more than the least populous State; they shall be in addition to those appointed by the States, but they shall be considered, for the purposes of the election of President and Vice President, to be electors appointed by a State; and they shall meet in the District and perform such duties as provided by the twelfth article of amendment.

Section 2 The Congress shall have power to enforce this article by appropriate legislation.

Amendment XXIV [1964]

Section 1 The right of citizens of the United States to vote in any primary or other election for President or Vice President, for electors for President or Vice President, or for Senator or Representative in Congress, shall not be denied or abridged by the United States or any State by reason of failure to pay any poll tax or other tax.

Section 2 The Congress shall have the power to enforce this article by appropriate legislation.

Amendment XXV [1967]

Section 1 In case of the removal of the President from office or his death or resignation, the Vice President shall become President.

Section 2 Whenever there is a vacancy in the office of the Vice President, the President shall nominate a Vice President who shall take the office upon confirmation by a majority vote of both houses of Congress.

Section 3 Whenever the President transmits to the President pro tempore of the Senate and the Speaker of the House of Representatives his written declaration that he is unable to discharge the powers and duties of his office, and until he transmits to them a written declaration to the contrary, such powers and duties shall be discharged by the Vice President as Acting President.

Section 4 Whenever the Vice President and a majority of either the principal officers of the executive departments, or of such other body as Congress may by law provide, transmit to the President pro tempore of the Senate and the Speaker of the House of Representatives their written declaration that the President is unable to discharge the powers and duties of his office, the Vice President shall immediately assume the powers and duties of the office as Acting President.

Thereafter, when the President transmits to the President pro tempore of the Senate and the Speaker of the House of Representatives his written declaration that no inability exists, he shall resume the powers and duties of his office unless the Vice President and a majority of either the principal officers of the executive departments, or of such other body as Congress may by law provide, transmit within four days to the President protempore of the Senate and the Speaker of the House of Representatives their written declaration that the President is unable to discharage the powers and duties of his office. Thereupon Congress shall decide the issue, assembling within 48 hours for that purpose if not in session. If the Congress, within 21 days after receipt of the latter written declaration, or, if Congress is not in session, within 21 days after Congress is required to assemble, determines by two-thirds vote of both houses that the President is unable to discharge the powers and duties of his office, the Vice President shall continue to discharge the same as Acting President; otherwise, the President shall resume the powers and duties of his office.

Amendment XXVI [1971]

Section 1 The right of citizens of the United States, who are 18 years of age or older, to vote shall not be denied or abridged by the United States or any state on account of age.

Section 2 The Congress shall have the power to enforce this article by appropriate legislation.

Amendment XXVII [1992]

No law varying the compensation for the service of Senators and Representatives shall take effect until an election of Representatives shall have intervened.

The Federalist Papers

The Federalist Papers is a collection of 85 essays written by Alexander Hamilton, John Jay, and James Madison under the pen name Publius. They were published in New York newspapers in 1787 and 1788 to support ratification of the Constitution. Federalist Nos. 10, 51, and 78 are reprinted here.

James Madison: Federalist No. 10

Among the numerous advantages promised by a well constructed Union, none deserves to be more accurately developed than its tendency to break and control the violence of faction. The friend of popular governments never finds himself so much alarmed for their character and fate as when he contemplates their propensity to this dangerous vice. He will not fail, therefore, to set a due value on any plan which, without violating the principles to which he is attached, provides a proper cure for it. The instability, injustice, and confusion, introduced into the public councils, have, in truth been the mortal diseases under which popular governments have everywhere perished; as they continue to be the favorite and fruitful topics from which the adversaries to liberty derive their most specious declamations. The valuable improvements made by the American constitutions on the popular models, both ancient and modern, cannot certainly be too much admired; but it would be an unwarrantable partiality, to contend that they have as effectually obviated the danger on this side, as was wished and expected. Complaints are everywhere heard from our most considerate and virtuous citizens, equally the friends of public and private faith, and of public and personal liberty, that our governments are too unstable; that the public good is disregarded in the conflicts of rival parties; and that measures are too often decided, not according to the rules of justice, and the rights of the minor party, but by the superior force of an interested and overbearing majority. However anxiously we may wish that these complaints had no foundation, the evidence of known facts will not permit us to deny that they are in some degree true. It will be found, indeed, on a candid review of our situation, that some of the distresses under which we labor, have been erroneously charged on the operation of our governments; but it will be found, at the same time, that other causes will not alone account for many of our heaviest misfortunes; and, particularly, for the prevailing and increasing distrust of public engagements, and alarm for private rights, which are echoed from one end of the continent to the other. These must be chiefly, if not wholly, effects of the unsteadiness and injustice, with which a factious spirit has tainted our public administrations.

By a faction, I understand a number of citizens, whether amounting to a majority or minority of the whole, who are united and actuated by some common impulse of passion, or of interest, adverse to the rights of other citizens, or to the permanent and aggregate interests of the community.

There are two methods of curing the mischiefs of faction: The one, by removing its causes; the other, by controlling its effects.

There are again two methods of removing the causes of faction: the one, by destroying the liberty which is essential to its existence; the other, by giving to every citizen the same opinions, the same passions, and the same interests.

It could never be more truly said, than of the first remedy, that it was worse than the disease. Liberty is to faction what air is to fire, an aliment, without which it instantly expires. But it could not be a less folly to abolish liberty, which is essential to political life because it nourishes faction, than it would be to wish the annihilation of air, which is essential to animal life, because it imparts to fire its destructive agency.

The second expedient is as impracticable, as the first would be unwise. As long as the reason of man continues fallible, and he is at liberty to exercise it, different opinions will be formed. As long as the connection subsists between his reason and his self-love, his opinions and his passions will have a reciprocal influence on each other; and the former will be objects to which the latter will attach themselves. The diversity in the faculties of men, from which the rights of property originate, is not less an insuperable obstacle to a uniformity of interests. The protection of those faculties is the first object of government. From the protection of different and unequal faculties of acquiring property, the possession of different degrees and kinds of property immediately results; and from the influence of these on the sentiments and views of the respective proprietors, ensues a division of the society into different interests and parties.

The latent causes of faction are thus sown in the nature of man; and we see them everywhere brought into different degrees of activity, according to the different circumstances of civil society. A zeal for different opinions concerning religion, concerning government, and many other points, as well of speculation as of practice; an attachment to different leaders, ambitiously contending for preeminence and power; or to persons of other descriptions, whose fortunes have been interesting to the human passions, have, in turn, divided mankind into parties, inflamed them with mutual animosity, and rendered them much more disposed to vex and oppress each other, than to cooperate for their common good. So strong is this propensity of mankind, to fall into mutual animosities, that where no substantial occasion presents itself, the most frivolous and fanciful distinctions have been sufficient to kindle their unfriendly passions, and excite their most violent conflicts. But the most common and durable source of factions has been the various and unequal distribution of property. Those who hold, and those who are without property, have ever formed distinct interests in society. Those who are creditors, and those who are debtors, fall under a like discrimination. A landed interest, a manufacturing interest, a mercantile interest, a moneyed interest, with many lesser interests, grow up of necessity in civilized nations, and divide them into different classes, actuated by different sentiments and views. The regulation of these various and interfering interests forms the principle task of modern legislation, and involves the spirit of party and faction in the necessary and ordinary operations of government.

No man is allowed to be a judge in his own cause; because his interest will certainly bias his judgment, and, not improbably, corrupt his integrity. With equal, nay, with greater reason, a body of men are unfit to be both judges and parties at the same time; yet what are many of the most important acts of legislation, but so many judicial determinations, not indeed concerning the rights of single persons, but concerning the rights of large bodies of citizens? And what are the different classes of legislators, but advocates and parties to the cause which they determine? Is a law proposed concerning private debts? It is a question to which the creditors are parties on one side, and the debtors on the other. Justice ought to hold the balance between them. Yet the parties are, and must be, themselves the judges; and the most numerous party, or, in other words, the most powerful faction, must be expected to prevail. Shall domestic manufactures be encouraged, and in what degree, by restrictions on foreign manufactures? are questions which would be differently decided by the landed and the manufacturing classes; and probably by neither with a sole regard to justice and the public good. . . .

It is in vain to say, that enlightened statesmen will be able to adjust these clashing interests, and render them all subservient to the public good. Enlightened statesmen will not always be at the helm; nor, in many cases, can such an adjustment be made at all, without taking into view indirect and remote considerations, which will rarely prevail over the immediate interest which one party may find in disregarding the rights of another, or the good of the whole.

The inference to which we are brought is, that the causes of faction cannot be removed; and that relief is only to be sought in the means of controlling its effects.

If a faction consists of less than a majority, relief is supplied by the republican principle, which enables the majority to defeat its sinister views, by regular vote. It may clog the administration, it may convulse the society; but it will be unable to execute and mask its violence under the forms of the constitution. When a majority is included in a faction, the form of popular government, on the other hand, enables it to sacrifice to its ruling passion or interest, both the public good and the rights of other citizens. To secure the public good, and private rights, against the danger of such a faction, and at the same time to preserve the spirit and the form of popular government, is then the great object to which our inquiries

are directed. Let me add, that it is the great desideratum, by which alone this form of government can be rescued from the opprobrium under which it has so long labored, and be recommended to the esteem and adoption of mankind.

By what means is this object attainable? Evidently by one of two only. Either the existence of the same passion or interest in a majority, at the same time must be prevented; or the majority, having such coexistent passion or interest, must be rendered, by their number and local situation, unable to concert and carry into effect schemes of oppression. If the impulse and the opportunity be suffered to coincide, we well know, that neither moral nor religious motives can be relied on as an adequate control. They are not found to be such on the injustice and violence of individuals, and lose their efficacy in proportion to the number combined together; that is in proportion as their efficacy becomes needful.

From this view of the subject, it may be concluded, that a pure democracy, by which I mean a society consisting of a small number of citizens, who assemble and administer the government in person, can admit of no cure from the mischiefs of faction. A common passion or interest will, in almost every case, be felt by a majority of the whole; a communication and concert, results from the form of government itself; and there is nothing to check the inducements to sacrifice the weaker party, or an obnoxious individual. Hence it is, that such democracies have ever been spectacles of turbulence and contention; have ever been found incompatible with personal security, or the rights of property; and have, in general been as short in their lives, as they have been violent in their deaths. Theoretic politicians, who have patronized this species of government, have erroneously supposed that by reducing mankind to a perfect equality in their political rights, they would, at the same time, be perfectly equalized and assimilated in their possessions, their opinions, and their passions.

A republic, by which I mean a government in which the scheme of representation takes place, opens a different prospect, and promises the cure for which we are seeking. Let us examine the points in which it varies from pure democracy, and we shall comprehend both the nature of the cure and the efficacy which it must derive from the union.

The two great points of difference, between a democracy and a republic, are, first, the delegation of the government, in the latter, to a small number of citizens elected by the rest; secondly, the greater number of citizens, and greater sphere of country, over which the latter may be extended.

The effect of the first difference is on the one hand, to refine and enlarge the public views, by passing them through the medium of a chosen body of citizens, whose wisdom may best discern the true interest in their country, and whose patriotism and love of justice, will be least likely to sacrifice it to temporary or partial considerations. Under such a regulation, it may well happen, that the public voice, pronounced by the representatives of the people, will be more consonant to the public good, than if pronounced by the people themselves, convened for the purpose. On the other hand, the effect may be inverted. Men of factious tempers, of local prejudices, or of sinister designs, may by intrigue, by corruption, or by other means, first obtain the suffrages, and then betray the interests, of the people. The question resulting is, whether small or extensive republics are most favorable to the election of proper guardians of the public weal; and it is clearly decided in favor of the latter by two obvious considerations.

In the first place, it is to be remarked, that however small the republic may be, the representatives must be raised to a certain number, in order to guard against the cabals of a few; and that however large it may be, they must be limited to a certain number, in order to guard against the confusion of a multitude. Hence, the number of representatives in the two cases not being in proportion to that of the constituents, and being proportionally greatest in the small republic, it follows that if the proportion of fit characters be not less in the large than in the small republic, the former will present a greater option, and consequently a greater probability of a fit choice.

In the next place, as each representative will be chosen by a greater number of citizens in the large than in the small republic, it will be more difficult for unworthy candidates to practice with success the vicious arts, by which elections are too often carried; and the suffrages of the people being more free, will be more likely to center in men who possess the most attractive merit, and the most diffusive and established characters. . . .

The other point of difference is, the greater number of citizens, and extent of territory, which may be brought within the compass of republican, than of democratic government; and it is this circumstance principally which renders factious combinations less to be dreaded in the former, than in the latter. The smaller the society, the fewer probably will be the distinct parties and interests composing it; the fewer the distinct parties and interests, the more frequently will a majority be found of the same party; and the smaller the number of individuals composing a majority, and the smaller the compass within which they are placed, the more easily they will concert and execute their plans of oppression. Extend the sphere, and you take in a greater variety of parties and interests; you make it less probable that a majority of the whole will have a common motive to invade the rights of other citizens; or if such a common motive exists, it will be more difficult for all who feel it to discover their own strength, and to act in unison with each other. . . .

Hence, it clearly appears, that the same advantage, which a republic has over a democracy, in controlling the effects of faction, is enjoyed by a large over a small republic—is enjoyed by the union over the states composing it. Does this advantage consist in the substitution of representatives, whose enlightened views and virtuous sentiments render them superior to local prejudices, and to schemes of injustice? It will not be denied, that the representation of the union will be most likely to possess these requisite endowments. Does it consist in the greater security afforded by a greater variety of parties, against the event of any one party being able to outnumber and oppress the rest? In an equal degree does the increased variety of parties, comprised within the union, increase this security? Does it, in fine, consist in the greater obstacles opposed to the concert and accomplishment of the secret wishes of an unjust and interested majority? Here, again, the extent of the union gives it the most palpable advantage. The influence of factious leaders may kindle a flame within their particular states, but will be unable to spread a general conflagration through the other states; a religious sect may degenerate into a political faction in a part of the confederacy; but the variety of sects dispersed over the entire face of it, must secure the national councils against any danger from that source; a rage for paper money, for an abolition of debts, for an equal division of property, or for any other improper or wicked project, will be less apt to pervade the whole body of the union, than a particular member of it; in the same proportion as such a malady is more likely to taint a particular country or district, than an entire state.

In the extent and proper structure of the union, therefore, we behold a republican remedy for the diseases most incident to republican government. And according to the degree of pleasure and pride we feel in being republicans, ought to be our zeal in cherishing the spirit, and supporting the character of Federalists.

James Madison: Federalist No. 51

To what expedient then shall we finally resort, for maintaining in practice the necessary partition of power among the several departments, as laid down in the constitution? The only answer that can be given is, that as all these exterior provisions are found to be inadequate, the defect must be supplied, by so contriving the interior structure of the government, as that its several constituent parts may, by their mutual relations, be the means of keeping each other in their proper places. . . .

In order to lay a due foundation for that separate and distinct exercise of the different powers of government, which, to a certain extent, is admitted on all hands to be essential to the preservation of liberty, it is evident that each department should have a will of its own; and consequently should be so constituted, that the members of each should have as little agency as possible in the appointment of the members of the others. . . .

It is equally evident, that the members of each department should be as little dependent as possible on those of the others, for the emoluments annexed to their offices. Were the executive magistrate, or the judges, not independent of the legislature in this particular, their independence in every other would be merely nominal.

But the great security against a gradual concentration of the several powers in the same department, consists in giving to those who administer each department, the necessary constitutional means, and personal motives, to resist encroachments of the others. The provision for defense must in this, as in all other cases, be made commensurate to the danger of attack. Ambition must be made to counteract ambition. The interest of the man must be connected with the constitutional rights of the place. It may be a reflection on human nature, that such devices should be necessary to control the abuses of government. But what is government itself, but the greatest of all reflections on human nature? If men were angels, no government would be necessary. If angels were to govern men, neither external nor internal controls on government would be necessary. In framing a government, which is to be administered by men over men, the great difficulty lies in this: You must first enable the government to control the governed; and in the next place, oblige it to control itself. A dependence on the people is, no doubt, the primary control on the government; but experience has taught mankind the necessity of auxiliary precautions.

This policy of supplying by opposite and rival interests, the defect of better motives, might be traced through the whole system of human affairs, private as well as public. We see it particularly displayed in all the subordinate distributions of power; where the constant aim is, to divide and arrange the several offices in such a manner, as that each may be a check on the other; that the private interest of every individual, may be a sentinel over the public rights. These interventions of prudence cannot be less requisite to the distribution of the supreme powers of the state.

But it is not possible to give to each department an equal power of self-defense. In republican government, the legislative authority necessarily predominates. The remedy for this inconvenience is, to divide the legislature into different branches; and to render them by different modes of election, and different principles of action, as little connected with each other, as the nature of their common functions, and their common dependence on the society will admit. It may even be necessary to guard against dangerous encroachments, by still further precautions. As the weight of the legislative authority requires that it should be thus divided, the weakness of the executive may require, on the other hand, that it should be fortified. An absolute negative on the legislature, appears, at first view, to be the natural defense with which the executive magistrate should be armed. But perhaps it would be neither altogether safe, nor alone sufficient. On ordinary occasions, it might not be exerted with the requisite firmness; and on extraordinary occasions, it might be perfidiously abused. May not this defect of an absolute negative be supplied by some qualified connection between this weaker department, and the weaker branch of the stronger department, by which the latter may be led to support the constitutional rights of the former, without being too much detached from the rights of its own department?

There are, moreover, two considerations particularly applicable to the federal system of America, which place that system in a very interesting point of view.

First. In a single republic, all the power surrendered by the people is submitted to the administration of a single government, and the usurpations are guarded against by a division of the government into distinct and separate departments. In the compound republic of America, the power surrendered by the people is first divided between two distinct governments, and then the portion allotted to each subdivided among distinct and separate departments. Hence a double security arises to the rights of the people. The different governments will control each other, at the same time that each will be controlled by itself.

Second. It is of great importance in a republic not only to guard the society against the oppression of its rulers, but to guard one part of the society against the injustice of the other part. Different interests necessarily exist in different classes of citizens. If a majority be united by a common interest, the rights of the minority will be insecure. There are but two methods of providing against this evil: the one by creating a will in the community independent of the majority—that is, of the society itself; the other, by comprehending in the society so many separate descriptions of citizens as will render an unjust combination of a majority of the whole very probable, if not impracticable. The first method prevails in all governments possessing an hereditary or self-appointed authority. This, at best, is but a precarious security; because a power independent of the society may as well espouse the unjust views of the major, as the rightful interests of the minor party, and may possibly be turned against both parties. The second method will be exemplified in the federal republic of the United States. Whilst all authority in it will be derived from and dependent on the society, the society itself will be broken into so many parts, interests and classes of citizens, that the rights of individuals, or of the minority, will be in little danger from interested combinations of the majority. In a free government the security for civil rights must be the same as that for religious rights. It consists in the one case in the multiplicity of interests, and in the other in the multiplicity of sects. The degree of security in both cases will depend on the number of interests and sects; and this may be presumed to depend on the extent of country and number of people comprehended under the same government. This view of the subject must particularly recommend a proper federal system to all the sincere and considerate friends of republican government, since it shows that in exact proportion as the territory of the Union may be formed into more circumscribed Confederacies, or States, oppressive combinations of a majority will be facilitated; the best security, under the republican forms, for the rights of every class of citizens, will be diminished; and consequently the stability and independence of some member of the government, the only other security, must be proportionately increased. Justice is the end of the government. It is the end of civil society. It ever has been and ever will be pursued until it be obtained, or until liberty be lost in the pursuit. In a society under the forms of which the stronger faction can readily unite and oppress the weaker, anarchy may as truly be said to reign as in a state of nature, where the weaker individual is not secured against the violence of the stronger; and as, in the latter state, even the stronger individuals are prompted, by the uncertainty of their condition, to submit to a government which may protect the weak as well as themselves; so, in the former state, will the more powerful factions or parties be gradually induced, by a like motive, to wish for a government which will protect all parties, the weaker as well as the more powerful. It can be little doubted that if the State of Rhode Island was separated from the Confederacy and left to itself, the insecurity of rights under the popular form of government within such narrow limits would be displayed by such reiterated oppressions of factious majorities that some power altogether independent of the people would soon be called for by the voice of the very factions whose misrule had proved the necessity of it. In the extended republic of the United States, and among the great variety of interests, parties, and sects which it embraces, a coalition of a majority of the whole society could seldom take place on any other principles than those of justice and the general good; whilst there being thus less danger to a minor from the will of a major party, there must be less pretext, also, to provide for the security of the former, by introducing into the government a will not dependent on the latter, or, in other words, a will independent of the society itself. It is no less certain than it is important, notwithstanding the contrary opinions which have been entertained, that the larger the society, provided it lie within a practical sphere, the more duly capable it will be of self-government. And happily for the republican cause, the practicable sphere may be carried to a very great extent, by a judicious modification and mixture of the federal principle.

Alexander Hamilton: Federalist No. 78

We proceed now to an examination of the judiciary department of the proposed government.

In unfolding the defects of the existing confederation, the utility and necessity of a federal judicature have been clearly pointed out. It is the less necessary to recapitulate the considerations there urged; as the propriety of the institution in the abstract is not disputed; the only questions which have been raised being relative to the manner of constituting it, and to its extent. To these points, therefore, our observations shall be confined.

The manner of constituting it seems to embrace these several objects: 1st. The mode of appointing the judges; 2nd. The tenure by which they are to hold their places;

3rd. The partition of the judiciary authority between courts, and their relations to each other.

First. As to the mode of appointing the judges: This is the same with that of appointing the officers of the union in general, and has been so fully discussed . . . that nothing can be said here which would not be useless repetition.

Second. As to the tenure by which the judges are to hold their places: This chiefly concerns their duration in office; the provisions for their support; the precautions for their responsibility.

According to the plan of the convention, all the judges who may be appointed by the United States are to hold their offices during good behavior; which is conformable to the most approved of the state constitutions. . . . The standard of good behavior for the continuance in office of the judicial magistracy is certainly one of the most valuable of the modern improvements in the practice of government. In a monarchy, it is an excellent barrier to the despotism of the prince; in a republic, it is a no less excellent barrier to the encroachments and oppressions of the representative body. And it is the best expedient which can be devised in any government, to secure a steady, upright, and impartial administration of the laws.

Whoever attentively considers the different departments of power must perceive, that, in a government in which they are separated from each other, the judiciary, from the nature of its functions, will always be the least dangerous to the political rights of the constitution; because it will be at least in a capacity to annoy or injure them. The executive not only dispenses the honors, but holds the sword of the community. The legislature not only commands the purse, but prescribes the rules by which the duties and rights of every citizen are to be regulated. The judiciary, on the contrary, has no influence over either the sword or the purse; no direction either of the strength or of the wealth of the society; and can take no active resolution whatever. It may truly be said to have neither force nor will, but merely judgment; and must ultimately depend upon the aid of the executive arm for the efficacious exercise even of this faculty.

This simple view of the matter suggests several important consequences: It proves incontestably, that the judiciary is beyond comparison, the weakest of the three departments of power, that it can never attack with success either of the other two: and that all possible care is requisite to enable it to defend itself against their attacks. It equally proves, that, though individual oppression may now and then proceed from the courts of justice, the general liberty of the people can never be endangered from that quarter; I mean so long as the judiciary remains truly distinct from both the legislature and executive. For I agree, that "there is no liberty, if the power of judging be not separated from the legislative and executive powers." It proves, in the last place, that as liberty can have nothing to fear from the judiciary alone, but would have everything to fear from its union with either of the other departments; that, as all the effects of such a union must ensue from a dependence of the former on the latter, notwithstanding a nominal and apparent separation; that as, from the natural feebleness of the judiciary, it is in continual jeopardy of being overpowered, awed or influenced by its coordinate branches; that, as nothing can contribute so much to its firmness and independence as permanency in office, this quality may therefore be justly regarded as an indispensable ingredient in its constitution; and, in a great measure, as the citadel of the public justice and the public security.

The complete independence of the courts of justice is peculiarly essential in a limited constitution. By a limited constitution, I understand one which contains certain specified exceptions to the legislative authority; such, for instance, as that it shall pass no bills of attainder, no ex post facto laws, and the like. Limitations of this kind can be preserved in practice no other way than through the medium of the courts of justice, whose duty it must be to declare all acts contrary to the manifest tenor of the constitution void. Without this, all the reservations of particular rights or privileges would amount to nothing.

Some perplexity respecting the right of the courts to pronounce legislative acts void, because contrary to the constitution, has arisen from an imagination that the doctrine would imply a superiority of the judiciary to the legislative power. It is urged that the authority which can declare the acts of another void, must necessarily be superior to the one whose acts may be declared void. As this doctrine is of great importance in all the American constitutions, a brief discussion of the grounds on which it rests cannot be unacceptable.

There is no position which depends on clearer principles than that every act of a delegated authority, contrary to the tenor of the commission under which it is exercised, is void. No legislative act, therefore, contrary to the constitution, can be valid. To deny this would be to affirm, that the deputy is greater then his principal; that the servant is above his master; that the representatives of the people are superior to the people themselves; that men, acting by virtue of powers, may do not only what their powers do not authorize, but what they forbid.

If it be said that the legislative body are themselves the constitutional judges of their own powers, and that the construction they put upon them is conclusive upon the other departments, it may be answered, that this cannot be the natural presumption, where it is not to be collected from any particular provisions in the constitution. It is not otherwise to be supposed that the constitution could intend to enable the representatives of the people to substitute their will to that of their constituents. It is far more rational to suppose that the courts were designed to be an intermediate body between the people and the legislature, in order, among other things, to keep the latter within the limits assigned to their authority. The interpretation of the laws is the proper and peculiar province of the courts. A constitution is, in fact, and must be, regarded by the judges as a fundamental law. It must therefore belong to them to ascertain its meaning, as well as the meaning of any particular act proceeding from the legislative body. If there should happen to be an irreconcilable variance between the two, that which has the superior obligation and validity ought, of course, to be preferred; in other words, the constitution ought to be preferred to the statute, the intention of the people to the intention of their agents.

Nor does this conclusion by any means suppose a superiority of the judicial to the legislative power. It only supposes that the power of the people is superior to both; and that where the will of the legislature declared in its statutes, stands in opposition to that of the people declared in the constitution, the judges ought to be governed by the latter, rather than the former. They ought to regulate their decisions by the fundamental laws, rather than by those which are not fundamental. . . .

It can be of no weight to say, that the courts, on the pretense of a repugnancy, may substitute their own pleasure to the constitutional intentions of the legislature. This might as well happen in the case of two contradictory statutes; or it might as well happen in every adjudication upon any single statute. The courts must declare the sense of the law; and if they should be disposed to exercise will instead of judgment, the consequence would equally be the substitution of their pleasure to that of the legislative body. The observation, if it proved anything, would prove that there ought to be no judges distinct from the body.

If then the courts of justice are to be considered as the bulwarks of a limited constitution, against legislative encroachments, this consideration will afford a strong argument for the permanent tenure of judicial officers, since nothing will contribute so much as this to that independent spirit in the judges, which must be essential to the faithful performance of so arduous a duty.

This independence of the judges is equally requisite to guard the constitution and the rights of individuals, from the effects of those ill-humors which are the arts of designing men, or the influence of particular conjunctures, sometimes disseminate among the people themselves, and which, though they speedily give place to better information, and more deliberate reflection, have a tendency, in the meantime, to occasion dangerous innovations in the government, and serious oppressions of the minor party in the community. . . . Until the people have, by some solemn and authoritative act, annulled or changed the established form, it is binding upon themselves collectively, as well as individually; and no presumption, or even knowledge of their sentiments, can warrant their representatives in a departure from it, prior to such an act. But it is easy to see, that it would require an uncommon portion of fortitude in the judges to do their duty as faithful guardians of the constitution, where legislative invasions of it had been instigated by the major voice of the community.

But it is not with a view to infractions of the constitution only, that the independence of the judges may be an

Glossary

active partisan People who identify with a party, vote in elections, and participate in additional party and party-candidate activities.

advocacy group An interest group organized to support a cause or ideology.

affirmative action Programs of private and public institutions favoring minorities and women in hiring and in admissions to colleges and universities in an attempt to compensate for past discrimination.

agenda setting Influencing what people consider important.

amicus curiae Latin for "a friend of the court"; describes a brief in which individuals not party to a suit may have their views heard.

Anti-Federalists Opponents of the Constitution during the fight over ratification.

appellate courts Courts that hear cases on appeal from other courts.

appropriation Legal authority for a federal agency to spend money from the U.S. Treasury.

Articles of Confederation The first constitution of the United States, adopted during the last stages of the Revolutionary War, created a system of government with most power lodged in the states and little in the central government.

axis of evil Three countries—Iraq, Iran, and North Korea—named by President Bush in 2002 as significant threats to the security of the United States because of their purported ties to terrorism and/or weapons of mass destruction.

balance of payments The annual difference between payments and receipts between a country and its trading partners.

beat The assigned location where a reporter regularly gathers news stories.

bias Deviation from some ideal standard, such as representativeness or objectivity.

bicameral As applied to a legislative body, consisting of two houses or chambers.

bill of attainder A governmental decree that a person is guilty of a crime that carries the death penalty, rendered without benefit of a trial.

Bill of Rights The first 10 amendments to the U.S. Constitution, concerned with basic liberties.

block grants Federal grants to the states to be used for general activities.

blog The common term for a weblog, a website on which an individual or group posts text, photos, audio files, and more, on a regular basis for others to view and respond to.

briefs Documents setting out the arguments in legal cases, prepared by attorneys and presented to courts.

budget deficit The amount by which annual government expenditures exceed revenues.

bureaucracy A large, complex organization characterized by a hierarchical set of offices, each with a specific task, controlled through a clear chain of command, and where appointment and advancement of personnel is based on merit.

bureaucrat A person who works in a bureaucratic organization.

capital crime Any crime for which death is a possible penalty.

casework Services performed by members of Congress for constituents.

categorical grants Federal aid to states and localities clearly specifying what the money can be used for.

caucus A regional, ethnic, racial or economic subgroup within the House or Senate.

caucus nominating system A system for selecting delegates to the national party conventions characterized by neighborhood and areawide meetings of party supporters and activists; used in only a handful of states.

checks and balances The constitutional principle that government power shall be divided and that the fragments should balance or check one another to prevent tyranny.

chief of staff A top adviser to the president who also manages the White House staff.

circuit courts The 12 geographical jurisdictions and one special court that hear appeals from the federal district courts.

civil disobedience Intentionally breaking a law and accepting the consequences as a way to publicize the unjustness of the law.

civil liberties Freedoms found primarily in the Bill of Rights that are protected from government interference.

civil rights Guarantees by government of equal citizenship to all social groups; guarantees of equal treatment by government officials regarding political rights, the judicial system, and public programs.

civil servants Government workers employed under the merit system; not political appointees.

civil service Federal government jobs held by civilian employees, excluding political appointees.

civil union A status in which same-sex couples have the same legal rights, benefits, and protections as married couples.

Civil War Amendments The Thirteenth, Fourteenth, and Fifteenth Amendments to the Constitution adopted immediately after the Civil War.

class action suit A suit brought on behalf of a group of people who are in a situation similar to that of the plaintiffs.

cloture A vote to end a filibuster or a debate; requires the votes of three-fifths of the membership of the Senate.

Cold War The period of tense relations between the United States and the Soviet Union from the late 1940s to the late 1980s.

collective public opinion The political attitudes of the public as a whole, expressed as averages, percentages, or other summaries of many individuals' opinions.

concurring opinion The opinion of one or more judges who vote with the majority on a case but wish to set out different reasons for their decision.

conditions Provisions in federal assistance requiring that state and local governments follow certain policies in order to obtain federal funds.

confederation A loose association of states or territorial units formed for a common purpose or in which very little power is lodged in the central government.

conference committees Ad hoc committees, made up of members of both the Senate and the House of Representatives, set up to reconcile differences in the provisions of bills.

Connecticut Compromise Also called the *Great Compromise;* the compromise between the New Jersey and Virginia plans formulated by the Connecticut delegates at the Constitutional Convention; called for a lower legislative house based on population size and an upper house based on equal representation of the states.

conservative The political position that holds that the federal government ought to play a very small role in economic regulation, social welfare, and overcoming racial inequality.

constituency The district of a legislator.

constituent A citizen who lives in the district of an elected official.

constitution The basic framework of law that prescribes how government is to operate.

constitutional courts Federal courts created by Congress under the authority of Article III of the Constitution.

contract clause The portion of Article I, Section 10, of the Constitution that prohibits states from passing any law "impairing the obligations of contracts."

convention A gathering of delegates who nominate a party's presidential candidate.

conventional participation Political activity related to elections (voting, persuading, and campaigning) or to contacting public officials.

cooperative federalism Federalism in which the powers of the states and the national government are so intertwined that public policies can happen only if the two levels of government cooperate.

core beliefs Individual's views about the fundamental nature of human beings, society, and economy; taken together, they comprise the political culture.

cost-benefit analysis A method of evaluating rules and regulations by weighing their potential costs against their potential benefits to society.

Council of Economic Advisers (CEA) An organization in the Executive Office of the President made up of a small group of economists who advise on economic policy.

dealignment A gradual reduction in the dominance of one political party without another party supplanting it.

delegate According to the doctrine articulated by Edmund Burke, an elected representative who acts in perfect accord with the wishes of his or her constituents.

democracy A system of rule by the people, defined by the existence of popular sovereignty, political equality, and political liberty.

depression A severe and persistent drop in economic activity.

deregulation The process of diminishing regulatory requirements for business.

descriptive representation Sometimes called *statistical representation;* means that the composition of a representative body reflects the demographic composition of the population as a whole.

devolution The delegation of power by the central government to state or local bodies.

direct democracy A form of political decision making in which the public business is decided by all citizens meeting in small assemblies.

discharge petition A petition signed by 218 House members to force a bill that has been before a committee for at least 30 days while the House is in session out of the committee and onto the floor for consideration.

discount rate The interest rate the Federal Reserve charges member banks to cover short-term loans.

dissenting opinion The opinion of the judge or judges who are in the minority on a particular case before the Supreme Court.

disturbance theory A theory that locates the origins of interest groups in changes in the economic, social, or political environment that threaten the well-being of some segment of the population.

divided government Control of the executive and legislative branches by different political parties.

dual federalism Federalism in which the powers of the states and the national government are neatly separated like the sections of a layer cake; also an interpretation of federalism in which the states and the national government have separate jurisdictions and responsibilities.

due process clause The section of the Fourteenth Amendment that prohibits states from depriving anyone of life, liberty, or property "without due process of law," a guarantee against arbitrary or unfair government action.

ear-marking Practice of appropriating money for specific pet projects of members of Congress.

economic conservatives People who favor private enterprise and oppose government regulations on spending.

economic liberals People who favor government regulation of business and government spending for social programs.

economic liberty The right to own and use property free from excessive government interference.

elastic clause Article I, Section 8, of the Constitution, also called the *necessary and proper clause;* gives Congress the authority to make whatever laws are necessary and proper to carry out its enumerated responsibilities.

electoral college Elected representatives of the states whose votes formally elect the president; the number of electors in each state is equal to the total number of its senators and representatives in the House.

electoral competition model A form of election in which parties seeking votes move toward the median voter or the center of the political spectrum.

electoral reward and punishment The tendency to vote for the incumbents when times are good and against them when times are bad.

electors Representatives who are elected in the states to formally choose the U.S. president.

entitlements Government benefits that are distributed automatically to citizens who qualify on the basis of a set of guidelines set by law; for example, Americans over the age of 65 are entitled to Medicare coverage.

enumerated powers Powers of the federal government specifically mentioned in the Constitution.

equal protection clause The section of the Fourteenth Amendment that provides equal protection of the laws to all citizens.

Equal Rights Amendment (ERA) Proposed amendment to the U.S. Constitution stating that equality of rights shall not be abridged or denied on account of a person's gender.

equal time provision The former requirement that television stations give or sell the same amount of time to all competing candidates.

establishment clause The part of the First Amendment to the Constitution that prohibits Congress from establishing an official religion; the basis for the doctrine of the separation of church and state.

European Union (EU) A common market formed by western European nations, with free trade and free population movement among them.

exclusionary rule A standard promulgated by the Supreme Court that prevents police and prosecutors from using evidence against a defendant that was obtained in an illegal search.

executive agreement An agreement with another country signed by the president that has the force of law, like a treaty; does not require Senate approval; originally used for minor technical matters, now an important tool of presidential power in foreign affairs.

Executive Office of the President (EOP) A group of organizations that advise the president on a wide range of issues; includes the Office of Management and Budget, the National Security Council, and the Council of Economic Advisers.

executive order A rule or regulation issued by the president that has the force of law, based either on the constitutional powers of the presidency or on congressional statutes.

executive privilege A presidential claim that certain communications with subordinates may be withheld from Congress and the courts.

ex post facto law A law that retroactively declares some action illegal.

externalities The positive and negative effects of economic activities on third parties.

faction Madison's term for groups or parties that try to advance their own interests at the expense of the public good.

fairness doctrine The former requirement that television stations present contrasting points of view.

federal Describing a system in which significant governmental powers are divided between a central government and smaller territorial units, such as states.

federal bureaucracy The totality of the departments and agencies of the executive branch of the national government.

federalism A system in which significant governmental powers are divided between a central government and smaller units, such as states.

Federalists Proponents of the Constitution during the ratification fight; also the political party of Hamilton, Washington, and Adams.

filibuster A parliamentary device used in the Senate to prevent a bill from coming to a vote by "talking it to death," made possible by the norm of unlimited debate.

fiscal policy Government efforts to affect overall output and incomes in the economy through spending and taxing policies.

framing Providing a context for interpretation.

franchise The right to vote.

franking privilege Public subsidization of mail from the members of Congress to their constituents.

free exercise clause That portion of the First Amendment to the Constitution that prohibits Congress from impeding religious observance or impinging upon religious beliefs.

free rider One who gains a benefit without contributing; explains why it is so difficult to form social movements and noneconomic interest groups.

General Agreement on Tariffs and Trade (GATT) An international agreement that requires the lowering of tariffs and other barriers to free trade.

general revenue sharing Federal aid to the states without any conditions on how the money is to be spent.

gerrymandering Redrawing electoral district lines to give an advantage to a particular party or candidate.

globalization The increasing worldwide integration of markets, production, and communications across national boundaries.

global warming The rise of mean global temperatures whether caused by human activities or naturally occurring cycles.

grand juries Groups of citizens who decide whether there is sufficient evidence to bring an indictment against accused persons.

grandfather clause A device that allowed whites who had failed the literacy test to vote anyway by extending the franchise to anyone whose ancestors had voted prior to 1867.

grants-in-aid Funds from the national government to state and local governments to help pay for programs created by the national government.

grassroots The constituents, voters, or rank-and-file of a party.

Great Depression The period of economic crisis in the United States that lasted from the stock market crash of 1929 to America's entry into World War II.

gross domestic product (GDP) Monetary value of all goods and services produced in a nation each year, excluding income residents earn abroad.

habeas corpus The legal doctrine that a person who is arrested must have a timely hearing before a judge.

hard money Regulated campaign contributions to candidate and party committees, as well as to political action committees.

hearings The taking of testimony by a congressional committee or subcommittee.

hegemon Term used to refer to the dominant power during various historical periods that takes on responsibilities maintaining and protecting a regional or global system.

hopper The box in the House of Representatives in which proposed bills are placed.

horizontal federalism Term used to refer to relationships among the states.

impeachment House action bringing formal charges against a member of the executive branch on the federal judiciary that may or may not lead to removal from office by the Senate.

incorporation The process by which the Supreme Court has made most of the provisions of the Bill of Rights binding on the states. See *nationalizing*.

inflation A condition of rising prices and reduced purchasing power.

in forma pauperis Describing a process by which indigents may file a suit with the Supreme Court free of charge.

infotainment The merging of hard news and entertainment in news presentations.

initiatives Procedures available in some states for citizens to put proposed laws and constitutional amendment on the ballot for voter approval or rejection.

institutional presidency The permanent bureaucracy associated with the presidency, designed to help the incumbent of the office carry out his responsibilities.

integration Policies encouraging the interaction between different races in schools or public facilities.

interest group A private voluntary association that seeks to influence public policy as a way to protect or advance some interest.

intermediate scrutiny A legal test falling between ordinary and strict scrutiny relevant to issues of gender; under this test, the Supreme Court will allow gender classifications in laws if they are *substantially* related to an *important* government objective.

interstate compacts Agreements among states to cooperate on solving mutual problems; requires approval by Congress.

iron triangle An enduring alliance of common interest among an interest group, a congressional committee, and a bureaucratic agency.

Jim Crow Popular term for the system of legally sanctioned racial segregation that existed in the American South until the middle of the twentieth century.

Joint Chiefs of Staff (JCS) The military officers in charge of each of the armed services.

joint committees Congressional committees with members from both the House and the Senate.

judicial activism Actions by the courts that go beyond the strict role of the judiciary as interpreter of the law and adjudicator of disputes.

judicial review The power of the Supreme Court to declare actions of the other branches and levels of government unconstitutional.

laissez-faire The political-economic doctrine that holds that government ought not interfere with the operations of the free market.

leak, news Inside or secret information given to a journalist or media outlet by a government official.

legislative courts Highly specialized federal courts created by Congress under the authority of Article I of the Constitution.

liberal The political position that holds that the federal government has a substantial role to play in economic regulation, social welfare, and overcoming racial inequality.

literacy test A device used by the southern states to prevent African Americans from voting before the passage of the Voting Rights Act of 1965, which banned its use; usually involved interpretation of a section of a state's constitution.

lobby An interest or pressure group that seeks to convey the group's interest to government decision makers; also, an action by a group or association to influence the behavior of a public official.

macroeconomic policy Policy that has to do with the performance of the economy as a whole.

majority-minority districts Districts drawn to ensure that a racial minority makes up the majority of voters.

majority rule The form of political decision making in which policies are decided on the basis of what a majority of the people want.

majority tyranny Suppression of the rights and liberties of a minority by the majority.

mandate A formal order from the national government that the states carry out certain policies.

markup   The process of revising a bill in committee.

mass mobilization   The process of involving large numbers of people in a social movement.

means-tested   Meeting the criterion of demonstrable need.

median household income   Household income number at which one-half of all households have more income and one-half have less income; the midpoint of all households ranked by income.

median voter   Refers to the voter at the exact middle of the political spectrum.

monetary policy   Government efforts to affect the supply of money and the level of interest rates in the economy.

multilateralist   The stance toward foreign policy that suggests that the United States should seek the cooperation of other nations and multilateral institutions in pursuing its goals; also those who believe the United States should use its military and diplomatic power in the world in cooperation with other nations and international organizations.

national debt   The total outstanding debt of the federal government; the sum total of all annual budget deficits and surpluses.

national interest   What is of benefit to the nation as a whole.

national security adviser   A top foreign policy and defense adviser to the president who heads the National Security Council.

National Security Council (NSC)   An organization in the Executive Office of the President made up of officials from the State and Defense Departments, the CIA, and the military, who advise on foreign and security affairs.

nationalist position   The view of American federalism that holds that the Constitution created a system in which the national government is supreme, relative to the states, and that granted to it a broad range of powers and responsibilities.

nationalizing   The process by which provisions of the Bill of Rights become incorporated. See *incorporation.*

nativist   Antiforeign; applied to political movements active in the nineteenth century.

necessary and proper clause   Article I, Section 8, of the Constitution, also known as the *elastic clause;* gives Congress the authority to make whatever laws are necessary and proper to carry out its enumerated responsibilities.

New Deal   The programs of the administration of President Franklin D. Roosevelt.

New Deal coalition   The informal electoral alliance of working-class ethnic groups, Catholics, Jews, urban dwellers, racial minorities, and the South that was the basis of the Democratic party dominance of American politics from the New Deal to the early 1970s.

New Jersey Plan   Proposal of the smaller states at the Constitutional Convention to create a government based on the equal representation of the states in a unicameral legislature.

newsworthy   Worth printing or broadcasting as news, according to editors' judgments.

nongovernmental organization (NGO)   A nonprofit advocacy group that tries to influence the public, national governments, and/or international organizations on issues of concern to it.

normal vote   The proportion of the votes that each party would win if party identification alone affected voting decisions.

North American Free Trade Agreement (NAFTA)   An agreement among the United States, Canada, and Mexico to eliminate nearly all barriers to trade and investment among the three countries.

nuclear proliferation   The spread of nuclear weapons to additional countries or to terrorist groups.

nullification   An attempt by states to declare national laws or actions null and void.

objective journalism   News reported with no evaluative language and with any opinions quoted or attributed to a specific source.

obscenity   As defined by the Supreme Court, the representation of sexually explicit material in a manner that violates community standards and is without redeeming social importance or value.

Office of Management and Budget (OMB)   An organization within the Executive Office of the President that advises on the federal budget, domestic legislation, and regulations.

open-seat election   An election in which there is no incumbent officeholder.

opinion   The explanation of the majority's reasoning that accompanies a court decision.

opinion of the Court   The majority opinion that accompanies a Supreme Court decision.

ordinary scrutiny   The assumption that the actions of elected bodies and officials are legal under the Constitution.

original intent   The doctrine that the courts must interpret the Constitution in ways consistent with the intentions of the framers rather than in light of contemporary conditions and needs.

original jurisdiction   The authority of a court to be the first to hear a particular kind of case.

oversight   Congressional responsibility for monitoring the actions of executive branch agencies and personnel to ensure conformity to federal statutes and congressional intent.

parliamentary system   A system of government in which authority is lodged in a legislative body (the parliament) that chooses, usually from within its own ranks, a prime minister and a cabinet to run the day-to-day affairs of state.

participation   Political activity, including voting, campaign activity, contacting officials, and demonstrating.

partisan   A committed member of a party; seeing issues from the point of view of the interests of a single party.

party conference   An organization of the members of a political party in the House or Senate.

party identification   The sense of belonging to one or another political party.

party platform   A party's statement of its positions on the issues of the day.

patronage   The practice of distributing government offices and contracts to the supporters of the winning party; also called the *spoils system*.

petit (trial) juries   Juries that hear evidence and sit in judgment on charges brought in civil or criminal cases.

plaintiff   One who brings suit in a court.

pluralist   A political scientist who views American politics as best understood in terms of the interaction, conflict, and bargaining of groups.

plurality   More votes than any other candidate but less than a majority of all votes cast.

pocket veto   Rejection of a bill if the president takes no action on it for 10 days and Congress has adjourned during that period.

podcast   Audio and visual digital files created for distribution over the Internet for use on personal computers and mobile devices.

policy preferences   Citizens' preferences concerning what policies they want government to pursue.

political action committee (PAC)   An entity created by an interest group whose purpose is to collect money and make contributions to candidates in federal elections.

political attitudes   Individual's views about public policies, political parties, candidates, government institutions, and public officials.

political efficacy   The sense that an individual can affect what government does.

political equality   The principle that says that each person carries equal weight in the conduct of the public business.

political ideology   A system of interrelated and coherently patterned beliefs and attitudes.

political liberty   The principle that citizens in a democracy are protected from government interference in the exercise of a range of basic freedoms, such as the freedoms of speech, association, and conscience.

political party   An organization that tries to win control of government by electing people to office who carry the party label.

political socialization   The process by which individuals come to have certain core beliefs and political attitudes.

poll tax   A tax to be paid as a condition of voting; used in the South to keep African Americans away from the polls.

popular sovereignty   The basic principle of democracy that the people ultimately rule.

pork   Also called *pork barrel;* projects designed to bring to the constituency jobs and public money for which the members of Congress can claim credit.

poverty line   The federal government's calculation of the amount of income families of various sizes need to stay out of poverty.

precedents   Rulings by courts that guide judicial reasoning in subsequent cases.

preemption   Exclusion of the states from actions that might interfere with federal authority or statutes.

presidential approval rating   A president's standing with the public, indicated by the percentage of Americans who tell survey interviewers that they approve a president's "handling of his job."

presidential popularity   The percentage of Americans who approve a president's handling of his job.

pressure group   An interest group or lobby; an association that brings pressure to bear on government decision makers.

primary election   Statewide elections in which voters choose delegates to the national party conventions; virtually all delegates are pledged to a specific candidate for the party's nomination.

prior restraint   The government's power to prevent publication, as opposed to punishment afterward.

private interest association   An interest group that seeks to protect or advance the material interests of its members.

privatization   The process of turning over certain government functions to the private sector.

privileges and immunities clause   The portion of Article IV, Section 2, of the Constitution that states that citizens from out of state have the same legal rights as local citizens in any state.

probable cause   legal doctrine that refers to a reasonable belief that a crime has been committed.

proportional representation   The awarding of legislative seats to political parties to reflect the proportion of the popular vote each party receives.

prospective voting model   A theory of democratic elections in which voters decide what government will do in the near future by choosing one or another responsible party.

provisional ballot   A vote that is cast but not counted until determination is made that the voter is properly registered.

public interest association   An interest group that advocates for a cause or an ideology.

public opinion   Political attitudes and core beliefs expressed by ordinary citizens as revealed by surveys.

pundits   Somewhat derisive term for print, broadcast, and radio commentators on the political news.

random sampling   The selection of survey respondents by chance, with equal probability, to ensure their representativeness of the whole population.

ranking minority member   The highest ranking member of the minority party on a congressional committee.

realignment   The process by which one party supplants another as the dominant party in a political system.

reapportionment   The reallocation of House seats among the states, done after each national census, to ensure that seats are held by the states in proportion to the size of their populations.

reciprocity Deferral by members of Congress to the judgment of subject-matter specialists, mainly on minor technical bills.

redistricting The redrawing of congressional district lines within a state to ensure roughly equal populations within each district.

red tape Overbearing bureaucratic rules and procedures.

referenda Procedures available in some states by which proposed state laws or constitutional amendments are submitted to the voters for approval or rejection.

regulations The issuing of rules by government agencies with the aim of reducing the scale of negative externalities produced by private firms.

remedy An action that a court determines must be taken to rectify a wrong.

representative democracy Indirect democracy, in which the people rule through elected representatives.

republicanism, eighteenth century A political doctrine advocating limited government based on popular consent, protected against majority tyranny.

reservation clause The Tenth Amendment to the Constitution, reserving powers to the states or the people.

responsible party A political party that takes clear, distinct stands on the issues and enacts them as policy when in office.

retrospective voting A form of election in which voters look back at the performance of a party in power and cast ballots on the basis of how well it did in office.

rule of four An *unwritten* practice that requires at least four justices of the Supreme Court to agree that a case warrants review by the Court before it will hear the case.

sample survey An interview study asking questions of a set of people who are chosen as representative of the whole population.

scope of conflict The number of groups involved in a political conflict; few groups mean a narrow scope of conflict, and many groups mean a wide scope of conflict.

secularization The spread of nonreligious values and outlooks.

select committees Temporary committees in Congress created to conduct studies or investigations; they have no power to report bills.

selective incorporation The gradual and piecemeal incorporation of the protections of the Bill of Rights by the U.S. Supreme Court.

senatorial courtesy The tradition that judicial nominations for federal district court appointments be cleared by the senior senator of the president's party from the relevant state.

seniority Length of service.

separate but equal doctrine The principle articulated in *Plessy* v. *Ferguson* (1896) that laws prescribing *separate* public facilities and services for nonwhite Americans are permissible if the facilities and services are *equal* to those provided for whites.

separation of powers The distribution of government legislative, executive, and judicial powers to separate branches of government.

sit-down strike A form of labor action in which workers stop production but do not leave their job site.

social contract A philosophical device, used by Enlightenment thinkers such as Locke, Rousseau, and Harrington, to suggest that governments are only legitimate if they are created by a voluntary compact among the people.

social insurance Government programs that provide services or income support in proportion to the amount of mandatory contributions made by individuals to a government trust fund.

social (lifestyle) conservatives People who favor traditional social values; they tend to support strong law-and-order measures and oppose abortion and gay rights.

social (lifestyle) liberals People who favor civil liberties, abortion rights, and alternative lifestyles.

soft money Unregulated expenditures by political parties on general public education, voter registration, and voter mobilization; often used to indirectly influence campaigns for elective office, until banned after 2002.

soft power Influence in world affairs that derives from the attractiveness to others of a nation's culture, products, and way of life.

spoils system The practice of distributing government offices and contracts to the supporters of the winning party; also called *patronage*.

standing Authority to bring legal action because one is directly affected by the issues at hand.

standing committees Relatively permanent congressional committees that address specific areas of legislation.

stare decisis The legal doctrine that says precedent should guide judicial decision making.

states' rights position The view of American federalism that holds that the Constitution created a system of dual sovereignty in which the national government and the state governments are sovereign in their own spheres.

stay acts Enactments postponing the collection of taxes or mortgage payments.

strict construction The doctrine that the provisions of the Constitution have a clear meaning and that judges must stick closely to this meaning when rendering decisions.

strict scrutiny The assumption that actions by elected bodies or officials violate constitutional rights.

suffrage The right to vote.

Sun Belt States of the Lower South, Southwest, and West, where sunny weather and often conservative politics prevail.

superpower A nation armed with nuclear weapons and able to project force anywhere on the globe.

supremacy clause The provision in Article VI of the Constitution that states that the Constitution and the laws and treaties of the United States are the supreme law of the land, taking precedence over state laws and constitutions.

suspect classification The invidious, arbitrary, or irrational designation of a group for special treatment by government.

terrorism The use of deadly violence against civilians to further some political goal.

test case A case brought to force a ruling on the constitutionality of some law or executive action.

trustee According to the doctrine articulated by Edmund Burke, an elected representative who believes that his or her own best judgment, rather than instructions from constituents, should be used in making legislative decisions.

trusts Large combinations of business corporations.

turnout The proportion of eligible voters who actually vote in a given election.

tyranny The abuse of power by a ruler or a government.

unanimous consent Legislative action taken "without objection" as a way to expedite business; used to conduct much of the business of the Senate.

unconventional participation Political activity in the form of demonstrations or protests.

unified government Control of the executive and legislative branches by the same political party.

unilateralist The stance toward foreign policy that suggests that the United States should "go it alone," pursuing its national interests without seeking the cooperation of other nations or multilateral institutions; also those who believe the United States should vigorously use its military and diplomatic power to pursue American national interests in the world, but on a "go it alone" basis.

unitary system A system in which a central government has complete power over its constituent units or states.

veto Presidential disapproval of a bill that has been passed by both houses of Congress. The president's veto can be overridden by a two-thirds vote in each house.

Virginia Plan Proposal by the large states at the Constitutional Convention to create a strong central government with power in the government apportioned to the states on the basis of population.

watchdog The role of the media in scrutinizing the actions of government officials.

weapons of mass destruction Nuclear, biological, or chemical weapons with the potential to cause vast harm to human populations.

welfare state The set of government programs that protects the minimum standard of living of families and individuals against loss of income.

whip A political party member in Congress charged with keeping members informed of the plans of the party leadership, counting votes before action on important issues, and rounding up party members for votes on bills.

whistle-blowers People who bring official misconduct in their agencies to public attention.

white-collar worker A person working at a service, sales, or office job.

white primaries Primary elections open only to whites.

World Trade Organization (WTO) An agency designed to enforce the provisions of the General Agreement on Tariffs and Trade and to resolve trade disputes between nations.

writ of certiorari An announcement that the Supreme Court will hear a case on appeal from a lower court; its issuance requires the vote of four of the nine justices.

writ of mandamus A court order that forces an official to act.

yellow journalism Sensational newspaper stories with large headlines and, in some cases, color cartoons.

Endnotes

CHAPTER 1

1. William H. Chafe, *The Unfinished Journey: America Since World War II* (New York: Oxford University Press, 1986), p. 304; Howard Zinn, *SNCC: The New Abolitionists* (Boston: Beacon Press, 1964), p. 64.

2. Chafe, *Unfinished Journey,* p. 305.

3. See summary of polls at Latinobarometro at **www.latinobarometro.org,** Asiabarometer at **http://avatoli.ioc.utokyo.ac.jp/~asiabarometer,** and the Pew Center for the People and the Press at **www.pewresearch.org.**

4. For a fuller treatment of the claims in this paragraph, as well as supporting evidence for them, see Robert A. Dahl, *Democracy and Its Critics* (New Haven, CT: Yale University Press, 1989); and Robert A. Dahl, *On Democracy* (New Haven, CT: Yale University Press, 1998). Also see Benjamin Radcliff, "Politics, Markets, and Life Satisfaction: The Political Economy of Human Happiness," *American Political Science Review,* 95 (December 2001), pp. 939–952.

5. Robert A. Dahl, "James Madison: Republican or Democrat?" *Perspectives on Politics,* 3, No. 3 (September 2005), pp. 439–448.

6. John Dewey, *The Public and Its Problems* (New York: Holt, 1927).

7. Dahl, *Democracy and Its Critics,* p. 13; Dahl, "James Madison: Republican or Democrat?"

8. Amartya Sen, *The Argumentative Indian: Writings on Indian History, Culture, and Identity* (New York: Farrar, Straus, and Giroux, 2005).

9. See Robert A. Dahl, *After the Revolution: Authority in the Good Society* (New Haven, CT: Yale University Press, 1970); Dahl, *Democracy and Its Critics;* Jane Mansbridge, *Beyond Adversary Democracy* (New York: Basic Books, 1980).

10. See Benjamin Barber, *Strong Democracy: Participatory Democracy for a New Age* (Berkeley, CA: University of California Press, 1984); Peter Bachrach, *The Theory of Democratic Elitism* (Boston: Little, Brown, 1967); Robert A. Dahl, *A Preface to Economic Democracy* (Berkeley, CA: University of California Press, 1985); Edward S. Greenberg, "Spillovers from Cooperative and Democratic Workplaces," in Brandon Sullivan and John Sullivan, eds., *Cooperation as the Basis of Individual and Group Functioning* (Minneapolis: University of Minnesota Press, 2006); Edward S. Greenberg, *Workplace Democracy: The Political Effects of Participation* (Ithaca, NY: Cornell University Press, 1986); C. B. MacPherson, *Democratic Theory: Essays in Retrieval* (Oxford, U.K.: Clarendon Press, 1973); Carole Pateman, *Participation and Democratic Theory* (London: Cambridge University Press, 1970).

11. Esther Dyson, *Release 2.0* (New York: Broadway Books, 1997); Lawrence K. Grossman, *The Electronic Republic: Reshaping Democracy in the Information Age* (New York: Viking Press, 1995).

12. On deliberation and democracy, see Jason Barabas, "How Deliberation Affects Policy Opinions," *American Political Science Review,* 98 (2004), pp. 687–701; Seyla Benhabib, "Toward a Deliberative Model of Democratic Legitimacy," in Seyla Benhabib, ed., *Democracy and Difference* (Princeton, NJ: Princeton University Press, 1996); John Dryzek, *Deliberative Democracy and Beyond: Liberals, Critics, Contestations* (Oxford: Oxford University Press, 2000); Nancy Fraser, "Rethinking the Public Sphere," in Craig Calhoun, ed., *Habermas and the Public Sphere* (New Brunswick, NJ: Rutgers University Press, 1992), pp. 109–142; Amy Guttman and Dennis Thompson, *Democracy and Disagreement* (Cambridge, U.K.: Belknap Press, 1996); Jurgen Habermas, *The Structural Transformation of the Public Sphere* (Cambridge, MA: MIT Press, 1989).

13. Kenneth May, "A Set of Independent, Necessary, and Sufficient Conditions for Simple Majority Decision," *Econometrical,* 20 (1952), pp. 680–684, shows that only majority rule can guarantee popular sovereignty, political equality, and neutrality among policy alternatives. See also Douglas W. Rae, "Decision Rules and Individual Values in Constitutional Choice," *American Political Science Review,* 63 (1969), pp. 40–53; Phillip D. Straffin, Jr., "Majority Rule and General Decision Rules," *Theory and Decision,* 8 (1977), pp. 351–360. On the other hand, Hans Gersbach argues in *Designing Democracy* (New York: Springer Publishers, 2005) that larger majorities ought to be required for more important decisions.

14. For a review of contemporary research on this issue, see Seymour Martin Lipset and Jason M. Lakin, *The Democratic Century* (Norman, OK: University of Oklahoma Press, 2004), ch. 5.

15. Dahl, A *Preface to Economic Democracy,* p. 68.

16. Robert A. Dahl, "On Removing Certain Impediments to Democracy in the United States," *Political Science Quarterly,* 92, no. 1 (Spring 1977), p. 14; Elaine Spitz, *Majority Rule* (Chatham, NJ: Chatham House, 1984), p. 83; Dahl, *Democracy and Its Critics,* p. 170.

17. See Marc Plattner, "Liberalism and Democracy," *Foreign Affairs* (March–April 1998), pp. 171–180.

18. David Caute, *The Great Fear* (New York: Simon & Schuster, 1978); Victor Navasky, *Naming Names* (New York: Viking, 1980); Michael Rogin, *The Intellectuals and McCarthy* (Cambridge, MA: MIT Press, 1967).

19. Fareed Zakaria, *The Future of Freedom: Illiberal Democracy at Home and Abroad* (New York: Norton, 2004).

20. See Bernard R. Berelson, Paul F. Lazarsfeld, and William N. McPhee, *Voting* (Chicago: University of Chicago Press, 1954); V. O. Key, Jr., *Public Opinion and American Democracy* (New York: Knopf, 1961); Herbert McClosky and Alida Brill, *Dimensions of Tolerance* (New York: Russell Sage Foundation, 1983); Robert Weissberg, *Polling, Policy, and Public Opinion: The Case Against Heeding the Voice of the People* (New York: Palgrave Press,

MacMillan, 2003); and Robert Weissberg, "Politicized Pseudo-Science," *PS* (January, 2006), pp. 39–42. But see, in rebuttal, James L. Gibson, "Political Intolerance and Political Repression During the McCarthy Red Scare," *American Political Science Review,* 82 (1988), pp. 511–529; Benjamin I. Page and Robert Y. Shapiro, *The Rational Public: Fifty Years of Trends in Americans' Policy Preferences* (Chicago: University of Chicago Press, 1992). See a summary of the debate and the supporting evidence in Carroll J. Glynn et al., *Public Opinion* (Boulder, CO: Westview Press, 1999).

21. Katherine Brandt, "Madisonian Majority Tyranny, Minority Rights, and American Democracy," paper presented at the annual meeting of the Midwest Political Science Association (April 2004).

22. Dahl, *Democracy and Its Critics,* p. 161.

23. Thanks to Professor Larry Martinez of the California State University, Long Beach for this insight.

24. Philip A. Klinkner with Rogers M. Smith, *The Unsteady March: The Rise and Decline of Racial Equality in America* (Chicago: The University of Chicago Press, 1999).

CHAPTER 2

1. Page Smith, A *People's History of the Young Republic: Vol. 3. The Shaping of America* (New York: McGraw-Hill, 1980), p. 25.

2. Quoted in Jackson Turner Main, *The Anti-Federalists* (Chapel Hill, NC: University of North Carolina Press, 1961), p. 62.

3. Richard Bushman, "Revolution," in Eric Foner and John A. Garraty, eds., *The Reader's Companion to American History* (Boston: Houghton Mifflin, 1991), p. 936; Gordon S. Wood, *The Creation of the American Republic* (New York: Norton, 1972), p. 12.

4. Joseph J. Ellis, *Founding Brothers: The Revolutionary Generation* (New York: Alfred A. Knopf, 2001), pp. 212–213.

5. Sarah M. Evans, *Born for Liberty: A History of Women in America* (New York: Free Press, 1997); John Hope Franklin and Alfred A. Moss, Jr., *From Slavery to Freedom* (New York: Knopf, 1967).

6. See Hannah Arendt, *On Revolution* (New York: Viking, 1965).

7. Smith, *Shaping of America,* pp. 8–9.

8. Richard Hofstadter, *The American Political Tradition* (New York: Vintage Books, 1948), p. 4.

9. Alexander Hamilton, James Madison, and John Jay, *The Federalist Papers,* ed. Clinton Rossiter (New York: New American Library, 1961), No. 10. (Originally published 1787–1788.)

10. See Gordon S. Wood, *The Radicalism of the American Revolution* (New York: Knopf, 1992).

11. Wood, *Creation of the American Republic,* pp. 311–318.

12. Ibid., ch. 8.

13. Samuel Elliot Morison, *The Oxford History of the American People* (New York: Oxford University Press, 1965), p. 274.

14. See Wood, *Creation of the American Republic,* p. 400.

15. David Brian Robertson, "Madison's Opponents and Constitutional Design," *American Political Science Review,* 99 (May 2006), pp. 225–243.

16. Melvin I. Urofsky, *A March of Liberty* (New York: Knopf, 1988), p. 89.

17. Quoted in *The Washington Post* (May 7, 1987). Also see Lee Epstein and Thomas G. Walker, *Constitutional Law for a Changing America* (Washington, D.C.: CQ Press, 2000), p. 6.

18. Charles Beard, *An Economic Interpretation of the Constitution* (New York: Macmillan, 1913). For a more recent work broadly supporting Beard's interpretation, see Robert A. McGuire, *To Form a More Perfect Union: A New Economic Interpretation of the United States Constitution* (New York: Oxford University Press, 2003).

19. See Robert Brown, *Charles Beard and the Constitution* (Princeton, NJ: Princeton University Press, 1956); Hofstadter, *The American Political Tradition;* Leonard Levy, *Constitutional Opinions* (New York: Oxford University Press, 1986); Robert A. McGuire and Robert L. Ohsfeldt, "An Economic Model of Voting Behavior over Specific Issues at the Constitutional Convention of 1787," *Journal of Economic History,* 66 (March 1986), pp. 79–111; James A. Morone, *The Democratic Wish* (New York: Basic Books, 1990); Forrest McDonald, *We the People: The Economic Origins of the Constitution* (Chicago: University of Chicago Press, 1958); Gordon S. Wood, *The Convention and the Constitution* (New York: St. Martin's Press, 1965); Wood, *Creation of the American Republic.*

20. Quoted in Wood, *Creation of the American Republic,* p. 473.

21. Ibid., p. 432.

22. Charles Stewart, "Congress and the Constitutional System," in Paul J. Quirk and Sarah A. Binder, eds., *The Legislative Branch* (New York: Oxford University Press, Institutions of American Democracy Series, 2005).

23. See Robertson, "Madison's Opponents and Constitutional Design," for more information on how the Great Compromise shaped the Constitution as a whole.

24. Ellis, *Founding Brothers,* p. 110.

25. Max Farrand, *The Records of the Federal Convention of 1787* (New Haven, CT: Yale University Press, 1937).

26. "The Invention of Centralized Federalism," in William H. Riker, ed., *The Development of Centralized Federalism* (Boston: Kluwer Academic, 1987).

27. Robert A. Dahl, "On Removing the Impediments to Democracy in the United States," *Political Science Quarterly,* 92 (Spring 1977), p. 5.

28. Hamilton, Madison, and Jay, *The Federalist Papers,* No. 51.

29. Thomas Jefferson, *Notes on the State of Virginia,* ed. Thomas Perkins Abernathy (New York: Harper & Row, 1964), p. 120.

30. See Main, *The Anti-Federalists;* Wood, *Creation of the American Republic;* Smith, *Shaping of America,* p. 99; Herbert Storing, *What the Anti-Federalists Were For* (Chicago: University of Chicago Press, 1981), p. 71; and Robertson, "Madison's Opponents and Constitutional Design."

31. Sven H. Steinmo, "American Exceptionalism Reconsidered: Culture or Institutions," in Lawrence C. Dodd and Calvin Jillson, eds., *The Dynamics of American Politics: Approaches and Interpretations* (Boulder, CO: Westview Press, 1994); Charles Noble, *The Collapse of Liberalism: Why America Needs a New Left* (Lanham, MD: Rowman and Littlefield, 2004), ch. 2.

32. Seymour Martin Lipset and Jason M. Lakin, *The Democratic Century* (Norman, OK: The University of Oklahoma Press, 2004), ch. 2.

CHAPTER 3

1. Material for this story is from "After the Flood," *The Economist* (September 3, 2005), pp. 27–31; "When Government Fails," *The Economist* (September 10, 2005), pp. 26–28; Bob Williams, "Blame Amid the Tragedy," *The Wall Street Journal* (September 6, 2005), p. A23; Eric Lipton, Christopher Drew, Scott Shane, and Dave Rohde, "Breakdowns Marked Path from Hurricane to Anarchy," *The New York Times* (September 11, 2005), p. A1.

2. William H. Riker, *The Development of American Federalism* (Boston: Kluwer Academic, 1987), pp. 56–60.

3. Daniel J. Elazar, *Federal Systems of the World: A Handbook of Federal, Confederal and Autonomy Arrangements* (Jerusalem: Jerusalem Center for Public Affairs, Online, **www.jcpa.org/dje/books/fedsysworld-intro.htm,** October 2005), p. 5.

4. Rodney Hero, *Faces of Inequality: Social Diversity in American Politics* (New York: Oxford University Press, 1998).

5. The study of the complex constitutional, legal, fiscal, and political links between states and the national government is often called the study of *intergovernmental relations* (the ever-changing constitutional, legal, fiscal, and political linkages among the states and the national government). For more on this, see B. G. Peters and J. Pierre, "Developments in Intergovernmental Relations: Towards Multi-Level Governance," *Policy and Politics* 29 (2001), pp. 131–141.

6. Thomas Gais and James Fossett, "Federalism and the Executive Branch," in Joel D. Aberbach and Mark A. Peterson, eds., *The Executive Branch* (New York: Oxford University Press, Institutions of American Democracy Series, 2005).

7. Hero, *Faces of Inequality,* pp. 31–34.

8. Robert G. McCloskey, *American Supreme Court,* 4th ed., ed. Sanford Levinsonn (Chicago: University of Chicago Press, 2004), pp. 49–51.

9. See the special "Symposium on Preemption" in *PS: Political Science and Politics* (Washington, D.C.: The American Political Science Association, July 2005), pp. 359–378.

10. McCloskey, *American Supreme Court,* pp. 104–107, 118–119.

11. "A Partisan Public Agenda: Opinion of Clinton and Congress Improves" (Washington, D.C.: Pew Research Center, 1997); "How Americans View Government: Deconstructing Distrust" (Washington, D.C.: Pew Research Center, 1998); "National Omnibus Survey" (Cambridge, MA: Cambridge Reports/Research International, 1982).

12. Ann O. M. Bowan and George A. Krause, "Power Shift: Measuring Policy Centralization in U.S. Intergovernmental Relations, 1947–1998," *American Politics Research,* 31, no. 3 (May 2003), pp. 301–313; B. Guy Peters, *American Public Policy: Promise and Performance* (Washington, D.C.: CQ Press, 2004), pp. 22–27; Robert Nagel, *The Implosion of American Federalism* (New York: Oxford University Press, 2002).

13. Morton Grodzins, *The American System* (New Brunswick, NJ: Transaction Books, 1983).

14. Riker, *The Development of American Federalism;* David B. Walker, *Toward a Functioning Federalism* (Cambridge, MA: Winthrop, 1981), pp. 60–63.

15. Paul E. Peterson, Barry G. Rabe, and Kenneth Wong, *When Federalism Works* (Washington, D.C.: Brookings Institution, 1986), p. 2.

16. Ed Gillespie and Bob Schellhas, eds., *Contract with America: The Bold Plan by Rep. Newt Gingrich, Rep. Dick Armey and the House Republicans to Change the Nation* (New York: Random House, 1994), p. 125.

17. "Symposium on Preemption," *PS.*

18. William H. Riker, *Federalism: Origin, Operation, Significance* (Boston: Little, Brown, 1964), ch. 6.

19. Paul E. Peterson, *City Limits* (Chicago: University of Chicago Press, 1981); Paul E. Peterson, *The Price of Federalism* (Washington, D.C.: Brookings Institution, 1995).

CHAPTER 4

1. "Now for the Reckoning," *The Economist* (October 15, 2005), pp. 71–73; "Industrial Metamorphosis," *The Economist* (October 1, 2005), pp. 69–70; Paul Ingrassia, "Showdown," *The Wall Street Journal Online* (**www.wsj.com,** October 13, 2005); Michael Maynard, "As Delphi Goes, So Goes G.M?" *The New York Times* (October 11, 2005), p. 1; Robert J. Samuelson, "Do American Manufacturers Have a Future?" *The Wall Street Journal Online* (**www.wsj.com**), October 19, 2005).

2. Jeremy W. Peters, "Once Set For Life, Autoworkers May Have to Gamble," *The New York Times* (March 23, 2006), p A1; "More Pain, Waiting for the Gain," *The Economist* (February 11, 2006), p. 58; Lee Hawkins, Jr., "GM Posts Massive Loss Amid North American Struggles," *The Wall Street Journal* (January 26, 2006), p. 1; Jeffery McCracken and John D. Stoll, "Ford Unveils Plan for Sweeping Cuts in '06 Production," *The Wall Street Journal* (August 19, 2006), p. 1.

3. Thomas L. Friedman, *The World Is Flat: A Brief History of the Twenty-First Century* (New York: Farrar, Straus and Giroux, 2005); Robert B. Reich, *The Work of Nations: Preparing Ourselves for the 21st Century* (New York: Alfred A. Knopf, 1991).

4. James O'Toole and Edward E. Lawler III, *The New American Workplace* (New York: Macmillan Palgrave, 2006).

5. William Julius Wilson, *When Work Disappears: The World of the New Urban Poor* (New York: Knopf, 1996); Louis

Uchitelle, "For Blacks, a Dream in Decline," *The New York Times* (October 23, 2005), section 4, p. 1.

6. U.S. Department of Homeland Security, *Yearbook of Immigration Statistics, 2003.*

7. U.S. Bureau of the Census, "2005 American Community Survey."

8. Richard Florida, *The Flight of the Creative Class* (New York: HarperBusiness, 2005).

9. "America's Immigration Quandary: No Consensus on Immigration Problem or Proposed Fixes," Pew Research Center for the People and the Press, March 30, 2006.

10. Samuel Huntington, *Who We Are: The Challenge to America's National Identity* (New York: Simon and Schuster, 2004).

11. Paul Magnusson, *"Mi Casa Es Su Casa?* Get Real," *BusinessWeek* (January 10, 2005), p. 25.

12. Daniel J. Tichenor, *Dividing Lines: The Politics of Immigration Control in the United States* (Princeton, NJ: Princeton University Press, 2002), p. 284.

13. "Not Here, Surely," *The Economist* (December 10, 2005), p. 31.

14. Based on purchasing power.

15. *Human Development Report, 2005* (New York: The United Nations, 2006).

16. U.S. Bureau of the Census.

17. "The Booming Economy: What Is It On?", *The Economist* (December 10, 2005), p. 37.

18. Stanley B. Greenberg, *Middle-Class Dreams* (New York: Times Books, 1995); Susan J. Tolchin, *The Angry American* (Boulder, CO: Westview Press, 1999). On the more general relationship between income growth and political mood see Benjamin M. Friedman, *The Moral Consequences of Economic Growth* (New York: Knopf, 2005).

19. "Income, Poverty, and Health Insurance in the United States, 2004," U.S. Bureau of the Census, 2005.

20. Peter Gottschalk, "Inequality, Income Growth and Mobility," *Journal of Economic Perspectives,* 11, no. 2 (Spring 1997), pp. 13–19; U.S. Bureau of the Census, 2005.

21. "Income, Poverty . . . ," U.S. Bureau of the Census, 2005.

22. Wilson, *When Work Disappears.*

23. Edward Wolff, "International Comparisons of Wealth Inequality," *Review of Income and Wealth,* 42, no. 4 (December 1996).

24. Michael Reich, "The Proletarianization of the Workforce," in Richard Edwards, Michael Reich, and Thomas A. Weisskopf, eds., *The Capitalist System* (Englewood Cliffs, NJ: Prentice Hall, 1966), p. 125.

25. See Edward S. Greenberg, *Capitalism and the American Political Ideal* (Armonk, NY: Sharpe, 1985), ch. 4.

26. On this history, see Thomas C. Cochran and William Miller, *The Age of Enterprise* (New York: Harper & Row, 1961); Louis M. Hacker, *American Economic Growth and Development* (New York: Wiley, 1970); Robert Wiebe, *The Search for Order* (New York: Hill & Wang, 1967).

27. U.S. Department of Commerce, *International Direct Investment* (Washington, D.C.: U.S. Government Printing Office, 1984), p. 1.

28. U.S. Bureau of the Census

29. G. Thomas Sims, "Northern Europe, U.S., East Asia Remain Tops in Competitiveness, *The Wall Street Journal* (September 28, 2005), p. 1.

30. Richard Florida, *The Rise of the Creative Class* (New York: Basic Books, 2002).

31. For entertaining yet highly informative critiques of extreme pro-globalization advocates and extreme anti-globalization advocates see Michael Veseth, *Selling Globalization: The Myth of the Global Economy* (Boulder, CO: Rienner, 1998); Michael Veseth, *Globaloney: Unraveling the Myths of Globalization* (Lanham, MD: Rowman & Littlefield Publishers, 2005).

32. Florida, *The Rise of the Creative Class.*

33. See Seymour Martin Lipset, *American Exceptionalism: A Double-Edged Sword* (New York: Norton, 1996); Jennifer L. Hochschild, *Facing Up to the American Dream* (Princeton, NJ: Princeton University Press, 1995), ch. 1; John Micklethwait and Adrian Wooldridge, *The Right Nation: Conservative Power in America* (New York: Penguin Press, 2004), part IV. For a contrary view— namely, that America is divided into distinct political cultural traditions—see Rogers M. Smith, *Civic Ideals: Conflicting Visions of Citizenship in American* (New Haven, CT: Yale University Press, 1997).

34. For a contrary view of the place of individualism in American life, see Desmond King, *The Liberty of Strangers: Making the American Nation* (New York: Oxford University Press, 2004).

35. See Jennifer L. Hochschild, *What's Fair? American Beliefs about Distributive Justice* (Cambridge, MA: Harvard University Press, 1981); Herbert McClosky and John R. Zaller, *The American Ethos: Public Attitudes Toward Capitalism and Democracy* (Cambridge, MA: Harvard University Press, 1984); Sidney Verba and Gary R. Orren, *Equality in America* (Cambridge, MA: Harvard University Press, 1985).

36. Verba and Orren, *Equality in America,* p. 255.

37. Alexis de Tocqueville, *Democracy in America* (1845).

38. On the domination of classical liberalism in America, see Louis Hartz, *The Liberal Tradition in America* (New York: Harcourt, Brace, 1955). But also see Rogers M. Smith, "Beyond Tocqueville, Myrdal, and Hartz: The Multiple Traditions of America," *American Political Science Review,* 87, no. 3 (September 1993), pp. 549–566.

39. John Kenneth Galbraith, *American Capitalism* (Boston: Houghton Mifflin, 1956); see also McClosky and Zaller, *The American Ethos,* pp. 270–271; John Micklethwait and Adrian Wooldridge, *The Right Nation* (New York: Penguin, 2004).

40. Russell Hanson, *The Democratic Imagination in America* (Princeton, NJ: Princeton University Press, 1985).

41. McClosky and Zaller, *The American Ethos,* p. 18; "Views of a Changing World 2003" (Washington, D.C.: Pew Research Center, 2003).

42. Gary Wills, *Under God: Religion and American Politics* (New York: Simon and Schuster, 1991); Micklethwait and Wooldridge, *The Right Nation;* Kevin Phillips, *American Theocracy: The Peril and Politics of Radical Religion, Oil, and Borrowed Money in the 21st Century* (New York: Viking, 2006).

43. "Views of a Changing World 2003."

44. Micklethwait and Wooldridge, *The Right Nation.*

CHAPTER 5

1. Joseph C. Goulden, *Truth Is the First Casualty: The Gulf of Tonkin Affair—Illusion and Reality* (Chicago: Rand McNally, 1969). Also see Scott Stane, "Vietnam War Intelligence Deliberately Skewed, Secret Study Says," *The New York Times* (December 2, 2005), p. A. 1.

2. All public opinion polls cited in this chapter-opening story are from John E. Mueller, *War, Presidents and Public Opinion* (New York: Wiley, 1973).

3. U.S. Department of Defense, OASD (Comptroller), *Selected Manpower Statistics* (Washington, D.C.: Government Publications, June 1976), pp. 59–60.

4. Alexander Hamilton, James Madison, and John Jay, *The Federalist Papers,* ed. Clinton Rossiter (New York: New American Library, 1961; originally published 1787–1788). See Benjamin I. Page and Robert Y. Shapiro, *The Rational Public: Fifty Years of Trends in Americans' Policy Preferences* (Chicago: University of Chicago Press, 1992), chs. 1 and 2.

5. Walter Lippmann, *Public Opinion* (New York: Macmillan, 1922), p. 127.

6. Philip E. Converse, "The Nature of Belief Systems in Mass Publics," in David Apter, ed., *Ideology and Discontent* (New York: Free Press, 1964), pp. 206–261; Philip E. Converse, "Attitudes and Non-Attitudes: Continuation of a Dialogue," in Edward R. Tufte, ed., *The Quantitative Analysis of Social Problems* (Reading, MA: Addison-Wesley, 1970), pp. 168–189.

7. Robert S. Erikson and Kent L. Tedin, *American Public Opinion: Its Origins, Content, and Impact,* 7th ed. (New York: Pearson Longman, 2006), table 2.1. This book offers an excellent introduction to how surveys are done.

8. Erickson and Tedin, *American Public Opinion,* p. 37.

9. George F. Bishop, *The Illusion of Public Opinion: Fact and Artifact in American Public Opinion Polls* (Lanham, MD: Rowman & Littlefield Publishers, 2004).

10. Shiraev and Sobel, *People and Their Opinions,* p. 95.

11. For a review of the research literature on political socialization see Erikson and Tedin, *American Public Opinion,* ch. 5.

12. Doris A. Graber, *Mass Media and American Democracy* (Washington, D.C.: CQ Press, 2006), pp. 185–188.

13. Paul Sniderman and Thomas Piazza, *Black Pride and Black Prejudice* (Princeton, NJ: Princeton University Press, 2002), pp. 175–179.

14. Laura R. Olson and John C. Green, "Introduction to the Symposium: Gapology and the Presidential Vote,"*PS* July 2006, pp. 443–446.

15. This and the votes of other democratic groups reported in this section are from "Edison/Mitofsky Exit Poll, 2004 Presidential Election," CNN.com, **www.cnn.com/ELECTION/2004,** November 2, 2004.

16. General Social Survey (Chicago: National Opinion Research Center; University of Chicago, 2002).

17. Stanley B. Greenberg, *The Two Americas: Our Current Political Deadlock and How to Break It* (New York: Thomas Dunne Books, St. Martins Press, 2004).

18. NBC News/*Wall Street Journal Poll,* 2003, cited in Erikson and Tedin, *American Public Opinion,* p. 188.

19. *Trends, 2005* (Washington, D.C.: The Pew Research Center for the People and the Press, 2005), p. 19.

20. Ibid., p. 87.

21. John A. Garcia, *Latino Politics in America: Community, Culture, and Interests* (Lanham, MD: Rowman and Littlefield Publishers, 2003), chs. 6 and 7.

22. Erickson and Tedin, *American Public Opinion,* p. 199.

23. General Social Survey, 2002.

24. Bernadette C. Hayes, "The Impact of Class on Political Attitudes," *European Journal of Political Research,* 27 (1995), p. 76.

25. Pew Research Center, "GOP Makes Gains Among the Working Class, While Democrats Hold On to the Union Vote," August 2, 2005.

26. Ibid, p. 4.

27. Erikson and Tedin, *American Public Opinion,* pp. 178–180.

28. Thomas B. Edsall, "The Shifting Sands of America's Political Parties," *The Washington Post, National Edition* (April 9–15, 2001), p. 11. Also see Richard Florida, *The Rise of the Creative Class* (New York: Basic Books, 2004). For a contrary view see Jeffrey M. Stonecash, *Class and Party in American Politics* (Boulder, CO: Westview, 2000).

29. General Social Survey, 2002.

30. Earl Black and Merle Black, *The Rise of Southern Republicans* (Cambridge, MA: Harvard University Press, 2002); The Pew Research Center for the People and the Press, *Evenly Divided: The 2004 Political Landscape* (Washington, D.C., 2003), ch. 1.

31. General Social Survey, 2002.

32. Morris P. Fiorina, *Culture War: the Myth of a Polarized American* (New York: Pearson Longman Publishers, 2005); Erikson and Tedin, *American Public Opinion,* pp. 202–205.

33. Erickson and Tedin, *American Public Opinion,* pp. 182–185.

34. Brigid C. Harrison, *Women in American Politics* (Belmont, CA: Thomson/Wadsworth Publishing, 2003), pp. 40–45.

35. M. Margaret Conway, Gertrude A. Steuernagel, and John R. Terocik, *Women and Political Participation* (Washington, D.C.: Congressional Quarterly Press, 1997).

36. Karen M. Kaufmann and John R. Petrocik, "The Changing Politics of American Men," *The American Journal of Political Science,* 43 (July 1999), pp. 864–887; Greenberg,

The Two Americas; Michael Lind, "Conservative Elites and Counterrevolutions Against the New Deal," in *Ruling America: A History of Wealth and Power in a Democracy* (Cambridge, MA: Harvard University Press, 2005).

37. Fiorina, *Culture War,* pp. 34–35, 66–76. For a contrary view see Janet M. Box-Steffensmeier, Suzanna De Boef, and Tse-Min Lin, "The Dynamics of the Partisan Gender Gap," *American Political Science Review,* 98, no. 3 (August 2004), pp. 515–528.

38. Mark Schlesinger and Caroline Heldman, "Gender Gap or Gender Gaps?" *The Journal of Politics,* 63, no. 1 (February 2001), pp. 59–92; Robert Y. Shapiro and Harpreet Mahajan, "Gender Differences in Policy Preferences: A Summary of Trends from the 1960s to the 1980s," *Public Opinion Quarterly,* 50 (1986), pp. 42–61; Curroll J. Glynn, Susan Herbst, Garrett J. O'Keefe, and Robert I. Shapiro, *Public Opinion* (Boulder, CO: Westview Press, 1999), pp. 235–238; American National Election Studies, 2003.

39. Richard Morin, "Defense Tops the List," *The Washington Post National Edition* (November 26–December 2, 2001), p. 34; General Social Survey, 2002.

40. Pew Research Center, *Evenly Divided,* p. 30.

41. Fiorina, *Culture War,* pp. 66–69.

42. Albert H. Cantril and Susan Davis Cantril, *Reading Mixed Signals: Ambivalence in American Public Opinion about Government* (Baltimore, MD: Johns Hopkins University Press, 1999), table 2.4, p. 22.

43. For a summary of statistics on how adherents of different religious traditions divide on party identification and on a range of policy issues, see Erikson and Tedin, *American Public Opinion,* pp. 195–201.

44. The data in this section is from *Trends, 2005* from the Pew Research Center.

45. Fiorina, *Culture War.*

46. Ibid., pp. 96–103.

47. The Gallup Poll, 2005.

48. Donald Green, Bradley Palmquist, and Eric Schickler, *Partisan Hearts and Minds: Political Parties and the Social Identity of Voters* (New Haven, CT: Yale University Press, 2002); Erikson and Tedin, *American Public Opinion,* pp. 77–83; Marjorie Randon Hershey, *Party Politics in America* (New York: Longman Classics, 2005), pp. 106–111; Fiorina, *Culture War,* pp. 34–35; Pew Research Center, *Evenly Divided:* Greenberg, *The Two Americas.*

49. Ibid.

50. Data are from 2004, reported in Alan Abramowitz and Kyle Saunders, "Culture War in American: Myth or Reality," *The Forum,* 3, no. 2 (2005), pp. 1–22.

51. Michael X Delli Carpini and Scott Keeter, *What Americans Know About Politics and Why It Matters* (New Haven, CT: Yale University Press, 1996); *American National Election Studies* (Ann Arbor, MI: University of Michigan Press, 2004).

52. Erikson and Tedin, *American Public Opinion;* Page and Shapiro, *The Rational Public,* pp. 9–14; calculations by the authors from the *American National Election Study,* 2004.

53. Paul M. Sniderman, Richard A. Brody, and Philip E. Tetlock, *Reasoning and Choice: Explorations in Political Psychology* (New York: Cambridge University Press, 1991). See also Carpini and Keeter, *What Americans know About Politics;* Samuel Popkin, *The Reasoning Voter* (Chicago: University of Chicago Press, 1991).

54. Robert E. Lane, *Political Ideology: Why the American Common Man Believes What He Does* (New York: Free Press, 1962); Jennifer L. Hochschild, *What's Fair? American Beliefs about Distributive Justice* (Cambridge, MA: Harvard University Press, 1986); Glynn et al., *Public Opinion,* ch. 8.

55. Page and Shapiro, *The Rational Public.* Also see Taeku Lee, *Mobilizing Public Opinion: Black Insurgency and Racial Attitudes in the Civil Rights Era* (Chicago: University of Chicago Press, 2002).

56. General Social Survey, 2002.

57. Harris Poll, June 2004.

58. Derek Bok, *The Trouble with Government* (Cambridge, MA: Harvard University Press, 2001); Joseph S. Nye, Jr., Philip D. Zelikow, and David C. King, eds., *Why People Don't Trust Government* (Cambridge, MA: Harvard University Press, 1997).

59. Robert Putnam, "Bowling Together: The United State of America," *The American Prospect* (February 11, 2002), pp. 20–22.

60. Pew Research Center, *Evenly Divided,* ch. 6.

61. *New York Times*/CBS News poll, May 10, 2006.

62. Samuel Kernell, "Explaining Presidential Popularity," *American Political Science Review,* 72 (June 1978), pp. 506–522; Richard A. Brody, *Assessing the President: The Media, Elite Opinion, and Public Support* (Stanford, CA: Stanford University Press, 1991).

63. Bruce E. Keith, David B. Magleby, Candice J. Nelson, Elizabeth Orr, Mark C. Westlye, and Raymond E. Wolfinger, *The Myth of the Independent Voter* (Berkeley, CA: University of California Press, 1992). Also see Marjorie Randon Hershey and Paul Allen Beck, *Party Politics in America,* 10th ed. (New York: Longman, 2003), pp. 120–121.

64. Walter Dean Burnham, "The Appearance and Disappearance of the American Voter," in Richard Rose, ed., *Electoral Participation: A Comparative Analysis* (Beverly Hills, CA: Sage, 1980), pp. 35–73; Jeffrey E. Cohen, *American Political Parties: Decline or Resurgence?* (Washington, D.C.: CQ Press, 2001); Michael B. MacKuen, Robert S. Erikson, and James A. Stimson, "Macropartisanship," *American Political Science Review,* 83 (1989), pp. 1125–1143.

65. *Beyond Red vs. Blue* (Washington, D.C.: Pew Research Center, 2005).

66. American National Election Studies, 2004.

67. Steven Kull, *Americans and Foreign Aid: A Study of American Public Attitudes* (Washington, D.C.: Program on International Policy Attitudes, 1995).

68. The General Social Survey, 1973–2002.

69. Gallup Poll, conducted for CNN and *USA Today,* February 2001.

70. William Caspary, " 'The Mood Theory': A Study of Public Opinion and Foreign Policy," *American Political Science Review,* 64 (1970), pp. 536–547; John E. Rielly, ed., *American Public Opinion and U.S. Foreign Policy, 1995* (Chicago: Chicago Council on Foreign Relations, 1995), p. 13; Princeton Survey Associates/Pew Research Center, October 1999.

71. *Time*/CNN Survey, December 7, 1994.

72. Gallup Poll, conducted for CNN and *USA Today,* September 2001.

73. Gallup Poll, October 28, 2005.

74. Summary of polls on American foreign policy reported at *The Public Agenda Online* at **www.publicagenda.org/**; Benjamin I. Page with Marshall M. Bouton, *The Foreign Policy Disconnect: What Americans Want from our Leaders But Do Not Get* (Chicago: University of Chicago Press, 2006).

75. For a summary of the evidence see Erikson and Tedin, *American Public Opinion,* pp. 302–308.

76. Alan D. Monroe, "Consistency Between Public Preferences and National Policy Decisions," *American Politics Quarterly,* 7 (January 1979), pp. 3–19; Benjamin I. Page and Robert Y. Shapiro, "Effects of Public Opinion on Policy," *American Political Science Review,* 77 (1983), pp. 175–190.

77. James A. Stimson, *Public Opinion in America: Moods, Cycles and Swings* (Boulder, CO: Westview Press, 1991).

78. Paul Burstein, "The Impact of Public Opinion on Public Policy: A Review and an Agenda," *Political Research Quarterly,* 56, no. 1 (March 2003). Also see Vincent L. Hutchings, *Public Opinion and Democratic Accountability: How Citizens Learn About Politics* (Princeton, NJ: Princeton University Press, 2003).

79. Summarized in Benjamin I. Page, "The Semi-Sovereign Public," in Jeff Manza, Fay Lomax Cook, and Benjamin I. Page, eds., *Navigating Public Opinion: Polls, Policy, and the Future of American Democracy* (New York: Oxford University Press, 2002).

80. Lawrence R. Jacobs and Robert Y. Shapiro, *Politicians Don't Pander: Political Manipulation and the Loss of Democratic Responsiveness* (Chicago: University of Chicago Press, 2000); John Zaller, *The Nature and Origins of Mass Opinion* (New York: Cambridge University Press, 1992).

81. Public opinion scholar Larry Bartels suggests that the 2001 tax cut (the largest in two decades, with tax relief going overwhelmingly to upper-income people) was supported by the public out of sheer ignorance and confusion about the impact of changes in the Tax Code. See Larry M. Bartels, "Homer Gets a Tax Cut: Inequality and Public Policy in the American Mind," *Perspectives on Politics,* 3, no. 1 (March 2005), pp. 15–29. In the same issue (pp. 33–53), Jacob Hacker and Paul Pierson disagree; they suggest in their article "Abandoning the Middle: the Bush Tax Cuts and the Limits of Democratic Control," that manipulation and deception were prominent in the successful effort to raise public support for the 2001 tax cuts.

82. Page with Bouton, *The Foreign Policy Disconnect.* Also see Lawrence R. Jacobs and Benjamin I. Page, "Who Influences Foreign Policy," *American Political Science Review,* 99, no. 1 (February 2005), pp. 107–124.

CHAPTER 6

1. Information for this story is from the following: Edward Morrissey, "Eason's Fable: Bloggers, the Old Media, and the Rise and Fall of CNN's Eason Jordan," *The Weekly Standard online* (**(www.weeklystandard.com),** February, 17, 2005; Jacques Steinberg and Katherine Q. Seelye, "CNN Executive Resigns Post Over Remarks," *The New York Times* (February 12, 2005), p. A1; Katherine Q. Seelye, "Bloggers as News Media Trophy Hunters," *The New York Times* (February 14, 2005), p. A1; Richard Posner, "Bad News," *The New York Times Book Review* (July 31, 2005), p. 1; Daniel W. Drezner and Henry Farrell, "Web of Influence," *Foreign Policy* (November/December, 2004), pp. 32–40.

2. Doris Graber, *Mass Media and American Politics,* 4th ed. (Washington, D.C.: Congressional Quarterly Press, 1993), p. 35.

3. Frances Hagopian, "Politics in Brazil," in Gabriel A. Almond, G. Bingham Powell, Jr., Daare Strom, and Russell J. Dalton, eds., *Comparative Politics Today* (New York: Pearson Longman Publishers, 2004), p. 240.

4. Graber, *Mass Media and American Politics,* ch. 3.

5. Joseph Cappella and Kathleen Hall Jamieson, *Spiral of Cynicism: The Press and the Public Good* (New York: Oxford University Press, 1997); Larry J. Sabato, Mark Stencel, and S. Robert Lichter, *Peepshow: Media and Politics in an Age of Scandal* (Boulder, CO: Rowman & Littlefield Publishers, 2000).

6. W. Lance Bennett, *News: the Politics of Illusion,* 6th ed. (New York: Pearson Longman Publishers, 2005), pp. 74–76.

7. Graber, *Mass Media and American Politics,* p. 38.

8. *Trends, 2005* (Washington, D.C.: Pew Research Center, 2004), ch. 3; Bill Kovach and Tom Rosenstiel, *Warp Speed: America in the Age of Mass Media* (New York: The Century Fund Press, 1999).

9. *Trends, 2005,* p. 45.

10. Ibid., p. 54; Diana Owen, "Talk Radio and Evaluations of President Clinton," *Political Communications,* 14 (1997), pp. 333–353.

11. *Talkers Magazine Online,* **www.talkers.com,** November 1, 2005.

12. Ibid.

13. See "Internet Penetration," Pew Research Center, April 5, 2006; *Trends, 2005,* p. 63.

14. *Ibid,* ch. 4, p. 58.

15. Kovach and Rosenstiel, *Warp Speed,* pp. 52–57; Samuel L. Popkin, "Changing Media, Changing Politics," *PS,* June 2006, pp. 327–341.

16. Robert S. Erikson and Kent L. Tedin, *American Public Opinion* (New York: Pearson Longman Publishers, 2005), p. 219.

17. Tom Lowry, "Antenna Adjustment," *BusinessWeek* (June 20, 2005), pp. 65–70.

18. Ben H. Bagdikian, *The New Media Monopoly* (Boston: Beacon Press, 2004); "Who Owns What?" *Columbia Journalism Review Online*, **www.cjr.org,** 2005.

19. Bennett, *News,* pp. 96–98.

20. Doug Underwood, "Market Research and the Audience for Political News," in Poris Graber, Denis McQuail, and Pippa Norris, eds., *The Politics of News; the News of Politics* (Washington, D.C.: CQ Press, 1998), p. 171; also see Bennett, *News,* pp. 96–98.

21. Edward Jay Epstein, *News from Nowhere: Television and the News* (New York: Vantage, 1973), p. 142. Also see Graber, *Mass Media and American Politics,* p. 43, on the important influence of the AP wire service.

22. Leon V. Sigal, *Reporters and Officials: The Organization and Politics of News Reporting* (Lexington, MA: Heath, 1973), p. 124.

23. Bennett, *News,* pp. 116–118; Steven Livingston and W. Lance Bennett, "Gatekeeping, Indexing, and Live Event News," *Political Communication,* 20, no. 4, (October–December, 2003), pp. 363–380.

24. Graber, *Mass Media and American Democracy,* pp. 76–77.

25. Mark Hertsgaard, *On Bended Knee* (New York: Farrar, Straus & Giroux, 1988), p. 5.

26. Anne E. Kornblut, "Administration Is Warned About Its News Videos," *The New York Times* (January 19, 2005), p. A9; Anne E. Kornblut, "Third Journalist Was Paid to Promote Bush Policies," *The New York Times* (January 29, 2005), p. A13; Charlie Savage and Alan Wirzbicki, "White House-Friendly Reporter Under Scrutiny," *The Boston Globe* (February 2, 2005), p. A1; "Source Watch," *Center for Media and Democracy* (**www.prwatch.org/cmd/index.html**) February 2005.

27. David Murray, Joel Schwartz, and S. Robert Lichter, *It Ain't Necessarily So: How Media Make and Unmake the Scientific Picture of Reality* (Lanham, MD: Rowan and Littlefield Publishers, 2001), pp. 29–30.

28. Graber, *Mass Media and American Democracy,* pp. 116–118, 335–336.

29. Eric Alterman, *What Liberal Media?* (New York: Basic Books, 2003).

30. Barnard Goldberg, *Bias in the News* (Washington, D.C.: Regnery, 2001).

31. *Trends, 2005,* p. 53.

32. Neal Hickey, "Is Fox News Fair?" *Columbia Journalism Review* (March/April, 1998), vol. 31; David Weaver and G. Cleveland Wilhoit, *The American Journalist* (Mahwah, NJ: Lawrence Erlbaum, 1996); Graber, *Mass Media and American Politics,* pp. 86–89.

33. Thomas E. Patterson and Wolfgang Donsbach, "News Decisions: Journalists as Partisan Actors," *Political Communications,* 13 (October–December 1996).

34. Bennett, *News,* pp. 27–28; Erikson and Tedin, *American Public Opinion,* pp. 220–224.

35. Fred Kaplan, *The Wizards of Armageddon* (New York: Simon & Schuster, 1983); Tom Gervasi, *The Myth of Soviet Military Supremacy* (New York: Harper & Row, 1986).

36. John Zaller, *A Theory of Media Politics* (Chicago: University of Chicago Press, 2004).

37. Kovach and Rosenstiel, *Warp Speed,* p. 66; Bennett, *News,* pp. 90–94.

38. Ibid.

39. Bennett, *News,* p. 27.

40. David L. Paletz, "The Media and Public Policy," in Graber, et al., *The Politics of News.*

41. Shanto Iyengar and Donald R. Kinder, *News That Matters* (Chicago: University of Chicago Press, 1987); also see Erikson and Tedin, *American Public Opinion,* pp. 230–231 for a review of the research on news media agenda setting.

42. G. Ray Funkhauser, "The Issues of the Sixties: An Exploratory Study in the Dynamics of Public Opinion," *Public Opinion Quarterly,* 37 (Spring 1973), pp. 62–75.

43. George C. Edwards, "Who Influences Whom? The President, Congress and the Media," *The American Political Science Review,* 93 (June 1999), pp. 327–344.

44. Shanto Iyengar, *Is Anyone Responsible? How Television News Frames Political Issues* (Chicago: University of Chicago Press, 1991); Kathleen Hall Jamieson and Paul Waldman, *The Press Effect* (Washington, D.C.: CQ Press, 2002).

45. Paul M. Kellstedt, *The Mass Media and the Dynamics of American Racial Attitudes* (Cambridge, England: Cambridge University Press, 2003).

46. Benjamin I. Page, Robert Y. Shapiro, and Glenn R. Dempsey, "What Moves Public Opinion?" *American Political Science Review,* 81 (1987), pp. 23–43.

47. Joseph Cappella and Kathleen Jamieson, *Spiral of Cynicism: The Press and the Public Good* (New York: Oxford University Press, 1997); Stephen C. Craig, ed., *Broken Contract: Changing Relations Between Americans and Their Government* (Boulder, CO: Westview Press, 1996); Mark J. Hetherington, "Declining Trust and Shrinking Policy Agenda," in Robert Hart and Daron R. Shaw, eds., *Communications in U.S. Elections* (Lanham, MD: Rowman & Littlefield, 2001); Bennett, *News;* Thomas E. Patterson, "Bad News, Period," *PS* (March 1996), pp. 17–20.

48. Daniel C. Hallin, *The "Uncensored War": The Media and Vietnam* (Berkeley, CA: University of California Press, 1989).

49. W. Lance Bennett and David L. Paletz, eds., *Taken by Storm: The Media, Public Opinion, and U.S. Foreign Policy in the Gulf War* (Chicago: University of Chicago Press, 1994).

50. Graber, *Mass Media and American Democracy,* pp. 333–335.

51. The Pew Research Center, "U.S. Image Up Slightly, But Still Negative: American Character Gets Mixed Reviews" (June 23, 2005).

52. See Graber, *Mass Media and American Politics,* pp. 43–47, for the extent of and limits on FCC powers to regulate.

53. Ibid. pp. 67–68.

54. Dan Schiller, *Digital Capitalism: Networking in the New Global Market System* (Cambridge, MA: MIT Press, 1999).

CHAPTER 7

1. Jackie Calmes, "How a Victorious Bush Fumbled Plan to Revamp Social Security: A Divided Republican Party, Strong Opposition Derails Push for Private Accounts," *The Wall Street Journal* (October 21, 2005), p. 1.

2. Alexander Hamilton, James Madison, and John Jay, *The Federalist Papers,* ed. Clinton Rossiter (New York: New American Library, 1961), No. 10. (Originally published 1787–1788.)

3. Arthur F. Bentley, *The Process of Government* (Chicago: University of Chicago Press, 1908); David Truman, *The Governmental Process* (New York: Knopf, 1951); V. O. Key, Jr., *Politics, Parties, and Pressure Groups* (New York: A. Crowell, 1952); Robert A. Dahl, *A Preface to Democratic Theory* (Chicago: University of Chicago Press, 1956); Robert A. Dahl, *Who Governs?* (New Haven, CT: Yale University Press, 1961). See also Jeffrey M. Berry, *The New Liberalism: The Rising Power of Citizen Groups* (Washington, D.C.: Brookings, 1999).

4. Roger H. Davidson and Walter J. Oleszek, *Congress and Its Members* (Washington, D.C.: CQ Press, 2006), p. 395.

5. The Center for Responsive Politics, based on required reports to the House and Senate, 2005.

6. Berry, *The New Liberalism,* pp. 20–21; Theda Skocpol, "Voice and Inequality: the Transformation of American Civic Democracy," *Perspectives on Politics,* 2, no. 1 (March 2004), pp. 3–20; Theda Skocpol, *Diminished Democracy: From Membership to Management in American Civic Life* (Norman, OK: University of Oklahoma Press, 2003).

7. "Lobby Watch," The Center for Public Integrity, 2005.

8. Truman, *The Governmental Process.*

9. Mancur Olson, *The Logic of Collective Action* (Cambridge, MA: Harvard University Press, 1965).

10. On Olson's theory, see Brian Barry and Russell Hardin, eds., *Rational Man and Irrational Society?* (Newbury Park, CA: Sage, 1982); Dennis Chong, *Collective Action and the Civil Rights Movement* (Chicago: University of Chicago Press, 1991); Russell Hardin, *Collective Action* (Baltimore: Johns Hopkins University Press); Terry Moe, *The Organization of Interests* (Chicago: University of Chicago Press, 1980).

11. Bruce Bimber, *Information and American Democracy* (New York: Cambridge University Press, 2003).

12. E. E. Schattschneider, *The Semi-Sovereign People* (New York: Holt, Rinehart & Winston, 1960).

13. Berry, *The New Liberalism;* Thomas Byrne Edsall, *The New Politics of Inequality* (New York: Norton, 1984); Michael Goldfield, *The Decline of Organized Labor in the United States* (Chicago: University of Chicago Press, 1987); Edward S. Greenberg, *Capitalism and the American Political Ideal* (Armonk, NY: Sharpe, 1985); David Vogel, *Fluctuating Fortunes: The Political Power of Business in America* (New York: Basic Books, 1989), ch. 8.

14. U.S. Bureau of Labor Statistics, 2005.

15. Jeffrey M. Berry, *Lobbying for the People* (Princeton, NJ: Princeton University Press, 1977), p. 7; Berry, *The New Liberalism,* p. 2.

16. Berry, *Lobbying for the People;* David Broder, *Changing the Guard* (New York: Simon & Schuster, 1980); Hugh Heclo, "Issue Networks and the Executive Establishment," in Anthony King, ed., *The New American Political System* (Washington, D.C.: American Enterprise Institute, 1978); Schlozman and Tierney, *Organized Interests;* Jack L. Walker, Jr., "The Origins and Maintenance of Interest Groups in America," *American Political Science Review,* 77 (1983), pp. 390–406; Skocpol, *Diminished Democracy.*

17. Skocpol, *Diminished Democracy;* Theda Skocpol, "Associations Without Members," *The American Prospect,* 10, no. 4 (July/August 1999), pp. 66–73; Skocpol, "Voice and Inequality."

18. Jack L. Walker, Jr., *Mobilizing Interest Groups in America* (Ann Arbor, MI: University of Michigan Press, 1991).

19. **(www.politicalmoneyline.com);** "The Lobbying Boom," CQ Researcher Online (**www.cqpress.com/ cqresearcher),** 2005.

20. "Pork and Scandals," *The Economist* (January 28, 2006), p. 29.

21. Leslie Wayne and Melody Petersen, "A Muscular Lobby Rolls Up Its Sleeves," *The New York Times* (November 4, 2001), Section 3, p. 1.

22. From the watchdog group Public Citizen, reported in "The Lobbying Boom."

23. Mark A. Smith, *Business and Political Power: Public Opinion, Elections and Democracy* (Chicago: University of Chicago Press, 2000).

24. Jeffrey M. Berry, *The Interest Group Society* (Glenview, IL: Scott, Foresman, 1989), p. 141.

25. Glen Justice, "New Rules on Fund-Raising Bring Lobbyists to the Fore," *The New York Times,* April 20, 2004, p. A1.

26. "The Lobbying Boom."

27. Kenneth M. Goldstein, *Interest Groups, Lobbying and Participation in America* (New York: Cambridge University Press, 1999), ch. 2; Kenneth Kollman, *Outside Lobbying* (Princeton, NJ: Princeton University Press, 1998).

28. E. E. Schattschneider, *The Semi-Sovereign People.*

29. Berry, *The New Liberalism.*

30. Schlozman and Tierney, *Organized Interests and American Democracy,* p. 175.

31. Bimber, *Information and American Democracy.*

32. Berry, *Lobbying for the People;* Skocpol, "Voice and Inequality"; Dara Strolovitch, "Closer to a Pluralist Heaven? Women's, Racial Minority, and Economic Justice Advocacy Groups and the Politics of Representation," paper presented at the annual meeting of the American Political Science Association, Philadelphia, Pennsylvania, August 2003.

33. Jim Drinkard, "Drugmakers Go Further to Sway Congress, *USA Today* (April 26, 2005), p. 2B; Leslie Wayne and Melody Petersen, "A Muscular Lobby Rolls Up Its Sleeves," *The New York Times* (November 4, 2001), Section 3, p. 1.

34. "Money Talks, Congress Listens," *The Boston Globe* (December 12, 1982), p. A24.

35. The Center for Public Integrity, October 18, 2004.

36. Derek Bok, *The Trouble with Government* (Cambridge, MA: Harvard University Press, 2001), pp. 81–94.

37. Scott H. Ainsworth, *Analyzing Interest Groups* (New York: W.W. Norton, 2002); Berry, *The New Liberalism;* Allan J. Cigler, "Interest Groups," in William Crotty, ed., *Political Science: Looking to the Future,* Vol. 4 (Evanston, IL: Northwestern University Press, 1991); Heclo, "Issue Networks"; Robert H. Salisbury, John P. Heinz, Edward O. Laumann, and Robert L. Nelson, "Triangles, Networks, and Hollow Cores," and Mark P. Petracca, "The Rediscovery of Interest Group Politics," both in Mark P. Petracca, ed., *The Politics of Interests: Interest Groups Transform* (Boulder, CO: Westview Press, 1992); Robert M. Stein and Kenneth Bickers, *Perpetuating the Pork Barrel: Policy Subsystems and American Democracy* (Cambridge, UK: Cambridge University Press, 1995).

38. Charles Lindblom, *Politics and Markets* (New York: Basic Books, 1977), p. 356.

39. Neil J. Mitchell, *The Conspicuous Corporation: Business, Public Policy and Representative Democracy* (Ann Arbor, MI: University of Michigan Press, 1997), p. 167.

40. Dan Clawson, Alan Neustadt, and Mark Weller, *Dollars and Votes* (Philadelphia: Temple University Press, 1998), pp. 26–28, 64–71, 97–99.

41. Vogel, *Fluctuating Fortunes,* p. 291.

42. David Rogers and Monica Langley, "Bush Set to Sign Landmark Bill on Class Actions," *The Wall Street Journal* (February 18, 2005), p. 1; Stephen Labaton, "Quick, Early Gains Embolden Business Lobby on Capitol Hill," *The New York Times* (February 18, 2005), p. A1.

43. Jeffrey Berry disagrees in *The New Liberalism.*

44. Walter Dean Burnham, *Critical Elections and the Mainsprings of American Politics* (New York: Norton, 1970), p. 133.

45. John E. Chubb and Paul E. Peterson, "American Political Institutions and the Problem of Governance," in John E. Chubb and Paul E. Peterson, eds., *Can the Government Govern?* (Washington, D.C.: Brookings Institution, 1989).

CHAPTER 8

1. James MacGregor Burns and Stewart Burns, *A People's Charter: The Pursuit of Rights in America* (New York: Knopf, 1991), ch. 5; E. McGlen and Karen O'Connor, *Women's Rights* (New York: Praeger, 1983), ch. 3; Sarah M. Evans, *Born for Liberty: A History of Women in America.* (New York: Free Press, 1997).

2. Sidney Tarrow, *Power in Movement* (New York: Cambridge University Press, 1998); David S. Meyer and Sidney Tarrow (eds.), *The Social Movement Society* (Lanham, MD: Rowman & Littlefield Publishers, 1997); Doug McAdams, John D. McCarthy, and Mayer N. Zald, "Social Movements," in Neil J. Smelser, ed., *Handbook of Sociology* (Newbury Park, CA: Sage, 1994); Joyce Gelb, *Feminism and Politics: A Comparative Perspective* (Berkeley, CA: University of California Press, 1989); Doug McAdams, *Political Process and the Development of Black Insurgency* (Chicago: University of Chicago Press, 1982).

3. Sidney Tarrow, "Social Movements as Contentious Politics," *American Political Science Review,* 90 (1996), pp. 853–866; Ronald R. Aminzade, Jack A. Goldstone, Doug McAdam, Elizabeth J. Perry, William H. Sewell Jr., and Sidney Tarrow, eds., *Silence and Voice in the Study of Contentious Politics* (New York: Cambridge University Press, Cambridge Studies in Contentious Politics, 2001)

4. Jackie Smith, "Globalizing Resistance: the Battle of Seattle and the Future of Social Movements," *Mobilization: An International Journal,* vol 6, no. 1 (2000), pp. 1–19.

5. CBS News telecast, February 16, 2003.

6. E. E. Schattschneider, *The Semi-Sovereign People* (New York: Holt, Rinehart & Winston, 1960), p. 142.

7. Richard Polenberg, *One Nation Divisible* (New York: Penguin, 1980), p. 268; Craig A. Rimmerman, *From Identity to Politics: The Lesbian and Gay Movements in the United States* (Philadelphia: Temple University Press, 2002), ch. 1.

8. Theodore J. Lowi, *The Politics of Disorder* (New York: Basic Books, 1971), p. 54.

9. Aminzade et. al., *Silence and Voice in the Study of Contentious Politics;* Meyer and Tarrow, *The Social Movement Society;* McAdams et al., "Social Movements"; Sidney Tarrow, *Social Movements, Collective Action, and Politics* (New York: Cambridge University Press, 1994).

10. Neil J. Smelser, *Theory of Collective Behavior* (New York: Free Press, 1962).

11. Barbara Sinclair Deckard, *The Women's Movement* (New York: Harper & Row, 1983); Ethel Klein, *Gender Politics: From Consciousness to Mass Politics* (Cambridge, MA: Harvard University Press, 1984), ch. 2.

12. Donald P. Haider-Markel, "Creating Change—Holding the Line," in Ellen D. B. Riggle and Barry L. Tadlock, eds., *Gays and Lesbians in the Political Process* (New York: Columbia University Press, 1999).

13. Rimmerman, *From Identity to Politics.*

14. William Gamson, *The Strategy of Social Protest* (Homewood, IL: Dorsey, 1975); John D. McCarthy and Mayer N. Zald, "Resource Mobilization and Social Movements: A Partial Theory," *American Journal of Sociology,* 82 (1977), pp. 1212–1241.

15. Jo Freeman, *The Politics of Women's Liberation* (New York: McKay, 1975); Nancy Burns, "Gender: Public Opinion and Political Action," in Ira Katznelson and Helen V. Milner, eds., *Political Science: The State of the Discipline* (New York: W.W. Norton, 2002), pp. 472–476.

16. Bruce Bimber, *Information and American Democracy: Technology and the Evolution of Political Power* (New York: Cambridge University Press, 2003), chs. 3 and 5.

17. McAdams, *Political Process;* Tarrow, *Social Movements, Collective Action, and Politics;* Peter K. Eisenger, "The Conditions of Protest Behavior in American Cities," *American Political Science Review,* 67 (1973), pp. 11–28.

18. Frances Fox Piven and Richard A. Cloward, *Poor People's Movements* (New York: Vintage, 1979), ch. 3.

19. Klein, *Gender Politics,* pp. 90–91.

20. National Opinion Research Center, General Social Survey, 1972.

21. The Pew Research Center for the People and the Press, *Evenly Divided and Increasingly Polarized: The 2004 Political Landscape* (Washington, D.C., 2003).

22. Carol A. Horton, *Race and the Making of American Liberalism* (New York: Oxford University Press, 2005), p. 140–141.

23. Rimmerman, *From Identity to Politics.*

24. Taylor Branch, *Parting the Waters: America in the King Years* (New York: Simon and Schuster, 1988); William H. Chafe, *The Unfinished Journey: America Since World War II* (New York: Oxford University Press, 2003).

25. Jane Mansbridge, *Why We Lost the ERA* (Chicago: University of Chicago Press, 1986).

26. Christian Davenport, Hank Johnson, and Carol Mueller, eds., *Mobilization and Repression* (Minneapolis, MN: University of Minnesota Press, 2005).

27. See David Caute, *The Great Fear* (New York: Simon & Schuster, 1978); Robert Justin Goldstein, *Political Repression in Modern America* (Cambridge, MA: Schenkman, 1978); Alan Wolfe, *The Seamy Side of Democracy* (New York: McKay, 1978).

28. Edward S. Greenberg, *Capitalism and the American Political Ideal* (Armonk, NY: Sharpe, 1985).

29. Mart Martin, *The Almanac of Women and Minorities in American Politics* (Boulder, CO: Westview Press, 2002).

30. William H. Chafe, *The Unfinished Journey: America Since World War II* (New York: Oxford University Press, 1986); Deckard, *The Women's Movement;* Klein, *Gender Politics,* ch. 2; Freeman, *Politics of Women's Liberation.* Also see debates on the relative progress of women in the United States collected in Dorothy McBride Stetson, *Women's Rights in the United States: Policy Debates and Gender Roles* (London: Routledge, 2004).

CHAPTER 9

1. Quotes in this story are from Richard W. Stevenson, "Bush Contends Partisan Critics Hurt War Effort," *The New York Times* (November 12, 2005), p. A.1; Elisabeth Bumiller, "Cheney Sees 'Shameless' Revisionism on War," *The New York Times* (November 22, 2005), p. A.1.

2. Robert A. Dahl, *On Democracy* (New Haven, CT: Yale University Press, 1998); Marjorie Randon Hershey, *Party Politics in America,* 11th ed. (New York: Pearson Longman, 2005), pp. 1–3.

3. E. E. Schattschneider, *Party Government* (New York: Holt, Rinehart & Winston, 1942), p. 208.

4. Ibid.

5. See Hershey, *Party Politics in America,* pp. 306–307; A. James Reichley, *The Life of the Parties: A History of American Political Parties* (Lanham, MD: Rowman and Littlefield, 2002), ch. 1.

6. Steven J. Rosenstone and John Mark Hansen, *Mobilization, Participation, and Democracy in America* (New York: Macmillan, 1993); Hershey, *Party Politics in America,* pp. 143–145.

7. E. E. Schattschneider, *The Semi-Sovereign People* (New York: Holt, Rinehart & Winston, 1960).

8. On realignment, see Walter Dean Burnham, *Critical Elections and the Mainsprings of American Politics* (New York: Norton, 1970); Jerome Clubb, William H. Flanigan, and Nancy H. Zingale, *Partisan Realignment* (Newbury Park, CA: Sage, 1980); V. O. Key, Jr., "A Theory of Critical Elections," *Journal of Politics,* 17 (1955), pp. 3–18; Hershey, *Party Politics in America,* ch. 7; David R. Mayhew, *Electoral Realignments* (New Haven, CT: Yale University Press, 2004); James L. Sundquist, *Dynamics of the Party System* (Washington, D.C.: Brookings Institution, 1973). For the special place that war has played in altering parties and party systems see David R. Mayhew, "Wars and American Politics," *Perspectives on Politics,* 3, no. 3 (September 2005), pp. 473–493.

9. C. Vann Woodward, *The Strange Career of Jim Crow* (New York: Oxford University Press, 1966).

10. John Aldrich and Richard Niemi, "The Sixth American Party System," in Stephen C. Craig, *Broken Contract: Changing Relationships Between Americans and Their Government* (Boulder, CO: Westview Press, 1996); Walter J. Stone and Ronald B. Rapoport, "It's Perot Stupid! The Legacy of the 1992 Perot Movement in the Major-Party System, 1994–2000," *PS: Political Science and Politics,* XXXIV, no. 1 (March 2001), pp. 49–56.

11. Thomas Byrne Edsall and Mary D. Edsall, *Chain Reaction: The Impact of Race, Rights and Taxes on American Politics* (New York: Norton, 1991); Stanley B. Greenberg, *Middle Class Dreams: The Politics and Power of the New American Majority* (New Haven, CT: Yale University Press, 1996).

12. Larry Sabato, *The Party's Just Begun* (Glenview, IL: Scott, Foresman, 1988); Sundquist, *Dynamics of the Party System;* Martin P. Wattenberg, *The Decline of American Political Parties* (Cambridge, MA: Harvard University Press, 1994); Greenberg, *Middle Class Dreams;* Everett C. Ladd, "The 1994 Congressional Elections," *Political Science Quarterly* 110 (1995), pp. 1–23.

13. Stanley B. Greenberg, *The Two Americas: Our Current Political Deadlock and How to Break It* (New York: Thomas Dunn Books, 2004).

14. The classic statement on electoral rules is Maurice Duverger, *Political Parties* (New York: Wiley, 1954).

15. Marjorie Randon Hershey, "Like a Bee: Election Law and the Survival of Third Parties," in Matthew J. Streb, ed., *Election Law and Electoral Politics* (Boulder, CO: Lynn Rienner, 2004).

16. Much of this discussion is drawn from Steven J. Rosenstone, Roy L. Behr, and Edward H. Lazarus, *Third Parties in America,* 2nd ed. (Princeton, NJ: Princeton University Press, 1996). Also see Paul S. Herrnson and John C. Green, *Multiparty Politics in America* (Lanham, MD: Rowman and Littlefield, 2002); John F. Bibby and Sandy Maisel, *Two Parties or More?* (Boulder, CO: Westview, 2003).

17. Marjorie Randon Hershey and Paul Allen Beck, *Party Politics in America,* 10th ed. (New York: Longman Publishers, 2003), pp. 102–104.

18. J. A. Schlesinger, "The New American Political Party," *American Political Science Review* 79 (1985), pp. 1152–1169; John Aldrich, *Why Parties?* (Chicago: University of Chicago Press, 1995).

19. David Menefee-Libey, *The Triumph of Campaign-Centered Politics* (New York: Chatham House Publishers, 2000).

20. Stephen Doyle, "The Very, Very Personal Is the Political," *The New York Times Magazine* (February 15, 2004), pp. 42–47.

21. Hershey, *Party Politics in America,* pp. 70–76.

22. Brian J. Brox, "The Development of Party Organizational Strength," paper presented at the Annual Meeting of the American Political Science Association, Washington, D.C., August 2003.

23. Roger H. Davidson and Walter J. Oleszek, *Congress and Its Members* (Washington, D.C.: CQ Press, 2006), chs. 3 and 4.

24. Jill Abramson, "A Law Survives. Now Let's Subvert It," *The New York Times* (December 14, 2003), Week in Review, p. 1.

25. Hershey, *Party Politics in America,* pp. 19–22.

26. Richard Florida, *The Rise of the Creative Class: How It's Transforming Work, Leisure, Communicy, and Everyday Life* (New York: Basic Books, 2002); Richard Florida, *The Flight of the Creative Class* (New York: Harper Business, 2005).

27. Hershey, *Party Politics in America,* pp. 287–291.

28. Greenberg, *The Two Americas;* Morris P. Fiorino, "Parties, Participation, and Representation in America," in Ira Katznelson and Helen V. Milner, eds., *Political Science: The State of the Discipline* (New York: W.W. Norton, 2002); Morris P. Fiorino, *Culture War? The Myth of a Polarized America* (New York: Pearson Longman, 2005), ch. 8; Hershey, *Party Politics in America,* ch. 15; Marc J. Hetherington, "Resurgent Mass Partisanship: The Role of Elite Polarization," *The American Political Science Review,* 95, no. 1 (September 2001), pp. 619–632; Gerald Pomper, "Parliamentary Government in the United States," in J. C. Green and D. M. Shea, eds., *The State of the Parties* (Lanham, MD: Rowman and Littlefield, 1999).

29. Lewis L. Gould, *Grand Old Party: A History of the Republicans* (New York: Random House, 2003); "When American Politics Turned European," *The Economist* (October 25, 2005), p. 74; Nils Gilman, "What the Rise of the Republicans as America's First Ideological Party Means for the Democrats," *The Forum,* 2, no. 1 (2004), pp. 1–4.

30. *National Election Studies,* 2004.

31. Ibid.

32. Pew Research Center for the People and the Press, *Evenly Divided and Increasingly Polarized* (Washington, D.C., 2003).

33. Alan D. Monroe, "American Party Platforms and Public Opinion," *American Journal of Political Science,* 27 (February 1983), p. 35; Gerald M. Pomper, *Elections in America* (New York: Longman, 1980), p. 169.

34. *New York Times*/CBS News, "Convention Delegate Polls," June 16–July 17, 2004, and August 3–23, 2004.

35. Jason M. Roberts and Steven S. Smith, "Procedural Contexts, Party Strategy, and Conditional Party Voting in the U.S. House of Representatives," *American Journal of Political Science,* 47 (2003), pp. 305–317; Douglas Hibbs, *The American Political Economy* (Cambridge, MA: Harvard University Press, 1987); Dennis P. Quinn and Robert Shapiro, "Business Political Power: The Case of Taxation," *American Political Science Review,* 85 (1991), pp. 851–874.

36. Hershey, *Party Politics in America,* pp. 290–291.

37. "Republican Fissures," *The Economist* (October 1, 2005), pp. 27–29; Sarah Lueck, "Cracks in a Republican Base," *The Wall Street Journal* (August 24, 2006), p. A1..

38. James MacGregor Burns, *Deadlock of Democracy* (Englewood Cliffs, NJ: Prentice Hall, 1967).

39. On the pernicious effects of divided government see Benjamin Ginsberg and Martin Shefter, *Politics by Other Means: The Declining Significance of Elections in America* (New York: Basic Books, 1990). For the contrary view see Morris P. Fiorina, *Divided Government* (New York: Macmillan, 1992); Gary Jacobson, *The Electoral Origins of Divided Government: Competition in U.S. House Elections* (Boulder, CO: Westview Press, 1990); David R. Mayhew, *Divided We Govern: Party Control, Lawmaking, and Investigations, 1946–1990* (New Haven, CT: Yale University Press, 1991).

CHAPTER 10

1. Federal Election Commission.

2. Campaign finance figures for this opening story are from Glen Justice, "Even with Campaign Finance Law, Money Talks Louder Than Ever," *The New York Times* (November 8, 2004), p. A16; Sharon Theimer, "Million Dollar-Plus Political Donors Rise," The Associated Press, October 29, 2004.

3. "527s in 2004," The Center for Public Integrity, press release December 16, 2004.

4. For further discussion, see Benjamin I. Page, *Choices and Echoes in Presidential Elections: Rational Man and Electoral Democracy* (Chicago: University of Chicago Press, 1978), ch. 2; Robert A. Dahl, *Democracy and Its Critics* (New Haven, CT: Yale University Press, 1989); Robert A. Dahl, *On Democracy* (New Haven, CT: Yale University Press, 1998); Hans Gersbach, *Designing Democracy* (New York: Springer Publishers, 2005).

5. See Austin Ranney, *The Doctrine of Responsible Party Government: Its Origins and Present State* (Urbana, IL: University of Illinois Press, 1962); E. E. Schattschneider, *Party Government* (New York: Holt, Rinehart & Winston, 1942); Marjorie Randon Hershey, *Party Politics in America* (New York: Pearson Longman Publishers, 2005), ch. 15.

6. Anthony Downs, *An Economic Theory of Democracy* (New York: Harper & Row, 1957); Otto Davis, Melvin Hinich, and Peter Ordeshook, "An Expository Development of a Mathematical Model of the Electoral Process," *American Political Science Review,* 64 (1970), pp. 426–448. Also see Allen Brierly, "Downs Model of Political Party Competition," paper presented at the annual meeting of the Midwest Political Science Association Palmer House Hilton, Chicago, IL (April 15, 2005).

7. Lawrence R. Jacobs and Robert Y. Shapiro, *Politicians Don't Pander: Political Manipulation and the Loss of*

Democratic Responsiveness (Chicago: University of Chicago Press, 2000).

8. See V. O. Key, Jr., *Public Opinion and American Democracy* (New York: Knopf, 1961); Morris P. Fiorina, *Retrospective Voting in American National Elections* (Cambridge, MA: Harvard University Press, 1981).

9. Katharine Q. Seelye, "Study Says 2000 Election Missed Millions of Votes," *The New York Times* (August, 10, 2001), p. A17.

10. David Stout, "Study Finds Ballot Problems Are More Likely for Poor," *The New York Times* (July 9, 2001), p. A9.

11. "Confusion Said to Create Invalid Ballots," Associated Press, reported on **WiredNews.com** February 22, 2005.

12. Dan Balz, "U.S. Panel Urges Reforms in Elections," *Washington Post* (September 19, 2005), p. 1.

13. Chilton Williamson, *American Suffrage* (Princeton, NJ: Princeton University Press, 1960), pp. 223, 241, 260. Also see Hershey, *Party Politics in America,* pp. 138–139.

14. See John Hope Franklin, *From Slavery to Freedom* (New York: Knopf, 1967); Leon Litwack, *North of Slavery* (Chicago: University of Chicago Press, 1961); Alexander Keyssar, *The Right to Vote: The Contested History of Democracy in the United States* (New York: Basic Books, 2001).

15. Walter Dean Burnham, "The Turnout Problem," in A. James Reichley, ed., *Elections, American Style* (Washington, D.C.: Brookings Institution, 1987), pp. 113–114.

16. Kay Lehman Schlozman, "Citizen Participation in America: What Do We Know? Why Do We Care?" in Ira Katznelson and Helen V. Milner, eds., *Political Science: The State of the Discipline* (New York: W. W. Norton, 2002), pp. 439–443; Martin P. Wattenberg, *Where Have All the Voters Gone?* (Cambridge, MA: Harvard University Press, 2002).

17. Peverill Squire, Raymond E. Wolfinger, and David P. Glass, "Residential Mobility and Voter Turnout," *American Political Science Review,* 81 (1987), pp. 45–65.

18. Nelson W. Polsby and Aaron Wildavsky, *Presidential Elections,* 11th ed. (Lanham, MD: Rowman and Littlefield, 2003), p. 17.

19. Ibid.; U.S. Bureau of the Census, 2002.

20. Wattenberg, *Where Have All the Voters Gone?* ch. 6.

21. Polsby and Wildavsky believe that barriers to registration are more important than alienation in explaining nonvoting. See *Presidential Elections,* p. 9. For an argument that registration laws are not very important in explaining low turnout see Benjamin Highton, "Voter Registration and Turnout in the United States," *Perspectives on Politics* (September 2004), pp. 507–516.

22. Joseph S. Nye, Jr., Philip D. Zelikow, and David C. King, eds., *Why People Don't Trust Government* (Cambridge, MA: Harvard University Press, 1997).

23. "Forum" in *The American Political Science Review,* 93 (December 1999), pp. 851–910; Richard R. Lau and Gerald M. Pomper, "Effects of Negative Campaigning on Turnout in U.S. Senate Elections, 1988–1998, *The Journal of Politics,* 63, no. 3 (August 2001), pp. 804–819.

24. Morris P. Fiorina, "Parties, Participation, and Representation in American: Old Theories Face New Realities," in Ira Katznelson and Helen V. Milner, *Political Science: The State of the Discipline* (New York: W. W. Norton, 2002).

25. Mark N. Franklin, *Voter Turnout and the Dynamics of Electoral Competition in Established Democracies Since 1945* (Cambridge: Cambridge University Press, 2004).

26. Fiorina, "Parties, Participation, and Representation in America."

27. Steven J. Rosenstone and John Mark Hansen, *Mobilization, Participation, and Democracy in American* (New York: Macmillan, 1993).

28. Alan S. Gerber and Donald M. Green, "The Effects of Canvassing, Telephone Calls, and Direct Mail on Voter Turnout," *American Political Science Review,* 94 (2000), pp. 653–663.

29. Russell Dalton, *Citizen Politics in Western Democracies* (Chatham, NJ: Chatham House, 1988), p. 42.

30. National Opinion Research Center, *The General Social Survey,* 2005.

31. Jack C. Doppelt and Ellen Shearer, *Non-Voters: America's No-Shows* (New York: Sage, 1999); Jeffrey Berry, *The New Liberalism* (Washington, D.C.: Brookings, 1999), pp. 39–40; Sidney Verba, Kay Lehman Schlozman, and Henry E. Brady, *Voice and Equality: Civic Volunteerism in American Politics* (Cambridge, MA: Harvard University Press, 1995).

32. Verba, Schlozman, and Brady, *Voice and Equality,* ch. 7; Sidney Verba and Norman H. Nie, *Participation in America* (New York: Harper & Row, 1972).

33. Susan A. MacManus, *Young v. Old* (Boulder, CO: Westview Press, 1996), ch. 2.

34. Thomas E. Patterson, "Young Voters and the 2004 Election," Working Paper: The Vanishing Voter Project, Harvard University (2005).

35. Margaret M. Conway, *Political Participation in the United States,* 3rd ed. (Washington, D.C.: CQ Press, 2000), p. 37.

36. E. J. Dionne, "If Nonvoters Had Voted: Same Winner, but Bigger," *The New York Times* (November 21, 1988), p. B16.

37. Sidney Verba, Kay Lehman Schlozman, Henry E. Brady, and Norman H. Nie, "Citizen Activity: Who Participates? What Do They Say?" *American Political Science Review,* 87 (1993), pp. 303–318; Robert S. Erikson and Kent L. Tedin, *American Public Opinion* (New York: Pearson Longman Publishers, 2005), ch. 7; Eric Shiraev and Richard Sobel, *People and Their Opinions* (New York: Pearson Longman Publishers, 2006), ch. 7–9.

38. Jacob Hacker and Paul Pierson, *Off Center* (New Haven: Yale University Press, 2005); Larry M. Bartels, "Is the Water Rising: Reflections on Inequality and American Democracy," *PS* (January 2006), pp. 39–42; Kay Lehman Schlozman, "On Inequality and Political Voice," *PS* (January 2006), pp. 55–57.

39. Polsby and Wildavsky, *Presidential Elections,* pp. 53–55, 57.

40. Ibid., pp. 92–93, 143–147.

41. Larry Bartels, *Presidential Primaries and the Dynamics of Public Choice* (Princeton, NJ: Princeton University Press, 1988); John H. Aldrich, *Before the Convention* (Chicago: University of Chicago Press, 1980).

42. Stephen J. Wayne, *The Road to the White House, 1992* (New York: Worth, 2000).

43. William G. Mayer, "Forecasting Presidential Nominations or, My Model Worked Just Fine, Thank You," *PS* (April 2003), pp. 153–157.

44. Polsby and Wildavsky, *Presidential Elections,* pp. 143–147.

45. Figures are from the National Election Commission.

46. Center for Responsive Politics (October 21, 2004).

47. Polsby and Wildavsky, *Presidential Elections,* pp. 62–67.

48. On this research see Thomas E. Mann, "Linking Knowledge and Action: Political Science and Campaign Finance Reform," *Perspectives on Politics,* 1, no. 1 (2003), pp. 69–83.

49. See Verba, Schlozman, and Brady, *Voice and Equality.*

50. Efforts to sort out their relative contributions include Benjamin I. Page and Calvin Jones, "Reciprocal Effects of Policy Preferences, Party Loyalties, and the Vote," *American Political Science Review,* 73 (1979), pp. 1071–1089; Gregory B. Markus and Philip E. Converse, "A Dynamic Simultaneous Equation Model of Public Choice," *American Political Science Review,* 73 (1979), pp. 1066–1070.

51. Carlos Elordi, "Ideology: Assessing Its Impact on Political Choices," *Public Perspective* (March/April 2000), pp. 34–35.

52. Erikson and Tedin, *American Public Opinion,* pp. 255–259.

53. Larry M. Bartels, "Partisanship and Voting Behavior, 1952–1996," *American Journal of Political Science,* 44 (January 2000), pp. 35–50; D. Sunshine Hillygus and Simon Jackman, "Voter Decision Making in Election 2000: Campaign Effects, Partisan Activation, and the Clinton Legacy," *American Journal of Political Science* 47 (2003), pp. 583–596.

54. Donald E. Stokes, "Some Dynamic Elements of Contests for the Presidency," *American Political Science Review,* 60 (1966), pp. 19–28.

55. Thomas B. Edsall, "The Shifting Sands of America's Political Parties," *The Washington Post National Edition* (April 9–15, 2001), p. 11.

CHAPTER 11

1. Polling and campaign finance information in this chapter opening story is from the following sources: Edison/Mitofsky Research for the National Election Pool, November 8, 2006; Frank Newport, Jeffrey M. Jones, and Lydia Saad, "Democrats Enlist Dissatisfied Voters to Build Congressional Victory," The Gallup News Service, press release, November 8, 2006; "Election Roundup," *The Wall Street Journal Online* (www.wsj.com), November 8, 2006; "Centrists Deliver for the Democrats," press release (Washington, D.C., Pew Research Center, November 8, 2006); "2006 Election Analysis," (Washington, D.C., The Center for Responsive Politics, November 9, 2006).

2. Sherly Gay Stolberg and Philip Shenon, "Elections Bring New Landscape to Capitol," *The New York Times* (November 8, 2006), p. A1.

3. Roger H. Davidson and Walter J. Oleszek, *Congress and Its Members,* 10th ed. (Washington, D.C.: Congressional Quarterly Press, 2006), pp. 17–18.

4. Ibid., pp. 24–25.

5. Quoted in Charles Warren, *The Supreme Court in U.S. History* (Boston: Little, Brown, 1919), p. 195.

6. Walter J. Oleszek, *Congressional Procedures and the Policy Process,* 6th ed. (Washington, D.C.: Congressional Quarterly Press, 2004), p. 4.

7. On this general question, see Jane Mansbridge, "Rethinking Representation," *American Political Science Review,* 97, no. 4 (2003), pp. 515–528.

8. Quoted in Charles Henning, *The Wit and Wisdom of Politics* (Golden, CO: Fulcrum, 1989), p. 235.

9. Abraham Lincoln, announcement in the *Sagamo Journal,* New Salem, Illinois (June 13, 1836).

10. For a dissenting view, one which suggests that senators, facing much more competitive elections than representatives, are just as likely as House members to lean toward the delegate style throughout their six-year term of office, see Charles Stewart III, "Congress and the Constitutional System," in Paul J. Quirk and Sarah A. Binder, eds., *The Legislative Branch* (New York: Oxford University Press, 2005).

11. The Inter-Parliamentary Union, Geneva, Switzerland, 2005.

12. Davidson and Oleszek, *Congress and Its Members,* pp. 118–119; "Guide to the New Congress," *CQ Today* (November 4, 2004), pp. 62–63.

13. Arturo Vega and Juanita Firestone, "The Effects of Gender on Congressional Behavior and the Substantive Representation of Women," *Legislative Studies Quarterly,* 20 (May 1995), pp. 213–222. Also see Michele L. Swers, *The Difference Women Make* (Chicago: University of Chicago Press, 2002); the collection of research on women's impact on the legislative process in Cindy Simon Rosenthal, ed., *Women Transforming Congress* (Norman, OK: University of Oklahoma Press, 2002).

14. Gary W. Cox and Jonathan Katz, "The Reapportionment Revolution and Bias in U.S. Congressional Elections," *American Journal of Political Science,* 43 (1999), pp. 812–840; Davidson and Oleszek, *Congress and Its Members,* pp. 47–50.

15. Ibid.; Charles S. Bulloch, III, "Two Generations of Redistricting: An Overview," *Extensions* (Fall 2004), pp. 12–13.

16. CQ Voting and Elections Collection Online **(http ://library.cqpress.com/elections),** 2005. Some have argued that districting is only one reason competitive elections have declined. Another may be that election districts are becoming more homogeneous as people increasingly move to areas where there are people like themselves. See the research of Bruce Oppenheimer and Alan Abramowitz, reported in Bill Bishop, "You Can't Compete With Voters' Feet," *Washington Post* (May 15, 2005), p. B2; Alan Abramowitz, Brad Alexander, and Matthew Gunning, "Drawing the Line on District Competition," *PS* (January 2006), pp. 95–97; Richard Florida, *The Flight of the Creative Class* (New York: Harper Business, 2005), pp. 217–222.

17. Davidson and Oleszek, *Congress and Its Members,* pp. 51–56.

18. Charles S. Bulloch, "Affirmative Action Districts: In Whose Face Will They Blow Up?" *Campaigns and Elections* (April 1995), p. 22.

19. Charles Cameron, David Epstein, and Sharon O'Halloran, "Do Majority-Minority Districts Maximize Black Representation in Congress?" *American Political Science Review,* 90 (1996), pp. 794–812; David Epstein and Sharon O'Halloran, "A Social Science Approach to Race, Districting and Representation," *American Political Science Review,* 93 (1999), pp. 187–191; David Lublin, *The Paradox of Representation: Racial Gerrymandering and Minority Interests* (Princeton, NJ: Princeton University Press, 1997); David T. Canon, "Representing Racial and Ethnic Minorities," in Paul J. Quirk and Sarah A. Binder, eds., *The Legislative Branch* (New York: Oxford University Press, 2005), pp. 185–186.

20. Federal Election Commission, Campaign Finance Reports and Data, 2005; Davidson and Oleszek, *Congress and Its Members,* pp. 67–68.

21. Gary W. Cox and Eric Magar, "How Much Is Majority Status in the U.S. Congress Worth?" *American Political Science Review,* 93 (1999), pp. 299–309.

22. Richard Hall and Frank W. Wayman, "Buying Time: Moneyed Interests and the Mobilization of Bias in Congressional Committees," *American Political Science Review,* 84 (1990), pp. 797–820.

23. See the classic work on this subject, David R. Mayhew, *Congress: The Electoral Connection* (New Haven, CT: Yale University Press, 1974). Also see Davidson and Oleszek, *Congress and Its Members,* ch. 5.

24. Malcolm Jewell, "Legislators and Their Districts," *Legislative Studies Quarterly,* 13 (1988), pp. 403–412.

25. Richard F. Fenno, Jr., *Home Style: House Members and Their Districts* (New York: Pearson Longman, 2003); Richard F. Fenno, Jr., *Senators on the Home Trail* (Norman, OK: University of Oklahoma Press, 1996).

26. Bruce Cain, John A. Ferejohn, and Morris P. Fiorina, *The Personal Vote: Constituency Service and Electoral Independence* (Cambridge, MA: Harvard University Press, 1987); Glenn Parker, *Homeward Bound: Explaining Change in Congressional Behavior* (Pittsburgh: University of Pittsburgh Press, 1986).

27. Robert S. Erikson, "Constituency Opinion and Congressional Behavior," *American Journal of Political Science,* 22 (1978), pp. 511–535; Robert S. Erikson and Gerald C. Wright, "Voters, Candidates, and Issues in Congressional Elections," in Lawrence C. Dodd and Bruce I. Oppenheimer, eds., *Congress Reconsidered,* 4th ed. (Washington, D.C.: Congressional Quarterly Press, 1989), pp. 91–116.

28. Alan Monroe, "Consistency Between Public Preferences and National Policy Decisions," *American Politics Quarterly,* 7 (1979), pp. 3–19; Benjamin I. Page and Robert Y. Shapiro, "Effects of Public Opinion on Policy," *American Political Science Review,* 77 (1983), pp. 175–190; Paul Burstein, "The Impact of Public Opinion on Public Policy: A Review and an Agenda," *Political Research Quarterly,* 56, no. 1 (March 2003).

29. Lawrence Jacobs and Robert Shapiro, *Politicians Don't Pander* (Chicago: University of Chicago Press, 2000).

30. Jacob S. Hacker and Paul Pierson, *Off Center: The Republican Revolution and the Erosion of American Democracy* (New Haven: Yale University Press, 2005).

31. Hacker and Pierson, *Off Center.*

32. Davidson and Oleszek, *Congress and Its Members,* p. 283–287.

33. Ibid., p. 285.

34. Quoted in Davidson and Oleszek, *Congress and Its Members,* p. 187.

35. On the transformation of the South in American politics and how it has affected Congress see Nelson W. Polsby, *How Congress Evolves: Social Bases of Institutional Change* (New York: New York University Press, 2004); Earl and Merle Black, *The Rise of Southern Republicans* (Cambridge, MA: Harvard University and Belknap Press, 2003); Stanley B. Greenberg, *The Two Americas* (New York: St. Martins Griffin, 2005).

36. Bill Marsh, "Wing-Tipped Migration: Five Prominent Men and How They Got From Congress to K Street," *The New York Times* (February 5, 2006), p. 14.

37. Davidson and Oleszek, *Congress and Its Members,* p. 185.

38. Ibid., pp. 290–292.

39. Alan I. Abramowitz and Kyle L. Saunders, "Ideological Realignment in the U.S. Electorate," *Journal of Politics,* 60 (1998), pp. 634–652; Keith T. Poole and Howard Rosenthal, *Congress: A Political-Economic History of Roll-Call Voting* (New York: Oxford University Press, 1997); *Evenly Divided and Increasingly Polarized: The 2004 Political Landscape* (Washington, D.C.: Pew Research Center, 2003); Nils Gilman, "What the Rise of the Republicans as America's First Ideological Party Means for the Democrats," *The Forum,* 2, no. 1 (2004), pp. 1–4.

40. Mickey Edwards, "Political Science and Political Practice," *Perspectives on Politics,* 1, no. 2 (June 2003), p. 352.

41. Richard Rose, "Giving Direction to Government in Comparative Perspective," in Joel D. Aberbach and Mark A. Peterson, eds., *The Executive Branch* (New York: Oxford University Press, 2005), pp. 79–81.

42. Ibid., pp. 77–79.

43. See John J. Kornacki, ed., *Leading Congress: New Styles, New Strategies* (Washington, D.C.: Congressional Quarterly Press, 1990); David W. Rohde, *Parties and Leaders in the Postreform Congress* (Chicago: University of Chicago Press, 1991).

44. Alan A. Abramowitz, "'Mr. Mayhew, Meet Mr. DeLay,' or the Electoral Connection in the Post-Reform Congress," *PS,* 34, no. 2 (June 2001), pp. 257–258.

45. Oleszek, *Congressional Procedures and the Policy Process,* p. 33; Davidson and Oleszek, *Congress and Its Members,* pp. 156–163.

46. This analogy is that of Congressman Tom DeLay reported in Jonathan Kaplan, "Hastert, DeLay: Political Pros Get Along to Go Along," *The Hill* (July 22, 2003), p. 8.

47. Bruce Oppenheimer, "Delayed Republican Revolution?

Testing the Limits of Institutional Constraints on the Senate Majority Party," *Extensions* (Spring 2005), p. 11.

48. Eric S. Heberlig, "Congressional Parties, Fundraising, and Committee Ambition," *Political Research Quarterly,* 56, no. 2 (June 2003), pp. 151–161.

49. Davidson and Oleszek, *Congress and Its Members,* pp. 203–214; David A. Rohde and Kenneth A. Shepsle, "Democratic Committee Assignments in the House of Representatives: Strategic Aspects of a Social Choice Process," in Matthew D. McCubbins and Terry Sullivan, eds., *Congress: Structure and Policy* (New York: Cambridge University Press, 1987).

50. Davidson and Oleszek, *Congress and Its Members,* pp. 213–214; Lawrence C. Dodd and Bruce I. Oppenheimer, "Revolution in the House: Testing the Limits of Party Government," in Lawrence C. Dodd and Bruce I. Oppenheimer, eds., *Congress Reconsidered,* 4th ed. (Washington, D.C.: Congressional Quarterly Press, 1989).

51. Jonathon Allen, "The Legacy of the Class of '94," *CQ Weekly* (September 4, 2004).

52. Davidson and Oleszek, *Congress and Its Members,* ch. 8; Donald R. Matthews, *U.S. Senators and Their World* (Chapel Hill, NC: University of North Carolina Press, 1960).

53. Robert Bendiner, *Obstacle Course on Capitol Hill* (New York: McGraw-Hill, 1964), p. 15.

54. Scott Shane, "Report Questions Legality of Briefings on Surveillance," *The New York Times* (January 19, 2006), p. A1.

55. Davidson and Oleszek, *Congress and Its Members,* pp. 486–489; John R. Hibbing and Elizabeth Theiss-Morse, *Congress as Public Enemy: Public Attitudes Toward American Political Institutions* (New York: Cambridge University Press, 1995); John Harwood, "Approval of Congress Erodes in Survey," *The Wall Street Journal* (May 19, 2005), p. A3.

56. Hibbing and Theiss-Morse, *Congress as Public Enemy,* p. 147.

CHAPTER 12

1. Harold J. Krent, *Presidential Powers* (New York: New York University Press, 2005)

2. U.S. Department of Commerce, *Historical Statistics of the United States, Colonial Times to 1970* (Washington, D.C.: U.S. Government Printing Office, 1971), pp. 8, 1143.

3. U.S. Bureau of the Census.

4. George C. Edwards III and Stephen J. Wayne, *Presidential Leadership: Politics and Policy Making* (Belmont, CA: Thomson Wadsworth, 2006), pp. 2–9.

5. On the contributions of particular presidents in shaping today's presidency, see Scott C. James, " The Evolution of the Presidency," in Joel D. Aberbach and Mark A. Peterson, eds., *The Executive Branch* (New York: Oxford University Press, 2005).

6. Quoted in Laurence J. Peter, *Peter's Quotations* (New York: Morrow, 1977), p. 405.

7. See Edwards and Wayne, *Presidential Leadership,* ch. 12.

8. Ibid, ch. 14.

9. *United States* v. *Curtiss-Wright* (1936). For more on judicial interpretations of presidential powers in foreign policy and war, see R. Shep Melnick, "The Courts, Jurisprudence, and the Executive Branch," in Joel D. Aberbach and Mark A. Peterson, eds., *The Executive Branch* (New York: Oxford University Press, 2005); Richard A. Brisbin, Jr., "The Judiciary and the Separation of Powers," in Kermit L. Hall and Kevin T. McGuire, eds., *The Judicial Branch* (New York: Oxford University Press, 2005).

10. Melnick, "The Courts, Jurisprudence, and the Executive Branch."

11. Edwards and Wayne, *Presidential Leadership,* p. 480.

12. Arthur Schlesinger, Jr, *The Imperial Presidency* (New York: Popular Library, Atlantic Monthly Press, 1973).

13. James P. Pfiffner, *The Modern Presidency* (New York: St. Martin's Press, 1998), ch. 4. Also see Edwards and Wayne, *Presidential Leadership,* ch. 6.

14. Edwards and Wayne, *Presidential Leadership,* p. 209.

15. Nathan Miller, *FDR: An Intimate History* (Lanham, MD: Madison Books, 1983), p. 276.

16. Thomas E. Cronin and Michael A. Genovese, *The Paradoxes of the American Presidency* (New York: Oxford University Press, 2004), ch. 10; Joseph A. Pika, "The Vice-Presidency: New Opportunities, Old Constraints," in Michael Nelson, ed., *The Presidency and the Political System,* 4th ed. (Washington, D.C.: Congressional Quarterly Press, 1995), pp. 496–528.

17. Edwards and Wayne, *Presidential Leadership,* p. 216.

18. Elizabeth Bumiller and Eric Schmitt, "In Indictment's Wake, A Focus on Cheney's Powerful Role in the White House," *The New York Times* (October 20, 2005), p. A1.

19. Richard E. Neustadt, *Presidential Power and the Modern Presidents: The Politics of Leadership from Roosevelt to Reagan* (New York: Free Press, 1990).

20. William G. Howell, *Power Without Persuasion: The Politics of Direct Presidential Action* (Princeton, NJ: Princeton University Press, 2003); Phillip J. Cooper, *By Order of the President: The Use and Abuse of Executive Direct Action* (Lawrence, KS: University of Kansas Press, 2002).

21. James, "The Evolution of the Presidency," pp. 28–31.

22. Graham T. Allison, *Essence of Decision: Explaining the Cuban Missile Crisis* (Boston: Little, Brown, 1971), pp. 141–142.

23. Neustadt, *Presidential Power and the Modern Presidents,* ch. 2.

24. Charles O. Jones, *Separate but Equal: Congress and the Presidency* (New York: Chatham House, 1999).

25. Andrew Rudalevige, "The Executive Branch and the Legislative Process," in Joel D. Aberbach and Mark A. Peterson, eds., *The Executive Branch* (New York: Oxford University Press, 2005), pp. 432–445.

26. Edwards and Wayne, *Presidential Leadership,* pp. 336–348; Jon R. Bond and Richard Fleisher, eds., *Polarized Politics: Congress and the President in a*

Partisan Era (Washington, D.C.: CQ Press, 2000); Jeffrey S. Peake, "Back on Track," *American Politics Research* (November 2004), pp. 679–697.

27. Terry Sullivan, "Headcounts, Expectations and Presidential Coalitions in Congress," *American Journal of Political Science,* 32 (1988), pp. 657–689.

28. Aaron Wildavsky, "The Two Presidencies," in Aaron Wildavsky, ed., *Perspectives on the Presidency* (Boston: Little, Brown, 1975), pp. 448–461.

29. Richard Brody, *Assessing the President: The Media, Elite Opinion, and Public Support* (Stanford, CA.: Stanford University Press, 1991); George C. Edwards III, *At the Margins: Presidential Leadership of Congress* (New Haven, CT: Yale University Press, 1989); George C. Edwards III, "Aligning Tests with Theory: Presidential Approval as a Source of Influence in Congress," *Congress and the Presidency,* 24 (Fall 1997), pp. 113–130.

30. Edwards and Wayne, *Presidential Leadership,* pp. 348–350.

31. Jeffrey K. Tulis, *The Rhetorical Presidency* (Princeton, NJ: Princeton University Press, 1987), chs. 2 and 3, esp. p. 64.

32. Woodrow Wilson, *Leaders of Men,* ed. T. H. Vail Motter (Princeton, NJ: Princeton University Press, 1952), p. 39; quoted in Tulis, *The Rhetorical Presidency,* ch. 4, which analyzes Wilson's theory at length and expresses some skepticism about it.

33. Tulis, *The Rhetorical Presidency,* pp. 138, 140.

34. Samuel Kernell, *Going Public: Strategies of Presidential Leadership,* 3rd ed. (Washington, D.C.: Congressional Quarterly Press, 1997), p. 92 and ch. 4.

35. Benjamin I. Page and Robert Y. Shapiro, "Presidents as Opinion Leaders: Some New Evidence," *Policy Studies Journal,* 12 (1984), pp. 649–661; Benjamin I. Page, Robert Y. Shapiro, and Glenn R. Dempsey, "What Moves Public Opinion," *American Political Science Review,* 81 (1987), pp. 23–43; but see Donald L. Jordan, "Newspaper Effects on Policy Preferences," *Public Opinion Quarterly,* 57 (1993), pp. 191–204.

36. Lawrence R. Jacobs and Robert Y. Shapiro, *Politicians Don't Pander: Political Manipulation and the Loss of Democratic Responsiveness* (Chicago: University of Chicago Press, 2000); Jacob Hacker and Paul Pierson, *Off Center* (New Haven, CT: Yale University Press, 2005).

37. Doris Graber, *Mass Media and American Politics* (Washington, D.C.: CQ Press, 2006), ch. 9; Lawrence R. Jacobs, "Communicating From the White House," Joel D. in Aberbach and Mark A. Peterson, eds., *The Executive Branch* (New York: Oxford University Press, 2005), pp. 189–205.

38. Benjamin I. Page and Mark P. Petracca, *The American Presidency* (New York: McGraw-Hill, 1983), p. 122. Also see Benjamin I. Page and Robert Y. Shapiro, "Effects of Public Opinion on Policy," *American Political Science Review,* 77 (1983), pp. 175–190.

39. Lawrence Jacobs and Robert Y. Shapiro, "The Rise of Presidential Polling: The Nixon White House in Historical Perspective," *Public Opinion Quarterly,* 59 (1995), pp. 163–195; Jacobs, "Communicating From the White House," pp. 178–189.

40. Edwards and Wayne, *Presidential Leadership,* pp. 112–123.

41. Brody, *Assessing the President.* See also John E. Mueller, "Presidential Popularity from Truman to Johnson," *American Political Science Review,* 64 (1970), pp. 18–34; Samuel Kernell, "Explaining Presidential Popularity," *American Political Science Review,* 72 (1978), pp. 506–522; George C. Edwards III, *Presidential Approval* (Baltimore, MD: Johns Hopkins University Press, 1990).

CHAPTER 13

1. David S. Broder, "So, Now Bigger Is Better," *The Washington Post National Weekly Edition* (January 20–26, 2003), p. 21.

2. See Charles T. Goodsell, *The Case for Bureaucracy,* 4th ed. (Washington, D.C.: CQ Press, 2003), p. 85; Kenneth J. Meier, "Representative Bureaucracy: An Empirical Analysis," *American Political Science Review,* 69 (June 1975), pp. 537–539.

3. Wallace Sayre, "Bureaucracies: Some Contrasts in Systems," *Indian Journal of Public Administration,* 10 (1964), p. 223. For contemporary evidence in support of this claim, see Gabriel A. Almond, G. Bingham Powell, Jr., Kaare Strom, and Russell J. Dalton, *Comparative Politics Today* (New York: Pearson Longman, 2004).

4. John A. Rohr, *Civil Servants and Their Constitutions* (Lawrence, KS: University of Kansas Press, 2002); Richard J. Stillman II, *The American Bureaucracy* (Chicago: Nelson-Hall, 1987), p. 18.

5. Rohr, *Civil Servants and Their Constitutions,* ch. 4.

6. B. Guy Peters, *American Public Policy: Policy and Performance,* 6th ed. (New York: CQ Press, 2004), pp. 97–98.

7. Daniel Carpenter, "The Evolution of National Bureaucracy in the United States," in Joel D. Aberbach and Mark A. Peterson, eds., *The Executive Branch* (New York: Oxford University Press, 2005), pp. 55–57.

8. Theodore J. Lowi, *The End of Liberalism,* 2nd ed. (New York: Norton, 1979).

9. Charles R. Shipan, "Congress and the Bureaucracy," in Paul J. Quirk and Sarah A. Binder, eds., *The Legislative Branch* (New York: Oxford University Press, 2005).

10. Christopher Lee, "An Overhaul, Not a Tuneup," *The Washington Post National Edition* (June 22, 2003), p. 30.

11. Patricia W. Ingraham, "The Federal Service: the People and the Challenge," in Joel D. Aberbach and Mark A. Peterson, eds., *The Executive Branch* (New York: Oxford University Press, 2005), pp. 290–291.

12. Ingraham, "The Federal Service," pp. 294–96.

13. See Samuel Krislov and David H. Rosenbloom, *Representative Bureaucracy and the American Political System* (New York: Praeger, 1981); Goodsell, *The Case for Bureaucracy;* Ingraham, "The Federal Service."

14. Goodsell, *The Case for Bureaucracy,* pp. 84–90; Stanley Rothman and S. Robert Lichter, "How Liberal Are Bureaucrats?" *Regulation* (November–December 1983), pp. 35–47.

15. Office of Personnel Management, 2005.

16. Ingraham, "The Federal Service," pp. 291–294.

17. Richard P. Nathan, *The Administrative Presidency* (New York: Wiley, 1983).

18. David E. Rosenbaum and Stephen Labaton, "Amid Many Fights on Qualifications, a Nomination Stalls," *The New York Times* (September 24, 2005), p. A12.

19. Hugh Heclo, *A Government of Strangers* (Washington, D.C.: Brookings Institution, 1977), p. 103.

20. Cornelius M. Kerwin, *Rulemaking: How Government Agencies Write Law and Make Policy* (Washington, DC: CQ Press, 2003), p. 183.

21. Richard E. Neustadt, *Presidential Power* (New York: Wiley, 1960); George C. Edwards III and Stephen J. Wayne, *Presidential Leadership: Politics and Policy Making* (Wadsworth, CA: Thomson Wadsworth, 2006), ch. 9.

22. Terry M. Moe, "Control and Feedback in Economic Regulation," *American Political Science Review,* 79 (1985), pp. 1094–1116; Richard W. Waterman, *Presidential Influence and the Administrative State* (Knoxville, TN: University of Tennessee Press, 1989); Edwards and Wayne, *Presidential Leadership,* pp. 295–303.

23. Richard W. Waterman and Kenneth J. Meier, "Principal-Agent Models: An Expansion?" *Journal of Public Administration Research and Theory,* 8 (April 1998), pp. 173–202; Edwards and Wayne, *Presidential Leadership,* pp. 305–307.

24. Roger H. Davidson and Walter J. Oleszek, *Congress and Its Members,* 10th ed. (Washington, D.C.: CQ Press, 2006), pp. 336–337, 354–361; Matthew D. McCubbins, "The Legislative Design of Regulatory Structure," *American Journal of Political Science,* 29 (1985), pp. 421–438.

25. Nolan McCarty and Rose Razahgian, "Advice and Consent: Senate Responses to Executive Branch Nominations, 1885–1996," *American Journal of Political Science,* 43 (October 1999), pp. 1122–1143.

26. Richard Fenno, *The Power of the Purse* (Boston: Little, Brown, 1966); Aaron Wildavsky, *The Politics of the Budgetary Process* (Boston: Little, Brown, 1964); Davidson and Oleszek, *Congress and Its Members,* pp. 357–359, 433–434.

27. John A. Ferejohn and Charles R. Shipan, "Congressional Influence on Administrative Agencies: A Case Study of Telecommunications Policy," in Lawrence C. Dodd and Bruce I. Oppenheimer, eds., *Congress Reconsidered,* 4th ed. (Washington, D.C.: Congressional Quarterly Press, 1989); Davidson and Oleszek, *Congress and Its Members,* p. 355.

28. Barry R. Weingast, "Caught in the Middle: The President, Congress, and the Political-Bureaucratic System," in Joel D. Aberbach and Mark A. Peterson, eds., *The Executive Branch* (New York: Oxford University Press, 2005), pp. 322–325.

29. See Derek Bok, *The Trouble with Government* (Cambridge, MA: Harvard University Press, 2001), ch. 9; Emanuel S. Savas, *Privatization: The Key to Better Government* (Chatham, NJ: Chatham House, 1987); Sheila B. Kamerman and Alfred J. Kahn, eds., *Privatization and the Welfare State* (Princeton, NJ: Princeton University Press, 1989); Lester M. Salamon, ed., *The Tools of Government: A Guide to the New Governance* (Oxford, England: Oxford University Press, 2002).

30. Paul Light, *The Size of Government* (Washington, D.C.: Brookings, 1999); Ingraham, "The Federal Public Service," pp. 301–303; Patricia Wallace Ingraham, "You Talking To Me? Accountability and the Modern Public Service," *PS* (January 2005), pp. 19–20.

31. Bok, *The Trouble with Government,* p. 233–234; Roberta Lynch and Ann Markusen, "Can Markets Govern?" *American Prospect* (Winter 1994), pp. 125–134; Dan Guttman, "Governance by Contract," *Public Contract Law Journal,* 33 (Winter 2004), pp. 321–360.

32. David Osborne and Ted Gaebler, *Reinventing Government* (Reading, MA: Addison-Wesley, 1992).

33. Bok, *The Trouble with Government,* pp. 234–239; Joel D. Aberbach and Bert A. Rockman, eds., *In the Web of Politics: Three Decades of the U.S. Federal Executive* (Washington, D.C.: Brookings Institution Press, 2000); Lester M. Salamon, "The New Governance and the Tools of Public Administration," in Lester M. Salamon, ed., *The Tools of Government* (Oxford, England: Oxford University Press, 2002).

34. Carpenter, "The Evolution of National Bureaucracy," pp. 63–64.

35. Terry M. Moe, "The Politics of Bureaucratic Structure," and John E. Chubb and Paul E. Peterson, "American Political Institutions and the Problem of Governance," p. 41, in John E. Chubb and Paul E. Peterson, eds., *Can the Government Govern?* (Washington, D.C.: Brookings Institution, 1989), James L. Sundquist, *Constitutional Reform and Effective Government* (Washington, D.C.: Brookings Institution, 1986).

CHAPTER 14

1. All quotes are from Neil A. Lewis, "Bitter Senators Divided Anew on Judgeships," *The Washington Post* (November 15, 2003), p. A1.

2. J. M. Sosin, *The Aristocracy of the Long Robe: The Origins of Judicial Review in America* (Westport, CT: Greenwood Press, 1989); William E. Nelson, "The Historical Foundations of the American Judiciary," Kermit L. Hall, "Judicial Independence and the Majoritarian Difficulty," and Cass R. Sunstein, "Judges and Democracy: the Changing Role of the United States Supreme Court," in Kermit L. Hall and Kevin T. McGuire, eds., *The Judicial Branch* (New York: Oxford University Press, 2005).

3. Robert G. McCloskey, *The American Supreme Court,* 4th ed. (Chicago: University of Chicago Press, 2005), pp. 12–13.

4. On *Marbury,* see Sylvia Snowmiss, *Judicial Review and the Law of the Constitution* (New Haven, CT: Yale University Press, 1990).

5. Linda Greenhouse, "The Imperial Presidency vs. the Imperial Judiciary," *The New York Times* (March 2, 2000), Week in Review sec., p. 1; Paul Gewirtz and Chad Golder, "So Who Are the Activists? *The New York Times* (July 6, 2005), p. A1.

6. Ran Hirschl, *Towards Juristocracy: The Origins and Consequences of the New Constitutionalism* (Cambridge, MA: Harvard University Press, 2004).

7. Ibid. pp. 6–10.

8. Donald P. Kommers, "American Courts and Democracy: A Comparative Perspective," in Kermit L. Hall and Kevin T. McGuire, eds., *The Judicial Branch* (New York: Oxford University Press, 2005), p. 209.

9. Ibid.

10. Robert A. Dahl, *How Democratic Is the American Constitution?* (New Haven, CT: Yale University Press, 2001), pp. 54–55.

11. Richard S. Randall, *American Constitutional Development* (New York: Longman, 2002), pp. 488–489.

12. Neil Lewis, "An Appeals Court That Always Veers to the Right," *The New York Times* (May 24, 1999), p. A1; Deborah Sontag, "The Power of the Fourth," *The New York Times Sunday Magazine* (March 9, 2003), pp. 38–44.

13. David M. O'Brien, *Storm Center: The Supreme Court in American Politics,* 7th ed. (New York: Norton, 2005), p. 73. Also see Joel B. Grossman, "Paths to the Bench," in Kermit L. Hall and Kevin T. McGuire, eds., *The Judicial Branch* (New York: Oxford University Press, 2005), p. 162. Also see Lee Epstein, Jack Knight, and Andrew D. Martin, "The Norm of Judicial Experience," *University of California Law Review,* 91 (2003), pp. 938–939.

14. Robert A. Carp and Ronald Stidham, *Judicial Process in America,* 6th ed. (Washington, D.C.: Congressional Quarterly Press, 2004), ch. 8; Grossman, "Paths to the Bench," pp. 160–161.

15. Grossman, "Paths to the Bench"; Lawrence Baum, "The Supreme Court in American Politics," in Nelson W. Polsby, ed., *Annual Review of Political Science* (Palo Alto, CA: Annual Reviews, 2003), pp. 161–180; Robert Dahl, "Decision-Making in a Democracy: The Supreme Court as a National Policy-Maker," *Journal of Public Law,* 6 (1957), pp. 279–295; Ronald Stidham and Robert A. Carp, "Judges, Presidents, and Policy Choices," *Social Science Quarterly,* 68 (1987), pp. 395–404; Carp and Stidham, *Judicial Process in America,* ch. 9.

16. See Bernard Schwartz, *Decision: How the Supreme Court Decides Cases* (New York: Oxford University Press, 2005).

17. Jeffrey Rosen, "So, Do You Believe in 'Super-Precedent'?" *The New York Times* (October 30, 2005), p. IV. 1.

18. Jeffrey A. Segal, Harold J. Spaeth, and Sara C. Benesh, *The Supreme Court in the American Legal System* (New York: Cambridge University Press, 2005), ch. 11.

19. For details, see H. W. Perry, Jr., *Deciding to Decide: Agenda Setting in the United States Supreme Court* (Cambridge, MA: Harvard University Press, 2005).

20. Ibid.

21. Segal, Spaeth, and Benesh, *The Supreme Court in the American Legal System,* pp. 318–323; David Adamany, "The Supreme Court," in John B. Gates and Charles A. Johnson, eds., *The American Courts* (Washington, D.C.: CQ Press, 1991), pp. 111–112; Baum, "The Supreme Court in U.S. Politics," pp. 162–168; Glendon Schubert, *The Judicial Mind* (Evanston, IL: Northwestern University Press, 1965); Jeffrey A. Segal and Harold J. Spaeth, *The Supreme Court and the Attitudinal Model* (New York: Cambridge University Press, 1993); John D. Sprague, *Voting Patterns of the United States Supreme Court* (Indianapolis: Bobbs-Merrill, 1968).

22. Walter Murphy, *Elements of Judicial Strategy* (Princeton, NJ: Princeton University Press, 1964).

23. Joel B. Grossman, "Social Backgrounds and Judicial Decision-Making," *Harvard Law Review,* 79 (1966), pp. 1551–1564; S. Sidney Ulmer, "Dissent Behavior and the Social Background of Supreme Court Justices," *Journal of Politics,* 32 (1970), pp. 580–589.

24. L. Epstein, J. Knight, and J. Martin, "The Supreme Court as a Strategic National Policy-Maker," *Emory Law Review,* 50 (2001), pp. 583–610.

25. Nicholas Wade, "A Mathematician Crunches the Supreme Court's Numbers," *The New York Times* (August 4, 2003), p. A21; Segal, Spaeth, and Benesh, *The Supreme Court in the American Legal System,* pp. 318–323.

26. John Harlan, "A Glimpse of the Supreme Court at Work," *University of Chicago Law School Record,* 1, no. 7 (1963), pp. 35–52.

27. Bob Woodward and Scott Armstrong, *The Brethren: Inside the Supreme Court* (New York: Simon & Schuster, 1979).

28. Lee Epstein and Jack Knight, "Mapping Out the Strategic Terrain: The Informational Role of Amici Curiae," in Cornell Clayton and Howard Gillman, eds., *Supreme Court Decision-Making* (Chicago: University of Chicago Press, 1999); Segal, Spaeth, and Benesh, *The Supreme Court in the American Legal System,* chs. 12 and 13.

29. Herbert Jacob, *Justice in America,* 3rd ed. (Boston: Little, Brown, 1978), p. 245. Also see Keith E. Whittington, "Judicial Review and Interpretation," in Kermit L. Hall and Kevin T. McGuire, eds., *The Judicial Branch* (New York, Oxford University Press, 2005).

30. McCloskey, *The American Supreme Court.* Also see James H. Fowler and Sangick Jeon, "The Authority of Supreme Court Precedent," University of California, Davis, Working Paper (June 29, 2005).

31. Carp and Stidham, *Judicial Process in America,* p. 28.

32. Ibid, p. 57.

33. Mark A. Graber, "From Republic to Democracy: the Judiciary and the Political Process," in Kermit L. Hall and Kevin T. McGuire, eds., *The Judicial Branch* (New York, Oxford University Press, 2005).

34. McCloskey, *The American Supreme Court.* Also see H. W. Perry, Jr., *The Transformation of the Supreme Court's Agenda: From the New Deal to the Reagan Administration* (Boulder, CO: Westview Press, 1991); Charles R. Epp, "The Supreme Court and the Rights Revolution," in Kermit L. Hall and Kevin T. McGuire, eds., *The Judicial Branch* (New York, Oxford University Press, 2005); Sunstein, "Judges and Democracy."

35. *Hamdi* v. *Rumsfeld* (2004).

36. Charles Lane, "A Mirror on the Nation's Mood," *The Washington Post National Edition* (July 14–20, 2003), p. 29; Linda Greenhouse, "In a Momentous Term, Justices Remake the Law, and the Court," *The New York Times*

(July 1, 2003), p. A1; "Affirmative Action," *The Economist* (June 28, 2003), p. 28.

37. Gewirtz and Golder, "So Who Are the Activists?", p. A29.

38. Ibid.

39. Baum, "The Supreme Court in American Politics," p. 167.

40. Linda Greenhouse, "Rehnquist Resumes His Call for Judicial Independence," *The New York Times* (December 31, 2004), p. A13.

41. See Roger H. Davidson and Walter J. Oleszek, *Congress and Its Members,* 10th ed. (Washington, D.C.: CQ Press, 2006), pp. 371–391, for a discussion of legislative checks on the judiciary.

42. Edward Lazurus, *Closed Chambers* (New York: Penguin, 1999), pp. 373–374.

43. Epstein and Knight, "Mapping Out the Strategic Terrain."

44. Dahl, "Decision Making in a Democracy," pp. 279–295; Thomas R. Marshall, "Public Opinion, Representation, and the Modern Supreme Court," *American Politics Quarterly,* 16 (1988), pp. 296–316; McCloskey, *The American Supreme Court,* p. 22; O'Brien, *Storm Center,* p. 325.

45. G. Caldeira, "Courts and Public Opinion," in Gates and Johnson, eds., *The American Courts;* Jay Casper, "The Supreme Court and National Policy Making," *American Political Science Review,* 70 (1976), pp. 50–63; Marshall, "Public Opinion, Representation, and the Modern Supreme Court"; William Mishler and Reginald S. Sheehan, "The Supreme Court as a Counter-Majoritarian Institution: The Impact of Public Opinion on Supreme Court Decisions," *American Political Science Review,* 87 (1993), pp. 87–101; Benjamin I. Page and Robert Y. Shapiro, "Effects of Public Opinion on Policy," *American Political Science Review,* 77 (1983), p. 183.

46. Segal, Spaeth, and Benesh, *The Supreme Court in the American Legal System,* pp. 326–328.

CHAPTER 15

1. These and other examples of campus speech codes, as well as an extended discussion of the controversies surrounding them, can be found in Donald Alexander Downs, *Restoring Free Speech and Liberty on Campus* (New York: Cambridge University Press, 2005).

2. Nat Hentoff, "Chilling Codes," *Washington Post,* Nexis: LEGI-SLATE Article No. 225/226.

3. On the "contract clause" see Lee Epstein and Thomas G. Walker, *Constitutional Law for a Changing America* (Washington, D.C.: CQ Press, 2005), ch. 9.

4. James E. Ely, Jr., "Property Rights and Democracy in the American Constitutional Order, " in Kermit L. Hall and Kevin T. McGuire eds., *The Judicial Branch* (New York: Oxford University Press, 2005); Richard Fallon, *The Dynamic Constitution: An Introduction to American Constitutional Law* (New York: Cambridge University Press, 2004), ch. 3, "Protection of Economic Liberties."

5. Laurence H. Tribe, *American Constitutional Law,* 3rd ed. (New York: Foundation Press, 2000), ch. 9.

6. Morton J. Horwitz, *The Transformation of American Law, 1780–1860* (Cambridge, MA: Harvard University Press, 1977); J. Willard Hurst, *Law and the Conditions of Freedom in the Nineteenth-Century United States* (Madison, WI: University of Wisconsin Press, 1956).

7. Epstein and Walker, *Constitutional Law for a Changing America,* pp. 438–431.

8. See Geoffrey R. Stone, *Perilous Times: Free Speech in Wartime* (New York: W.W. Norton, 2004).

9. See Stanley I. Kutler, *The American Inquisition: Justice and Injustice in the Cold War* (New York: Hill & Wang, 1982).

10. See Fred W. Friendly, *Minnesota Rag* (New York: Vintage, 1981).

11. See Charles Rembar, *The End of Obscenity* (New York: Harper & Row, 1968).

12. Fallon, *The Dynamic Constitution,* p. 48.

13. Ibid., pp. 61–67.

14. Ibid., p. 63.

15. *Katz* v. *United States* (1967).

16. *United States* v. *Leon* (1984); *Massachusetts* v. *Sheppard* (1984).

17. *Nix* v. *Williams* (1984).

18. *Harris* v. *New York* (1971); *New York* v. *Quarles* (1984).

19. *Arizona* v. *Fulminate* (1991).

20. Jim Yardley, "A Role Model for Executions," *The New York Times* (January 9, 2000), p. A1, IV–5.

21. Linda Greenhouse, "Court's Term a Turn Back to the Center," *The New York Times* (July 4, 2005), p. A1; Linda Greenhouse, "Supreme Court Rules for Texan on Death Row," *The New York Times* (June 14, 2005), p. A1; Adam Liptak and Ralph Blumenthal, "Death Sentences in Texas Cases Try Supreme Court's Patience," *The New York Times* (December 5, 2004), p. A1.

22. Bureau of Judicial Statistics (December 2005).

23. Adam Liptak, "Juries Reject Death Penalty in Nearly All Federal Trials," *The New York Times* (November 21, 2003), p. A1.

24. "The Death Penalty: An International Perspective," The Death Penalty Information Center (**www .deathpenaltyinfo.org),** 2006.

25. Geoffrey R. Stone, *Perilous Times: Free Speech in Wartime* (New York: W.W. Norton, 2004); Fallon, *The Dynamic Constitution,* ch. 12.

26. Former Chief Justice William Rehnquist believed that each successive American war involved fewer and less serious violations of civil liberties. See *All the Laws But One: Civil Liberties in Wartime* (New York: Knopf, 1998).

27. Barton Gellman, "The FBI's Secret Scrutiny," *The Washington Post* (November 6, 2005), p. A1.

28. David A. Yalof, "Courts and the Definition of Defendants Rights," in Kermit L. Hall and Kevin T. McGuire, eds., *The Judicial Branch* (New York: Oxford University Press, 2005), pp. 452–454.

29. "Security Trumps Civil Liberties," a report of a poll conducted by National Public Radio, the Kennedy School of Government of Harvard University, and the Kaiser Family Fund (November 30, 2001).

30. Robert Block, "Bush Antiterror Plans Irk Big Business," *The Wall Street Journal* (November 28, 2005), p. A1; Richard S. Dunham, "The Patriot Act: Business Balks," *BusinessWeek* (November 21, 2005), pp. 124–126.

31. Pew Research Center, "Americans Taking Abramoff, Alito, and Domestic Spying in Stride" (January 11, 2006).

CHAPTER 16

1. Greg Winter, "Schools Resegregate, Study Finds," *The New York Times* (January 21, 2003), p. A14.

2. Gary Orfield and Chungmei Lee, *Brown at 50: King's Dream or Plessy's Nightmare?* (Cambridge, MA: Harvard University—The Civil Rights Project, 2004), p. 1.

3. Ibid., p. 20.

4. Ibid., p. 27. Also see Gary Orfield and Chungmei Lee, *Racial Transformation and the Changing Nature of Segregation* (Cambridge, MA: Harvard University—The Civil Rights Project, 2006); Charles T. Clotfelter, *After Brown: The Rise and Retreat of School Desegregation* (Princeton, NJ: Princeton University Press, 2004).

5. Richard H. Fallon, *The Dynamic Constitution: An Introduction to Constitutional Law* (New York: Cambridge University Press, 2004), pp. 109–110.

6. James MacGregor Burns and Stewart Burns, *A People's Charter: The Pursuit of Rights in America* (New York: Knopf, 1991), p. 37.

7. On why the courts were such an attractive target for people seeking to expand civil rights, see Charles R. Epp, "The Courts and the Rights Revolution," in Kermit L. Hall and Kevin T. McGuire, eds., *The Judicial Branch* (New York: Oxford University Press, 2005).

8. William H. Chafe, *The Unfinished Journey: America Since World War II* (New York: Oxford University Press, 1986), p. 149.

9. Fallon, *The Dynamic Constitution,* pp. 118–120.

10. Ibid., pp. 119–122.

11. Epp, "The Courts and the Rights Revolution."

12. Richard Morin and Michael H. Cottman, "The Invisible Slap," *The Washington Post National Edition* (July 2–8, 2001), p. 5.

13. Gallup Poll, June 12–15, 2003.

14. Pew Research Center, "The Black and White of Public Opinion," October 31, 2005.

15. Amnesty International, "Threat and Humiliation: Racial Profiling, Domestic Security, and Human Rights in the United States" (September 2004).

16. This section is based on Richard D. Kahlenberg, *The Remedy: Class, Race, and Affirmative Action* (New York: Basic Books, 1996); Fallon, *The Dynamic Constitution,* ch. 5.

17. Sam Howe Verhovek, "In Poll, Americans Reject Means But Not the Ends of Racial Diversity," *The New York Times* (December 14, 1997), p. A1; Martin Gilens, Paul M. Sniderman, and James H. Kuklinski, "Affirmative Action and the Politics of Realignment," *British Journal of Political Science,* 28 (January 1998), pp. 159–184; Jack Citrin, David O. Sears, Christopher Muste, and Cara Wong, "Multiculturalism in American Public Opinion," *British Journal of Political Science* 31 (2001), pp. 247–275.

18. The Gallup Survey (August 2001; June 2003).

19. The Pew Research Center for the People and the Press, "Evenly Divided and Increasingly Polarized" (Washington, D.C., 2003), p. 45, and "Conflicted Views of Affirmative Action" (Washington, D.C, 2004), p. 1.

20. Ibid., p. 46.

21. George M. Fredrickson, "Still Separate and Unequal," *The New York Review of Books* (November 17, 2005), p. 13.

22. In *Hunt* v. *Cromartie* (1999), the Court ruled in favor of the redrawn Twelfth Congressional District in North Carolina, presumably because race was not the only consideration in drawing district lines.

23. Opinion of the Court, *Grutter* v. *Bollinger* (2003).

24. William H. Chafe, *The Unfinished Journey: America Since World War II* (New York: Oxford University Press, 1986); Barbara Sinclair Deckard, *The Women's Movement* (New York: Harper and Row, 1975); Ethel Klein, *Gender Politics* (Cambridge, MA: Harvard University Press, 1984), ch. 2; J. Freeman, *Politics of Women's Liberation* (New York: McKay, 1975).

25. See Epp, "Courts and the Rights Revolution"; Fallon, *The Dynamic Constitution,* pp. 129–133.

26. See Marian Faux, *Roe v. Wade* (New York: Macmillan, 1988).

27. Ibid., p. 45.

28. Eva R. Rubin, *Abortion, Politics, and the Courts* (Westport, CT: Greenwood Press, 1982), ch. 2.

29. Kristen Luker, *Abortion and the Politics of Motherhood* (Berkeley: University of California Press, 1984), ch. 2.

30. *Newsweek* (October 21, 1991), p. 34.

31. Linda Greenhouse, "Justices Give the States Immunity from Suits by Disabled Workers," *The New York Times* (February 22, 2001), p. A1.

32. Kenneth Sherrill and Alan Yang, "From Outlaws to In-Laws," *Public Perspectives* (January/February 2000), pp. 20–23; "The Agony and the Ecstasy," *The Economist* (July 2, 2005).

33. ABC News/*Washington Post* Poll (January 15–18, 2004); CBS News/*New York Times* Poll (December 10–13, 2003); *The Los Angeles Times* Poll (November 15–18, 2003); *Time*/CNN Poll conducted by Harris Interactive (November 18–19, 2003).

34. *Los Angeles Times* Poll, May 2004, reported in "Another Thirty Years War in the Making"? *The Economist* (May 22, 2004), p. 24. Also see "Reading the Polls on Gay Marriage and the Constitution," Pew Research Center (July 13, 2004).

35. Pew Research Center (July 13–17, 2005).

CHAPTER 17

1. David Firestone, "Dizzying Dive to Red Ink Poses Stark Choices for Washington," *The New York Times* (September 14, 2003), p. A1.

2. *The Budget and Economic Outlook, 2006–2016* (Washington, D.C.: The Congressional Budget Office, January 26, 2006), summary tables of baseline projections.

3. Mark Mazzetti and Joel Havemann, "Bush's Bill for War Is Rising," *Los Angeles Times* (February 3, 2006), p. A1.

4. Fred C. Pampel, *Age, Class, Politics, and the Welfare State* (New York: Cambridge University Press, 1989), p. 16; Harold Wilensky, *The Welfare State and Equality* (Berkeley, CA: University of California Press, 1975).

5. Robert E. Goodin, "Reasons for Welfare," in J. Donald Moon, ed., *Responsibility, Rights, and Welfare: The Theory of the Welfare State* (Boulder, CO: Westview Press, 1988); Wilensky, *The Welfare State and Equality*. See also Clark Kerr, John T. Dunlop, Fredrick H. Harbison, and Charles A. Myers, *Industrialism and Industrial Man* (New York: Oxford University Press, 1964).

6. This discussion is based largely on B. Guy Peters, *American Public Policy: Promise and Performance,* 6th ed. (New York: CQ Press, 2004), pp. 193–203.

7. Ibid, pp. 128–130.

8. Ibid., pp. 130–138.

9. All budget numbers in this section are from the *Budget of the United States Government, 2007* (Washington, D.C.: Office of Management and Budget, February 2006).

10. "The Bush Budget Proposal," *The Wall Street Journal* (February 6, 2006), p. 1.

11. "Bush to Ask for More War Funding," *The Wall Street Journal* (February 3, 2006), p. 1.

12. *The Budget of the United States, Fiscal 2007.*

13. Peters, *American Public Policy*, pp. 234–235.

14. Edmund L. Andrews, "Conflicts Seen in Bush Tax Initiative," *The New York Times* (October 5, 2005), Week in Review, p. 1.; David Cay Johnston, *Perfectly Legal: The Covert Campaign to Rig Our Tax System to Benefit the Super Rich—and Cheat Everybody Else* (New York: Penguin, 2003), pp. 309–311. For the first evidence showing a shift in tax burdens favoring the wealthiest Americans, see David Cay Johnston, "Big Gains for Rich Seen in Tax Cuts for Investment," *The New York Times* (April 5, 2006), p. A1.

15. Benjamin Friedman, *Day of Reckoning: The Consequences of American Economic Policy Under Reagan and After* (New York: Random House, 1989), p. 90.

16. David Wessel, "Deficit Debate Makes for Strange Bedfellows," *The Wall Street Journal On-line* at **www.wsj.com** (October 20, 2005).

17. George J. Stigler, "The Theory of Economic Regulation," *Bell Journal,* 2 (Spring 1971), pp. 3–21. Also see Gabriel Kolko, *The Triumph of Conservatism* (Chicago: Quadrangle, 1967); James Weinstein, *The Corporate Ideal in the Liberal State* (Boston: Beacon Press, 1968).

18. See Richard Harris and Sidney Milkis, *The Politics of Regulatory Change* (New York: Oxford University Press, 1989); Marc Allen Eisner, *Regulatory Politics in Transition* (Baltimore: Johns Hopkins University Press, 2000).

19. See G. William Domhoff, *The Higher Circles* (New York: Random House, 1970); Edward S. Greenberg, *Capitalism and the American Political Ideal* (Armonk, NY: Sharpe, 1985); Kolko, *The Triumph of Conservatism;* Weinstein, *The Corporate Ideal in the Liberal State.*

20. Frances Fox Piven and Richard A. Cloward, *Poor People's Movements* (New York: Vintage, 1979).

21. Marver Bernstein, *Regulation by Independent Commission* (Princeton, NJ: Princeton University Press, 1955); Grant McConnell, *Private Power and American Democracy* (New York: Vintage Books, 1966); Theodore J. Lowi, *The End of Liberalism,* 2nd ed. (New York: Norton, 1979).

22. David Vogel, *Fluctuating Fortunes: The Political Power of Business in the United States* (New York: Basic Books, 1989), pp. 59, 112.

23. James Buchanan and Gordon Tullock, "Polluters, Profits and Political Responses: Direct Control versus Taxes," *American Economic Review,* 65 (1975), pp. 139–147; L. Lave, *The Strategy of Social Regulation* (Washington, D.C.: Brookings Institution, 1981); Murray Weidenbaum, *The Costs of Government Regulation of Business* (Washington, D.C.: Joint Economic Committee of Congress, 1978).

24. See Thomas Byrne Edsall, *The New Politics of Inequality* (New York: Norton, 1984); Vogel, *Fluctuating Fortunes;* Kevin P. Phillips, *The Politics of Rich and Poor: Wealth and the American Electorate in the Reagan Aftermath* (New York: Random House, 1990); Thomas Ferguson and Joel Rogers, *Right Turn: The Decline of the Democrats and the Future of American Politics* (New York: Farrar, Straus & Giroux, 1986).

25. Peters, *American Public Policy,* ch. 11; "Historical Tables," in *The Budget of the United States, Fiscal 2007.*

26. *The 2005 OASDI Trustees Report* (Washington, DC: The Social Security Administration, 2005).

27. Roger Lowenstein, "A Question of Numbers," *New York Times Magazine* (January 16, 2005), pp. 42–47.

28. Benjamin I. Page and James R. Simmons, *What Government Can Do: Dealing with Poverty and Inequality* (Chicago: University of Chicago Press, 2000), ch. 3; Edmund L. Andrews, "4 Ways That Might Save the Government Trillions," *The New York Times* (February 4, 2006), p. A7.

29. Paul Krugman, "Confusions About Social Security," *The Economists' Voice,* 2 (no. 1) (2005), pp. 1–9 Article 1; Edward P. Lazear, "The Virtues of Personal Accounts for Social Security," *The Economists' Voice,* 2 (no. 1) (2005), pp. 1–7, article 2.

30. John Harwood, "Republicans Risk Losing Key Voting Bloc," *The Wall Street Journal* (December 15, 2005), p. A4.

31. "U.S. Pensions Found to Lift Many of the Poor," *The New York Times* (December 28, 1989), p. A1. See also Theodore R. K. Marmor, Jerry L. Mashaw, and Philip L. Harvey, *America's Misunderstood Welfare State* (New York: HarperCollins, 1990), ch. 4.

32. U.S. Bureau of the Census, *Statistical Abstracts of the United States, 2006.*

33. "Americans Dissatisfied with Government's Efforts on Poverty," *The Gallup Poll* (October 25, 2005).

34. Hugh Heclo, "The Political Foundations of Anti-Poverty Policy," in Sheldon Danziger and Daniel Weinberg, eds., *Fighting Poverty: What Works and What Doesn't?* (Cambridge, MA: Harvard University Press, 1986); Fay Lomax Cook and Edith J. Barrett, *Support for the American Welfare State: The Views of Congress and the Public* (New York: HarperCollins, 1990), ch 4.

35. David T. Ellwood, *Poor Support: Poverty in the American Family* (New York: Basic Books, 1988); Martin Gilens, *Why Americans Hate Welfare: Race, Media, and the Politics of Antipoverty Policy* (Chicago: The University of Chicago Press, 1999).

36. John E. Schwarz, *America's Hidden Success: A Reassessment of Public Policy from Kennedy to Reagan* (New York: Norton, 1988), p. 37.

37. Peters, *American Public Policy*, p. 314; Christopher Howard, *The Hidden Welfare State* (Princeton, NJ: Princeton University Press, 1999), ch. 3.

38. Robert Greenstein, *The Earned Income Tax Credit* (Washington, D.C.: The Center for Budget Priorities, September 2005).

39. "From Welfare to Work," *The Economist* (July 29, 2006), pp. 27–30; Lauren Etter, "Welfare Reform: Ten Years Later," *The Wall Street Journal* (August 26, 2006), p. A9; Robert Pear and Erik Eckholm, "A Decade After Welfare Reform," *The New York Times* (August 21, 2006), p. A12.

40. Ibid.

41. Gosta Esping-Andersen, "The Three Political Economies of the Welfare State," *Canadian Review of Sociology and Anthropology*, 26 (1989), pp. 10–36; Jonas Pontusson, "The American Welfare State in Comparative Perspective," *Perspectives on Politics* 4, no. 2 (June 2006); pp. 315–326.

42. Vincent A. Mahler and Claudio J. Katz, "Social Benefits in Advanced Capitalist Countries: A Cross-National Assessment," *Comparative Politics*, 21 (1988), pp. 37–50. See also Arnold J. Heidenheimer, Hugh Heclo, and Carolyn Teich Adams, *Comparative Public Policy: The Politics of Social Choice in America, Europe, and Japan*, 3rd ed. (New York: St. Martin's Press, 1990).

43. Peter Lindert, *Growing Public: Social Spending and Economic Growth Since the 18th Century* (Cambridge, England: Cambridge University Press, 2004); U.S. Bureau of the Census, *Statistical Abstracts of the United States, 2006.*

44. Christopher Howard, *The Hidden Welfare State: Tax Expenditures and Social Policy in the United States* (Princeton, NJ: Princeton University Press, 2001); Christopher Howard, "Is the American Welfare State Unusually Small?" *PS* (July 2003), pp. 411–416.

45. U.S. Bureau of the Census, *Poverty in the United States, 1998.*

46. Andrea Brandolini and Timothy Smeeding, "Patterns of Economic Inequality in Western Democracies: Some Facts on Levels and Trends," *PS* (January 2006), pp. 21–26; Lee Kenworthy and Jonas Pontusson, "Rising Inequality and the Politics of Redistribution in Affluent Countries," *Perspectives on Politics*, 3, no. 3 (September 2005), pp. 449–472.

47. *Income, Poverty, and Health Insurance Coverage in the United States, 2005* (Washington, D.C.: U.S. Bureau of the Census, 2005).

48. Nathan Glazer, *The Limits of Social Policy* (Cambridge, MA: Harvard University Press, 1988), pp. 187–188. See also W. Sombart, *Why There Is No Socialism in the United States* (Armonk, NY: Sharpe, 1976).

49. Gilens, *Why Americans Hate Welfare;* Jeff Manza, "Race and the Underdevelopment of the American Welfare State," *Theory and Society*, 29 (2000), pp. 819–832. Also see Alberto Alesina and Edward L. Glaeser, *Fighting Poverty: in the US and Europe: A World of Difference* (Oxford, England: Oxford University Press, 2004).

50. Wilensky, *The Welfare State and Equality;* John Micklethwait and Adrain Wooldridge, *The Right Nation: Conservative Power in America* (New York: Penguin, 2004).

51. Francis G. Castles, *The Impact of Parties: Politics and Policies in Democratic Capitalist States* (Newbury Park, CA: Sage, 1982); Gosta Esping-Andersen, *Politics Against Markets* (Princeton, NJ: Princeton University Press, 1985); Korpi, *Democratic Class Struggle;* John Stephens, *The Transition from Capitalism to Socialism* (London: Macmillan, 1979).

CHAPTER 18

1. President George W. Bush, The State of the Union Address, The United States Capitol, Washington, D.C. (January 29, 2002).

2. Both quotations are from *The National Security Strategy of the United States* (Washington, D.C.: The White House, September, 2003), ch. V, p. 1.

3. Steven Erlanger, "Europe Seethes as the U.S. Flies Solo in World Affairs," *The New York Times* (February 22, 2002), p. A10; David E. Sanger, "Allies Hear Sour Notes in 'Axis of Evil' Chorus," *The New York Times* (February 17, 2002), p. A1.

4. David E. Sanger, "In a Global Shift, Bush Rethinks Going It Alone," *The New York Times* (March 13, 2006), p. A1.

5. Benjamin I. Page with Marshall M. Bouton, *The Foreign Policy Disconnect: What Americans Want from Our Leaders but Don't Get* (Chicago: University of Chicago Press, 2006).

6. Niall Ferguson, *Colossus: The Price of America's Empire* (New York: Pengum, 2004); William E. Odom and Robert Dujarric, *America's Inadvertent Empire* (New Haven: Yale University Press, 2004); Chalmers Johnson, *The Sorrows of Empire* (New York: Metropolitan Books, 2004).

7. Statistics are from the *CIA World Factbook, 2005,* **www.cia.gov/cia/publications/factbook.**

8. Gregg Easterbrook, "American Might Moves Beyond Superpower," *The New York Times* (April 27, 2003), Week in Review Section, p. 1; The Center for Defense Information, **www.cdi.org** (2006); the Center for Arms Control and Non-Proliferation, **www.armscontrolcenter.org** (2006).

9. Johnson, *The Sorrows of Empire.*

10. "The Dragon Comes Calling," *The Economist* (September 3, 2005), p. 25; "Aphorisms and Suspicions," *The Economist* (November 19, 2005), pp. 23–25.

11. Ibid.

12. Joseph S. Nye, Jr., "Redefining the National Interest," *Foreign Affairs* (July/August 1999), pp. 22–35. Also see Richard Florida, *The Rise of the Creative Class* (New York: Basic Books, 2002), chs. 3 and 14.

13. Ibid; Thomas L. Friedman, *The Lexus and the Olive Tree* (New York: Farrar, Straus, Giroux, 1999).

14. Pew Research Center for the People and the Press, "War with Iraq Further Divides Global Publics" (June 3, 2003), "A Year After Iraq War: Mistrust of America in Europe Ever Higher, Muslim Anger Persists" (March 16, 2004).

15. "Global Opinion: The Spread of Anti-Americanism," *Trends, 2005* (Washington, DC: Pew Research Center for the People and the Press, 2005), p. 106; "America's Image Slips, But Allies Share U.S. Concern Over Iran, Hamas," *Survey Report* (Washington, D.C.: Pew Research Center for the People and the Press, June 13, 2006); "The Great Divide: How Westerners and Muslims View Each Other," *Global Attitudes Project Report* (Washington, D.C.: Pew Research Center, June 22, 2006).

16. Pew, "War with Iraq Further Divides Global Publics."

17. Pew, "Global Opinions," p. 108.

18. Kagan, *Of Paradise and Power;* Richard Bernstein, "Foreign Views of U.S. Darken After Sept. 11," *The New York Times* (September 2003), p. A1.

19. Fouad Ajami, "The Falseness of Anti-Americanism," *Foreign Policy* (September/October 2003), pp. 52–61; Dominique Moisi and Hubert Vedrine, *France in an Age of Globalization* (Washington, D.C.: Brookings Institution Press, 2001); Bernard Lewis, *What Went Wrong? Western Impact and Middle Eastern Response* (Oxford: Oxford University Press, 2001).

20. Michael Mandelbaum, *The Case for Goliath: How America Acts as the World's Government in the Twenty-First Century* (Baltimore, MD: The Johns Hopkins University Press, 2006).

21. Melvyn P. Leffler, "Bush's Foreign Policy," *Foreign Policy* (September/October, 2004), p. 23.

22. Robert O. Keohane and Joseph S. Nye, Jr., *Power and Interdependence: World Politics in Transition* (Boston: Little Brown, 1977); Robert Gilpin, *The Political Economy of International Relations* (Princeton: Princeton University Press, 1987).

23. Mandelbaum, *The Case for Goliath;* Ferguson, *Colossus;* Odom and Dujarric, *America's Inadvertent Empire.* Also see Robert Gilpin, *The Challenge of Global Capitalism: The World Economy in the 21st Century* (Princeton: Princeton University Press, 2000).

24. John Lewis Gaddis, "A Grand Strategy," *Foreign Policy* (November/December 2002), pp. 50–57; Ivo H. Daalder and James M. Lindsay, *America Unbound: The Bush Revolution in Foreign Policy* (Washington, D.C.: Brookings Institution Press, 2003).

25. Emily Eakin, "All Roads Lead to D.C.," *The New York Times* (March 31, 2002), Week in Review, p. 3.

26. Arab Human Development Report 2003, *Building a Knowledge Society* (New York: The United Nations, 2003).

27. Lewis, *What Went Wrong?*

28. Samuel P. Huntington, "The Clash of Civilizations," *Foreign Affairs,* 72 (1993).

29. Mario F. Bognanno and Kathryn J. Ready, eds., *The North American Free Trade Agreement: Labor, Industry, and Government Perspectives* (Westport, CT: Praeger, 1993).

30. See "Liberty's Great Advance," *The Economist* (June 28, 2003), pp. 5–9; Jagdish Bhagwati, *In Defense of Globalization* (New York: Oxford University Press, 2004); Jagdish Bhagwati and Marvin H. Kosters, eds., *Trade and Wages: Leveling Down Wages?* (Washington, D.C.: AEI Press, 1994); Martin Wolf, *Why Globalization Works* (New Haven: Yale University Press, 2004); Michael Veseth, *Globaloney: Unraveling the Myths of Globalization* (Lanham, MD: Rowman and Littlefield Publishers, 2005). Dani Rodrik, among others, disagrees. See his *Has Globalization Gone Too Far* (Washington, D.C.: The Institute of International Economics, 1997). Also see E. Stiglitz, *Globalization and Its Discontents* (New York: W. W. Norton and Company, 2003).

31. Jerry Mander and Edward Goldsmith, eds., *The Case Against the Global Economy* (San Francisco: Sierra Club Books, 1996).

32. *The United Nations Annual Report,* World Health Organization, 2005.

33. "The $25 Billion Question," *The Economist* (July 2, 2005), p. 24.

34. Budget of the United States, 2007 (Washington, D.C.: Office of Management and Budget, 2006); Organization for Economic Cooperation and Development (OECD), International Development Statistics, 2006.

35. Jeffrey Ball, "Kyoto Questioned as U.S. Moves on Coal," *The New York Times* (December 6, 2005), p. A1.

36. Bob Woodward, *Plan of Attack* (New York: Simon and Schuster, 2004).

37. Charles W. Kegley, Jr., and Eugene R. Wittkopf, *American Foreign Policy: Pattern and Process,* 6th ed. (Belmont, CA: Wadsworth Publishing, 2002), p. 387.

Credits

TEXT, FIGURES, AND TABLES

Page 69: Figure 3.3, From Morris P. Fiorina and Paul E. Peterson, *New American Democracy,* 2nd ed. (New York: Longman Publishers, 2001) p. 81. Reprinted by permission of Pearson Education, Inc.; **p. 73:** By the Numbers box, Chapter 3, "Educated Guesses: Sampling Is Taboo, But the Census Does Plenty of 'Imputing'—It Fills in Missing Answers on Race, Sex, Age—Even Postulates Whole People—Whatever the Neighbors Say," by Glenn R. Simpson, *The Wall Street Journal,* August 30, 2001. Copyright © 2001 Dow Jones & Company, Inc. Reproduced by permission of Dow Jones & Company, Inc., in the format Textbook via Copyright Clearance Center; **p. 97:** By the Numbers box, Chapter 4, From *Perspectives on Politics,* vol. 3, no. 3, 2005. Copyright © 2005. Reprinted with the permission of Cambridge University Press; **p. 209:** Table 7.2, From "Money in Politics Databases", *PoliticalMoneyLine*, July 13, 2005. Copyright © 2005. Reprinted with permission; **p. 421:** Figure 14.3, From *Storm Center: The Supreme Court in American Politics,* Third Edition, by David M. O'Brien. Copyright © 1993, 1990, 1986 by David M. O'Brien. Used by permission of W. W. Norton & Company, Inc.

PHOTOS

Page v: © Chip East/Reuters/CORBIS; **p. 1:** © Alan Schein/Zefa/CORBIS; **p. 2:** © Alan Schein/Zefa/CORBIS; **p. 3:** Jeff Greenberg/PhotoEdit Inc.; **p. 5:** Farnood/SIPA Press; **p. 6:** The Granger Collection, New York; **p. 9:** Bob Daemmrich/The Image Works; **p. 12:** ITTC Productions/The Image Bank/Getty Images; **p. 13:** ITTC Productions/The Image Bank/Getty Images; **p. 14:** The Granger Collection, New York; **p. 15:** The Granger Collection, New York; **p. 18:** AP Images; **p. 23:** © Chip East/Reuters/CORBIS; **p. 24:** © Chip East/Reuters/CORBIS; **p. 25:** The Granger Collection, New York; **p. 28 (left):** The Granger Collection, New York; **p. 28 (right):** Library of Congress; **p. 30:** Library of Congress; **p. 32:** Scala/Art Resource, NY; **p. 35:** The Signing of the Constitution by Howard Chandler Christy. Art Resource, NY; **p. 41:** Alex Wong/Getty Images; **p. 47:** Mark Peterson/CORBIS; **p. 52:** © Chip East/Reuters/CORBIS; **p. 53:** Larry Downing/Reuters/Landov; **p. 55:** Wathiq Khuzaie/Getty Images; **p. 61:** AP Images; **p. 64:** Timothy O. Sullivan/Library of Congress; **p. 65:** Russell Lee/Library of Congress; **p. 67:** Tyrone Turner/Black Star/Stockphoto.com; **p. 72:** Comstock Royalty Free; **p. 74:** David Young-Wolff/PhotoEdit Inc.; **p. 75:** Ralph A. Clevenger/CORBIS; **p. 78:** Mark Richards/PhotoEdit Inc.; **p. 82:** © Chip East/Reuters/CORBIS; **p. 83:** Rebecca Cook/Reuters/CORBIS; **p. 87:** AP Images; **p. 88:** Robert Brenner/PhotoEdit Inc.; **p. 92:** Copyright © 2002/VisionsofAmerica.com; **p. 95:** Bettmann/CORBIS; **p. 96:** © Royalty-Free/CORBIS; **p. 98:** Shen Yu/Imaginechina/ZUMA Press; **p. 100:** AP Images;

p. 101: Faleh Kheiber/Reuters/CORBIS; **p. 105:** Fujifotos/The Image Works; **p. 109:** David Young-Wolff/PhotoEdit Inc.; **p. 113:** © Kevin Fleming/CORBIS; **p. 114:** © Kevin Fleming/CORBIS; **p. 115:** Philip Jones Griffiths/Magnum Photos, Inc.; **p. 117:** AP Images; **p. 119:** Mark Richards/PhotoEdit Inc.; **p. 120:** Bettmann/CORBIS; **p. 122:** Kent Meireis/The Image Works; **p. 125:** Bob Daemmrich/PhotoEdit Inc.; **p. 127:** Anthony Bolante/Reuters/Landov; **p. 130:** © 1976 Matt Herron/Take Stock; **p. 131:** AP Images; **p. 136:** Alex Wong/Getty Images for Meet the Press; **p. 137:** Wally McNamee/CORBIS; **p. 139:** AP Images; **p. 144:** Mark Mainz/Getty Images; **p. 152:** © Kevin Fleming/CORBIS; **p. 153:** AP Images; **p. 158:** Scott Gries/Getty Images; **p. 160:** SuperStock; **p. 161:** SuperStock; **p. 164:** AP Images; **p. 166:** AP Images; **p. 167:** Time Life Pictures/Getty Images; **p. 170:** CBS/Landov; **p. 172:** Vasily Fedosenko/Reuters/CORBIS; **p. 173:** Alex Wong/Getty Images for Meet the Press; **p. 174:** Alex Brandon/Newshouse News Servicce/Landov; **p. 176:** Facelly/SIPA Press; **p. 179:** AP Images; **p. 182:** Tim Page/CORBIS; **p. 184:** Getty Images; **p. 185:** AP Images; **p. 187:** Michael L. Abramson/Time Life Pictures/Getty Images; **p. 189:** © Kevin Fleming/CORBIS; **p. 190:** AP Images; **p. 192:** Library of Congress; **p. 195:** Chris Hondros/Getty Images; **p. 196:** Ken Cedeno/CORBIS; **p. 201:** Bill Grenblatt/UPI/Landov; **p. 203:** Paul Conklin/PhotoEdit Inc.; **p. 205:** Allan Tannenbaum; **p. 206:** Ted Spiegel/CORBIS; **p. 207:** Ted Spiegel/CORBIS; **p. 213:** Melanie Stetson Freeman/The Christian Science Monitor/Getty Images; **p. 215:** Jeff Greenberg/PhotoEdit Inc.; **p. 220:** © Kevin Fleming/CORBIS; **p. 221:** The Granger Collection, New York; **p. 226:** David Butow/CORBIS SABA; **p. 227:** Edgar Mata/SIPA Press; **p. 230:** Susan McCartney/Photo Researchers, Inc.; **p. 231:** AP Images; **p. 233:** Bettmann/CORBIS; **p. 234:** AP Images; **p. 235:** Jim Ruymen/UPI/Landov; **p. 236:** AP Images; **p. 239:** Susan Van Etten/PhotoEdit Inc.; **p. 242:** © Kevin Fleming/CORBIS; **p. 243:** Shawn Thew/AFP/Getty Images; **p. 245:** Stringer/AFP/Getty Images; **p. 247:** Pearson Education U.S. ELT/Scott Foresman; **p. 250:** Bettmann/CORBIS; **p. 254:** J. Albert Diaz/Miami Herald/SIPA Press; **p. 256:** AP Images; **p. 259:** Matthew Polak/CORBIS SYGMA; **p. 260:** Mark Peterson/CORBIS SABA; **p. 261:** Brian Snyder/Reuters/Landov; **p. 269:** © Kevin Fleming/CORBIS; **p. 270 (left):** AP Images; **p. 270 (right):** Greg Whitesell/UPI/Landov; **p. 274:** Bob Daemmrich/AFP/Getty Images; **p. 277:** Rob Crandall/The Image Works; **p. 280:** The County Election by George Caleb Bingham, 1852. The St. Louis Art Museum. Museum Purchase; **p. 283:** Jean-Paul Pelissier/REUTERS; **p. 284:** Ed Kashi/CORBIS; **p. 287:** Syracuse Newspapers/Jim Commentucci /The Image Works; **p. 290:** Mike Segar/Reuters/CORBIS; **p. 291 (left):** Bettmann/CORBIS; **p. 291 (right):** CORBIS; **p. 293:** AP Images; **p. 297:** Arnaldo Magnani/Getty Images; **p. 300:** AP Images; **p. 302:** AFP/Getty Images; **p. 303:** AFP/Getty

Index

C-SPAN, 342
Cuba, 156, 401
Cuban Missile Crisis, 368
Culture. *See* Political culture
Cunningham, Randy "Duke," 202
Czech Republic, 416

Dahl, Robert, 10–11, 16, 41–42
The Daily Show, 157, 158
DaimlerChrysler, 83
Darfour, 180
Dartmouth College v. *Woodward* (1819), 429, 449
Daschle, Tom, 173
Davidson, Roger H., 328, 329
Days of Rage vandalism, 225
Dealignment, 251
Dean, Howard, 161–162, 192, 290
Death penalty. *See* Capital punishment
Death with Dignity Act (Oregon), 463
Declaration of Independence
    drafting of, 27–28
    key ideas in, 28–29
    omissions in, 29
    text of, A-2–A-3
Declaration of Sentiments and Resolutions, 480
Deep Throat, 169
Defense Department (DOD), 170, 386, 387, 558
Defense of Marriage Act (1996), 58, 498
DeLauro, Rosa, 326
DeLay, Tom
    campaign finance irregularities and, 177, 202
    leadership style of, 332
    Texas redistricting conflict and, 318–319
Delegates
    to convention of 2004, 264
    explanation of, 313
    to national conventions, 290
Dell Computer, 99
Delphi, 83
Democracy
    bureaucracy and, 408
    civil liberties and, 474
    direct, 6–7
    elections and, 271–272, 304
    as evaluative standard, 16–17
    explanation of, 5
    federalism and, 79
    foreign policy and, 538–539
    George W. Bush and spread of, 536, 537, 546
    imperfect electoral, 275
    inequality and, 96
    interest groups and, 192–193, 204, 217
    judicial review and, 416–417
    news media and, 154, 155, 186
    nomination politics and, 292
    objections to, 14–16
    origins of, 5–6
    overview of, 4–5
    political culture and, 107
    political equality and, 9–13

political parties and, 244–245, 267
popular sovereignty and, 7–9
public opinion and, 117, 147
representation and, 313–326
representative, 7–16 (*See also* Representative democracy)
republicanism and, 31–32
republic vs., 49
Supreme Court and, 439
trade and, 102–103
Democratic Leadership Council, 264
Democratic party. *See also* Political parties
    African Americans and, 123, 124, 131, 251, 261–262, 298
    civil rights and, 250–251
    control of Congress by, 327–328, 370
    core supporters of, 261–262
    geographic region and, 128
    Hispanic vote and, 124, 125, 310
    historical background of, 247–251
    ideology and policies of, 262–264
    internal divisions within, 264
    Iraq war and, 243, 244, 350
    Jews and, 130–131, 298
    labor unions and, 126
    organization of, 257–261
    party identification and, 133–134, 139–140
    policy positions of, 133–134
    religious beliefs and, 130–131
    Social Security and, 520
    socioeconomic status and, 126, 127
Democratic Republicans, 247, 248
Democratic Whig party, 248
Demographics. *See* United States
Department of Homeland Security (DHS)
    establishment of, 195, 383, 387
    mandate of, 383
    operation of, 391
    spending by, 404–405, 512
Departments, 386. *See also specific departments*
Deportation hearings, 472, 475
Depressions, 505. *See also* Great Depression
De Priest, Oscar, 314
Deregulation, 183, 517. *See also* Government regulation
Descriptive representation, 313
Desegregation, school, 204, 233, 425, 435, 478–479, 484
Desert Storm. *See* Gulf War
Devolution, 67
Dewey, Thomas, 120
Dickerson v. *United States* (2000), 465
Direct democracy, 6–7. *See also* Democracy
Director of National Intelligence, 558
Direct TV, 164
Disabled individuals, 495–496
Discharge petition, 341
Discount rate, 509
Discrimination. *See also* Civil rights
    age, 432
    commerce clause and, 66

against individuals with disabilities, 495–496
    racial, 484–485
    against women, 492
Disney, 99, 164, 165
Dissenting opinion, 428
District of Columbia, 280
Disturbance theory, 195
Diversity. *See also* Ethnicity
    federalism and, 56–57
    political participation and, 123–126, 285–286
    social welfare programs and, 529–530
    in United States, 85–89
Divided government
    explanation of, 265
    in late 20th and early 21st century, 266
    problem of, 401–402
DNA evidence, in death penalty cases, 467, 469
Dobson, James, 260
Dole, Elizabeth, 289
Dole, Robert, 209, 293
"Don't ask, don't tell" policy, 237, 497
Dot-com bust, 99
Douglas, William, 428
Dowell v. *Oklahoma City* (1991), 478
Dred Scott v. *Standford* (1857), 449–450, 480, 481
Drug companies
    lobbyists for, 208–209
    Medical prescription drug program and, 210
Dual federalism, 61–62, 68
Due process clause
    corporations and, 430
    explanation of, 64, 403, 481
    Supreme Court and, 450
Dukakis, Michael, 300
Duke, David, 257–258

Ear-marking, 202
Earned Income Tax Credit, 525
Easongate, 153
East Timor, 175
eBay, 99
An Economic Interpretation of the Constitution (Beard), 34
Economic conservatives, 141
Economic liberals, 141
Economic liberty, 448–450
Economic policy. *See also* Federal budget
    budget deficit and, 514–515
    Congress and, 360
    federal budget and, 509–515
    federal spending and, 503, 504, 511–512
    goals of, 506–508
    government spending and, 503, 504
    macroeconomic, 508–509
    president and, 360
    public opinion on, 531
    responsibility for, 505
    taxes and, 512–514
Economic recessions, 99, 379, 503
Economic theory of regulation, 516